The New
Historical Dictionary of the
American Film Industry

Anthony Slide

The Scarecrow Press, Inc.
Lanham, Maryland, and London
2001

SCARECROW PRESS, INC.

Published in the United States of America by Scarecrow Press, Inc.
4720 Boston Way, Lanham, Maryland 20706
www.scarecrowpress.com

4 Pleydell Gardens, Folkestone
Kent CT20 2DN, England

Distributed by National Book Network

Copyright © 1998 by Anthony Slide
First paperback edition 2001

British Library Cataloguing-in-Publication Information Available

Library of Congress Cataloging-in-Publication Data

The hardback edition of this book was previously cataloged by the Library of Congress as follows:

Slide, Anthony.
    The new historical dictionary of the American film industry / Anthony Slide.
      p. cm.
    Rev. ed. of : The American film industry, 1986.
    Includes bibliographical references and index.
    ISBN 0-8108-3426-X (cloth : alk. paper)
    1. Motion picture industry—United States—Dictionaries. I. Slide, Anthony. American film industry. II. Title.
PN1993.5.U6S539 1998
384'.8'0973—dc21   97-35737
                                                  CIP

ISBN 1-57886-015-6 (pbk. : alk. paper)

for Ann and
Andre de Toth

Contents

Preface

The New Historical Dictionary of the American Film Industry is a revised and updated version of my 1986 book, *The American Film Industry: A Historical Dictionary.* More than 200 new entries have been added, and other entries have been updated where appropriate. Like its predecessor, *The New Historical Dictionary of the American Film Industry* is unique in that it is not a "Who's Who" of the American film industry, of which there are many, but rather a "What's What," a dictionary of American producing and releasing companies, technical innovations, industry terms, studios, genres, and organizations. Included here are more than 800 entries on everything from the Academy of Motion Picture Arts and Sciences to the zoom lens, from Astoria Studios to Zoetrope. There are entries on more than 100 companies active in the second decade of the twentieth century, as well as major studios, such as Metro-Goldwyn-Mayer and 20th Century-Fox. The various color systems, such as Technicolor, Kinemacolor, Prizma Color, and Eastman Color, are described in this volume, as are CinemaScope, Todd-AO, Dolby Sound, and Panavision.

Following many of the entries is an address (if the company or organization is still active), a short bibliography, and, where appropriate, information—under the heading "Resources"—as to institutional holdings of the subject's films, papers, photographs, and scripts. An asterisk (*) following a name in any of the entries indicates that there is a separate entry for that subject.

Headings are based on the best-known name of a company, studio, or technical innovation and are not necessarily the final name by which the subject was known. However, cross-references within the text will immediately indicate the heading used. Cross-references have also been used to refer researchers to a studio or company outside of a major film community, where the researcher is only familiar with the town or city in which the company was located but is not aware of its name. Thus, under Lake Placid, New York, will be found a cross-reference to Excelsior Feature Film Company, Inc., and under Providence, Rhode Island, will be found a cross-reference to Eastern Film Company. The index includes the names of all individuals associated with a particular company, thus enabling a researcher, yet again, to track down a company without prior knowledge of the name. Wherever possible in the text, birth and death years are provided for such individuals.

Space does not permit my acknowledging the countless individuals, companies, and institutions that have helped in the research for this and the earlier volume. However, I would like to note a special debt to Alan Gevinson and to the staff of the Margaret Herrick Library of the Academy of Motion Picture Arts and Sciences.

A BAND APART PRODUCTIONS was founded in 1991 by Quentin Tarantino (born 1963) and producer Lawrence Bender, and named after the 1964 French feature film directed by Jean-Luc Godard. Its first production was *Pulp Fiction* (1994). A subsidiary, A Band Apart Commercials, was created in 1995.

ABC MOTION PICTURES, INC. Formed in May 1979 by the American Broadcasting Company, ABC Motion Pictures, Inc., was the network's second attempt to become involved in feature film production. Under Brandon Stoddard's presidency, the company waited almost two years before commencing production on its first feature, *Young Doctors in Love* (1982). The best known of ABC Motion Pictures' productions, all of which were released by 20th Century-Fox*, is *Silkwood* (1983). The division closed in October 1985.

BIBLIOGRAPHY

Kilday, Gregg. "ABC Motion Pictures Comes of Age." *Los Angeles Herald-Examiner,* July 16, 1982, p. D4.

ACADEMY OF MOTION PICTURE ARTS AND SCIENCES. The concept for the Academy of Motion Picture Arts and Sciences was first discussed at a dinner hosted in January 1927 by M-G-M* production head Louis B. Mayer. On January 11, 1927, a meeting was held at the Ambassador Hotel in Los Angeles, and the Academy of Motion Picture Arts and Sciences was officially formed. Among its founders were Louis B. Mayer, Mary Pickford, Douglas Fairbanks (who became the first president), Frank Lloyd, Joseph M. Schenck, Fred Niblo, and Cedric Gibbons. It was granted a charter as a nonprofit California organization on May 4, 1927, and an organizational banquet was held at the Biltmore Hotel, Los Angeles, on May 11, 1927.

The Academy was formed to fend off attacks against the industry, to promote unity among the various groups of workers within the industry, to advance the power and influence of the motion picture, and—for what it is best known—to "encourage the improvement and advancement of the arts and sciences of the profession by the interchange of constructive ideas and by awards of merit for distinctive achievement."

To this end the Academy gives annual awards of merit—first presented at the Hollywood Roosevelt Hotel on May 16,

1929, for the year August 1, 1927–July 31, 1928—which became known by the late thirties as "Oscars." The Oscar statuette, which has never changed (except for the height of its base) stands 13.5 inches tall and weighs 8.5 pounds. It is manufactured from Britannium and is gold-plated. Conrad Nagel, one of the Academy's founders, urged that the award be a "symbol of continuing progress—militant, dynamic." Art director Cedric Gibbons sketched a knight, holding a crusader's sword and standing on a reel of film, and the figure was molded by sculptor George Stanley. The name "Oscar," according to the Academy, was given to the statuette by the organization's first librarian, Margaret Herrick (then Margaret Gledhill), who claimed it looked like her Uncle Oscar. Other stories have the name originating with Bette Davis.

Awards for Best Actor, Actress, Art Direction, Picture, Cinematography, Directing, and Writing have been given since the first year. Special Awards—from 1950 onward called Honorary Awards—have also been part of the Academy Awards ceremony since its conception. Sound was added to the Awards schedule in 1929/1930; Scientific or Technical Awards were added in 1930/1931; Short Subjects were added in 1931/1932; Assistant Director Awards were given from 1932/1933 to 1937; Music and Film Editing were added in 1934; Dance Direction was given from 1935 to 1937; Best Supporting Actor and Actress were introduced in 1936; the Irving G. Thalberg Memorial Award was introduced in 1937; Special Effects was first given an Award in 1939; Documentary Awards were first given in 1942; Costume Design was added in 1948, and that same year the Foreign Language Film Award was given as a Special Award—it did not become a regular category until 1956; the Jean Hersholt Humanitarian Award was introduced in 1956.

Initially the Academy was heavily involved in labor relations and disputes within the industry. Because it was quickly branded as a producers' tool, it lost much of its membership, and the March 5, 1936, Awards Banquet was boycotted by the majority of filmmakers; at that ceremony Dudley Nichols became the first man to refuse an Oscar—for Best Screenplay. The following year, the Academy completely removed itself from the area of labor relations responsibilities and, today, has no concern with either economic or political matters.

Another area in which the Academy immediately became involved was that of technical research, about which it remained concerned until its Research Council went under the aegis of the Association of Motion Picture Producers in January 1948.

It has always been concerned with educational and cultural matters, cosponsoring, with the University of Southern California, a 1928 course on "Introduction to the Photoplay." On January 31, 1944, the Academy Foundation was incorporated, and under its aegis the Academy has presented major retrospective film screenings and tributes, as well as lectures and seminars. Its Student Film Awards have been an annual event since 1973. It provides scholarships and grants and regularly sends members to talk on college campuses. The Academy's Margaret Herrick Library, named for its first librarian and one-time executive director (1943–1970), is considered one of the finest film-related research libraries in the country, with access by mail available through the National Film Information Service.

Through the *Screen Achievement Records Bulletin,* first published in 1933, the Academy provides valuable documentation on screen credits. The *Academy Players Directory,* first published as the *Players Directory Bulletin* in 1937, is considered the casting director's bible, with its photographs of players, broken down by category, and with the agents' names and telephone numbers.

During the Second World War, the Academy administered a War Film Library, securing prints of documentaries produced by the Allies and making them available to studios and for nontheatrical screenings. The Academy has also maintained a film archives, which, in 1994, announced a new policy of preserving and safeguarding documentaries.

In the fall of 1975, the Academy moved to a new seven-story office building (8949 Wilshire Boulevard, Beverly Hills, Calif. 90211), in which is housed its Samuel Goldwyn Theatre. The library and film archives are housed in the Center for Motion Picture Study (333 South La Cienega, Beverly Hills, Calif. 90211), which opened in January 1992.

The activities of the Academy are almost exclusively funded by membership subscriptions—membership is by invitation only and remains constant at around 4,000—and through revenues from the Academy Awards presentations.

BIBLIOGRAPHY

Holden, Anthony. *Behind the Oscars: The Secret History of the Academy Awards.* New York: Simon & Schuster, 1993.

Levy, Emanuel. *And the Winner Is . . . The History and Politics of the Oscar Awards.* New York: Ungar, 1987.

Mason, Wiley, and Damien Bora. *Inside Oscar: The Unofficial History of the Academy Awards.* New York: Ballantine Books, 1993.

Sands, Pierre Norman. *A Historical Study of the Academy of Motion Picture Arts and Sciences.* New York: Arno Press, 1973.

Shale, Richard. *The Academy Awards Index.* Westport, Conn.: Greenwood Press, 1993.

ACETATE FILM. Although it is really a misnomer, as film today is generally triacetate, acetate film is the term used to describe safety or noninflammable filmstock, which has an estimated life span of 200 years or more. Eastman Kodak* first introduced acetate film in 1908, and, although it was crucial in the development of 16mm and 8mm film, it was not generally used for 35mm film production by the industry. However, in the late forties, Eastman Kodak introduced an improved safety-base motion picture film—for which in 1949 the company received a Class I (Oscar statuette) Scientific or Technical Award; this new safety film superseded nitrate film*, and from 1950/1951 all film has been shot and processed on safety stock.

ACME VIDEOTAPE AND FILM LABORATORIES. See CONSOLIDATED FILM INDUSTRIES

ACTOPHONE COMPANY, formed in New York by Mark Dintenfass, produced one-reel comedies and dramas on a weekly basis, beginning with *The Third Degree,* released on February 23, 1910. It ceased production after being sued by the Motion Picture Patents Company*, and its last film, *Love's Great Tragedy,* was released on May 25, 1910. Dintenfass subsequently formed the Champion Film Company, whose first film, *Abernathy Kids to the Rescue,* was released on July 13, 1910, and which became part of Universal* in 1912.

"THE ACTOR'S BIBLE" was an early nickname for *Variety* (first published December 16, 1905). It was perhaps used before 1905 in reference to another trade paper, the *New York Clipper.*

THE ACTORS STUDIO, INC. The home of a style known as "method acting," which had its origins in the Russian theatre at the turn of the century and in the work of Constantin Stanislavski, the Actors Studio, Inc., was opened in September 1947 by Cheryl Crawford and Elia Kazan, with classes taught by Kazan and Robert Lewis. A "workshop for professional actors," the Studio includes among its graduates Paul Newman, Joanne Woodward, Karl Malden, Lee Grant, Kim Hunter, and Marlon Brando. Lee Strasberg became involved with the Studio in 1949, and, in 1952, was named its artistic director, a title he held until his death in 1982. Al Pacino and Ellen Burstyn were named co-artistic directors in 1982; Pacino resigned in 1984 and Burstyn in 1988. Since 1987, the Actors Studio has been plagued with financial problems, and in 1994, it became allied with the New School. A West Coast operation, Actors Studio West, was formed in Los Angeles in 1966.

BIBLIOGRAPHY

Garfield, David. *A Player's Place: The Story of the Actors Studio.* New York: Macmillan, 1980.

Hethman, Robert H., ed. *Strasberg at the Actors Studio.* New York: Viking Press, 1965.

Hirsch, Foster. *A Method in Their Madness.* New York: W. W. Norton, 1984.

Kaufman, Joanne. "Studio System." *Vanity Fair,* November 1992, pp. 230–39, 273.

THE ADULT FILM ASSOCIATION OF AMERICA was founded in Kansas City on January 14, 1969, as a non-profit corporation set up to protect and promote the interests of its member producers, distributors, and exhibitors, all of whom were involved in what they described as "sexually explicit" films. On July 14, 1977, the Association presented the first annual Erotic Film Awards, and from 1971–1986, it published *The AFAA Bulletin.* The name was changed to the Adult Film and Video Association of America, Inc., in July 1986; it is now defunct.

BIBLIOGRAPHY

Friedman, David. "A History of the AFAA." *Boxoffice,* March 1982, pp. 20, 22, 24, 26.

Knight, Arthur. "Adult Film Group in Quest to Gain Respect." *Los Angeles Times* Calendar, February 17, 1984, pp. 14, 17.

ADIRONDACKS. See ARTIC FILM STUDIOS

AFFILIATED DISTRIBUTORS' CORPORATION, incorporated in May 1918, was formed to serve exhibitors as a national clearinghouse to ensure that the various exhibitor booking associations in different states would get a consistent supply of high-quality films. The exhibitor-controlled organization was led by Frank Rembusch, Sydney Cohen, and general counsel Charles C. Pettijohn. In November 1918, Affiliated acquired 51 percent of the Mutual Film Corporation*. With headquarters established in Grand Rapids, Michigan, the exhibitors planned to divide the country into five sections and cooperatively book films directly from the producer to the exhibitor. The plan took effect on November 20, 1918, when the Robertson-Cole Company* made a long-term contract to furnish all films for the new organization, which had changed its name to Exhibitors' Mutual Distributing Corporation.

BIBLIOGRAPHY

"Affiliated Distributors Are Incorporated." *The Moving Picture World.* May 11, 1918, p. 1003.

"Affiliated Takes Over Mutual Film." *The Moving Picture World.* November 23, 1918, p. 809.

AGENTS. William Morris* is the oldest surviving and most famous of the entertainment-oriented agents. Abe Lastfogel (1898–1984) joined William Morris in 1912, and came out to Hollywood in 1932 to expand its involvement in the representation of film talent; Lastfogel became president of William Morris in 1952 and its chairman of the board in 1969. Another top agent at William Morris was Stan Kamen (1926–1986), who joined the company in 1950. Michael

Ovitz (born 1946) was an agent with William Morris from 1965 to 1975, before co-founding Creative Artists Agency*. Music Corporation of America, founded in Chicago in 1924 by Jules Stein (1896–1981) as a booking agency for dance bands eventually became the parent company of Universal*. The best known name associated with it is Lew Wasserman (born 1913), who joined MCA in 1936. Irving "Swifty" Lazar began his show business career as an attorney with MCA, also in 1936. Nicknamed "Swifty" by Humphrey Bogart because of the speed with which he put together deals, Lazar was a prominent independent agent from the 1940s onward, noted in later years for the star-studded Oscar night parties that he hosted, beginning in the 1970s at the Bistro Garden in Beverly Hills, and continuing in the 1980s through 1993 at Spago.

The brother of David O. Selznick, Myron Selznick (1898–1944) became an agent in the twenties, initially in partnership with Felix Young and later Frank Joyce. The first top female agent was Sue Mengers, who came to Hollywood in 1968, working with International Creative Management*, which she quit in 1986. So well known is Mengers that she appears as a character in the 1973 film, *The Last of Sheila,* played by Dyan Cannon.

BIBLIOGRAPHY

Lazar, Irving, with Annette Tapert. *Swifty: My Life and Good Times.* New York: Simon & Schuster, 1995.

Rose, Frank. *The Agency: William Morris and the Hidden History of Show Business.* New York: HarperCollins, 1995.

Small, Edgar. *From Agent to Actor: An Unsentimental Education, or What the Other Half Knows.* Los Angeles: Samuel French, 1991.

Swanson, H. N. *Sprinkled with Ruby Dust.* New York: Warner Books, 1989.

AIP. See AMERICAN INTERNATIONAL PICTURES

THE AKELEY "PANCAKE" CAMERA was invented in 1919 by Dr. Carl Akeley, a curator at the American Museum of Natural History in New York, and designed as a compact, circular-shaped camera for use on his expeditions to Africa. Because of its compactness and its ease of operation, it quickly became the camera of choice for newsreelmen and for those involved in location shooting. Robert Flaherty's *Nanook of the North* (1922) was filmed using an Akeley camera.

ALBUQUERQUE FILM MANUFACTURING COMPANY, INC., organized in the fall of 1913 with G. P. Hamilton as its president and general manager, specialized in the production of three-reel Westerns, written by and starring Dot Farley. Milton H. Fahrney directed at the company's inception and his wife appeared in the films. The company used the studios at the J.A.C. plant on Broadway in downtown Los Angeles and released its product through

Warners Features, Inc. In October 1913, the company was reincorporated as the Albuquerque Film Company of Los Angeles with a capitalization of $200,000. At this point the company began releasing one-reel comedies and comedy dramas with United Films* under the brand name of Luna Films and starring Dot Farley. Augustus Carney, known as "Alkali Ike," appeared in Albuquerque productions at this time. In July 1915, the company occupied temporary studios on Allesandro Street in Los Angeles and produced two reels a week, the one being a comedy-drama written by Dot Farley and supervised by Hamilton and the other a comedy directed by Nick Cogley. In early 1918, Hamilton declared bankruptcy.

BIBLIOGRAPHY

"New Western Film Company." *The New York Dramatic Mirror,* November 12, 1913, p. 27.

ALCO FILM CORPORATION. Al Lichtman, former sales manager for Famous Players Film Company, formed the Alco Film Corporation in August 1914 with newspaperman Walter Hoff Seeley to distribute films to their own exchanges* throughout the country. Lichtman's idea was to organize a circuit of the largest theatres in the country, one in each city of over 200,000 people, which would book through Alco at the highest justifiable price in return for exclusive rights in that city for a certain period. The system would enable exhibitors to charge higher admissions without the fear of competition. After a week's run, the film would not be shown again in that city for six months, then it would play in smaller towns, distributed through Alco exchanges. Lichtman, by engaging the feature film companies of All-Star Feature Company*, California Motion Picture Corporation*, Popular Plays and Players, Inc.*, Favorite Players Film Co.*, Excelsior Feature Film Co.*, Tiffany Film Corporation*, B. A. Rolfe*, and Life Photo*, set up distribution centers in 20 cities to take their entire output for five years. Alco executives were to approve all scenarios and casts and all production plans. On October 1, 1914, Alco began to issue one film per week. Lichtman left the corporation in November 1914. Bankruptcy proceedings were initiated early in 1915 because of internal dissension.

BIBLIOGRAPHY

"Alco Another Big Combine." *The Moving Picture World,* September 5, 1914, p. 1383.
"For Film Distribution." *The New York Dramatic Mirror,* July 22, 1914, p. 24.

ALCOHOLISM. From its earliest beginnings, the film industry has sent out mixed signals with regard to the positive and negative aspects of drinking alcohol. During the Prohibition era, it paid little attention to the law, both on screen and in private, with all studios having their own private bootleggers. However, as early as February 1937, Joseph I.

Breen of the Production Code Administration placed a ban on "excessive or unnecessary drinking" on screen. As late as January 1983, the Caucus of Producers, Writers, and Directors issued a policy statement against the depiction of alcohol abuse. Negative depictions of alcohol were provided by Fredric March in *A Star Is Born* (1937), Ray Milland in *The Lost Weekend* (1945), Burt Lancaster in *Come Back, Little Sheba* (1952), Bing Crosby in *The Country Girl* (1954), Susan Hayward in *I'll Cry Tomorrow* (1955), Jack Lemmon and Lee Remick in *Days of Wine and Roses* (1962), and Albert Finney in *Under the Volcano* (1984).

John Barrymore and Peter O'Toole are two actors who have become closely associated with the pleasures of alcohol. In *The Great Gabbo* (1929), Erich von Stroheim orders Veuve Clicquot. In *The Thin Man* series, William Powell and Myrna Loy were seldom without a martini. Thomas Mitchell was an alcoholic doctor in *Stagecoach* (1939). James Stewart's Elwood P. Dowd is frequently drunk in *Harvey* (1950). Veuve Clicquot was the champagne of choice for Sean Connery's James Bond, while Timothy Dalton, in the same role, preferred Bollinger. Alcoholic pleasures have been depicted by Dudley Moore in *Arthur* (1981) and Tom Cruise in *Cocktail* (1988). It is perhaps ironic that it was a drunk driver who nearly killed actresses Janet Gaynor and Mary Martin on a San Francisco street on September 5, 1982, while the latter's son, Larry Hagman, was seldom seen without a glass of bourbon on the television series *Dallas*.

ALDRICH STUDIOS. Built in 1913, consisting of two sound stages and production offices, and formerly known as the Sutherland and Occidental Studios, the Aldrich Studios were located at 201–225 North Occidental Boulevard, Los Angeles. Director Robert Aldrich (1918–1983) acquired the complex in January 1968 for a reported $1,150,000, using profits from his feature *The Dirty Dozen*. The studios became the headquarters for the director's company, Associates & Aldrich (formed in 1954). The first three features filmed by Aldrich at his new studios were *The Killing of Sister George* (1968), *Whatever Happened to Aunt Alice* (1969), and *Too Late the Hero* (1970). The studios were sold to Video Cassette Industries (VCI) in July 1973.

ALHAMBRA MOTION PICTURE COMPANY was formed in November 1914 to produce comedies and dramas written by and starring Betty Harte. In January 1915, it commenced releasing under the Kriterion* brand. Directors included L. B. Carleton and Sidney Debray (who also played starring roles), and actors included E. J. Peil, Master Edward Peil, and Etta Raynor. In September 1915, Alhambra joined the Associated Film Manufacturers, consisting of eight West Coast producers.

ALIVE FILMS was formed in 1983 by show business entrepreneur Shep Gordon and producer Carolyn Pfeiffer as an offshoot of the former's management company, Alive Enterprises (founded in 1966). Gordon had previously created Enigma, in association with David Puttnam in 1978, to produce *The Duellists*. Initially, Alive produced and distributed in association with Island Pictures* under the name Island/Alive, but the partnership was dissolved in 1985. Alive Films ceased operations in 1989, with one of its last productions being *The Whales of August* (1987).

AL JENNINGS PRODUCTION COMPANY. Al Jennings formed the Al Jennings Production Company in July 1918 to make films about his exploits as an outlaw and his later struggles to become a respectable citizen after he joined the Baptist church. Both he and his brother, Frank, an attorney who also had been an outlaw, were to appear in the films. Jennings, the president and general manager of the company, promised that the films would contain real banditry and no idle sentimentality about the West. He hoped that by showing the outlaw's life realistically, and emphasizing the grimness, privation, and dangers, the films would teach audiences the futility of crime. The Jennings's company studios were in both Tucson and Los Angeles. W. S. Van Dyke was the director of productions, and the company's first film was *The Lady in the Dugout* with Corinne Grant. Jennings's films were distributed by Ernest Shipman.

BIBLIOGRAPHY

"Jennings Forms Company to Film His Experiences." *The Moving Picture World,* July 13, 1918, p. 232.

ALL-AMERICAN NEWS. See NEWSREELS

ALL-CELTIC FILM COMPANY, incorporated early in 1915, produced the *Peaceful Rafferty* series. Charles J. O'Hara wrote and directed the series and also was the president of the company, which used the Physioc Studios at 624 West 24th Street, New York.

"ALLEN SMITHEE" is the name invented by the Directors Guild of America* to be given directorial credit when the actual director, for whatever reason, does not want his or her name associated with the film or television production. It was first used on the Richard Widmark Western, *Death of a Gunfighter* (1969), directed in part by Robert Totten and in part by Don Siegel. Other films and made-for-television movies on which it has been seen include *Fade-In* (1970), *City in Fear* (1980), *Student Bodies* (1981), *Moonlight* (1982), *Dune* (1984 television version), *Stitches* (1985), *Let's Get Harry* (1986), *Riviera* (1987), *I Love N.Y.* (1988), and *Fatal Charm* (1992). The 1997 production, *An Alan (sic) Smithee Film* became an Allen Smithee film, when its director, Arthur Hiller, asked for his name to be removed.

BIBLIOGRAPHY

Lazar, Jerry. "Hollywood's Worst Director." *Reader's Digest,* May 1988, pp. 171–72.

Redman, Nick. "The Well Known, the Not-So-Known, and the Virtually Unknown." *DGA News,* August/September 1992, pp. 13–15, 22–23.

Roberts, Jerry. "A Name That Will Live in Infamy." *Daily Variety,* November 20, 1996, pp. 18, 38.

Shapiro, Eben. "Despite Disdain, a Legendary Director Endures." *The Wall Street Journal,* April 19, 1996, pp. B1, B3.

"The Strange, Faceless Tale of Allen Smithee, Man of Mystery." *Los Angeles Times* Calendar, September 13, 1987, pp. 24, 88.

ALLIANCE FILMS CORPORATION was formed in September 1914 as an organization of exchanges. A rotating committee appointed by the exchange decided whether to purchase films from selected manufacturers. The organization received its profits from a percentage of the bookings of the films selected. Its goal was to eliminate states rights* buying and to secure high-quality films. The first film to be released by Alliance was *At the Crossroads,* produced by the Select Photoplay Producing Company. Andrew J. Cobe, Hector J. Streyckmans, and P. P. Craft were involved in the company.

BIBLIOGRAPHY

"The Alliance Program." *The Moving Picture World,* October 10, 1914, p. 166.

ALLIED ARTISTS was formed by Steve Broidy (1905–1991) in November 1946 as a wholly owned subsidiary of Monogram Pictures,* which, in November 1953, changed its name to Allied Artists. It was initially intended that the Allied Artists name would be used on better quality productions, beginning with *It Happened on Fifth Avenue* in 1947. The company was in poor financial shape until 1965, when it released the Elvis Presley vehicle, *Tickle Me.* By the mid-sixties, Allied Artists was renting out its studio, which it eventually sold in 1967 (and which is now KCET). After the studio sale, the company concentrated on releasing foreign films, such as *Belle de Jour* (1968), but returned to active production in the seventies under Emanuel L. Wolf (who took over the company in 1967), with its best-known films including *Cabaret* (1972) and *The Man Who Would Be King* (1975). The last was *The Wild Geese* (1978).

In January 1976, the consumer products groups, Allied Artists Industries, Inc., was created with the merger of Allied Artists Pictures Corporation, Kalvex, Inc., and PSP, Inc. In May 1979, it filed for reorganization under Chapter XI of the bankruptcy laws, but was unsuccessful, and in 1980, Allied Artists—with its library of 450 films—was sold for $7 million to Lorimar Productions.* From 1949 to 1959, Stratford Pictures Corporation distributed foreign films on behalf of Monogram and Allied Artists, and in 1951, a TV division, Interstate Television Corporation, was formed.

BIBLIOGRAPHY

Martin, Len D. *The Allied Artists Checklist: The Feature Films and Short Subjects of Allied Artists Pictures Corporation, 1947–1978.* Jefferson, N.C.: McFarland, 1993.

Penn, Stanley. "How 'Little Guy' Allied Artists Tumbled from Moviemaking Role into Chapter 11." *The Wall Street Journal,* May 4, 1979, p. 40.

ALLIED PICTURES CORPORATION was founded in 1931 by M. H. "Max" Hoffman (1881–1937), and was active through 1934. In all, it produced some 22 features, of which ten were Westerns starring Hoot Gibson. The company was also responsible for a modernized version of *Vanity Fair* (1932), starring Myrna Loy, and the Ginger Rogers vehicle, *A Shriek in the Night* (1933).

ALLIED STATES ASSOCIATION OF MOTION PICTURE EXHIBITORS. See NATIONAL ASSOCIATION OF THEATRE OWNERS, INC.

ALL-SCOPE PICTURES, INC., was a Los Angeles-based producer of 35mm and 16mm industrial and educational films. Founded in 1946 by Gordon S. Mitchell, the former manager of the Research Council of the Academy of Motion Picture Arts and Sciences; it ceased operations in 1957.

ALL-STAR FEATURE COMPANY, incorporated in Albany, New York, in 1913, had Harry Raver as its president, Archibald Selwyn as vice president, and Augustus Thomas as director-general. Its first production was *Arizona*, a six-reel feature version of Thomas's play. Its studio was on Fox Hill, near Fort Wadsworth, Staten Island. All-Star also used the old Lee Lash scenic studio in Mount Vernon, New York. Among the performers who made their screen debuts with All-Star are Ethel Barrymore, William Faversham, and Lew Dockstader. The Exclusive Supply Corporation* distributed All-Star's product from its inception, as Raver was president and general manager of that concern. As of August 25, 1914, Alco Film Corporation* distributed the All-Star product. In December 1914, Harry Raver and Augustus Thomas withdrew, and John Dunlap became head. Alco secured the complete control of All-Star, and George Foster Platt became the company's new director-general. Like Alco, All-Star went bankrupt in early 1915. Among the more important All-Star features were *The Nightingale* (1914), starring Ethel Barrymore, and *The Jungle* (1914), based on the novel by Upton Sinclair. Sol Lesser was the president and general manager of All-Star Feature Distributors of San Francisco, Los Angeles, Denver, Seattle, and Portland.

BIBLIOGRAPHY

"Alco Absorbs All-Star," *The Moving Picture World.* December 19, 1914, p. 1699.

"All-Star Feature Company." *The New York Dramatic Mirror,* July 19, 1913, p. 25.

ALPHAVILLE is an independent production company founded in March 1992 by Sean Daniel and Jim Jacks, and initially based at Universal.* It moved to the Paramount* lot in 1997. Caldecott Chubb (who had formed the independent production company Chubco in 1992) became president of production in July 1994. The company's films include *Hard Target, Tombstone, CB4,* and *Dazed and Confused,* all released in 1993.

Address: 5300 Melrose Avenue, Suite 204, Los Angeles, Calif. 90038.

BIBLIOGRAPHY

Parker, Donna. "Pizza with Jacks/Daniel," *The Hollywood Reporter*, March 17, 1994, pp. S-9, S-19.

AMBASSADOR, PICTURES, INC., formed by Maurice Conn, was active as a Western producer from 1934 to 1938, with the majority of its features starring Kermit Maynard. Also during the same period, Maurice Conn launched Conn Pictures Corp., Conn Productions, Inc., Conn Studios, and Melody Pictures Corp.

AMBLIN ENTERTAINMENT is a privately owned company, created in 1984 as his production base by Steven Spielberg (born 1947) in close association with Kathleen Kennedy (who served as its president through 1992) and her husband, Frank Marshall. Housed on the Universal* lot, the company takes its name from the title of a 1969 short subject, *Amblin'*, made by Spielberg, and which led to his first contract with Universal. A television division was formed in June 1988.

Address: 100 Universal City Plaza, Universal City, Calif. 91608.

AMERICAN CINEMA EDITORS, INC., is a professional group of film editors from Los Angeles Local 776 and New York Local 551. The group's stated objectives and purposes are "to advance the art and science of the film editing profession; to increase the entertainment value of motion pictures by attaining pre-eminence and scientific achievement in the creative art of film editing; to bring into close alliance those Film Editors who desire to advance the prestige and dignity of the film editing profession." Members are permitted to use the initials "A.C.E." after their names for screen credit purposes.

The society was first discussed by a small group of editors on October 26, 1950, formal plans for its creation were made on November 28, 1950, and the first general membership meeting took place on January 9, 1951. American Cinema Editors publishes a newsletter, *Cinemeditor,* and presents annual awards, Eddies, for best-edited features, documentaries, television episodes, and television specials.

Address: 1041 N. Formosa Avenue, Los Angeles, Calif. 90046.

AMERICAN CONGRESS OF EXHIBITORS. See COMPO

AMERICAN CORRESPONDENT FILM COMPANY, INC., was formed in mid–1915 to produce films of the war in Europe. President M. B. Clausson planned to arrange for his newspapers to hire halls in various cities in which to screen the films. He had cameramen and correspondents at the German-Austrian war fronts, the Italian frontier, and the German front. The company's "factory" was located in Stamford, Connecticut, and it had offices in the Candler Building at 222 West 42 Street, New York. Its first film, *The Battle and Fall of Przemsyl,* was released in August 1915. According to Terry Ramsaye, in *A Million and One Nights* (p. 690), the company later admitted having made an arrangement to propagandize for Germany and Austria, and after the United States entered the war, some officials of the company were sentenced to prison terms for violation of war laws.

BIBLIOGRAPHY

"American Correspondent Film Company, Inc." *The Moving Picture World,* July 3, 1915, p. 67.

Dopperen, Ron van. "Shooting the Great War: Albert Dawson and the American Correspondent Film Company, 1914–1918." *Film History,* vol. 4, no. 2, 1990, pp. 123–29.

AMERICAN DOCUMENTARY FILMS. See FRONTIER FILMS

AMERICAN EXHIBITORS' ASSOCIATION (AEA) was a short-lived offshoot of the Motion Picture Exhibitors' League of America (MPELA)*, formed in August 1917 by 85 delegates to the MPELA's convention when they felt they were not getting a fair deal from president Lee Ochs. The president of the AEA was Jack Wells and general manager was Charles Pettijohn. The AEA fought to end the system whereby exhibitors were required to make an advance deposit for films that they wished to screen.

BIBLIOGRAPHY

"Exhibitors Form New Association." *The Moving Picture World,* August 21, 1917, p. 798.

THE AMERICAN FEDERATION OF ARTS, founded in 1909, is a nonprofit, national museum service, intended to broaden the knowledge and appreciation of the arts of the past and present. It has produced a number of traveling programs devoted to film as art.

Address: 41 East 65th Street, New York, N.Y. 10021.

THE AMERICAN FILM FOUNDATION is a nonprofit, educational media corporation, founded in 1974 by Frieda Lee Mock and Terry Sanders. Its first production was *Copland Portrait* (1975), a 30-minute documentary on composer Aaron Copland. The American Film Foundation has produced the Emmy Award-winning *Lillian Gish: The Actor's Life for Me* (1988); the Oscar-nominated short subjects *Rose Kennedy: A Life to Remember* (1990) and *Never Give Up: The 20th Century Odyssey of Herbert Zipper* (1995), and the Academy Award-winning feature *Maya Lin: A Strong Clear Vision* (1994).

Address: 1333 Ocean Avenue, Santa Monica, Calif. 90401.

AMERICAN FILM INSTITUTE. On September 29, 1965, President Lyndon B. Johnson signed the National Arts and Humanities Act, at which time he announced plans for the creation of an American Film Institute. However, it was not until June 5, 1967, that the Institute was founded as a nonprofit, nongovernmental corporation, with headquarters in Washington, D.C. The Institute's basic premise was "to advance and preserve the art of the moving image."

With establishing grants from the National Council of the Arts, the Ford Foundation, and the Motion Picture Association of America, the Institute allocated (on December 11, 1967) $1.2 million for a nitrate film rescue program, established (on January 23, 1968) a $500,000 production fund for student and independent filmmakers, announced (on April 3, 1968) the commencement of a National Film Catalog project, and financed (on June 15, 1968) an oral history program in film begun by UCLA.

The most promoted of the Institute's activities is its film preservation program, whereby films are preserved in the National Film Collection at the Library of Congress. The Institute has no film archives itself and, in recent years, only a minute portion of its budget has actually been spent on film preservation. In reality, it siphons money received from the National Endowment for the Arts to the various American organizations active in film preservation.

In September 1969, the Institute's Center for Advanced Film Studies, located at the Greystone Mansion in Beverly Hills, became operational. The Center initially accepted both filmmaking and research fellows, but for more than a decade now has limited its activities to working with independent and young filmmakers. A Directing Workshop for Women was created in 1974, and the Center also receives funding from the Academy of Motion Picture Arts and Sciences* for a chair in screenwriting. In August 1980, the Institute purchased the former Immaculate Heart College campus in Hollywood, and, on October 3, 1980, it was opened as the new headquarters for the Center, officially known as the American Film Institute-West.

The National Film Catalog project has as its aim the documentation of all American films from the 1890s onward.

Catalogs documenting the beginnings, the teens, twenties, thirties, forties, and sixties have already been published.

The oral history program continued for a number of years, with funding from the Louis B. Mayer Foundation, but is no longer pursued by the Institute.

On March 3, 1973, the American Film Institute presented the first of its Life Achievement Awards to John Ford, at a ceremony attended by President Richard Nixon, a presence that resulted in much negative comment and picketing. Thanks to its television coverage, the Life Achievement Award has become the best known of the Institute's activities. Second in importance to the Award was the Institute's journal, *American Film*, (1975–1992).

George Stevens, Jr., was the founding director of the Institute. He resigned in 1979 to become its co-chairman with Charlton Heston—Gregory Peck was the Institute's first chairman of the Board of Trustees—and on January 1, 1980, Jean Firstenberg became the Institute's new director.

The American Film Institute has long been the subject of much controversy and adverse publicity. There have been frequent complaints that it is too much concerned with self-promotion and little interested in performing any of the functions—particularly film preservation—for which it actively seeks funding. Its Education Department has repeatedly been closed down and its staff fired. George Stevens, Jr., was severely criticized in 1972 for utilizing $300,000 of the Center's production budget for an unreleased feature film titled *In Pursuit of Treasure*. Stevens came under even stronger fire in 1973, when he cancelled one of the opening films at the Institute's new AFI Theatre at the Kennedy Center. The film was *State of Siege,* which Stevens denounced as rationalizing assassination. As a result of Stevens's action, many filmmakers withdrew their films from the opening program.

National Film Day, first held on October 23, 1973, was organized to raise funds for the Institute's activities, but it proved to be a disastrous failure and was cancelled after a few years. The Institute has repeatedly had problems in funding its various programs. Sustaining grants from both the Ford Foundation and the Motion Picture Association of America* ended in 1974, and in December of that year Congress voted against direct federal funding, forcing the Institute to apply, as must other organizations, for funds from the National Endowment for the Arts.

According to its various publicity brochures, "the American Film Institute is concerned with the motion picture in American life—in theatres, homes, libraries, classrooms and wherever films are found. To bring cinema to its fullest stature in the country of its birth, to preserve, stimulate, enrich and nurture the art of film in America—these are the Institute's goals." There are many who would question if the American Film Institute has achieved much progress toward such goals.

Addresses: John F. Kennedy Center for the Performing Arts, Washington, D.C. 20566; 2021 North Western Avenue, Hollywood, Calif. 90027.

BIBLIOGRAPHY

The American Film Institute. *The First Ten Years.* Washington, D.C.: The Author, 1977.

Farber, Stephen. "Alienation and Success for AFI." *Los Angeles Times Calendar*, September 2, 1973, pp. 1, 16, 22–23.

Gold, Ronald. "Rundown of Issues under Dispute, American Film Institute vs. Dissenters." *Variety,* July 7, 1971, pp. 13, 21.

Harmetz, Aljean. "Custodian for Cinema Culture." *Show,* August 20, 1970, pp. 16–19.

"The Journal Looks at AFI and other Film Institutes." *Journal of the Producers Guild of America* (September 1967), entire issue.

McBride, Joseph, ed. *Filmmakers on Filmmaking: The American Film Institute Seminars on Motion Pictures and Television.* Los Angeles: J. P. Tarcher, 1983.

McCarty, Todd. "George Stevens Jr. Reviews 12 Years of AFI Progress." *Daily Variety,* January 22, 1980, pp. 12, 15.

Shales, Tom, ed. *The American Film Heritage: Impressions from the American Film Institute Archives.* Washington, D.C.: Acropolis Books, 1972.

Stevens, George, Jr.. "About the American Film Institute." *Film Quarterly,* Winter 1971–72, pp. 36–42.

Yoffe, Emily. "Popcorn Politics." *Harper's,* December 1983, pp. 17–22.

AMERICAN FILM MANUFACTURING COMPANY. The announcement of the formation of the American Film Manufacturing Company appeared in the October 8, 1910, edition of *The Moving Picture World.* Organized by exchangemen John R. Freuler, Harry E. Aitken, Charles J. Hite, and Samuel S. Hutchinson to furnish their exchanges* with films after the Motion Picture Patents Company* cut off their supply, American—with headquarters in Chicago—succeeded in snatching players and staff of the nearest member of the Patents Company, Essanay Film Manufacturing Company*, thus acquiring such players as J. Warren Kerrigan and Dot Farley; scenarist Allan Dwan; directors Thomas Ricketts, Sam Morris, and Frank Beal; technical expert Charles Ziebath; and executives Aubrey M. Kennedy and Gilbert P. Hamilton. With a "Flying A" as its symbol and nickname, American copied Essanay's product and established three companies making comedies, dramas, and Westerns*. Frank Beal took a company West in the spring of 1911. Dwan followed and relieved Beal of directorial duties, as it located in San Juan Capistrano, later in La Mesa, California, and, finally, in June 1912, in an abandoned ostrich farm in Santa Barbara. American made two reels per week at this time.

In June 1912, American joined Harry Aitken's newly formed Mutual Film Corporation* and began producing its entire output in Santa Barbara. Early in 1913 American built a well-equipped studio on Mission and Chapala streets in

Santa Barbara, and according to cameraman Roy Overbaugh, this was the first time a glass stage was used on the West Coast for staging interior scenes. Wallace Reid began directing society dramas in 1913, and, when Dwan left in May 1913, Lorimer Johnston became the leading director. In January 1914, American began releasing the weekly "Beauty" brand of comedies. When the Santa Barbara Motion Picture Company*, a neighbor newly formed by Aubrey M. Kennedy and former Santa Barbara mayor Elmer J. Boeseke, hired away Johnston, Overbaugh, and assistant cameraman Victor Fleming in mid–1914, Sydney Ayres became American's chief director.

American made its first feature film, *The Quest,* with Margarita Fischer, directed by her husband Harry Pollard, in 1915, and it was soon followed by its first serial, *The Diamond from the Sky,* with Lottie Pickford, directed by Jacques Jaccard and William Desmond Taylor. In the next year, American added more brands, including "Vogue" comedies, "Mustang" Westerns, and "Clipper" dramas, starring Harold Lockwood and May Allison. In 1917, American began producing features exclusively and became Mutual's chief producer, with its stars Mary Miles Minter, William Russell, and Margarita Fisher (who dropped the Germanic "c" after the United States entered the First World War).

When Mutual ended in mid–1918, American began distributing through Pathé*. The number of its productions decreased until Fisher left the company in 1921, after which it soon disbanded.

Other directors of note with American were Lloyd Ingraham, Henry King, Frank Borzage, and Edward Sloman.

BIBLIOGRAPHY

"The American Studio." *The Moving Picture World,* July 10, 1915, p. 255.
"American's Santa Barbara Plant." *The Moving Picture World,* February 8, 1913, p. 559.
Birchard, Robert S. "Roy Overbaugh, ASC." *American Cinematographer,* May 1984, pp. 34–38.
Lyons, Timothy J. *The Silent Partner: The History of the American Film Manufacturing Company 1910–1921.* New York: Arno Press, 1974.

AMERICAN FILM MARKET, held in Los Angeles each spring, is a showcase and sales market for primarily English-language films, attended by more than 1,000 distributors from more than 60 countries. It was first held March 21–31, 1981.

Address: 12424 Wilshire Boulevard, Suite 600, Los Angeles, Calif. 90025.

AMERICAN FILM THEATRE. The American Film Theatre project was conceived in 1972 by Ely A. Landau (1920–1993), working in association with American Express Films and the Ely Landau Organization. Landau's idea was to provide "a national theatre on film," offering screen versions of major contemporary stage classics to film audiences on a subscription basis. Each film would be produced at a minimal cost of $750,000, with directors, stars, and production staff working at minimum rates. Four hundred and fifty American theatres were signed to participate in the first season of films, 1973/1974, which consisted of *The Iceman Cometh, Rhinoceros, The Homecoming, A Delicate Balance, Luther, Butley, Lost in the Stars,* and *Three Sisters.*

Unfortunately, the concept was not successful. Critics considered the idea neither film nor theatre and were basically negative in their comments. Further, the subscription idea meant that theatres were required to set aside one or two days a month for the American Film Theatre productions, and the major film distributors made it very clear that they would boycott those theatres that elected to interrupt the run of one of their films for an American Film Theatre presentation.

Despite problems and the loss of 35 percent of participating theatres, a second season was presented for 1974/1975, consisting of *The Maids, The Man in the Glass Booth, Galileo, Jacques Brel Is Alive and Well and Living in Paris,* and *In Celebration.* In June 1975, Landau announced a year's intermission for the American Film Theatre, and the concept was never revived. Worldwide distribution rights to the features were subsequently acquired by Telepictures Corporation.

BIBLIOGRAPHY

Kerr, Walter. "The Score is Theatre 7, Movies 1." *The New York Times,* April 7, 1974, section 2, pp. 1, 15.
McKee, Allen. "Will These 'New Era' Movies Bring Out the Snob in You?" *The New York Times,* October 28, 1973, p. D13.
Pennington, Ron. "Ely Landau Reveals Details of American Film Theatre." *The Hollywood Reporter,* April 21, 1972, pp. 1, 3.
Rich, Frank. "A Discouraging Word or Two about the American Film Theatre." *New Times,* December 14, 1975, pp. 60–61.

AMERICAN FOTOFONE COMPANY. See POWERS COMPANY

AMERICAN GENERAL PICTURES was a poverty row* production company, founded by David L. Hewitt. Its first film was *Spider Baby* (1964) and its last, *Fiend with the Electronic Brain* (1969). It ceased operations in 1970.

BIBLIOGRAPHY

Ray, Fred Olen. *The New Poverty Row: Independent Filmmakers as Distributors.* Jefferson, N.C.: McFarland, 1991.

AMERICAN INDEPENDENT PRODUCTIONS, INC., was a poverty row* production company, founded in 1986 by Fred Olen Ray. Its first film was *The Phantom Empire* (1986) and its last, *Demon Cop* (1991).

BIBLIOGRAPHY

Ray, Fred Olen. *The New Poverty Row: Independent Film-makers as Distributors*. Jefferson, N.C.: McFarland, 1991.

AMERICAN INTERNATIONAL PICTURES (AIP) began as American Releasing Corporation in 1954, founded by James H. Nicholson (1916–1972) and Samuel Z. Arkoff (born 1918) with $3,000. Their announced plans were to release eight films in 1955, to be sold either as a block or film by film. In March 1956, American Releasing changed its name to American International Pictures and announced a schedule of 14 films to be delivered by five independent producers, among whom was Roger Corman.

AIP's films were sold for flat fees to exhibitors since they were invariably relegated to the bottom half of double bills. To combat this problem and to increase its rentals, AIP decided to send its films out as paired double bills. The company started this policy in 1956, with *The Day the World Ended* and *The Phantom from 10,000 Leagues*. The success of the idea led other companies to copy AIP; as a result, it was in danger of losing its share of the market. In 1959 the company decided it would have to distribute more expensive films if it was to compete with other releasing organizations and so decided to make its films in color and CinemaScope*. *The House of Usher* (1960) was the first film to be made after this change in policy, and it was the first AIP film to play by itself at most theatres and to be booked on a percentage basis.

The cycle of horror films based on the Edgar Allen Poe stories was a success for the company and was followed in 1963 by a cycle of teen films beginning with *Beach Party*. The company was successful enough that, in February 1964, it was planning to produce a television series based on *Beach Party* and was also thinking of purchasing theatres around the country. The latter did not happen, but in November 1965 AIP did set up Trans American Films to distribute its foreign and art features.

In 1966, thanks to the success of *The Wild Angels* (1966), it started a cycle of protest films. Business was going so well that, in March 1966, AIP purchased an office building in Beverly Hills, which became its corporate headquarters. In June 1969, after many years of refusing to consider the idea, Nicholson and Arkoff took the company public.

In January 1972 Nicholson resigned as president to become an independent producer. In June of that same year, Arkoff became president as well as chairman of the board. The company continued to be profitable, and in 1974 it took over distributing the films of Cinerama*.

In 1975, Arkoff announced plans to change the philosophy of AIP and to begin the production of big-budget films costing between $3 and $4 million each. In that same year the company reported profits of $3.5 million, the best ever.

Plans were announced for a merger with Filmways*, the reasons having to do with the need for more money to fund the big-budget films that AIP was making and wished to make. The merger was called off in December 1978, but talks began again in March 1979. In May 1979, AIP announced the first loss—$1.5 million—in its history, and, in July 1979, it merged with Filmways.

BIBLIOGRAPHY

American International Pictures: Twenty-Five Years. New York: Museum of Modern Art, 1979.
Arkoff, Sam, and Richard Trubo. *Flying through Hollywood by the Seat of My Pants*. New York: Carol, 1992.
Harmetz, Aljean. *Rolling Breaks and Other Movie Breaks*. New York: Alfred A. Knopf, 1983.
McGee, Mark Thomas. *Faster and Furiouser: The Revised and Fattened Fable of American International Pictures*. Jefferson, N.C.: McFarland, 1996.
Ottoson, Robert L. *American International Pictures: A Filmography*. New York: Garland, 1985.

AMERICAN MUTOSCOPE AND BIOGRAPH COMPANY. See BIOGRAPH COMPANY

AMERICAN MUTOSCOPE COMPANY. See BIOGRAPH COMPANY

AMERICAN NATIONAL ENTERPRISES. See JENSEN-FARLEY PICTURES, INC.

AMERICAN RELEASING CORPORATION. See AMERICAN INTERNATIONAL PICTURES

AMERICAN SOCIETY OF CINEMATOGRAPHERS. In 1913, a group of West Coast cameramen formed a group called The Static Club of America*, which published a newspaper-style journal, titled *Static Flashes,* and which served as a meeting place for the exchange of ideas. The Static Club was disbanded in 1918, and a group of its members—Charles Rosher, Arthur Edeson, Victor Milner, L. Guy Wilky, Philip Rosen, Homer Scott, William Foster, Dal Clawson, Eugene Gaudio, Walter Griffin, Roy Klaffki, Joseph August, Fred Granville, Deveral Jennings, and Robert Newhard—founded a new organization, the American Society of Cinematographers, which was incorporated on January 18, 1919.

The Society's motto, "Loyalty, Progress, and Artistry," sums up the aims and ideals of the organization, membership in which is by invitation only. The initials "ASC" after a cinematographer's name indicates that he or she is a member of the Society; it is generally considered a mark of quality. Since November 1, 1920, the Society has published *American Cinematographer;* it maintains a museum in its clubhouse and, in recent years, has embarked on a publication program. The American Society of Cinematographers provides monthly meetings for its members, at which the latest developments in all aspects of film and television production are discussed. It is the oldest extant motion picture organization in Los Angeles.

Address: 1782 North Orange Drive, Hollywood, Calif. 90028.

BIBLIOGRAPHY

Broening, H. Lyman. "How It All Happened." *American Cinematographer,* November 1, 1921, p. 13.

Mitchell, George. "The ASC Is an Honor Society, Not a Trade Union, of Cinematographers." *Films in Review.* August-September 1967, pp. 385–97.

"Six Decades of 'Loyalty, Progress, Artistry'." *American Cinematographer.* June 1979, pp. 576–77, 580–81, 600–601.

Williams, Whitney. "Society of Cinematographers Marks 50 Years of Achievement." *Daily Variety.* January 17, 1969, pp. 10, 16.

AMERICAN TALKING-PICTURE COMPANY. See KINETOPHONE

AMERICAN WOMAN FILM COMPANY, financially backed almost entirely by wealthy society women of Los Angeles, was formed in May 1916 to produce ten-reel features. Mrs. Mary Whitney Emerson was president. J. Farrell MacDonald was to be in charge of production at a studio located at 1339 Gordon Street in Hollywood, with the first film to be *Saul of Tarsus.* As far as can be ascertained, the company did not actually produce any films.

BIBLIOGRAPHY

"Women Start Something." *The Moving Picture World.* May 27, 1916, p. 1515.

AMERICAN ZOETROPE. See ZOETROPE

AMKINO CORPORATION. See ARTKINO PICTURES, INC.

ANAGLYPHIC PROCESS. See THREE-DIMENSIONAL FILMS

ANALYSIS FILM RELEASING was a New York-based distributor, founded by president Paul E. Cohen, Robert J. Kaplan, and banker Paul Leeman. Its releases included such diverse foreign titles as *My Brilliant Career* (1979) and *Caligula* (1980). The company gained some notoriety in 1981, when it threatened legal action against the *Los Angeles Times* for its refusal to print an advertisement for its horror release, *Maniac.* Also in 1981, Analysis formed a production unit, Grand Slam. The company ceased operations in the mid eighties.

"ANDY HARDY" SERIES. Arguably the most popular, the most commercially successful, and the most wholesome group of films ever produced in the history of the American motion picture, the "Andy Hardy" series began in 1937 with *A Family Affair,* based on the 1928 play, *Skidding,* by Mrs. Aurania Rouverol. In that first film, Andy Hardy's father, Judge Hardy, was played by Lionel Barrymore, his mother by Spring Byington, Andy Hardy by Mickey Rooney, Aunt Milly by Sara Haden, and Marian Hardy by Cecilia Parker. Only the last three continued in the series, with Judge Hardy subsequently played by Lewis Stone and Mrs. Hardy by Fay Holden. George Seitz directed all but three films in the series, and the scripts were generally by Kay Van Riper, William Ludwig, and Agnes Christine Johnston.

Set in Carvel, Idaho, the films were concerned with Andy Hardy's exploits. Judy Garland was featured in three of the films, *Love Finds Andy Hardy, Andy Hardy Meets a Debutante,* and *Life Begins for Andy Hardy.* Lana Turner was featured in *Love Finds Andy Hardy.* Ostensibly the series ended in 1946, with *Love Laughs at Andy Hardy,* but a final film, *Andy Hardy Comes Home,* was released in 1958, with Mickey Rooney, Fay Holden, Sara Haden, and Cecilia Parker essaying their former roles. The following is a complete list of all the films in the series, all of which were produced and released by M-G-M*: *A Family Affair* (1937), *You're Only Young Once* (1937), *Judge Hardy's Children* (1938), *Love Finds Andy Hardy* (1938), *Out West with the Hardys* (1938), *The Hardys Ride High* (1939), *Andy Hardy Gets Spring Fever* (1939), *Judge Hardy and Son* (1939), *Andy Hardy Meets a Debutante* (1940), *Andy Hardy's Private Secretary* (1941), *Life Begins for Andy Hardy* (1941), *Courtship of Andy Hardy* (1942), *Andy Hardy's Double Life* (1942), *Andy Hardy's Blonde Trouble* (1944), *Love Laughs at Andy Hardy* (1946), and *Andy Hardy Comes Home* (1958).

BIBLIOGRAPHY

Jordan, Don, and Edward Connor. "Judge Hardy and Family." *Films in Review,* January 1974, pp. 1–10.

APOGEE, INC., was formed in September 1978 by a group of special effects experts, led by John Dykstra, who had first come together to work on *Star Wars.* The first major project on which Apogee worked was *Battlestar Galactica* (1979). In 1989, following the bankruptcy of FilmDallas* the previous year, Sam Grogg and Ernest G. Fausto joined Apogee to form the independent production company, Magic Pictures, Inc. Dykstra closed his company in 1993 and went on to work independently on productions such as *Batman Forever* (1995).

APOLLO PICTURES, INC., was incorporated late in 1916. Harry R. Raver was its president. It was affiliated with Art Dramas, Inc.*, a combination of independent producers modeled on Metro Pictures Corporation's* system of distribution.

Apollo's first film, *The God of Little Children* (1917), starred Alma Hanlon and was directed by Richard Ridgley. In 1917, Apollo leased the Solax* plant at Fort Lee*, New Jersey. Stars appearing in Apollo productions included Bigelow Cooper and Viola Dana, who made *Rosie O'Grady* in 1917 under the direction of John H. Collins.

AQUARIUS RELEASING, INC., founded by Terry Levene in 1971, distributes primarily exploitation fare.

Address: 321 West 45th Street, 9th Floor, New York, N.Y. 10036.

ARGOSY PICTURES CORPORATION was John Ford's production company—he was its chairman of the board and Merian C. Cooper was its president—during the late forties and early fifties. Argosy produced *Mighty Joe Young* (1949), directed by Ernest B. Schoedsack, and seven John Ford features: *The Fugitive* (1947), *Fort Apache* (1948), *3 Godfathers* (1948), *She Wore a Yellow Ribbon* (1949), *Wagon Master* (1949), *Rio Grande* (1950), and *The Quiet Man* (1952).

ARMY PICTORIAL CENTER/SERVICE. See ASTORIA STUDIOS

AROMARAMA AND SMELL-O-VISION were two systems introduced in the 1959–1960 period, whereby theatre patrons could smell a film as well as see and hear it. AromaRama basically utilized a theatre's existing air-conditioning system to filter smells to the audience, while Smell-o-Vision required the installation of piping to bring the smells to individual seats.

AromaRama was invented by Charles Weiss in 1958 and the system cost between $3,500 and $7,500 to install in individual theatres. Its scents were developed by Rhodia, Inc., and the air purification system necessary to remove each odor was created by American Statronic Corporation. The first, and last, feature in AromaRama was *Behind the Great Wall,* a documentary on China, which received its New York premiere at the Mayfair Theatre on December 2, 1959.

Smell-o-Vision, initially called Scentovision, was created by a Swiss osmologist, Professor Hans Laube, who demonstrated it to showman Mike Todd in 1954. The system was explained in the February 1960 issue of *American Cinematographer:*

The heart of the process is an electrically controlled dispensing machine which acts as the "smell-brain." Made of stainless steel, specially treated rubber, and glass, it looks like something out of an Atomic plant. Installed in the depths of the theatre, this mechanical monster is equipped with a series of metal vials containing essences of every aroma to be projected during the run of the film. It also has a central panel with a bank of dials for regulating the concentration of odors.

The machine begins to operate as soon as the projectionist starts the 70mm* picture print running through the projector. A precisely synchronized separate track cued with electronic signals for each odor triggers the smell mechanism and the almost-human machine moves into action selecting in order and dispensing over 30 different scents from the circular tray of vials.

The process was utilized for only one feature, *Scent of Mystery,* first screened at the Cinestage, Chicago, on January 12, 1960, and which was subsequently released, without Smell-o-Vision, as *Holiday in Spain.*

Neither process was greeted with much enthusiasm by the general public, and contemporary reports indicate that the major problem was disposing of one smell from the auditorium before the arrival of the next.

BIBLIOGRAPHY

Alpert, Hollis."Aromatics." In *The Dream and the Dreamers.* New York: Macmillan, 1962, pp. 178–81.
Lightman, Herb A. "The Movie Has Scents!" *American Cinematographer,* February 1960, pp. 92–93, 120.
"Nose Opera." *Time,* February 29, 1960, p. 98.

ARROW FILM CORPORATION began its existence in July 1915 as a producer for the Pathé* Exchange. It made the *Who Is Guilty?* series, featuring Emmy Wehlen, and a five-reel feature with baseball star Mike Donlin titled *Right Off the Bat*. In late 1915 it reorganized and incorporated in Virginia with a capitalization of $350,000. Arrow contracted with Pathé to produce ten five-reel Gold Rooster features a year. W. E. Shallenberger was the president and Albert S. Le Vino was the head of the scenario department. In 1916, it was producing five-reel features, seven- and eight-reel specials, and serials. Henry Cronjager was the chief cameraman at this time.

By the late part of the second decade of the twentieth century, Arrow was a distributor of films for the states rights* market. It remained active through the mid-twenties.

ART CINEMA CORPORATION was formed by Joseph M. Schenck (1877–1961) in July 1926 to take over his earlier Art Finance Corporation, a financial entity that in turn had organized Feature Productions, Inc. (Both Art Finance and Feature Productions were created in 1925 and were responsible for three features, *The Eagle* [1925], *The Bat* [1926], and *The Son of the Sheik* [1926]). In existence through 1933, Art Cinema Corporation produced a number of features at what became known as the Samuel Goldwyn Studios in Hollywood, among which were *Topsy and Eva* (1927), *The Beloved Rogue* (1927), *Lady of the Pavements* (1929), *Lummox* (1930), *Be Yourself* (1930), *Abraham Lincoln* (1930), *The Bat Whispers* (1931), *Kiki* (1931), *Street Scene* (1931), *Rain* (1932), and *Hallelujah, I'm a Bum* (1933).

BIBLIOGRAPHY

Balio, Tino. *United Artists*. Madison, Wis.: University of Wisconsin Press, 1976.

ARTCLASS PICTURES CORP. was a New York-based producer/distributor, active intermittently from 1922 to 1932. It was founded initially by three brothers, Adolph, Max, and Louis Weiss.

ARTCOLOR PICTURES COMPANY was formed in April 1918 to market and produce films by L. J. Dittmar, the president of the Majestic Amusement Company of Louisville, who earlier was active in the Kinemacolor Company* and was one of the incorporators of the Natural Color Picture Company. With offices at 1600 Broadway in New York, the company planned to build a manufacturing plant at Whitestone, Long Island, to produce its own features and educational shorts or to cooperate in the production of other manufacturers' films. The company claimed to use a new color process, perfected by W. Francis Fox and A. G. Waddington of England, based on the Kinemacolor* process, which used no dyes or coloring matters but rather involved chemical reaction on the film's emulsion; projection of the films could be accomplished using standard equipment.

BIBLIOGRAPHY

"L. J. Dittmar Forming New Company." *The Moving Picture World,* April 13, 1918, p. 227.
"New Color Concern Starts Work on Commercial Lines." *The Moving Picture World,* January 25, 1919, p. 481.

ARTCO PRODUCTIONS, INC., entered the producing field in February 1919, after producer Harry Raver received an option from author Augustus Thomas for the rights to some of his old plays and a contract for Thomas to write a series of original screenplays. Raver called the resulting films "Four Star Productions," to emphasize the four essential production elements: author, star, director, and producer. Artco's first production, *As a Man Thinks*, was directed by George Irving and starred Leah Baird, whose husband, Arthur Beck, was an executive with the company. When Raver left the company in August 1919, four old plays by Thomas stayed with Artco, while Raver kept the rights to one new play. In September 1919, Artco took out a long lease on the Kalem* studios.

BIBLIOGRAPHY

"Four Star Combination Enters Field." *The Moving Picture World,* February 15, 1919, p. 874.

ART DIRECTION. The art director, along with the director of photography and the director, is ultimately responsible for the "look" of the film on which he is working, be it naturalistic or imaginative. He must have a basic understanding of the principles of architecture and painting and of cinematography. As Leo K. Kuter wrote in 1957, "An art director conceives, designs, and completes a film's settings with no thought other than to help tell the story in every way commensurate with the production values indicated in the budget." The art director's department will include set dressers and designers and scenic artists. The costume designer also works closely with the art director, and, indeed, during the silent era, many art directors were also responsible for the costume design on the film.

Wilfred Buckland is generally considered to have been America's first art director, having started his film career with the Jesse L. Lasky Feature Play Company early in the second decade of the twentieth century. Previous to Buckland's hiring, the "look" of the film was haphazardly decided by the director, the cinematographer, and the propman, taking into account whatever furnishings might be available. During the silent era, the art director was often referred to as the technical director. In the thirties, William Cameron Menzies or David O. Selznick introduced the title of production designer, implying that the art director's work in certain cases was on a par with that of the director, which in the case of William Cameron Menzies and director Sam Wood was undoubtedly true.

It was customary for the head of the art department to take credit for all of a studio's films, no matter which individual actually happened to be responsible for the art direction. Thus, the art director on M-G-M* films for almost three decades was always Cedric Gibbons, just as the art director on all Fox* and 20th Century-Fox* features was William Darling. In the fifties, there was a unique journal, *Production Design,* devoted to the art and craft of art direction and published by the Society of Motion Picture and Television Art Directors*.

Academy Awards have been given for art direction since their inception in 1927–1928, with the first award going to William Cameron Menzies for his work on *The Dove* and *Tempest.* From 1941 onward, the Art Direction Award has gone to both the art director and the set decorator (initially called the interior decorator).

BIBLIOGRAPHY

Affron, Charles, and Mirella Jona Affron. *Sets in Motion: Art Direction and Film Narrative.* New Brunswick, N.J.: Rutgers University Press, 1995.
Barsacq, Leon, and Elliot Stein. *Caligari's Cabinet and Other Grand Illusions.* Boston: New York Graphic Society, 1976.
Heisner, Beverly. *Hollywood Art: Art Direction in the Days of the Great Studios.* Jefferson, N.C.: McFarland, 1990.
Kuter, Leo K. "Art Direction." *Films in Review,* June–July 1957, pp. 248–58.

Larson, Orville, ed. *Scene Design for Stage and Screen.* East Lansing, Mich.: Michigan State University Press, 1961.

Lobrutto, Vincent. *By Design: Interviews with Film Production Designers.* New York: Praeger, 1992.

Marner, Terence St. John. *Film Design.* New York: A. S. Barnes, 1974.

Olson, Robert. *Art Direction for Film and Video.* Boston: Focal Press, 1993.

Sennett, Robert S. *Setting the Scene: The Great Hollywood Art Directors.* New York: Harry N. Abrams, 1994.

Surowiec, Catherine A. *Accent on Design: Four European Art Directors.* London: British Film Institute, 1992.

Thames Television Ltd. *The Art of Hollywood.* London: Thames Television, 1979.

Wiard, Preston. *What an Art Director Does: An Introduction to Motion Picture Production Design.* Los Angeles: Silman-James Press, 1994.

ART DRAMAS, INC., was a grouping of independent manufacturers formed in late 1916 to distribute 52 five-reel features a year. The production companies associated with Art Dramas included Apollo*, Van Dyke Film Productions Company, Erbograph*, and William L. Sherrill Feature Corporation. Sherrill was the company's first president, with Herbert Blaché its treasurer. With a distribution system patterned after that of Metro*, with direct cooperation between producers and the exchanges, Art Dramas announced it would emphasize stars and its primary concern would be with the storylines. Harry R. Raver became president of Art Dramas in 1917, resigning later that same year.

BIBLIOGRAPHY

"New Group of Independent Manufacturers." *The Moving Picture World,* October 7, 1916, p. 60.

ART FILM COMPANY, whose offices and studio were located at 25 and Lehigh avenues in Philadelphia, was formed in April 1915 to release to states rights* buyers one five-reel film a month, based on a popular book or play and with a well-known star. Broadway star Laura Nelson Hall appeared in the first film, *The Stubbornness of Geraldine,* with Marie Empress and Vernon Steele. Gaston Mervale was the general manager for all productions and William S. Forsythe was the chief cameraman.

ART FINANCE CORPORATION. See ART CINEMA CORPORATION

ART HOUSES. Although the art house or "little cinema" movement is said to have originated in France, there were art houses specializing in critically acclaimed films of an artistic or noncommercial nature as early as 1925 in the United States.

Symon Gould (who died in 1963 at the age of 70) founded the International Film Arts Guild in October 1925 and organized screenings on Sundays at the George M. Cohan and Central Theatres in New York City. In 1926, the International Film Arts Guild inaugurated regular screenings at the Cameo Theatre on 42nd Street. The Guild presented an Ernst Lubitsch retrospective, and, during 1926, screened *The Birth of a Nation, Intolerance, The Last Laugh,* and other classics. The last film to be screened at the Cameo under the sponsorship of the International Film Arts Guild was *Stark Love* on February 28, 1927. In 1927, Symon Gould founded the Film Guild Cinema at 52 West 8th Street in New York (now the 8th Street Playhouse) and two years later opened the Film Art Cinema (formerly the Regent Theatre) at 16 and Market streets in Philadelphia.

Michael Mindlin (who died in 1946 at the age of 54) was founder of the 5th Avenue Playhouse Group, nicknamed "The Aristocrats of the Cinema." He was managing director and founder of the 5th Avenue Playhouse at 66 Fifth Avenue, New York, which was designed by his wife, Betty. The theatre opened on October 9, 1926, with *The Cabinet of Dr. Caligari.* Mindlin also opened the 55th Street Playhouse in New York, on May 20, 1927 (and which changed its name in the early thirties to the Europa), and the Little Carnegie Playhouse on 57th Street in New York, which opened on November 2, 1928, with *Ten Days That Shook the World.* Mindlin also operated the St. George Theatre in Brooklyn, the Chicago Playhouse, the Buffalo Playhouse, and the Rochester Playhouse.

Nathan Machet's Motion Picture Guild opened the first art house in Washington, D.C., the Wardman Park Theatre, which was active from 1926 to 1929. The Film Mutual Benefit Bureau opened the Little Picture House, at 151 East 50th Street in New York, on December 23, 1929, with the British feature, *The Unwritten Law.* The Film Mutual Benefit Bureau also published *The Film Bulletin* from 1923 to 1929. Another organization of the art house movement was Film Associates, founded in 1925, which sponsored screenings at the Klaw Theatre in New York in the mid-twenties.

Art houses survive through the present, but they are as much concerned with the screening of popular revivals as with what may be classified as "art" films. Landmark Theatres of Southern California* and Laemmle Theatres* are two circuits that operate a number of art houses. In more recent years, the best-known art houses in New York have been the Bleeker Street Theatre, the Carnegie Hall Cinema, the New Yorker, and the Thalia; in Chicago, the Walnut Street Theatre; and in Washington, D.C., the Biograph, the Circle, and the Key theatres.

BIBLIOGRAPHY

Larkin, John, Jr. "The Guild Movie Is Here." *Theatre,* May 1926, pp. 32, 62.

Mindlin, Michael. "The Little Cinema Movement." *Theatre,* July 1928, pp. 18, 62.

Weinberg, Herman G. "The Fallacy of the 'Art' Theatre." *Motion Picture Herald,* March 30, 1935, pp. 75–76.

ARTHUR MAYER & JOSEPH BURSTYN, INC. See JOSEPH BURSTYN, INC.

ARTIC CITY STUDIOS opened in January 1919 at Port Henry in the Adirondacks for use by independent producers. Managed by Edward Small, Inc., the studio boasted a complete zoo of trained animals under the charge of Michael Schliesser.

BIBLIOGRAPHY

"Edward Small Agent for Artic City Studio." *Motion Picture News,* January 4, 1919, p. 102.

ARTKINO PICTURES, INC., was the official distributor of Soviet features, shorts, documentaries, and newsreels in both North and South America from 1940 through 1980. It was the successor to Amkino Corporation, founded in 1927 and official distributor of Soviet films in the United States through February 1940. Amkino imported 15 to 20 feature films a year, plus short subjects, and also acquired films for Soviet outlets. Artkino ceased operations when there became sufficient interest in Soviet films to warrant their release by any number of commercial American distributors.

BIBLIOGRAPHY

"Red Russia Liquidates Its U.S. Film Company." *Motion Picture Herald,* February 10, 1940, p. 16.

RESOURCES

Papers and Scripts: Museum of Modern Art.

ARTLEE. See LEE-BRADFORD CORPORATION

ASBURY PARK, NEW JERSEY. See Sawyer, Inc.

ASC. See AMERICAN SOCIETY OF CINEMATOGRAPHERS

ASPEN PRODUCTIONS, INC., was formed in the mid fifties by directors Robert Wise (born 1914) and Mark Robson (1913–1978). It produced only two films: Wise's *The Captive City* (1952) and Robson's *Return to Paradise* (1953).

THE ASSISTANCE LEAGUE OF SOUTHERN CALIFORNIA FILM BUREAU lined up private estates for location shooting, with fees going to specific charities. It closed down in April 1955 after 30 years of operation.

ASSOCIATED CINEMA STARS was a short-lived organization of early film personalities formed by J. Stuart Blackton in 1936. The group organized a dinner dance at the Los Angeles Biltmore Hotel in the summer of 1936, which was attended by D. W. Griffith, Clara Kimball Young, Agnes Ayres, Maurice Costello, Mrs. Wallace Reid, Florence Lawrence, and others.

BIBLIOGRAPHY

"Blackton Founds Organization of Screen Pioneers." *Motion Picture Herald,* September 5, 1936, p. 36.

ASSOCIATED DISTRIBUTORS PRODUCTIONS, INC., was a poverty row* production company, founded by Jerry Warren. Its first release was *Man Beast* (1956) and its last, *The Wild World of Batwoman* (1966). Production was sporadic, and in all, the company produced 13 films.

BIBLIOGRAPHY

Ray, Fred Olen. *The New Poverty Row: Independent Filmmakers as Distributors.* Jefferson, N.C.: McFarland, 1991.

ASSOCIATED FILM SALES CORPORATION. A group of eight West Coast manufacturers combined in mid–1915 under the name of "The Associated Service" (more formally known as Associated Film Sales Corporation) to distribute their own product. The companies involved were the Empire Film Manufacturing Company, Santa Barbara Motion Picture Company*, Liberty Film Company, Burke Film Manufacturing Company, Navajo Film Manufacturing Company*, Federal Film Company, and Alhambra Motion Picture Company*.

BIBLIOGRAPHY

"Associated Service Enters Field." *The Moving Picture World,* June 5, 1915, p. 1590.

ASSOCIATED FIRST NATIONAL PICTURES INCORPORATED. See FIRST NATIONAL PICTURES, INC.

ASSOCIATED INDEPENDENT MANUFACTURERS. See MOTION PICTURE DISTRIBUTING AND SALES COMPANY

ASSOCIATED MOTION PICTURE ADVERTISERS, INC. Active in the second and third decades of the twentieth century, Associated Motion Picture Advertisers, Inc., was formed August 2, 1916, "to voluntarily foster the interests of motion picture advertisers and to promote a more enlarged and friendly intercourse between persons connected with the business of advertising motion pictures and general motion picture advertisers and to reform abuses relative thereto; and to voluntarily diffuse accurate and reliable information affecting the standing of persons engaged in, and with reference to the conditions, customs and usages of the trade or business of motion picture advertising, as well as affecting and relating to the motion picture industry."

ASSOCIATED PICTURES, INC., was formed in June 1918 to produce, market, and exploit Ralph Ince Film Attractions, a series of "big" features based on stage successes and books by famous authors. Along with Ince, Arthur H. Sawyer, Herbert Lubin, and Louis Joseph Vance (who functioned as production analyst and writer) were involved.

BIBLIOGRAPHY

"Ralph Ince at Head of New Company." *The Moving Picture World,* June 8, 1918, p. 1417.

ASSOCIATED PRODUCERS, INC. On November 8, 1919, Thomas H. Ince announced the formation of Associated Producers, Inc., to organize a distribution chain of offices to handle the films made by himself, Maurice Tourneur, Allan Dwan, Mack Sennett, Marshall Neilan, and George Loane Tucker. The organization planned to take effect September 1920, when all the above producers would have been free of their present contracts. Ince was the president and Sennett was the treasurer. B. P. Schulberg and Walter Greene were rumored to have been involved with the formation of the company. All films were to be rented on an open-booking plan. The organization remained active through 1921.

ASSOCIATES & ALDRICH. See ALDRICH STUDIOS

ASTORIA STUDIOS. Located in the Astoria Section of the Queens Borough of New York, on Long Island, the Astoria Studios opened on September 20, 1920, as the new East Coast production center for Famous Players-Lasky (better known as Paramount*). More than 100 silent features were shot there—including all the Paramount films of D. W. Griffith and many of Gloria Swanson's productions—and the studio was also utilized for the testing of potential film personalities from the New York stage. In 1925, Jesse L. Lasky opened on the lot the Paramount Acting School, whose members included Charles "Buddy" Rogers and Thelma Todd, and the school's pupils were featured in a 1926 feature, *Fascinating Youth,* directed by Sam Wood and also filmed at Astoria.

Astoria closed briefly in 1927 but was reopened a year later, and among the early Paramount sound features filmed on the lot were *The Letter, Glorifying the American Girl, The Cocoanuts, and Applause,* all released in 1929. In the thirties, the studio was utilized as an independent production center, and among the films shot there were *The Emperor Jones* (1933) and the Ben Hecht–Charles MacArthur features of 1934–1936. The last two features of the thirties to be filmed at Astoria were *Backdoor to Heaven* and *One Third of a Nation* (both released by Paramount in 1939).

Between 1940 and 1946, Astoria was taken over by the War Department and became the U.S. Army Pictorial Center, at which worked directors such as Frank Capra, George Cukor, and John Huston and at which such mundane series as the *Army-Navy Screen Magazine* were produced. The U.S. Army Pictorial Service continued to utilize Astoria through 1970, although from 1946 onward it was also available as a rental facility.

In 1976, a nonprofit organization, the Astoria Motion Picture and Television Center Foundation, was created to take over the studio, and *Thieves* (1977) became the first commercial feature to be made at Astoria since before the Second World War. Among other films shot at Astoria were *The Wiz* (1977), *Hair* (1979), *All That Jazz* (1979), *Eyewitness* (1981), *Arthur* (1981), *Author, Author* (1982), *The World According to Garp* (1982), and *Daniel* (1983).

In addition to operating as a major East Coast studio facility, Astoria also offers a regular screening program of classic and important new films and has announced plans for the opening of a museum devoted to East Coast motion picture and television production.

The studios are also known as the Kaufman Astoria Studios, after its chairman of the board, George S. Kaufman.

Address: 34–31 35th Street, Astoria, N.Y. 11106.

BIBLIOGRAPHY

Brady, Frank. "Astoria Lives Again." *American Film,* December 1979, pp. 42–48.
Koszarski, Richard. *The Astoria Studio and Its Fabulous Films.* New York: Dover, 1983.
Krista, Charlene. "Kaufman Astoria Studios." *Films in Review,* August/September 1985, pp. 398–403.
Reilly, Charles Phillips. "Astoria Film Studio." *Films in Review,* January 1976, pp. 59–60.

ASTOR PICTURES CORPORATION advertised itself as "where all the big major company releases go for reissue," and it is for its reissue of such classic films as *Tumbleweeds* (1925, reissued 1939), *Hell's Angels* (1930), *The Bat Whispers* (1931), *Front Page* (1931), *Street Scene* (1931), *Scarface* (1932), and *Rain* (1932) that the company is best remembered. Formed in 1925, Astor also released many new features and short subjects. In the thirties, it operated three subsidiary companies, Vigilant Pictures Corporation, B 'n' B Film Corporation, and Promotional Films, Inc., and in 1936 formed a Hollywood production company, Astor Productions, Inc. In the fifties, Astor formed Atlantic Television Corporation to sell its product to television. The New York-based corporation was headed by Robert M. Savini, until his death at the age of 71 in 1956. Astor Pictures was purchased by Franklin F. Bruder in 1959 and filed for bankruptcy on January 31, 1963.

ASTRA FILM CORPORATION. Louis J. Gasnier formed Astra Film Corporation as a producer of serials and comedies in March 1916 and became its president. George Baker was vice president, and George B. Seitz was secretary. Astra's productions were released through Pathé, and the company leased the Pathé Studios in Jersey City, New Jersey. In 1919, it purchased a studio on Verdugo Road in Glendale, California, which had formerly been occupied by the Diando Film Company*.

ATLANTIC RELEASING CORPORATION was founded in 1975 by Thomas J. Coleman and David Altschuler. It was initially a distributor, but following the success of its first production, *Valley Girl* (1983), Atlantic expanded heavily into the production field. In 1985, it created Clubhouse Pictures to produce and distribute family-oriented films. Originally located in Boston, the company moved to Los Angeles in 1987. In March 1989, Atlantic was acquired by Saffron Associates, Inc., and in July of the same year, it filed for Chapter XI bankruptcy protection with reported debts of $45 million. The company ceased operations, and in 1991, its library was taken over by Island Pictures*.

ATLANTIC TELEVISION CORPORATION. See ASTOR PICTURES CORPORATION

AVCO EMBASSY PICTURES CORPORATION. See EMBASSY COMMUNICATIONS

AVENUE PICTURES was founded in September 1987 by Cary Brokaw and Michael Eliasberg. Its first feature was *Pascali's Island* (1988).

Address: 11111 Santa Monica Boulevard, Los Angeles, Calif. 90025.

AYWON FILM CORPORATION. Nathan Hirsch, former general manager and president of Pioneer Film Corporation, formed Aywon Film Corporation in early 1919. He purchased 16 negatives of five-reel features, each of which he planned to distribute to states rights* exchanges after they were retitled and reedited, sometimes with new material shot and added. Its first film to be released was *The Eternal Penalty,* which was a reedited version of the 1915 Triumph Film Corporation production of *The Warning,* although Aywon in releasing the film made no mention of the earlier title. Aywon's offices were located at 729 Seventh Avenue in New York, and the company remained in existence through 1929. It is probably best remembered for its reissue of the D. W. Griffith Biograph* short subjects, many of which it managed to change from one- to two-reelers by the addition of lengthy and often unnecessary subtitles*.

AZTECA FILMS. Now defunct, Azteca Films was a leading American distributor of Mexican films from its inception in 1932. In the sixties, 90 percent of all Hispanic theatres in the United States were supplied by Azteca, but by 1985—at which time the company reported it controlled the rights to more than 5,000 Spanish-language films—the number had dropped to between 40 and 60 percent.

BACON-BACKER FILM CORPORATION, owned by George Backer, who supervised productions, and Gerald F. Bacon, began production on February 17, 1919. *The Havoc,* directed by Perry Vekroff, was its first production. The company's three-story studio was located at 230 West 38th Street, New York.

BALABAN & KATZ was the most successful of the early theatre chains, merging with the Paramount* theatres in 1925 to form the Publix Theatres Corporation*. The company was formed in 1916 when two brothers, Barney and Abraham "A. J." Balaban, linked their theatres with those of Sam Katz; the Balabans had opened their first nickelodeon theatre in Chicago in 1908, and Katz his first Chicago theatre in 1912. Balaban & Katz opened its first major theatre, the Central Park, in Chicago, on October 27, 1917, and it was the first mechanically air-cooled theatre in the world. The Central Park was followed in Chicago by the Riviera, the Tivoli, the Chicago, the Uptown, the Norshore, and the Oriental. From its Chicago base, the company expanded with the May 1924 acquisition of Midwest Theatres, with houses in Wisconsin and Illinois.

BIBLIOGRAPHY

Gomery, Douglas. *Shared Pleasures: A History of Movie Presentation in the United States.* Madison, Wis.: University of Wisconsin Press, 1992.

BALBOA AMUSEMENT PRODUCING COMPANY, with capital of $7,000, began work on May 23, 1913, at its studio located at 6th and Alamitos streets in Long Beach, California, a studio formerly utilized by J. Searle Dawley of the Edison Manufacturing Company*. H. M. Horkheimer, a former ticket seller for a circus, was president and general manager, while his brother, Elwood, was secretary and treasurer. In 1914, Balboa contracted to release all its films through Box Office Attractions Company*. In 1917, it claimed to have the largest glass studio in the industry.

William Desmond Taylor was with Balboa until November 1914. Henry B. Walthall and Ruth Roland made films for the company, some of which were released under the "Panama" brand. In 1917, it contracted with the General Film Company to produce Knickerbocker Star Features*. The Balboa studios were turned over to creditors on March 25, 1918, for liquidation, and early in 1919 the Master Pictures Corporation purchased the real estate, studio, and other company property.

BIBLIOGRAPHY

"Balboa Continues to Grow." *The Moving Picture World,* September 4, 1915, p. 1653.
"The Balboa Enterprise." *The Moving Picture World,* July 10, 1915, p. 245.
"Balboa's Plant Growing Steadily." *The Moving Picture World,* September 23, 1916, p. 1977.
Fernett, Gene. "Balboa Studios Brought Fame to Long Beach." *Classic Images,* no. 82, April 1982, pp. 50–51.

RESOURCES

Papers: Historical Society of Long Beach (scrapbook for 1913 and 1914).

BANANA PEEL PRATFALLS. The joke of an individual slipping on a discarded banana peel is a film cliché, but one that has not been used as much as might be imagined. In *By the Sea* (1915), Charlie Chaplin falls on a banana peel, which he has just thrown away, and in *The Pilgrim* (1923), both Chaplin and Mack Swain slip on a banana peel dropped by a young boy. *The Battle of the Century* (1927) involves extensive gags with Laurel and Hardy, originating with the pair's slipping on a banana peel. In *From Soup to Nuts* (1928), Oliver Hardy enters carrying a large cake and slips on a banana peel, and in *The Hollywood Revue of 1929* (1929), Hardy slips on a banana peel and somersaults into a gigantic cake. Harold Lloyd slips on a banana peel in *Feet First* (1930). In *Sleeper* (1973), Woody Allen has a gag with a giant banana peel.

BANK NIGHTS were introduced as a box office stimulant by theatres in the Depression era of the late twenties and early thirties. On these nights, patrons had the opportunity to win prizes for the price of an admission ticket. The concept of bank nights fell afoul of the law in the mid-thirties, with many states declaring them nothing more than illegal lotteries.

BANK OF AMERICA is the pioneering institution in the loan of funds for film production. It provided initial funding for the creation of Columbia Pictures*, Twentieth Century Pictures*, and Walt Disney Productions*, and has financed the films of many major Hollywood producers, including Charlie Chaplin, Samuel Goldwyn, David O. Selznick, and Walter Wanger. Between 1936 and 1949, it financed the production of some 330 feature films for a total cost in excess of $123 million. In April 1945, *Coronet* reported that Bank of America had loaned the film industry some $150 million.

Bank of America was founded in San Francisco in 1904 as the Bank of Italy by A. P. Giannini, who was soon joined in the enterprise by his brother, A. H. "Doc" Giannini (who served as vice president). It was A. H. Giannini who made the Bank's first film-related loan, supposedly in 1908, to future producer Sol Lesser. In 1919, Doc Giannini moved to New York to become president of the East River National Bank, at which he funded a number of film productions, including Chaplin's *The Kid* (1921). After taking over a number of New York banks, Doc Giannini merged his banking empire with Bank of Italy to create Bank of America, of which he became chairman. From 1936 to 1938, Doc Giannini served as president of United Artists*, with Bank of America making loans for the production of most of its releases.

Among the films financed by Bank of America are *The Best Years of Our Lives* (1946), *Cat Ballou* (1965), *Dr. Doolittle* (1967), *Dodsworth* (1936), *Fantasia* (1940), *Foreign Correspondent* (1940), *From Russia with Love* (1963), *Gone with the Wind* (1939), *It Happened One Night* (1934), *It's a Wonderful Life* (1946), *Lawrence of Arabia* (1962), *Macbeth* (1948), *Meet John Doe* (1941), *The Misfits* (1961), *Queen Kelly* (1928), *The Quiet Man* (1952), *Showboat* (1936), *Snow White and the Seven Dwarfs* (1937), *Stagecoach* (1939), *The Ten Commandments* (1923), *The Third Man* (1949), *West Side Story* (1961), and *Wuthering Heights* (1939).

BIBLIOGRAPHY

Carleton, Jack. "The Films Are Financed Here!" *Los Angeles Times Sunday Magazine,* April 21, 1935, pp. 4, 16.
"Dr. Giannini Sees New Expansion Coming in Amusement Industry." *The Wall Street Journal,* September 12, 1935, p. 1.
Giannini, Dr. Attilio H. "Financial Aspects." In *The Story of the Films,* ed. Joseph P. Kennedy. Chicago: A. W. Shaw Company, 1927, pp. 77–98.
Kann, Red. "Loans $50,000,000; Losses Zero, Giannini's Balance." *Motion Picture Daily,* May 17, 1934.

BANNER FILM COMPANY, formed in 1915 and located in San Mateo, California, made "Banner" brand comedies starring Bill Stinger, who was the president of the company. It banded together with seven other companies to form the Associated Service in mid–1915. In October 1915, its president was Miss Sadie Lindblom.

BANTHA MUSIC. See LUCASFILM, LTD.

B. A. ROLFE PHOTOPLAYS, INC. Benjamin A. Rolfe, Charles B. Maddox, and Maxwell Karger were directors of the B. A. Rolfe Photoplays, Inc., which was incorporated in New York in July 1914 with offices at 1493 Broadway. Its first production, *Satan Sanderson,* was released by the Alco Film Corporation*. In December 1914, the company changed its name to simply Rolfe Photoplays, Inc. It soon dropped Alco because of doubts concerning the regularity of Alco's releases and began to release with the newly formed Metro Pictures Corporation*, which owned part of Rolfe. Edwin Carewe and John H. Collins were among Rolfe's directors, and its players included Ethel Barrymore, William Faversham, and Viola Dana. In June 1915, Rolfe bought the Dyreda Art Film Corporation* and occupied its studio at 3 West 61st Street, New York. On May 25, 1917, Rolfe was completely absorbed by Metro, along with Columbia and Popular Plays and Players*, with B. A. Rolfe becoming the general manager of the three producers. B. A. Rolfe left the Metro organization in April 1918 to form Rolfe Productions, Inc., which made a Houdini serial and films starring Marguerite Marsh and directed by Burton King. In August 1919, Rolfe signed a contract to make films exclusively for A. H. Features, Inc., and occupied the Thanhouser* studios in New Rochelle, New York.

BIBLIOGRAPHY

"B. A. Rolfe Company Incorporated." *The New York Dramatic Mirror,* July 22, 1914, p. 24.

BATJAC PRODUCTIONS, INC., was formed in 1951 by John Wayne (1907–1979) and Robert Fellows (1903–1969) as Wayne-Fellows Productions. Batjac was the name of the trading company owned by Luther Adler in *Wake of the Red Witch* (1948). It produced the following John Wayne features: *Blood Alley* (1955), *Legend of the Lost* (1957), *The Alamo* (1960), *McLintock!* (1963), *Cast a Giant Shadow* (1966), *War Wagon* (1967), and *The Green Berets* (1968). The company, which remains in existence under the presidency of Wayne's son, Michael, also produced some non-Wayne features such as *Track of the Cat* (1954).

Address: 9595 Wilshire Boulevard, Suite 610, Beverly Hills, Calif. 90212.

BIBLIOGRAPHY

Zolotow, Maurice. *Shooting Star.* New York: Simon and Schuster, 1974.

BAYONNE, NEW JERSEY. See CENTAUR FILM COMPANY and DAVID HORSLEY PRODUCTIONS

B.B. FEATURES. See ROBERTSON-COLE COMPANY

B.B.S. PRODUCTIONS was formed in 1969 by Berton J. Schneider, Robert J. Rafelson, and J. Stephen Blauner. The most prominent member of the trio was Bert Schneider, a former Columbia Pictures-Screen Gems executive, who had earlier—in 1975—formed, with Robert Rafelson, the television production company of Raybert, which was responsible for the popular series *The Monkees*. BBS produced five features, which were all released by Columbia: *Easy Rider* (1969), *Five Easy Pieces* (1970), *The Last Picture Show* (1971), *Drive, He Said* (1971), and *A Safe Place* (1971). Columbia refused to release BBS's controversial feature-length documentary on the Vietnam War, *Hearts and Minds* (1974), and this led, indirectly, to the breakup of the company. All BBS stock was purchased in December 1971 by Columbia Pictures*. "There was no corporate ideology," Schneider told *The New York Times* (May 4, 1975). "The only philosophy we had was backing particular people." The result was BBS's producing the most important independent American feature films from 1969 to 1971.

BEACH MOVIES. Although beach movies are commonly thought to have begun with *Beach Party* (1963), the roots of the cycle are in *Gidget* (1959) and *Where the Boys Are* (1960). These two films set out the basic situation of teenagers on vacation falling in love away from adult supervision. With *Beach Party,* however, American International Pictures* pushed the basic situation to an extreme: the vacation became permanent, falling in love did not mean marriage but permanent courtship, any problems from real life were banished, and adults had no power. As William Asher, the director of most of the films in the cycle, remarked, "There was no real fruition of sex. There was no booze. No cigarettes. The nucleus of the beach gang just weren't in trouble. . . . The theme was almost like a Doris Day picture I guess."

This formula of pretty girls, no problems, music, and broad comedy proved very popular, and it led to a series that includes *Bikini Beach* (1964), *Muscle Beach Party* (1964), *Pajama Party* (1964), *Beach Blanket Bingo* (1965), and *How to Stuff a Wild Bikini* (1965). The cycle proved popular enough that another studio, aside from American International Pictures, made a beach film, but when Paramount* produced *Beach Ball* in 1965, it met with little success. This was an indication that the formula was beginning to erode, as was the fact that American International Pictures began attempting variations on the formula with *Dr. Goldfoot and the Bikini Machine* (1965), *Ski Party* (1965), and *The Ghost in the Invisible Bikini* (1966). Consequently, in 1966, American International Pictures announced it would commence producing a new cycle of films that it dubbed "protest" films. As Sam Arkoff said, "If our public wants more serious subjects, we'll supply them."

The beach film was not entirely dead, for it enjoyed a slight comeback with *Malibu Beach* (1978) and *The Beach Girls* (1982). Despite the interest of the genre's best-known stars, Frankie Avalon and Annette Funicello, in making a comeback, it is doubtful that the cycle will return.

BIBLIOGRAPHY

"AIP: Action, Youth, Older O'Seas Fans; Let TV Gravy Bubble Up by Itself." *Variety,* June 22, 1966, p. 24.

Ehrlich, Henry. "Hollywood's Teen-Age Gold Mine." *Look,* November 3, 1964, pp. 59–66.

Funicello, Annette, and Patricia Romanowski. *A Dream Is a Wish Your Heart Makes: My Story.* New York: Hyperion, 1994.

Levy, Alan. "Peekaboo Sex, or How to Fill a Drive-In." *Life,* July 16, 1965, pp. 81–88.

Lewis, Richard Warren. "Those Swinging Beach Movies." *The Saturday Evening Post,* July 31, 1965, pp. 83–87.

McGee, Mark Thomas. *Fast and Furious: The Story of American International Pictures*. Jefferson, N.C.: McFarland, 1984.

Penn, Jean Cox. "'Hey, Annette . . . Those Surfers Are Actually Getting into the Water." *Los Angeles,* March 1978, pp. 78–88.

BEACON PRODUCTIONS, INC., was active from 1933 through 1935, and founded by Max Alexander (1904–1964), in association with his brother Arthur. Its primary output consisted of Guinn "Big Boy" Williams Westerns.

BEHIND THE LENS is an association of professional camerawomen, based in Santa Monica, California. Founded informally in the summer of 1983, it was officially established in April 1984.

BELL & HOWELL CO. What was once a leading manufacturer of cameras and projectors for both the professional and the amateur is now a diversified information products and services company with no involvement in the field that made it famous. The company was founded in 1907 by projectionist Donald H. Bell and camera repairman Albert S. Howell with an initial investment of $5,000. Its precision-built cameras and projectors soon became well known in the film industry, with the company's claiming it had taken "the flick out of flickers." Bell sold out in 1921 to Joe Hector McNabb, who became the head of the company and the man largely responsible for Bell & Howell's ongoing success. The company entered the amateur movie field in 1922, after agreeing with Eastman Kodak* that 16mm should be the standard for amateurs; it introduced its popular Filmsound 16mm projector in 1932 and its first double-run 8mm camera in 1936. A wholly-owned subsidiary is University Microfilms Inc., the largest microform publisher in the world.

Address: 5215 Old Orchard Road, Skokie, Ill. 60077.

BIBLIOGRAPHY

"Elegant Bell & Howell." *Fortune,* July 1948, pp. 150, 153–55.

"Half-a-Hundred . . . The Bell & Howell Story." *Film News,* Summer 1957, pp. 7, 11.

BENNETT PICTURES CORP. was founded in 1931 by actress Constance Bennett (1905–1965) and her then-husband, Henri de la Falaise. It produced only two feature films, *Legong: Dance of the Virgins* and *Kliou/The Tiger* (1936), shot in Bali and Indo-China, respectively, which are of importance in that they are the last two features to be released in the two-color Technicolor* process.

BETZWOOD FILM COMPANY. Early in 1918, the Betzwood Film Company bought the 400-acre Lubin plant in Betzwood, Pennsylvania, on the Schuylkill River, one mile from Valley Forge and 20 miles from Philadelphia. Clarence Wolf was the president and Ira M. Lowry was the general manager of the plant. The company's first two stars were Louis Bennison and Tsen Mei. J. Allen Dunn was the scenarist. The banking establishment of Wolf Brothers and Company backed Betzwood, whose first film was *For the Freedom of the East* (1918).

THE BIG BROADCAST SERIES consists of four features produced by Paramount* between 1932 and 1938, each with a radio background. The first, titled simply *The Big Broadcast* (1932), featured a number of popular radio personalities of the day: Bing Crosby, Arthur Tracy ("The Street Singer"), Kate Smith, George Burns and Gracie Allen, Cab Calloway, Vincent Lopez and His Orchestra, the Mills Brothers, and the Boswell Sisters. It was followed by *The Big Broadcast of 1936, The Big Broadcast of 1937,* and *The Big Broadcast of 1938.* In the last, Bob Hope and Shirley Ross introduced what was to become Hope's signature tune, "Thanks for the Memory."

BIOGRAPH COMPANY. There can be little argument that the Biograph Company is the best known of all early American production companies, thanks entirely to its being the studio where D. W. Griffith (1875–1948) began his directorial career (with *The Adventures of Dollie* in 1908) and where he remained through 1913, creating the entire grammar and syntax of filmmaking. At Biograph, Griffith built up a stock company of players, including Mary Pickford, Blanche Sweet, Lillian and Dorothy Gish, Mae Marsh, Henry B. Walthall, and Robert Harron, all of whom enjoyed major success after leaving the company.

The Biograph Company was founded in 1895 by Henry Norton Marvin as the American Mutoscope Company, with financial backing from Abner McKinley and the New York Security and Trust Company. Its initial purpose was to manufacture a peep-show machine, the Mutoscope, along with a series of flipped photographs for use therein. With the help of Edison associate W. K. L. Dickson, the company manufactured a camera that did not infringe on Thomas Edison's patents and presented its first film program, on October 12, 1896, at Hammerstein's Olympia Music Hall, New York. At that time, the company became the American Mutoscope and Biograph Company and by 1909 had shortened its name simply to the Biograph Company. In 1908, with Edison, it helped set up the Motion Picture Patents Company* and released its films through that organization's General Film Company.

The best-known studio of the Biograph Company was a brownstone mansion at 11 East 14th Street in New York, where the company made the bulk of its films from 1908 to 1912. In 1913, it moved to a new studio in the Bronx, at 807 East 175th Street, where it remained until 1917. In addition, Biograph operated two studios in Los Angeles; the first (from January to April 1910) was located at Grand Avenue and Washington Street, and the second (from 1911 to 1915) was at Georgia Street and Girard Street.

In 1913, Biograph signed a contract with the theatrical firm of Klaw & Erlanger (K & E), to produce five-reel features, based on its plays, with such films being screened at K & E theatres. The venture was not particularly successful.

When D. W. Griffith left Biograph in 1913, largely out of frustration at the company's refusal to allow him to direct feature-length productions, not to mention its attitude regarding the nonpublicity of either himself as director or the names of his players, Biograph lost its importance. It remained active through 1917, producing new films for a short period, but basically reissuing its old Griffith productions. One of the last releases from Biograph was a six-reel version of D. W. Griffith's only Biograph film, *Judith of Bethulia,* retitled *Her Condoned Sin* by the company in 1917.

BIBLIOGRAPHY

Bowser, Eileen, ed. *Biograph Bulletins: 1908–1912.* New York: Octagon Books, 1973.

Dickson, W. K. L. *The Biograph in Battle.* London: T. Unwin Fisher, 1901.

Graham, Cooper C., Steven Higgins, Elaine Mancini, and João Luiz Vieira. *D. W. Griffith and the Biograph Company.* Metuchen, N.J.: Scarecrow Press, 1985.

Gunning, Tom. *D. W. Griffith and the Origins of American Narrative Films: The Early Years at Biograph.* Urbana, Ill.: University of Illinois Press, 1991.

Henderson, Robert M. *D. W. Griffith: The Years at Biograph.* New York: Farrar, Straus and Giroux, 1970.

Jesionowski, Joyce E. *Thinking of Pictures: Dramatic Structure in D. W. Griffith's Biograph Films.* Berkeley, Calif.: University of California Press, 1987.

Niver, Kemp R. *Mary Pickford, Comedienne.* Los Angeles: Locare Research Group, 1969.

———, ed. *Biograph Bulletins: 1898–1908.* Los Angeles: Locare Research Group, 1971.

———. *D. W. Griffith: His Biograph Films in Perspective.* Los Angeles: n.p., 1974.

Pearson, Roberta E. *Eloquent Gestures: The Transformation of Performance Style in the Griffith Biograph Films.* Berkeley, Calif.: University of California Press, 1992.

Stern, Seymour. "11 East 14 Street." *Films in Review,* October 1952, pp. 399–406.

RESOURCES

Films: Library of Congress; Museum of Modern Art.
Papers: Museum of Modern Art.

THE BIOSCOPE FILM COMPANY was founded early in 1920 by a group of local businessmen at Goldstein's

Springs, near Tampa, Florida, to produce slapstick comedies. A. B. McMullen was the president, Bert Tracy handled direction, and Via Kadz was the company's leading lady. Its first production was *Introduce Me Quick.*

BIRNS & SAWYER, INC., founded in 1954 by Jack Birns and Cliff Sawyer, is Hollywood's leading rental agency for anything relating to cinematography, including cameras, dollies, grip equipment, lenses, blimps, batteries, and lights.

Address: 1026 North Highland Avenue, Hollywood, Calif. 90038.

BLACK FILMMAKERS HALL OF FAME, INC. A nonprofit California corporation, the Black Filmmakers Hall of Fame, Inc. organizes an annual tribute to black filmmakers each February in Oakland, California, consisting of special screenings and the Oscar Micheaux Awards Ceremony. Founded in 1974 under the sponsorship of the Cultural and Ethnic Affairs Guild of the Oakland Museum Association, the organization has been an independent corporation since 1977.

Among the inductees into the Hall of Fame are Ossie Davis, Sammy Davis, Jr., Clarence Muse, Gordon Parks, Sr., Stepin Fetchit, and Paul Robeson (all 1974); Eddie "Rochester" Anderson, Ruby Dee, Rex Ingram, Quincy Jones, Butterfly McQueen, Hattie McDaniel, Sidney Poitier (all 1975); Josephine Baker, Louise Beavers, Harry Belafonte, Eubie Blake, the Nicholas Brothers, Ethel Waters (all 1976); Dorothy Dandridge, James Earl Jones, Cicely Tyson (all 1977); William "Count" Basie, Nat "King" Cole, Ella Fitzgerald, Nina Mae McKinney, Bill "Bojangles" Robinson (all 1978); Paul Winfield (1979); Woody Strode (1980); Maya Angelou, Lou Gossett, Jr. (both 1981); and Cab Calloway (1982). In 1993, it established the Sidney Poitier Fellowships to support African-American film/video artists.

Address: 1212 Broadway, Suite 830, Oakland, Calif. 94612.

BLACKS IN AMERICAN FILM. Black Americans have been appearing in films from the 1890s, originally in the capacity of servants or as comic relief. In the silent era, it was not uncommon to have a white actor portray a Negro in blackface, as in *The Birth of a Nation* (1915). When the great black vaudeville performer Bert Williams appeared in a 1916 one-reel short, *A Natural Born Gambler,* he was also required to don blackface makeup. Black Americans were seldom permitted major roles in white-produced American films of the silent era, one exception being James E. Lowe, who was featured as Uncle Tom in Universal's 1927 production of *Uncle Tom's Cabin.*

In the thirties, a number of black actors and actresses were featured in Hollywood productions, and notable among them were Bill "Bojangles" Robinson, Clarence Muse, Stepin Fetchit, Nina Mae McKinney, Willie Best, Louise Beavers, and Hattie McDaniel (who was the first black performer to receive an Academy Award, for Best Supporting Actress for her work in the 1939 feature *Gone with the Wind*). Paul Robeson, who had been seen in the 1924 Oscar Micheaux* production of *Body and Soul,* as well as *The Emperor Jones* (1933) and *Show Boat* (1937), achieved greater fame in European films, beginning with *Borderline* (1928) and including *King Solomon's Mines* (1937), *Song of Freedom* (1938), and *The Proud Valley* (1941).

There were two all-black features produced in Hollywood in the forties—*Cabin in the Sky* (1942) and *Stormy Weather* (1943)—but outside of these films, blacks still found themselves relegated to supporting roles of a menial nature or, as with Lena Horne and similar performers, to cameo parts that could easily be cut from films for consumption by southern audiences.

A new black image began to be projected in American films of the fifties, such as *Carmen Jones* (1954), *Island in the Sun* (1957), and *Take a Giant Step* (1958). The new "look" continued into the sixties with *Lilies of the Field* (1967), *Guess Who's Coming to Dinner* (1968), and *In the Heat of the Night* (1968), among other features. At the same time producers began to realize the box office potential of black heroes, such as Jim Brown, Calvin Lockhart, Godfrey Cambridge, Pamela Grier, and Richard Roundtree, who introduced the black private detective, Shaft, in the 1971 feature of the same name. Black heroes came of age with *Superfly* (1972), directed by Gordon Parks, Jr., one of America's few black directors. There were new black stars, including Ossie Davis, Ruby Dee, Brock Peters, Beah Richards, and, most important of all, Sidney Poitier.

Blacks have starred in *Lady Sings the Blues* (1972), *Sounder* (1972), *Claudine* (1972), and *The Wiz* (1978). A new market has opened up for black exploitation films, such as *Blacula* (1972), and *Super Fly T.N.T.* (1973).

Independent black films produced for and by black Americans date back to the second decade of the twentieth century. They include films produced by the Lincoln Motion Picture Company* and the Micheaux Film Corporation* and features such as *The Scar of Shame* (1927), produced by the Colored Players Film Corporation of Philadelphia; *Chicago after Dark* (1946), *Boarding House Blues* (1948), and *Killer Diller* (1948), all produced by All American News, Inc.; *Go Down, Death!* (1944) and *Juke Joint* (1947), from Sack Amusement Enterprises*; *Harlem on the Prairie,* an all-black musical Western; and Clarence Muse's *Broken Strings* (1940).

A gay black cinema emerged with Marlon Riggs's *Tongues United* (1989) and Isaac Julien's *Looking for Langston* (1989). Black women found a place in the industry thanks to the pioneering work of Kathleen Collins (1942–1986), whose first feature was *The Cruz Brothers and Mrs. Malloy* (1980); she was followed by Julie Dash, best known for *Daughters of the Dust* (1992). Spike Lee is the best known of modern black filmmakers. He directed his first feature, *She's Gotta Have It,* in 1986, and it was followed by *Do the Right Thing* (1989), *Mo Better Blues* (1990), *Jungle Fever* (1991), and *Malcolm X* (1992). Other prominent black filmmakers and their features include Robert Townsend and *Hollywood Shuffle* (1987), Mario Van Peebles and *New Jack City* (1991), and Tony Singleton and *Boyz N the Hood* (1991). Ironically, the most praised and award winning of recent "black" features is *The Color Purple* (1985), directed by Steven Spielberg, and with masterful performances by Whoopi Goldberg, Oprah Winfrey, and Danny Glover. The most prominent of black actors in mainstream cinema today is Eddie Murphy, who made his debut in *48 Hrs.* (1982), and unsuccessfully directed *Harlem Nights* (1989).

Hattie McDaniel was the first black to receive an Academy Award. She was followed by James Baskett (who received a Special Award in 1947 "for his able and heartwarming characterization of Uncle Remus, friend and story teller to the children of the world" in *Song of the South*), Sidney Poitier (who received the 1963 Academy Award for Best Actor for his work in *Lillies of the Field*), and Isaac Hayes (who received the 1971 Academy Award for Best Music—Song for "Theme from *Shaft*").

BIBLIOGRAPHY

Bogle, Donald. *Toms, Coons, Mulattoes, Mammies, and Bucks*. New York: Viking Press, 1973.

———. *Blacks in American Film and Television: An Encyclopedia*. New York: Garland, 1988.

Cripps, Tom. *Slow Fade to Black*. New York: Oxford University Press, 1977.

———. *Black Films as Genre*. Bloomington, Ind.: Indiana University Press, 1978.

———. *Making Movies Black: The Hollywood Message Movie from World War II to the Civil Rights Era*. New York: Oxford University Press, 1993.

Diawara, Manthia, ed. *Black American Cinema*. New York: Routledge, 1993.

Guerrero, Ed. *Framing Blackness: The African American Image in Film*. Philadelphia: Temple University Press, 1993.

Harris, Erich Leon. *African-American Screenwriters Now: Conversations with Hollywood's Black Pack*. Los Angeles: Silman-James Press, 1996.

Jones, G. William. *Black Cinema Treasures: Lost and Found*. Denton, Tex.: University of North Texas Press, 1991.

Kisch, John, and Edward Mapp. *A Separate Cinema: Fifty Years of Black-Cast Posters*. New York: Noonday Press, 1992.

Landay, Eileen. *Black Film Stars*. New York: Drake, 1973.

Leab, Daniel J. *From Sambo to Superspade*. Boston: Houghton Mifflin, 1975.

Mapp, Edward. *Blacks in American Films: Today and Yesterday*. Metuchen, N. J.: Scarecrow Press, 1972.

Nelson, George. *Blackface: Reflections on African-Americans and the Movies*. New York: HarperCollins, 1994.

Noble, Peter. *The Negro in Films*. London: Skelton Robinson, 1948.

Null, Gary. *Black Hollywood from 1970 to Today*. New York: Carol Publishing, 1993.

Ogle, Patrick. *Facets African-American Video Guide*. Chicago: Academy Chicago, 1994.

Parish, James Robert. *Black Action Films*. Jefferson, North Carolina: McFarland, 1989.

———. *Today's Black Hollywood*. New York: Pinnacle Books, 1995.

Patterson, Lindsay, ed. *Black Films and Film-Makers*. New York: Dodd, Mead, 1975.

Powers, Ann, compiler. *Blacks in American Film: A Selected Bibliography*. Metuchen, New Jersey: Scarecrow Press, 1974.

Reid, Mark A. *Redefining Black Film*. Berkeley, Calif.: University of California Press, 1993.

Rhines, Jesse Algernon. *Black Film, White Money*. New Brunswick, New Jersey: Rutgers University Press, 1996.

Sampson, Henry T. *Blacks in Black and White: A Source Book on Black Films*. Metuchen, New Jersey: Scarecrow Press, 1995.

Snead, James. *White Screens, Black Images: Hollywood from the Dark Side*. New York: Routledge, 1994.

BLANEY-SPOONER FEATURE FILM COMPANY, established in mid–1913, produced films starring Cecil Spooner, based on her highly successful plays. In October 1914, the company, which had changed its name to the Charles E. Blaney Feature Play Company, was purchased by Lewis J. Selznick for the World Film Corporation*. The Blaney studio was located between Clason's Point and Throgg's Neck, New York. The films that it produced, along with the other Blaney plays, became the property of World.

BLAZED TRAIL PRODUCTIONS, INC., began in 1919 to produce a series of films with subjects set in the Canadian North Woods. The films, distributed by Arrow Film Corporation*, were written by L. Case Russell, directed by Joseph J. Barry, photographed by Joseph Settle, starred John Lowell, and were shot in the Adirondacks. The Blazed Trail studio was located in Gloversville, New York.

BLIND BIDDING or selling is the practice by which distributors rent a group of films to exhibitors before the majority of the films have been produced. Thus, the exhibitors are renting a block of films about which they know next to nothing—not the stars, the story, the title, or the release date.

This practice, a necessary complement to block booking*, was prohibited by the 1940 consent decree*. The major distributors agreed to trade show their completed films in each exchange district so that an exhibitor had the opportunity to see the film and decide whether to rent it.

The distributors continued to trade show their films even after the terms of the consent decree had expired. Since the trade shows were so poorly attended by exhibitors, the 1946 court decision that forced divestiture of theatres and banned block booking did not prohibit blind bidding or selling, so that it is legal to this day. However, there have been attempts by individual states to outlaw the practice.

BIBLIOGRAPHY

"Court Decision in the New York Equity Suit." *Film Daily Year Book, 1947*, pp. 848–63.

Machetti, Roger. *Law of the Stage, Screen and Radio.* San Francisco: Suttonhouse, 1936.

"A Review of the New York Equity Suit and the Consent Decree." *Film Daily Year Book, 1941*, pp. 636–49.

Valenti, Jack, and A. Alan Friedberg. "Blind Bidding: Two Sides of the Box Office Dollar." *Premiere,* vol. 2, no. 1, July 15, 1980, pp. 16–19, 26.

BLOCK BOOKING is the practice of renting one group of films on the condition that the exhibitor, during the same period, also rents another group of films. The second group was usually designated "B" movies*, as it would not feature the stars and production values of the films in the first group. Though not called such, the practice of block booking was common from the early history of the American film industry, as exhibitors would contract for the total output from the General Film Company, Universal*, or Mutual*.

It was only with the dominance of feature films and the attempt by Paramount's Adolph Zukor to control the industry that block booking became a problem for the independent exhibitor. In 1921, the Federal Trade Commission filed suit against Famous Players-Lasky (Paramount*), charging restraint of trade and unfair methods of competition. Block booking was one of the methods prohibited, but this ban was overturned by a court of appeals in 1932.

In July 1938, the federal government filed suit against Paramount and the other major producers and distributors. Under the consent decree* of November 1940, the government agreed not to press for the divorcement of theatres from producers for three years, and in return the studios agreed to modify their trade practices, including block booking. Instead of selling a year's worth of films, the distributors agreed to sell films in blocks of five or fewer.

In August 1944, the government reactivated the case, and, in June 1946, a court ruled a large number of distribution practices illegal, including block booking. On appeal, the Supreme Court, in 1948, affirmed the lower court ruling and thus signaled the end of block booking. Unofficially, however, the practice still survives, as was seen when 20th Century-Fox* was fined in 1978 for forcing exhibitors to take *The Other Side of Midnight* in order to show *Star Wars. See also* Blind Bidding.

BIBLIOGRAPHY

Conant, Michael. *Antitrust in the Motion Picture Industry.* Berkeley, Calif.: University of California Press, 1960.

"Fed Grand Jury Indicts, 20th Pleads No Contest, Is Fined 25G, Costs of Investigation." *Variety,* September 13, 1978, pp. 1, 19.

BLOCKBUSTER ENTERTAINMENT CORP., the world's largest video chain, was founded in 1975 with one store in Dallas, Texas. In 1987, H. Wayne Huizenga gained control of the company and began its expansion. Aside from its more than 2,600 video stores, Blockbuster also co-owns the music store chains of Sound Warehouse and Music Plus. It entered film and television production and distribution in 1993 with the partial acquisition of Republic Pictures* and the total acquisition of Spelling Entertainment Group.* In January 1994, the company agreed to be acquired by and merge with Viacom*, and that merger was finally approved on September 29, 1994.

Address: One Blockbuster Plaza, Fort Lauderdale, Fla. 33301.

BIBLIOGRAPHY

Bates, James. "Wayne's World." *Los Angeles Times,* June 6, 1993, pp. D1, D5, D7.

"B" MOVIES is a term used to describe films of a secondary or lesser nature, usually produced to fill the second half of a double bill. The features of many of the so-called poverty row* studios, such as Monogram*, Republic*, Mascot*, and Grand National*, were always—often quite erroneously—described as "B" movies. Some of the smaller of the major studios, notably Columbia* and Universal*, operated production units exclusively involved in the making of "B" movies, as did the major studios starting around 1935. With the demise of the two-feature program at most theatres in the fifties, the "B" movie ceased to be produced, and although there are many films today of a minor nature, none can be legitimately referred to as "B" movies. Among the best-known producers of "B" movies are Sam Katzman, Nat Levine, Herbert J. Yates, Trem Carr, Bryan E. Foy, Sol Wurtzel, Albert Zugsmith, and Val Lewton.

BIBLIOGRAPHY

McCarthy, Todd, and Charles Flynn, eds. *King of the Bs.* New York: E. P. Dutton, 1975.

Miller, Don. *"B" Movies.* New York: Curtis Books, 1973.

B 'N' B FILM CORPORATION. See ASTOR PICTURES CORPORATION

BOARD OF CENSORSHIP. See NATIONAL BOARD OF CENSORSHIP OF MOTION PICTURES

BODYBUILDING IN THE CINEMA was first considered as a genre in December 1989, following a London National Film Theatre retrospective on the subject. The films of Steve Reeves and Arnold Schwarzenegger are obvious examples of the genre. Others include *Arrivano i Titani/Sons of Thunder* (1962, with Serge Nubret), *A Kid for Two Farthings* (1965, with Joe Robinson), *Will Success Spoil Rock Hunter?* (1957, with Mickey Hargity), and *Don't Make Waves* (1967, with David Draper). Joseph Strick's and Irving Lerner's *Muscle Beach* (1948) also belongs to the genre, as do the physique films of Richard Fontaine and others.

BOLEY, OKLAHOMA. See NORMAN FILM MANUFACTURING COMPANY

BOOTS AND SADDLES PICTURES, INC. See CALIFORNIA STUDIOS

BORDER FEATURE FILM CORPORATION, based in Bisbee, Arizona, and with studios in Bisbee and Tombstone, was active early in the twenties, producing two-reel Westerns. Its leading man was Grant Merrill, its leading lady Peggy Parkan, and the two directors under contract were Therdo Joos and Harry Moody.

BORIS THOMASHEFSKY FILM COMPANY. Boris Thomashefsky, a leading Yiddish actor, formed the Boris Thomashefsky Film Company early in 1915 to produce film versions of modern Yiddish stage successes. Sidney M. Goldin was engaged to direct the films, which starred Thomashefsky.

BIBLIOGRAPHY

"Producing Primarily for the Jews." *The Moving Picture World,* February 6, 1915, p. 809.

BOSS FILM CORPORATION was founded in the summer of 1983 as a major special effects company by Richard Edlund, and grew out of Edlund's partnership with Douglas Trumbull in the Entertainment Effects Group. Boss Film's first project was *Ghostbusters* (1984).

Address: 13335 Maxella Avenue, Marina Del Rey, Calif. 90292.

BIBLIOGRAPHY

Block, Alex Ben. "Make-Believe Millions." *Forbes,* November 18, 1985, p. 268.

BOSTOCK JUNGLE AND FILM COMPANY. In July 1915, David Horsley formed the Bostock Jungle and Film Company after having bought the entire Bostock collection of animals and transported them to a five-acre site he secured in Los Angeles. Horsley had six stages erected and proceeded to produce two reels per week of animal films, which were released through Mutual Film Corporation*.

BOSTON. See HOLLAND FILM MANUFACTURING COMPANY, MASTERCRAFT PHOTO-PLAY CORPORATION, and PURITAN SPECIAL FEATURES COMPANY

BOSWORTH, INC. In August 1913, Hobart Bosworth (1867–1943), an actor who had previously worked with the Selig Polyscope Company*, encouraged by W. W. Hodkinson, formed Bosworth, Inc., with H. T. Rudisill and a California capitalist and sportsman, Frank A. Garbutt. The primary object of the new company was to produce films based on the Jack London stories, after the author had declared that an earlier contract with Balboa* was nullified by reason of that company's failure to produce any films by a specified date. The first Bosworth film was *The Sea Wolf*, which featured Hobart Bosworth and was filmed, in seven reels, at Truckee, California, and at the J.A.C. Studios in Los Angeles. It was followed by film versions of other Jack London stories: *John Barleycorn, The Valley of the Moon,* and *Martin Eden.*

Phillips Smalley and Lois Weber joined Bosworth as actor-directors in June 1914, and Oscar Apfel was added to the directorial staff early in 1915. When Paramount Pictures* was formed in May 1914, it distributed the Bosworth films. In November 1914, Bosworth became associated with the Oliver Morosco Photoplay Company*, and both companies shared a studio at 201 North Occidental Boulevard in Los Angeles. Hobart Bosworth left the company in March 1915, and, by October 1916, Bosworth, Inc., was no longer part of the Paramount program, its productions having been taken over by Morosco and Pallas Pictures.

BIBLIOGRAPHY

"Bosworth, Inc." *The Moving Picture World,* August 13, 1913, p. 848.
"Morosco-Bosworth." *The Moving Picture World,* July 10, 1915, p. 242.

RESOURCES

Films: Library of Congress.

BOUND BROOK, NEW JERSEY. See PATHÉ

BOX OFFICE ATTRACTIONS COMPANY. In January 1914, William Fox (1879–1952) formed Box Office Attraction Film Rental Company, which owned the exclusive exhibition rights in New York City, New York state, and New England of the films produced by Solax*, Blaché, American Film Manufacturing Company*, Film Releases of America, Ramo*, Electric, Great Northern Special Features, and Great Northern Preferred Features. In May 1914, the name was shortened to the Box Office Attractions Company, and it began distributing films nationally on a states rights* basis. At the time, an arrangement was made with Balboa* to have Box Office Attractions sell all of Balboa's features to exchanges.

The company was located at 130 West 46th Street in New York, with Fox as president and Winfield R. Sheehan as general manager. In September 1914, Frank Powell and Edgar Lewis were hired to direct films for the company, the first of which was Powell's *The Children of the Ghetto.* Other directors were to include J. Gordon Edwards and Lloyd B. Carleton, and the company's stars included Theda Bara and Betty Nansen. Box Office Attractions was replaced by the Fox Film Corporation* when the latter was incorporated in February 1915.

BIBLIOGRAPHY

"Fox Starts Feature Exchange." *The Moving Picture World,* January 10, 1914, p. 182.
"Fox to Sell State Rights." *The Moving Picture World,* May 16, 1914, p. 977.

BOY CITY FILM CORPORATION. Judge Willis Brown, who presided over a juvenile court in Salt Lake City, and established a boys' city, dramatized typical problems of the boys in half-hour films produced by his company, Boy City Film Corporation. Brown hired King Vidor, who had earlier worked with Brown when he was a newsreel cameraman, to direct the films, which were made at a Culver City, California, studio and a self-governed boys' town that was set up. The company produced some 10 to 12 films in 1918 before it stopped production because of financial problems. General Film Company released the films.

BIBLIOGRAPHY

"Judge Says His Stories Are Designed for Adult Appeal." *The Moving Picture World,* June 1, 1918, p. 1304.

BRAY STUDIOS, INC. J. R. Bray, formerly a newspaper and journal cartoonist, spent six years studying animal movements at the Bronx Zoo and experimenting with animation processes before he signed a contract with Pathé* in 1912 to release his animated cartoons on its program. Bray Studios, Inc., produced the popular "Colonel Heeza Liar" and "Police Dog" series for Pathé in its New York studios before Bray signed with Paramount* to produce one reel of animated cartoons per week as well as cartoons to be included in Paramount's news weekly, to begin in January 1916. Bray patented his work-saving methods in 1914 and 1915, involving the use of backgrounds on translucent paper that could be laid over the paper on which the part of the picture that would appear to move would be drawn. Later, Bray formed the Bray-Hurd Patent Trust with Earl Hurd, a holder of a patent for the use of cels in animation, and studios using cels had to pay license fees to the Trust.

Bray sold his cartoons in 1916 for $2 a foot. The Paramount-Bray Pictograph screen magazine began in 1916 and incorporated live action with the animation. Max Fleischer created his "Out of the Inkwell" series for these pictographs. During the First World War, the Bray Studios produced training films for the military. In June 1919, the company enlarged to become a million-dollar corporation, the Bray Pictures Corporation, and began production of its "Greater Bray Pictographs." In September 1919, it produced color-animated cartoons, which were released by the Goldwyn Distributing Corporation. Bray closed his animation studio in 1927, but his company continued producing documentaries and educational filmstrips. In addition to Max Fleischer, Paul Terry and Walter Lantz also worked at Bray early in their careers.

BIBLIOGRAPHY

"Animated Cartoons in Motion Pictures." *The Moving Picture World,* April 3, 1915, p. 54.
"Bray Studios, Inc. to Reorganize." *The Moving Picture World,* June 21, 1919, p. 1784.
"Cartoonist Bray with Paramount." *The Moving Picture World,* December 11, 1915, p. 1988.
Crafton, Donald. *Before Mickey.* Cambridge, Mass.: MIT Press, 1982.

BRENTWOOD FILM CORPORATION was formed in 1918 by nine doctors in the Los Angeles area to produce feature-length films directed by King Vidor "that will stir the emotions with stories of every-day life and its problems, every-day drama and every-day comedy." Brentwood leased a studio, located at 4811 Fountain Street in Hollywood, formerly occupied by the Mena Film Corporation, whose plans to produce biblical stories shot both in Hollywood and Palestine were interrupted by the First World War. Later, Brentwood purchased outright the three-and-one-half acres fronting Fountain Street, between Berendo and Catalina streets. Lloyd C. Hughes was Brentwood's first president.

Brentwood's first production, *The Turn in the Road,* with Helen Jerome Eddy, Ben Alexander, and George Nichols, opened at a small theatre in Los Angeles and attracted overflow crowds for 11 weeks, until Brentwood contracted with the Robertson-Cole Company* to distribute it nationally. The film, a critical and financial success, launched Vidor's career and made him a much sought-after director, but he felt obligated to remain with Brentwood for a year, with his second film being *Better Times,* with ZaSu Pitts in her first starring role.

When Vidor signed with the First National* Exhibitors Circuit in September 1919, after writing, producing, and directing four films for Brentwood, the company hired Henry Kolker to replace him as director but planned to keep the basic Christian Science philosophy that Vidor's films exemplified. Although Kolker made *Bright Skies,* with ZaSu Pitts, Brentwood soon disbanded.

BIBLIOGRAPHY

Vidor, King. *A Tree Is a Tree.* New York: Harcourt, Brace, 1952.

BRIDGEPORT, CONNECTICUT. See NATIONAL CAMERAPHONE COMPANY

"BROADWAY FAVORITES." See KALEM COMPANY, INC.

BRONSON CANYON AND CAVES, located just north of Hollywood Boulevard in the heart of Hollywood, is a popular location for filmmakers. Originally called Brush Canyon, the area was developed by the Union Rock Company in 1907. The earliest documented use of Bronson Canyon and Caves is in the 1919 Western *Lightning Bryce*. Other films shot there include *Hurricane Express* (1932), *The Phantom Empire* (1935), *Flash Gordon* (1936), *Superman* (1948), *Invasion of the Body Snatchers* (1956), *Lost Horizon* (1972), *Raise the Titanic!* (1980), and *Star Trek VI: The Undiscovered Country* (1992).

BIBLIOGRAPHY

Henderson, Jan Alan. "Bronson Caves: A Hollywood Spelunker's Dream." *American Cinematographer,* vol. 74, no. 6, June 1993, pp. 86–90.

BROOKSFILMS LIMITED is the production company of actor/writer/director Mel Brooks (born 1926), founded in 1979. The company's first film was *The Elephant Man* (1980).
Address: P.O. Box 900, Beverly Hills, Calif. 90213.

BIBLIOGRAPHY

Kristal, Marc. "Brooks' Bookshop." *Saturday Review,* July-August 1983, pp. 25–28.

THE BRYNA COMPANY, also known as Bryna Productions, was formed in 1955 by Kirk Douglas—Bryna is his mother's name—to produce *Spartacus,* which was not completed until 1960. Bryna has produced or co-produced the following Kirk Douglas features: *The Indian Fighter* (1955), *The Vikings* (1958), *The Devil's Disciple* (1959), *Strangers When We Meet* (1960), *Spartacus* (1960), *The Last Sunset* (1961), *Cast a Giant Shadow* (1966), *A Gunfight* (1971), *The Light at the Edge of the World* (1971), *Catch Me a Spy* (1971), *Scalawag* (1973), and *Posse* (1975). During the sixties, Douglas also owned Joel Productions.
Address: 141 El Camino Drive, Beverly Hills, Calif. 90212.

B. S. MOSS MOTION PICTURE COMPANY was incorporated in New York in mid–1915 to maintain a theatrical and vaudeville agency and to engage in motion picture business. Benjamin S. Moss, a manager of theatres in New York, had been president of an earlier production company, the Reliance Feature Film Corporation, formed late in 1914, which produced the five-reel *Three Weeks* from Elinor Glyn's novel. The Moss Company did not begin production until September 1916, at which time it released, on the states rights* market, George Bronson Howard's *The Power of Evil.* The company gave first-run privilege to the Moss theatre chain. It practiced block booking* arrangements but allowed purchasers to see at least 4 of its features before they agreed to purchase up to 12. The company ceased operations in 1918.

BIBLIOGRAPHY

"B. S. Moss Enters the Production Field." *The Moving Picture World,* July 29, 1916. p. 771.

BUD BARSKY PRODUCTIONS, also known as Bud Barsky Corp., was active from 1924 to 1927. Founded by independent producer Bud Barsky (1891–1967), who was active in both the twenties and thirties, the company specialized in the production of "B" pictures starring Kenneth McDonald, Al Hoxie, and Frank Merrill, and short comedies with Jimmy Valentine. In 1925, it produced *The Coast Patrol,* the first feature to star Fay Wray, whose name Barsky tried to change to June Darling. Circa 1931, Barsky purchased a troupe of chimpanzees, which he named Barsky's Chimps, and which he rented out to various studios, including to M-G-M* for the first Tarzan features.

RESOURCES

Papers: Academy of Motion Picture Arts and Sciences.

BUENA VISTA DISTRIBUTION COMPANY, LTD., was formed in 1953 as a wholly owned subsidiary of Walt Disney Productions* to distribute the company's films theatrically. It took its name from the street upon which the studios were built. From 1930 to 1932, all Walt Disney films had been distributed theatrically in the United States by Columbia Pictures*. From 1932 to 1937, distribution was handled by United Artists Corporation*, but with the release of Disney's first feature-length cartoon, *Snow White and the Seven Dwarfs,* in 1937, distribution of all films was taken over by RKO Radio Pictures* (except *Victory through Air Power* in 1942, which was released by United Artists). The first Disney film to be released by Buena Vista was *The Living Desert* in 1953. The next Disney release, *Rob Roy, the Highland Rogue* (1954), was distributed by RKO, but from the following production, *20,000 Leagues under the Sea* (1954), onward, all films were Buena Vista releases.
Address: 350 South Buena Vista Street, Burbank, Calif. 91521.

BULLS EYE FILM CORPORATION, formed in 1918, was a producer of short comedies for the states rights* market. Billy West was Bulls Eye's first star, and he was supported by Ethel Gibson. Gale Henry, formerly with Universal*, began starring in Bulls Eye comedies in February 1919. The company's offices were located in New York, but its studio was in Hollywood. Charles Parrot was the company's director and Milton L. Cohen its president. Bulls Eye ceased production in 1920.

THE BURBANK STUDIOS (TBS) were created in 1972, when Warner Bros.* invited Columbia Pictures* to share its production facilities in Burbank. When Columbia moved to the former M-G-M* studios in Culver City in 1989, the name was dropped, and the studio complex became known simply as the Warner Bros. Studios.

BURTON HOLMES TRAVELOGUES. The best known of all travelogues—indeed, Burton Holmes is credited with coining the word in 1904—the Burton Holmes Travelogues began with the use of projected slide photographs in 1891. Holmes made his first motion pictures in 1897, forming the Burton Holmes Corporation, with Oscar DePue, a year later. Initially, Holmes would present his slides and films in person, but by the twenties he was producing travelogue shorts for release by Paramount*, and, in 1931, he produced a series of sound shorts for M-G-M*. Burton Holmes (1870–1958) said that his credo was "to satisfy that universal yearning to see and know the wonders and the beauty of that world of Otherwhere—the earth-wide realm of modern travel." In 1952, there were abortive plans for Sol Lesser to edit the Burton Holmes travelogues for a television series.

BIBLIOGRAPHY

"And Now It's Travel Lecturer Burton Holmes in Film." *Motion Picture News,* January 8, 1916, p. 50.

Barber, X. Theodore. "The Roots of Travel Cinema: John L. Stoddard, E. Burton Holmes and the Nineteenth Century Illustrated Travel Lecture." *Film History,* vol. 5, no. 1, 1993, pp. 68–84.

Caldwell, Genoa, ed. *The Man Who Photographed the World.* New York: Harry N. Abrams, 1977.

Evans, Delight. "An Invincible Violet." *Photoplay,* July 1919, pp. 73–74.

Holmes, Burton. *The World Is Mine.* Culver City, Calif.: Murray & Gee, 1953.

"Holmes's Happy Days." *Life,* August 11, 1958, pp. 8–9.

Scully, Sir Francis. "The Noble Neighbor." *Variety,* January 7, 1959, pp. 46, 86.

Stewart, Leslie. "The Roving Eye." *Westways,* November 1979, pp. 32–36.

BUSTER KEATON PRODUCTIONS, INC., was founded in March 1922 by Joseph M. Schenck (1877–1961) as a successor company to Comique*. Main stockholders, aside from Schenck, were Marcus Loew and A. H. Giannini. The company was located at the former Lone Star studios on the corner of Lillian Way and Eleanor Avenue in Hollywood. It produced the following features and short subjects starring Buster Keaton (1895–1966): *The Frozen North* (1922), *The Electric House* (1922), *Daydreams* (1922), *The Balloonatic* (1923), *The Love Nest* (1923), *The Three Ages* (1923), *Our Hospitality* (1923), *Sherlock Jr.* (1924), *The Navigator* (1924), *Seven Chances* (1925), *Go West* (1925), *Battling Butler* (1926), *The General* (1927), and *Steamboat Bill, Jr.* (1928). It was dissolved by Schenck in 1928.

BIBLIOGRAPHY

Kline, Jim. *The Complete Films of Buster Keaton.* New York: Citadel Press, 1993.

Meade, Marion. *Buster Keaton: Cut to the Chase.* New York: HarperCollins, 1995.

Rapf, Joanna, and Gary L. Green. *Buster Keaton: A Bio-Bibliography.* Westport, Conn.: Greenwood Press, 1995.

THE CADDO COMPANY, INC., was Howard Hughes's production company, releasing through Paramount* or United Artists*, from 1927 to 1932; he was president and Noah Dietrich was vice president. (Caddo was incorporated in Louisiana in 1912.) Hughes (1905–1976) produced nine features with Caddo: *Two Arabian Knights* (1927), *The Racket* (1928), *The Mating Call* (1928), *Hell's Angels* (1930), *The Front Page* (1931), *This Age for Love* (1931), *Cock of the Air* (1932), *Scarface* (1932), and *Sky Devils* (1932). In 1932, he became bored with filmmaking, and Caddo became inoperative. Caddo had maintained headquarters in Hollywood at 1040 North Las Palmas Avenue, at the United Artists Studios, and at 7000 Romaine Street. Its films are now controlled by Universal.*

RESOURCES

Papers: Academy of Motion Picture Arts and Sciences (Collection of publicist Lincoln Quarberg).

CALIFORNIA MOTION PICTURE CORPORATION. Opera singer Beatriz Michelena (1890–1942) was the featured star of the California Motion Picture Corporation, which was formed early in 1914. Its offices were in San Francisco, while its studios were located near San Raphael, California. Some of the state's best-known businessmen and capitalists financed the new company, and among them were Charles Temple Crocker, the owner of the St. Francis Hotel in San Francisco, and Herbert Scott, president of the Mercantile Bank. Herbert Payne was president of the company, Alexander E. Beyfuss the vice president and general manager, George E. Middleton (Michelena's husband) the production manager and director, and Louis Hutt the chief cameraman and head of its laboratory.

California's first release was *Salomy Jane,* based on the Bret Harte novel, and it was followed by other adaptations of books, plays, and operas, including *Mrs. Wiggs of the Cabbage Patch, Mignon,* and *The Lily of Poverty Flat.* Beginning August 25, 1914, California's productions were distributed by Alco Film Corporation*. In December 1914, the World Film Corporation* began distributing the films, and, in February 1916, California began selling to the states rights* market because it claimed it would not be hampered by set release dates or contracts. Michelena and Middleton left the company in November 1916 when, during the production of *Faust,* California asked Michelena to continue without compensation.

She refused, she said, because the company already owed her $12,000. California went out of business soon thereafter.

BIBLIOGRAPHY

Bell, Geoffrey. "The Rise and Fall of the California Motion Picture Company." *American Classic Screen,* May/June 1981, pp. 16–24.
———. *The Golden Gate and the Silver Screen.* New York: Cornwall Books, 1984.
"California Motion Picture Company's First Release." *The Moving Picture World,* July 4, 1914, p. 68.
"California Motion Picture Corporation." *The Moving Picture World,* July 10, 1915, p. 252.
"A Prima Donna of the Screen." *The New York Dramatic Mirror,* July 1, 1914, p. 25.

CALIFORNIA PICTURES CORPORATION. See CALIFORNIA STUDIOS

CALIFORNIA STUDIOS, formerly the Tec-Art Studio*, were also known as the Prudential Studios (1933–1936), although they were the home of California Studio's owner, Harry Sherman, from 1934 onward. Sherman utilized the studios, which he leased from the Clune family, for the production of the Hopalong Cassidy Westerns, featuring William Boyd, and for the Edward Finney productions made under the Boots and Saddles Pictures, Inc., banner.

In 1944, California Pictures Corporation was formed on the lot by Howard Hughes, with Preston Sturges as president, for the production of Sturges's *Mad Wednesday* (1947), starring Harold Lloyd. Sherman leased the studios to Enterprise Productions, Inc.*, in 1946, and it was renamed Enterprise Studio through 1948. In the fifties, California Studios was the home of Albert Zugsmith Productions (from 1952), Horizon Productions (from 1952), and Stanley Kramer Productions (from 1955), and was utilized for many television series, notably *Superman*. In February 1961, the studio was acquired by Producers Studios Incorporated, which renamed it Producers Studios, and, as a rental lot, it was used by Jack Lemmon, Richard Quine, and American International Pictures*. In 1980, Raleigh Enterprises, Inc., purchased the studio and renamed it the Raleigh Studios. The studio has utilized three different postal addresses: 5360 Melrose Avenue, 650 N. Bronson Avenue, and 5255 Clinton Street, Los Angeles, Calif. 90004.

"CAMEO" COMEDIES. See COLONIAL MOTION PICTURE CORPORATION

CAMERAPHONE. See NATIONAL CAMERAPHONE COMPANY

"CANNED SHOWS" is an early term for motion pictures, coined by *Variety,* because films were always shipped in cans.

THE CANNON GROUP, INC., has its origins in Cannon Films, formed in 1967 by Dennis Friedland and Chris Dewey. The company's earliest films were little more than sex exploitation subjects, but it gained a reputation in 1970 with the low-budget feature *Joe.* In 1979, a majority holding in the company was acquired by two Israelis, Menahem Golan (chairman of the board) and Yoram Globus (president). The two men began an aggressive policy of producing films for independent distribution throughout the world at a logical budget and with pre-licensing to ensure immediate profits. An Italian production arm, Cannon Italia, S.R.L., was formed in 1982, in which year London-Cannon Films, Ltd., was established in the United Kingdom, and the company acquired the Classic Cinema chain, with 130 screens in the British Isles.

By 1983, Cannon was California's fastest growing corporation, with more films in production than many of the major studios. *Forbes* (March 26, 1984) described Cannon as "one of Hollywood's more prolific and profitable film finance and production houses." Among Cannon's productions were *That Championship Season* (1982), *Death Wish II* (1982), *Treasure of the Four Crowns* (1983), *The Wicked Lady* (1983), *Revenge of the Ninja* (1983), *Sahara* (1984), and *Bolero* (1984).

In 1987, Giancarlo Parretti acquired the Cannon Group and, in 1989, renamed it Pathé Entertainment*.

BIBLIOGRAPHY

Barnett, Chris. "Israelis Invade Hollywood." *OTC Review,* July 1983, pp. 18–23.
Ilott, Terry. "Five Years On, Golan and Globus Make Cannon a Major Force." *Screen International,* March 10, 1984, pp. 61–62.
Malan, Rian. "Two Guys from Israel." *California Magazine,* November 1983, pp. 109–10.
Minard, Lawrence. "Givebacks, Hollywood Style." *Forbes,* March 26, 1984, pp. 182–83.
Murnane, Tom. "The Cannon Group, Inc." *California Business,* September 1983, pp. 79–80.
Rehfeld, Jerry. "Cannon Fathers." *Film Comment,* December 1983, pp. 20–24.

CANNON PICTURES INC. should not be confused with the Cannon Group*, although the companies are interrelated. In 1989, Giancarlo Parretti purchased the New York based-21st Century Distribution and renamed it Cannon Pictures. It was acquired from Parretti's Pathé Entertainment* in 1990 by CEO Christopher Pearce, and two years later, it was announced that Cannon would merge with Yoram Globus's Melrose Entertainment to form the Cannon Entertainment Group. The company filed for Chapter XI bankruptcy protection in December 1994, and distribution of its films was taken over by MCEG Sterling.

CANON CITY, COLORADO. See COLORADO MOTION PICTURE COMPANY

CAPITAL FILM COMPANY, incorporated on February 27, 1918, with $2.5 million capital stock, was backed by bankers and financiers throughout the state of Indiana. With headquarters in the Merchants Building in Indianapolis, Capital planned to manufacture and distribute a regular program of 21 reels a week. Production began in mid-May 1918 in a studio on the outskirts of the city. Grain dealer William H. Miller, the first president, was soon succeeded by Ike Schlank of New York, who headed the company for a year. In June 1918, Capital began releasing a portion of the Selig* output. It ended operations in 1924.

BIBLIOGRAPHY

"Capital Film Incorporates in Indiana." *The Moving Picture World,* March 23, 1918, p. 1647.

CARDINAL FILM COMPANY was formed by Paramount Pictures* in 1916 to handle the special release and exploitation of *Joan the Woman,* directed by Cecil B. DeMille and starring Geraldine Farrar as Joan of Arc, supported by Raymond Hatton, Hobart Bosworth, Theodore Roberts, and Wallace Reid.

CARLOS PRODUCTIONS, headed by president A. Carlos, was active from 1923 to 1926, primarily responsible for a series of "B" features, starring action hero Richard Talmadge (1896–1981).

CAROLCO PICTURES, INC., is known as the producer/distributor of the "Rambo" series, starring Sylvester Stallone. It began life in 1977 as Carolco Service Inc., a financing and foreign distribution company, founded by Mario Kassar and Andy Vajna (who sold out to Kassar in November 1989). Carolco's first production was *First Blood* (1982), starring Sylvester Stallone (who joined Carolco's board in 1987). The company went public in November 1986, and the following year, it acquired Orbis Communications and International Video Entertainment Inc. In the early 1990s, despite severe financial problems, it continued lavishly to promote its films and pay outrageous sums of money to its stars, including Arnold Schwarzenegger (*Total Recall*). In 1992, certain television rights to Carolco's library were sold to Spelling Entertainment Inc.* for

$64 million. In 1994, the company's net loss was $43.5 million.

In November 1995, Carolco filed for Chapter XI bankruptcy protection, and chairman Mario Kassar resigned. Canal Plus Distribution purchased Carolco's film library for $58 million, and in September 1996, the remaining assets of the company were auctioned.

BIBLIOGRAPHY

Hammer, Joshua. "From Rambo to Riches." *Newsweek,* July 30, 1990, p. 41.
———. "Total Free Fall." *Newsweek,* March 9, 1992, pp. 50–52.

RESOURCES

Photographs: University of Southern California.

CAROLCO STUDIOS. See DEG STUDIOS

CARTHAY CIRCLE THEATRE, designed by architect Dwight Gibbs, combined both modern and Spanish styles to become one of the most impressive and important of Los Angeles's theatres. It opened on May 18, 1926, with Cecil B. DeMille's *The Volga Boatman,* and was the site of many Los Angeles premieres, including *Sunrise, What Price Glory,* and *Gone with the Wind;* when *The Heiress* had its premiere there in 1949, a publicity stunt involved the invitation of stars from 26 earlier films that had received their premieres at the Carthay Circle. During the silent era and through the early thirties, Carli Elinor was conductor at the theatre, and he composed the scores for the silent features screened there. Also known as the Fox Carthay Circle Theatre and located at Wilshire Boulevard and Camarillo Drive, with a postal address of 6316 San Vicente Boulevard, the Carthay Circle closed in April 1969 following the West Coast premiere of *Shoes of the Fisherman* and was demolished shortly thereafter.

CASABLANCA FILM WORKS. See POLYGRAM N.V.

CASINO STAR COMEDIES. See GAUMONT COMPANY

CASTLE ROCK ENTERTAINMENT is a highly successful production company—*When Harry Met Sally* (1989), *City Slickers* (1991), *A Few Good Men* (1992), etc.—founded on October 12, 1987, by Rob Reiner, Alan Horn, Andrew Scheinman, Glenn Padnick, and Martin Shafter, with a reported $270 million in funding provided by the entertainment division of the Coca-Cola Co. Aside from its film production, Castle Rock is also responsible for the television series *Seinfeld* (first seen on NBC in 1990). On August 17, 1993, Castle Rock was purchased by the Turner Broadcasting System, at which time 44 percent of the company was owned by Sony*, 15 percent by Westinghouse, and the remaining 41 percent by the original partners. When Time Warner* acquired the Turner Broadcasting System, it tried unsuccessfully to sell off the company—in large part because of the financial failure of the Demi Moore vehicle *Striptease* (1996). However, as of December 1996, Time Warner announced it would retain ownership of Castle Rock, seeking outside financing for five productions a year.

Address: 335 North Maple Drive, Suite 135, Beverly Hills, Calif. 90210.

BIBLIOGRAPHY

Eller, Claudia. "When Castle Rock Met Ted Turner." *Los Angeles Times,* November 8, 1993, pp. F1, F5.
Weinraub, Bernard. "Castle Rock Raises the Stakes." *New York Times,* December 20, 1992, p. F12.
Welkos, Robert W. "Between a Rock and a Reiner Stand a Few Other Guys." *Los Angeles Times* Calendar, December 6, 1992, pp. 21, 25–29, 32.

C.B.C. FILM SALES CORPORATION. See COLUMBIA PICTURES

THE CATHOLIC MOTION PICTURE GUILD was founded in March 1923 by the Rev. Michael J. Mullins, with the approval and authorization of the Right Reverend John J. Cantwell, Bishop of Los Angeles and San Diego, "for the spiritual and economic aid of the Catholics engaged in the motion picture industry." John W. Considine was the Guild's first president, and early members included Ruth Clifford, Bebe Daniels, Dolores Del Rio, Joseph P. Kennedy, May McAvoy, Colleen Moore, and Eddie Quillan. The Guild was responsible for the production of the annual *Motion Picture Gambol.*

CENSORSHIP. Unlike most countries, the United States of America has shied away from official censorship of motion pictures, relying on the film industry to regulate itself by way of the Production Code* or on private bodies, such as the National Board of Review of Motion Pictures*, to provide a seal of approval.

Although films were the subject of considerable complaint regarding moral content, theme, and lurid advertising from the turn of the century onward, the first film to experience widespread censorship was D. W. Griffith's *The Birth of a Nation* (1915), which has been the subject of at least 100 challenges as to its presentation and continues to arouse demands for censorship because of its depiction of blacks and of the Ku Klux Klan (curiously, not from conservative elements, but from liberals, those who historically have abhorred censorship and limitations on freedom of speech). D. W. Griffith was a staunch opponent of censorship, always available to speak in states considering censorship laws, and the author of a 1915 pamphlet, *The Rise and Fall of Free Speech in America.* Racial tension was also the reasoning behind a curious federal law that, from 1912 to 1940, banned the importation and transportation across state lines of any film picturing a prize fight, a law that had its origin in black-white violence created by the 1909 Jeffries-Johnson fight.

On November 4, 1907, Chicago passed the first local censorship ordinance, "prohibiting the exhibition of obscene and immoral pictures and regulating the exhibition of pictures of the classes and kinds commonly shown in mutoscope, kinetoscopes, cinematographs and penny arcades." Pennsylvania was the first state to approve a film censorship law (on July 19, 1911); it was followed by Kansas (1913), Ohio (1913), Maryland (1916), New York (1921), Florida (1921), Virginia (1922), Massachusetts (1922), Connecticut (1925), and Louisiana (1935). The film industry was very familiar with the workings of local censorship boards and tried to avoid the depiction of anything that might offend them. It knew that Ohio was opposed to brutality and it limited the number of punches in a fist fight accordingly. New York was strict on immorality.

The constitutionality of such state censorship laws was increasingly questioned, and gradually the states—as much on the ground of cost as of legality—gave up their rights to censor. Despite the U.S. Supreme Court's quashing of the conviction of a Maryland exhibitor who, in 1964, screened *Revenge at Daybreak* without a state license, Maryland continued as the only state with local censorship laws until it finally closed down its Censor Board on June 30, 1981.

In 1915, the Supreme Court had ruled that films were not constitutionally protected from censorship—in the cases of *Mutual Film Corp. v. Industrial Commission of Ohio* and *Mutual Film Corp. of Missouri v. Hodges*—and it did not grant such protection until 1952, in a case involving the Italian film *The Miracle,* which was declared "officially and personally blasphemous" by the commissioner of licenses for New York City, following condemnation of the film by Cardinal Spellman. The Supreme Court ruled that "sacrilege was not a justifiable ground of censorship" and that motion pictures constituted a form of expression protected by the First Amendment.

The federal government has been able to prevent the import of foreign films into the United States if they are considered immoral, subversive, or obscene. In 1935, the Czech film *Extase,* which featured a lengthy nude bathing scene with Hedy Lamarr, was refused entry by New York customs officials, as was a 1965 Swedish film, *491.* Generally, local antiobscenity and antipornography laws have offered the only opportunity for the continued censorship of motion pictures.

BIBLIOGRAPHY

Berman, Lamar Taney, ed. *Selected Articles on Censorship of the Theatre and Moving Pictures.* New York: H. W. Wilson Company, 1931.

Carmen, Ira H. *Movies, Censorship, and the Law.* Ann Arbor, Mich.: University of Michigan Press, 1966.

Cline, Victor B., ed. *Where Do You Draw the Line?* Provo, Utah: Brigham Young University Press, 1974.

De Grazia, Edward, and Roger K. Newman. *Banned Films.* New York: R. R. Bowker, 1982.

Devol, Kenneth S., ed. *Mass Media and the Supreme Court.* New York: Hastings House, 1971.

Ernst, Morris L. *The First Freedom.* New York: Macmillan, 1946.

Ernst, Morris L., and Pare Lorentz. *Censored: The Private Life of the Movie.* New York: Jonathan Cape and H. Smith, 1930.

Ernst, Morris L., and Alan U. Schwartz. *Censorship: The Search for the Obscene.* New York: Macmillan, 1964.

Ernst, Morris L., and William Seagle. *To the Pure . . .* New York: Viking Press, 1928.

Gardiner, Harold C. *Catholic Viewpoint on Censorship.* Garden City, N.Y.: Hanover House, 1958.

Griffith, D. W. *The Rise and Fall of Free Speech in America.* Los Angeles: The Author, 1915 (reprinted by Larry Edmunds Book Shop, 1967).

Hunnings, Neville March. *Film Censors and the Law.* London: George Allen & Unwin, 1967.

Inglis, Ruth A. *Freedom of the Movies.* Chicago: University of Chicago Press, 1947.

Jacobs, Lea. *The Wages of Sin: Censorship and the Fallen Woman Film, 1928–1942.* Madison, Wis.: University of Wisconsin Press, 1991.

Kuhn, Annette. *Cinema, Censorship and Sexuality, 1909–1925.* New York: Routledge, 1988.

Miles, William E. *Damn It!* Evanston, Ill.: Regency, 1963.

Phelps, Guy. *Film Censorship.* London: Victor Gollancz, 1975.

Randall, Richard S. *Censorship of the Movies.* Madison, Wis.: University of Wisconsin Press, 1968.

Roeburt, John. *The Wicked and the Banned.* New York: Macfadden, 1963.

Schumach, Murray. *The Face on the Cutting Room Floor.* New York: William Morrow, 1964.

Vizzard, Jack. *See No Evil.* New York: Simon and Schuster, 1970.

Wistrich, Enid. *"I Don't Mind the Sex It's the Violence": Film Censorship Explored.* London: Marion Boyars, 1978.

RESOURCES

Papers: New York State Archives (New York State Censorship Board records); Ohio Historical Society (Ohio State Censorship Board records).

CENTAUR FILM COMPANY. David Horsley decided to become a film manufacturer after he lost a few hundred dollars when he opened a small motion picture theatre in 1907. With former Biograph* player Charles Gorman, Horsley, who believed he could make better films than any manufacturer except for Biograph and Pathé*, prepared to shoot his first film early in 1908 at a building he owned in Bayonne, New Jersey (where he constructed an open-air stage). When his cameraman decided not to jeopardize his own career, Horsley (who had no previous experience in filmmaking) decided to shoot the film himself. Knowing that the Motion Picture Patents Company* was forming, Horsley would not wait the eight to nine weeks that it would take for a camera to be sent from England, and so he decided to design his own camera.

His company, the Centaur Film Manufacturing Company, later shortened to the Centaur Film Company, was located at 900 Broadway in Bayonne. It released its first film, *A Cowboy Escapade,* on September 19, 1908, but since this was a few weeks after the Kalem Company* released its first film, Kalem, and not Centaur, was selected to be a member of the Motion Picture Patents Company, while Centaur achieved the distinction of becoming the first independent company. Horsley discontinued production until Ludwig G. B. Erb bought a half interest in the company. After production recommenced, the partners quarreled and Horsley purchased Erb's interest. Erb subsequently formed the Crystal Film Company*.

Centaur went out of existence in 1910 as Horsley's new company, the Nestor Film Company, also located at 900 Broadway, Bayonne, was formed with his brother William. A series based on the "Mutt and Jeff" comic strip and another series with the comic villain "Desperate Desmond" were among its earliest productions. Players included Violet and Claire Mersereau, Dorothy Davenport, Alice Davenport, and cowboy Art Acord. Al E. Christie was Nestor's chief of production.

In October 1911, Nestor became the first motion picture company to locate in Hollywood, when it rented a building at Sunset Boulevard and Gower Street. By 1912, most of Nestor's films were being produced in Los Angeles, and it was the first producer to bring three companies to California. Thomas Ricketts directed the dramas, Milton Fahrney the Westerns*, and Al Christie the comedies.

Nestor released through the Motion Picture Distributing and Sales Company*, the distribution company for the independents formed in April 1910 to compete with the Motion Picture Patents Company. When Universal* was formed, Nestor began releasing through that company. Because of a fight for control of Nestor with Universal, in which Horsley had stock, Horsley returned to Bayonne in 1913 and erected a new studio at Avenue E and East 43d Street, where the Centaur productions resumed, with the company now being called the Centaur Film Company. In 1914, Horsley proclaimed that the feature film had seen its day, and, although Centaur produced a six-reel version of *Il Trovatore,* it began to specialize in one-reel comedies under the "Ace" brand. Chester Beecroft was general manager of Centaur in 1915. The "Nestor" brand, which had become part of Universal, ceased to exist in 1919.

BIBLIOGRAPHY

"Centaur's New Building Well Equipped." *The Moving Picture World,* March 7, 1914, p. 1239.
"David Horsley, 'How the First Independent Started.'" *The Moving Picture World,* March 10, 1917, pp. 1518–19.
"Picture Personalities: David Horsley." *The Moving Picture World,* July 2, 1910, p. 117.
von Harleman, G. P. "Motion Picture Studios of California." *The Moving Picture World,* March 10, 1917, pp. 1601–2.

CENTRAL CASTING CORPORATION. Following a study by the Russell Sage Foundation, the major Hollywood producers comprising the Association of Motion Picture Producers decided to establish their own organization to provide extras for their films. Central Casting Corporation was established on December 4, 1925, with the purchase of the Screen Service Agency, one of the largest of the independent casting agencies. No "bit" players, only extras, were handled by Central Casting, which required that individuals register with them and check on a daily basis if work was available. Central Casting was entirely funded by the Association of Motion Picture Producers (later Association of Motion Picture & Television Producers), of which it was a wholly owned subsidiary, and extras were not required to pay commissions.

Central Casting Corporation was able to provide any type of extra—man, woman, child, or handicapped—and through the forties extras were divided by Central Casting into four distinct types: "atmosphere," "character," "specialized," and "dress." Despite the small percentage of extras who actually found employment in the industry, the numbers registered with Central Casting were substantial. In 1929, 17,541 were registered; in 1935, 15,000; in 1946, 5,500; but by 1976 only 2,200 were on register. From 1929 onward, Central Casting published a Call Bureau Cast Service sheet for each feature, providing invaluable information as to the "bit" and extra players in such films. In 1975, the Call Bureau Cast Service became the Actors Agency Directory.

Initially located at 5504 Hollywood Boulevard, at the intersection with Western Avenue, Central Casting moved in the sixties to 8480 Beverly Boulevard. In 1976, Central Casting ceased to be a service for the studios and was sold to Production Payments, Inc.

BIBLIOGRAPHY

Facts about Extra Work. Hollywood, Calif.: Central Casting, August 1, 1936.
Herbert, Ray. "Want to Act? Maybe This'll Dissuade You." *Los Angeles Times,* June 10, 1957, pp. 1, 9.
MacCulloch, Campbell. *Motion Picture "Extra" Work.* Hollywood, Calif.: Central Casting, 1935.

CENTURY COMEDIES, formed in 1917 and active through the mid-twenties, was operated by two brothers,

Julius and Abe Stern, with a studio at 6100 Sunset Boulevard (at the southwest corner of Sunset and Gower Street). Century Comedies were two reels in length; featured the Century Dog, Baby Peggy, Harry Sweet, and Charles Dorety; and were released by Universal*. The Sterns also operated the Great Western Producing Company.

CHADWICK PICTURES CORPORATION, active from 1924 to 1928, was an independent producer of feature films, founded by I. E. Chadwick. The company's best-known film was *The Wizard of Oz* (1925), starring Larry Semon, Dorothy Dwan, and Oliver Hardy.

CHAPLIN STUDIOS occupied a five-acre site bounded on three sides by De Longpre Avenue, La Brea Avenue, and Sunset Boulevard, with a postal address at 1416 N. La Brea Avenue in Hollywood. Ground breaking for the new studios took place in November 1917, and Chaplin (1889–1977) made his first film there, *A Dog's Life,* in 1918. The following Chaplin films were shot at the studio: *The Bond* (1918), *Shoulder Arms* (1918), *Sunnyside* (1919), *A Day's Pleasure* (1919), *The Kid* (1921), *The Idle Class* (1921), *Pay Day* (1922), *The Pilgrim* (1923), *A Woman of Paris* (1923), *The Gold Rush* (1925), *The Circus* (1928), *City Lights* (1931), *Modern Times* (1936), *The Great Dictator* (1940), *Monsieur Verdoux* (1947), and *Limelight* (1952).

The studio was designed in the style of an English village and built for a reported sum of $35,000. At one corner of the studio, at the junction of Sunset and La Brea, stood the McClelan Mansion, which was occupied by Chaplin's brother Sydney. This house was later demolished and on the site stands a Safeway supermarket.

Chaplin sold his studios in September 1953 to the New York real estate company of Weber & Knapp for $650,000. The company announced plans to demolish the studio but instead leased it, in December 1953, to Kling Studios of Chicago for television production. In 1958, Red Skelton's Van Bernard Productions acquired the lot, and in 1962 it was purchased by CBS, Inc., as a production facility for Paisano Productions' television series *Perry Mason*. Finally, in August 1966, the present owners, Herb Alpert and Jerry Moss's A & M Record Company and Tijuana Brass Enterprises, Inc., purchased the studios. The Chaplin Studio was declared a Historic-Cultural Monument by the Los Angeles Cultural Heritage Board on February 5, 1969.

CHARIOT FILM COMPANY, with offices at 110 West 40th Street, New York, released its first production, the four-reel *The God of Vengeance,* in April 1914. Alex Yokel was the president and general manager of the company, which planned to release one film every three weeks.

BIBLIOGRAPHY

"Chariot Film Company Enters the Arena." *The Moving Picture World,* April 11, 1914, p. 225.

THE CHARLES AIDIKOFF SCREENING ROOM is the best-known private screening facility in the Los Angeles area. Charles Aidikoff, a former New York projectionist, opened his first screening room in 1966 in a building at Sunset and Doheny in West Hollywood; in 1992, it moved to 150 S. Rodeo Drive in Beverly Hills. The original theatre had 26 seats, and the present one has 53.

BIBLIOGRAPHY

Johnson, Quendrith. "The Room Where the Industry Unspools Its Films." *Los Angeles Times,* February 23, 1994, p. F4.

CHARLES E. BLANEY FEATURE PLAY COMPANY. See BLANEY-SPOONER FEATURE FILM COMPANY

CHARLES K. HARRIS FEATURE FILM COMPANY, a company that produced films based on the songs of Charles K. Harris (1865–1930), was incorporated in New York on February 10, 1915. It released with the World Film Corporation*. Charles K. Harris was one of the directors of the company, and among the players who appeared in its films were Edwin August, Grace Washburn, and Muriel Ostriche.

CHASE-PARK CITRON. See INTERNATIONAL CREATIVE MANAGEMENT, INC.

CHAS. K. FELDMAN'S GROUP PRODUCTIONS was formed in the mid-forties by Charles K. Feldman (1904–1968) to produce a small series of quality features, including *Uncle Harry* (1945), *The Red Pony* (1949), *The Glass Menagerie* (1950), *A Streetcar Named Desire* (1951), and *The Seven Year Itch* (1955), released through various distributors. All Group Productions properties were sold in 1955 to 20th Century-Fox* for a reported $1 million. Feldman was also president of Famous Artists Corporation, a talent agency that he formed in 1932 and whose clients included Tyrone Power, Kirk Douglas, Max Steiner, Salvador Dali, John Wayne, Lauren Bacall, George Stevens, Ava Gardner, and Charles Boyer. (The agency was sold in 1962 to Ashley-Steiner and became Ashley-Famous.)

RESOURCES

Papers: American Film Institute.

CHEMICAL FADE is a term introduced in the silent era to describe an effect created in the laboratory rather than in the camera.

CHESTERFIELD MOTION PICTURE CORPORATION, a low-budget producer, was active from circa 1925 to 1936. Films were initially shot on the Universal* lot, and, in the thirties, at what became Republic Pictures Corporation* in Studio City. George R. Batcheller was president of the corporation, whose best-known director—under contract in the early thirties—was Richard Thorpe. In the thirties, Chesterfield was associated with Invincible Pictures Corporation (whose president was Maury Cohen).

CHICAGO INTERNATIONAL FILM FESTIVAL. First held November 4–11, 1965, the Chicago International Film Festival remains under the directorship of Michael Kutza, Jr. It is a competitive festival, held each November, offering a Golden Hugo for best film, with a Silver and Bronze Hugo for runners-up; there are also awards for Best First Feature, Best Actor, Best Actress, and a Special Jury Prize.

Address: 415 North Dearborn Street, Chicago, Ill. 60610.

CHILD LABOR LAWS. Current child labor laws within the motion picture industry govern the number of hours a minor may work, the times during which he or she may work, and the schooling to be provided by the production company. (Schooling is handled by Studio Teachers, Local No. 884 of IATSE*.) Such laws date back to 1927, when an informal agreement was worked out between teachers' groups and the State Labor Commission governing the use of children in films from both a safety and a morality viewpoint. The question of the use of children in films became a major public issue with the deaths of two children and actor Vic Morrow on the set of *The Twilight Zone* on July 23, 1982; the two children were working during hours when the employment of minors in film production was forbidden.

The best known of child labor laws concerns the holding in trust of a minor's earnings until he or she gains maturity. On April 11, 1938, former child star Jackie Coogan filed suit against his mother and stepfather to recover his earnings dating back to the early twenties. Coogan was successful in his suit, but it transpired that the bulk of the money had already been spent. As a result, the State Assembly in Sacramento, California, passed a Child Actor's Bill, commonly known as "The Coogan Act," under Section 36 of the California Civil Code. The bill gave the court authority to approve all contracts between minors and the entertainment industry and provided that at least one-half of the minor's earnings had to be paid by the studio or other employer directly into a trust fund established for the minor's benefit. Deanna Durbin was the first child star to become subject to the new bill.

BIBLIOGRAPHY

Cary, Diana Serra. *Hollywood's Children.* Boston: Houghton Mifflin, 1979.
Silverberg, Herbert T. "Status of Minors in Hollywood." *Daily Variety,* October 24, 1938, p. 74.
Zierold, Norman J. *The Child Stars.* New York: Coward-McCann, 1965.

CHILD STARS. Just as the American public has been fascinated by the image of the child-woman, as exemplified by Mary Pickford, Mary Miles Minter, Audrey Hepburn, and others, so has it had a long and lasting appreciation of child stars, beginning in the early teens. The box office appeal of children reached its zenith between 1915 and 1917, when films featured Ida and Ella Mackenzie, Viola Dana, Billy Jacobs, Clara Horton, Baby Marie Osborne, Thelma Salter, and many other children. The Thanhouser Film Corporation* had a veritable stable of child performers, including Leland Benham; Helen Badgley, billed as the Thanhouser Kidlet; Marie Eline, known as the Thanhouser Kid; and Marion and Madeline Fairbanks, the Thanhouser Twins. Jane and Katherine Lee first came to the public's attention in *A Daughter of the Gods* (1916). They joined Fine Arts* and were featured, along with Charles Spofford, Francis Carpenter, and Virginia Lee Corbin, in *Let Katie Do It* (1916). From Fine Arts, the children moved over as a group to the Fox Film Corporation*, where they were billed as the Fox Kiddies and featured in a series of films, most based on fairy tales, directed by Sidney and Chester Franklin.

Jackie Coogan achieved stardom with his performance in the title role of Charle Chaplin's *The Kid* (1921). Producer Sol Lesser helped advance his career, and Lesser is also responsible for the success of another child star of the twenties, Baby Peggy (Montgomery). In 1922, Hal Roach introduced the "Our Gang" series*.

The thirties saw a new wave of child stars, including dramatic actor Freddie Bartholomew, who was featured in *David Copperfield* (1934) and *Little Lord Fauntleroy* (1937); Mickey Rooney and Judy Garland, who were teamed in a series of M-G-M* musicals; Shirley Temple, who became the biggest box office star at 20th Century-Fox*; Deanna Durbin, who helped save Universal* from bankruptcy with her cheery musicals; boy soprano Bobby Breen; Jackie Cooper, who made a name for himself in *Skippy* (1930) and *The Champ* (1931); Jane Withers, who was 20th Century-Fox's other major child star; Gloria Jean, whom Universal introduced as a second Deanna Durbin; Baby LeRoy, who infuriated W. C. Fields; Bonita Granville, who starred as Nancy Drew; as well as many others.

Margaret O'Brien, Peggy Ann Garner, and Claude Jarman, Jr., were the best of the forties child stars, all of them featured as dramatic rather than musical performers. In more recent years, Tatum O'Neal won an Academy Award for Best Supporting Actress for her work in *Paper Moon* (1973). Ricky Schroder followed in the footsteps of Jackie Cooper in a 1979 remake of *The Champ,* and that same year Justin Henry was nominated for an Oscar, for Best Supporting Actor, for his work in *Kramer vs. Kramer.*

Sue Lyon presented an unusual child heroine in *Lolita* (1962). Modern child stars, some of whom have already proved adept at adult roles, include Christina Applegate, Drew Barrymore, Maccauley Culkin, and Brooke Shields.

In 1935, the Academy of Motion Picture Arts and Sciences presented a miniature statuette to Shirley Temple, "in grateful recognition of her outstanding contribution to screen entertainment during the year 1934." Beginning with the 1938 awards year, the Academy presented Special

Awards to child performers: Deanna Durbin and Mickey Rooney (1938), Judy Garland (1939), Margaret O'Brien (1944), Peggy Ann Garner (1945), Claude Jarman, Jr. (1946), Ivan Jandl (1948), Bobby Driscoll (1949), Jon Whiteley and Vincent Winter (1954), and Hayley Mills (1960).

BIBLIOGRAPHY

Aylesworth, Thomas G. *Hollywood Kids: Child Stars of the Silver Screen from 1903 to the Present.* New York: E. P. Dutton, 1987.

Best, Marc. *Those Endearing Young Charms.* New York: A. S. Barnes, 1971.

———. *Their Hearts Were Young and Gay.* New York: A. S. Barnes, 1975.

Cary, Diana Serra. *Hollywood's Children.* Boston: Houghton Mifflin, 1979.

Chandler, Suzanne. *Children of Babylon.* Stamford, Conn.: Longmeadow Press, 1993.

Coghlan, Frank. *They Still Call Me Junior: Autobiography of a Child Star.* Jefferson, N.C.: McFarland, 1993.

Darvi, Andrea. *Pretty Babies: An Insider's Look at the World of the Hollywood Child Star.* New York: McGraw-Hill, 1983.

Dye, David. *Child and Youth Actors: Filmographies of Their Entire Careers, 1914–1985.* Jefferson, N.C.: McFarland, 1988.

Holmstrom, John. *The Moving Picture Boy: An International Encyclopedia from 1895 to 1995.* Wilby, Norwich, U.K.: Michael Russell, 1996.

Maltin, Leonard, ed. *Hollywood Kids.* New York: Popular Library, 1978.

Moore, Dick. *Twinkle, Twinkle, Little Star.* New York: Harper & Row, 1984.

Slide, Anthony. "Child Stars." In *Aspects of American Film History Prior to 1920.* Metuchen, N.J.: Scarecrow Press, 1978, pp. 16–25.

Zierold, Norman. *The Child Stars.* New York: Coward-McCann, 1965.

CHRISTIE FILM COMPANY. Al E. Christie (1886–1951), who was earlier the head of production at the Nestor Film Company, along with his brother Charles leased the old Nestor studio, at Sunset Boulevard and Gower Street, from the Quality Pictures Corporation* on January 1, 1916, and formed the Christie Film Company, to produce comedies for release through Universal* under the "Nestor" brand. Al was president and director of production, and Charles was the general manager. In May 1916, Fred L. Porter became the vice president and secretary.

In July 1916, Christie severed his connection with Universal and began offering his weekly release to independent exchanges on the open market. Christie doubled its output in October 1916 by adding director Horace G. Davey. Among the players at Christie were Billie Rhodes, Dorothy Devore, Stella Adams, Eddie Barry, and Harry Ham. Laura La Plante and Betty Compson were two major stars of the twenties who made their screen debuts in Christie comedies.

In April 1918, Christie began releasing its comedies with First National*, and, in 1920, Educational began to distribute the films.

Christie turned to feature-length production in the twenties, notably with two versions of *Charley's Aunt.* The first, in 1925, starred Syd Chaplin, and the second, in 1930, featured Charlie Ruggles. The relationship with Educational continued, and, when Christie ceased to be an independent producer, he worked for Educational as a producer of its musical and comedy shorts. Al Christie retired in the late thirties.

BIBLIOGRAPHY

"Al Christie's Comedy Checkerboard." *Photoplay,* May 1925, p. 81.

Christie, Al E. *The Elements of Situation Comedy.* Los Angeles: Palmer Photoplay Corporation, 1920.

Weir, Hugh S. "Al Christie's Recipe for a Successful Movie Picture Company." *Moving Picture Weekly,* July 24, 1915, p. 46.

"THE CHRONICLES OF AMERICA" is a series of short historical subjects, produced by Yale University Press in 1923–1924, and distributed by Pathé*. The first in the series was *Columbus,* directed by Edwin L. Hollywood, and the last, *Dixie.* The films are preserved at both the Library of Congress and the Museum of Modern Art.

BIBLIOGRAPHY

Slide, Anthony. "The Chronicles of America." In *Before Video: A History of the Non-Theatrical Film.* Westport, Conn.: Greenwood Press, 1992, pp. 75–87.

CIGARETTE SMOKING was an integral element in Hollywood films; it was both a substitute for sex and a sign of a liberated or perhaps "bad" woman. "Cigarette smoking has . . . long been one of the theater's most powerful means of expression," wrote Walter Kerr in the *New York Times* (January 30, 1981), a comment that might just as well be applied to motion pictures. A shared cigarette is a basic part of the film scene, as witness Paul Henreid and Bette Davis in *Now Voyager* (1942), with Henreid's lighting of two cigarettes and his comment, "Shall we just have a cigarette on it?" Robert Walker expresses his love for Jennifer Jones with a cigarette in *Since You Went Away* (1944). Humphrey Bogart is first seen in *Casablanca* (1942) with a cigarette in his mouth. Lauren Bacall makes her entrance in *To Have and Have Not* (1944), demanding that Bogart light her cigarette.

William Holden chain-smoked in *The World of Suzie Wong* (1960). Tom Cruise lit up in *Rain Man* (1988). In *Lethal Weapon 2* (1989), Mel Gibson is a police detective lighting up in defiance of the "No Smoking" signs. *The*

Client (1994) opens with a ten-year-old teaching an eight-year-old how to smoke, and later, Susan Sarandon relaxes with a cigarette.

It was routine in the golden age of Hollywood for film stars to promote cigarette smoking. As late as the fifties, Liggett & Myers published advertising stating that "Rosalind Russell says L&M filters are just what the doctor ordered." At the same time, Jack Webb was inviting Americans to join him in smoking L&Ms.

The promotion of cigarette smoking on screen may be more subtle, but it is still there. Philip Morris paid $42,500 to have Lois Lane smoke in *Superman* (1978), despite the character's not smoking in the comic books. In 1989, Philip Morris paid $350,000 to have Timothy Dalton as James Bond smoke a Lark in *License to Kill*.

Cigarette advertising has been banned on television since 1971, but while some programs—such as *Cheers*—are smoke-free environments, others are not. For example, *Prime Suspect,* with Helen Mirren, features an ongoing fight over cigarettes.

A study in the *American Journal of Public Health* (June 20, 1994) noted that tobacco use had not declined on screen, despite a reduction in Americans who smoke. The journal pointed out that the adopted mother of *E.T.* (1982) smoked, as did the crew of *Ghostbusters* (1984). Cigar smoking in the entertainment industry has also been on the increase. There are, of course, classic examples, such as George Burns with his trademark cigar, Orson Welles in *Citizen Kane* (1941), Sidney Greenstreet in *The Maltese Falcon* (1941), Henry Hull in *Lifeboat* (1944), Charles Laughton in *Witness for the Prosecution* (1957), and Jeff Bridges in *Jagged Edge* (1985). In the nineties, cigar smoking was taken up by a highly publicized group of women, including Whoopi Goldberg, Madonna, Demi Moore, and Sharon Stone. The characters are defined by what they smoke in Wayne Wang's *Smoke* (1995), and in 1996, Alex Trebek introduced a line of celebrity cigars.

The ultimate tribute to cigarette smoking—what might be described as "smoxploitation"—is the 1995 video, *Paula,* which is nothing more than 30 minutes of footage of a woman smoking.

BIBLIOGRAPHY

Dutka, Elaine. "Force of Habit." *Los Angeles Times,* September 5, 1996, pp. F1, F10, F11.
Gary, Juliann. "Blame It on Bizet." *Los Angeles Times* Calendar, June 17, 1994, pp. 25, 27, 28.
Harmetz, Aljean. "History Is Written in Smoke." *New York Times,* November 8, 1992, pp. 13, 16.
Lane, Anthony. "Where There's Fire." *The New Yorker,* March 21, 1994, pp. 203–6.
"Lights, Camera, Cigar!" *Philip Morris Magazine,* March/April 1989, pp. 22–24.
Matsumoto, Nancy, Carolyn Ramsay, and Karen Jackovich. "Hollywood Goes Up in Smoke." *People,* September 12, 1994, pp. 114–16.

CINECOLOR. Introduced in 1932, and a descendent of Prizma Color* and Multicolor, Cinecolor utilized a bipack system of photography, in which two negatives were run through the camera, emulsion to emulsion, and exposed simultaneously. One negative recorded the red-orange portion of the spectrum and the other the blue-green. Prints were made on duplitized positive film with an emulsion coated on both sides—one toned blue-green, the other red-orange. Because it was less expensive than Technicolor* and did not require the three-strip Technicolor camera, Cinecolor was very popular with low-budget feature producers and with producers of short subjects. A similar two-color system, Trucolor, was developed by Consolidated Film Industries* for Republic Pictures*. All of these two-color systems were superseded by Eastman Color*. Cinecolor, Inc., was reorganized in 1944 as Cinecolor Corp.; the name was changed to Color Corp. of America in 1953, and in 1970, the company merged with Image Systems, Inc.

THE CINEMA AUDIO SOCIETY (CAS) was founded in 1964 to enable sound professionals in the film and television industries to share information. It hosts an annual awards banquet and publishes a journal and directory.

Address: 12414 Huston Street, Valley Village, Calif. 91607.

CINEMA CORPORATION OF AMERICA. See PRODUCERS DISTRIBUTING CORPORATION

CINEMA EDUCATIONAL GUILD. See COMMUNISM

CINEMA 5 was a leading independent distributor of critical and artistic successes under the guidance of its founder—in 1963—Donald S. Rugoff (1927–1989). Rugoff's family had operated a theatre chain, Rugoff and Becker, since 1921, and Rugoff became the company's president in 1957; among the theatres that he opened was New York's Cinema I and II in 1962, and believed to be America's first twin theatre. Rugoff lost control of the company in 1979, when it was taken over by William R. Forman, and it left the distribution field until 1981. In 1982, the distribution arm (100 features) was sold to the Almi Group, which merged it with Libra Films Corp. to form Libra Cinema 5 Films, and in 1985, RKO Century Warner Theatres, Inc., acquired Cinema 5 Ltd. and changed its name to Cinema 5 Theatres.

THE CINEMA GUILD is a major distributor of independent documentary films and videotapes, founded in 1975.

Address: 1697 Broadway, Suite 506, New York, N.Y. 10019.

CINEMASCOPE. A widescreen process that utilizes an anamorphic camera and projector lens—and needs only one camera and projector—CinemaScope was introduced by 20th Century-Fox* with *The Robe,* which opened at the

Roxy Theatre*, New York, on September 16, 1953. The CinemaScope lens, which was manufactured in the United States by Bausch & Lomb, was the invention of the Frenchman Henri Chrétien and dates back to 1927. The British Rank Organization had an option on the use of the lens, but when that option expired, it was taken up by 20th Century-Fox, which saw CinemaScope as a solution to its falling profits brought on, in part, by television.

Wholly owned by 20th Century-Fox, the CinemaScope process was subsequently licensed to M-G-M* in March 1953. Warner Bros.* had come up with an anamorphic lens similar to CinemaScope, which it initially called WarnerSuperScope, and RKO* introduced its system, SuperScope. However, late in 1953, Warner Bros. abandoned its widescreen process and signed a license agreement with 20th Century-Fox. By the end of 1953, every major studio—with the exception of Paramount*, which had its VistaVision* process—was licensed to use CinemaScope. All CinemaScope productions of 1953 were in stereophonic sound, but by 1954 20th Century-Fox had commenced producing prints with monaural soundtracks for those theatres not equipped for stereo. By November 1, 1954, it was reported that some 9,000 theatres in the United States and Canada were able to screen CinemaScope prints.

To improve the quality of its 35mm release prints, 20th Century-Fox introduced CinemaScope 55 in 1956, which utilized a film in the camera 55mm wide. The first film to be shot in CinemaScope 55 was *Carousel,* but the process was abandoned by 20th Century-Fox after *The King and I* (1956).

In 1953, Henri Chrétien, Earl Sponable, Sol Halprin, Lorin Grignon, Herbert Bragg, and Carl Faulkner of the 20th Century-Fox studios received a Class I Scientific or Technical Award (Oscar statuette) "for creating, developing and engineering the equipment, processes, and techniques known as CinemaScope." 20th Century-Fox utilized CinemaScope for all its features through 1967.

BIBLIOGRAPHY
Belton, John. *Widescreen Cinema.* Cambridge, Mass.: Harvard University Press, 1992.
Carr, Robert E., and R. M. Hayes. *Wide Screen Movies: A History and Filmography of Wide Screen Gauge Filmmaking.* Jefferson, North Carolina: McFarland, 1988.

CINEMIRACLE, developed by National Theatres, was similar to Cinerama*. It utilized three projectors and three cameras, with the right and left cameras photographing their images through mirrors. The "joins" between the three strips of film were eliminated through the use of "vignetting" in the cameras and in the laboratory printing. The right- and left-hand projectors also used mirrors, and the three projectors could be placed in the same booth, unlike Cinerama, which required three separate booths. The seven-track stereophonic sound was heard through five speakers placed behind the deeply curved screen and two speakers to the right and left of the auditorium. Both the Roxy* in New York and Grauman's Chinese Theatre in Hollywood were refurbished for the premiere of the one and only feature to be shot in Cinemiracle, *Windjammer.* The world premiere of *Windjammer* took place at Grauman's Chinese Theatre on April 8, 1958, with the Roxy opening following a day later.

BIBLIOGRAPHY
"Cinemiracle with 'Windjammer' Opens Big, Wide View of the World." *The Film Daily,* April 7, 1958, pp. 5–13.
Smith, P. Stanley. "The Cinemiracle Camera and Its Development." *American Cinematographer,* February 1958, pp. 100–101, 118–119.
Zunser, Jesse. "Cinemiracle." *Cue,* April 5, 1958, p. 12.

CINERAMA gave the effect of reality to a presentation by utilizing three synchronized projectors showing the three 35mm images, slightly overlapping, on a wide, curved screen, made up of 1,100 vertical strips of perforated tape. To add to the effect, the system also utilized multitrack stereophonic sound. Theatres screening Cinerama were required to install special projectors (each of which required a separate projectionist) and a new screen. The Cinerama camera unit utilized three films and three 27mm lenses set at 48 degree angles to each other, with the left lens filming the right hand side of the picture and the right lens filming the left. To project Cinerama, the complete film—at least up to a break or intermission—needed to be loaded on one single reel, each for three projectors, and projected at one-and-a-half times the normal speed to allow for the increased size of the film frame.

The process was invented by Fred Waller (1886–1954) and was first seen at the 1937 New York World's Fair, where it was known as Vitarama. Waller explained Cinerama as quoted in the *Journal of the British Film Academy* (Autumn 1954) as "the medium of subjective participation, the only true 'I am a camera' system. Every single scene, every single shot must be conceived *within* the medium; the audience must be brought into the picture. The Cinerama screen is not a mirror of life, but life itself, and is an extension of the physical world, with the spectator at the centre of it." The patent on the Cinerama process was controlled by Vitarama Corporation, jointly owned by Waller and Laurance Rockefeller. The process was exploited by Cinerama, Inc. (formerly Cinerama Corporation), formed by Lowell Thomas and others and which remained in existence as a distribution company, often financially troubled, through the present.

The first Cinerama presentation, *This Is Cinerama,* opened at the Broadway Theatre, New York, on September 30, 1952, and caused such a sensation that even *the New York Times* covered the event as a front-page news story. Eventually problems with the overlapping image of the three projectors and the cost of installation of the special equipment led to Cinerama's being presented, using a single projector, with a single 70mm* film.

BIBLIOGRAPHY

"Cinerama—the Broad Picture." *Fortune,* January 1953, pp. 92–93, 144–46, 148, 150.
Halas, John. "Discovering Cinerama." *Journal of the British Film Academy* (Autumn 1954): pp. 2–6.

CINERGI PRODS. INC. was launched as an independent producer by Andrew G. "Andy" Vajna in December 1989 after he left Carolco Pictures.* Its first release was *Tombstone* (1993). In August 1990, Cinergi signed a five-year contract with the Walt Disney Productions* for the latter to distribute its films, and, in October 1992, it acquired the library of Sovereign Pictures. The company went public in June 1994. Cinergi has been responsible for a number of successful productions, including *Nixon* (1995), *Die Hard with a Vengeance* (1995, co-produced with 20th Century-Fox*), and *Evita* (1996), as well as such box-office failures as *Judge Dredd* and *The Scarlet Letter*, both released in 1995. Early in 1997, it abruptly closed down production on the Bruce Willis vehicle *Broadway Brawler*. Between 1989 and 1993, Cinergi lost approximately $27 million, and in April 1997, it was forced to turn over the bulk of its library to Disney as compensation for the more than $38 million that Disney had loaned the company.

Address: 2308 Broadway, Santa Monica, Calif. 90404.

BIBLIOGRAPHY

Bates, James. "Cinergi to Pay Disney Debt by Turning over Its Library." *Los Angeles Times*, April 4, 1997, p. D1.
Brown, Colin. "Seeing Scarlet." *Screen International*, November 10, 1995, p. 12.
Citron, Alan. "Andy Vajna Returns to the Front Lines." *Los Angeles Times*, December 10, 1993, p. D5.

CINEVISTA, INC., founded in 1982, distributes foreign- and English-language feature films for the art house market, including *Taxi Zum Klo, Caravaggio,* and number of titles directed by Pedro Almodovar.

Address: 560 West 42d Street, Suite 8J, New York, N.Y. 10036.

CITY ISLAND. See RYNO FILM COMPANY, INC.

C.K.Y. FILM CORPORATION was formed in August 1917 to market and distribute the films of popular star Clara Kimball Young (1890–1960).

CLARK-CORNELIUS CORP. was organized in 1919, with William J. Clark as president and H. C. Cornelius as vice president, by the controlling interests of Exhibitors' Mutual Distributing Corporation to purchase the negatives of 12 Charlie Chaplin Mutual comedies. It continued in business after the sale of the Exhibitors' Mutual Distributing exchanges.

CLAY ANIMATION is a form of three-dimensional animation that owes its existence to William Harbutt's invention of plasticine in the late 1890s. The earliest known clay animation film is *Fun in a Bakery Shop,* produced in 1902. The "Gumby" television series (NBC, 1957) introduced clay animation to modern audiences, and the technique was improved by Will Vinton in the seventies. Vinton trademarked Claymation in 1981, and in 1986, he introduced the "California Raisins," utilizing the process, in television commercials. The most impressive example of clay animation, or more precisely clay painting, is Joan Gratz's short, *Mona Lisa Descending a Staircase,* which won the 1993 Academy Award for Best Animated Short Film.

BIBLIOGRAPHY

Frierson, Michael. *Clay Animation: American Highlights 1908 to the Present.* New York: Twayne, 1994.

CLAYMATION. See CLAY ANIMATION

CLEVELAND. See JUVENILE FILM COMPANY

CLIFFSIDE, NEW JERSEY. See JESTER COMEDY COMPANY and SERIAL FILM COMPANY

CLUNE STUDIO. See TEC-ART STUDIO

CODE. See PRODUCTION CODE

THE COLD WAR, the struggle for power between the West and the Communist bloc immediately following the Second World War, led to the production of a number of propagandistic films by Hollywood, warning of the danger of Communism in Russia and, to a lesser extent, in China. Beginning with *The Iron Curtain,* produced by 20th Century-Fox in 1948, these films were an obvious response by Hollywood studios to the House Un-American Activities Committee investigation of the film industry, which had begun in earnest in 1947. The insidious activities of Communist spies and sympathizers—often depicted as little more than gangsters—in the United States was the subject matter of such films as *The Red Menace* (1949), *I Was a Communist for the FBI* (1951), *My Son John* (1952), and *The Manchurian Candidate* (1962). The work of Communists abroad was documented in *Rogue's Regiment* (1948), *The Big Lift* (1950), *Diplomatic Courier* (1952), *Target Hong Kong* (1953), *Blood Alley* (1955), *China Gate* (1957), *The Beast of Budapest* (1958), *The Quiet American* (1958), and *Satan Never Sleeps* (1962).

The approach was often heavy-handed, with producers often insisting that it was the patriotic duty of all Americans to see these films (and coincidentally enrich their makers), but there were a handful of comedies with a Cold War theme. Bob Hope starred in *My Favorite Spy* (1951) and *The Iron Petticoat* (1956), while Donald O'Connor and Francis the Talking Mule did their bit with *Francis Goes to West Point* (1952) and *Francis Joins the WACS* (1954).

Composer/singer Floyd Tillman took the subject to heart with his 1949 song "This Cold War with You." On the musical stage, the Cold War was celebrated in *Silk Stockings,* with music and lyrics by Cole Porter and a book by George S. Kaufman, Leueen MacGrath, and Abe Burrows, which opened at New York's Imperial Theatre on February 24, 1955. A satire of Soviet Russia, based on the 1939 Greta Garbo film, *Ninotchka, Silk Stockings* told of a female commissar (played by Hildegarde Neff) who is transformed into a romantic woman as a result of a visit to Paris. One of the songs listed the joys of being sent to "Siberia," where one never had to phone for ice and where there is no unemployment. Two years after its Broadway success, *Silk Stockings* was filmed by M-G-M*, under the direction of Rouben Mamoulian, and starring Fred Astaire and Cyd Charisse.

BIBLIOGRAPHY

Shain, Russell E. "Hollywood's Cold War" and "Cold War Films, 1948–1962: An Annotated Filmography." *Journal of Popular Film* vol. 3, no. 4, (Fall 1974): pp. 334–50 and 365–72.

COLLECTIVE FILM PRODUCERS, INC., was founded in New York in the summer of 1937 by Roman Rebush to produce Yiddish-language films. Rebush hired Edgar G. Ulmer as his director, and the first production was *Grine Felder/Green Fields,* released in October 1937, and based on the classic play by Peretz Hirschbein. It was follwed by *Der Zingendiker Shmid/The Singing Blacksmith* (1938).

BIBLIOGRAPHY

Goldman, Eric A. *Visions, Images, and Dreams: Yiddish Film Past and Present.* Ann Arbor, Mich.: UMI Research Press, 1983.

COLONIAL MOTION PICTURE CORPORATION was formed late in 1913 after having secured the rights to the writings of various novelists. James D. Law was the president, and Frederick S. Dudley was vice president and general manager of the company. Its first production, the nine-reel *Seats of the Mighty,* written by Sir Gilbert Parker, was directed by T. Hayes Hunter and starred Millicent Evans, Lionel Barrymore, and Lois Meredith. In 1915, Colonial began producing "Cameo" brand comedies featuring Harry Kelley.

COLONY PICTURES, INC., founded by brothers Max and Arthur Alexander, was active from 1936 through 1940 as a producer of Westerns starring Rex Bell, Ken Maynard, and Gene Austin.

COLORADO MOTION PICTURE COMPANY began production in October 1913 and was located at 1444 Stuart Street in Denver. It specialized in military and Western* films. Otis B. Thayer was the company's first director, until he left, late in 1914, to go to the Pike's Peak Film Company*. In March 1914, Colorado built a new studio in Canon City, Colorado. It was a regular contributor to Warner's Features, Inc.

COLORADO SPRINGS, COLORADO. See PIKE'S PEAK FILM COMPANY

COLORIZATION is the generic term used to describe a computerized process that transforms black-and-white films into color; it was developed by Ralph Weinger, an electronics engineer, in 1978. Weinger's process is used by Color Systems Technology of Los Angeles. An electronic scanner breaks down each frame of film into 525,000 dots. An art director examines the first and last frames of each scene and determines the color for each object in the frame. A computer then colorizes the scene, selecting the colors by comparing each frame with the one preceding it. A similar system was also utilized by Colorization, Inc., a subsidiary of Hal Roach Studios, Inc.*

Film and television distributors were particularly interested in the process, believing it would give new life to black-and-white subjects, for which it is hard to find playing time on television. The process also, from a legal viewpoint, creates new films that can be recopyrighted. However, most creative people within the industry have denounced colorization as a form of vandalization of films that were shot and meant to be seen only in black-and-white. A major controversy arose in 1989, when Ted Turner announced plans to colorize *Citizen Kane,* but director Orson Welles's original contract prevented such tampering with his masterwork. In January 1994, Turner announced no future plans to colorize beyond the 120 films already done, noting there was no marketplace to justify the expense. As of the mid nineties, only two colorization companies, CST Entertainment in Culver City and American Film Technologies in San Diego, remained active. At that time, it was reported that the average cost of colorizing a feature film was $110,000 and a 30-minute television show was $24,000.

BIBLIOGRAPHY

Slide, Anthony. "Colorization." In *Nitrate Won't Wait: A History of Film Preservation in the United States.* Jefferson, North Carolina: McFarland, 1992, pp. 122–33.

COLUMBIA LICENSED MOTION PICTURES. See POWERS COMPANY

COLUMBIA PICTURES CORPORATION (TEENS). See METRO PICTURES CORPORATION

COLUMBIA PICTURES. A humble yet spirited company, Columbia Pictures was virtually the only "poverty row"* studio to transform its image and become a major corporation, thanks entirely to the vigor of its cofounder, Harry Cohn (1891–1958). It was Cohn who personally supervised all studio production and who was responsible for signing Columbia's best-known director, Frank Capra (1897–1991). Capra was active at Columbia from the late twenties through the late thirties, and his films for the studio included *That Certain Thing* (1928), *Platinum Blonde* (1931), *Lady for a Day* (1933), *It Happened One Night* (1934), *Mr. Deeds Goes to Town* (1936), *Lost Horizon* (1937), and *Mr. Smith Goes to Washington* (1939).

Aside from the Capra features, Columbia produced some of the best screwball comedies* of the thirties, including *Twentieth Century* (1934), *Theodora Goes Wild* (1936), *The Awful Truth* (1937), and *His Girl Friday* (1939). Grace Moore was one of Columbia's first major stars, followed by Rita Hayworth, Kim Novak, William Holden, Glenn Ford, and Judy Holliday. Among the "classic" Columbia features were *Gilda* (1946), *The Jolson Story* (1946), *The Lady from Shanghai* (1948), *Jolson Sings Again* (1949), *All the King's Men* (1949), *Born Yesterday* (1950), *On the Waterfront* (1955), *The Bridge on the River Kwai* (1957), *Lawrence of Arabia* (1962), *A Man for All Seasons* (1966), and *Guess Who's Coming to Dinner* (1968). Columbia also released the first group of major youth-oriented quality features, such as *Easy Rider* (1969), *Five Easy Pieces* (1970), and *The Last Picture Show* (1971).

Columbia was founded in 1922 by Harry Cohn, Joe Brandt, and Jack Cohn as C.B.C. Film Sales Corporation, which produced cheap Westerns*, comedies starring the Hall Room Boys, and the "Screen Snapshots" series on Hollywood, which Columbia continued to produce through 1958. C.B.C. changed its name when Columbia Pictures was incorporated on January 10, 1924. *More to Be Pitied Than Scorned* is usually referred to as Columbia's first feature. In fact, this six-reel melodrama, directed by Edward Le Saint and starring Rosemary Theby, was a Waldorf Production, produced by Harry Cohn and released by C.B.C. in 1922. Arguably the first Columbia feature is *Yesterday's Wife;* directed by Le Saint and starring Irene Rich, it was produced by Columbia but released by C.B.C. in August 1923. The first major Columbia feature is generally considered to have been *Blood Ship,* directed by George B. Seitz and starring Hobart Bosworth; it opened at the Roxy Theatre* in 1927.

Following Cohn's death, Leo Jaffe (1909–1997) maintained a link with Columbia's past; he had joined the studio in 1930, becoming its president in 1967, president of Columbia Pictures in 1969, chairman of the board in 1973, and chairman emeritus for life in 1981.

Columbia was the first of the major studios to become actively involved in television. It formed Screen Gems in 1952 to produce programs for television and to distribute the studio's product to the new medium. In 1968, Columbia Pictures Corporation was reorganized as Columbia Pictures Industries, Inc. It weathered a major scandal when David Begelman (who had been appointed president of its Motion Picture Division as of September 4, 1973) resigned in 1978, after admitting that he had embezzled $61,000 from the studio. In 1982, the studio was acquired by Coca-Cola Co. as part of its entertainment division, and a year later Frank Price, the company's chief executive officer since 1979, was replaced by Guy McElwaine. That same year Columbia enjoyed two major box office hits with *Tootsie* and *Gandhi.*

In 1972, Columbia left its original studios at Sunset Boulevard and Gower Street in Hollywood to share the newly named Burbank Studios* with Warner Bros.* In 1986, British producer David Puttnam (born 1941) began a short and controversial reign as chairman and CEO (replacing Guy MacElwaine); he quit a year later, replaced by Dawn Steel (who left in 1990). Also in 1987, Columbia merged with TriStar* to create Columbia Pictures Entertainment. In September 1989, Sony USA acquired Columbia for $3.4 billion, and named Peter Gruber and Jon Peters to head the studio (at the same time, acquiring the Gruber-Peters Company, formed in 1987). As part of a litigation deal with Warner Bros., to whom Gruber and Peters were under contract, Columbia gave up its share of the Burbank Studios and moved in 1980 to the former M-G-M* lot that Warner Bros. has acquired from Lorimar.* In 1991, Jon Peters resigned as cochairman, and Stanley R. Jaffe was named president and CEO. That same year, on August 7, the company was renamed Sony Pictures Entertainment. It continues to use the Columbia name on its films and the Columbia trademark of the lady with the torch.

Address: 10202 W. Washington Boulevard, Culver City, Calif. 90232.

BIBLIOGRAPHY

Dick, Bernard. *Columbia Pictures: Portrait of a Studio.* Lexington, Kentucky.: University Press of Kentucky, 1992.

———. *The Merchant Prince of Poverty Row: Harry Cohn of Columbia Pictures.* Lexington, Kentucky: University Press of Kentucky, 1993.

Griffin, Nancy, and Kim Masters. *Hit and Run: How Jon Peters and Peter Gruber Took Sony for a Ride in Hollywood.* New York: Simon & Schuster, 1996.

Hirschhorn, Clive. *The Columbia Story.* New York: Crown, 1990.

Kipps, Charles. *Out of Focus: Power, Pride and Prejudice—David Puttnam in Hollywood.* New York: William Morrow, 1989.

Larkin, Rochelle. *Hail Columbia.* New Rochelle, New York: Arlington House, 1975.

Martin, Len D. *The Columbia Checklist: The Feature Films, Serials, Cartoons and Short Subjects of Columbia Pictures Corporation, 1922–1988.* Jefferson, N.C.: McFarland, 1991.

McClintick, David. *Indecent Exposure.* New York: William Morrow, 1982.

Okuda, Ted, and Edward Watz. *The Columbia Comedy Shorts: Two-Reel Hollywood Film Comedies, 1933–1958.* Jefferson, North Carolina: McFarland, 1986.

Yule, Andrew. *Fast Fade: David Puttnam, Columbia Pictures, and the Battle for Hollywood.* New York: Delacorte Press, 1989.

RESOURCES

Papers: Academy of Motion Picture Arts and Sciences (Set List/Set Budget Collection); University of Wyoming (Telegrams).

COMBINED PHOTOPLAY PRODUCERS, INC. See UNITED FILM SERVICE

COMET PRODUCTIONS, INC. Established in 1945 by Mary Pickford (she was its president) as a production company, releasing through United Artists, for her husband Charles "Buddy" Rogers (he was vice president), Comet Productions was responsible for a handful of minor features beginning with *Little Iodine* (1946). Rogers produced but did not star in any of the Comet features, which included *Susie Steps Out* (1946), *Stork Bites Man* (1947), and *Sleep My Love* (1948). Although inactive, the company remained in existence through the sixties. A related production company, also controlled by Pickford and Rogers, during this same period, was Triangle Productions, Inc.

RESOURCES

Papers: Academy of Motion Picture Arts and Sciences (Mary Pickford Collection).

COMING ATTRACTION TRAILERS. See TRAILERS

COMIQUE FILM CORPORATION was created by Joseph M. Schenck in the spring of 1917 to produce the films of Roscoe "Fatty" Arbuckle and Buster Keaton, for release through Paramount*. The first comedy, *The Butcher Boy*, was released on April 23, 1917, and the last, *The Garage*, on January 11, 1920. The first films were shot at the studios of the Norma Talmadge Film Corporation at 318 East 48th Street, New York. Comique later moved to the Balboa* studios in Long Beach, California, and finally to the Diando* studios in Glendale.

COMMAND PERFORMANCE. See HOLLYWOOD VICTORY COMMITTEE

COMMERCIAL ADVERTISING BUREAU. See VITAGRAPH COMPANY OF AMERICA

COMMITTEE FOR THE FIRST AMENDMENT. See COMMUNISM

COMMODORE PICTURES CORP. was a New York-based distributor, headed by William Steiner. It was active from 1935 to 1936.

COMMONWEALTH UNITED CORP. was a real estate holding company, formed in 1961 as Real Properties Corp. It changed its name in 1965, and, in 1967, became involved in film with the acquisition of Harold Goldman's Television Enterprises Corp. and Landau-Unger-Goldman (founded in July 1963 by Ely Landau, Oliver A. Unger, and Harold Goldman, former staffers with National Telefilm Associates*). By 1968, Commonwealth United had 17 films ready for production and distribution, and had also entered the music publishing and recording business. Among its films are *Eve* (1968), *The Madwoman of Chaillot* (1969), *That Cold Day in the Park* (1969), *Paranoia* (1969), *The Magic Christian* (1970), *Dorian Gray* (1970), and *Julius Caesar* (1970). In September 1971, the company reported losses of $81 million, and plans for major refinancing never materialized. The U.S. rights to Commonwealth's films were acquired by American International Pictures* in 1970, and the foreign rights, in 1972, by National Telefilm Associates.

COMMUNISM. The spectre of Communists infiltrating the film industry is one that has led to extraordinary efforts by government and private individuals to stifle freedom of speech and to purge anyone with even the slightest hint of left-wing leanings.

Communists were active in Hollywood in the thirties in organizations such as the Hollywood Anti-Nazi League* and the Motion Picture Democratic Committee* and in the formation of the Screen Writers Guild. To young men and women in the entertainment industry during the grim days of the Depression, communism sparked a social consciousness that was lacking in much of American society. As early as September 16, 1933, *Variety* carried the headline "Pinks Plan to Stalinize Studios." Just as the studios worked vigorously against Upton Sinclair's campaign for governorship of California—with its motto "End Poverty in California" (EPIC)—so did many intellectuals within the industry actively support this socialistic candidate.

The Spanish Civil War galvanized many left-wingers and Communists within the film industry. The Motion Picture Artists Committee was formed by Lewis Milestone, Gale Sondergaard, Luise Rainer, John Garfield, Fredric March, and others to aid Republican Spain. Joris Ivens's documentary *The Spanish Earth* (1937) was funded by many within the Hollywood community, including John Cromwell, Fredric March, Paul Muni, Frank Tuttle, and James Cagney.

The signing of a nonaggression pact between Hitler and Stalin in August 1939 temporarily destroyed whatever popularity communism might have had within the film community. It was not until the Nazi invasion of the Soviet Union that communism once more found favor within the film industry. In 1943, Goldwyn* produced *The North Star,* scripted by Lillian Hellman and directed by Russian-born Lewis Milestone; M-G-M* produced *Song of Russia;* and Warner Bros.* filmed *Mission to Moscow,* based on the book by the former American ambassador to the Soviet Union, Joseph E. Davies.

Active organization against communism from within the film industry began in the mid-forties, with the formation of the Motion Picture Alliance for the Preservation of American Ideals* by such right-wingers as King Vidor, Clarence Brown, Walt Disney, and Gary Cooper. Screenwriter John Lee Mahin announced that the Alliance would "turn off the faucets which dripped red water into film scripts." As early as 1944, the Alliance urged a congressional investigation of communism in the film industry.

Attacks on communism within the industry were seen by many as a way of bringing the film unions, particularly the Conference of Studio Unions*, into line.

On May 7, 1947, the House Un-American Activities Committee (HUAC), under the chairmanship of J. Parnell Thomas, held closed hearings in Los Angeles, at which Robert Taylor, Adolphe Menjou, Leo McCarey, and others told of "Communist subversion" within the industry. Initially, the studio heads were uncooperative in their dealings with the Committee, but their attitudes changed in September 1947, when subpoenas were issued to 47 members of the film community, ordering their appearance at hearings in Washington, D.C.

Among the "unfriendly" group of 19 witnesses were Donald Ogden Stewart, Larry Parks, Dalton Trumbo, and Edward Dmytryk. To defend the rights of these witnesses, the Committee for the First Amendment—which did not permit membership by Communists—was formed by Philip Dunne, Alexander Knox, and John Huston, a group that held its first meeting at Ira Gershwin's home. Sadly, the Committee and public opinion went against the unfriendly witnesses. Ten who refused to answer the Committee's questions became known as "The Hollywood Ten."* They were denied employment in the industry and subsequently served jail sentences for their belief in the First Amendment.

What became of the Hollywood Ten was only the beginning as far as the search for Communists within the film industry was concerned. The House Un-American Activities Committee, now under the chairmanship of John S. Wood and spurred on by the anti-Communist campaigns of Senator Joseph McCarthy, issued more subpoenas. Guilds and unions demanded loyalty oaths from their members. The Screen Actors Guild* refused to defend one of its members, Gale Sondergaard, against blacklisting. Larry Parks was forced to apologize publicly for his political beliefs. Lucille Ball was able to persuade the Committee and the public that she had only registered as a Communist in 1936 to please her grandfather.

As a result of the HUAC hearings, held through 1953, many within the film industry were blacklisted. Others were forced to find employment abroad or in the New York theatre. Organizations such as Myron C. Fagan's Cinema Educational Guild reminded the public of those film personalities with supposedly Communist backgrounds. Gossip columnist Hedda Hopper made sure that her readers never forgot who was a loyal American and who was not. A publication called *Red Channels,* produced by American Business Consultants, was available to motion picture and television executives, listing the names of Communists within the community. Blacklisting was always subtle, and never did any executive admit to its existence. It was not until 1960, when Otto Preminger and Kirk Douglas began to employ openly those who had been branded as Communists, that the blacklist period in the American film industry came to a close.

The political beliefs of film personalities have never since been that important to film audiences, except during the Vietnam War, when the activities of actress Jane Fonda created a considerable outcry. Perhaps symbolic of the laissez-faire attitude of the film industry toward communism is Paramount's financing of the 1981 film, *Reds,* directed by and starring Warren Beatty, which glorified the life of American Communist John Reed.

BIBLIOGRAPHY

Belfrage, Cedric. *The American Inquisition 1945–1960.* Indianapolis: Bobbs-Merrill, 1973.

Bentley, Eric, ed. *Thirty Years of Treason.* New York: Viking Press, 1971.

Ceplair, Larry, and Steven Englund. *The Inquisition in Hollywood.* Garden City, N.Y.: Anchor Press/Doubleday, 1980.

Cogley, John. *Report on Blacklisting, I. The Movies.* New York: The Fund for the Republic, 1956.

Donner, Frank J. *The Un-Americans.* New York: Ballantine Books, 1961.

Fagan, Myron C. *Red Treason in Hollywood!* Hollywood, Calif.: Cinema Educational Guild, 1949.

———. *Documentation of the Red Stars in Hollywood.* Hollywood, Calif.: Cinema Educational Guild, 1950.

Faulk, John Henry. *Fear on Trial.* New York: Simon and Schuster, 1964.

Kanfer, Stefan. *A Journal of the Plague Years.* New York: Atheneum, 1973.

McWilliams, Carey. *Witch Hunt.* Boston: Little, Brown, 1950.

Miller, Merle. *The Judges and the Judged.* Garden City, N.Y.: Doubleday, 1952.

Navasky, Victor S. *Naming Names.* New York: Viking Press, 1980.

Red Channels. New York: American Business Consultants, 1950.

Taylor, Telford. *Grand Inquest*. New York: Ballantine Books, 1955.

Trumbo, Dalton. *The Time of the Toad*. New York: Harper & Row, 1972.

Vaughn, Robert. *Only Victims*. New York: G. P. Putnam's Sons, 1972.

COMPASS INTERNATIONAL PICTURES was a Los Angeles-based distributor and producer, founded by Irwin Yablans (born 1934) in collaboration with Moustapha Akkad and incorporated on January 3, 1978. It was noted for its release of horror titles, such as *Halloween* (1978), *Fade to Black* (1980), and *Hell Night* (1981). It ceased operations in the late eighties.

COMPO (the Council of Motion Picture Organizations), which remained active through the seventies, was formed in Washington, D.C., in December 1949, by the Conference Committee of the Motion Picture Industry to "plan, organize and supervise a comprehensive, continuous public relations program representing the maximum coordination of all member organizations, such program to include not only projects in the general public relations field, but also those which affect better box office, those which pertain more particularly to the relationship of the 238,000 people in the motion picture industry to one another, and those which are related to discriminatory taxation and restrictive regulations, and to conduct the necessary basic research prerequisite to the initiation and fulfillment of such a program." Funding was from payment by exhibitors and distributors of ten cents on each $100 of film rentals. Among the ten founding organizations were Variety Clubs, International; Allied States Association; Motion Picture Association of America*; and the Committee of Trade Press Publishers.

A similar organization, ACE (American Congress of Exhibitors), was formed in 1958, with its concerns being the sale of pre–1948 films to television, pay television, producer-distributor-exhibitor relations, industry-government relations, ways and means of increasing production, and industry research. COMPO worked with ACE as an industry spokesperson in fighting censorship and in developments in the public relations field.

COMPUTER ANIMATION. In his book, *Computers for Animation,* Stan Hayward writes, "The field of computer graphics and animation is a no man's land somewhere between visual arts and data processing." It has also been described as a new art form, with obvious relevance in the area of special effects*. Computer animation provides for new styles of computer-generated images and offers a cost-efficient method of producing animated films. It involves the transfer of artwork to a computer, a process known as "digitizing" (in other words, converting the artwork to binary digital form). The drawings must be translated into numbers, which can be done automatically through a scanning device.

The computer can subsequently change the size, color, speed, and movement of the drawings. It can also complement or change the voice and other sounds to be utilized. The first feature film generated completely on computers was *Toy Story* (1995), directed by John Lasseter and produced by Walt Disney* in partnership with Pixar.

BIBLIOGRAPHY

Baker, Christopher W. *Computer Illusion in Film & TV*. Indianapolis: Alpha Books, 1994.

Beckerman, Howard. "Animation Kit: Computer Animation." *Filmmakers Newsletter,* February 1978, pp. 53–54.

Catmull, Edwin E. "New Frontiers in Computer Animation." *American Cinematographer,* October 1979, pp. 1000–1003, 1049–53.

Harden, Fred. "The Computer in Animation." *Cinema Papers,* November–December 1981, pp. 470–77.

Hayward, Philip, and Tana Wollen, eds. *Future Visions: New Technologies of the Screen*. London: British Film Institute, 1993.

Hayward, Stan. *Computers for Animation*. Boston: Focal Press, 1984.

MacNicol, Gregory. *Desktop Computer Animation: A Guide to Low-Cost Computer Animation*. Boston: Focal Press, 1992.

McKenna, Sherry. "The Future of Computer Generated Animation." *On Location,* January 1982, pp. 78–87, 90–91.

CONCORDE PICTURES CORPORATION. When he sold New World Pictures*, Roger Corman had agreed not to become involved in film distribution except with his own films. However, following an out-of-court settlement with New World, Corman and his wife, Julie, formed Concorde Pictures Corporation as a cooperative distributorship to handle Corman's own films and those produced by others willing to share distribution costs. Concorde was organized in March 1985, and its first release, in May 1985, was *Streetwalkin',* which marked a directorial debut for Joan Freeman.

The settlement with New World also gave Corman and Concorde distribution rights to all New World features produced and/or distributed by Corman, a library of 120 titles. In addition, Corcorde distributes features produced by Corman's other company, New Horizon Pictures Corporation. In July 1985, Concorde and Cinema Group formed a new organization, Concorde/Cinema Group, an independent distribution alliance with announced plans to release between 15 and 20 features a year.

In February 1997, Roger Corman announced the sale of his company to producer Elliott Kastner for $100 million. Included in the sale was the library of 387 titles, a studio in Venice, California, the company's Los Angeles headquarters, and a number of office buildings in Southern California.

Address: 11600 San Vicente Boulevard, Los Angeles, Calif. 90049.

BIBLIOGRAPHY

"Corman Launches Concorde Pictures Co-op Distrib Outfit." *Variety,* March 27, 1985, pp. 5, 106.
Crosby, Joan. "Roger and Julie Corman Form Concorde Pictures." *Drama-Logue,* April 18, 1985, pp. 1, 20.
Klein, Richard. "Roger Corman's Concorde, Cinema Group Join to Form New Distribution Alliance." *Daily Variety,* July 18, 1985, pp. 1, 30.

CONDOR PICTURES. See VAN BEUREN CORPORATION

CONEY ISLAND. See RELIANCE MOTION PICTURE COMPANY AND MAJESTIC MOTION PICTURE COMPANY

CONFERENCE OF STUDIO UNIONS. In 1941, militant trade unionist Herb Sorrell (1897–1973) began organizing locals in Hollywood that were not members of the then-discredited IATSE*. Following a successful 1941 strike against the Walt Disney Studios*, the Conference of Studio Unions (CSU) was formed by Sorrell, including office workers, publicists, set decorators, painters, cartoonists, and laboratory technicians. The producers, however, preferred to deal with IATSE, and a violent, 30-week strike broke out in the spring of 1945. It reached its peak on October 5, 1945, during a violent confrontation outside the Warner Bros.* studios in Burbank, which became known as "The Battle of Warner Bros." Fire hoses were turned on the demonstrators and pickets, the police threw tear gas grenades, and Warner Bros. executives hurled whatever was at hand at the pickets from the studio rooftop. Eventually, that same year, the producers, IATSE, and the Conference of Studio Unions came to an agreement, known as "The Treaty of Beverly Hills." A year later, violence again broke out as the producers and IATSE tried to "lock out" CSU members from studios. IATSE's Roy Brewer denounced the CSU as a Communist organization, and he was aided in his efforts by the new president of the Screen Actors Guild*, Ronald Reagan. The Teamsters Local 399 also turned against the CSU, and by 1947, the Conference of Studio Unions was left with only a handful of members.

RESOURCES

Papers: University of California at Los Angeles (papers of Herb Sorrell).

CONSENT DECREE. Prior to 1940, five major studios—M-G-M*, Paramount*, RKO*, 20th Century-Fox*, and Warner Bros.*—effectively controlled the film industry, being producers, distributors, and exhibitors. With ownership of the theatres in which their product was to be shown, these five studios were blatantly in violation of American antitrust laws. The first consent decree was signed between the studios and the Justice Department in November 1940, and under it the five major producers agreed to end blind bidding* and to modify their block booking* activities. The decree was filed in Federal District Court for the Southern District of New York and expired on November 20, 1943, at which time the studios asked for drastic changes in the decree, and the matter dragged on through the legal system for most of the decade.

In the meantime, in 1946, the Justice Department filed suit, again in New York, against Paramount Pictures. The decree of December 1946 basically confirmed the 1940 decree but did not require, as the government had asked, that the studios divest themselves of their theatre chains. However, on appeal to the Supreme Court, in 1948, such divestiture was ordered, and the five independent theatre chains so created were prohibited from acquiring additional theatres if such acquisitions would restrain free trade, and they were given until the early fifties to separate their production and distribution arms from exhibition. Naturally, the studios fought against the consent decree, and it was not until October 16, 1960, that the Supreme Court refused to reconsider the decisions rendered against Loew's Inc. (M-G-M), Warner Bros., and 20th Century-Fox.

With theatre chains freed of restraint, there was an immediate increase in independent film production. Although some theatre chains have since become involved in film production—notably Stanley Warner Corp.* with Cinerama* and National General Corp.*—the Justice Department has effectively ruled against any major changes in the consent decree when they were requested in 1971 and 1984.

BIBLIOGRAPHY

Conant, Michael. *Antitrust in the Motion Picture Industry.* Berkeley, Calif.: University of California Press, 1960.
———. "The Paramount Decrees Reconsidered." In *The American Film Industry,* ed. Tino Balio. Madison, Wis.: University of Wisconsin Press, 1985, pp. 537–73.
Mayer, Arthur L. "Dissent with Consent Decree." *Variety,* January 9, 1957, p. 25.

CONSOLIDATED FILM CORPORATION was formed in June 1916 to produce the 16-part serial *The Crimson Stain Mystery,* which Metro Pictures Corporation* distributed. O. E. Goebel of the St. Louis Motion Picture Company was the president, and Ludwig G. B. Erb, owner of the Erbograph Company*, was also involved. Maurice Costello and Ethel Grandin were the serial's stars, with Albert Payson Terhune as scenarist and T. Hayes Hunter as director.

CONSOLIDATED FILM INDUSTRIES began as a film-processing laboratory 1924. It was acquired by Herbert J. Yates (1880–1966), best known as the head of Republic

Pictures*, who had begun his film career by acquiring Hedwig Film Laboratories and Republic Film Laboratories in the second decade of the twentieth century. In the twenties, Consolidated acquired two New York laboratories, Erbograph and Craftsman. Its long-time head, for 33 years, was Sidney Solow.

The laboratory claims to have been the first to process film for television and the first to produce a kinescope on the West Coast. It continued its expansion by acquiring Paramount Laboratory in New York in 1950; in 1971, it acquired Acme Videotape and Film Laboratories, and a year later acquired Glen Glenn Sound*.

Address: 959 Seward Street, Hollywood, Calif. 90038.

CONSOLIDATED NATIONAL FILM EXCHANGES. See TODDY PICTURES COMPANY

CONTINENTAL DISTRIBUTING. See WALTER READE ORGANIZATION

CONTINENTAL FEATURE FILM COMPANY. See MUTUAL FILM CORPORATION

CONTEMPORARY FILMS, INC., was founded in New York in March 1948 as a 16mm film distributor, concentrating on "art" and foreign films. It was acquired in 1972 by publisher McGraw-Hill.

"THE COOGAN ACT." See CHILD LABOR LAWS

COOPER-HEWITT lights were some of the earliest used by the film industry, installed at the Biograph studios as early as 1905. They were electric lights in which mercury was employed instead of a carbon, and they gave off a bluish light, producing a soft, diffused effect. The lights were manufactured by the Cooper-Hewitt Elec. Co. of Los Angeles.

COPYRIGHT. Prior to 1912, motion pictures were not referred to in copyright legislation. The 1912 copyright act gave motion pictures copyright protection for 28 years, after which the copyright could be renewed for a further 28-year period. The Copyright Act of 1976 (which went into effect on January 1, 1978) gave motion pictures copyright for 75 years from the first publication of the work, or 100 years from its creation, if the work was "made for hire." Where the motion picture was not a "work for hire," the copyright lasts for the life of the author plus 50 years. The 1976 Copyright Act was not retroactive. It did not affect any works that had already fallen into the public domain through failure to copyright or to renew copyright. It requires that those motion pictures in their first 28 years of copyright protection must be renewed to gain further protection of 28 years, plus 19 years, giving a total of 75 years if the motion picture is a work "made for hire" (as is virtually always the case with

motion pictures). The new law also requires that a copyright notice, consisting of the symbol © or the word copyright or the abbreviation copr., the year of first publication, and the name of the copyright owners be placed on all publicly distributed copies of the motion picture. Full information as to copyright procedure is given in Circular R45, available at no charge from the Library of Congress Copyright Office.

The copyright laws also provide that copies of motion pictures be deposited with the Library of Congress, but from 1912 to 1942 the Library did not enforce this as part of the copyright process. However, the Library does now request the deposit of one copy of all important motion pictures, and such copies may be viewed on the premises of the Library of Congress at no charge.

Many films are no longer protected by copyright, in other words they are part of the public domain, because their distributors or producers either failed to copyright the films in the first place or failed to renew such copyrights. This is particularly true of films from minor producers and films produced abroad. Occasionally, a major studio will forget to renew a copyright, but in many cases the copyright has not been renewed because the producer's rights to the literary or musical materials used in the film were limited to a certain number of years. Although a film is in the public domain, it may well be that underlying literary or musical rights in the film are still subject to copyright protection. Further, the copyright status of a film applies to the United States only and may be, and usually is, considerably different in Europe or Canada.

The only "safe" way to check the copyright status of a specific film is through a copyright search at the Library of Congress (Washington, D.C. 20559). 7 Arts Press has published *Film Superlist: 20,000 Motion Pictures in the Public Domain* and *Film Superlist for 1940–1949,* which is a reprint of three volumes of the Library of Congress Copyright Catalogs (1894–1949), marked with renewals of copyright where appropriate.

Both the General Agreement on Tariffs and Trades (GATT) and the North American Free Trade Agreement will have a profound effect on U.S. copyright law, restoring to copyright many films once considered in the public domain. *Public Domain Report* (P.O. Box 3102, Margate, N.J. 08402) provides a monthly guide to significant works in the public domain.

BIBLIOGRAPHY

Hurst, Walter E., and William Storm Hale. *Film Superlist for 1940–1949.* Hollywood, Calif.: 7 Arts Press, 1982.

Minus, Johnny, and William Storm Hale. *Film Superlist: 20,000 Motion Pictures in the Public Domain.* Hollywood, Calif.: 7 Arts Press, 1973.

Strong, William S. *The Copyright Book.* Cambridge, Mass.: MIT Press, 1993.

COQUILLE FILM COMPANY. René Plaisetty, a director who left France to produce films in the United States because of the First World War, contracted with Pathé Freres to make films for them in this country. He formed the Coquille Film Company in New Orleans in January 1915, built a glass-enclosed studio, and released three- and five-reel films under the brand name "Nola." Leatrice Joy Zeidler, later known as Leatrice Joy, called at that time "a social favorite of New Orleans," was the leading lady. In December 1915, the company became known as the Nola Film Company. Captain William J. Hannon was the president and general manager, Walter Morton was the director, Norton Travis was the cameraman, and William Morgan Hannon was the scenario editor and assistant director. Leatrice Joy continued as the star, along with Madelyn Nichols. Its films were released through the Associated Service. In September 1917, the Diamond Film Company took over the Nola plant.

BIBLIOGRAPHY

"New Southern Film Company." *The Moving Picture World,* January 30, 1915, p. 651.

CORONADO, CALIFORNIA. See LUBIN MANUFACTURING COMPANY

CORRIGANVILLE, a 1,611-acre ranch on Highway 118 near Chatsworth on the outskirts of Los Angeles, was so named by Western actor Ray "Crash" Corrigan (1903–1976), who purchased the property in 1937 for $11,354. Corriganville was utilized for innumerable Westerns and television series. The property was sold, as part of a divorce settlement by Corrigan, in 1964 for $2.5 million. The following year, Bob Hope acquired the property and renamed it Hopetown. The ranch's continued use as a film location was halted a year later, and, in November 1979, fire destroyed the last of the standing sets. From 1948 onward, Corriganville was also open to the public as a Western-style amusement park. The property was acquired for real estate development in 1985.

COSMOFOTOFILM COMPANY began operations in 1914 as an importer of films from England. Paul H. Cromelin was its head. Cosmofotofilm Company was the sole American distributor of films from the London Film Company, which at that time employed two American producer/directors, Harold Shaw and George Loane Tucker.

COSMOPOLITAN PRODUCTIONS. William Randolph Hearst's personal production company, Cosmopolitan Productions was formed in 1918 to produce the features of his mistress, actress Marion Davies. All of Davies's films, from *Cecilia of the Pink Roses* (1918) through her last feature, *Ever Since Eve* (1937), were Cosmopolitan Productions. In addition to Cosmopolitan, Hearst also owned International Film Service Company, which produced the 1918 Marion Davies feature *Beatrice Fairfax,* and whose best-known film was *Humoresque* (1920), starring Alma Rubens.

In 1918, Cosmopolitan productions were released by Graphic Film*. From 1918 to 1919, they were released by Select. Paramount* released the productions from 1919 to 1922. In 1923, they were Goldwyn* releases. From 1924 to 1934, the films were released by M-G-M*, and, finally, from 1935 to 1937 by Warner Bros.* In addition to the Marion Davies features, Cosmopolitan also produced a number of other major features, including *Enchantment* (1921), *The Valley of Silent Men* (1922), *The Temptress* (1926), *Our Dancing Daughters* (1928), *White Shadows in the South Seas* (1928), *The Big House* (1930), *Gabriel over the White House* (1933), and *Oil for the Lamps of China* (1935).

BIBLIOGRAPHY

Guiles, Fred Lawrence. *Marion Davies.* New York: McGraw-Hill, 1972.

COSTUME DESIGNERS GUILD. All major Los Angeles-based costume designers are members of the Costume Designers Guild, which was formed in 1953 and became a recognized negotiating body with its 1976 joining of IATSE*. It is IATSE Local 892. The Costume Designers Guild should not be confused with Motion Picture Costumes, which is IATSE Local 705, or with IATSE Local 829, which takes care of the interests of New York-based costumers.

Address: 13949 Ventura Boulevard, Suite 309, Sherman Oaks, Calif. 91423.

COUNCIL OF MOTION PICTURE ORGANIZATIONS. See COMPO

COUNTERATTACK, a private, independent organization, was founded in May 1947 by former FBI agents "to publish the newsletter *Counterattack,* which exposes the most important aspects of Communist activity in America each week. To compile factual information on Communists, Communist fronts, and other subversive organizations. To assist, consult with, and provide factual information on Communist activities to responsible individuals and organizations." Located in New York, in 1950, the group published *Red Channels: The Report of Communist Influence in Radio and Television,* containing an alphabetical listing of the names of those with supposed Communist ties or sympathies.

COYTESVILLE, NEW JERSEY. See KALEM COMPANY, INC.

CRAFTSMAN LABORATORY. See CONSOLIDATED FILM INDUSTRIES

CREATIVE ARTISTS AGENCY was founded in 1975 by its majority stockholder, Michael Ovitz, and four colleagues,

Ron Meyer, Bill Haber, Michael Rosenfeld, and Rowland Perkins. All founders were formerly with the William Morris Agency*. Under the leadership of Ovitz, who has been described as "the most powerful man in Hollywood," the agency became one of the most prominent in the industry, handling the sale of Columbia Pictures* and Tri-Star* to Sony Corporation, and the sale of MCA, Inc*, to Matsushita and later Seagram Co. It negotiated three of the largest recording contracts in history for clients Michael Jackson, Madonna, and Barbra Streisand. One of its few failures was the 1990 acquisition of a 10 percent interest in Century City Mercantile National Bank. In August 1995, Michael Ovitz left Creative Artists Agency to become president of Walt Disney*. As of 1997, Creative Artists Agency's clients included Warren Beatty, Glenn Close, Robert De Niro, Dustin Hoffman, Ron Howard, Bette Midler, Robert Redford, Martin Scorsese, and Steven Spielberg.

Address: 9830 Wilshire Boulevard, Beverly Hills, Calif. 90212.

THE CREATIVE FILM SOCIETY, a nonprofit, 16mm distributor dedicated to the promotion of film as an art form, was created in Burbank, California, in the spring of 1958.

CRESCENT PICTURES CORP., founded by E. B. Derr, was a production company, located at the Talisman Studios* in Los Angeles, and active from 1936 to 1941.

CREST PICTURE COMPANY, controlled by Colorado capitalists C. F. Rickey and B. W. Davies, began production in June 1917 for the states rights* market. Judge Lyman Henry, who wrote its first film, *The Chosen Prince,* an eight-reel biblical subject, was also the company's president. William V. Mong was director-general. The company, which produced at Monrovia, California, went out of business in 1920.

CRIME DOES NOT PAY. A series of two-reel short subjects that concluded with proof of the basic premise that "Crime Does Not Pay," these films were produced by M-G-M* from 1935 to 1947. The first was *Buried Loot* and the last *Luckiest Guy in the World.*

BIBLIOGRAPHY

Maltin, Leonard. *The Great Movie Shorts.* New York: Crown, 1972.

CROWN CITY FILM MANUFACTURING COMPANY. Prominent Pasadena, California, businessmen formed the Crown City Film Manufacturing Company in October 1914. Located at 40 West Mountain Street in Pasadena, the company produced comedies under the "Thistle" brand, one of which was a two-reeler about the Pasadena Tournament of Roses, and dramas under the "Paragon" brand. Bruce Mitchell directed Allan Fralick, Rena Rogers, and Ralph McComas in the comedies, while Donald Mac-

Donald directed Dorothy Davenport, Joe Singleton, and Lee Hill in the dramas. Anthony W. Coldeway was the studio manager and scenario editor. The company released on the Kriterion* program.

CROWN INTERNATIONAL PICTURES. Founded in 1959 by Newton P. "Red" Jacobs, Crown International Pictures is an independent distributor that has also produced an average of three or four films a year. Crown specializes in exploitation features, such as *Chain Gang Women* (1971), *The Pom Pom Girls* (1976), *Hustler Squad* (1978), *Coach* (1978), *Dracula's Dog* (1979), and *Satan's Slave* (1979), but it has also released Mae West's last film, *Sextette* (1978), and the critically successful British feature *McVicar* (1981). According to *Boxoffice* (October 15, 1973), Crown is "known for its tailor-made campaigns for individual pictures and trendsetting concepts." Mark Tenser took over as president of the company in 1974 and, in 1985, announced that Crown would be spending $40 million in the next two years on distribution, production, and marketing.

Address: 8701 Wilshire Boulevard, Beverly Hills, Calif. 90211.

BIBLIOGRAPHY

Auerbach, Alexander. "Growth Gives Added Sparkle to Crown." *Boxoffice,* April 1983, pp. 8–9.

CRYSTAL FILM COMPANY, formed in the latter part of 1912 by Ludwig G. B. Erb to be a producer of weekly split-reel comedies for the Universal* program, was located at Wendover and Park avenues, New York. Pearl White starred in the comedies, the first two of which, *The Girl in the Next Room* and *The Man from the North Pole,* were released on October 6, 1912. Crystal later added dramas but discontinued them in 1914. Joseph A. Golden was the company's first director, and Vivian Prescott and Charles De Forrest appeared in later Crystal films.

At the end of 1914, Crystal severed its connections with Universal and became part of United Motion Picture Producers, Inc., formed by Erb to provide a daily service of one- and two-reel films to the United Film Service*. Crystal began at this time making one-reel comedies with De Forrest under the "Superba" brand. H. M. "Ben" Goetz was the general manager until April 1915.

When the United Film Service failed in June 1915, Crystal joined a new combination of producers, Combined Photoplay Producers, Inc., of which Erb was also president. Standard Photoplay Distributors, Inc., handled the product of the new combination. Crystal films were later released on the states rights* market by the Triumph Film Corporation. On October 8, 1917, Joseph A. Golden, previously the company's vice president, succeeded Julius Steger as president. Crystal ended operations in June 1919.

CUB. See DAVID HORSLEY PRODUCTIONS

"CUCKOO COMEDIES" — "Every One's a Bird" was its slogan — was created in 1919 by Mark Dintenfass to produce a series of blackface short subjects.

CUSTARD PIE GAG. The earliest known instances of a custard pie being thrown in a film are in Keystone's *The Ragtime Band,* released on May 1, 1913, with Mabel Normand at the receiving end, and in Keystone's *A Noise from the Deep,* released on July 17, 1913, with Roscoe "Fatty" Arbuckle at the receiving end and Mabel Normand doing the throwing. The largest custard pie fight ever staged is in the Laurel and Hardy short subject *The Battle of the Century,* released on December 31, 1927, in which more than 3,000 pies from the Los Angeles Pie Company were thrown. *The Great Race* (1965) featured a Technicolor custard pie fight, staged by Blake Edwards, and the custard pie gag became familiar on television thanks to Soupy Sales.

D

DANUBIA PICTURES, INC., was the major, if not the exclusive, distributor of Hungarian-produced films in the United States from 1934 to 1940. The company, which was located at 729 Seventh Avenue, New York, was headed by Eugene J. Lang. It was revived after the Second World War and remained active through the sixties, distributing both Hungarian and Soviet films.

DARMOUR PRODUCTIONS. See MAJESTIC PICTURES CORPORATION

DAVID HORSLEY PRODUCTIONS. In July 1914, pioneer producer David Horsley (1872–1933) declared that the feature film had had its day. He announced that his nearly completed studio and factory in Bayonne, New Jersey, would produce seven one-reel comedies per week. In October 1914, Horsley became the first producer invited to join the Motion Picture Patents Company* since its formation. The invitation came after Pathé* Freres severed its connection with the company. After a competition to select the name of Horsley's new brand of films, "MinA" was selected, a name that stood for "Made in America." Horsley advertised the invention of a new double exposure camera that made two exposures and produced two separate negatives at once, which was to be used in MinA productions. Circus clown Harry La Pearl was MinA's first leading comedian.

About this time, Horsley acquired the Bostock animals—together with their London trainer Harry Tudor—which were sold because of the war. The subsequent Bostock Jungle and Film Company animal pictures were made at Horsley's new studios located at Main and Washington streets in Los Angeles. Other Horsley brands included Ace, of which Milton H. Fahrney was director-in-chief, and Cub. Horsley was also the producer of various serials.

In July 1915, Horsley cancelled his contract to release with General Film Company, and contracted to release with the Mutual Film Corporation*. At that time, the brand name of MinA was retained by the General Film Company.

BIBLIOGRAPHY

"Horsley in Licensed Group." *The Moving Picture World,* October 3, 1914, p. 71.
"Horsley's Animal Studios." *The Moving Picture World,* July 10, 1915, pp. 253–54.
"Horsley's Big Plans." *The New York Dramatic Mirror,* July 8, 1914, p. 24.
"Horsley's Camera Used for MinA Pictures." *The Motion Picture News,* February 6, 1915, p. 36.
"MinA Film Here." *The New York Dramatic Mirror,* December 16, 1914, p. 40.

DAVID MILES, INC. David Miles formed his own company, variously called David Miles, Inc., David Miles Corporation, and David Miles Production Company, with T. Hayes Hunter in August 1914. Miles directed a stock company of actors he had worked with previously, including Linda Arvidson Griffith, John G. Brammall, and Charles Perley, in one-reel comedies. Charles Fleming also directed. David Miles, Inc., released two films per week through Sawyer, Inc.*, until Miles died in 1915.

DEATH VALLEY has proved an impressive location for films as varied as *Greed* (1924) and *Zabriskie Point* (1970). Other films shot there include *Chimmie Fadden Out West* (1915), *Death Valley* (1927), *The Three Godfathers* (1948), *The Gunfighter* (1950), and *One-Eyed Jacks* (1961).

DE FOREST PHONOFILM. Responsible for the audion tube, a key invention in the development of the sound motion picture, Dr. Lee De Forest created a sound-on-film system, the Phonofilm. Through the De Forest Phonofilm Corporation, founded in November 1922, Dr. De Forest exploited his invention, presenting the first public performance of his films before the New York Electrical Society on April 12, 1923. Among the celebrities who appeared in De Forest Phonofilms were Eddie Cantor, DeWolf Hopper, and Fannie Ward; Calvin Coolidge appeared in what is probably the first sound newsreel, produced by De Forest, in 1924. Phonofilms were also produced and marketed in England and Australia.

The system was not commercially successful because it required the installation of new projection equipment, and the subjects were only one reel or less in length. From the mid-twenties onward, De Forest's invention was successfully advanced by two former associates of his, E. I. Sponable and Theodore Case, and the sound-on-film system that they developed became Fox Movietone.

BIBLIOGRAPHY

Carneal, Georgette. *A Conqueror of Space.* New York: Horace Liveright, 1930.
De Forest, Lee. "Pioneering in Talking Pictures." *American Cinematographer,* April 1941, pp. 164, 201–2.

Geduld, Harry. *The Birth of the Talkies.* Bloomington, Ind.: Indiana University Press, 1975.

Griggs, I. C. "De Forest Phonofilms (Australia) Ltd." *Cinema Papers,* June-July 1976, pp. 16–20, 91.

"Pictures That Talk." *Photoplay,* July 1924, p. 78.

RESOURCES

Films: Library of Congress.

DEG STUDIOS were opened in Wilmington, North Carolina, by Dino De Laurentiis (born 1919) in March 1984, with *Firestarter* (1984) the first film to be shot there. In 1987, the studio was sold to Carolco* and renamed Carolco Studios, Inc. (1223 North 23d Street, Wilmington, N.C. 28405); the studio was also known as the North Carolina Film Studios, Inc. With the bankruptcy of Carolco, the studio was sold to EUE/Screen Gems for $3.4 million in July 1996.

DEITRICH-BECK, INC. Theodore C. Deitrich and Arthur F. Beck formed Deitrich-Beck, Inc., in July 1919 to produce four to six films a year from the novels of Louis Joseph Vance. Doris Kenyon was the star. The first film of the company was *The Bandbox,* directed by Roy William Neill, released through the W. W. Hodkinson Corporation*.

BIBLIOGRAPHY

"New Producing Company Organized." *The Moving Picture World,* July 12, 1919, p. 192.

DE LAURENTIIS ENTERTAINMENT GROUP was incorporated in October 1985, following producer Dino De Laurentiis's acquisition of Embassy Communications*. The films produced and distributed by the group were remarkably unsuccessful—notably *King Kong Lives* (1986)—and despite going public in May 1986, the company filed for Chapter XV bankruptcy protection on April 16, 1988. On April 27, 1990, the U.S. Bankruptcy Court approved purchase of the group's assets by Carolco Pictures*, but in the meantime, De Laurentiis had formed a partnership with Giancarlo Parretti and formed Dino De Laurentiis Communications (8670 Wilshire Boulevard, Beverly Hills, Calif. 90211). A production subsidiary, Onyx Entertainment, was created in October 1988.

BIBLIOGRAPHY

Behar, Richard. "Star of His Own Dubious Epic." *Time,* April 9, 1990, p. 63.

Lieberman, Jane. "DEG." *Daily Variety,* March 1, 1989, pp. F5, F41.

DeLUXE LABORATORIES, INC., for many years a wholly owned subsidiary of 20th Century-Fox*, claims to be one of the three largest processing laboratories in the world. Founded in 1915 in Fort Lee, New Jersey*, and incorporated in 1932, DeLuxe was for a long time a New York-based laboratory, located at 850 Tenth Avenue, with a Hollywood branch at 1546 North Argyle Street. The credit DeLuxe Color or Color by DeLuxe on a film indicates that the production was processed by the laboratory but is, in reality, in Eastman Color. In December 1990, DeLuxe was acquired by the Rank Organization PLC for a reported $150 million.

Address: 1377 North Serrano Avenue, Hollywood, Calif. 90027.

DE LUXE PICTURES, INC. Theodore C. Deitrich, the publicity director of the International Film Service*, formed De Luxe Pictures, Inc., on November 1, 1917, and became its president and general manager. With offices at 516 Fifth Avenue, New York, the company planned to produce four to eight features a year starring Doris Kenyon. Its first film, *The Street of Seven Stars*, was directed by John B. O'Brien and released through the William Sherry Feature Film Company.

BIBLIOGRAPHY

"Deitrich Forms New Company." *The Moving Picture World,* December 8, 1917, p. 1506.

DeMILLE FOUNDATION FOR POLITICAL FREEDOM. In 1944, Cecil B. DeMille was informed by the American Federation of Radio Artists (AFRA), to which he belonged, that he must, along with all other members, pay one dollar to help fight a California ballot proposition that provided that no man should be required to belong to a union in order to work to support his family. DeMille decided to support the proposition, refused to pay the one dollar, and was suspended by AFRA, resulting in his being unable to work in radio, with which AFRA had a closed-shop contract.

Dropped as host of *Lux Radio Theatre*, DeMille received many letters of support on his stand. These, along with financial contributions, led to his forming the DeMille Foundation for Political Freedom, which fought for the right to work in some 16 states. Incorporated in September 1945, the foundation had as its trustees DeMille, Neil McCarthy, and Sidney Biddell. William M. Jeffers was the first chairman of the board, succeeded by Y. Frank Freeman. The DeMille Foundation for Political Freedom was dissolved in February 1959.

BIBLIOGRAPHY

Hayne, Donald, ed. *The Autobiography of Cecil B. DeMille.* Englewood Cliffs, N.J.: Prentice-Hall, 1959.

DEMOCRACY FILM COMPANY was incorporated in June 1919 by prominent blacks in California. It planned to make a patriotic feature to show the part that black Americans had played in the First World War and to eliminate racial prejudice. Captain Leslie T. Peacocke, a white American, was signed to write and supervise the film, for which the E & R Studio* near Eastlake Park, Los Angeles, was leased.

BIBLIOGRAPHY

"Democracy Film Company Is All-Negro Organization." *The Moving Picture World*, June 7, 1919, p. 1491.

DENVER. See COLORADO MOTION PICTURE COMPANY

DETROIT. See JAM HANDY ORGANIZATION and WILDING PICTURE PRODUCTIONS

DIANA PRODUCTIONS was founded in 1945 by Walter Wanger, Joan Bennett, and Fritz Lang (who was in charge of production), and produced *Scarlet Street* (1945) and *Secret Beyond the Door* (1948). The company ceased operations when Wanger pulled out in May 1948.

DIANDO FILM COMPANY began making five-reel features for Pathé* in December 1917. It had two producing companies at that time, one featuring the child star Baby Marie Osborne, the other featuring Bryant Washburn. W. A. S. Douglas was the president, and L. T. Osborne, Baby Marie's father, was vice president. In 1918, Diando produced the serial *The Wolf-Faced Man,* starring George Larkin and directed by Stuart Paton, for Pathé release. The company went out of business in 1919.

DIES COMMITTEE INVESTIGATION. The Dies Committee, or the House Un-American Activities Committee, as it was formally known, began its investigations in 1938. Congressman Martin Dies first announced that he would hold hearings in Hollywood in September 1938 to investigate the participation in Communist activities by members of the film industry. In particular, he was attacking the Anti-Nazi League and its members as being, at best, stooges for the Communists. The Anti-Nazi League led the opposition to these hearings in Hollywood, and they were cancelled with an explanation of a "lack of funds and time."

Perhaps assuming that Dies was no longer interested in Hollywood after this retreat, the congressman was feted at a luncheon at 20th Century-Fox* in August 1939, where he spoke to the leaders of the industry (including, among others, Louis B. Mayer, Harry and Jack Warner, Y. Frank Freeman, and Sam Goldwyn) and warned them about subversive elements. Nothing had changed, however, and, in November, Dies was urging the House to re-fund the Committee to investigate the charges that Communists were being financially assisted by Hollywood radicals.

These charges were set down in a report, and on December 27, 1939, *Daily Variety* reported that the Committee was split as to releasing the report, which was supposed to name prominent members of the film industry with Communist ties. Since there had been no investigation of the charges, members of the Committee were reluctant to release it, but Dies pushed to have it released anyway and used the conditions described in the report as justification for the House to extend the life of the Committee (which was to expire on January 3, 1940) and to fund it for another two years.

This report was the basis for an article by Dies, which was published in the February issue of *Liberty* magazine. Dies charged that there were 42 or 43 prominent members of the Hollywood community who were Communists or Red sympathizers and blamed them for the propaganda appearing in *Juarez, Blockade,* and *Fury.* This article again provoked a reaction from the industry, and *Daily Variety* editorialized on February 9, 1940, that the charges were not new and that the industry would welcome any honest investigation. *The Hollywood Reporter* reacted more cholerically and attacked Dies's motives, charging that there had been no investigation, only one investigator who had a shady past and may have used his position for shakedowns. Finally, a mass meeting was held on February 21, 1940, at which the Committee's motives were attacked by Donald Ogden Stewart, Mary McCall, and Dorothy Parker, among others.

Once again there was a retreat by Dies, and, in June 1940, he announced that the Committee had decided to postpone the Hollywood investigation because of the political situation. Yet hearings were held in Beaumont, Texas, in July, and a former member of the Communist party named 42 members of the industry as "active in promotion of communism." (This witness, John L. Leech, later testified before a Los Angeles Grand Jury in August and named people, such as Humphrey Bogart, James Cagney, and Fredric March, whom Dies himself stated were not Communists or tied to communism*.)

As before, the Dies Committee did nothing with the information it received, except to use it to argue for money and extension of its life, and on February 23, 1941, the House re-funded the Committee for 15 months. Yet, if the Dies Committee was basically just bluster, its attacks led to a climate where investigations of Hollywood were acceptable (the Los Angeles Grand Jury in August 1940 and the California legislature in 1941) and it showed how easily attacks against communism in the industry could be launched with almost no evidence. That was a lesson that a later chairman of the Committee took to heart.

BIBLIOGRAPHY

"Cagney, Others Cleared in Dies Statement." *Daily Variety,* August 21, 1940, p. 4.

Ceplair, Larry, and Steven Englund. *The Inquisition in Hollywood: Politics in the Film Community, 1930–1960.* Garden City, N.Y.: Anchor Press/Doubleday, 1980.

"Dies the Politician." *The Hollywood Reporter,* February 12, 1940, pp. 1, 4.

"Fite [sic] Looms on Pic Red Charges." *Daily Variety,* December 27, 1939, pp. 1, 4.
"42 Filmites Aiding Reds Named before Dies Body." *Daily Variety,* July 18, 1940, pp. 1, 4.
Rosten, Leo C. *Hollywood: The Movie Colony, the Movie Makers.* New York: Harcourt, Brace, 1941.

DIMENSION PICTURES was a poverty row* producer and distributor, founded by Laurence H. Woolner. Its first film was *Twilight People* (1973) and its last, *Skycopter Summer* (1981). Its most important releases were the 1975 documentary, *Brother Can You Spare a Dime?,* produced by Sandy Lieberson and David Puttnam, and *Ruby* (1977), directed by Curtis Harrington.

BIBLIOGRAPHY

Ray, Fred Olen. *The New Poverty Row: Independent Filmmakers as Distributors.* Jefferson, N.C.: McFarland, 1991.

DIRECT CINEMA LTD., founded in 1975 by Mitchell Block, is a major distributor of independent films and documentaries, with more than 600 titles in its library.

Address: P.O. Box 10003, Santa Monica, Calif. 90410.

DIRECTORS FILM CORPORATION. See RAMO FILMS, INC.

DIRECTORS GUILD OF AMERICA, INC., was organized as the Screen Directors Guild Incorporated on January 16, 1936, to represent the interests of some 75 directors. A year later, assistant directors were admitted to the Guild, which had become recognized as a bargaining agent after a strike threat and which signed its first agreement with the Hollywood producers in May 1939. The first contract covering television direction was signed in 1950.

In 1960, the Screen Directors Guild Incorporated merged with the Radio and Television Directors Guild (formed in 1947) and became the Directors Guild of America. That same year the Guild established a pension plan. In 1963, Assistant Directors IATSE* Local 161 (formed in New York in 1944) merged with the Guild; a year later the Unit Production Managers became part of the Guild; and, in 1965, the Screen Directors International Guild (formed on the East Coast in 1957) merged with the Directors Guild.

The Guild presents annual awards, notable among which are the D. W. Griffith Award (first presented to Cecil B. DeMille in 1953) and the Frank Capra Achievement Award (presented to an assistant director or unit production manager, and first given to Emmett Emerson in 1980).

Address: 7920 Sunset Boulevard, Los Angeles, Calif. 90046; 400 North Michigan Avenue, Suite 307, Chicago, Ill. 60611; 110 West 57th Street, New York, N.Y. 10019; 4000 Hollywood Boulevard, Suite 265-S, Hollywood, Fla. 33021.

DISCINA INTERNATIONAL FILMS CORP. The American branch of André Paulvé's French company, Discina International Films Corp., distributed all of its sister company's productions, including Jean Cocteau's *Beauty and the Beast* (1947) and *Orpheus* (1950), as well as other foreign-language films, mainly French. The company was active in the forties and fifties.

DISNEYLAND. See WALT DISNEY PRODUCTIONS

DIVISION OF FILMS. See UNITED STATES GOVERNMENT COMMITTEE ON PUBLIC INFORMATION: DIVISION OF FILMS

DIXIE FILM EXCHANGE. See TODDY PICTURES COMPANY

"DR. KILDARE" SERIES. Produced by M-G-M* and set in the mythical Blair Hospital, the "Dr. Kildare" series starred Lew Ayres in the title role, with Lionel Barrymore as the crotchety Dr. Leonard Gillespie. Samuel S. Hinds and Emma Dunn portrayed James Kildare's parents, and Alma Kruger and Nell Craig were featured as nurses. The series had its origins in a 1937 Paramount feature, *Interns Can't Take Money,* in which Joel McCrea portrayed James Kildare, a character created by Max Brand. Lew Ayres and Lionel Barrymore were starred in nine M-G-M Dr. Kildare features: *Young Dr. Kildare* (1938), *Calling Dr. Kildare* (1939), *The Secret of Dr. Kildare* (1939), *Dr. Kildare's Strangest Case* (1940), *Dr. Kildare Goes Home* (1940), *Dr. Kildare's Crisis* (1940), *The People vs. Dr. Kildare* (1941), *Dr. Kildare's Wedding Day* (1941), and *Dr. Kildare's Victory* (1942). When America entered the Second World War, Lew Ayres registered as a conscientious objector, and the studio, fearing adverse public reaction, hastily dropped the Kildare character, continuing the series for six more features with Lionel Barrymore as the lone star.

BIBLIOGRAPHY

Zinman, David. *Saturday Afternoon at the Bijou.* New Rochelle, N.Y.: Arlington House, 1973.

DOCUMENTARIES. The term "documentary" is used to refer to a factual film, of any length, dealing with actual events or people. Film documentaries have their origins in both newsreels* and the actuality subjects shot in the 1890s by the earliest filmmakers. The word was first used by John Grierson in a review of *Moana* in a 1926 issue of the *New York Sun* and comes from the French "documentaire," first used in the January 1914 issue of *Cinéopse.*

Although documentary features were not uncommon in the second decade of the twentieth century, the father of the American documentary is generally considered to have been Robert Flaherty (1884–1951), who made *Moana* and whose other films included *Nanook of the North* (1922), *Man of Aran* (1934), *The Land* (1942), and *Louisiana Story* (1948). The leader of the documentary film movement is the man who coined the word, John Grierson (1898–1972), who was active in his native Britain, founded the National Film Board of Canada, and produced some documentaries in the United States for his company, The World Today, Inc., in the mid-forties.

Some of the best American documentaries were those sponsored by the U.S. government in the late thirties and through the Second World War, including *The Plow That Broke the Plains* (1936), *The River* (1937), *The City* (1939), *The Forgotten Village* (1941), *The Battle of Midway* (1942), *Prelude to War* (1943), *The Battle of Russia* (1943), *The Memphis Belle* (1944), *The Fighting Lady* (1944), and *The Battle of San Pietro* (1945).

Prior to the Second World War, documentaries were shot in 35mm, but by the fifties 16mm* was the medium used by most documentary filmmakers. Because of its lightweight portability, 16mm allowed filmmakers to get closer to their subjects and to document their lives more feasibly on a daily basis. This led to the "cinema verité" movement of the sixties, which has its origins in Soviet cinema, but which was pioneered in the United States by Richard Leacock, D. A. Pennebaker, Albert and David Maysles, and Haskell Wexler.

In the eighties and nineties, documentaries began to garner a wider, theatrical audience. Among these are Obie Benz's *Heavy Petting* (1988), Errol Morris's *The Thin Blue Line* (1988), Michael Moore's *Roger and Me* (1989), Jennie Livingston's *Paris Is Burning* (1990), Michael Apted's *35 Up* (1991), Alek Keshishian's *Madonna: Truth or Dare* (1991), and Errol Morris's *A Brief History of Time* (1992).

Although the Academy of Motion Picture Arts and Sciences* has given Academy Awards for Best Short Subjects since 1931–1932 (short subjects that would usually include a novelty subject and might well be considered a documentary), it was not until 1941 that it gave three special awards in the documentary category, to *Churchill's Island* (produced by the National Film Board of Canada), to Rey Scott (for *Kukan,* his documentary on China), and to the British Ministry of Information (for *Target for Tonight*). The categories of best Documentary Feature and Short Subjects were not introduced by the Academy until 1964, when the winners were *Jacques-Yves Cousteau's World without Sun* (feature) and *Nine from Little Rock* (short subject). The Academy's rules governing documentary nominations were the subject of considerable criticism in 1994 and 1995, after such popular 1994 theatrical releases as *Hoop Dreams* and *Crumb* failed to be nominated.

BIBLIOGRAPHY

Barnouw, Erik. *Documentary*. New York: Oxford University Press, 1974.
Barsam, Richard M. *Nonfiction Film: A Critical History*. Bloomington, Ind.: Indiana University Press, 1992.
Hardy, Forsyth, ed. *Grierson on Documentary*. Berkeley, Calif.: University of California Press, 1966.
Jacobs, Lewis, ed. *The Documentary Tradition*. New York: W. W. Norton, 1971.
MacCann, Richard Dyer. *The People's Films*. New York: Hastings House, 1973.
Rabinger, Michael. *Directing the Documentary*. Boston: Focal Press, 1992.
Rotha, Paul *Documentary Film*. London: Faber and Faber, 1936.
Slide, Anthony. *Before Video: A History of the Non-Theatrical Film*. Westport, Conn.: Greenwood Press, 1992.

DOLBY SOUND. The patented Dolby sound system both enhances the sound and reduces the level of "hiss" on the soundtrack, the "hiss" being inherent to all magnetic tape recording. The system was developed by Ray Dolby as a noise reduction system for the recording industry in 1965. It was first commercially used in the motion picture industry by Stanley Kubrick for *A Clockwork Orange* (1971). Later, Dolby developed a four-channel stereo-optical track, which also utilized its noise reduction system. However, use of the Dolby system did require the installation of a special decoding device in theatres. The use of Dolby on 35mm stereo-optic release prints of *Star Wars* (1977) encouraged theatres to install the equipment and, as of October 1984, some 6,000 U.S. theatres were equipped to screen Dolby sound. The Dolby sound system is available in theatres in some 45 countries, and the majority of American films are today released with the potential of Dolby sound.

Address: Dolby Laboratories, Inc., 100 Potrero Avenue, San Francisco, Calif. 94103.

BIBLIOGRAPHY

Barry, David. "Let's Hear It for Dolby Sound." *Los Angeles Times,* Calendar, April 30, 1978, p. 40.
Stetter, Elmar. "Sound Becoming More Important as Integral Part of Motion Pics." *Variety,* January 12, 1983, pp. 147–48.

"DOMINO" BRAND. See NEW YORK MOTION PICTURE COMPANY

DOTY-DAYTON PRODUCTIONS was formed as a general partnership in 1973 by Lyman D. Dayton (born 1941) and his father-in-law, Dr. George E. Doty. The company was incorporated in March 1974, and in 1975, a subsidiary, Doty-Dayton Releasing, Inc., was founded. Based in North Hollywood, California, but with strong ties to Utah, Doty-Dayton produced four films—*Where the Red Fern Grows* (1974), *Seven Alone* (1974), *Against a Crooked Sky* (1975), and *Baker's Hawk* (1977)—all stressing the family, moral values, and Americanism. After suffering heavy losses, it filed for Chapter XI bankruptcy protection in February 1977, and ceased operations in 1979; a successor company is Dayton Stewart Productions of St. George, Utah.

BIBLIOGRAPHY

Grant, Lee. "Film-Maker Proves Virtue Is Profitable." *Los Angeles Times*, part 4, September 2, 1976, pp. 1, 16.

RESOURCES

Papers, Photographs, Scripts: Brigham Young University.

DOUGLASS NATURAL COLOR FILM COMPANY, LTD.

Leon F. Douglass, one of the patentees of the Victor Talking Machine, developed a color process for motion picture films that had its first public exhibition at the Wurlitzer Fine Hall in New York on February 12, 1918. The invention, which involved a small device that could be attached to any camera, could reproduce every hue, shade, and tint of nature. The projection of the films did not involve the use of a rotary colored shutter, as did previous attempts to make color films. According to contemporaneous news items, the attached device to the camera gave several color values to the negative. A positive print then was made by a chemical process. The films, which were projected at a speed of 24 frames per second, also were reputed to give a stereoscopic effect. The first exhibition included shots of the sunset, a rainbow, a forest fire, and Nevada Falls. Reviews commented on the brilliant reds and greens obtained. In May 1918, after a public showing at the Kinema Theatre in Los Angeles, W. W. Hodkinson* announced plans to distribute shorts made by the company, among which was *Cupid Angling,* starring Ruth Roland.

BIBLIOGRAPHY

"Douglass Color Process." *The Moving Picture World,* March 1, 1918, p. 1231.

DRACO FILM COMPANY, INC., began producing early in 1915 with George L. Sargent as chief director and releasing through Mutual Film Corporation*. In December 1915, a company named Dra-Ko Film Company, which may have been the same as Draco, produced a five-reel feature, *The York State Follies,* which was released on the Premier program. J. Snyder was the general manager, and Joseph A. Richmond was the director of the studio at Tappan, New York.

DRA-KO FILM COMPANY. See DRACO FILM COMPANY, INC.

DRAMATIC FEATURE FILM COMPANY. Frank J. Baum and Francis Power were the co-presidents of the Dramatic Feature Film Company, which filmed its first production, *The Little Grey Nun of Belgium,* starring Cathrine Countiss, at the Oz Studio in Hollywood in April 1915. David Proctor was the leading man and Francis Power the film's director. *The Little Grey Nun of Belgium* was released on the Alliance program.

DREAMWORKS SKG is the two billion dollar production and distribution studio created by Steven Spielberg (born 1947), David Geffen (born 1943), and Jeffrey Katzenberg (born 1950), officially announced on October 12, 1994 as the unnamed studio. In December 1994, Dreamworks announced an alliance for television production with Capital Cities/ABC; in March 1995, it revealed a ten-year agreement with Home Box Office and a $30 million joint venture with Microsoft; and in March 1996, it acquired a 40 percent interest in Pacific Data Images, a computer animation company. As of 1996, Dreamworks had lined up two billion dollars in financing, had more than 560 employees, and was planning studio complexes in Playa Vista in West Los Angeles (bitterly opposed by environmentalists and others) and in the city of Glendale (for animation work).

BIBLIOGRAPHY

Corliss, Richard. "A Studio Is Born." *Time,* October 24, 1994, pp. 68–70.
———. "Hey, Let's Put on a Show!" *Time,* March 27, 1995, pp. 54–60.
Meyer, Michael, and Charles Fleming. "Hollywood Poker." *Newsweek,* October 24, 1994, pp. 40–41.
Sloan, Allan. "Pennies from Heaven." *Newsweek,* April 3, 1995, pp. 44–45.
Weinraub, Bernard, and Geraldine Fabrikant. "A Hollywood Recipe: Vision, Wealth. Ego," *The New York Times,* October 16, 1994, pp. 1, 32.

DRIVE-IN THEATRES. The concept of a drive-in theatre can be traced back to 1911, when David S. Hulfish in *The Motion Picture Cyclopedia* first mooted the idea for an open-air movie theatre or airdrome. The first drive-in theater per se was opened by Richard M. Hollingshead, Jr., in Camden, New Jersey, on June 6, 1933, with a capacity for 400 cars. Hollingshead opened a second drive-in, on Pico Boulevard, Los Angeles, in July of the following year.

Drive-in theatres gradually gained in number. In 1948, there were 743; in 1949, 1,000; in 1956, 5,000. The number of drive-in theatres in the United States reached an all-time high in 1961, with a total of 6,000. By 1969, the number was reduced to 3,700, and in 1985 there were only 2,800. As the number of regular movie theatres diminished in the forties and fifties, the number of drive-ins increased. The success of the drive-in theatre had much to do with the baby boom after the Second World War; drive-in theatres provided cheap entertainment for large families, all members of which could fit into one vehicle. The decline in the number of drive-in theatres can be linked to the increased value of real estate and the increase in "R"- and "X"-rated films, which most local authorities barred drive-in theatres from screening.

In *Boxoffice* (May 1984), Dr. Bruce A. Austin wrote, "The drive-in has been credited with providing an exhibition outlet for the product of smaller, independent film producers and distributors. It also proved to be the means for drawing back to the movies the 'lost audience' of the 1950s. Today, the drive-in is the only form of moviegoing for many patrons, and a few industry observers suggest that, at least in warm weather locales, it will survive and prosper as an alternative to the pay TV competition in the home."

Among the stranger versions of the drive-in was a "fly-in, drive-in" theatre, opened in June 1948 at Asbury Park, New Jersey, which could accommodate 500 cars and 25 planes from an adjoining airstrip. The largest drive-in ever to open was one at Copiague, New York, with a capacity for 2,500 cars.

BIBLIOGRAPHY

Segrave, Kerry. *Drive-In Theaters: A History from Their Inception in 1933.* Jefferson, North Carolina: McFarland, 1992.

DRUGS. Hollywood has always adopted a negative corporate attitude toward drugs, even if some of its better-known names have taken a different viewpoint. Unfortunately, the industry's antidrug message has often been held up to ridicule and become a source of entertainment for those into rather than opposed to many forms of drugs. Even that all-American genre, the Western, could not escape the insidious reach of marijuana. As early as 1924, *Notch Number One* featured a scene in which the all-American hero went beserk after smoking marijuana, or "loco weed." The 1929 Yakima Canutt vehicle, currently in distribution as *High on the Range* but originally released under a different title, implies that marijuana was firmly entrenched as part of American social behavior. At one point, a character comments, "There's too much marijuana smoking on this ranch." The antidrug sentiment of the 1936 features *Reefer Madness* and *Marijuana* (subtitled "The Weed with Roots in Hell") was so heavy-handed that the reissue of these films in the 1970s proved popular with marijuana-smoking American college students.

As early as 1894, Thomas Edison copyrighted *Chinese Opium Den.* The emphasis in this and other early films was on opium rather than other types of drugs, and generally they warned against the danger of smoking. A notable exception was D. W. Griffith's *Broken Blossoms* (1919), in which the Richard Barthelmess character is seen enjoying opium as a blessed relief from the discrimination he, as a Chinese immigrant, experiences in London's Limehouse District.

Douglas Fairbanks, Sr., demonstrated the effects of cocaine addiction in *The Mystery of the Leaping Fish* (1916), in which he plays Coke Ennyday, a detective whose boundless energy and verve are the result of a daily dose of the drug. Ultimately, the film denigrates the recreational use of cocaine, and pictures foreigners, rather than Americans, as purveyors of the drug. Around the same time as the release of this film, composer W. C. Powell wrote two songs whose titles leave no doubt as to their subject matter: "Dope" and "The Dopey Rag."

One of the two leading ladies in *The Mystery of the Leap-*

ing Fish was Alma Rubens, who died at the age of 33, in 1931, of drug addiction. Other silent stars whose early deaths were the result of overindulgence in drugs include Barbara La Marr, Mabel Normand, and Wallace Reid. Later Hollywood stars whose names were linked to drugs include River Phoenix, John Belushi, Bela Lugosi, and Errol Flynn. In 1948, Robert Mitchum was charged with possession of marijuana and served a brief jail term; in the 1960s, he remarked disingenuously, "I've been smoking it since 1945 and it never got to be a habit with me." In 1960, Cary Grant, childless, discontented, and apparently unable to fall in love, took to experimenting with L.S.D. He told the fan magazines that L.S.D. had made him "ready for life, ready for love," and *Modern Screen* (June 1960) avidly informed its readership, "The daring experiment with the drug called L.S.D. has proved to be a success."

The two best-known exponents of the drug craze of the 1970s were Cheech and Chong, a comedy team formed in January 1970 by Richard Marin (born 1946) and Tommy Chong (born 1938). Noted for their jokes on the subject of pot, the couple told *Rolling Stone* (December 14, 1978), "We want to be the Bob Hopes of the doper generation, smoking onstage." Cheech and Chong appeared in live concerts throughout the United States and Canada, and were particularly popular with campus audiences. They released their first album, "Cheech & Chong," in September 1971, and made their first feature film, *Up in Smoke,* for Paramount in 1978, under the direction of Lou Adler. *Up in Smoke* was the first major Hollywood feature with a sympathetic approach to marijuana use, as Cheech and Chong go in search of pot, pursued by narcotics detective Stacy Keach. Since 1985, Cheech and Chong have gone their separate ways, and both have mellowed as the political climate has turned to the right.

Drug use was virtually ignored in Hollywood in the forties, but was the subject of critical examination in the fifties with *The Man with the Golden Arm* (1955), *Monkey on My Back* (1957), and *A Hatful of Rain* (1957). The drug scene of the sixties led to a number of films promoting a positive approach to the subject, including *The Trip* (1967), *I Love You, Alice B. Toklas* (1968), *Easy Rider* (1969), *Bob & Carol & Ted & Alice* (1969), *Zabriskie Point* (1970), and *The Magic Garden of Stanley Sweeetheart* (1970). Since then, the only individuals who have had fun with drugs have been the characters of Edina Monsoon and Patsy Stone, as played by Jennifer Saunders and Joanna Lumley, in the BBC television series *Absolutely Fabulous* (1992–1995).

The American tribal love-rock musical of the 1960s, *Hair,* emulated the youth culture of the decade, advocating free love and free drugs, and including in its repertoire a song titled "Hashish." With book and lyrics by Gerome Ragni and James Rado, and music by Galt MacDermot, *Hair* opened off-Broadway as a New York Shakespeare Festival Public Theater (Joseph Papp) presentation at the Anspacher Theatre on October 17, 1967. With a cast that included both

Ragni and Rado, the show opened on Broadway at the Biltmore Theatre on April 29, 1968. It was filmed by director Milos Forman in 1979, and seemed as dated as the hippy generation it glorified.

"Hashish" was not the only song on the subject of marijuana. African-American orchestra leader Cab Calloway popularized two similar numbers, "The Wail of the Reefer Man" by Ted Koehler and Harold Arlen, introduced in the 1932 New York revue *Cotton Club Parade;* and "Reefer Man" by J. Russell Robinson, first heard in the 1933 Paramount feature *International House.* Two other songs from the same period are "Smokin' Reefers" by Howard Dietz and Arthur Schwartz, introduced in the New York revue *Flying Colors* in 1932; and "Marahuana" (sic) by Sam Coslow and Arthur Johnson, introduced by Gertrude Michael in the 1934 Paramount feature *Murder at the Vanities.*

No discussion of the power of drugs could fail to include Sherlock Holmes, whose drug of choice was cocaine in the stories and novels of Sir Arthur Conan Doyle. Only one classic Sherlock Holmes feature film makes reference to Holmes's chemical nemesis, and that is the 1939 version of *The Hound of the Baskervilles,* which ends with Basil Rathbone, as Holmes, saying to Nigel Bruce, "Watson —the needle!"

BIBLIOGRAPHY

Starks, Michael. *Cocaine Fiends and Reefer Madness: An Illustrated History of Drugs in the Movies.* New York: Cornwall Books, 1982.

DU ART FILM LABORATORIES, INC., founded in 1922, is a major New York organization, providing full-service 16mm* and 35mm* black-and-white and color film processing. It specializes in the Frame Count Cueing System, which minimizes the handling of negative film; offers a computer program whereby the work print can be conformed with the original negative in the camera of an optical printer; and is noted for the blow-up of 16mm to 35mm film, utilizing a computerized cueing and timing system.

Address: 245 West 55th Street, New York, N.Y. 10019.

DUDLEY MOTION PICTURE MANUFACTURING COMPANY. M. B. Dudley was the president of the Dudley Motion Picture Manufacturing Company, which produced Western* dramas at its studio in Redlands, California. In September 1916, the company arranged to release one five- or six-reel feature a month with Unity Sales Corporation. The company was reorganized in November 1916.

DUDLEY PICTURES CORPORATION was founded in Los Angeles in 1947 by Carl W. Dudley (1910–1973). The latter was a veteran producer of travel films—he was responsible for the Cinerama* release *Cinerama—South Seas Adventure* (1968)—and a former shorts screenwriter for M-G-M* and Warner Bros.*, and his company produced travel films for airlines, tourist agencies, and others. Among the series created by Dudley were *It's a Wonderful World*, *Wide, Wide World* and *This World of Ours.* Dudley Television Corporation was created, as a subsidiary, in 1951. Dudley Pictures Corporation ceased operations shortly after the death of its founder.

DUQUESNE AMUSEMENT SUPPLY COMPANY. See WARNER BROS. PICTURES, INC.

DYREDA ART FILM CORPORATION. Frank L. Dyer, J. Parker Read, Jr., and J. Searle Dawley combined the first two letters of their last names to form the name of their new production company, the Dyreda Art Film Corporation, formed in October 1914. Dyer was president, Read vice president and treasurer, and Dawley, a director since 1907 with Edison and Famous Players Film Company, was given full charge of production. The company leased from the Mutual Film Corporation* the studio erected on the Clara Morris estate on the Hudson by the Reliance Company for D. W. Griffith. Dyreda's first two productions were *One of Millions*, with Laura Sawyer and Robert Broderick, and *In the Name of the Prince of Peace,* an antiwar subject. Dyreda released its product with World Film Corporation* from October 1914 until April 1915. In December 1914, World purchased the rights to two Charles K. Harris songs, "Always in the Way" and "Break the News to Mother," and contracted with Dyreda to produce them. After April 1915, Dyreda released exclusively with the Metro Film Corporation*. In May 1915, its studios were located at 3 West 61st Street, New York. On May 27, 1915, the B. A. Rolfe organization, which was owned in part by Metro, purchased Dyreda. C. M. Maddox of Rolfe became the general manager of the new company.

BIBLIOGRAPHY

"Dyreda—New Producing Company." *The Moving Picture World,* October 3, 1914, p. 69.

EACO FILMS, INC. Edwin August and Edward E. Anderson, the brother of Gilbert M. "Broncho Billy" Anderson, formed Eaco Films, Inc., in September 1914. August supervised the production of three reels per week, which included two-reelers in which he played the lead, one-reel comedies with Hal August, and Westerns* with Edward Piel. With offices in the World Tower Building in New York, Eaco used the Pathé* studios in Jersey City and filmed on location in Bermuda and Florida. David Santarelli was the company cameraman and supervised the laboratory work. Eaco's first film, which was released by Apex Film Corporation, was *Below the Dead Line*. In October 1914, Eaco produced its first three-reel production, *The Millionaire Detective*, released by the Strand Film Company, which had secured exclusive rights to Eaco's films. In December 1914, August left Eaco to join the Kinetophote Film Corporation*.

BIBLIOGRAPHY

"Edwin August a Manufacturer." *The Moving Picture World*, September 26, 1914, p. 1786.

EAGLE FEATURE FILM COMPANY was located at 5 East 14th Street, New York. It produced the four-reel feature *Hawkshaw, the Detective*, in July 1913. Charles Streamer was the company's manager.

EAGLE FILM MANUFACTURING AND PRODUCING COMPANY, formed in late 1915, was located at 109 North Dearborn Street in Chicago. William J. Dunn was the general manager and director of the company, which produced *The Adventures of Duffy*, a comedy detective series, and the six-reel feature, *The Pirates of the Sky*. In June 1916, the company relocated to Jacksonville, Florida, and changed its name to the Eagle Film Company. It produced comedies released through Unity Sales Corporation*, including the "Tweedledum and Tweedledee" series. Fernandez Perez was the featured comedian. In August 1918, the Jacksonville plant was purchased by a hardware company after Eagle went into bankruptcy.

EAGLE-LION FILMS, INC. The name Eagle-Lion was first introduced by British film magnate J. Arthur Rank, in February 1944, as a worldwide distributor of British films. However, the name was subsequently taken by Arthur Krim and Robert Young (a railroad magnate) for a production company, which had its basis in P.R.C.* and which was officially formed on April 24, 1946. (The British Eagle-Lion became part of Rank's General Film Distributors but was still utilized in some countries for several years.) Bryan Foy became the new company's production chief, and Eagle-Lion's first film was the Kenny Delmar comedy vehicle, *It's a Joke, Son* (1947).

Although it was little more than a "B" movie* producer, Eagle-Lion's films were quite well regarded critically, particularly those directed by Anthony Mann. Writing of Eagle-Lion's crime melodramas, Don Miller has commented, "Its influence was felt long after the organization had ceased to function, but particularly during the early part of the fifties. Eventually, this influence predominated in American television crime shows, for better or worse." In 1950, Eagle-Lion merged with Film Classics to become Eagle-Lion Classics, and the following year production ceased and the company's product was taken over by the new United Artists Corporation* organization.

BIBLIOGRAPHY

Miller, Don. "Eagle-Lion: The Violent Years." *Focus on Film*, no. 31, November 1978, pp. 27–38.

EARL OWENSBY STUDIOS. See E. O. CORP.

EASTERN FILM COMPANY, a Providence, Rhode Island, production company, was organized in September 1915 by three men from Providence: Elwood F. Bostwick, who became the general manager, Frederick S. Peck, the president and one of the wealthiest men in New England and vice president of the National Exchange Bank of Providence, and Benjamin L. Cook. The company capitalized at $300,000 and had no stock for sale. It produced under the "Pelican" brand four one-reel films per week, in addition to two-reel comedies and two five-reel features per month. Directors for Eastern included Frederick Esmelton, Lambert Hillyer, George Lessy, Hamilton Crane, Dan Mason, Charles Pitt, and Allen Crolius. Eastern's first film was *Peaceful Valley*, with Frederick Burton, which was followed by *Next*, with Helen Lowell, and *The Red Petticoat*, with John Bunny's brother George, all produced in 1915.

BIBLIOGRAPHY

"New Producing Company." *The Moving Picture World*, September 4, 1915, p. 1624.

EASTMAN COLOR. Eastman color negative and color print film was introduced by Eastman Kodak* in 1950; in 1952, the company received an Academy Award (Scientific or Technical Award, Class I) for the film. The new film was immediately successful and in effect became the industry standard, particularly when the Technicolor* three-strip process became obsolete in the mid-fifties. Unfortunately, the new Eastman color film does not have the stability of Technicolor dye transfer prints and many prints and negatives have faded, resulting in an outcry in the early eighties from filmmakers and archivists. In response, Eastman Kodak introduced a new "low fade" film stock. Virtually every film today is photographed in Eastman color, despite the use of such patented names as Metrocolor, Warnercolor, and Color by De Luxe*. As Technicolor has not printed any original Technicolor dye transfer prints outside of China since 1975, all films presently identified as in Technicolor are in fact printed on Eastman color film but by the Technicolor Corporation.

EASTMAN KODAK COMPANY was formed as the Eastman Dry Plate Company by George Eastman (1854–1932) and Henry A. Strong on January 1, 1881. It became the Eastman Dry Plate and Film Company in 1884, the Eastman Company in 1889, and the Eastman Kodak Company in 1892. The present company was organized in 1901. The company's name is synonymous with film and with still cameras. It introduced the first transparent roll film in 1889; the first acetate* film in 1908; 16mm film in 1923; X-ray film in 1924; 16mm Kodacolor film in 1928; 8mm film and cameras in 1932; 35mm microfilm in 1934; Kodachrome film in 1935; its first 16mm sound-on-film projector, the Koda-scope, in 1937; acetate film for general use in the motion picture industry in 1948; and Super 8mm in 1965. Its trademarks are Kodak, Eastman, Recordak, Brownie, Kodachrome, Instamatic, Ektaprint, Colorburst, and Kodel.

The name "Kodak" was invented by George Eastman in 1888. He wanted a short word that could be spelled and pronounced simply in any language, and after studying many combinations of letters, he selected a word that began and ended with his favorite letter, "K."

Address: Rochester, N.Y. 14650.

BIBLIOGRAPHY

Collins, Douglas. *The Story of Kodak*. New York: Harry N. Abrams, 1990.
Eastman Kodak. *Eastman Professional Motion Picture Films*. Rochester, N.Y.: Eastman Kodak Company, 1982.
———. *The Book of Film Care*. Rochester, N.Y.: Eastman Kodak Company, 1983.
———. *Eastman Kodak Company: A Brief History*. Rochester, N.Y.: Eastman Kodak Company, 1983.
Simmons, Dr. Norwood L "Kodak: Innovator behind the Scenes." *Movie/TV Marketing*, March 1970, pp. 9–13.
Smith, Frederick James. "The Man behind the Films—George Eastman." *Motion Picture Magazine,* September 1918, pp. 79–81, 128.
Solbert, O. N. *George Eastman*. Rochester, N.Y.: Eastman Kodak Company, n.d. (reprinted from the November 1953 issue of *Image*).

EAVES COSTUME CO. For many years advertised as "the largest manufacturers of theatrical costumes in the East," the New York-based Eaves Costume Co. provided the costumes for virtually all of the silent films produced in and around the city, including D. W. Griffith's *Way Down East* (1920), *Orphans of the Storm* (1921), *One Exciting Night* (1922), and *The White Rose* (1923); Marion Davies's *When Knighthood Was in Flower* (1922) and *Little Old New York* (1923); Rudolph Valentino's *Monsieur Beaucaire* (1924); George Arliss's *Disraeli* (1921); John Barrymore's *Dr. Jekyll and Mr. Hyde* (1920); Norma Talmadge's *Smilin' Through* (1922); and William Fox's *If I Were King* (1920) and *Over the Hill* (1920). The company later became the Eaves-Brooks Costume Company, and its historical collection of costumes was donated to the Astoria* Motion Picture and Television Foundation.

EBONY PICTURES CORPORATION of Chicago began releasing films with the General Film Company on April 15, 1918. It made one-reel slapstick comedies with all-black casts. L. J. Pollard was the president and general manager of the company and Bob Horner its scenario editor. In May 1918, the company of 150 persons, which had previously filmed at Oshkosh, Wisconsin, obtained lakefront property on which to erect a studio at Fort du Lac, Wisconsin. Ralph Phillips and Charles N. David directed for the company. Actors included Sam Robinson, Yvonne Junior, Samuel Jacks, and Mattie Edwards. In July 1918, casts comprised of both black and white actors began appearing in Ebony productions. After a short hiatus, the company resumed production in September 1919, producing its first two-reel film, which starred Samuel Jacks, surrounded by a white cast. Late in 1919, Ebony made a six-reel dramatic feature, dealing with spiritualism and titled *Do the Dead Talk?* The company went out of existence in 1922, largely, one suspects, because of opposition from black newspapers, which objected to this white-owned company's depiction of blacks and its exploitation of black audiences.

The best known of Ebony comedies was *Spying the Spy* (1918), which is preserved in the National Film Collection at the Library of Congress.

BIBLIOGRAPHY

Sampson, Henry T. *Blacks in Black and White: A Source Book*. Metuchen, N.J.: Scarecrow Press, 1995.

ECLAIR COMPANY. Charles Jourjon, the president of the Eclair Company in Paris, came to the United States to open the company's American branch in Fort Lee, New Jersey*, in the fall of 1911, to "give the trade an American picture made the Eclair way." This meant, Jourjon specified, using American players and French cameramen and technicians trained in Paris. A factory and two glass studios, designed by French experts, were erected, each with the capacity for shooting four scenes simultaneously. Harry Raver, formerly with circus, carnival, and other motion picture enterprises, was business manager of the American branch. Jules Brulatour was the political and financial advisor; M. Maire, the chief cameraman; C. DeMoos, in charge of the technical end of the plant; Lawrence McGill, George Le Soir, and Joseph Smiley were the directors; Will S. Rising was the scenarist; and Wray Physioc was the scenic artist. The first American-made film was the two-reel *Hands across the Sea in '76,* released November 7, 1911.

Eclair began releasing with the Universal Film Manufacturing Company at its inception in 1912. In November 1913, Eclair sent Webster Cullison to establish a permanent western branch of Eclair in Tucson, Arizona, with a company of 23. A studio and plant were set up there, and, after a disastrous fire at the Fort Lee plant in March 1914 (which destroyed Eclair's laboratory), the entire American producing force was sent to Tucson.

After the fire, some of the Eclair company stayed in Fort Lee and joined the newly created Peerless Feature Film Company, which Brulatour headed. Eclair began releasing with Warner's Features, and, late in 1914, formed Features Ideal, Inc., sometimes called the Ideal Company of Hollywood, as its Hollywood branch. Robert Levy was the general manager; the three directors were Frank Beal, Webster Cullison, and Carl Levinus; and the players included Dolly and George Larkin, Edna Payne, and Fred Hearn. Other players of note who appeared in Eclair's American films were Barbara Tennant, Fred Truesdell, Alec B. Francis, Muriel Ostriche, Clara Horton, and John Adolfi. Other cameramen included René Guissart and Lucien Andriot. Ben Carré was an Eclair scenic artist. Maurice Tourneur came to the United States in 1914 to direct at Eclair's Fort Lee plant.

BIBLIOGRAPHY

"American Eclair Studio." *The Moving Picture World,* October 7, 1911, pp. 24–25.
"Charles Jourjon, 'Concerning Eclair Enterprises.'" *The Moving Picture World,* July 11, 1914, p. 207.
"Cullison Is New Managing Director of Eclair Productions." *The Universal Weekly,* August 22, 1914, pp. 8–9.

ECLECTIC FILM COMPANY, located at 110 West 40th Street, New York, began distributing European films in the United States early in 1913 with the two-reel *Lucretia Borgia.* In April 1913, the company distributed the 12-reel *Les Miserables,* followed by *The Mysteries of Paris.* In mid–1914, it jointly produced the Pearl White serial *The Perils of Pauline,* whose story was presented in the Hearst newspapers, with Pathé* Freres. Compared to the usual 25 to 30 made for most previous serials, 147 prints of the serial were struck, so that exhibitions across the country could be coordinated with the newspaper stories. In January 1915, the staffs of Eclectic and Pathé Freres were combined under a new name, Pathé Exchange, Inc.

BIBLIOGRAPHY

"Expediting Service." *The Moving Picture World,* July 11, 1914, p. 284.
"First Eclectic Film." *The New York Dramatic Mirror,* January 15, 1913, p. 60.

EDISON MANUFACTURING COMPANY, also known as Thomas A. Edison, Inc., had its origins in the primitive films photographed by Edison's associates in the Black Maria studio at Edison's laboratory in West Orange, New Jersey, built in 1891. Here Edison's associate, W. K. L. Dickson, produced the first films to be copyrighted—in 1893. The first public performance of Edison films, under the name of Edison Vitascope, took place at Koster and Bial's Music Hall, Herald Square, New York, on April 23, 1896.

Although Thomas Edison himself took little, if any, interest in film production, his company flourished, and, in 1908, the Edison Company erected a new studio at 2826 Decatur Avenue, Bedford Park, the Bronx, New York. The new studio replaced a makeshift studio at 41 East 21st Street, New York, where Edwin S. Porter (1869–1941) had been in charge of production and had produced and directed some of the first, and certainly most important, narrative films, including *The Great Train Robbery* and *Life of an American Fireman,* both released in 1903. It was Porter's associate, J. Searle Dawley, who directed D. W. Griffith's first screen appearance, in the 1907 Edison short, *Rescued from an Eagle's Nest.*

A fire at the Edison studio on March 27, 1914, caused extensive damage, and for a while the company was forced to utilize the 11 East 14th Street studios of the Biograph Company*.

Among the players making up the Edison stock company were Viola Dana, Mary Fuller, Charles Ogle, Mabel Trunnelle, Marc McDermott, Gertrude McCoy, Bessie Learn, and Herbert Prior. Charles Ogle was the star of Edison's 1910 production of *Frankenstein,* and Mary Fuller was featured in the first serial*, Edison's *What Happened to Mary?* (1912).

As the most important member of the Motion Picture Patents Company*, the Edison Company enjoyed considerable success from 1908 through 1912, but as the power of the Patents group dissipated, and as Edison failed to embark on an adequate production schedule for feature-length films, the company lost its importance. The last Edison production was *The Unbeliever,* directed by Alan Crosland in 1918.

BIBLIOGRAPHY

Baldwin, Neil. *Edison: Inventing the Century.* New York: Hyperion, 1995.
Crosland, Alan. "How Edison's 'Black Maria' Grew." *Motography,* April 22, 1916, pp. 911–14.

Dickson, Antonia, and W. K. L. Dickson. *Edison's Invention of the Kineto-Phonograph.* Los Angeles: Pueblo Press, 1939.

————. *History of the Kinetograph, Kinetoscope and Kineto-Phonograph.* New York: Arno Press, 1970.

"Edisonia." *Exhibitors' Times,* August 30, 1913, pp. 1, 4.

"Edison's Pictures and Players." *The New York Dramatic Mirror,* January 31, 1912, p. 54.

"Edison Progress." *The Moving Picture World,* December 11, 1909, pp. 833–35.

Harrison, Louis Reeves. "Studio Saunterings." *The Moving Picture World,* April 13, 1913, pp. 127–31.

Hendricks, Gordon. *The Edison Motion Picture Myth.* Berkeley, Calif.: University of California Press, 1961.

Musser, Charles. *Before the Nickelodeon: Edwin S. Porter and the Edison Manufacturing Company.* Berkeley, Calif.: University of California Press, 1991.

————. *Thomas A. Edison and His Kinetographic Motion Pictures.* New Brunswick, N.J.: Rutgers University Press, 1995.

Spehr, Paul C. "Edison Films in the Library of Congress." *The Quarterly Journal of the Library of Congress* (January 1975): pp. 34–50.

Svejda, George J. *The Black Maria Site Study.* Washington, D.C.: Office of Archeology and Historic Preservation, 1969.

RESOURCES

Papers: Edison National Historic Site; Museum of Modern Art (scripts).

EDISON VITAGRAPH COMPANY. See VITAGRAPH COMPANY OF AMERICA

EDITDROID. See LUCASFILM, LTD.

EDITING. Editing is the art and craft of joining together the various pieces of film shot by the cinematographer into a lucid, dramatic, and emotional whole. Some directors work closely with the editor, selecting each shot and deciding exactly where a cut should take place, while others recognize the editor's expertise and leave many of the decisions to him or her. Similarly, some directors shoot a minimum of footage, which virtually prevents the editor from making creative decisions, while other directors shoot excessive footage to give the editor tremendous choice and variety.

The Soviet theorist and director V. I. Pudovkin has argued that editing is the one crucial and creative art in film production. Certainly the editor can, at times, save a film that might otherwise be mediocre. He can also add much to a film's dramatic or emotional impact. Edwin S. Porter was, arguably, the first filmmaker to recognize the importance of editing, but it was D. W. Griffith who displayed the first true understanding of editing as a creative tool with *The Birth of a Nation* (1915) and *Intolerance* (1916).

During much of the silent era, film editors were called simply cutters, who, using little more than their own two eyes and a pair of scissors, would, literally, cut the film into shape. Although the art of editing is an American invention, it was the Russians who recognized it as such. Many editors, including Dorothy Arzner, Edward Dmytryk, and Robert Wise, were able to make a successful transition to directing. The British David Lean continued both to edit and direct his features up to and including *A Passage to India* (1984).

Editing includes both the cutting of the picture and the soundtrack, and, in recent years, the work of sound effects editors has come to be recognized as a separate craft. Editors work with a "work print" made specifically for editing purposes. Once the work print has been cut, it is turned over to a negative cutter, responsible for matching the work of the editor on the work print with the camera negative.

Academy Awards for Best Film Editing have been given since 1934. The first winner was Conrad Nervig for his work on *Eskimo.*

BIBLIOGRAPHY

Ash, René L. *The Motion Picture Film Editor.* Metuchen, N.J.: Scarecrow Press, 1974.

Balmuth, Bernard. *Introduction to Film Editing.* Boston: Focal Press, 1989.

Dancyger, Ken. *The Technique of Film and Video Editing.* Boston: Focal Press, 1993.

Dymtryk, Edward. *On Film Editing.* Boston: Focal Press, 1984.

Hollyn, Norman. *The Film Editing Room Handbook.* New York: Arco, 1984.

LoBrutto, Vincent. *Selected Takes: Film Editors on Editing.* New York: Praeger, 1991.

Oldham, Gabriella. *First Cut: Conversations with Film Editors.* Berkeley, Calif.: University of California Press, 1992.

Reisz, Karel, and Gavin Millar. *The Technique of Film Editing.* New York: Hastings House, 1968.

Roseblum, Ralph, and Robert Karen. *When the Story Stops—the Cutting Begins: A Film Editor's Story.* New York: Viking Press, 1979.

Thompson, Roy. *Grammar of the Edit.* Boston: Focal Press, 1993.

EDUCATIONAL PICTURES, INC. The Educational Films Corporation claimed to have begun operations in 1914 as a distributor of short educational and entertainment subjects. In the 1918–1919 season, it released three films per week, in weekly series, including Robert C. Bruce's *Scenics of Adventure in the Northwest;* Raymond L. Ditmars's *The Living Book of Nature;* George D. Wright's *Mexico Today;* Dwight L. Elmendorf's foreign travel pictures; E. M. Newman's Far East films, *Newman Travels;* and cartoons featuring Happy Hooligan and Tad's Silk Hat Harry, made by Gregory La Cava (who later became a leading comedy director).

George A. Skinner was the president and Earl Wooldrige Hammons (1882–1962) was the vice president and general manager of Educational, which had 15 exchanges* across the country. By the twenties, Educational was releasing many series of comedies, and by the end of the decade it was the major independent distributor of short subjects. Lloyd Hamilton and Lupino Lane were the company's leading comedians.

In 1927, Educational reorganized to produce under the new Educational Pictures, Inc., name and distributed through Educational Film Exchanges, Inc. Hammons was the president, Jack White was director-general, and E. H. Allen was general manager.

In the thirties, Educational set up its production headquarters at the Astoria Studios*, and its short subjects featured comedy greats on the way down, such as Buster Keaton and Harry Langdon, and would-be film comedians, such as Danny Kaye, Bert Lahr, Joe Cook, Tom Patricola, and Tom Howard. Educational's short subjects were never of a particularly high quality; film historian Leonard Maltin has written that "Educational films almost always looked cheap, even though they were made in most cases by seasoned veterans." Educational, with its familiar trademark of Aladdin's lamp and its slogan, "The Spice of the Programme," disappeared in 1940.

BIBLIOGRAPHY

"Educational Enthusiastic." *The Moving Picture World,* March 26, 1927, p. 384.
"Educational Films Branching Out." *The Moving Picture World,* August 31, 1918, p. 1244.
"Educational to Enlarge Program." *Motion Picture News,* October 18, 1919, p. 2996.
Maltin, Leonard. "The Spice of the Programme." *The Silent Picture,* no. 15, Summer 1972, pp. 19–25.
————. *The Great Movie Shorts.* New York: Crown, 1972.
"Putting Sugar on the Pill." *Photoplay,* June 1919, pp. 90, 93.

EDWARD SMALL PRODUCTIONS, INC. Edward Small's (1891–1977) first involvement with the film industry was as head of his own talent agency, the Edward Small Agency, which he opened in 1924, and which later became the Small Agency and the Small-Landau Agency. Small became an independent producer in the mid-twenties, and, in 1932, organized Reliance Pictures, Inc., with Harry M. Goetz, the company responsible for *I Cover the Waterfront* (1933), *The Count of Monte Cristo* (1934), and several other features. Reliance advertised itself as "Producers of Box-Office Entertainment for United Artists Release."

Edward Small Productions, Inc., was incorporated on January 25, 1938, initially to produce five features for United Artists release, commencing with *The Duke of West Point* (1938).

Among the company's films were *The Corsican Brothers* (1941), *Up in Mabel's Room* (1944), *Getting Gertie's Garter* (1945), *Valentino* (1951), *Lorna Doone* (1951), and *Monkey on My Back* (1957). Small's last feature was *The Christine Jorgensen Story* (1970). Aside from Edward Small Productions, the producer also had a television production company, Television Productions of America, Inc., organized in 1953.

RESOURCES
Papers: University of Southern California.

EDWARDS THEATRES CIRCUIT is a family-owned chain, formed by James Edwards, Sr., with 140 screens in Southern California. It opened its first theatre, the Monterey, in Monterey Park on October 9, 1930.

Address: 300 Newport Center Drive, Newport Beach, Calif. 92660.

BIBLIOGRAPHY

LaGanda, Maria. "Edwards' 58-Year Run." *Los Angeles Times,* Part 4, January 17, 1988, pp. 1, 4.

8mm. The first 8mm cameras, projectors, and film were introduced by Eastman Kodak* in 1932. It was intended primarily for amateur, or home, use, but by the sixties was also used for teaching and other educational purposes. With the introduction of Super 8mm*, standard 8mm—as it came to be known—was gradually phased out. 8mm in width, standard 8mm film has perforations down one side of the film only, with 80 frames to one foot of film.

Eastman Kodak introduced an 8mm magazine Cine-Kodak camera in 1940, with the low-priced Brownie 8mm movie camera appearing on the scene in 1951 (followed a year later by the 8mm Brownie projector).

BIBLIOGRAPHY

Callenbach, Ernest. "The State of 8." *Film Quarterly,* Summer 1966, pp. 36–39.
Film News. February 1966. Special issue devoted to 8mm.
Provisor, Henry. *8mm/16mm Movie-Making.* New York: Amphoto, 1970.

ELECTRICAL RESEARCH PRODUCTS, INC. A major name in the design, improvement, sale, and service of sound equipment during the pioneering years of the sound motion picture, Electrical Research Products, Inc. (ERPI), was a subsidiary of the Western Electric Company. It published a newsletter, *The Erpigram,* conducted and coordinated much of the research into sound on film and sound on disc on behalf of Western Electric and the Bell Telephone System, and was the recipient of five Scientific or Technical Awards from the Academy of Motion Picture Arts and Sciences between 1930/1931 and 1935. Western Electric discontinued the division in the summer of 1937, but ERPI continued as a licensor and recipient of royalties from equipment covered by ERPI patents.

ELECTRONOVISION, developed by H. W. (Bill) Sargent, and hailed in 1964 as a major effort to bring stageplays direct to film audiences, utilized multiple cameras to "film" electronically a stage production with only available light. The images were transmitted to a monitoring board and converted to the correct size and shape for projection by Theatrofilm. The first production to be shot in Electronovision was Richard Burton's *Hamlet* (1964). It was followed by *The TAMI Show* (1964) and *Harlow* (1965). Electronovision's combination of film and television techniques failed to achieve an adequate audience—despite the low cost of production—and, by the middle of 1965, Sargent's company, Electronovision, Inc., was in financial difficulty.

BIBLIOGRAPHY

Scheuer, Philip K. "Hollywood's Newest Threat." *Los Angeles Times,* Calendar, November 1, 1964, pp. 1, 35.

XI PRODUCTIONS was a company created by Mickey Rooney (born 1920). It was acquired by Universal Coverage Co., an insurance holding company, in April 1969.

THE ELTON CORP. was the production company of Douglas Fairbanks, Sr. (1883–1939)—Elton is his middle name—responsible for *Don Q, Son of Zorro* (1925), *The Black Pirate* (1926), *The Gaucho* (1928), *The Iron Mask* (1929), *Taming of the Shrew* (1929), *Around the World in Eighty Minutes with Douglas Fairbanks* (1931), and *Mr. Robinson Crusoe* (1932).

EMBASSY COMMUNICATIONS was formed after Norman Lear and Jerry Parenchio purchased Avco Embassy Pictures Corporation on November 30, 1981, for a reported $25 million. Avco Embassy had begun life as Joseph E. Levine's Embassy Pictures Corporation in the late fifties. Under Levine (born 1905), Embassy was noted for the American release of such foreign films as *Divorce—Italian Style* (1962), *8 1/2* (1963), and *Marriage Italian Style* (1964) and for *Long Day's Journey into Night* (1962), *The Carpetbaggers* (1964), *Harlow* (1965), *John F. Kennedy: Years of Lightning, Days of Drums* (1966), *The Oscar* (1966), *The Producers* (1967), and *The Graduate* (1967).

Avco Corp. acquired Embassy in 1968, and Joseph E. Levine left the company to form his own independent organization, in 1974. Tom Laughlin tried to purchase the new company, Avco Embassy, early in 1981, but considered the asking price too high. It was subsequently acquired by Lear and Parenchio, who controlled the television production companies of Tandem and T.A.T. Communications, and the television syndication organization P.I.T.S. (which stands for "Pie in the Sky"). Embassy Communication's theatrical film division, Embassy Pictures, released the Ingmar Bergman feature *Fanny and Alexander,* in 1983. Embassy Television continued to handle the former Tandem productions, *The Jeffersons, One Day at a Time, The Facts of Life, Silver Spoons,* and *Diff'rent Strokes.* Embassy Home Entertainment handled home videotape sales of Embassy's own films, as well as feature films controlled by Janus and the Samuel Goldwyn Company*. Embassy moved its production activities to the Universal* lot in May 1982, while maintaining corporate offices in Century City. In June 1985, the Coca-Cola Company acquired Embassy for $485 million, subsequently selling Embassy Communications to Dino De Laurentiis in September 1985 and Embassy Home Entertainment to Nelson Entertainment in August 1986.

BIBLIOGRAPHY

Harmetz, Aljean. "Lear Plans 8 to 10 Films a Year from His New Embassy Studio." *The New York Times,* January 20, 1982, p. C19.
Kerr, James R. "Billions Make a Nice Cushion." *Variety,* November 13, 1968, p. 31.
Pollock, Dale. "A New Team Gives a New Look to Embassy Communications." *Los Angeles Times.* Calendar, January 20, 1982, pp. 1, 4.

EMBASSY PICTURES CORPORATION. See EMBASSY COMMUNICATIONS

EMERALD PRODUCTIONS. See FILMAKERS, INC.

EMINENT AUTHORS PICTURES, INC. See GOLDWYN PICTURES CORPORATION

EMPIRE FEATURE FILM COMPANY. See MONROVIA FEATURE FILM COMPANY

ENTERPRISE PRODUCTIONS, INC., formed by David Loew and Charles Einfeld on February 14, 1946, was located at the California Studios* and was responsible for more than a dozen memorable features, beginning with *Ramrod,* directed by Andre de Toth in 1947; that same year, de Toth also directed *The Other Love* for Enterprise. Lewis Milestone directed a comedy, *No Minor Vices* (1948), for Enterprise, and he also directed for the company its most prestigious feature, *Arch of Triumph* (1948), an adaptation of the Erich Maria Remarque novel, starring Charles Boyer and Ingrid Bergman, which proved such a disaster at the box office—it had cost a reported $4 million to produce—that Enterprise was forced to cease operations in September 1948. David Lewis served as vice president and as producer for the Enterprise features, which were released through United Artists. In 1951, the Bank of America, which had put up much of the money for the Enterprise operation, foreclosed its mortgages on eight of the Enterprise pictures, which eventually were released to television through the new Republic Pictures*.

BIBLIOGRAPHY

"Einfeld and Loew Form Enterprise." *Motion Picture World,* March 9, 1946, p. 26.

E. O. CORP. is a production company founded by Earl Owensby (born 1935) in 1974 with a studio facility in Shelby, North Carolina, which is the largest outside of Los Angeles. An extraordinary figure in non-Hollywood film production, Owensby has been called "the Cecil B. DeMille of North Carolina," producing and starring in a group of features beginning with *Challenge* (1974), which have found audiences outside of the usual Hollywood exhibition and distribution field. In February 1990, the studio was sold to Atlantic Pacific Group for $25 million, but in July 1991, Owensby recovered ownership and occupation. Aside from E. O. Corp., Owensby formed a distribution company, Maverick Pictures International, which he sold to McCoy Industries International in 1980.

Address: P.O. Box 184, Shelby, N.C. 28150.

BIBLIOGRAPHY

Auerbach, Alexander. "Earl Owensby Stepping Out from behind Country Boy Image." *Boxoffice,* June 1981, pp. 12, 15.

Bergman, Andrew. "A Very Minor Movie Mogul." *Esquire,* November 1980, pp. 82–87.

Copeland, Jeff B., and Peter McAlevey. "A Down-Home Mogul." *Newsweek,* January 22, 1987, p. 41.

Harris, Art. "The Dixie De Mille." *GQ,* August 1986, pp. 170–73, 212–15.

Honeycutt, Kirk. "Maverick of the Movies—Regional Filmmakers." *The New York Times,* November 9, 1980, pp. D1, D23.

McCarthy, Todd. "Earl Owensby Undertaking $5 Mil Expansion of His North Carolina Studio." *Daily Variety,* May 26, 1981, pp. 1, 11.

Owensby, Earl. "Grass Roots, Grits and Now, BIG TIME." *Daily Variety,* June 15, 1977, p. 36.

———. "North Carolina's 'Hollywood'; Producer Acts as His Own Star; 11 Films to Date, None in Red." *Variety,* January 3, 1979, p. 36.

EQUITABLE MOTION PICTURE CORPORATION. See WORLD FILM CORPORATION

EQUITY PICTURES CORPORATION, a New York-based distributor of independent productions from 1919 to 1924, was chiefly associated with the films of actress Clara Kimball Young, produced by Harry Garson at his Garson Studios (located at 1845 Glendale Avenue in Los Angeles).

ERBOGRAPH COMPANY, headed by Ludwig G. B. Erb, was formed in 1916 and released its productions through Art Dramas, Inc.* In April 1917, it added a second company, headed by Marion Swayne with Joseph Levering as director. Erbograph closed down that same year.

ERBOGRAPH LABORATORY. See CONSOLIDATED FILM INDUSTRIES

ERPI. See ELECTRICAL RESEARCH PRODUCTS, INC.

ESSANAY FILM MANUFACTURING COMPANY was incorporated on February 5, 1907, by George K. Spoor and G. M. Anderson, with the company's name being composed of the first letters of their names. Anderson, born Max Aronson, was a vaudeville performer, who, after appearing as a train robber in Edison's *The Great Train Robbery* in 1903, continued acting in dramatic films made by Vitagraph* and Selig*. Spoor, a proprietor of the Kinodrome Circuit, which showed motion pictures in the Orpheum vaudeville theatres of the West, and the growing National Film Renting Company, which rented the films his circuit showed, needed more productions to meet growing demands for them. Essanay's first production, *An Awful Skater, or The Hobo on Rollers,* was announced in *The Moving Picture World* on July 27, 1907. Essanay's first plant was located at 501 Wells Street in Chicago. According to Robert Grau (in *The Theatre of Science*), Essanay was the first company to turn out 1,000-foot films. On September 8, 1909, Anderson, his cameraman Jesse J. Robbins, and a company of players left Chicago to go West. Along the way, they filmed Essanay's first film shot in the West, *The Best Man Wins.* After stopping in Denver, El Paso, and Santa Barbara, the company settled in Niles, California, near Oakland, where it produced a series of "Broncho Billy" Westerns* starring G. M. Anderson for the next seven years.

Essanay was a member of the Motion Picture Patents Company* and its films were released by the General Film Company. In 1915, it joined with Vitagraph, Lubin*, and Selig to form V-L-S-E* to release longer pictures.

Early in 1910, J. Warren Kerrigan made his debut in motion pictures under the Essanay brand. Kerrigan and most of Essanay's staff and players went to the independent American Film Manufacturing Company* in October 1910, a company that began to copy Essanay's successful formula of producing comedies, dramas, and Westerns. Francis X. Bushman began his motion picture career with Essanay in 1911, and Beverly Bayne followed the next year. William F. "Buffalo Bill" Cody signed with Essanay in 1913 to appear in films depicting the pioneer days of the West. On January 2, 1915, Essanay announced that it had signed Charles Chaplin, but Spoor let the comedian go to Mutual* after his contract had run out in 1916. Shortly thereafter, Spoor bought out Anderson, and, although he hired Max Linder to make films in 1917, the company declined. Late in 1918 it stopped production, and in mid–1919 Victor Kremer purchased the Essanay negatives and prints and began reissuing them.

BIBLIOGRAPHY

"Essanay Chaplin Comedies." *The Moving Picture World,* July 10, 1915, p. 238.

"The Essanay Company Out West." *The Moving Picture World,* December 4, 1909, pp. 801–2.

"Essanay's New Studio." *The Moving Picture World,* March 4, 1916, p. 1452.

"Essanay's Western Plant." *The Moving Picture World,* July 10, 1915, pp. 237–38.

Parsons, Louella O. "The Essanay Days." *Theatre Arts,* July 1951, pp. 33, 96.

"Some Prominent Essanay Players." *The Moving Picture World,* July 11, 1914, pp. 234–35.

Spoor, George K. "Remarkable Growth of Motion Picture Industry." *The Moving Picture World,* July 11, 1914, p. 191.

ESTEE STUDIOS, located at 561–562 125 Street, New York, were operational from 1918 to 1919 under the presidency of Eugene Spritz.

EXACTUS PHOTO-FILM CORPORATION OF PALO ALTO, CALIFORNIA, incorporated on August 28, 1914, would appear to be the first film company organized solely for the production of educational subjects. Its president was Thomas Kimmwood Peters and the company boasted a number of educators as consultants. Its films received two gold medals and one bronze medal at the 1915 Panama-Pacific International Exposition. However, by 1916, the company had auctioned off its assets, and its remaining property was taken over by the Palo Alto Film Company (organized in 1915).

RESOURCES

Papers: Stanford University.

EXCELSIOR FEATURE FILM COMPANY, INC., began production in April 1914 at its Lake Placid, New York, studio. Harry Handworth was the company director and Gordon de Maine its leading man. Other actors included Octavia Handworth, Tom Tempest, and William A. Williams, who was also the company's vice president. Excelsior's first film was *The Toil of Mammon.* It distributed with Alco Film Corporation* as of August 25, 1914, but as of October 10, 1914, it released through the Alliance Films Corporation*. Handworth resigned in January 1915.

BIBLIOGRAPHY

"A New Film Organization." *The Moving Picture World,* April 11, 1914, p. 199.

EXCHANGES take their name from their primary function, which is to supply exhibitors with a continuing change of films. In the early years of the film industry, exhibitors acquired their films directly from the producer, but it soon became necessary to set up exchanges on a local level, from which exhibitors could obtain features or shorts. There have always been two types of exchanges, those operated by the producers and those independently owned. Prior to 1910, there were fewer than a dozen exchanges operating in the United States, but by 1930 there were more than 500, with the biggest increase taking place between 1914 and 1924 (during which time 72 percent of all the exchanges operating in the United States by 1929 came into existence).

EXCLUSIVE SUPPLY CORPORATION, located at 220 West 42d Street, New York, was formed in May 1913 when the Film Supply Corporation of America, which distributed films associated with the Mutual Film Corporation*, was disbanded. Herbert Blaché was the president; I. C. Oes was Exclusive's vice president. Harry R. Raver was the secretary and treasurer; Joseph R. Miles was the general manager. By July 1914, the company's name had changed to Exclusive Supply Corporation. It was opposed to the "forced program" (whereby theatres were forced to book complete programs as a package) and while it distributed mainly shorts at the beginning, by July 1914, it was handling features by All-Star Feature Company*, Blaché-American, F.R.A., Gaumont*, Great Northern, Itala, Lewis Pennant, Ramo*, Solax, and Films Lloyd. It released five features weekly to the states rights* market. Although it planned to increase to handling seven pictures per week, and intended in the future to deal directly with exhibitors, Exclusive went out of business in October 1914.

EXHIBITORS' MUTUAL DISTRIBUTING CORPORATION. See MUTUAL FILM CORPORATION

EXPLOITATION FILMS. *Exploitation films* is a term used to describe productions that exploit a popular social phenomenon. Such films are almost as old as the motion picture itself and can be dated back at least to 1913, when the Universal* feature *Traffic in Souls* exploited the then current public interest in "white slavery." There is no rule as to what is or is not an exploitation film, and certainly what one critic labels as such may not be so called by another. Low-budget horror films, such as *Night of the Living Dead* (1969) and *Texas Chainsaw Massacre* (1974), are generally considered to be exploitation films.

Low budgets and low production values are common among most exploitation films. Bad taste as evidenced in *Pink Flamingos* (1974) can also be the mark of an exploitation film. A subgenre is sex exploitation films, which are not hardcore pornographic in content but are mildly salacious, or softcore, dealing with usually taboo subjects, such as lesbianism or prostitution. The features of erotic film producer Russ Meyer can easily be classified as sex exploitive, dealing as they do with drug abuse and sexual perversion (for example, *Beyond the Valley of the Dolls,* 1970). Films that go beyond exploitation to "camp," such as *Myra Breckinridge* (1970), are outside of the genre.

One major group of exploitation films from the late forties and early fifties was those dealing with the dangers of communism*, such as Republic Pictures' *The Red Menace* (1949), which claimed to be performing a public service, but which was produced purely for the profit of its maker. Indeed, it might well be argued that any American feature with a social message is an exploitation film in that it exploits its audience for the financial benefit of its producer.

BIBLIOGRAPHY

Karr, Katherine. "The Long Square-Up: Exploitation Trends in the Silent Film." *Journal of Popular Film* 3.2, (Spring 1974): pp. 107–28.

Keckes, David. *Killing for Culture: An Illustrated History of Death Film from Mondo to Snuff.* San Francisco: Creation Books, 1995.

McCarty, John. *The Sleaze Merchants: Adventures in Exploitation Filmmaking.* New York: St. Martin's Griffin, 1995.

Maitland, McDonagh. *Filmmaking on the Fringe: The Good, the Bad, and the Deviant Directors.* New York: Carol Publishing, 1995.

Quarles, Mike. *Down and Dirty: Hollywood's Exploitation Filmmakers and Their Movies.* Jefferson, N.C.: McFarland, 1993.

Taylor, John Russell. "Beyond the Taste Barrier." *Sight and Sound,* Winter 1976/77, pp. 37–39.

Weldon, Michael J. *The Psychotronic Video Guide.* New York: St. Martin's Griffin, 1996.

EXTRAS. See CENTRAL CASTING CORPORATION and SCREEN EXTRAS GUILD

FACETS MULTIMEDIA, INC., founded in 1975, is the largest general distributor of films for the home video market, with more than 26,000 titles in its library.

Address: 1517 West Fullerton Avenue, Chicago, Ill. 60614.

FAIRFAX, CALIFORNIA. See UNITED KEANOGRAPH FILM MANUFACTURING COMPANY

FAMILY FILMS was a Los Angeles-based production company, founded in 1948 by Sam Hersh. By 1962, it claimed to be the largest producer and distributor of religious films in the United States. It ceased operations in 1964.

FAMOUS ARTISTS CORPORATION. See CHAS. K. FELDMAN'S GROUP PRODUCTIONS

FAMOUS ATTRACTIONS CORPORATION. See PREFERRED PICTURES

FAMOUS PLAYERS FILM COMPANY. See PARAMOUNT PICTURES, INC.

FAMOUS PLAYERS-LASKY FILM CORPORATION. See PARAMOUNT PICTURES, INC.

FANTASOUND. Experiments with Fantasound began in 1937, and the process was successfully utilized for Walt Disney's *Fantasia* (1941). As an early form of stereophonic sound, Fantasound was both a critical and commercial success, but the cost of installation plus America's entry into the Second World War hindered its later use.

BIBLIOGRAPHY

Garity, William E., and J. N. A. Hawkins. "Fantasound." *Journal of the Society of Motion Picture and Television Engineers* (August 1941): pp. 127–46.

FAVORITE PLAYERS FILM COMPANY. Carlyle Blackwell formed the Favorite Players Film Company in August 1914 to produce films starring himself, to be distributed by Alco Film Corporation*. William Desmond Taylor was in charge of production at its new studio in Edendale, California. As of October 10, 1914, Favorite Players released through Alliance Films Corporation*. Its first release was *The Key to Yesterday,* with Edna Mayo. The company disbanded in April 1915, when Blackwell went to the Jesse L. Lasky Feature Play Company.

FBO. See RKO RADIO PICTURES, INC.

THE F. B. WARREN CORP. was a short-lived distributor, of interest in that the three feature films it released were all directed by women: Lois Weber's *The Blot* (1921), Nell Shipman's *The Girl from God's Country* (1921), and May Tully's *The Old Oaken Bucket* (1921).

FEATURE PRODUCTIONS, INC. See ART CINEMA CORPORATION

FEATURES AND SHORTS. See SHORTS AND FEATURES

FEDERAL FEATURE FILMS CORPORATION of New York was said to have the largest motion picture studio in the world when it became affiliated with Metro Pictures Corporation* in September 1915. The studio was located at Rocky Glen, Pennsylvania, between Scranton and Wilkes-Barre. Arthur Jans was the company's president, and Merritt Crawford was secretary. The company made productions to sell to small exhibitors before the Metro takeover. It was reorganized in January 1917.

FICTION PICTURES, INC., was a short-lived producing company of 1915, which was formed by novelist Louis Joseph Vance (1879-1933) after he came to Los Angeles to help with the preparation of a series that Universal* was producing from his works. Vance engaged Wilfred Lucas as his director-general, Gilbert Warrenton as his cameraman, and he put together a company that included Cleo Madison, Joe King, and Edward Sloman. Its first film, Vance's *The Spanish Jade,* starred Betty Bellairs. Fiction's studio was located first in Glendale and later at Melrose Avenue and Bronson Street in Hollywood. In June 1915, Fiction went out of business and sold its studio to the Famous Players Film Company.

5TH AVENUE PLAYHOUSE GROUP. See ART HOUSES

FILM ADVISORY BOARD, INC., was incorporated on July 19, 1975, when Elayne Blythe broke away from the Southern California Motion Picture Council*, of which she had been president for 11 years. The Film Advisory Board (FAB) presents monthly awards to films, television programs, and individuals that promote family entertainment.

Address:1727-1/2 N. Sycamore Avenue, Hollywood, Calif. 90028.

FILMAKERS, INC., an independent production company noted for its low-budget features dealing with social issues, was organized in 1949 by producer Collier Young (1908–1980) and his then wife—they were divorced in 1951—Ida Lupino (1918-1995). The company had previously been known as Emerald Productions, which was responsible for one feature, *Not Wanted* (1949), which gave Lupino her first opportunity to direct. Filmakers produced five features, directed by Lupino: *Never Fear* (1950), *Outrage* (1950), *Hard, Fast and Beautiful* (1951), *The Hitchhiker* (1953), and *The Bigamist* (1954). It also produced *Private Hell* (1954), starring Ida Lupino, and *Mad at the World* (1955).

FILM ALLIANCE OF THE U.S., INC. See TRANS-LUX CORPORATION

FILM AND PHOTO LEAGUE. See NATIONAL FILM AND PHOTO LEAGUE

FILMARTE THEATRE, NEW YORK. See LENAUER INTERNATIONAL FILMS, INC.

FILM CLASSICS, INC., was founded in 1943 by Irving Shapiro (1907–1989) to handle U.S. distribution of Gaumont British features; later it acquired distribution rights to the Selznick* films. In 1945, Shapiro organized Film Rights International Ltd., and another of his companies was Films Around the World.

FILM COMMISSIONS serve to promote the film production potential of a city or a state. The first state film commission was the Colorado Motion Picture and Television Commission, founded in 1969 by Karol Smith (who was its director until his retirement in 1989). A complete listing of state and film commissions appears each year in *Motion Picture Almanac*.

FILMDALLAS was founded as a limited partnership by Sam L. Grogg in August 1984 as FilmDallas Investment Fund 1, and helped finance a number of specialized features, including *Kiss of the Spider Woman* and *The Trip to Bountiful* (both 1985). In 1986, FilmDallas Pictures, Inc., was formed with New World Entertainment*, but the latter pulled out of the venture in 1988. The company was the subject of an involuntary bankruptcy action in December 1988, was reorganized in February 1990, but ultimately failed. While in bankruptcy, Grogg and his partner, Ernest Fausto, formed Grogg Entertainment Inc. and Magic Pictures.

FILMEX is the name by which the Los Angeles International Film Exposition was best known. Created by George Cukor, Philip Chamberlin, and Garry Essert (1938–1992), the first Filmex was held under the last's directorship, November 4–14, 1971. A noncompetitive festival for features and shorts, Filmex never had a permanent home; the first exposition was held at the Chinese Theatre in Hollywood, and the majority of times it was held at the two Plitt Century Plaza Theatres in Century City.

Gary Essert's flamboyant and often abrasive manner aroused much controversy, and, finally, in the summer of 1983, he resigned from Filmex amid much rancor. He was replaced by Suzanne McCormick, as executive director, and Ken Wlaschin, from the London Film Festival, as artistic director. After a brief hiatus, Filmex reemerged as the AFI Festival, headed by Wlaschin. Essert announced plans for an American Cinematheque in Los Angeles in 1984. Best known for its annual fundraising Moving Picture Ball, the Cinematheque plans to open a theatre complex at the former Grauman's Egyptian Theatre in Hollywood.

Address: AFI Los Angeles International Film Festival, 2021 North Western Avenue, Los Angeles, Calif. 90027; American Cinematheque, 7000 Hollywood Boulevard, 3rd Floor, Hollywood, Calif. 90028.

FILM FINANCES, INC., was founded in London in 1950 as a completion bond guarantor. Independent producers seeking a bond come to Film Finances, Inc., which examines the script, budget, shooting schedule, and crew and cast list, and determines that the film is a viable one. Film Finances, Inc., then guarantees that the film will be made on time and on budget. If it is not, Film Finances, Inc., will pay the additional costs involved. Through its offices in the United Kingdom, the United States, Australia, France, Italy, and Canada, Film Finances, Inc., has bonded many hundreds of feature films, including *The African Queen, Dr. No, Cabaret, The Rocky Horror Picture Show, An American Werewolf in London, Platoon, Robocop, The Last Emperor, Rain Man, Mississippi Burning, Thelma and Louise,* and *Howard's End.* Film Finances, Inc., is the oldest company of its type in existence.

Address: 9000 Sunset Boulevard, Los Angeles, Calif. 90069.

BIBLIOGRAPHY

"Celebrating 40 Years: Film Finances." *The Hollywood Reporter,* special supplement, April 25, 1991.

THE FILM FUND was formed in 1977 by three men with inherited wealth—David Crocker, George Pillsbury, and Obie Benz—and by filmmaker Barbara Kopple, who was enjoying financial success from her documentary feature, *Harlan County U.S.A.* (1977). According to its then director, Terry Lawler, in an interview with the *Los Angeles Times* (January 14, 1982), the purpose of the Film Fund was "to create a mechanism and a staff through which people can support independent, social issue films, films that can be used by groups organizing for social change."

A service organization for filmmakers and community groups, the Film Fund was best known for its grants to socially aware documentaries. In 1978, it selected the first 22 projects for funding, out of 420 applications. The Film Fund also published the quarterly *News from the Film Fund,* and on October 23, 1985, it presented its first annual Arts and Justice Award to Harry Belefonte. The Film Fund ceased operations as of June 20, 1986.

FILM MARKET, INC., was a brokerage company formed by Robert W. Priest, in August 1918, to handle productions from independent producers. Its offices were located in the Times Building, New York.

FILM MUTUAL BENEFIT BUREAU. See ART HOUSES

FILM NOIR. *Film Noir* was first used as a critical term in France in the fifties and became established after the publication, in 1955, of *Panorama du Film Noir Americain* by Raymond Borde and Etienne Chaumeton. The term was used to designate a group of films that was different from the usual crime and gangster films, both visually and structurally. Visually, the high-key lighting used in most Hollywood* films was replaced by a repeated use of low-key lighting, so that the screen was often literally in the dark. Structurally, the redemptive elements of the gangster and crime film—the police win; the city is cleaned up; the gangster dies—are replaced by a narrative in which no one is able to win, especially not the hero.

The visual style of these films was derived from the German expressionist films and was a blend of chiaroscuro, unusual camera angles, and extreme close-ups. This type of style worked to compress space and give the viewer a disorienting view of the action. It also helped establish a mood in which the characters in the film were trapped by the encroaching darkness and the extreme close-ups, without there being any place to escape.

This mood was intensified by the narrative structure of *film noir,* in which the straight-ahead drive of the classic gangster film (from rise to fall) is replaced by a twisting, retrogressive narrative. Flashbacks become crucial for *film noir,* as a mood of hopelessness and fatality is established by beginning the film with the protagonist defeated (*The Killers*), on the run (*Out of the Past*), in the most extreme case, dead but still moving (*D.O.A.*) and then flashing back to see how this state was brought about.

Since the films that make up *film noir* do not have the thematic coherence of Westerns* or gangster films*, there has been an argument as to whether *film noir* is a genre. If the films do not have common themes, they do share a common perception of the world and of life, a view in which life is nasty and bleak and where there is no escape except through the blackness of death.

Films of the genre date, basically, from 1945 to 1957, with Orson Welles's *Touch of Evil* (1958) arguably the last film of the genre.

BIBLIOGRAPHY

Cameron, Ian, ed. *The Book of Film Noir.* New York: Continuum, 1992.

Copjec, Joan, ed. *Shades of Noir: A Reader.* New York: Verso, 1993.

Crowther, Bruce. *Film Noir: Reflections in a Dark Mirror.* New York: Continuum, 1989.

Hirsch, Foster. *The Dark Side of the Screen: Film Noir.* San Diego: A. S. Barnes, 1981.

Karimi, A. M. *Toward a Definition of the American Film Noir (1941–1949).* New York: Arno Press, 1976.

Ottoson, Robert. *A Reference Guide to the American Film Noir (1940–1958).* Metuchen, N.J.: Scarecrow Press, 1981.

Palmer, R. Barton. *Hollywood's Dark Cinema: The American Film Noir.* New York: Twayne, 1994.

Richardson, Carl. *Autopsy: An Element of Realism in Film Noir.* Metuchen, N.J.: Scarecrow Press, 1992.

Selby, Spender. *Dark City: The Film Noir.* Jefferson, N.C.: McFarland, 1984.

Silver, Alain, and James Ursini, ed. *Film Noir Reader.* New York: Limelight, 1996.

Stephens, Michael L. *Film Noir: A Comprehensive, Illustrated Reference to Movies, Terms and Persons.* Jefferson, N.C.: McFarland, 1995.

Telotte, J. P. *Voices in the Dark: The Narrative Patterns of Film Noir.* Urbana, Ill.: University of Illinois Press, 1989.

Tuska, Jon. *Dark Cinema: American Film Noir in Cultural Perspective.* Westport, Conn.: Greenwood Press, 1984.

FILM RIGHTS INTERNATIONAL LTD. See FILM CLASSICS, INC.

FILMS AROUND THE WORLD. See FILM CLASSICS, INC.

FILM SECURITY OFFICE. See MOTION PICTURE ASSOCIATION OF AMERICA

FILM SERVICE ASSOCIATION. See MOTION PICTURE PATENTS COMPANY

FILMS FOR DEMOCRACY, a group sponsored by Walter Wanger, Dudley Nichols, Marc Connelly, Sherwood Anderson, Fritz Lang, and Fredric March, was founded in 1938. In 1939, it merged with Film Audiences to become Film Audiences for Democracy. Films for Democracy was cited as a Communist front organization in the report of the House Committee on Un-American Activities, March 29, 1944.

FILMS INCORPORATED was the largest nontheatrical (or 16mm*) film distributor in the United States, with more than 10,000 features listed in its catalog as of 1985. It includes the former independent 16mm film libraries of Audio Brandon (which began in 1924 as Ideal Film Centers and was consolidated by Macmillan, Inc., in the sixties with the merger of Audio Film Center and Brandon Films, Inc.), Janus Films (a prestigious distributor noted for its classic foreign-language and British features), and Texture Films (which specializes in short subjects and films for children).

The company was founded in 1927 by Orton Hicks (born 1900) as Home Film Libraries Incorporated, the first major distributor of 16mm films for home use. Paramount* was the first major studio to allow 16mm distribution of its films by the company, followed in 1936 by Universal* and in 1941 by 20th Century-Fox* (whose films continue to be distributed by Films Incorporated). On May 1, 1938, Home Film Libraries, Incorporated, was acquired by Eric Haight and the name changed to Films Incorporated. Films Incorporated was subsequently purchased by Encyclopedia Films in 1951. In 1956, it acquired 16mm, nontheatrical rights, in perpetuity, to all pre–1948 RKO* features, including such classics as *King Kong* and *Citizen Kane*. On May 1, 1968—exactly 30 years after the company became Films Incorporated—it was acquired by Charles Benton, who continues to head the organization.

Among Films Incorporated's other activities have been the 1975 launching of educational sound filmstrips called "Moviestrips," the 1976 publication of *Rediscovering the American Cinema* catalogs, and its first major entry into the field of 35mm distribution in 1978 with a retrospective devoted to 20th Century-Fox.

Films Incorporated is now a division of Charles Benton's Public Media Incorporated, created in 1968. Public Media also controlled Lionheart Television International, a worldwide television distribution company, which represents both the British Broadcasting Corporation and the Australian Broadcasting Commission in the United States, which was taken over by the BBC in 1986. It was founded on May 1, 1981, with the dissolution of Time-Life Films*, which had previously distributed BBC product in the United States. Also part of the Public Media "family" is Quartet Films (which merged with Films Incorporated in 1979), which distributes quality features and foreign-language films theatrically in the United States.

Address: 5547 North Ravenswood Avenue, Chicago, Ill. 60640.

FILMS MADE FOR TELEVISION. The first feature-length film made specifically for television was *The Three Musketeers,* produced by Hal Roach, Jr., in 1950, and seen on CBS under the sponsorship of Magnavox, which paid $25,000 for all rights to the production. A few weeks later, Peter N. Rathvon produced *The Pharmacist's Mate,* directed by Irving Pichel and starring Gene Raymond and Brian Donlevy, which was hailed as the most expensive single film to be made for television. It cost the sponsor, Schlitz Beer, $30,000.

According to Alvin H. Marill, in his definitive reference work, *Movies Made for Television,* the first feature to be produced for television and which heralded the advent of the made-for-television movie on a regular basis was *See How They Run,* directed by John Lowell Rich; starring John Forsythe, Senta Berger, and Jane Wyatt; produced by Universal; and aired on NBC on October 7, 1964.

The made-for-television film may be one feature or a feature-length episode in a mini-series. "It quickly has caught up with its bigger [theatrical] brother," writes Marill, "in its approach to virtually any subject, limited on the network merely by 'viewer sensibilities' and other considerations and guidelines that eliminate nudity, profanity and explicit mayhem." An average of 120 features are now produced annually strictly for television, although some are also released theatrically overseas. Because made-for-television films rise to a climax at a commercial break, their theatrical release is often precluded because the transition from one segment to the next without a break can often seem jarring. Some made-for-television features have, however, received a theatrical release in the United States, notably *Brian's Song* (1972), *Duel* (1983), and *My Sweet Charlie* (1970). There have even been a few made-for-television films—such as *Warning Shot* (1967) and *Scott Joplin* (1976)—that received a theatrical release prior to their television debut.

Although directors of made-for-television features tend to be a breed unto themselves, some have been able to make the transition to theatrical features, notably James L. Brooks. Similarly, a few respected directors of theatrical features have later worked in television, particularly George Cukor with *Love Among the Ruins* (1975) and *The Corn Is Green* (1979) and Nicholas Meyer with *The Day After* (1983).

One of the best, continuing sources for information on made-for-television films is the monthly column "The Television Scene," in *Films in Review.*

BIBLIOGRAPHY

Allen, Tom. "The Semi-Precious Age of TV Movies." *Film Comment,* July–August 1979, pp. 21–23, 47.

Battison, John H. *Movies for TV.* New York: Macmillan, 1950.

Canton, Maj. *Maj Canton's the Complete Reference Guide to Movies and Miniseries Made for TV and Cable, July 1, 1989 to September 1, 1992.* Santa Monica, Calif.: Hollywood Creative Directory, 1992.

Champlin, Charles. "TV: The End of the Beginning." *American Film,* October 1975, pp. 60–63.

Marill, Alvin H. *Movies Made for Television: The Tele-Feature and the Mini-Series, 1964–1986.* New York: Zoetrope, 1987.

McGilligan, Patrick. "Movies Are Better Than Ever—on Television." *American Film,* March 1980, pp. 50–54.

Menaker, Daniel. "Television Apposite Reactions." *Film Comment,* July–August 1980, pp. 76–77.

FILMS ON TELEVISION. In the September 29, 1948, edition of *The Hollywood Reporter*, Eugene F. McDonald, Jr., president of Zenith Radio Corporation, predicted that "television will soon be using motion pictures for more than half of its programs and commercials." However, the initial reaction of the film industry toward television was a totally negative one. Without dissension, the major studios refused to allow their features to be aired on television; further, the companies refused to permit contract stars and technicians to work in the new medium.

In 1948, Film Classics released 24 features produced by the British filmmaker Alexander Korda to Los Angeles station KTLA, which was the first major sale of feature films to television and which heralded increased sales of foreign films to independent stations. (That same year, KTLA screened Vittorio de Sica's 1946 Italian feature, *Shoeshine*.) Television was to herald the demise of the "B" movie*, and it is perhaps not surprising that it was the smaller independent producers that specialized in "B" pictures, such as Republic*, that were the first to make their product available to television.

In July 1951, Roy Rogers was able to obtain a temporary injunction preventing the sale of his Republic* features to television, and, at the same time, the various guilds and unions were fighting television sales, demanding additional, supplemental fees from the producers. However, beginning with a November 25, 1952, ruling against the writers, the courts ruled unanimously that those involved in the original production of the films had no control over them.

Universal-International was the first major company to allow its players to work in television, and it was quickly followed by RKO*, Paramount*, M-G-M*, and Columbia*. Producers began to realize the promotional potential of television when CBS, on April 13, 1952, had Edward R. Murrow take viewers behind the scenes of the making of Goldwyn's *Hans Christian Andersen*. Eventually, a 1952 antitrust suit filed by various television companies against the major studios forced the release of feature films to television.

Sales of films to television were initially limited to pre-1948 titles, but following a January 1960 strike by actors, which led to a guarantee that they would share in television sales of films made after January 31, 1960, the studios, beginning with Warner Bros.*, started to release post-August 1948 features to television.

The cutting of films for television for both space and censorship* reasons did not become a problem until the late sixties. Both Otto Preminger (with regard to his 1966 feature, *Anatomy of a Murder*) and George Stevens (with regard to his 1965 feature, *A Place in the Sun*) brought unsuccessful lawsuits against the cutting of their films for television. Alfred Hitchcock was able to work out a special contract with NBC to prevent the editing of *Rear Window* for its 1966 and 1967 network screenings. In 1985, Warren Beatty was able to prevent ABC from screening his film *Reds* except in the version and at the length at which the film was theatrically released in the United States.

According to the Guinness book of *Movie Facts and Feats* (Sterling, 1980), the first film to be shown on television was *The Bride* (1929), experimentally transmitted from the Baird Television Studios in London on August 19, 1929. The first feature-length film to be shown on television was *Police Patrol* (1925), transmitted in six daily episodes by W2XCD of Passaic, New Jersey, April 6–11, 1931. The first feature film to receive its premiere on television was *African Journey* (1947), broadcast on WNBT-New York on January 1, 1948.

In recent years, television has taken to retitling feature films to imply that they have been made for television. For example, *Sometimes a Great Notion* (1971) was aired on television as *Never Give an Inch, Bloodbrothers* (1978) as *Fathers and Sons, September 30, 1955* (1978) as *24 Hours of the Rebel,* and *Hurricane* (1979) as *Forbidden Paradise.*

The most famous film to be aired on television was, of course, *Gone with the Wind*, which was first shown on Japanese television in 1975. Its first American airing was on Home Box Office, on June 14, 1976. *Gone with the Wind* was first seen on network television, in two parts, on NBC, on November 7 and 8, 1976. It was subsequently aired on CBS in 1979, 1981, 1983, and 1984, and was seen again on Japanese television in 1979.

BIBLIOGRAPHY

Brown, Saul. "How Television Cuts the Bleep Out of Shows." *TV Guide,* May 5, 1973, pp. 6–10.

Canby, Vincent. "Major Films on TV Emerging as Vital Problem for Two Industries." *Motion Picture Herald,* January 19, 1957, pp. 13, 17.

Champlin, Charles. "TV Off and Running in High-Paying Movie Stakes." *Los Angeles Times,* Calendar, September 5, 1965, p. 10.

Kael, Pauline. "Movies on Television." *The New Yorker,* June 3, 1967, pp. 120–34.

Maltin, Leonard. "The 75 Best and 25 Worst Movies on TV." *Esquire,* December 1968, pp. 148–49, 266–72.

———. "Show It Again, Sam." *TV Guide,* March 31, 1973, pp. 20–23.

———, ed. *Movie & Video Guide.* New York: Signet Books, 1997.

Markfield, Wallace. "'Play It Again, Sam'—And Again." *The Saturday Evening Post,* April 22, 1967, pp. 72–78.

Sarris, Andrew. "The Primal Screen." *The Village Voice,* July 10, 1984, p. 43.

Scheuer, Steven H. *Movies on TV.* New York: Bantam Books, 1983.

Schlossheimer, Michael. *The Films You Don't See on Television.* New York: Vantage Press, 1979.
Shain, Sam. "Movies Ruling Television's Roost." *Motion Picture Exhibitor,* October 18, 1967, pp. 8, 19.
Spilker, Eric. "The Movies You Don't See on Television." *TV Guide,* April 9, 1966, pp. 6–8.

FILM SUPPLY COMPANY OF AMERICA. See MOTION PICTURE DISTRIBUTING AND SALES COMPANY

FILMUSIC COMPANY was formed in 1918 to produce music rolls that could be synchronously connected to a motion picture projector. A demonstration in Los Angeles of the apparatus, arranged under the auspices of Jesse L. Lasky, Cecil B. DeMille, Thomas H. Ince, H. D. Davis, Robert Brunton, Reginald Barker, and Raymond B. West, attracted 600 people. An electric device called a "synchron-o-meter" kept the music in sync with the picture, and two rolls of music were required for each reel of film. Filmusic had a factory at 1729 Highland Avenue in Hollywood, where it produced master rolls from which copies were produced. It was claimed that the Filmusic rolls could be played on any mechanical musical instrument. C. P. Bradshaw was president and general manager of Filmusic, and W. A. Bishop was director of musical production.

BIBLIOGRAPHY

"Filmusic Company Makes Its Bow." *The Moving Picture World,* June 8, 1918, p. 1420.

FILMWAYS, INC. See ORION PICTURES CORPORATION

FINE ARTS CORPORATION came into existence on September 4, 1915, when Harry E. Aitken announced that the films to be supervised by D. W. Griffith for release by Aitken's Triangle Film Corporation* would be known as Fine Arts productions. The Fine Arts Corporation studios were located at 4500 Sunset Boulevard in Hollywood, a site that had previously been designated as the Reliance-Majestic Studios and from which D. W. Griffith had directed *The Birth of a Nation.* The company also operated an East Coast studio—formerly the Reliance Studios—at 537 Riverdale Avenue in Yonkers.

Players under contract to Fine Arts included Douglas Fairbanks, DeWolf Hopper, Lillian and Dorothy Gish, Margery Wilson, Mae Marsh, Robert Harron, Elmer Clifton, Wilfred Lucas, and Owen Moore. Directors included Eddie Dillon, W. Christy Cabanne, Paul Powell, Lloyd Ingraham, Jack Conway, Allan Dwan, Sidney and Chester Franklin, and John Emerson. Frank Woods was in charge of the studio. D. W. Griffith was credited as supervisor of all Fine Arts productions, but his role in most of the productions appears to have been minimal at most, as much of the time Fine Arts was in existence Griffith was shooting *Intolerance.* The first Fine Arts film was *The Lamb,* released on November 7, 1915, directed by W. Christy Cabanne and starring Douglas Fairbanks and Seena Owen.

A major event in Fine Arts history came with the signing of Sir Herbert Beerbohm Tree in 1915 to star in a film version of *Macbeth,* released in 1916, with Constance Collier as Lady Macbeth, and directed by John Emerson. When D. W. Griffith resigned from Fine Arts, in March 1917, most of the directors and players followed suit—Douglas Fairbanks had already left for Paramount*—and all future Fine Arts productions were taken over by Thomas H. Ince. The last film to be shot at the Los Angeles Fine Arts studio was *Madame Bo-Peep,* directed by Chester Withey and starring Seena Owen.

By 1921, the Fine Arts Studios had become the Arthur H. Gooden rental studios, and in the later years the complex was utilized as an annex by Columbia Pictures*.

BIBLIOGRAPHY

Duncan, Robert C. "The Fine Arts Studios." *Picture Play,* September 1916, pp. 88–94.
Slide, Anthony. *The Kindergarten of the Movies: A History of the Fine Arts Company.* Metuchen, N.J.: Scarecrow Press, 1980.

FINE LINE FEATURES is the specialized distribution division of New Line Cinema*, acquiring and marketing films for a sophisticated audience, such as *The Player* (1992) and *Hoop Dreams* (1994). Founded in December 1990 and based in New York, the company was initially headed (until 1995) by Ira Deutchman. In 1991, Fine Line also entered co-production, beginning with *Waterland* (1992).

BIBLIOGRAPHY

Eller, Claudia. "New Line Cinema Expands Base." *Daily Variety,* December 6, 1990, pp. 1, 23.

FIRES. Because of its use of nitrate film* and because most movie sets are built of wood, the film industry has suffered more than its share of fires. The first major studio fire took place at the Thanhouser Film Corporation* studios in New Rochelle at 1:30 P.M. on January 13, 1913. The fire created so much publicity that the company produced a short film exploiting the event titled *When the Studio Burned.* The remaining sets—except for one church—on the Inceville* site were destroyed by fire in 1924. That same year, on July 8, a fire caused $175,000 worth of damage at the Hal Roach Studios* in Culver City.

A $200,000 fire took place at the 20th Century-Fox studio on January 25, 1937. Damage totaling $350,000 occurred at the Metro-Goldwyn-Mayer* backlot on November 24, 1940, when fire destroyed storage buildings that held, among other things, many of the props brought over from

China for the filming of *The Good Earth* (1937). Two years later, a second fire, on October 14, 1942, caused $100,000 worth of damage at M-G-M. On July 19, 1945, fire swept part of the Universal* backlot, causing $250,000 worth of damage and destroying a number of Western sets and 70 "ancient wagons and vehicles."

On May 16, 1952, a fire destroyed eight acres of sets and caused some $1.5 million worth of damage at the Warner Bros.* studio in Burbank. The studios of Samuel Goldwyn, Inc.*, were the site of a number of fires, beginning with two small ones in 1972. A $1 million fire hit the lot in May 1974, followed by a $3 million fire in December 1975, and a much smaller fire in June 1976. Major arson fires occurred on the Universal* backlot in September 1987 and November 1990, and there were two minor fires on the lot in September and November 1992. The Universal fire of November 6, 1990, caused a reported $20 million in damage, destroying the New York Street and Court House Square standing sets.

The worst motion picture-related fire took place at the Charity Bazaar in Paris on May 4, 1897. The 1926 edition of *Film Daily Year Book* lists some 20 film-related fires in America, which occurred between October 1924 and September 1925. The worst occurred at Fort Lee, New Jersey, where a nitrate fire claimed two lives and injured many on February 7, 1925. Silent film star Martha Mansfield was burned to death on November 20, 1923, when the dress she was wearing caught fire during the production of *The Warrens of Virginia*.

FIRST ARTISTS PRODUCTION COMPANY, LTD.,

was the first major production company to be created by film industry principals since United Artists* in 1919. It was formed by Barbra Streisand, Sidney Poitier, and Paul Newman in June 1969 as a Delaware company with production offices in both New York and Los Angeles. Steve McQueen joined the company in 1971, and a year later he was followed by Dustin Hoffman. The first president of First Artists was Patrick Kelley, followed in 1973 by Jay Kanter, in 1975 by Phil Feldman, and in 1980 by Erwin E. Holly.

Despite the favorable critical reception of the majority of First Artists films, the company never generated sufficient income for a healthy cash flow. By 1979, it was in severe financial difficulties and involved in a stormy legal suit with Dustin Hoffman. Despite reported assets of $24 million—along with 201 employees—in 1979, the company could not continue, and, in 1982, it merged with the Australian-based Mascot Industries, Inc.

Among First Artists productions were *Pocket Money* (1971), *The Getaway* (1972), *Up the Sandbox* (1972), *The Life and Times of Judge Roy Bean* (1972), *A Warm December* (1973), *Uptown Saturday Night* (1974), *The Drowning Pool* (1975), *A Star Is Born* (1976), *Straight Time* (1978), *Agatha* (1979), *The Main Event* (1979), *Tom Horn* (1980), and *An Enemy of the People* (1981).

BIBLIOGRAPHY

Hollie, Pamela G. "First Artists—Star-Crossed Child of the 1960's." *The New York Times,* December 23, 1979, p. F3.
Marks, Marlene Adler. "First Artists on the Rocks." *Los Angeles Magazine,* October 1979, pp. 180–85, 286–88.

FIRST NATIONAL PICTURES, INC.,

FIRST NATIONAL PICTURES, INC., was created as a circuit of independent exhibitors under the initial title of First National Exhibitors Circuit, Inc., on April 25, 1917. Thomas L. Tally and J. D. Williams were the two men responsible for its formation, and they were joined by 25 other founding exhibitors, including Frederick Dahnken of the Turner and Dahnken Circuit in San Francisco, Harry O. Schwalbe of Philadelphia, John H. Kunsky of Detroit, S. L. Rothapfel of New York, Nathan H. Gordon of Boston, Tom Saxe of Milwaukee, and Earl H. Hulsey of Dallas.

Because of problems involved in obtaining films from producers, the high cost of rental, block booking*, and the inferior quality of some prints, these exhibitors decided to pool their purchasing power and to obtain films directly from the stars and directors. Its original motto was "The Good Guys Get, by Getting Together." One of the first features the new circuit was able to obtain directly was the Warner Bros.* production of *My Four Years in Germany* (1918). First National's biggest coup was the signing of a million-dollar contract with Charlie Chaplin, whereby the comedian made six films for the new organization: *A Dog's Life* (1918), *Shoulder Arms* (1918), *Sunnyside* (1919), *A Day's Pleasure* (1919), *The Kid* (1920), and *The Pilgrim* (1922).

Adolph Zukor of Paramount* tried various means to cripple the First National organization, which he saw as a very real threat to his organization. The company reformed as Associated First National Pictures Incorporated and Associated First National Theatres Incorporated. It was able to sign contracts with Norma and Constance Talmadge, Marshall Neilan, Allan Dwan, Maurice Tourneur, J. Parker Reade, Jr., Frank Borzage, and others. In 1921, First National imported the German feature *Du Barry,* retitled it *Passion,* and successfully launched it in the United States, while at the same time creating American careers for its director Ernst Lubitsch and its star Pola Negri.

In 1922, First National decided that it needed to create its own production organization and opened studios in Burbank, California. Two years later, the company took over the former American Biograph* studios in New York but, by 1926, had consolidated production on the West Coast.

In 1928, First National was acquired by Warner Bros. through the latter's obtaining control of the Stanley Company, a theatre circuit that was a majority stockholder in First National. Warner Bros. moved its studio facilities to Burbank, although as part of the acquisition agreement certain Warner Bros. films were called "First National Pictures." Warner Bros. films were later designated as First

National productions well into the forties, and the First National name appeared on some Warner Bros. films as late as 1956.

BIBLIOGRAPHY

Einfeld, S. Charles. "The History of First National." *Variety*, June 25, 1930, p. 28.
"First National Exchange Armoured." *The Moving Picture World*, October 27, 1917, p. 513.
"First National Issues Handsome Booklet." *The Moving Picture World*, May 4, 1918, p. 705.
"FNEC of New York at 507 5th Ave." *The Moving Picture World*, March 23, 1918, p. 1669.
Jobes, Gertrude. *Motion Picture Empire*. Hamden, Conn.: Archon Books, 1966.

FISHER'S COSTUME HOUSE. See WESTERN COSTUME CO.

FLAMINGO FILM COMPANY was formed in October 1914 as the result of an alliance between the distribution company Sawyer, Inc.*, Chartered Theaters Corporation, and the stock exchange house of Gilbert Elliott & Company. Flamingo planned to produce two- and three-reel comedies and five-reel dramatic features. Fred Mace was in charge of production, and Roy McCardell and Elaine Sterne wrote for the company. Frederick Upham Adams was the president, A. H. Sawyer was the secretary, and A. H. Hallett was the vice president and general manager. Offices were in the Meece Building at 48th Street and Broadway, New York.

Flamingo's first release was the four-reel comedy *Without Hope*, starring Marguerite Loveridge. The company released its product with Sawyer, Inc., until February 1915, when Sawyer left Flamingo and it began releasing with World Film Corporation*. In 1915, Flamingo made the farce series "The Feats of Felix" with Charles Mason, directed by J. A. Murphy and shot at the Imperial Studio on New York's East 48th Street.

BIBLIOGRAPHY

"Flamingo Company Organizes." *The Moving Picture World*, October 31, 1914, p. 618.

FLUSHING, NEW YORK. See KNICKERBOCKER STAR FEATURES

FLYING A. See AMERICAN FILM MANUFACTURING COMPANY

FORDART PRODUCTIONS was formed by Francis Ford (1882–1953), in April 1918, to produce films for the states rights* market. *Berlin via America* was the first film that it produced. The company had offices in New York and leased space at the Christie* Studios in Hollywood. Fordart planned to make six features a year plus a series of one- and two-reel shorts. Edna Emerson was Ford's leading lady and Elsie Van Name his scenario writer.

FOREIGN PRESS ASSOCIATION OF HOLLYWOOD. See HOLLYWOOD FOREIGN PRESS ASSOCIATION, INC.

FORT DU LAC, WISCONSIN. See EBONY PICTURES CORPORATION

FORT LEE, NEW JERSEY. With its close proximity to New York City, Fort Lee, New Jersey, offered a variety of scenery for early filmmakers, notably the Palisades on the Hudson River and the many types of country settings. D. W. Griffith made a number of films in the neighborhood for the American Biograph Company*. Indeed, by 1910, one trade paper was complaining of the relentless use by filmmakers of the "Jersey scenery." Early in the second decade of the twentieth century, the town became a major center of filmmaking as various studios were built: Champion, Eclair*, Willat, Peerless/World, Paragon, and Solax*. These studios were utilized by many of the major producers, including William Fox*, Metro Pictures Corporation*, and Goldwyn*. Among the stars who worked at the Fort Lee studios on a regular basis were Theda Bara, Ethel Barrymore, Alice Brady, June Caprice, Ethel Clayton, Madge Evans, Geraldine Farrar, Elsie Ferguson, Pauline Frederick, Madge Kennedy, Mabel Normand, Olga Petrova, Pearl White, and Clara Kimball Young.

BIBLIOGRAPHY

Altomara, Rita Ecke. *Hollywood on the Palisades*. New York: Garland, 1983.
Spehr, Paul C. *The Movies Begin*. Newark, N.J.: The Newark Museum, 1977.

FOUR STAR PRODUCTIONS. See ARTCO PRODUCTIONS, INC.

FOX CARTHAY CIRCLE THEATRE. See CARTHAY CIRCLE THEATRE

FOX FILM CORPORATION. Although the Fox Film Corporation was officially incorporated on February 1, 1915, the company's roots stretch back to 1904. In that year, William Fox (1879–1952), a New York City exhibitor who bought his first theatre in 1903, began the Greater New York Film Rental Company to distribute films. The company prospered, and, after surviving a legal battle with the General Film Company (settled in Fox's favor in 1912), William Fox decided to go into production and changed the name of his company in 1913 to Box Office Attractions Film Rental Company. At first, Fox used the Balboa Amusement Producing Company* to supply the films but soon began to produce films by himself, beginning with his first feature, *Life's Shop Window*, in 1914. In 1915, the name of the company was changed to represent its increased activities.

In 1914, the company made its first film in Los Angeles and, in 1915, decided to establish a permanent studio in California. Fox leased the old Selig* studio in Edendale until its own studio, at Sunset Boulevard and Western Avenue, opened in 1916. In 1919, offices were opened in Paris, Rome, Berlin, London, and Dublin to distribute Fox films and to aid in the making of newsreels (as *Fox News* was established that same year).

Buoyed by profits and the need to compete with Adolph Zukor's Paramount Pictures* and the other major studios, the company began to expand in several ways during the twenties. In 1924, Fox owned 24 theatres in New York City, New Jersey, Chicago, Oakland, and Detroit. In 1925, West Coast Theatres was acquired and the Fox Theatre Corporation was incorporated in November 1925. In 1927, the Roxy Theatre* was purchased by William Fox, and, in March 1929, he acquired majority control of Loew's, Inc., for some $50 million.

At the same time the company was acquiring theatres, it was also building a new studio in Los Angeles. Construction began on the Westwood Studio (now part of Century City) in 1924, and it was officially dedicated in October 1928. At the same time, the company was making plans for the introduction of sound motion pictures. In July 1925, the rights to the Case-Sponable system were purchased and the system renamed Movietone. This system was later buttressed by the purchase, in July 1927, of the U.S. rights to the German Tri-Ergon patents.

To pay for this expansion and experimentation, Fox Film Corporation went public in 1925 with an offering of one million shares. This did not provide enough money for all the acquisitions that William Fox wanted to make, and so, in 1929, to purchase Loew's, Inc., he borrowed over $40 million from AT&T, two banks, and his New York investment house, Halsey, Stuart & Co. Loew's was bought, but antitrust questions raised by the government prevented Fox from taking control of the company. In addition, William Fox was injured in an automobile accident in July 1929, and by the time he had recovered from his injuries the stock market had started to slide and the loans he had taken out to purchase Loew's were becoming due. With no one willing to loan him any money, William Fox was forced out of the company in 1930 by AT&T and Halsey, Stuart & Co. The new president was Harley Clarke, president of General Theatres Equipment Corporation, which took control of Fox in April 1930.

Under Clarke's leadership the company began to lose a great deal of money. From a profit of $8 million in 1930, the company reported losses of $2 million in 1931 and $9.5 million in 1932. After a year as president, Harley Clarke was followed by Edward R. Tinker, who, also after only one year, was followed by Sidney R. Kent. In March 1933, a stockholder filed suit to have the company put into receivership, and, on April 1, 1933, the company was reorganized. Finances did not improve very much and, on May 29,

1935, a merger with Twentieth Century Pictures* was announced. On August 15, 1935, the name of the company was officially changed to 20th Century-Fox Film Corporation*.

BIBLIOGRAPHY

Allvine, Glendon. *The Greatest Fox of Them All*. New York: Lyle Stuart, 1969.
Sinclair, Upton. *Upton Sinclair Presents William Fox*. Los Angeles: The Author, 1933.
Thomas, Tony, and Aubrey Solomon. *The Films of 20th Century-Fox*. Secaucus, N.J.: Citadel Press, 1979.

RESOURCES

Films: Museum of Modern Art; UCLA Film and Television Archive.
Photographs: Academy of Motion Picture Arts and Sciences (set reference photographs); UCLA.

FOX GRANDEUR. See GRANDEUR

FOX MOVIETONE NEWS. See NEWSREELS

FOX NEWS. See NEWSREELS

FOX WEST COAST THEATRES CORPORATION. The best known of the 20th Century-Fox-owned theatre chains dating back to the twenties, Fox West Coast Theatres Corporation was a subsidiary of National Theatres Corporation. Other subsidiaries of National Theatres Corporation (which was, in turn, a wholly owned subsidiary of 20th Century-Fox*) were Evergreen State Amusement Corporation, Fox Intermountain Theatres, Fox Michigan Corporation, Fox Midwest Amusement Corporation, Fox Philadelphia Building, Inc., and Fox Wisconsin Amusement Corporation. Following the consent decree*, the 549 theatres owned by National Theatres Corporation in 1951 were transferred to the ownership of the newly formed National Theatres, Inc.

FRANK A. KEENEY PICTURES CORPORATION. Frank A. Keeney, formerly a theatrical promoter and owner of a string of vaudeville houses in various eastern cities, was the head and sole financial backer for Frank A. Keeney Pictures Corporation, which was founded in January 1918 to produce films starring Catherine Calvert. James Kirkwood was the director and Benjamin S. Kutler the scenario editor. It used the Pathé* studios in the Bronx at Park Avenue and 134th Street, and its offices were in the Putnam Building at 1493 Broadway. The William L. Sherry Service* distributed the films, the first of which was *A Romance of the Underworld*.

BIBLIOGRAPHY

"Frank A. Keeney." *The Moving Picture World*, January 12, 1918, p. 247.

FRAZEE FILMS PRODUCTIONS. Edwin A. Frazee, formerly a director with Keystone and Fox*, formed Frazee Films Productions in July 1918 to exploit the trick methods of cinematography that he had developed and perfected, including underwater photography at low cost on a stage. Frazee had a studio in the Boyle Heights section of Los Angeles, and his first film, *The Haunted House,* was distributed by Ernest Shipman.

FREDERICK DOUGLASS FILM COMPANY, an early black production company located in Jersey City, New Jersey, was created to present blacks in positive, successful roles, in contrast to the depictions of them in *The Birth of a Nation.* Traverse Sprague was the company's director. Its first production, *The Colored American Winning His Suit,* which received its premiere in Jersey City on July 14, 1916, in six reels, later cut to four, was criticized for its lack of technical expertise. It produced the three-reel *The Scapegoat* in 1917, from a story by Paul Lawrence Dunbar, and a documentary about black soldiers during the First World War, but it soon ended operations because of financial problems and inability to get bookings for its films.

FRENCH RESEARCH FOUNDATION was founded in Hollywood by actor Charles Boyer (1897–1978). It opened on October 15, 1940, to provide film producers with research materials and documentation for features dealing with the work of the French "underground" during the Second World War. Later, it served as a research center for anyone in the film industry requiring general information on France and French customs. The Foundation received its first screen credit on the 1948 Lewis Milestone production of *Arch of Triumph.* In January 1970, it donated its assets to the UCLA Theatre Arts Department.

FRIES ENTERTAINMENT, INC., was formed in 1975 as Charles Fries Productions by Charles W. "Chuck" Fries (born 1928 and pronounced "Freeze"). One of the largest producers of films for television, it went public in January 1984, but filed for Chapter XI bankruptcy protection on October 16, 1991, after posting losses for four out of the last five fiscal years. With a library of 230 television programs and films, the company has languished in bankruptcy while unsecured creditors and Credit Lyonnais argue over its fate.

Address: 6922 Hollywood Boulevard, Hollywood, Calif. 90028.

BIBLIOGRAPHY

Lippman, John. "Fries Entertainment Seeks Bankruptcy Shield." *Los Angeles Times,* October 17, 1991, pp. D2, D4.
———. "Flawed Script." *Los Angeles Times,* November 24, 1991, pp. D1, D7.

FROHMAN AMUSEMENT CORPORATION. Gustave Frohman, the brother of stage impresarios Daniel and Charles Frohman, followed his brothers into the world of film when he established the Frohman Amusement Corporation, in November 1914, with William L. Sherrill and S. H. Boynton. Its policy was to produce only original scenarios, preferably non-slapstick comedies. George Irving was the director, Ralph Dean the technical director, Jacques Monteron the cameraman, and Frank Norcross the manager of the studio that the company leased and that had formerly belonged to the Gene Gauntier Players. Its first film was *The Fairy and the Waif,* starring Mary Miles Minter. Frohman distributed through World Film Corporation*.

By October 1916, Frohman himself was no longer involved in the company, and Sherrill became its president. The company went out of business in 1920.

"FRONTIER" BRAND. See ST. LOUIS MOTION PICTURE COMPANY

FRONTIER FILMS was formed in March 1937 as a nonprofit production company, with its origins in the Nykino Collective and the New York branch of the National Film and Photo League*. It was concerned with the production of documentaries* with a left-wing viewpoint, and its original members included Paul Strand, Leo Hurwitz, Ralph Steiner, Willard Van Dyke, Lionel Berman, Ben Maddow, Sidney Meyers, Irving Lerner, and Jay Leyda. The organization's films were funded by liberal and left-wing sympathizers. Its best-known production was the feature-length *Native Land* (1942); its other films were *Heart of Spain* (1937), *China Strikes Back* (1937), *People of the Cumberland* (1938), *Return to Life* (1938), *History and Romance of Transportation* (1939), and *White Flood* (1940).

Ralph Steiner and Willard Van Dyke left Frontier Films early in 1939 to form American Documentary Films, which produced the classic documentary *The City* (1939), and Frontier Films was disbanded in 1941.

BIBLIOGRAPHY

Alexander, William. "Frontier Films, 1936–1941: The Aesthetics of Impact." *Cinema Journal* 15, 1 (Fall 1975): pp. 16–28.
Campbell, Russell. *Cinema Strikes Back.* Ann Arbor, Mich.: UMI Research Press, 1982.

FUJIYAMA FEATURE FILM COMPANY was formed in Los Angeles, in October 1916, to produce a series of Japanese films for release in the United States. It planned to build a studio in Redlands, California, and to send a company of actors to film in Japan. Mrs. E. L. Greer was the head of the company.

THE GANGSTER FILM. A very American film genre, the gangster film is generally dated from 1912 when D. W. Griffith directed *Musketeers of Pig Alley*. The modern story of Griffith's *Intolerance* (1916) depicts gangsterism at work in an American city. Arguably the best silent film with a gangster theme is Josef von Sternberg's *Underworld* (1927), starring George Bancroft as a mobster and Evelyn Brent as his moll. The first all-talking Vitaphone* feature, *Lights of New York* (1928), introduced many of the cliches that have come to be associated with the genre; Warner Bros.*, which produced the feature, became the studio most associated with the gangster film in the thirties and forties, through films such as *The Public Enemy* (1931), *Little Caesar* (1931), *G-Men* (1935), *The Petrified Forest* (1936), *Angels with Dirty Faces* (1938), *The Roaring Twenties* (1939), *Key Largo* (1948), and *White Heart* (1949). Many of these films feature Edward G. Robinson, James Cagney, and Humphrey Bogart, the studio's best-known exponents of the gangster genre. Other major gangster melodramas of the period include Rouben Mamoulian's *City Streets* (1931) and Howard Hawks's *Scarface: The Shame of a Nation* (1932).

Gangsters have been shown in a favorable light in Frank Capra's *Lady for a Day* (1933) and *Pocketful of Miracles* (1961). The musical *Guys and Dolls* (1955) is concerned with gangsters. The British have tried to emulate the American gangster feature with *No Orchids for Miss Blandish* (1948), *Night and the City* (1950), and *The Lavender Hill Mob* (1950).

Real-life gangsters have been portrayed in many films. Mickey Rooney played Baby Face Nelson in the 1957 film of the same title. Al Capone was portrayed by Rod Steiger in the 1959 film of the same name, by Neville Brand in *The George Raft Story* (1961) and in the television series, *The Untouchables,* by Jason Robards in *The St. Valentine's Day Massacre* (1967), and by Ben Gazzara in *Capone* (1975). John Ericson played "Pretty Boy" Floyd in the 1959 film of that title; Fabian played the gangster in *A Bullet for Pretty Boy* (1970). Ma Barker was portrayed by Shelley Winters in *Bloody Mama* (1970). Bonnie Parker and Clyde Barrow were played by Dorothy Provine and Jack Hogan in *The Bonnie Parker Story* (1958) and by Faye Dunaway and Warren Beatty in *Bonnie and Clyde* (1967). Dillinger was portrayed by Lawrence Tierney in *Dillinger* (1945), by Nick Adams in *Young Dillinger* (1965), and by Warren Oates in *Dillinger* (1973). Charles Bronson was *Machine Gun Kelly* (1958), and Ray Danton played the title role in *The Rise and Fall of Legs Diamond* (1959). Three 1991 films were based on the life of Bugsy Siegel: *The Marrying Man* (with Armande Assante), *Mobsters* (with Richard Grieco), and *Bugsy* (with Warren Beatty).

More recent gangster films have concentrated on the Mafia, notably Francis Ford Coppola's *The Godfather* (1972) and its sequels, together with *The Sicilian Connection* (1973), *Mafia Junction* (1973), *Once Upon a Time in America* (1984), *Prizzi's Honor* (1985), and *The Freshman* (1990). Robert Mitchum took on the Japanese mob in *The Yakuza* (1975), and it is also the subject of *Black Rain* (1989). Later gangster films have emphasized violence: Martin Scorsese's *Goodfellas* (1990), Abel Ferrara's *Bad Lieutenant* (1992), and Quentin Tarantino's *Pulp Fiction* (1994).

BIBLIOGRAPHY

Bookbinder, Robert. *Classics of the Gangster Film.* Secaucus, N.J.: Citadel Press, 1985.

Brode, Douglas. *Money, Women and Guns: Crime Movies from Bonnie and Clyde to the Present.* New York: Carol Publishing, 1995.

Lee, Raymond, and B. C. Van Hecke. *Gangster and Hoodlums.* New York: A. S. Barnes, 1971.

McArthur, Colin. *Underworld U.S.A.* New York: Viking Press, 1972.

McCarthy, John. *Hollywood Gangland: The Movies' Love Affair with the Mob.* New York: St. Martin's Press, 1993.

Parish, James Robert, and Michael R. Pitts. *The Great Gangster Pictures.* Metuchen, N.J.: Scarecrow Press, 1976.

———. *The Great Gangster Pictures II.* Metuchen, N.J.: Scarecrow Press, 1987.

Rosow, Eugene. *Born to Lose.* New York: Oxford University Press, 1978.

Sklar, Robert. *City Boys: Cagney, Bogart, Garfield.* Princeton, N.J.: Princeton University Press, 1992.

Stephens, Michael L. *Gangster Films: A Comprehensive, Illustrated Reference to People, Films and Terms.* Jefferson, N.C.: McFarland, 1996.

THE GARDEN OF ALLAH, one of the best-known hotels among many in the literary and intellectual film communities, was a favorite of F. Scott Fitzgerald, Dorothy Parker, Robert Benchley, Errol Flynn, and Orson Welles. The modern

Hollywood equivalent is the Chateau Marmont, across Sunset Boulevard and slightly to the west of the site of the Garden of Allah, which opened in 1929 as an apartment hotel. The Garden of Allah operated as a hotel, with 25 bungalows, all with a minimum of three rooms, on a three-acre site at 8152 Sunset Boulevard, the former home of actress Alla Nazimova (1879–1945). Originally controlled by the Garden of Allah Corporation, under the presidency of Maurice Barber, the hotel opened in January 1927, and was demolished in 1959. A bank, and later a shopping mall, occupy the site. The Garden of Allah was recreated by Herman Wouk, as Rainbow's End, in his novel *Youngblood Hawke.*

BIBLIOGRAPHY

Graham, Sheilah. *The Garden of Allah.* New York: Crown, 1970.
Link, Tom. "The Last Days of Hollywood's Rowdiest Watering Hole." *Los Angeles,* August 1979, pp. 100–103.
"Nazimova's Old Home Site of 25 New Villas." *Exhibitors Herald,* section 3, December 25, 1926, p. 9.

GARSON STUDIOS. See EQUITY PICTURES CORPORATION

GASPARCOLOR, a three-color process, required the printing of the three negatives directly in their appropriate colors. The colored emulsions were coated on the film, with the magenta and yellow layers on one side and the blue-green layer on the other. Unlike Technicolor*, Gasparcolor prints could be developed at any standard black-and-white laboratory. Developed prior to the Second World War in Europe by Dr. Bela Gaspar, the color system became known to American audiences through George Pal's Puppetoons*. In 1941, Colorfilm Laboratory in Burbank began the processing of Gasparcolor in the United States, and, in 1955, Eastman Kodak* obtained a license to utilize Gasparcolor patent nos. 2,344,084 and 2,312,543.

BIBLIOGRAPHY

Klein, Adrian. "The Gasparcolor Process." *The Journal of the Association of Cine-Technicians* (February 1936): pp. 83–84.
Wyckoff, Alvin. "Gasparcolor Comes to Hollywood." *American Cinematographer,* November 1941, pp. 510–11.

THE GAUMONT ANIMATED WEEKLY. See NEWSREELS

GAUMONT COMPANY. The American branch of the Gaumont Company, which brought over films made by the parent company in France, released its first film made in the United States, *The Faithful Servitor,* on September 15, 1913. Herbert Blaché was at the time Gaumont's vice president and American representative. It distributed through the Exclusive Supply Corporation*, of which Blaché was president. In January 1915, Gaumont began producing one-reel comedies under the "Empress" brand, featuring Marion Swayne, Joseph Levering, and Arthur Hill and released through the United Film Service.

By October 1915, Gaumont was releasing its entire output with the Mutual Film Corporation*. At that time, it produced Rialto Star Features and Casino Star Comedies in Flushing, New York, and Jacksonville, Florida. In April 1918, after a period of inactivity, Gaumont began to produce features for the states rights* market at its Flushing studio.

BIBLIOGRAPHY

"First American Gaumont." *The New York Dramatic Mirror,* September 10, 1913, p. 27.
"Foreign Films in the American Market." *The New York Dramatic Mirror,* February 12, 1913, p. 29.

GAYETY COMEDIES, INC., a minor Los Angeles-based production company, active in 1919 and 1920, produced short subjects featuring comedian George Ovey.

G.C.C. THEATRES, INC. See GENERAL CINEMA CORPORATION

THE GEFFEN FILM CO. was founded in 1982 by David Geffen (born 1943) to produce films financed and to be distributed by Warner Bros.* The first production was *Risky Business* (1983), and other features include *Little Shop of Horrors* (1986), *Beetlejuice* (1988), and *Interview with a Vampire* (1994). Earlier, Geffen had founded Asylum Records in 1970 (sold to Warner Bros. in 1976) and Geffen Records in 1980 (sold to MCA in 1990 for $700 million).

Address: 9130 Sunset Boulevard, Los Angeles, Calif. 90069.

THE GENE GAUNTIER FEATURE PLAYERS was formed in December 1912, when actress-screenwriter Gene Gauntier (1880–1966) left Kalem. According to *The New York Dramatic Mirror* (January 18, 1913), the company consisted of Gauntier, director Sidney Olcott, Jack J. Clark, Arthur Donaldson, Robert Walker, John Vincent, Allen Farnham, Herbert Tracy, Helen Lynn, Florence Donaldson, Herman Obrock (cameraman), Ross Fisher, and William Bailey. The company spent the winter of 1912–1913 filming in Florida at 737 Talleyrand Avenue, Jacksonville, with Allen Farnham serving as studio manager. Its first production was the three-reel *A Daughter of the Confederacy,* released by Warner's Features in February 1913. In the summer of 1913, the company filmed in Killarney, Ireland, producing *For Ireland's Sake* (1914) and *Come Back to Erin* (1914). In the spring of 1915, the Gene Gauntier Feature Players was disbanded, when Gauntier and her husband, Jack J. Clark, joined Universal.*

GENERAL CINEMA CORPORATION controlled some 1,500 theatre screens, chiefly in suburban shopping malls. It was also involved in various diversified operations, notably as the country's largest independent bottler of Pepsi Cola products.

The corporation was founded in 1922 by Philip Smith, a former Pathé* film salesman, with the acquisition of the National Theatre in Boston. The economic depression forced Smith to dispose of most of the more than 20 theatres he controlled in the twenties, and, by 1933, he had only three theatres in his company. However, Smith took the major step of becoming involved in the drive-in theatre* movement, and by the outbreak of the Second World War controlled more than half of the drive-in theatres operational in the United States. In 1947, the company began to move away from drive-in theatres and into the acquisition of theatres in shopping malls. In 1960, the company made its first public offering and changed its name from General Drive-In Corporation to General Cinema Corporation. Philip Smith died in 1961, and the corporation was taken over by his son, Richard A. Smith. General Cinema Corporation tried, unsuccessfully, to become involved in film production in 1979, when it attempted to acquire 20 percent of the stock of Columbia Pictures*.

In 1989, General sold its bottling business to Pepsico for $1.77 billion. In January 1989, it agreed to purchase publisher Harcourt Brace Jovanovich in a $1.4 billion deal, subsequently changing its name to Harcourt General, Inc. In September 1993, GC Company, Inc., was incorporated to handle its theatres operation, reduced by 1996 to 196 theatres.

Address: 27 Boylston Street, Chestnut Hill, Mass. 02167

BIBLIOGRAPHY

Harris, Kathryn. "General Cinema More Wall St. Than Hollywood." *Los Angeles Times,* August 11, 1985, business section, pp. 1, 5–6.

GENERAL FILM COMPANY. See MOTION PICTURE PATENTS COMPANY

GENERAL SERVICE STUDIOS. See HOLLYWOOD GENERAL STUDIOS

GEORGE KLEINE OPTICAL COMPANY. A manufacturer of optical equipment, lenses, cameras, projectors, and film, the George Kleine Optical Company was incorporated in Chicago in 1907 and founded by George Kleine (1864–1931). Kleine (pronounced Cline-ee) was one of the founders of the Kalem Company* and of the Motion Picture Patents Company*; in 1910, he sold his company to the General Film Company arm of the Patents Company but retained the majority of the stock in the company, of which he was vice president and later president.

George Kleine was best known for the importation of foreign films, such as *Quo Vadis, Othello,* and *The Last Days of Pompeii,* all of which were brought from Italy in 1913. In 1919, he released *Deliverance,* starring Helen Keller in her only feature-film appearance. From 1919 onward, Kleine operated as an individual rather than as a company. In the early twenties he served as chairman of the board of Ritz-Carlton Pictures and was active in the field of educational films.

BIBLIOGRAPHY

Horwitz, Rita, and Harriet Harrison. *The George Kleine Collection of Early Motion Pictures in the Library of Congress: A Catalog.* Washington, D.C.: Library of Congress, 1980.

RESOURCES

Films and Papers: Library of Congress.

A GIMBALLED ROOM is a special effects set built inside a cylindrical drum with the furniture and fixtures bolted down. The drum is turned to give the impression that the actors are walking first on the floor and then on the walls and ceiling. The effect was used by Fred Astaire in his 1951 feature, *Royal Wedding.*

GLASS SHOT is the term used to describe a type of special effect* whereby a portion of a scene is painted on glass. Years ago, the glass was positioned in front of the camera and the sequence was filmed with the scene on the glass becoming part of the overall shot. Today, the painting on glass is done following the live-action scene in the studio but utilizing the same negative. Theoretically, it is impossible to tell where the live-action scene and the glass shot join. By utilizing a scene painted on glass, the necessity of building expensive sets is eliminated. A related term is *matte shot,* for which a portion of the frame is matted out to permit the later insertion of another shot.

GLEN ALDEN CORP. See RKO THEATRES CORPORATION and STANLEY WARNER CORPORATION

GLENDALE, CALIFORNIA. See LIBERTY MOTION PICTURE COMPANY

GLENDALE, LONG ISLAND. See MIRROR FILMS, INC.

GLEN GLENN SOUND COMPANY, INC., a familiar name in all areas of sound recording for both film and television, was founded in 1937 by Harry Eckles and Glen Glenn (1908–1960). The company, which was acquired by Todd-AO in 1986, moved to a new sound center in 1983; this new center has served as post-production headquarters for such major features as *Star Trek—The Motion Picture, Raiders of the Lost Ark, Indiana Jones and the Temple of Doom, Under the Volcano,* and *Purple Rain.*

Address: 900 North Seward Street, Hollywood, Calif. 90038.

BIBLIOGRAPHY

"Glen Glenn a 'Resounding' Success Brought Up to Date." *On Location,* June 1985, pp. 184–85.

GLOBE PRODUCTIONS. See SOUNDIES

"GOLD DIGGERS" SERIES was Warner Bros.* most popular group of musicals* in the thirties. Warner Bros. produced the first film, titled simply *The Gold Diggers,* in 1923; it was based on the 1919 Avery Hopwood play of the same title, as was the Warner Bros. 1929 remake, titled *Gold Diggers of Broadway.*

There were three musicals in the thirties: *The Gold Diggers of 1933, The Gold Diggers of 1935,* and *The Gold Diggers of 1937.* All three starred Dick Powell and are best remembered for their musical numbers staged by Busby Berkeley. In addition, Warner Bros. filmed *Gold Diggers in Paris* (1938), starring Rudy Vallee and again with musical numbers by Busby Berkeley.

GOLDEN STATE MOTION PICTURE COMPANY OF CALIFORNIA was a production company of 1913. James K. Hackett, after starring in *The Prisoner of Zenda* for the Famous Players Film Company, directed himself as Jean Valjean in *The Bishop's Candlesticks* for Golden State. Ernest Shipman and H. M. Russell were associated with the company. In July 1913, it produced *One Hundred Years of Mormonism* for the states rights* market.

BIBLIOGRAPHY

"Another Hackett Film." *The New York Dramatic Mirror,* July 2, 1913, p. 26.

GOLDWYN PICTURES CORPORATION was the first production company to bear the name of Samuel Goldwyn (1882–1974), although he had earlier been associated with the Jesse L. Lasky Motion Picture Company (of which he was treasurer and general manager). It was founded in December 1916 by Samuel Goldfish and Edgar and Archibald Selwyn; Goldwyn adopted the name of the company as his own in 1918. The Goldwyn Corporation continued the concept introduced earlier by Adolph Zukor of utilizing famous names from the theatrical world for its productions. Placed under contract were playwrights such as Bayard Veiller, Avery Hopwood, and Margaret Mayo; actresses such as Madge Kennedy, Maxine Elliott, and Jane Cowl; and opera singers Mary Garden and Geraldine Farrar. Of the group only Farrar and Kennedy proved to have any popularity with filmgoers, as the former had already shown when she was under contract to Famous Players-Lasky. One other stage personality who began what was to be a successful film career under Goldwyn was Will Rogers.

Realizing the need for recognized film personalities, Goldwyn placed under contract Mabel Normand and Mae Marsh, but neither proved particularly successful under the producer's guidance. Equally unsuccessful was Eminent Authors Pictures, Inc., introduced by Goldwyn in 1919, whereby popular writers, including Rex Beach, Gertrude Atherton, Gouverneur Morris, Rupert Hughes, and Mary Roberts Rinehart, would adapt their works for the screen. Because the eminent authors resolutely refused to understand film technique, the experiment proved a failure, although it did lead to Goldwyn's producing one superior feature, *The Penalty* (1920), starring Lon Chaney and based on a story by Gouverneur Morris.

In 1922, Goldwyn was removed as president of his company by a vote of the stockholders. Goldwyn Pictures Corporation merged with Metro Pictures Corporation* and Louis B. Mayer's independent production company to form Metro-Goldwyn-Mayer*, with Goldwyn's Culver City studios becoming the studios for the new organization. In 1924, Goldwyn formed a new company, Samuel Goldwyn, Inc.*

BIBLIOGRAPHY

Berg, A. Scott. *Goldwyn: A Biography.* New York: Alfred A. Knopf, 1989.
Goldwyn, Sam. *Behind the Screen.* New York: George H. Doran, 1923.
"Goldwyn Gets Big Playwrights." *The Moving Picture World,* December 30, 1916, p. 1943.
"Goldwyn Pictures Enters Field." *The Moving Picture World,* December 16, 1916, p. 1627.
Hughes, Rupert. "Early Days in the Movies." *The Saturday Evening Post,* April 6, 1935, pp. 18–19, 37, 39–40, 43–44; and April 13, 1935, pp. 30–31, 118, 120–23.
"Life Inside the Goldwyn Gate." *Photoplay,* July 1922, pp. 38–39.

THE GORDON SAWYER AWARD is presented annually by the Academy of Motion Picture Arts and Sciences* to individuals for their contributions to the advancement of film sciences or technology. The award, which is voted by the Academy's board of governors, was first given in 1981 to Joseph B. Walker. Under the supervision of Gordon Sawyer (1905–1980), the sound department at the Samuel Goldwyn* studio became the most highly regarded in the industry; Sawyer joined Goldwyn in 1928 and retired 42 years later. In 1973, the Sawyer Sound Building on the lot was named in his honor.

GOSSIP COLUMNISTS. Now usurped in function by tabloid television news programs, such as *Hard Copy* and *Inside Edition,* gossip columnists once wielded incredible power, manipulating their readership to love or hate different celebrities. Feared and hated by the film industry, their power waned in the 1960s. The two most influential of gossip columnists were Hedda Hopper (1885–1966) and Louella Parsons (1893–1972), whose combined readership totaled more than 75 million. Louella Parsons, born Louella Oettinger, is generally considered to have originated the gossip column with the *Chicago Record-Herald* in 1915. She moved to the *New York Morning Telegraph* in 1918, but it was when she joined the staff of the Hearst-owned newspapers and magazines becoming motion picture editor of the *New York American* on November 19, 1923, that Parsons became a power broker. Born Elda Furry, Hedda Hopper took her name from one-time husband, actor De Wolf Hopper; she became a syndicated columnist in 1937 after a lengthy career as a minor screen actress, and was first published in the *Los Angeles Times* on February 14, 1938. Hopper continued to write a syndicated column for the *Times* and other newspapers until her death. After she became old and infirm, Louella Parson's column was taken over by her assistant, Dorothy Manners, on December 1, 1964.

Other syndicated gossip columnists active during the same period include Sheilah Graham, Sidney Skolsky, and Jimmy Starr. Later gossip columnists include Rona Barrett, Marilyn Beck, and Liz Smith (who is arguably the last major syndicated gossip columnist). *Daily Variety*'s gossip columnist, Army Archerd, has been writing a column since April 27, 1953. *The Hollywood Reporter* has published a number of gossip columns, including "Rambling Reporter," written by Hank Grant and later Robert Osborne, "Broadway Ballyhoo" by Radie Harris (who earlier wrote for *Variety*), and George Christy's "Great Life" column.

BIBLIOGRAPHY

Bacon, James. *Made in Hollywood.* Chicago: Contemporary Books, 1977.
Barrett, Rona. *Miss Rona.* Los Angeles: Nash Publishing, 1974.
Beck, Marilyn. *Marilyn Beck's Hollywood.* New York: Hawthorn Books, 1973.
Fairey, Wendy W. *One of the Family.* New York: W. W. Norton, 1992.
Graham, Sheilah. *The Rest of the Day.* New York: Coward-McCann, 1964.
———. *College of One.* London: Weidenfeld and Nicholson, 1966.
———. *The Late Lily Shiel.* New York: Grosset & Dunlap, 1978.
———. *Hollywood Revisited.* New York: St. Martin's Press, 1985.
Graham, Sheilah, and Gerold Frank. *Beloved Infidel: The Education of a Woman.* New York: Henry Holt, 1958.
Harris, Radie. *Radie's World: The Memoirs of Radie Harris.* New York: G. P. Putnam's Sons, 1975.
Hopper, Hedda. *From Under My Hat.* Garden City, N.Y.: Doubleday, 1952.
Hopper, Hedda, and James Brough. *The Whole Truth and Nothing But.* Garden City, N.Y.: Doubleday, 1963.
Muir, Florabel. *Headline Happy.* New York: Henry Holt, 1950.
Parsons, Louella O. *The Gay Illiterate.* Garden City, N.Y.: Doubleday, Doran, 1944.
———. *Tell It to Louella.* New York: G. P. Putnam's Sons, 1961.
Skolsky, Sidney. *Don't Get Me Wrong—I Love Hollywood.* New York: G. P. Putnam's Sons, 1975.
Wilson, Earl. *I Am Gazing into My 8-Ball.* Garden City, N.Y.: Doubleday, Doran, 1945.
———. *The Show Business Nobody Knows.* Chicago: Cowles, 1971.
———. *Show Business Laid Bare.* New York: G. P. Putnam's Sons, 1974.
———. *Hot Times: True Stories of Hollywood and Broadway.* Chicago: Contemporary Books, 1984.

RESOURCES

Papers: Academy of Motion Picture Arts and Sciences (Hedda Hopper, Louella Parsons, and Sidney Skolsky); Arizona State University (Jimmy Starr).

GOTHAM FILM COMPANY was incorporated on April 24, 1915, to produce and distribute its own and other companies' productions. It had a studio at 237 Lafayette Street in New York and offices at 1600 Broadway. Its first production, *The Man Who Beat Dan Dolan,* starred former lightweight boxing champion Willie Ritchie. Gotham soon contracted with Reel Photoplay Company to release its product on the Gotham program, with Reel's first production being *Love and the Pennant,* featuring baseball star Mike Donlin. Marshall W. Taggart was the president of Gotham.

"GOWER GULCH" was the nickname given to the area at the junction of Gower Street and Sunset Boulevard in Hollywood, where "cowboys" would gather both to socialize and to look for work in the film industry of the twenties. They gathered there much as Chicanos are drawn in the eighties to the intersection of Sepulveda and Pico boulevards in Los Angeles, seeking elusive employment. At the junction of Gower and Sunset stood the Century Studios, where many "B"* Western* productions were filmed, but by the thirties most Western production was centered in the San Fernando Valley.

GRACIE FILMS was formed in 1984 by James L. Brooks (born 1940), and is primarily noted for two television programs produced for the Fox network, *The Tracey Ullman Show* (1987–1990) and *The Simpsons* (first aired 1990). Its most prominent feature film is *Broadcast News* (1987). In 1990, Gracie Films signed a seven-year exclusive distribution deal with Columbia Pictures.

Address: 10202 West Washington Boulevard, Culver City, Calif. 90232.

GRANDEUR, also known as Fox Grandeur, was a widescreen system, utilizing 70mm* film, with a frame size 48mm by 22.5mm and a soundtrack 10mm wide. It was first exhibited at the Gaiety Theatre, New York, on September

17, 1929, with a scenic short on Niagara Falls, a Grandeur version of *Fox Movietone News,* and the feature *Fox Movietone Follies of 1929.* The system was developed by the Fox Film Corporation in association with Harley L. Clarke and his company, General Theatres Equipment, Inc. It was utilized for two further features, *Happy Days* (1929) and *The Big Trail* (1930), but due to the cost to theatres of installing new projectors and new screens (at a time when theatre owners had been forced to meet the cost of new sound equipment), it was not successful.

BIBLIOGRAPHY

Vischer, Peter. "Fox Grandeur Films Make New History at First Public Show." *Exhibitors Herald-World,* September 28, 1929, p. 19.

GRAND NATIONAL FILMS, INC., was organized on April 16, 1936, by former Pathé* executives and with Pathé financing. Its major coup, in the summer of 1936, was the signing of James Cagney, who was involved in a contract dispute with Warner Bros.* and who starred in two films for Grand National, *Great Guy* (1936) and *Something to Sing About* (1937). The company's first president was Edward L. Alperson and its first feature was *Devil on Horseback* (1936). Grand National began operations on the RKO-Pathé lot in Culver City but, in April 1937, took over the Educational Studios lot at 7250 Santa Monica Boulevard in Hollywood.

In 1938, Grand National was the subject of bankruptcy proceedings and reorganized as Grand National Pictures, Inc., with E. W. Hammons as the new president. Following continued financial problems, the company collapsed in 1940, and its assets were sold to Mohawk Film Corporation in March 1940. Grand National's trademark was always a clock tower with the company name on its face. It had no financial interest in the British production company, Grand National Pictures, Ltd.

BIBLIOGRAPHY

Fernett, Gene. *Poverty Row.* Satellite Beach, Fla.: Coral Reef Publications, 1973.
Okuda, Ted. *Grand National, Producers Releasing Corporation, and Screen Guild/Lippert: Complete Filmographies with Studio Histories.* Jefferson, North Carolina: McFarland, 1989.
Robison, Robert J. "A Short History of Grand National Pictures." *The Films of Yesteryear,* July 1977, entire issue.

GRAND NATIONAL PICTURES, INC. See GRAND NATIONAL FILMS, INC.

GRANTWOOD, NEW JERSEY. See LIFE PHOTO FILM CORPORATION

GRAPHIC FILM CORPORATION. After leaving Ivan Film Productions, Inc.*, which he founded and named after

himself, Ivan Abramson formed a new company, Graphic Film Corporation, on December 3, 1917, and became its president and director-general. Its first production was *Moral Suicide,* starring John Mason and Anna Luther. Gail Kane and Tallulah Bankhead also appeared in Graphic films. The company, whose offices were located at 729 Seventh Avenue, New York, existed until 1922.

BIBLIOGRAPHY

"Ivan Abramson Creates Own Firm." *The Moving Picture World,* December 22, 1917, p. 1812.

GRAUMAN'S THEATRES. Sidney Patrick Grauman (1879–1950) was, undoubtedly, Hollywood's best-known showman. He was noted for the prologues that accompanied feature films at his theatres from the latter half of the second decade of the twentieth century through the mid-thirties and for the handprints and footprints of the stars in the forecourt of his Chinese Theatre.

He began his theatrical career in the Yukon in the late 1890s. Prior to the San Francisco earthquake, he had opened the Unique Theatre there, and, immediately following the earthquake and fire, he opened a tent theatre, called the Canvas Theatre. Grauman opened a number of theatres in northern California and one in New York, and, by 1915, he was hailed as "one of the liveliest exhibitors on the Pacific Coast."

Sid Grauman opened his first Los Angeles theatre, the Million Dollar, on February 1, 1918, with the William S. Hart feature, *The Silent Man.* In 1919, he acquired the Rialto Theatre, also in downtown Los Angeles, and reopened it, on November 20, 1919, with the Gloria Swanson/Cecil B. DeMille film, *Male and Female.* A third downtown theatre, the Metropolitan, opened on January 26, 1923. These three theatres were all acquired, in 1924, by Paramount*.

The first of Grauman's two Hollywood theatres, the Egyptian, opened on October 18, 1922, with the premiere of *Robin Hood,* starring Douglas Fairbanks. The Egyptian was also the site of the first dual premiere—on May 14, 1926—of the Mary Pickford vehicle, *Sparrows,* and the Douglas Fairbanks feature, *The Black Pirate.* On October 27, 1926, Hollywood was introduced to the first commercial use of sound in a feature film, at the Egyptian, with the West Coast premiere of *Don Juan,* starring John Barrymore. The Chinese Theatre, located as is the Egyptian on Hollywood Boulevard, opened on May 19, 1927, with the world premiere of Cecil B. DeMille's *King of Kings.* The current owners of the Chinese opened two additional, adjacent theatres, the Chinese I and II, on April 12, 1979.

BIBLIOGRAPHY

Beardsley, Charles. *Hollywood's Master Showman.* New York: Cornwall Books, 1983.
Endres, Stacy, and Robert Cushman. *Hollywood at Your Feet: The Story of the World-Famous Chinese Theatre.* Los Angeles: Pomegranate Press, 1992.

GREAT AUTHORS' PICTURES, INC. Benjamin Hampton and George H. Perry formed Great Authors' Pictures, Inc., in February 1919, to produce adaptations of works by well-known authors. Its first production, *The Westerners,* was produced at the Robert Brunton Studios in Hollywood. The company made note of the fact that it would use no stars in its productions. The W. W. Hodkinson Corporation* distributed Great Authors' Pictures through Pathé exchanges*.

BIBLIOGRAPHY

"Hampton and Perry Form Great Authors' Pictures, Inc." *The Moving Picture World,* February 22, 1919, p. 1020.

"GREATER BRAY PICTOGRAPHS." See BRAY STUDIOS, INC.

GREATER NEW YORK FILM RENTAL COMPANY. See FOX FILM CORPORATION

"GREAT EVENTS" was a series of dramatic short subjects, produced in color by the Technicolor Corporation* and released by M-G-M*: *The Flag* (1927), directed by Arthur Maude and starring Francis X. Bushman (as Washington) and Enid Bennett (as Betsy Ross); *The Lady of the Victories* (1927), directed by William R. Neill and starring Otto Matiesen and Agnes Ayres (as Napoleon and Josephine); *The Virgin Queen* (1928), directed by Roy William Neill and starring Dorothy Dwan (as Elizabeth I); *Madame Du Barry* (1928), directed by William Dieterle and starring Priscilla Dean (in the title role); *The Czarina's Secret* (1928), directed by Roy William Neill and starring Olga Baclanova (as Catherine II of Russia); *Cleopatra* (1928), directed by Roy William Neill and starring Dorothy Revier (in the title role); *Victorious Defeat* (1928), directed by Roy William Neill and starring Barney Sherry (as Robert E. Lee); *Frontier Romance* (1929), directed by Elmer Clifton and starring Allan Simpson (as George Rogers Clark); *Light of India* (1929), directed by Elmer Clifton and starring Harold Goodwin (as Captain Jack Dunlap); *Manchu Love* (1929), directed by Elmer Clifton and starring Sojin (as Su Shun) and Etta Lee (as the Empress Tzu Hsi); and *A Princess of Destiny* (1929), directed by Tom Terriss and starring Anders Randolph (as Henry VIII) and Doris Lloyd (as Anne Boleyn).

GREAT NORTHERN FILM COMPANY, located in Copenhagen, Denmark, claimed that it was the first concern to introduce a feature-length film in the United States when it released the three-reel *Temptations of a Great City* in the early spring of 1911. O. Olsen was the president, and Ingvald C. Oes was the American representative. In 1913, its product was distributed in the United States by Universal*. Charles (Feature) Abrams was the company's American manager at that time. In 1914, it released its product through the Exclusive Supply Corporation*. In 1915, it produced a series called "Polar Bear Features," which were selected to meet the demands of the American public.

BIBLIOGRAPHY

Bergsten, Bebe. *The Great Dane and the Great Northern Film Company.* Los Angeles: Locare Research Group, 1973.

GREAT WESTERN PRODUCING COMPANY. See CENTURY COMEDIES

GREENAWAY PRODUCTIONS. See RAMPART PRODUCTIONS, INC.

GREENWICH STUDIO CITY. See IVAN TORS STUDIO

GRIP is the name given to a stagehand who works closely with the film crew, moving equipment, and so named because he needed a strong grip. The first grip to receive screen credit was Morris Rosen, the boom and dolly operator on Alfred Hitchcock's *Rope* (1948); according to *The Hollywood Reporter* (July 2, 1948), "Hitchcock decided he was entitled to it for plotting as many as 30 camera movements in a single shot."

GROSSES. A film's gross is the amount it accrues in rentals from individual theatres or theatre chains. A theatre's gross is the amount it accrues in box office receipts. Each year, *International Motion Picture Almanac* publishes a listing, from 1942, of U.S. box office receipts in relation to personal consumption expenditures. Each January, in its anniversary issue, *Variety* publishes a listing of the "Big Rental Films" of the previous year and a listing of the "All-Time Film Rental Champs," with total rentals for every film included.

GROSSMONT, CALIFORNIA. See MONROVIA FEATURE FILM COMPANY

GROUP PRODUCTIONS. See CHAS. K. FELDMAN's GROUP PRODUCTIONS

GUARANTEED PICTURES COMPANY, INC., was organized in 1918 by Mortimer D. Sackett (died 1965) and Samuel Goldstein (1897–1950). The New York-based company specialized in the distribution of reissues and the import of European features. In 1938, it created Commonwealth Pictures for 16mm and nontheatrical releases, and a television division, Commonwealth Film & TV, Inc., was formed in 1947. The company ceased operation in 1974.

GULF + WESTERN INDUSTRIES, INC., was founded in 1958 by Charles G. Bludhorn (1927–1983) as a

Michigan-based auto parts company. It became a major U.S. conglomerate, whose Entertainment and Communications Group controlled Madison Square Garden, Paramount Pictures* (which it acquired in 1966), *Esquire* magazine, and the publishing houses of Simon & Schuster and Prentice-Hall. On April 7, 1989, its board decided to change the corporate name to Paramount Communications, Inc., and it was that company that was acquired by Viacom* on July 7, 1994.

HALLMARK PICTURES CORPORATION. In September 1919, the Hallmark Pictures Corporation was formed, representing a merger of Frank G. Hall's enterprises, which included Film Clearing House, Independent Sales Corporation, Film Finance Corporation, Hobart Henley Productions, Inc., and Charles Miller Productions, Inc. Hallmark planned to release 26 films per year in its "Famous Directors' Pictures" series, which were to be booked by exhibitors on one contract, allowing the exhibitor to view the film before booking and to cancel the contract after two pictures. Hallmark also planned to release 12 films from the British-American Finance Corporation and 12 special features per year. Its first release was the serial *The Trail of the Octopus.* Hallmark took over Triangle* Distributing Corporation in 1920, and was itself taken over by Robertson-Cole* at the end of the same year.

BIBLIOGRAPHY

"Hallmark Merges Hall's Interests." *The Moving Picture World,* September 6, 1919, p. 1500.

HALLMARK PRODUCTIONS, INC., was organized in 1945 by veteran Ohio showman Kroger Babb (1907–1980) to produce and release exploitation films*, features that he described as "Triple-E Presentations: Enlightenment, Education, Entertainment." Hallmark's first release was *Mom and Dad,* filmed by Babb's Hygenic Productions, which dealt, among other things, with childbirth, and was screened before segregated male and female audiences. In 1948, Hallmark filmed a version of the Passion Play, *Prince of Peace,* in Lawton, Oklahoma. Other Hallmark productions—dates for which are obscure—included *Half-Way to Hell, One Too Many, Monika: The Story of a Bad Girl, She Shoulda Said No,* and *Walk the Walk.* Hallmark also released, in 1972, a German version of *Uncle Tom's Cabin.* The company's headquarters were initially located in Wilmington, Ohio, but Hallmark eventually moved to Los Angeles.

BIBLIOGRAPHY

Turan, Kenneth. "You've Got to Tell 'Em to Sell 'Em Said Kroger Babb, and Did He Sell 'Em." *The Washington Post,* August 1, 1977, pp. B1, B3.

RESOURCES

Papers: Academy of Motion Picture Arts and Sciences (Kroger Babb Collection).

HAL ROACH STUDIOS, INC. Hal Roach (1892–1992) entered the film industry in 1912 and by 1915 had formed his own company, the Rolin Film Company, with a partner, Dan Linthicum, to produce Harold Lloyd one-reel comedies under the series name of "Phun-Philms." In 1919, Roach formed Hal Roach Studios and built his own production facility at 8822 West Washington Boulevard in Culver City. Here, Roach produced the comedies that made him a household name, with a stable of stars that included Harold Lloyd, Laurel and Hardy, Charley Chase, Our Gang, Thelma Todd and Patsy Kelly, and Will Rogers.

As historian Leonard Maltin has commented, "Probably no producer's work has brought the world more laughter than that of movie producer Hal Roach." However, the Hal Roach Studios were responsible not only for comedy shorts and features but also for feature-length dramas, such as *Captain Fury* (1939), *Of Mice and Men* (1939), and *One Million Years B.C.* (1940).

During the Second World War, the Hal Roach Studios were leased to the U.S. government for the production of training films and became known as Fort Roach. Hal Roach appeared to lose interest in film production after the war, and his studios were rented out for the shooting of features such as *Joan of Arc* (1948). The studios became the first major production center to become actively involved in television production in 1948, and among the series filmed there were *My Little Margie, The Life of Riley, Oh Susannah,* and *Amos 'n' Andy.*

Hal Roach entered semiretirement in 1955, and his studios were taken over by his son, Hal Roach, Jr. (1921–1972). In May 1958, Roach's stock was acquired by the Scranton Corporation, and a year later—in April 1959—the studio was closed when Scranton asked for federal receivership. On December 20, 1962, the 15-acre studios were sold, for $1,326,000, to Ponty-Fenmore Realty Fund, which renamed them the Landmark Studios and promised that they would be renovated. However, the contents of the studio were put up for public auction on August 1, 1963, and in September of the same year the studios were demolished.

When the original company was reorganized, following its bankruptcy, it became Hal Roach Studios, Inc., a Toronto-based organization with which Hal Roach had no association. The new company co-produced *The Groundstar Conspiracy* (1972), *Starship Invasions* (1978), and *Children of the Corn* (1984), among other films, and was chiefly involved in the exploitation of the colorization* process. In

1980, it merged with RHI Entertainment, Inc.*, to form Quintex Entertainment, Inc.

BIBLIOGRAPHY
Everson, William K. *The Films of Hal Roach.* New York: Museum of Modern Art, 1971.
Slide, Anthony. "Hal Roach on Film Comedy: An Interview." *The Silent Picture,* no. 6, Spring 1970, pp. 3–7.

RESOURCES
Papers: University of Southern California.

HANNA-BARBERA PRODUCTIONS was formed in 1957 by William Hanna (born 1911) and Joseph Barbera (born 1905). The two men had joined M-G-M* in 1937 and are generally considered the creative force behind that studio's "Tom and Jerry" cartoons. Before setting up their own animated production company, Hanna and Barbera had, in 1955, become joint heads of the cartoon department at M-G-M.

Hanna-Barbera claims to be the "world's largest producer of family entertainment" for television, with its highly successful animated and live-action series and specials. Among its best-known series are *Huckleberry Hound* (1958–1962), *Yogi Bear* (1960–1962), *The Flintstones* (1960–1966 and 1979–1980), *Shazzam* (1967–1968), *The Smurfs* (1981 to present) and *Pac-Man* (1982–1984). Its features and movies for television included *A Man Called Flintstone* (1966), *Charlotte's Web* (1973), *The Gathering* (1977), and *Heidi's Song* (1982). The company's animated subjects are chiefly known for their inexpensive methods of production, which usually ignore the details to be found in cartoons from Hollywood's golden age of animation. Hanna-Barbera's first television series was *Ruff and Ready*, aired on NBC from 1957 to 1960. In December 1967, the company was acquired by Taft Broadcasting Company, but Hanna and Barbera remained with the company, with Barbera as president and Hanna as senior vice president. In December 1991, Turner Broadcasting System, Inc., and the Apollo Investment Fund purchased Hanna-Barbera for $320 million; David Kirschner, who had been the company's CEO, was named president of the production division. In December 1993, Turner acquired Apollo's stake in the company. Following the acquisition of Turner by Time Warner*, as of November 1996, oversight of Hanna-Barbera was the responsibility of the president of Warner Bros. Television Animation. Since 1993, Hanna-Barbera has sponsored a "Storyboard Talent Search" for young, amateur animators.

Address: 3400 Cahuenga Boulevard, Hollywood, Calif. 90068.

BIBLIOGRAPHY
Lenberg, Jeff. "Hanna and Barbera." In *The Great Cartoon Directors.* Jefferson, N.C.: McFarland, 1983.
Street, Rita. "H-B Is Sharing Its Initiatives Literally." *Daily Variety,* March 22, 1996, pp. A18, A20.

HARMAN-ISING. Hugh Harman (1903–1982) and Rudolf Ising (1903–1992) first became partners in 1923 in Kansas City, 1992 where earlier Harman had worked for the young Walt Disney. It was Disney who brought the pair to Los Angeles, where, in 1929, Harman-Ising was formed to produce animated shorts for release through Warner Bros.* The first cartoon from the new company was *Sinkin' in the Bathtub* (1930), featuring Bosko. For Warner Bros., Harman-Ising created "Looney Tunes" and "Merrie Melodies," which became the studio's best-known cartoon series. In 1934, Harman-Ising left Warner Bros. for M-G-M*, for which they worked as independent producers until 1938, when the Harman-Ising unit became a wholly owned M-G-M company. In 1941, Harman formed Hugh Harman Productions, and Ising became involved in government film production. As late as 1958, Harman-Ising was revived and signed a co-production agreement with Toei Motion Picture Company of Japan.

BIBLIOGRAPHY
McCaskill, Marney. "Harman-Ising." In *The Film Daily Cavalcade,* New York: The Film Daily, 1939, p. 302.

THE HAROLD LLOYD FILM CORPORATION was founded in 1924 by the comedian (1893–1971), with William R. Fraser as secretary and general manager and John L. Murphy as production manager. The company retained office space and filmed at the Hollywood General Studios*. Its first production was *Girl Shy* (1924), followed by *Hot Water* (1924), *The Freshman* (1925), *For Heaven's Sake* (1926), *The Kid Brother* (1927), *Speedy* (1928), *Welcome Danger* (1929), *Feet First* (1930), *Movie Crazy* (1932), and *The Cat's Paw* (1934). Paramount* financed its production of *The Milky Way* (1936) and *Professor Beware* (1938). The corporation became inactive in 1939.

BIBLIOGRAPHY
D'Agostino, Annette M. *Harold Lloyd: A Bio-Bibliography.* Westport, Conn.: Greenwood Press, 1994.

HARRY RAVER, INC. See RAVER FILM CORPORATION

HARVEY ENTERTAINMENT CO. was founded in New York in 1939 by three brothers, Alfred, Leon, and Robert Harvey, who owned the comic-book rights to Casper the Friendly Ghost and Baby Huey, and who later created Richie Rich, Hot Stuff, and others. In July 1989, the company was acquired by a young entrepreneur, Jeffrey Montgomery (born 1964). He revived the failing organization, renamed it Harvey Entertainment Co., and began exploiting the company-owned characters in television series. He also sold 20 percent of Harvey Entertainment Co. in 1990 to MCA*, which, in 1995, released the feature-length *Casper.* In June 1993, the company went public.

Address: 1919 Avenue of the Stars, Suite 2050, Los Angeles, Calif. 90067.

BIBLIOGRAPHY

Krieger, Todd. "Yes, the Movie's Opening, But His Mind's on T-Shirts." *New York Times,* December 18, 1994, p. F10.

Natale, Richard. "Friendly Takeover." *Los Angeles Times,* May 26, 1995, pp. D1, D4.

O'Brien, Timothy L. "Casper Will Fly Again—Or So Small Company Hopes." *Wall Street Journal,* September 19, 1994, pp. B1, B2.

Schmuckler, Eric. "Ghost of a Chance." *The Hollywood Reporter,* August 8, 1995, pp. S14–S15.

HAWORTH PICTURES CORPORATION. See ROBERTSON-COLE COMPANY

HEARST-METROTONE NEWS. See NEWSREELS

HEARST-PATHÉ NEWS. See NEWSREELS

THE HEARST-SELIG NEWS PICTORIAL. See NEWSREELS

HECHT-HILL-LANCASTER was one of the major independent film production companies of the late fifties, founded in December 1956 by producer Harold Hecht, screenwriter-director James Hill, and actor Burt Lancaster, as an extension of the former Hecht-Lancaster company, founded a couple of years earlier. In *The New York Times* (January 6, 1958), Thomas M. Pryor wrote, "Its principal assets are ownership in film negatives, ownership of literary properties and the fact that it has first call on Mr. Lancaster's services as an actor." Throughout its life, Lancaster also worked independently of the company. Hecht and Hill did not, but, in the spring of 1959, all three partners began to take on personal projects outside of their corporate productions, and by the summer of that same year Hecht-Hill-Lancaster had been effectively dismantled as a production operation. With headquarters in Beverly Hills, California, the company released its features through United Artists*, among which were *Sweet Smell of Success* (1957), *Run Silent, Run Deep* (1958), *Separate Tables* (1958), *The Devil's Disciple* (1959), and *Take a Giant Step* (1959).

HECHT-LANCASTER. See HECHT-HILL-LANCASTER

HECTOR FILM CORPORATION, formed in mid-1914 by Hector J. Streyckmans, made five-reel features, starring Beulah Poynter and directed by Wray Physioc.

HEDWIG FILM LABORATORIES. See CONSOLIDATED FILM INDUSTRIES

HELICOPTER SHOTS. Although aerial photography dates back to the second decade of the twentieth century, the first use of a helicopter for filming was by cinematographer Paul Ivano in 1947, utilizing a Mitchell camera, for RKO's *They Live by Night* (1948).

BIBLIOGRAPHY

Lacy, Madison S. "The First Helicopter Used." *International Photographer,* vol. 47, no. 8, August 1975, pp. 8–9, 21–22.

HEMISPHERE PICTURES, INC., was a poverty row* production company, founded by Kane Lynn. Its first film was *The Raiders of the Leyte Gulf* (1963) and its last, *Mysteries of the Gods* (1977).

BIBLIOGRAPHY

Ray, Fred Olen. *The New Poverty Row: Independent Filmmakers as Distributors.* Jefferson, N.C.: McFarland, 1991.

HERALD PICTURES, INC., was founded by Jack Goldberg in 1946 to produce musicals and other films with Negro casts "which have registered favorably in night clubs and bands." Its first two productions were *Boy! What a Girl* (1946) and *Sepia Cinderella* (1947). A subsidiary company, Federal Studios, Inc., was created late in 1946.

HIRLICOLOR was a two-color process, which did not require additional lighting during the shooting process and which could be developed at any color film laboratory, patented by Hollywood producer and entrepreneur George Hirliman in 1936. Hirliman was associated with Consolidated Film Industries* and his color process was later called Magnacolor.

BIBLIOGRAPHY

"Hirliman to Patent a New Color Process." *Motion Picture Herald,* March 28, 1936, p. 66.

HISTORICAL FILM COMPANY was a production company located in New York and London, formed, in April 1913, to produce three- and four-reel historical scenarios written by Edward S. Ellis for the open market and states rights* exchanges. Eustache Hale Bennett was the general manager and Garfield Thompson the director. The New York offices were located at One Madison Avenue and the studio was on East 23d Street. In addition to producing features, Historical planned to make educational films with eastern universities, government films, and industrial subjects.

HOFFBERG PRODUCTIONS, a New York-based producer/distributor of minor films and foreign imports was founded by Jack H. Hoffberg (1895–1969) in 1924 as the J. H. Hoffberg Company. It changed its name in 1940, and ceased operations in 1970. The film assets were acquired by Raymond Rohauer.

HOLLAND FILM MANUFACTURING COMPANY, located at 105 Lawrence Avenue in the Roxbury district of Boston, claimed to be the first motion picture production company in the city. Organized in October 1914 by Herbert B. Holland, the company acquired the services of director William F. Haddock, formerly with Edison*, Eclair*, and All-Star*, who produced the one-reel *Mary Jane's Burglar,* written by and starring Maude Fealy. In February 1915, the company went bankrupt, and its assets, including the above-mentioned film and five others, were sold at public auction.

BIBLIOGRAPHY

"Maude Fealy Starring for Hub Company." *The Moving Picture World,* October 24, 1914, p. 469.

HOLLYWOOD. The July 1927 issue of *Hi-Hat,* published "for the Hollywood Country Gentleman," came up with a number of still applicable definitions for Hollywood: "Not a place but a mental assumption. . . . Hollywood isn't a place; it's a condition of mind. . . . Hollywood isn't a town. It's a national obsession."

Hollywood came into existence in 1886, when Harvey Wilcox purchased a tract of land, which his wife named Hollywood because she liked the sound of it. There are no woods and no holly in Hollywood. The community first became known as the residence of French-born painter Paul DeLongpre (who moved there in 1901). Hollywood became a city in 1903, but it was annexed by Los Angeles in 1910. The Hollywood Hotel (1902–1956), which lent its name to Louella Parsons's popular radio program, was the city's best-known landmark; other notable Hollywood institutions include the Hollywood Bowl (which opened in 1920), the Brown Derby (1929–1985), Grauman's Chinese Theatre*, and the Griffith Park Observatory (opened 1935).

Despite being synonymous with the motion picture industry, Hollywood had only three major studios ever located in its geographic area—Columbia*, Paramount*, and RKO*—and, today, only Paramount remains. However, many smaller independent and rental studios were, and continue to be, situated in Hollywood.

Today, Hollywood consists of 1,700 acres, bounded, approximately, by Western Avenue, La Brea Avenue, Franklin Avenue, and Santa Monica Boulevard. The postal code for the Hollywood post office is 90028. It has a population of 140,000, many of whom are foreign-born and can be defined as low-earning, working class. The community has declined in recent years and has become increasingly known for prostitution—both female and male—drug-related crimes, and as a basically unsafe neighborhood.

Hollywood's Santa Claus Parade, held the first Sunday af-ter Thanksgiving, is widely televised. Hollywood is the home of three major legitimate theatres—the Pantages (opened as a movie theatre, June 4, 1930), the Henry Fonda, and the Huntington Hartford—and of two major hotels—the Holiday Inn and the Dolittle. (Former important Hollywood hotels were the Plaza, the Knickerbocker, and the Christie.) Its major thoroughfare, Hollywood Boulevard—famous for the Hollywood Walk of Fame*—was initially known as Prospect Avenue. Aside from Grauman's theatres, the most historically important of film theatres in Hollywood is the Warner Theatre, on Hollywood Boulevard, which opened on April 26, 1928, with *Glorious Betsy,* and had a seating capacity of 2,742; it closed in 1994.

BIBLIOGRAPHY

Alleman, Richard. *The Movie Lover's Guide to Hollywood.* New York: Harper and Row, 1985.
Cini, Zelda, and Bob Crane. *Hollywood, Land and Legend.* Westport, Conn.: Arlington House, 1980.
Friedrich, Otto. *City of Nets: A Portrait of Hollywood in the 1940s.* New York: Harper and Row, 1986.
Lamparski, Richard. *Lamparski's Hidden Hollywood.* New York: Simon and Schuster, 1981.
Palmer, Edwin O. *History of Hollywood.* Los Angeles: Arthur H. Cawston, 1937.
Thomas, Bob. *The Heart of Hollywood.* New York: Berkeley Publishing, 1994.
Torrence, Bruce. *Hollywood: The First 100 Years.* Hollywood, Calif. : Hollywood Chamber of Commerce, 1979.

HOLLYWOOD ANTI-NAZI LEAGUE came about as a result of the efforts of Prince Hubestus zu Loewenstein, the former leader of the German Center Party, who hosted a dinner in Hollywood in April of 1936, at which plans for the League were formulated by Dorothy Parker, Donald Ogden Stewart, Fritz Lang, Fredric March, and Oscar Hammerstein. The League was officially organized on July 23, 1936. It fought fascism through rallies, demonstrations, and picketing of the German consulate. In the late thirties, the Hollywood Anti-Nazi League was denounced as a Communist front organization by the Dies Committee*. It was dissolved when the United States entered the Second World War.

HOLLYWOOD CANTEEN. Inspired by New York's Stage Door Canteen and cofounded by Bette Davis, John Garfield, J. K. (Spike) Wallace, and Carroll Hollister, the Hollywood Canteen was a "home away from home" for servicemen during the Second World War. There, the stars entertained, provided meals, washed dishes, and contributed in any way possible toward the well-being of the men and women in uniform. Only two major Hollywood stars—Charlie Chaplin and Greta Garbo—failed to participate. The Hollywood Canteen opened, in a building that had formerly been a little theatre and a livery stable, at 1451 North Cahuenga Boulevard, in Hollywood, on October 17, 1942. It closed on November 22, 1945. Warner

Bros.* produced the 1944 feature *Hollywood Canteen* to raise funds for the organization's work.

Following its closure, the Hollywood Canteen Foundation was established to supervise and distribute the large amount of money that the Canteen had accrued. The Foundation continues its charitable work through the present, and the Hollywood Canteen continues to exist, to a certain extent, as the Bob Hope USO (at 1641 Ivar Avenue in Hollywood). The building that housed the Hollywood Canteen was demolished in 1966.

HOLLYWOOD COORDINATING COMMITTEE. See HOLLYWOOD VICTORY COMMITTEE

THE HOLLYWOOD DEMOCRATIC COMMITTEE was organized in late 1942 to promote the reelection of Culbert Olson as governor of California. It changed its name in June 1945 to the Hollywood Independent Citizens Committee of the Arts, Sciences, and Professions, and on June 27, 1945, it presented the play, *The American Caravan,* starring Bette Davis, Danny Kaye, Edward G. Robinson, and Orson Welles, in support of the United Nations. It was branded a Communist front organization by the extreme right wing in Hollywood, and disbanded in 1947.

THE HOLLYWOOD FILM & BROADCAST LABOR COUNCIL was created in September 1989 with the merger of the Hollywood Film Council (founded 1946) and the Hollywood Broadcast Labor Council (formed 1978). The new organization coordinates the activities of the various film and television unions.

HOLLYWOOD FILM ENTERPRISES, INC., founded in 1907, is the oldest operating film laboratory in the United States. In the eighties, it changed its name to Hollywood Film & Video, Inc.

Address: 6060 Sunset Boulevard, Hollywood, Calif. 90028.

HOLLYWOOD FOREIGN CORRESPONDENTS ASSOCIATION. See HOLLYWOOD FOREIGN PRESS ASSOCIATION, INC.

HOLLYWOOD FOREIGN PRESS ASSOCIATION, INC., was formed in October 1943 as the Hollywood Foreign Correspondents Association, with William Mooring as its first president. The Association presented its first awards in 1944 and two years later introduced the Golden Globes, the name by which its awards ceremony became known. In 1950, a disagreement broke out within the organization, and it split into two, the Hollywood Foreign Correspondents Association and the Foreign Press Association of Hollywood. The former continued to present the Golden Globes, while the latter awarded Henriettas, named after its president, Henry Gris.

The two groups rejoined in October of 1955, and the new Hollywood Foreign Press Association was created. It

is an organization of professional journalists and photographers who cover Hollywood film and television production for various foreign publications. The membership, which never drops or increases much beyond 75, is open to anyone who can document their work as a foreign-film correspondent. The organization has been embroiled in considerable controversy through the years, both in terms of the makeup of its membership and the presentation of its awards. However, thanks to the televising of the Golden Globes, the Hollywood Foreign Press Association has been able to make donations of $140,000 a year to a variety of industry organizations, including the American Film Institute*, the Motion Picture and Television Fund*, and various AIDS-related charities. Because of a 1996 grant, it became official sponsor of the Sundance Film Festival.

In April 1996, a breakaway group, the International Press Academy, was founded, headed by former Hollywood Foreign Press Association president, Marijana Van Blaricom.

Address: 292 South La Cienega Boulevard, Suite 316, Los Angeles, Calif. 90211.

BIBLIOGRAPHY

Borie, Marcia. "Golden Globes Growth Great." *The Hollywood Reporter,* January 30, 1976, p. 28.
Grant, Lee. "Foreign Press: See How They Work." *Los Angeles Times,* Calendar, January 25, 1981, pp. 1, 6–7.
Nugent, John Peer. "And in the Category 'Most Curious Awards Show,' the Winner Is . . . " *Los Angeles,* January 1978, pp. 60–68.
Willman, Chris. "Beyond the Buffet Table." *California,* March 1991, pp. 58–61.

THE HOLLYWOOD FOR ROOSEVELT COMMITTEE was part of the industry's 1944 presidential campaign; it was chaired by Jack L. Warner, Katharine Hepburn, and Samuel Goldwyn, and its members included Ronald Reagan, Edward G. Robinson, and Gene Kelly.

HOLLYWOOD GENERAL STUDIOS, a studio with many names, was built in the spring of 1919 by architect John Jasper (who was also responsible for the Chaplin Studios*) as a "unitized" studio. In other words, it offered office space and a production space for four filmmaking units. The first producers to move on to the lot were Marshall Neilan and Hunt Stromberg, followed, in 1921, by Harold Lloyd.

Al Christie acquired the studio in 1925 and renamed it the Hollywood Metropolitan Studios. Also in the twenties, Howard Hughes moved his production company to the lot. When Al Christie's company went into receivership, following the Wall Street crash, the studio was taken over, in 1932, by Eastern Service (a division of Electrical Research Products*) and renamed General Service Studios. It was utilized as a rental studio by both Paramount* and United Artists*, and among those filming there were Walter Wanger, Edward Small*, Mae West, Bing Crosby, and Gary Cooper.

In 1947, the studio changed hands again, when it was purchased by James and George Nasser and renamed the Hollywood General Studios. Several production companies, including United Artists, Benedict Bogeaus, James Cagney, Sam Bischoff, Hunt Stromberg, Charles R. Rogers, Golden Productions, and Hopalong Cassidy Productions, remained on the lot. In 1978, Glenn Speidel and Ellison Miles, with their Esquire Holding Co., purchased the lot, and in 1980, it changed hands again, when Francis Ford Coppola took over Speidel's mortgage and renamed the studio Zoetrope*.

At a bankruptcy auction in 1984, the studio was purchased for $12.3 million by Canadian investor Jack Singer, who set up his office in Harold Lloyd's original studio bungalow. Singer renamed the lot Hollywood Studio Center. One of the oldest tenants on the lot was George Burns, who had maintained an office there since the early fifties and in whose honor, in 1979, Stage One was dedicated as the George Burns Stage, in honor of George Burns, who maintained an office on the lot from the fifties until his death in 1996. Originally 15 acres, the studio now occupies some 10.5 acres.

Address: 1040 North Las Palmas Avenue, Hollywood, Calif. 90038.

BIBLIOGRAPHY

Farley, Ellen. "Canadian Investor Turns to Films." *Los Angeles Times,* business section, May 14, 1984, pp. 1, 5.

HOLLYWOOD METROPOLITAN STUDIOS. See HOLLYWOOD GENERAL STUDIOS

HOLLYWOOD MUSEUM. A museum devoted to the history of film and television and located in Hollywood has long been a dream of many in the industry. Through the enthusiasm of Sol Lesser, the Los Angeles County Board of Supervisors unanimously voted to created such a museum on June 16, 1959. The Board appointed an interim commission, headed by Lesser, and approved a site for the museum across from the Hollywood Bowl on Highland Avenue. Groundbreaking for the new museum took place on October 20, 1963, with Rosalind Russell, Jack L. Warner, Walt Disney, and Gene Autry among the celebrities present.

In the meantime, the County of Los Angeles began acquiring property standing on the proposed museum site through the expediency of condemnation. One of the homes condemned was that of a former marine, Steve E. Anthony, located at 6655 Alta Loma Terrace. Anthony fought the county, first with legal action and eventually by refusal to move. The former marine's fight created a considerable amount of negative publicity for the museum, particularly when the house was seized on April 13, 1964, as Anthony and approximately 100 demonstrators battled with police.

In December 1964, the Board of Supervisors froze funding for the museum amidst criticism that the museum was a private institution and should not be funded with taxpapers' money. Sol Lesser urged, unsuccessfully, that the film and television industry raise the $5 million needed, and, ultimately, in August 1965, resigned as chairman of the commission.

The site for the museum became a parking lot for the Hollywood Bowl, and the many artifacts collected were housed by the Los Angeles City Recreation and Parks Department in Lincoln Heights Jail. The city refused to return donations and insisted that all artifacts could be displayed only in a museum situated in the geographic area of Hollywood. Many plans for a new Hollywood Museum were formulated by Debbie Reynolds, the Hollywood Chamber of Commerce, Jane Withers, and others, but to no avail. In 1981, the city agreed that all paper materials donated to the Museum should be given on a 25-year loan to the Academy of Motion Picture Arts and Sciences*, the American Film Institute*, the University of California at Los Angeles, and the University of Southern California.

From 1984 to 1986, a privately funded Hollywood Museum, chiefly utilizing costumes from the John LeBold collection, was opened on Hollywood Boulevard.

BIBLIOGRAPHY

Elvenstar, Diane. "The Hollywood Museum Fades to Black." *Los Angeles Magazine,* September 1981, pp. 148–56.
Luft, Herbert G. "Hollywood's Museum." *Films in Review,* February 1962, pp. 65–70.
Miller, Jonathan. "A Museum for Hollywood: At Long Last?" *Los Angeles Times,* Calendar, September 23, 1984, pp. 18–22.

HOLLYWOOD PICTURES was formed in 1989 by the Walt Disney* organization as an independent production arm within the company, creating films that would be not appropriate to the Disney image.

Address: 500 South Buena Vista Street, Burbank, Calif. 91521.

THE "HOLLYWOOD" SIGN is probably the best known and most enduring of Hollywood landmarks. It was erected in 1923, at which time it read "Hollywoodland," to promote a real estate development on Beechwood Canyon. The sign was placed on land that was originally owned by Mack Sennett (and is now owned by the City of Los Angeles) on top of Mount Lee. It cost $21,000 to build, with each letter 30 feet wide and 50 feet tall, and each of the letters was studded with 20-watt electric light bulbs.

Stage actress Peg Entwistle, who had come to Hollywood with an RKO* contract, committed suicide by jumping from the "H" of the sign on September 16, 1932. Maintenance of the sign was ended in 1939, and it was severely damaged by vandals. After threats from the city that it would be demolished, the sign was restored by the Hollywood Chamber of Commerce in 1949, at which time it was shortened to read simply "Hollywood." Vandalism continued to plague the sign, as did the ravages of the weather. It was declared a Historic-Cultural Monument in 1973. Eventually, through private donations, a new "Hollywood" sign was erected and officially unveiled on November 11, 1978.

BIBLIOGRAPHY

Reed, Rochelle. "Hollywood Has a New Act." *California,* November 1977, pp. 94–99, 106–7, 111.

Robinson, C. E., and Bruce T. Torrence. *The Hollywood Sign.* Hollywood, Calif.: First Federal Savings and Loan Association of Hollywood, 1976.

Simross, Lynn. "Hullywood [*sic*] Sign Broken—and Broke." *Los Angeles Times,* part 4, December 28, 1977, pp. 1, 6.

HOLLYWOOD STUDIO CENTER. See HOLLYWOOD GENERAL STUDIOS

HOLLYWOOD STUDIO CLUB was founded in 1916, at the suggestion of librarian Eleanor Jones, by the Young Women's Christian Association (YWCA) to provide low-cost housing for young women trying to enter the film industry. It was originally located at 6129 Carlos Avenue in Hollywood. A new building, at 1215 Lodi Place, was erected in 1926, with funds raised by Mrs. Cecil B. DeMille and others. Sponsored by the Motion Picture Producers Association and run by the YWCA, the Club was organized along the lines of a sorority house. By 1953, a reported 8,000 women had been residents there, among whom were Marilyn Monroe, Barbara Hale, Donna Reed, Helen Jerome Eddy, Evelyn Keyes, Linda Darnell, and ZaSu Pitts. The Club closed in February 1975.

BIBLIOGRAPHY

Crivello, Kirk. "The Hollywood Studio Club." *Film Fan Monthly,* no. 127, January 1972, pp. 25–29.

Muir, Jean. "Boardinghouse of Broken Hearts." *The Saturday Evening Post,* September 19, 1953, pp. 41, 135–38.

Simross, Lynn. "Studio Club Closes Doors on Memories." *Los Angeles Times,* View section, February 9, 1975, pp. 1, 18–20.

Smith, Bradley. "Gateway to Glamor," *Collier's,* March 9, 1946, pp. 22–23.

THE HOLLYWOOD TEN were Alvah Bessie (1904–1985), Herbert Biberman (1900–1971), Lester Cole (1905–1985), Edward Dmytryk born in 1908, Ring Lardner, Jr. born in 1915, John Howard Lawson (1894–1977), Albert Maltz (1908–1985), Samuel Ornitz (1891–1957), Adrian Scott (1912–1973), and Dalton Trumbo (1905–1976). The majority of these writers or directors were minor figures in the film industry who achieved a fame that would not have been theirs had not history placed them in a unique and tragic position. The Hollywood Ten were also dubbed the Unfriendly Ten, and

it was Billy Wilder who joked, "Of the Unfriendly Ten, only two had any talent, the other eight were just unfriendly."

These men, along with Bertolt Brecht, appeared before the House Un-American Activities Committee in the fall of 1947. All refused to answer questions concerning Communist affiliations put to them by the Committee. Brecht fled the country the day following his inquest, but the remaining ten were voted in contempt by Congress on November 24, 1947. They were tried in federal court the following year and found guilty, with each being sentenced to a year in jail and a thousand-dollar fine. In the spring of 1950, the U.S. Supreme Court refused to review the convictions, and the ten went to prison (although Dmytryk later agreed to cooperate with the Committee and was released prior to serving his entire sentence). The wives of the Hollywood Ten published a 4-page pamphlet titled *For Justice and Peace,* and Gale Sondergaard (Biberman's wife) and Albert Maltz published a 14-page pamphlet, *On the Eve of Prison.*

With the exception of Dmytryk, the group was blacklisted by the film community and could gain work only by utilizing pseudonyms. The best known of such pseudonyms was "Robert Rich," used by Dalton Trumbo, under which he won an Academy Award for Best Screenplay for *The Brave One* (1956). *See also* Communism.

BIBLIOGRAPHY

Cole, Lester. *Hollywood Red.* Palo Alto, Calif.: Ramparts Press, 1982.

Dick, Bernard F. *Radical Innocence: A Critical Study of the Hollywood Ten.* Lexington, Kentucky: University Press of Kentucky, 1989.

Keerdoja, Eileen. "After the Blacklist." *Newsweek,* January 24, 1977, p. 10.

Navasky, Victor S. *Naming Names.* New York: Viking Press, 1980.

Trumbo, Dalton. *The Time of the Toad.* New York: Harper & Row, 1972.

HOLLYWOOD VICTORY COMMITTEE, organized on December 10, 1941, with its New York affiliate called the United Theatrical War Activities Committee, was responsible for sending out screen personalities to bond drives, to entertain the troops at USO-camp shows and on the front lines, and for other morale-boosting purposes. During the Second World War, the Committee arranged for 56, 037 free appearances by 4,147 individuals at 7,700 events. The Hollywood Victory Committee provided stars to perform on *Command Performance,* a short-wave radio transcription broadcast over 18 international stations each Sunday; it also provided celebrities for similar shows, such as *Mail Call, Anchors Aweigh, Soldiers with Wings, Yarns for Yanks, Main Street U.S.A.,* and *America Speaks.* Personal appearances by stars were also arranged throughout America for charity drives on behalf of the Red Cross, USO, Community Chests, and the relief activities of the United Nations.

The Hollywood Victory Committee's most ambitious venture took place in September 1942, when, on behalf of the U.S. Treasury Department, screen personalities traveled some 21,000 miles to attend bond rallies in 368 cities, raising more than $206 million. This particular campaign, called "Stars over America," also took celebrities to Canada to assist in its Victory Bond Drive and female stars to various cities to participate in "Women at War Week."

At the war's close, the Hollywood Victory Committee became the Hollywood Coordinating Committee, concerned with coordinating appearances by screen personalties at charitable and other events.

RESOURCES

Papers: Academy of Motion Picture Arts and Sciences (Edward Manson Collection).

HOLLYWOOD WALK OF FAME extends along Hollywood Boulevard from Gower to Sycamore and along Vine Street from Sunset to Yucca. It is a gray terrazzo sidewalk, in which are embedded coral stars bearing the names of personalities from the worlds of film, television, radio, and the recording industry. A different symbol is utilized for each aspect of the entertainment industry, and many celebrities have more than one star if they have been involved in more than one area of entertainment.

The concept of a Walk of Fame was first proposed by E. M. Stuart, then head of the Hollywood Chamber of Commerce, in 1953. It was part of the 1956 Hollywood beautification project, but ground breaking did not take place until February 8, 1960, with civic dignitaries and Linda Darnell, Gigi Perreau, Francis X. Bushman, and Charles Coburn in attendance. The Hollywood Walk of Fame, with 1,500 personalities represented, was officially dedicated on November 23, 1960.

The project was immediately the subject of controversy with its refusal to name a "star" in honor of Charlie Chaplin, an omission that was not corrected until 1972—the Chaplin "star" is at 6751 Hollywood Boulevard. The Hollywood Walk of Fame continues to be criticized for its failure to honor many pioneers of the industry and for its blatant commercialism in terms of demanding a fee from a sponsor and approval by an unidentified committee of the Hollywood Chamber of Commerce. Generally, if a star is unwilling to appear at the unveiling of his "star," then the committee will not honor that personality.

BIBLIOGRAPHY

Morino, Marianne. *The Hollywood Walk of Fame.* Berkeley, Calif.: Ten Speed Press, 1987.

HOLLYWOOD WRITERS' MOBILIZATON, consisting of representatives of the Screen Writers Guild, Radio Writers Guild, Screen Publicists Guild, Screen Readers Guild, Screen Cartoonists Guild, American Newspaper Guild, Independent Publicists, and the Song Writers Protective Association, was established during the Second World War to provide scripts and other written materials for government and war-related productions—motion picture or radio—at no charge. In October 1945, in association with the University of California, the Hollywood Writers' Mobilization established *The Hollywood Quarterly,* which was to become *Film Quarterly.*

HORIZON PICTURES was founded by Sam Spiegel (born 1903) and John Huston (1906–1987) in 1947, and initially housed on the Goldwyn studios lot. It produced its first film, *We Were Strangers,* directed by Huston, in 1949, and among the company's major successes were *The African Queen* (1952) and *Bridge on the River Kwai* (1957). As late as 1981, Horizon produced *Betrayal.*

HORROR FILMS. The horror film had its beginning in the French and German cinemas. One of the first, and certainly best known, American "horror" films—the term is used loosely—is Edison's 1910 production of *Frankenstein,* starring Charles Ogle. D. W. Griffith adapted Edgar Allan Poe's *The Tell-Tale Heart* as *The Avenging Conscience* (1914), but the director's only other venture into the horror genre was *One Exciting Night* (1922).

Lon Chaney (1883–1930) was the chief acting exponent of the horror genre in the silent era, beginning with *The Hunchback of Notre Dame* (1923) and *The Phantom of the Opera* (1925) at Universal* and continuing at M-G-M* with *The Unholy Three* (1925), *The Black Bird* (1926), *London After Midnight* (1927), and *The Unholy Three* (1930), among others. Chaney's best-known director was Tod Browning (1882–1962), and, aside from the Chaney features, Browning was responsible for *Freaks* (1932), *Mark of the Vampire* (1935), *The Devil Doll* (1936), and, of course, *Dracula* (1931), starring Bela Lugosi in a recreation of his stage role.

Director Paul Leni brought the Germanic vision of horror to the United States with *The Cat and the Canary* (1927), *The Man Who Laughs* (1928), and *The Last Warning* (1929). Other American films that illustrated a German influence include *The Bat* (1926) and *The Bat Whispers* (1931), both directed by Roland West.

No studio is more associated with the horror genre than Universal*. James Whale (1896–1957) directed three classic horror films there: *Frankenstein* (1931), *The Invisible Man* (1933), and *The Bride of Frankenstein* (1935). The first and last featured Boris Karloff, who is to the sound horror film what Lon Chaney was to the genre in the silent era. Boris Karloff (1887–1969) includes among his American horror films *The Mask of Fu Manchu* (1932), *The Mummy* (1932), *The Black Cat* (1934), *The Raven* (1935), *The Walking Dead* (1936), *Son of Frankenstein* (1939), *Tower of London* (1939), *House of Frankenstein* (1944), *Bedlam* (1946), *Frankenstein 1970* (1958), *The Raven* (1963), and *Mad Monster Party* (1967).

The Universal horror features continued into the forties and fifties, with Lon Chaney, Jr., appearing as the Son of Dracula, the Mummy, and the Wolf Man. By the early fifties, Universal was no longer taking the genre too seriously, with titles such as *Abbott and Costello Meet Frankenstein* (1948), *Abbott and Costello Meet the Invisible Man* (1951), and *Abbott and Costello Go to Mars* (1953). However, honorable mention should be made of some Universal features of the fifties: *It Came from Outer Space* (1953), *Creature from the Black Lagoon* (1954), *Revenge of the Creature* (1955), *The Incredible Shrinking Man* (1957), and *Curse of the Undead* (1959).

Paramount's one major contribution to the horror genre in the thirties was *Dr. Jekyll and Mr. Hyde* (1931), directed by Rouben Mamoulian and starring Fredric March in the title role. Robert Louis Stevenson's novel has been filmed many times: in 1912, by Thanhouser* with James Cruze in the title role; in 1913, by Universal with King Baggot in the title role; in 1920, by Famous Players-Lasky with John Barrymore in the title role; and in 1941, by M-G-M* with Spencer Tracy in the title role, to mention a few.

Other horror films of the thirties worth noting are two directed by Michael Curtiz at Warner Bros.*: *Doctor X* (1932) and *The Mystery of the Wax Museum* (1933), both of which were filmed in two-strip Technicolor* and starred Lionel Atwill and Fay Wray. *White Zombie* (1932), featuring Bela Lugosi and Madge Bellamy, has a considerable cult following, as does another feature, also directed by Victor Halperin, *Supernatural* (1933). Halperin tried unsuccessfully to repeat the popularity of *White Zombie* with *Revolt of the Zombies* (1936). A far more memorable production dealing with the "living dead" is Jacques Tourneur's *I Walked with a Zombie* (1943).

The "living dead" was the subject of George Romero's *Night of the Living Dead* (1969). It heralded a new era of explicit and graphic horror films that were to replace films such as Alfred Hitchcock's *Psycho* (1960), which terrified without showing the viewer a knife actually slashing human flesh. Graphic horror films of a more recent vintage are exemplified by the "Halloween" series, which commenced with *Halloween* (1978), and the "Friday the 13th" series, which began with *Friday the 13th* (1980).

More recent horror films that have gained a lasting reputation are *The Texas Chainsaw Massacre* (1974), *The Hills Have Eyes* (1977), *Alien* (1979), *The Fly* (1986), *The Blob* (1988), *Child's Play* (1988), *The Silence of the Lambs* (1991), *The People Under the Stairs* (1991), and *The Hand That Rocks the Cradle* (1992). Among "newer" directors associated with the genre are Clive Barker, Wes Craven, and John Cronenberg.

BIBLIOGRAPHY

Brunas, Michael, John Brunas, and Tom Weaver. *Universal Horrors: The Studio's Classic Films, 1931–1946.* Jefferson, N.C.: McFarland, 1990.

Butler, Ivan. *The Horror Film.* New York: A. S. Barnes, 1967.

Clarens, Carlos. *An Illustrated History of the Horror Films.* New York: G. P. Putnam's Sons, 1967.

Clover, Carol J. *Men, Women and Chain Saws: Gender in the Modern Horror Film.* Princeton, N.J.: Princeton University Press, 1992.

Dettman, Bruce. *The Horror Factory.* New York: Gordon Press, 1976.

Douglas, Drake. *Horror!* New York: Macmillan, 1996.

Everman, Welch. *Cult Horror Films: From Attack of the 50 Foot Woman to Zombies of Mora Tau.* New York: Carol Publishing, 1993.

Everson, William K. *Classics of the Horror Film.* Secaucus, N.J.: Citadel Press, 1974.

Fischer, Dennis. *Horror Film Directors, 1931–1990.* Jefferson, N.C.: McFarland, 1991.

Gifford, Denis. *A Pictorial History of Horror Movies.* New York: Hamlyn, 1973.

Glut, Donald F. *The Dracula Book.* Metuchen, N.J.: Scarecrow Press, 1975.

————. *The Frankenstein Catalog.* Jefferson, N.C.: McFarland, 1984.

Grant, Barry Keith, ed. *Planks of Reason: Essays on the Horror Film.* Metuchen, N.J.: Scarecrow Press, 1984.

Guttmacher, Peter. *Legendary Horror Films: Essential Genre History, Offscreen Anecdotes, Special Effects Secrets, Ghoulish Facts.* New York: MetroBooks, 1995.

Halliwell, Leslie. *The Dead That Walk: Dracula, Frankenstein, the Mummy, and Other Favorite Movie Monsters.* New York: Continuum, 1988.

Hanke, Ken. *A Critical Guide to Horror Film Series.* New York: Garland, 1991.

Hardy, Phil, ed. *The Encyclopedia of Horror Movies.* New York: Harper and Row, 1986.

Kinnard, Roy. *Horror in Silent Films: A Filmography, 1896–1929.* Jefferson, N.C.: McFarland, 1995.

Mank, Gregory William. *Hollywood's Cauldron: Thirteen Horror Films from the Genre's Golden Age.* Jefferson, N.C.: McFarland, 1994.

McCarty, John. *Pyschos: Eighty Years of Mad Movies, Maniacs, and Murderous Deeds.* New York: St. Martin's Press, 1986.

————. *The Modern Horror Film: 50 Contemporary Classics from The Curse of Frankenstein to The Lair of the White Worm.* New York: Carol Publishing, 1990.

————. *Movie Pyschos and Madmen: Film Psychopaths from Jekyll and Hyde to Hannibal Lecter.* New York: Carol Publishing, 1993.

————, ed. *The Fearmakers: The Screen's Directorial Masters of Suspense and Terror.* New York: St. Martin's Press, 1994.

Paul, William. *Laughing, Screaming: Modern Hollywood Horror and Comedy.* New York: Columbia University Press, 1994.

Pitts, Michael R. *Horror Film Stars.* Jefferson, N.C.: McFarland, 1991.

Schoell, William. *Stay Out of the Shower: 25 Years of Shocker Films Beginning with Psycho.* New York: December Books, 1985.

Senn, Bryan. *Fantastic Cinema Subject Guide: A Topical Index to 2500 Horror, Science Fiction, and Fantasy Films.* Jefferson, N.C.: McFarland, 1992.

Skal, David J. *The Monster Show: A Cultural History of Horror.* New York: W. W. Norton, 1993.

Sternfield, Jonathan. *The Look of Horror: Scary Moments from Scary Movies.* Philadelphia: Courage Books, 1990.

Svehla, Gary J., and Susan Svehla, eds. *Bitches, Bimbos and Virgins: Women in the Horror Film.* Baltimore, Md.: Midnight Marquee Press, 1996.

————, eds. *Cinematic Hauntings.* Baltimore, Md.: Midnight Marquee Press, 1996.

————, eds. *Guilty Pleasures of the Horror Film.* Baltimore, Md.: Midnight Marquee Press, 1996.

Turner, George E., and Michael H. Price. *Human Monsters: The Bizarre Psychology of Movie Villains.* Northampton, Mass.: Kitchen Sink Press, 1995.

Ursini, James, and Alain Silver. *More Things Than Are Dreamt Of: Masterpieces of Supernatural Horror—from Mary Shelley to Stephen King—in Literature and Film.* New York: Limelight, 1994.

Waller, Gregory A. *The Living and the Undead from Stoker's Dracula to Romero's Dawn of the Dead.* Urbana, Ill.: University of Chicago Press, 1986.

————, ed. *American Horrors: Essays on the Modern American Horror Film.* Urbana, Ill.: University of Chicago Press, 1987.

Weaver, Tom. *Poverty Row Horrors!: Monogram, PRC and Republic Horror Films of the Forties.* Jefferson, N.C.: McFarland, 1993.

————. *Attack of the Monster Movie Makers: Interviews with 20 Genre Giants.* Jefferson, N.C.: McFarland, 1994.

Wiater, Stanley. *Dark Visions: Conversations with the Masters of the Horror Film.* New York: Avon Books, 1992.

Wills, Donald C. *Horror and Science Fiction Films: A Checklist.* Metuchen, N.J.: Scarecrow Press, 1972.

————. *Horror and Science Fiction Films: A Checklist II.* Metuchen, N.J.: Scarecrow Press, 1982.

————. *Horror and Science Fiction Films: A Checklist III.* Metuchen, N.J.: Scarecrow Press, 1984.

Wolf, Leonard. *Horror: A Connoisseur's Guide to Literature and Film.* New York: Facts on File, 1989.

Wright, Bruce Lanier. *Nightwalkers: Gothic Horror Movies, the Modern Era.* Dallas, Tex.: Taylor Publishing, 1995.

Wright, Gene. *Horrorshows: The A-Z of Horror in Film, TV, Radio and Theater.* New York: Facts on File, 1986.

HOTEX FILM MANUFACTURING COMPANY. King Vidor, John Boggs, and Ed Sedgwick formed this short-lived company of 1914, located in Texas, which produced two one-reel comedies directed by Sedgwick. Although Vidor succeeded in contracting with Sawyer, Inc.*, in October 1914, to release the comedies, when Sawyer went bankrupt shortly thereafter, the prints, negatives, and royalties were never retrieved. The company produced a film starring Vidor's wife, Florence, about the manufacture and marketing of sugar, before its disbandment when the Vidors left Galveston.

BIBLIOGRAPHY

"Hotel [*sic*] Will Release through Sawyer." *The Moving Picture World,* October 17, 1914, p. 315.

Vidor, King. *A Tree Is a Tree.* New York: Harcourt, Brace, 1952.

HOWARD A. ANDERSON COMPANY, which specializes in post-production special effects and opticals, was founded in 1927. It became involved in video with the 1988 establishment of Anderson Video and the 1989 building of a facility on the Universal* lot. (The company has a close relationship with Universal following Universal Title & Opticals becoming Howard A. Anderson Title & Opticals.)

Address: 100 Universal City Plaza, Universal City, Calif. 91608.

HUGH HARMAN PRODUCTIONS. See HARMANISING

HUMANOLOGY FILM PRODUCING COMPANY of Medford, Massachusetts, produced films in 1913, released by United Film Service*. Jack Rose was the president, and Reginald Wright Kaufmann was hired to write scenarios for the company.

HYGENIC PRODUCTIONS. See HALLMARK PRODUCTIONS, INC.

I

IATSE. See INTERNATIONAL ALLIANCE OF THE-ATRICAL STAGE EMPLOYES AND MOVING PICTURE MACHINE OPERATORS OF THE UNITED STATES AND CANADA

IMAGEN AWARDS are given to film and television programs that portray Latinos in a positive light. Created in 1985 by the Hispanic Media Task Force of the National Conference of Christians and Jews, the awards are now presented by the Imagen Foundation.

Address: 3000 West Alameda Avenue, Room 3355, Burbank, Calif. 91523.

IMAGINE FILMS ENTERTAINMENT, INC., is a successful production company—*Parenthood* (1989), *Backdraft* (1991), *Far and Away* (1992), *Apollo 13* (1995), etc.—formed by former actor Ron Howard (born 1954) and Brian Grazer (born 1951) in May 1986. A public company, it is 25 percent owned by MCA/Universal*.

Address: 1925 Century Park East, Suite 2300, Los Angeles, Calif. 90067.

IMAX—short for "maximum image"—was developed for Expo 70 in Osaka, Japan. It is a sophisticated widescreen system, which utilizes 70mm* film fed through the camera horizontally and, therefore, is ten times the width of 35mm* film. The projector uses a rolling loop movement to advance the film horizontally. The latter was invented by P. R. W. Jones, and the former by William C. Shaw. The Imax system was developed in Canada, as was a similar system, Omnimax, which is designed for use on a domed theatre screen, rather than a curved screen as in Imax. Omnimax was introduced to the United States at the Reuben H. Fleet Space Theater in San Diego in 1973.

Address: Imax Systems Corporation, 38 Isabella Street, Toronto, Ontario, Canada M4Y 1N1.

BIBLIOGRAPHY

Jones, P. R. W. "The Rolling Loop—a New Concept of Film Transport." *Journal of the SMPTE* (January 1968): pp. 21–23.

Shaw, William C. "New Large-Screen and Multi-Image Motion-Picture System." *Journal of the SMPTE* (September 1970): pp. 782–87.

IMP. See UNIVERSAL PICTURES

IMPERIAL DISTRIBUTING CORP. was active from 1931 through 1938, handling "B" movies and foreign imports. New York based, it was founded by William M. Pizor.

INCE CULVER CITY STUDIOS. See LAIRD INTERNATIONAL STUDIOS

INCEVILLE. The Miller Bros. 101 Ranch, situated where Sunset Boulevard joins the ocean in Los Angeles, became known as Inceville when it was taken over by pioneer producer Thomas H. Ince (1882–1924) late in 1911. The rugged terrain was used not only for the production of Westerns but also for shooting all types of films. Numerous standing sets were built, many directly on the beach.

The following description of the lot appeared in the October 9, 1915, edition of *The Moving Picture World:*

> Like many of the Western studios, the establishment is made up of a confusion of frame buildings, small and large, each additional structure marking the expansion of the company's business. It has a main stage 175 × 220 feet; a new glass stage 360 × 160 and two auxiliary stages 50 × 80 feet; an administrative building, a restaurant, a commissary, a wardrobe building, a property building, a scene building, 200 dressing rooms, an arsenal where weapons, ammunition and explosives are kept, a power house furnishing light for stages and buildings, a reservoir furnishing fresh water, six stables and corrals and a number of other structures. In addition to the inexhaustible supply of natural settings for exteriors, Inceville has a Spanish Mission, a Dutch village with a genuine canal, old windmill, etc., a Japanese village with jinrikshaws, an Irish village, a Canadian village, an East Indian street and a Sioux camp.

When Ince moved his operation to Culver City in 1915, Inceville continued to be used to a lesser extent until 1922. A 1924 fire destroyed the remaining standing sets except for one church.

BIBLIOGRAPHY

Duncan, Robert C. "The Ince Studios." *Picture Play,* March 1, 1916, pp. 26–39.

"Ince to Move to Culver City." *The Moving Picture World,* October 9, 1915, p. 272.

INDEPENDENT-INTERNATIONAL PICTURES was a poverty row* production company, founded by Sam Sherman.

Its first film was *Satan's Sadists* (1970), and its last, *The Texas Hill Killings* (1987).

BIBLIOGRAPHY

Ray, Fred Olen. *The New Poverty Row: Independent Filmmakers as Producers.* Jefferson, N.C.: McFarland, 1991.

INDEPENDENT MOTION PICTURE CORPORATION. See UNIVERSAL PICTURES

INDEPENDENT PRODUCTIONS CORPORATION was founded in 1951 by Herbert Biberman, along with Paul Jarrico and Simon Lazarus, after Biberman had served time in a federal penitentiary for contempt of Congress as a member of the Hollywood Ten*. It announced plans for various films, including one on Paul Robeson, one on the trial of Helen Johnson, and a feature on the life of Frederick Douglas's titled *The House on Cedar Hill.* The company actually made only one film, *Salt of the Earth,* about the striking miners of New Mexico, which eventually was shown publicly, in 1954, but never gained a commercial release because of the blacklisting of Biberman by the film industry.

INDEPENDENT SALES CORPORATION began December 1, 1918, as a booking organization distinct from producers and exchange organizations. With a New York headquarters and salesmen in every territory of the country, Independent Sales, headed by Frank G. Hall, contracted with Film Clearing House, Inc., to handle the physical distribution of its films. Film Clearing House, incorporated on May 6, 1918, by Colonel Julian Ruppert, a brewer and the owner of the New York Yankees, was formed to eliminate the overhead costs of many exchanges by doing the shipping portion of distribution and leaving the sales end to the individual distributors utilizing their own services. Distributors housed their sales staff in Film Clearing House offices and were able to operate at much lower costs because they did not have to provide the overhead necessary physically to ship the films. One of the organizers of Film Clearing House, William M. Seabury, was the vice president of Independent Sales, and Frank G. Hall was Film Clearing House's supervising director. After Film Clearing House bought and remodeled the Kleine* exchanges, it contracted to handle films of Blackton Productions, Bacon-Backer*, and the William L. Sherry Service*. Although Independent Sales was not a producer, it did at times put up cash advances on finished negatives and financed printing and advertising. In September 1919, Independent Sales and Film Clearing House merged with other of Frank G. Hall's interest to form Hallmark Pictures Corporation*.

BIBLIOGRAPHY

"Independent Company to Direct Film Salesmen." *The Moving Picture World,* December 7, 1918, p. 1103.
"Ruppert Plans a Film Clearing House." *The Moving Picture World,* June 29, 1918, p. 1822.

INDIANAPOLIS. See CAPITAL FILM COMPANY

INDUSTRIAL FILM COMPANY, said to be the first company to specialize in making and distributing films for industrial exploitation, commercial education, advertising, and historical recording, was organized in December 1909 in Chicago by Carl Laemmle, Watterson R. Rothacker, and R. H. Cochrane. Rothacker, who was subsequently in the trade paper field, became president, succeeding Laemmle in 1913, when Laemmle sold his stock and left to concentrate his efforts with the Universal Film Manufacturing Company*. Some of the companies for which Industrial produced films included H. J. Heinz Company, du Pont Powder Company, Postum Cereal Company, Winchester Repeating Arms Company, Northern Pacific Railway Company, Imperial Oil Company, and the U.S. Brewers Association. In addition, Industrial made a film for the state of Michigan, showing its natural resources and industrial activities, for the Panama-Pacific Exposition of 1915, and a film of Vernon and Irene Castle dancing on the Orpheum vaudeville circuit. In mid-1916, Industrial was succeeded by the Rothacker Film Manufacturing Company, located at Diversey Parkway and Ward Street in Chicago.

BIBLIOGRAPHY

"Laemmle Sells Stock. " *The New York Dramatic Mirror,* September 24, 1913, p. 35.
"The Rothacker Film Manufacturing Company." *The Moving Picture World,* June 3, 1916, p. 1720.
"Watterson R. Rothacker." *The Moving Picture World,* December 5, 1914, p. 1370.

INDUSTRIAL FILMS AND POSTER SERVICE. See UNITED PRODUCTIONS OF AMERICA

INDUSTRIAL LIGHT & MAGIC. See LUCASFILM, LTD.

IN-FLIGHT MOVIES. According to the Guinness record book of *Movie Facts and Feats,* the first in-flight movie was *The Lost World* (1925), shown on a scheduled Imperial Airways flight from London to the Continent in April 1925. The first American in-flight film presentation was of a Universal newsreel and two short subjects, shown on a transcontinental Air Transport, Inc., Ford transport aircraft on October 8, 1929.

There is a documentary record of a screening of the 1928 Harold Lloyd feature, *Speedy,* on an American passenger plane, possibly a TAT (later TWA) flight from Los Angeles to New York on an unspecified date but presumably within a year or two of *Speedy*'s release. As a publicity stunt, the 1933 Columbia feature *Air Hostess* was screened for reporters on a plane flying over New York. According to the *Motion Picture Herald*, the documentary feature *Baboona* was previewed on board a plane in December 1934. The film's producers, Mr. and Mrs. Martin Johnson, announced they were equipping one of their planes with a sound projector in order to screen the film for African natives in the summer of 1935. At the same time, Captain Eddie Rickenbacker announced, "The big transatlantic flying boats and the long distance cross-country planes will be equipped with movies before long."

Early in 1946, Pan-Am began test-screening films on its North Atlantic runs, and announced regular 16mm screenings the following year. TWA was the first airline to begin regular in-flight movie presentations on July 19, 1961, with the screening of *By Love Possessed*, on a regular flight between New York and Los Angeles. The film was seen by first-class passengers only.

BIBLIOGRAPHY

"Regular Film Fare Seen for Airliners." *Motion Picture Herald*, January 12, 1935, p. 24.

INSPIRATION PICTURES, INC., a major producer from 1921 to 1931, was founded by Charles H. Duell (its first president) and J. Boyce Smith, Jr. (its first vice president). Walter Camp, Jr., became president in the mid-twenties. Releasing through United Artists*, First National*, or Paramount*, Inspiration rightly boasted that its films were "always on the best programs." Richard Barthelmess was the company's first major star, in *Tol'able David* (1921), followed by *The Fighting Blade* (1923), *The Enchanted Cottage* (1924), *Soul-Fire* (1925), and other features. Dorothy Gish was also under contract to Inspiration, appearing in *The Bright Shawl* (1923), *Fury* (1923), and *The Beautiful City* (1925). She also costarred with her sister, Lillian, in *Romola* (1925), and it was Inspiration that sent Lillian to Italy to make *The White Sister* (1923). Director Henry King spent most of the twenties directing at Inspiration, where he made ten features, from *Tol'able David* in 1921 to *Hell Harbor* in 1930.

RESOURCES

Photographs: Lincoln Center

INTER-CONTINENT FILM COMPANY began in January 1914 as the American distributor for the Verafilm Company of Rome as well as two Copenhagen-based companies. It planned to produce one feature per month and a series of educational films to export to Japan and China. F. Baske Yamado, a Japanese-American artist, was hired to supervise these productions. Offices for Inter-Continent were in the World's Tower Building at 110–112 West 40th Street, New York.

BIBLIOGRAPHY

"Inter-Continent Film Company Begins." *The Moving Picture World*, January 10, 1914, p. 177.

INTERNATIONAL ALLIANCE OF THEATRICAL STAGE EMPLOYES [*sic*] AND MOVING PICTURE MACHINE OPERATORS OF THE UNITED STATES AND CANADA, commonly known as IATSE, was organized on July 17, 1893, as the International Alliance of Theatrical Stage Employes. It affiliated as an international union on October 1, 1902, and affiliated with the American Federation of Labor and Congress of Industrial Organizations on December 5, 1955.

IATSE, along with the United Brotherhood of Carpenters and Joiners, the International Brotherhood of Electrical Workers, the International Brotherhood of Painters and Paperhangers, and the American Federation of Musicians, was one of the signatories to the first Hollywood film industry recognition of unions, the so-called Studio Basic Agreement, which was signed by nine major producers on November 29, 1926. The Studio Basic Agreement divided work in the industry between various crafts, but with the coming of sound, and resultant new technology and new jobs, jurisdictional disputes broke out. A bitter dispute evolved in the late thirties and early forties between IATSE and the Congress of Industrial Organizations (CIO) and the Conference of Studio Unions*, throughout much of which IATSE branded the last two as Communist front organizations. It was not until 1947 that IATSE finally consolidated its control over film industry labor matters.

Address: 1515 Broadway, New York, N.Y. 10036.

BIBLIOGRAPHY

Ross, Murray. *Stars and Strikes: Unionization of Hollywood.* New York: Columbia University Press, 1941.
———. "Labor Relations in Hollywood." In *The Annals of the American Academy of Political and Social Science: The Motion Picture Industry* ed. Thorsten Sellin. Philadelphia: The American Academy of Political and Social Science, 1947, pp. 58–64.

INTERNATIONAL CREATIVE MANAGEMENT, INC. One of the three largest of the Hollywood agents, representing individuals in all areas of film and television production, International Creative Management (ICM), Inc., was created in 1975 with the merger of Creative Management Associates (founded in 1960) and International Famous Agency. Creative Management Associates had an antecedent in General Amusements Corporation. International Creative Management is a subsidiary of Josephson International (formerly Marvin Josephson Associates, Inc.). In the summer of 1984, it assimilated Chase-Park Citron, which had been formed in 1962 and acquired by Josephson in 1973. In 1985, International Creative Management acquired ATI Equities, Inc., a talent agency that represents many contemporary music groups. In March 1995, four agents from ICM defected to form the independent Endeavor agency. In May 1996, ICM completed a refinancing through City National Bank of Beverly Hills, allowing it to remain a private company; ICM has been in debt since it was taken private in 1988. ICM has been headed by president Jeff Berg since 1980. As of 1997, it had more than 150 individual agents worldwide (with 90 in Los Angeles), and its clients included Woody Allen, Mel Gibson, Eddie Murphy, Arnold Schwarzenegger, Barbra Streisand, and Denzel Washington.

Address: 8942 Wilshire Boulevard, Beverly Hills, Calif. 90211.

THE INTERNATIONAL DOCUMENTARY ASSOCIATION (IDA) was founded in 1982 as a nonprofit organization, supporting the efforts of nonfiction film and video producers, and to increase public support and demand for documentaries. Since 1985 it has presented annual awards in the field.

Address: 155 South Robertson Blvd., Los Angeles, Calif. 90035.

INTERNATIONAL FILM SERVICE, INC. William Randolph Hearst formed the International Film Service, Inc., which was incorporated on December 3, 1914, following the success of the serial* *The Perils of Pauline,* whose story appeared in the Hearst newspapers. After sponsoring subsequent serials, *The Exploits of Elaine, The Goddess,* and *The Adventures of Wallingford,* International became more directly involved in the production and distribution of the serials *The Mysteries of Myra, Beatrice of Fairfax,* and *Patria* and began production of the Hearst-International News Pictorial, an antecedent to the Hearst-Selig and Hearst-Vitagraph newsreels. In April 1916, Hearst opened exchanges in cities where the Hearst papers were the strongest, and through them he released his own newsreels*, serials, cartoons, and feature productions. Hearst was the president and Edward A. McManus was the general manager. On January 1, 1917, International began distributing its product through the Pathé* exchanges and it combined its newsreel with that of Pathé to form the Hearst-Pathé News. In March 1919, International began releasing with the Famous Players-Lasky Corporation. It remained in existence through 1922.

BIBLIOGRAPHY

"Hearst Opens Exchanges." *The Moving Picture World,* April 8, 1916, p. 230.

INTERNATIONAL MOTION PICTURE ASSOCIATION. See MOTION PICTURE EXHIBITORS' LEAGUE OF AMERICA

THE INTERNATIONAL NEWSREEL. See NEWSREELS

INTERNATIONAL PHOTOPLAY CORPORATION, based in Chicago, with John Wojtalewicz as president, was active in the latter half of the second and the third decades of the twentieth century producing a series of one- and two-reel comedies, featuring Art Bates and Lou Tops.

INTERNATIONAL PICTURES. See UNIVERSAL PICTURES

THE INTERNATIONAL PICTURE SHOW CO. was founded in 1977 by Lloyd N. Adams, Jr., as an Atlanta-based producer and distributor. It released some minor U.S. features, as well as the British films *The Thirty-Nine Steps* (1978) and *Tarka the Otter* (1979). It went public in August 1980, and in September 1984, the company sought Chapter XI bankruptcy protection.

INTER-OCEAN FILM CORPORATION, active in the second and third decade of the twentieth century as a distributor of and agent for American films abroad, was organized by Paul H. Cromelin. According to the 1921 edition of *Motion Picture Studio Directory,* "In the efficient execution of foreign film transactions, the American producer needs the co-operation of an export organization equipped with the necessary resources, facilities and experience to render a genuine foreign service—profitably. The tireless efforts of Paul H. Cromelin to bring into being such an organization have been amply rewarded."

INTERSTATE FEATURE FILM COMPANY, with headquarters in Middletown, Connecticut, was formed in April 1915 by New England businessmen to produce two feature films per month. Kenneth MacDougall was the vice president and general manager. Its first feature, the four-reel *Bulldogs of the Trail,* starred leading lady Snyder Shields. Interstate released with the Picture Playhouse Film Company*.

BIBLIOGRAPHY

"Interstate Feature Film Company Founded." *The Moving Picture World,* April 17, 1915, p. 370.

INTERSTATE TELEVISION CORPORATION. See ALLIED ARTISTS

INVINCIBLE PICTURES CORPORATION. See CHESTERFIELD MOTION PICTURE CORPORATION

ISLAND PICTURES, noted for the distinctive independent films that it produced and distributed, was created in 1982 by Chris Blackwell as one of the Island Group of Companies (including Island Records) that he owned. From 1983 to 1985, the company was associated with Alive Films* under the name Island/Alive. A specialty distribution subsidiary, Fourth & B'Way Films, was created in 1988. The company ceased its distribution activities in January 1990, and in December 1994, it was purchased by Polygram NV*, which had acquired Island Records in 1989.

Address: 8920 Sunset Boulevard, Los Angeles, Calif. 90069.

ITALA FILM COMPANY OF AMERICA was organized in July 1915 by Harry R. Raver to produce an eight-reel film with "Maciste," the character created by Gabrielle D'Annunzio in the earlier Italian success, *Cabiria.* Ernest Pagano, who played the role in *Cabiria,* continued in subsequent productions. Agnes L. Bain was the company's scenarist.

BIBLIOGRAPHY

"Itala Company's Plans." *The Moving Picture World,* July 31, 1915, p. 800.

ITHACA, NEW YORK. See WHARTON, INC.

IVAN FILM PRODUCTIONS, INC. Ivan Abramson (1872–1934), formerly the manager of the largest traveling opera organization and a manager of Yiddish theatre stars, founded Ivan Film Productions, in 1914, and acted as director-general and writer for the company. Some of his films include *Forbidden Fruit, A Fool's Paradise, Concealed Truth,* and *The Immortal Flame.* His best-known production is probably *Enlighten Thy Daughter* (1917). When Abramson left the company late in 1917 and formed the Graphic Film Corporation*, I. E. Chadwick became the new head, and Ivan continued production with F. J. Grandon and Edmund Lawrence as directors.

BIBLIOGRAPHY

"Ivan Abramson, Master Craftsman." *The Moving Picture World,* March 4, 1916, p. 1455.

IVAN TORS STUDIO was founded in 1964 when producer Ivan Tors (1916–1983) purchased and enlarged United Studios in the city of North Miami. A year earlier, he had formed Ivan Tors Films, Inc., and utilized the studio for feature film production and the making of the television series *Flipper* (NBC, 1964–1967). The studio was later acquired by Stanley Markofsky and renovated as the Greenwich Studio City (with four sound stages). In 1989, producer Matthew Hayden acquired rights to Ivan Tors's name, and the following year, he formed Ivan Tors Entertainment.

Address: 11111 Biscayne Boulevard, North Miami, Fla. 33161.

IVERSON RANCH. Located in the Chatsworth area of the San Fernando Valley, on the outskirts of Los Angeles, the Iverson Ranch has been used as a location site for more than 2,000 films from 1912 onward. According to the *New York Herald Tribune* (September 10, 1950), the ranch "offers ten different types of location sites, including jungle, mountain, desert, and open range, and they are so isolated from one another that five companies can be shooting without conflicting with one another." In particular, the 600-acre ranch offered rock formations and rugged scenery making it an ideal venue for Westerns*. The ranch was founded by Karl Iverson and purchased by Bob Sherman, in 1982, from Iverson's son, Joe. Among the films shot in part at the Iverson Ranch were *Tell It to the Marines* (1927), *Noah's Ark* (1929), *Morocco* (1930), *The Lives of a Bengal Lancer* (1935), *Trail of the Lonesome Pine* (1936), *Wee Willie Winkle* (1937), *The Flying Deuces* (1939), *Stagecoach* (1939), and *Cattle Queen of Montana* (1954). It has also been used in the production of many television series.

BIBLIOGRAPHY

Sherman, Robert G. *Quiet on the Set!* Chatsworth, Calif.: Sherway Publishing Company, 1984.

J

J.A.C. See ZODIAK FILM MANUFACTURING COMPANY

JACKSONVILLE, FLORIDA. See GENE GAUNTIER FEATURE PLAYERS and KALEM COMPANY, INC.

JACK WRATHER PICTURES, INC. See WRATHER CORPORATION

THE JAM HANDY ORGANIZATION, INC., was founded in 1910 by Jamison Handy and Herbert Kaufman, and operated under a variety of names until 1929, when it became the Jam Handy Picture Service. A major producer of industrial and educational film, it was responsible for the first Technicolor* industrial film, *Refreshment through the Years,* sponsored by the Coca-Cola Company in 1937. Jamison Handy died in 1983, and his company went out of existence in 1988. For most of its life, it was located in Detroit.

THE JAMES AGEE FILM PROJECT was established in 1974 as a nonprofit organization to distribute films to the nontheatrical market, with the emphasis on documentaries dealing with social justice and the South.

Address: 316 East Main Street, Johnson City, Tenn. 37601.

JANS PRODUCTIONS, INC., founded in 1920 by Herman F. Jans, remained active through 1926 as a minor producer of society dramas and melodramas.

JAPANESE-AMERICAN FILM COMPANY. Claiming to be the first company in the United States to be owned, controlled, and operated by Japanese, the Japanese-American Film Company was formed in October 1914 by Japanese businessmen, after existing for the previous two years in Japan as a producer of commercial, educational, and industrial features. The company had a stock company of 40 actors and actresses from Japan. Its first production, *The Oath of the Sword,* was said to have treated Japanese themes and customs with fidelity. It was distributed by Sawyer, Inc.* The company planned to make dramatic films part of the year in Japan and also in Hawaii. K. Numamoto was the president, Tomi Morri and Hisa Numa were the leading players, and Kohano Akashi and Jack Y. Abbe also acted in the company.

BIBLIOGRAPHY

"Japanese-American Film Company." *The Moving Picture World,* October 17, 1914, p. 314.

JAPANESE PHOTOPLAYERS' CLUB OF LOS ANGELES was organized, in October 1917, to see that its members did not appear in films reflecting badly upon the Japanese people. Members were asked to use their influence to urge producers to portray the Japanese race in a dignified manner. Sessue Hayakawa and Frank Tokanaga were the club's leaders.

JASPER HOLLYWOOD STUDIOS. See HOLLYWOOD GENERAL STUDIOS

JENSEN-FARLEY PICTURES, INC. The distribution company of Jensen-Farley Pictures, Inc., was formed in 1981 by Raylan Jensen and Clair Farley with the purchase of Taft International Pictures, Inc., a subsidiary of Taft Broadcasting. Taft International Pictures had been created, in 1980, with the acquisition of the library of Sunn Classics, which was well known for its marketing of such exploitation features as *In Search of Noah's Ark* (1977), *Chariots of the Gods* (1974), and *The Outer Space Connection* (1975). At the time of its acquisition by Taft, Sunn Classics had a library of 22 features and 57 television productions. Sunn Classics had its origins in American National Enterprises, formed in Salt Lake City in 1966 by Robert Crosier. The company became Sunn Classics in 1971, when it was acquired by the Schick Razor Company. It filed for Chapter XI bankruptcy protection on December 30, 1983.

BIBLIOGRAPHY

Hollinger, Hy. "Jensen Farley Pictures Wants to Fill Niche Once Held by Avco and Filmways." *Daily Variety,* November 18, 1982, pp. 1, 22.

JERRY FAIRBANKS PRODUCTIONS. A production house dating back to the thirties, Jerry Fairbanks Productions is best known for three series of short subjects that it produced for Paramount: *Popular Science* (1935–1949), *Unusual Occupations* (1937–1949), and *Speaking of Animals* (1941–1949). In more recent years, the company had been involved in television production. Subsidiary companies were Western Audio Visual Enterprises and Yukon Pictures, Inc. Largely inactive for a number of years, the company ceased operations with the death of its owner Jerry Fairbanks (1905–1995).

RESOURCES
Films: UCLA Film and Television Archive.

JERSEY CITY, NEW JERSEY. See FREDERICK DOUGLASS FILM COMPANY and PATHÉ

JESSE D. HAMPTON FEATURE CORP. See ROBERTSON-COLE COMPANY

JESTER COMEDY COMPANY. William Steiner formed the Jester Comedy Company, in December 1917, to make two-reel comedies starring the European Fernandez Perez as the character "Twede-Dan." The Jester studios were located in Cliffside, New Jersey, and its first production was titled *The Recruit*. William A. Seiter was the company's director.

JEWEL PRODUCTIONS, INC. With the slogan "It's a Jewel" to advertise its films, Jewel Productions, Inc., was formed on August 26, 1917, to release "the biggest and best special features," which it would purchase outright with cash. It released approximately one film per month. Harry M. Berman, formerly with Artcraft, was the head of the New York exchange, while Leon J. Bamburger was the general supervisor for all the exchanges. Some films that Jewel released include *Come Through* and *The Heart of Humanity*, both purchased from Universal*. In June 1919, Jewel consolidated its offices with those of Universal, and "Jewel" became a brand name for certain Universal releases.

BIBLIOGRAPHY
"Jewel Productions, Inc." *The Moving Picture World,* August 25, 1917, p. 1206.

JEWISH TALKING PICTURES was a Yiddish-language production company, founded in New York in 1935 by Joseph Seiden. It produced the following features: *Yidishe Kinig Lir/Jewish King Lear* (1935), *Libe un Laydnshaft/Love and Passion* (1936), *Ikh Vil Zayn a Pansyoner/I Want To Be a Boarder* (1937), *Kol Nidre* (1939), *Motl der Operator/Motel the Operator* (1939), *Der Groyser Eytse Geber/The Greater Advisor* (1940), *Der Yidishe Nigun/The Jewish Melody* (1940), *Eli, Eli/My God, My God* (1940), *Is Tsveyte Mame/Her Second Mother* (1940), and *Mazl Tov Yidn/Mazel Tov, Jews* (1941).

BIBLIOGRAPHY
Goldman, Eric A. *Visions, Images, and Dreams: Yiddish Film Past and Present.* Ann Arbor, Mich.: UMI Research Press, 1983.

JOEL PRODUCTIONS. See THE BRYNA COMPANY

JOSEPH BURSTYN, INC. Although Joseph Burstyn died in 1953 at the age of 53, the company that bears his name continued in operation as one of the best known and most highly respected of importers and distributors of foreign films.

Burstyn entered film distribution in 1930 with the feature *A Jew at War*. He organized his company in 1935 and the following year joined forces with Arthur Mayer to form Arthur Mayer & Joseph Burstyn, Inc., which remained in existence until September 1949, when Burstyn bought out his partner. Although the company did distribute some American features, such as *The Little Fugitive* (1953), Burstyn is more closely associated with the original American release of classic foreign-language films, such as *The New Gulliver, Open City, Paisan, The Bicycle Thief,* and, of course, *The Miracle,* which involved Burstyn in a lengthy and successful fight against film censorship. The company ceased operations in 1985.

JUDEA PICTURES was formed in New York in 1929 by Joseph Seiden to produce a series of two-reel Yiddish-language films, beginning with *Style and Class,* a filmed record of a musical revue. In all, Judea produced some 18 short subjects, together with three features: *Mayne Yidishe Mame/My Jewish Mother* (1930), *Eybike Naronim/Eternal Fools* (1930), and *The Voice of Israel* (1931).

BIBLIOGRAPHY
Goldman, Eric A. *Visions, Images, and Dreams: Yiddish Film Past and Present.* Ann Arbor, Mich.: UMI Research Press, 1983.

JUNGLE FILM COMPANY, located at Eastlake Park in Los Angeles, was formed in July 1914 to make only wild animal films. It was often referred to as the E. & R. Jungle Film Company, after its owners J. S. Edwards and John Rounan. Paul Machette was the company director, and Irvin Willatt was the head of the camera department. Its best-known films were a series of more than 40 one-reel comedies featuring chimpanzees Sally and Napoleon (who were married on stage, as part of a vaudeville act, at the Pantages Theatre, Los Angeles, on December 25, 1913).

BIBLIOGRAPHY
"Napoleon and Sally, the Only Chimpanzees in Motion Pictures Have Romped through Forty E. & R. Comedies." *Motion Picture News Studio Directory,* October 21, 1916, p. 9.

JUNO FILMS. See LOPERT FILMS DISTRIBUTING COMPANY

JUVENILE FILM COMPANY, located in Cleveland, was formed in 1915 to produce children's films. James A. Fitz-Patrick—formerly a reporter, acting student, and instructor of child actors—directed, wrote, and acted in the films, which featured child performers Janethal and Joseph Monahan in leading roles.

BIBLIOGRAPHY
"Fitz-Patrick with Juvenile Film Company." *The Moving Picture World,* March 4, 1916, p. 1454.

K & R FILM COMPANY was formed in April 1915 by R. R. Roberts, Pierce Kingsley, and Frances Kell. Kingsley wrote and starred in its first production, *Silver Threads among the Gold*. Leon Victor was the general manager of the company, which had offices in the Putnam Building at 1493 Broadway, New York.

KALEM COMPANY, INC., was organized early in 1907 by George Kleine, Samuel Long, and Frank Marion, who created the name from the first letters of their last names. Kleine, the president, was the owner of the Kleine Optical Company of Chicago, which handled films from leading foreign manufacturers as well as projection machines. Long, the vice president, was formerly the superintendent of the Biograph* factory. Marion, Kalem's secretary and treasurer, was formerly in charge of the Biograph studio and responsible for selling the company's films. Kalem's first production, *A Runaway Sleighbelle,* was directed by Sidney Olcott, who had earlier been associated with Marion at Biograph. The early Kalem films contained subtitles in the form of cartoons drawn by a newspaper artist. Its studio and headquarters were at 131 West 24th Street, New York.

According to Kalem's general manager, William Wright, Marion created a stock company early in Kalem's history, and this may have been the first such motion picture stock company. Wright also claimed that Kalem was the first producer to exploit the names of its players.

After Kalem produced *Ben-Hur* in a one-reel version late in 1907, it was sued by the publishers of the book, the author's estate, and the producers of the stage production in what was the first case dealing with the right to make motion pictures from dramatic or literary sources. A few years later, the U.S. Supreme Court handed down a decision against Kalem, which established the precedent that rights to properties must be obtained by companies prior to the properties being made into films.

Kalem joined the Motion Picture Patents Company* and released its films on the General Film Company program. Olcott made Westerns* in Coytesville, New Jersey, and then, in the fall of 1908, went with a company of 12 players to Jacksonville, Florida, and secured an estate complete with a mansion, cabins, wharf, boats, and a grove. Kalem's first Florida film, *A Florida Feud,* or *Love in the Everglades,* was released in December 1908. Later films shot in Florida included Civil War dramas sympathetic to the South.

Sidney Olcott, of Irish descent, took a small company to Ireland in August 1910. Included were Gene Gauntier, who, in addition to being the leading lady, was also the company's scenarist; Robert Vignola; and cameraman George K. Hollister. The company settled in Beaufort, County Kerry, and returned there the following year with a larger company. After Olcott and Gauntier left Kalem, in 1912, to form the Gene Gauntier Feature Players, they continued to return to Beaufort.

Olcott, Gauntier, Vignola, Jack Clarke, and others traveled to Palestine in the fall of 1912 to film the six-reel *From the Manger to the Cross,* which William Wright claimed to be the first film, other than topical subjects, of that length. Although the film was very successful, Kalem refused to continue producing long films and preferred to go out of business once the industry norm was the feature film, rather than take the risks that feature production involved.

Director Kenean Buell took a company of players to the West Coast with William Wright. They established a studio at Verdugo Canyon, Glendale, on December 11, 1910. Included in the company were Alice Joyce, Mr. and Mrs. George Melford, and Jane Wolfe. Early in 1911, Carlyle Blackwell and William H. West joined the Glendale studio, which produced a one-reel Western every week. Later in 1911, P. C. Hartigan opened a Kalem studio in Santa Monica, at which worked Ruth Roland, Marin Sais, Ed Coxen, and Marshall Neilan, who assisted Hartigan and later became the Santa Monica company's chief director. George Melford took over chief directing chores at the Glendale studio when Buell replaced Olcott in Jacksonville, taking with him Miriam Cooper, Anna Q. Nilsson, Guy Coombs, and Hal Clements. In 1913, Carlyle Blackwell became chief director at the new Kalem studios in Hollywood. Neilan joined him and initiated the "Ham and Bud" comedy series, featuring Lloyd Hamilton and Bud Duncan. J. P. McGowan went West shortly thereafter and produced *The Hazards of Helen* serial, starring Helen Holmes. Later, Helen Gibson was featured in the railroad series.

In 1915, Kalem made a series of three-reel "Broadway Favorites" released with General, at a new studio in Cliffside, New Jersey. In 1916, Kalem ended production. Early in 1919, Vitagraph* purchased Kalem's properties, films, and laboratory equipment, as William Wright became associated with Vitagraph. Later that same year, it was announced that Kalem's films would be reissued.

BIBLIOGRAPHY

Blaisdell, George. "Mecca of the Motion Picture." *The Moving Picture World,* July 10, 1915, p. 218.

Condon, Mabel. "Hot Chocolate and Reminiscences at Nine of the Morning." *Photoplay*, January 1915, pp. 69–72.

Gauntier, Gene. *Blazing the Trail*. Manuscript in the files of the Museum of Modern Art, December 16, 1928.

"Kalem Company (Inc.)." *The Moving Picture World*, June 8, 1907, p. 223.

"Kalem Players Combine in Search for Picturesque Locations." *Motion Picture News*, March 31, 1917, p. 2021.

"Kalem Railroad Films Have Seven Years' History." *Motion Picture News*, January 8, 1916, p. 81.

"Kalem's Achievements as Pioneer." *The Moving Picture World*, March 10, 1917, pp. 1504–5.

Slide, Anthony. "The Kalem Serial Queens." *The Silent Picture*, no. 1, Winter 1968–69, pp. 8–11.

———. "The O'Kalems." In *Aspects of American Film History prior to 1920*. Metuchen, N.J.: Scarecrow Press, 1978, pp. 87–97.

RESOURCES:

Scrapbooks: Lincoln Center Library of the Performing Arts.

KAUFMAN ASTORIA STUDIOS. See Astoria Studios

K. C. BOOKING COMPANY. See KINETOPHOTE FILM CORPORATION

KELLUM TALKING PICTURES, similar to Edison's Kinetophone*, was developed in Los Angeles by Orlando E. Kellum in 1913. Kellum recorded the action and sound simultaneously, utilizing a device to synchronize the recording phonograph and the camera. Electrical impulses from a commutator connected to the phonograph turntable were sent by wires to a series of electromagnets in the synchronizing device used for either the camera or the projector. The electromagnets were linked by pistons to a crankshaft that rotated the projector mechanism in exact synchronization with the phonograph.

Although not particularly successful from a commercial standpoint, Kellum Talking Pictures were important because the process was utilized by D. W. Griffith for his 1921 feature, *Dream Street*, which included a title song performed by leading man Ralph Graves and an introduction by the director. Accompanying *Dream Street* at its initial screenings in New York, Brooklyn, and Chicago were a series of short subjects produced by Kellum, with such personalities as labor leader Samuel Gompers, the Van Eps Trio, Sam Moore and His Singing Saw, and singer Ruby Norton.

BIBLIOGRAPHY

Hoffman, Hugh. "A New Talking Picture Device." *The Moving Picture World*, November 1, 1913, p. 483.

RESOURCES

Films: UCLA Film and Television Archive.

KENNEDY FEATURES, INC. Aubrey M. Kennedy formed Kennedy Features, Inc., early in 1914 to produce one three- to five-reel feature, starring English tragedienne Constance Crawley and Arthur Maude, every two weeks. Kennedy was vice president and general manager, while Irving C. Ackerman was the president. Offices for the company were located in the World's Tower Building at 110 West 40th Street in New York. The name of the cinematographer, William F. Alder, was given equal prominence in the main titles of its films as those of the director and scenarist. Its films were shot on the Pacific Coast and released through the Criterion Feature Film Manufacturing Company. Its first productions were *The Bride of Lammermoor* and *Mary Magdalen*, both three-reel features.

BIBLIOGRAPHY

"New Picture Concern." *The Moving Picture World*, January 17, 1914, p. 300.

KEYSTONE FILM COMPANY, formed in 1912 by former Biograph* player and comedy director Mack Sennett (1880–1960) and the owners of the New York Motion Picture Company, Adam Kessel, Jr., and Charles O. Baumann, released its first two films, *Cohen Collects a Debt* and *The Water Nymph*, on September 23, 1912, and continued to release a weekly split-reel on Mondays on the Mutual* program. Its offices were located at 150 East 14th Street, New York.

Mabel Normand, Fred Mace, Ford Sterling, and Sennett were featured in the comedies, which Sennett directed. Productions were, at first, shot at Fort Lee, New Jersey*, and in September 1912 the company went West and settled at the old Bison studio in Edendale, California. The demand for Keystone comedies grew, and soon Mabel Normand began directing a second company. Charles Chaplin made his motion picture debut in Keystone's *Making a Living* early in 1914. Before he left the company at the end of that year, Chaplin had developed his Tramp character and was directing and writing his own films, in addition to starring in them. On November 14, 1914, the feature-length *Tillie's Punctured Romance*, featuring Mabel Normand, Marie Dressler, and Chaplin, was released, and it was a huge success.

In 1915, Keystone, along with D. W. Griffith's and Thomas H. Ince's companies, formed the Triangle Film Corporation*. At that time Keystone was comprised of three production companies. In 1917, Keystone began releasing with Paramount*. That same year Keystone officially went out of existence, although it might be argued that it continued until Mack Sennett Productions went bankrupt in 1933. (In 1928, Sennett moved to new studios in Studio City, California, studios that later became known as Republic*.)

BIBLIOGRAPHY

Bartlett, Randolph. "Why Aren't We Killed?" *Photoplay,* April 1916, pp. 81–84.

Lahue, Kalton C. *Mack Sennett's Keystone.* South Brunswick, N.J.: A. S. Barnes, 1971.

Lahue, Kalton C., and Terry Brewer. *Kops and Custards.* Norman, Okla.: University of Oklahoma Press, 1967.

"The Psychology of a Laugh." *The Moving Picture World,* July 10, 1915, p. 236.

Todd, Stanley W. "Putting the Key in Keystone." *Motion Picture Classic,* November 1917, pp. 27–31.

"Where Laughs Are Made." *The Moving Picture World,* July 10, 1915, pp. 233–36.

RESOURCES

Papers, Photographs, and Scripts: Academy of Motion Picture Arts and Sciences (Mack Sennett Collection).

KILLIAM SHOWS, INC., was possibly the best-known supplier of silent film footage to television. It was formed by Paul Killiam (born 1916), who, in 1946, opened the Old Knick Music Hall on New York's Second Avenue and included as part of the entertainment early silent films. Killiam began acquiring rights to early films, including the Biograph* and Edison* productions, and the films of D. W. Griffith. He was involved in the restoration of many films in cooperation with the Museum of Modern Art. Killiam was first seen on television, on a regular basis, on CBS in 1952 with *The Paul Killiam Show,* which utilized Edison films strictly for laugh value. His first major television series (produced in collaboration with Saul Turrell) was *Movie Museum* (1954–1955). It was followed by *Silents Please* (released nontheatrically as *The History of the Motion Picture*), which Killiam again produced in collaboration with Saul Turrell and which consisted of 39 30-minute programs. Killiam Shows began screening silent films in their entirety on television with the series *The Silent Years,* first seen on PBS. Killiam Shows was also involved in *The Legend of Valentino* (1961) and *The Great Chase* (1962).

Address: 6 East 39th Street, New York, N.Y. 10016.

KINEMACOLOR, the earliest commercially successful natural color film process, was a two-color additive system, involving photography through a red-orange and a blue-green gelatin filter and projection through filters of the same colors at 32 frames per second. It was invented by Edward R. Turner and F. Marshall Lee and exploited by American Charles Urban (1867–1942). The first Kinemacolor demonstration was given in London on May 1, 1908, and it was in the United Kingdom that the process gained popularity. Its greatest success came with the filming of the 1911 *Delhi Durbar.* Kinemacolor was first exhibited in the United States, at New York's Madison Square Garden, on December 11, 1909; the Kinemacolor Company of America was established in 1910, and, by 1913, Kinemacolor had reached the height of its American popularity. By the middle of the second decade of the twentieth century, the process had been discarded, largely because of complaints from the audience that the color hurt their eyes.

BIBLIOGRAPHY

Allbee, Burton H. "Impressions of Kinemacolor Films." *The Moving Picture World,* December 25, 1909, pp. 915–16.

"All Eyes Are on Kinemacolor." *Motography,* July 12, 1913, p. 6.

Brown, Theodore. "My Impressions of 'Kinemacolor.' " *The Moving Picture World,* May 28, 1910, p. 886.

Harrison, Louis Reeves. "Sauntering with Kinemacolor." *The Moving Picture World,* February 15, 1913, pp. 661–62.

Thomas, D. B. *The First Colour Motion Pictures.* London: Her Majesty's Stationery Office, 1969.

KINEMACOLOR COMPANY OF AMERICA. Following the 1909 New York presentation of Kinemacolor films, Gilbert H. Aymar, a businessman from Allentown, Pennsylvania, secured an exclusive option on the equipment. With James K. Bowen, Aymar formed the Kinemacolor Company of America in April 1910, with offices in Allentown. By July 1911, the company's offices had moved to 145 West 45th Street, New York, and J. J. Murdock had become the general manager.

In May 1912, the company, then headed by Henry J. Brock, hired Thomas L. Cochrane to superintend the organization of a plant and stock company to produce dramatic and comedy films with the Kinemacolor process. Since the films had to be taken by sunlight, it was appropriate that among the first pictures planned were a travel series to be taken by Alfred G. Gosden of various national parks, called "See America First," and films of U.S. naval battleships. Brock engaged David Miles as the head of Kinemacolor's dramatic production units. Miles worked with three companies at Kinemacolor's Whitestone, Long Island, plant, and on location throughout the eastern states.

In the fall of 1912, he formed three more companies of 70 people and took one to the Grand Canyon and the remaining two to Hollywood, where they moved into a studio at 4500 Sunset Boulevard, previously the Revier Laboratories and later the Fine Arts* studio. Some of those going east were leading lady Linda Arvidson Griffith, Mabel Van Buren, Stella Razetto, Clara Bracy, Ruby Ross, Ethel Davis, Gaston Bell, Charles Fleming, Jack Brammell, Charles Haydon, Guy Oliver, Robert Broderick, Murdock McQuarrie, and Mahlon Hamilton. Frank Woods also directed with the Hollywood company, and Lee Dougherty was the scenario editor. William Haddock directed the company in New York. Lillian Russell was engaged for two weeks at the end of 1912.

Although Kinemacolor obtained a license from the Motion Picture Patents Company* in August 1913, permitting it to install its service in any licensed theatre, the company was failing because of the high cost of the process and the limited number of theatres equipped to exhibit it.

Its Hollywood studio closed in June 1913. Miles returned to New York with director Charles Fleming, Gaston Bell, Jack Brammell, Charles Perley, Guy Oliver, and Linda Griffith, while other members stayed in California, joining other companies. In October 1913, Kinemacolor built a studio at Lowville, New York, near the St. Lawrence River. Also in October, Miles left the company for Biograph* and took most of the stock company with him. Theodore Marston replaced Miles and formed a new company. In November 1913, Kinemacolor formed the Weber-Fields-Kinemacolor Company to make comedies with the famous vaudeville team. Roy McCardell was hired to write scenarios. Rumors circulated that the Kinemacolor plant at Whitestone would again be used for production and that it would make a five-reel feature, but by 1915 Kinemacolor was effectively dead.

BIBLIOGRAPHY

"Demonstration of Kinemacolor." *The Moving Picture World,* August 6, 1910, pp. 291–92.

"Kinemacolor Closed." *The New York Dramatic Mirror,* June 11, 1913, p. 25.

"Kinemacolor Company Branches Out." *The Moving Picture World,* May 26, 1912, p. 716.

"Kinemacolor Company Now Releasing." *The Moving Picture World,* October 12, 1912, p. 231.

"Kinemacolor in America." *The Moving Picture World,* April 16, 1910, p. 605.

KINETOGRAPH AND KINETOSCOPE. The Kinetograph is the name of Thomas Alvah Edison's first practical motion picture camera, developed by Edison employee W. K. L. Dickson, in principle if not in practical form, in 1891 and patented in 1893. Film photographed by the Kinetograph was first viewed on a peep-show device called a Kinetoscope, a coin-operated machine inside a wooden box. The first commercial presentation of motion pictures in the United States took place in a kinetoscope parlor at 1155 Broadway, New York, on April 14, 1894.

These first films, known as Kinetoscopic records, were produced at a studio built of wood and tar paper at Edison's West Orange laboratory and nicknamed by the inventor's staff as the "Black Maria." (The "Black Maria" presently on view at the Edison National Historic Site in Orange, New Jersey, is a re-creation.) The first film to be copyrighted, on January 7, 1894, was *Edison Kinetoscopic Record of a Sneeze,* which showed Edison employee Fred Ott sneezing.

BIBLIOGRAPHY

Hendricks, Gordon. *The Edison Motion Picture Myth.* Berkeley, Calif.: University of California Press, 1961.

KINETOGRAPH COMPANY was organized by J. J. Kennedy, of the Biograph* Company, and P. L. Waters, former general manager of General Film Company, early in 1913. It obtained a license from the Motion Picture Patents Company* to lease licensed pictures and established distribution offices in New York, Atlanta, and New Orleans. It began distribution on February 9, 1913, but went out of business two months later following a dispute over the distribution rights to the Detective Burns film *Exposure of the Land Swindlers.* All of Kinetograph's stock and assets were sold to General Film Company.

BIBLIOGRAPHY

"Kinetograph Company Quits Business." *The Moving Picture World,* April 26, 1913, p. 359.

KINETOPHONE. The concept of combining a phonograph with a film projector and thus creating synchronized sound motion pictures was conceived by Thomas Edison in 1887. His assistant, W. K. L. Dickson, worked on the project, which was called a Kineto-Phonograph, and by 1895 may have come up with a workable machine. The project was subsequently shelved until 1911, when Edison's staff developed a method of amplification that permitted the phonograph recorder to pick up sounds from a distance of more than 20 feet. Following various modifications, the Kinetophone—one of the first commercial sound film projects—was launched in 1913. The films that were screened in vaudeville houses rather than motion picture theatres were released by the American Talking-Picture Company, which also leased the projection-sound machines and which was formed by B. F. Keith and E. F. Albee's United Booking Offices of America. Kinetophone films were seen spasmodically during 1913 and 1914 but were not successful, largely because of problems with keeping the phonograph record in synchronization with the film and because the performers in the films were minor entertainers and audiences had little reason for paying to see such performers on film when, for the same amount of money, they could see vaudeville headliners in person.

BIBLIOGRAPHY

Rogoff, Rosalind. "Edison's Dream: A Brief History of the Kinetophone." *Cinema Journal* 15, 2 (Spring 1976): pp. 58–68.

Shifrin, Art. "The Trouble with Kinetophone." *American Cinematographer,* September 1983, pp. 50–54, 115–25.

RESOURCES

Films: Library of Congress; Museum of Modern Art.
Papers: Edison National Historic Site

KINETOPHOTE FILM CORPORATION and the K. C. Booking Company, Inc., were established in November 1914 to work in conjunction with one another in the release of

American and foreign-made films in the United States. Offices for both companies were at 126–133 West 46th Street, New York. Ira H. Simmons was the general manager of Kinetophote. Some of its releases included films from the Ambrosia Company of Italy and the Hollandia Film Company.

BIBLIOGRAPHY

"Tips from Kinetophone." *The Moving Picture World,* November 7, 1914, p. 800.

KINETOSCOPE PARLORS provided Americans with their first opportunity to view motion pictures as a peep show attraction. The first was opened in New York, at 1155 Broadway, by Andrew Holland on April 14, 1894. The first films were Edison* productions.

KING-BEE FILMS CORPORATION. Louis B. Burstein, one of the organizers of the New York Motion Picture Company* and the Reliance Stock Company, formed King-Bee Films in 1917 to make Billy West comedies. Its studio was located in Jacksonville, Florida. Other players in the films included Ethel Gibson and Oliver Hardy.

KING BROS. PRODUCTIONS, INC. See KING INTERNATIONAL CORPORATION

KING INTERNATIONAL CORPORATION. On April 15, 1942, three brothers, Frank, Maurice (who died in 1977), and Herman King, organized King Bros. Productions as a low-budget production company, whose best-known features were *Gun Crazy/Deadly Is the Female* (1950), *The Brave One* (1956), and *Return of the Gunfighter* (1966). The name of the company was changed to King International Corporation in 1970. It ceased operations in 1992.

KINNEY NATIONAL SERVICES, INC. See WARNER BROS. PICTURES, INC.

KINOGRAMS. See NEWSREELS

KINO INTERNATIONAL CORPORATION was formed, as a Denver-based corporation, by William Pence in 1975. At that time, it handled the 35mm distribution of Janus Films and some productions from Samuel Goldwyn*, Walter Wanger, and RKO*. The company was acquired in 1977 by Donald Krim (who had earlier created the Classics Division of United Artists), and he added the libraries of Charles Chaplin, Alexander Korda, David O. Selznick, Harold Lloyd, and Grove Press. In 1982, Kino acquired Walter Reade's Continental Films Library, along with some Samuel Bronston productions and George Stevens's *Giant.* The following year, Kino released the "restored" versions of the Louise Brooks/G. W. Pabst features, *Pandora's Box* and *Diary of a Lost Girl.* In 1984, it announced worldwide distribution of a restored version of Erich von Stroheim's unfinished 1928 feature, *Queen Kelly,* starring Gloria

Swanson. As of January 1, 1989, Kino lost the rights to the Chaplin films. In 1986, it took over the library of Horizon Releasing. Kino created a video division in the 1980s, and continues as a prominent independent distributor.

Address: 333 West 39th Street, Suite 503, New York, N.Y. 10018.

KIT PARKER FILMS, INC., founded in 1971, distributes the classic films of Warner Bros.*, Orion*, Republic*, and others in 35mm*, and, for many years, has been a leading 16mm* distributor.

Address: P.O. Box 16022, Monterey, Calif. 93942.

KLEINE-EDISON FEATURE SERVICE began operations in June 1915 to distribute features produced by the two member companies of the Motion Picture Patents Company*. It claimed to have abolished the advance deposit system. Beginning September 2, 1916, the Kleine-Edison-Selig-Essanay Service replaced the previous company and released its members' products through the George Kleine* exchanges.

BIBLIOGRAPHY

"Kleine-Edison Merger Formed." *The Moving Picture World,* July 24, 1915, p. 626.

KLEVER KOMEDIES, starring Victor Moore and directed by either Harry Jackson or Chester M. Vonde, were produced between 1916 and 1919 by New York-based Klever Pictures, Inc.

BIBLIOGRAPHY

Webb, Stephen R. "Klever Komedies in the Great War: One Studio's Contribution to the War Effort." *Film History,* vol. 3, no. 2, 1989, pp. 105–13.

KLIEG LIGHTS were carbon arc lamps utilized in film studios from the first half of the second decade of the twentieth century onward. Because of the intensity of the ultraviolet rays given off by the lamps, many actors and actresses in the silent era suffered from what was called "Klieg eyes," the symptoms of which were painful inflammation and partial blindness that often lasted for several days. Carbon arc lighting of studios was eventually superceded by tungsten lighting, with the first feature film entirely lit by tungsten being Universal's *Broadway* (1929). Klieg lights were manufactured by the Kliegl Bros. (hence the name) of 321 West 50th Street, New York, later renamed the Kliegl Bros. Universal Electric Stage Lighting Co. Today, the term Klieg lights is closely associated with the giant searchlights at Hollywood premieres and other Los Angeles events.

KNICKERBOCKER STAR FEATURES began producing three-reel pictures in May 1915 for release every other Wednesday with the General Film Company service. Stanner E. V. Taylor was the head of the directorial staff. Players making Knickerbocker films included Ralph Stuart, Alice Brady, J. Forbes Robertson, Mary Nash, Lenore Ulrich, Florence Rockwell, Walter Hampden, and Marion Leonard (Taylor's wife). Knickerbocker had a studio in Flushing, New York In February 1917, the company went out of business, and the Balboa Amusement Producing Company* began producing Knickerbocker Star Features for General's program.

BIBLIOGRAPHY

"Knickerbocker Star Features Successful." *The Moving Picture World,* September 25, 1915, p. 2189.

KRITERION FILM CORPORATION was incorporated in November 1914 by H. F. Rhatigan, E. H. Reilly, and C. H. Ayres as a successor to the Mica Film Company. With offices at the Mecca Building, 1600 Broadway, New York, Kriterion began, in January 1915, releasing films of West Coast companies Crown City Film Manufacturing Company*, Navajo Film Manufacturing Company*, Monarch Producing Company*, Alhambra Motion Picture Company*, Robin's Photoplays, Inc., Santa Barbara Motion Picture Company*, Liberty Film Company*, and the Nash Motion Picture Company, Inc.*

Its projected releasing output was to be 21 reels per week, including six one-reel subjects and six two-reelers. Aubrey M. Kennedy, the general manager of the Santa Barbara Motion Picture Company, was general representative of the company and had complete authority over the productions of the companies associated with Kriterion. Although each producing company had its own scenario department, Kriterion retained "cooperative jurisdiction" over scenarios and all matters pertaining to each company. Also, the laboratories for the companies were on the East Coast.

The financial difficulties of Kriterion were reported as early as January 1915; the companies associated with Kriterion complained that they could not pay their actors' and employees' back salaries. In May 1915, the Alhambra Motion Picture Company and four minor creditors made an application for receivership of Kriterion, which was accepted. The Associated Film Service Corporation began releasing the product of most of Kriterion's former producing companies in October 1915. Although news items in August 1915 announced that the new Kriterion Sales Company was in the process of reforming the old Kriterion program, the effort never materialized.

BIBLIOGRAPHY

"Kriterion to Release January First." *The Moving Picture World,* November 21, 1914, p. 1052.

LABADIE-DETROIT MOTION PICTURE COM-PANY, active in 1915 and 1916, was founded by Oliver Labadie, and located on Labadie Island, Kent Lake, New Hudson, Michigan.

LACLEDE WESTERN FEATURES. See LLOYD FILMS, INC.

THE LADD COMPANY was formed in 1979 as a "mini studio" when Alan Ladd, Jr., (born 1937) left as president of 20th Century-Fox*. Two other Fox employees joined Ladd in the creation of the new company: Jay Kanter and Gareth Wigan. For his logo, Ladd selected a spreading and luxuriantly green oak tree. The Ladd Company was financed in part by Warner Bros.*, with which it had an exclusive distribution deal from 1979 to 1984, and on whose Burbank Studios* lot the company made its headquarters. Sandy Lieberson served as London head of the Ladd Company until the British office was closed in January 1984, and it was Lieberson who was responsible for bringing *Chariots of Fire* (1981) to Ladd's attention. The Ladd Company acquired American rights to the feature, which was released through Warner Bros. *Chariots of Fire* and *Police Academy* (1984) were the only two major "hits" of the Ladd Company, although *The Right Stuff* (1983) enjoyed limited success. The organization ended its relationship with Warner Bros. in April 1984, and with Alan Ladd, Jr., occupied elsewhere, it was inactive from 1984 through 1994, when it became involved in the production of *Braveheart* (1995). When Ladd signed a production deal with Paramount* in August 1993, the company moved to that studio's lot.

Address: 5555 Melrose Avenue, Hollywood, Calif. 90038.

BIBLIOGRAPHY

Waters, Harry F. "The Ladd Co's Wrong Stuff." *Newsweek,* December 12, 1983, p. 88.

LAEMMLE FILM SERVICE. See UNIVERSAL PICTURES

LAEMMLE THEATRES. The Laemmle Theatre chain is a small, Los Angeles-based operation with little more than a dozen theatres, specializing in foreign-language films. It is important because of its location in the American film production capital and because so many shorts* and documentaries* nominated for Academy Award consideration rely on Laemmle theatres for eligibility screenings. (The Academy Awards rules are such that most shorts and documentaries must play seven consecutive days in the Los Angeles area to be eligible for consideration.) *Screen International* (August 27, 1983) described the Laemmle theatres as "the most respected art and foreign film houses in the U.S." The chain was founded by Max Laemmle, a distant nephew of Carl Laemmle, who became an American exhibitor in 1939. He acquired the first of his theatres, the Los Feliz, in 1947, and it became the flagship for his chain. As of 1997, the chain consisted of the Royal in West Los Angeles, the Monica (five screens) in Santa Monica, the Town Center (five screens) in Encino, the Esquire and the Colorado in Pasadena, the Sunset-5 (five screens) in West Hollywood, the Music Hall (three screens) in Beverly Hills, and the Grande (four screens) in downtown Los Angeles.

Address: 11523 Santa Monica Boulevard, Los Angeles, Calif. 90025.

BIBLIOGRAPHY

"Max Laemmle: Laemmle Theatres." *Los Angeles,* March 1981, p. 181.
Thomas, Kevin. "Cultivating the Foreign Film Market." *Los Angeles Times,* Calendar, December 30, 1979, pp. 31–32.
Williams, Dick. "Max Laemmle Devotee of Both Movies and Art." *Los Angeles Mirror,* July 29, 1961, pp. 2, 4.

LAIRD INTERNATIONAL STUDIOS. One of the oldest—as late as 1996, a glass-topped stage dating from late in the second decade of the twentieth century still stands on the lot—and the most familiar of all American studio lots, the Laird International Studios opened in 1919 as the new studios, on Washington Boulevard in Culver City, California, of producer Thomas H. Ince. Some of the first films to be shot there were *Behind the Door* (1920) and *Homer Comes Home* (1920). In 1925, following Ince's unexpected death, the studios were acquired by Cecil B. DeMille and utilized for the production of features for Producers' Distributing Corporation*. In 1928, DeMille disposed of his interest in the studio and it became the Pathé* Studios, becoming the RKO-Pathé Studios, in 1930, with the merger of the two companies. Among the major RKO* productions filmed on the lot were *What Price Hollywood* (1932), *A Bill of Divorcement* (1932), *King Kong* (1933), *The Informer* (1935), *Top Hat* (1935), and *Citizen Kane* (1941). The first three-strip Technicolor* feature, *Becky Sharp,* was shot there.

In 1935, while still used by RKO, the studio was leased by David O. Selznick and the name was changed to the Selznick International Studios. The colonial-style administration building at the front of the studio, built by Thomas H. Ince in 1919, became the trademark for Selznick International Pictures*. Here Selznick filmed many of his greatest productions, beginning with *Little Lord Fauntleroy* (1936) and including *The Garden of Allah* (1936), *A Star Is Born* (1937), *Rebecca* (1940), *Spellbound* (1945), *Duel in the Sun* (1946), and *Portrait of Jennie* (1948). The sets from *King of Kings* (1927) and *King Kong* were burned by Selznick for the burning-of-Atlanta sequence from *Gone with the Wind* (1939).

With RKO's demise, the studios were taken over by Desilu Productions and utilized for a number of independent features and television programs, with 20th Century-Fox* filming a number of productions there. Perfect Film and Chemical acquired the lot in 1968; in 1969, it was purchased by OSF Industries, Ltd., and, in 1970, renamed the Culver City Studios. Laird International purchased the lot in December 1977 and renamed it Laird International Studios. In 1986, the studio again changed hands, when it was purchased for $24 million by Grant Tinker Gannet Entertainment. In June 1991, Sony Corp. acquired the studio for $84 million, to serve as the headquarters for Columbia's television operations.

Address: 9336 West Washington Boulevard, Culver City, Calif. 90232.

LAKE ARROWHEAD in California's San Bernardino Mountains is a favorite film location, seen to advantage in F. W. Murnau's *Sunrise* (1927). It was utilized by Cecil B. DeMille as early as 1913 for *The Squaw Man,* and has also been seen in *Of Human Hearts* (1938), *Untamed* (1940), and *The Yearling* (1946), among many others.

LAKE PLACID, NEW YORK. See EXCELSIOR FEATURE FILM COMPANY, INC.

LA MESA, CALIFORNIA. See SAN DIEGO.

LANDMARK THEATRE CORP. was created by Kim Jorgensen in 1974 with the opening of the Nuart Theatre in West Los Angeles. In December 1988, the theatre chain was sold to Heritage Entertainment, Inc., at which time it had 42 screens in 22 locations, and in 1991, it merged with the Samuel Goldwyn Company*.

Address: 2222 South Barrington Avenue, Los Angeles, Calif. 90064.

BIBLIOGRAPHY

Harris, William. "See It Again, Sam." *Forbes,* May 10, 1982, pp. 164–66.

LASALIDA FILMS, INC. (the name means "light of the sun"), was formed in April 1917 to produce eight films a year starring the four-year-old Baby Marie Osborne. The films were to be released by the Pathé* Exchange. W. A. S. Douglas, formerly with Pathé, was the vice president and general manager of the company, which used the David Horsley* studio in Los Angeles. Lasalida's first films were *When Baby Forgot* and *Miss Captain Kidd.* The company went out of existence at the end of 1917 when the Diando Film Company* was formed by Douglas and Baby Marie's father to produce her films.

BIBLIOGRAPHY

"Lasalida Films, Inc. Formed." *The Moving Picture World,* April 14, 1917, p. 259.

LA SALLE FILM COMPANY released one-reel comedies on the Mutual* program in 1917. Marion De La Parelle was the company's director, with King Vidor as codirector and scenarist. Studios for the company were initially located in Hollywood and later in Culver City.

"THE LASKY BARN" originally stood approximately at the junction of Hollywood Boulevard and Vine Street in Hollywood and is purportedly where Cecil B. DeMille and Oscar Apfel began shooting *The Squaw Man* in Hollywood in December 1913. (*The Squaw Man* is erroneously considered to have been the first feature-length film to be shot in Hollywood.) The building is called "The Lasky Barn" because Jesse L. Lasky was one of the producers of *The Squaw Man* and the creative genius behind Paramount Pictures*, whose first studio was located next to the barn.

When Paramount moved to its present location, the barn also moved—in 1927. The barn was utilized by Paramount as a gymnasium for many years and was also used as part of the set for the *Bonanza* television series. On December 26, 1956, it was declared California Historical Landmark No. 554, the first state landmark connected with the film industry. Paramount gave the barn to the Hollywood Historic Trust in October 1979, and the building was moved to a temporary site adjacent to the Palace Theatre on Vine Street. During the night of November 11, 1982, the barn was moved to its permanent site, at 2100 North Highland Avenue, in the parking lot of the Hollywood Bowl, where it opened as the Hollywood Studio Museum in November 1985. On September 18, 1995, an arson fire damaged part of the structure, and since then the Museum has been closed.

The history of the barn is clouded in mystery, and most historians agree that the present building was almost entirely rebuilt—it is a wooden structure—in the thirties or forties.

LAUGH-O-GRAM FILMS. See WALT DISNEY PRODUCTIONS

LEE-BRADFORD CORPORATION (sometimes known as Artlee) was a minor distributor of independent productions of the twenties, formed by Arthur A. Lee, the company's president, and F. G. Bradford, its vice president. None of the more than 30 features released by this New York-based organization are memorable.

LEGION OF DECENCY. See NATIONAL LEGION OF DECENCY

LENAUER INTERNATIONAL FILMS, INC., active from 1935 to 1940, was formed by Jean H. Lenauer (who died in 1983 at the age of 79) to distribute foreign-language films, mainly French, in the United States. Contrary to published reports at the time of Lenauer's death, he did not initially distribute such classic French films as *La Grande Illusion* or *Carnival in Flanders,* but, rather, he distributed lesser features such as Sacha Guitry's *Pearls of the Crown* (1937). Lenauer also leased the Filmarte Theatre at 202 West 58th Street in New York and made it the East Coast home of the best in foreign-language films. Lenauer appeared as the waiter in the critically acclaimed 1981 feature *My Dinner with André.*

LENTICULAR FILM was an early system for color photography in 16mm, introduced by Eastman Kodak in 1928 and in use through the mid 1930s. It is a normal black-and-white film stock with a series of bands, or lenticules, embossed into the base of the film. During exposure, a color-banded lens in conjunction with these lenticules generates multiple black-and-white images in the film emulsion. During projection, the lenticules in combination with a color-banded projection lens combine the black-and-white images into a single full-color image.

LEO THE LION was the first, and best known, animal to serve as the Metro-Goldwyn-Mayer* trademark, turning his head and roaring at the opening of each of the studio's films. The massive lion, weighing 734 pounds, was captured, at the age of one year, in the Nubian desert, and brought to Los Angeles in 1921 to appear in jungle films. Following his debut as the M-G-M logo, Leo was exhibited around the country, touring in a specially designed and constructed car, the first lion to be transported in an airplane, and with his handler giving out autographed photographs signed, "Growlingly yours, Leo." Leo died at the Philadelphia Zoo, at the age of 20, in April 1935. Following his death, the animal was buried at his handler's, Captain Volney Phifer's, farm in Long Hill, New Jersey. In 1994, plans were announced to turn Leo's grave into a parking lot, and various local residents campaigned to have the site named an historic monument or to rebury Leo's bones in a purpose-built mausoleum.

BIBLIOGRAPHY

Langley, William. "Roaring Trade." *The Sunday Times* (London), Style section, November 6, 1994, p. 20.
"Leo, Metro's Lion, Is Dead at Twenty." *Motion Picture News,* May 2, 1935, p. 35.

LEWIS J. SELZNICK PRODUCTIONS, INC., was incorporated early in April 1916 after Selznick left his position as vice president and general manager of the World Film Corporation* and created the Clara Kimball Young Corporation with World's leading star. World was not the only party upset at the new development. Young's husband, James, sued Selznick for alienation of his wife's affection, a charge that Selznick dismissed by stating that the troubles with their marriage started long before he became interested in Clara Kimball Young's artistic success. Young herself, later in 1917, sued Selznick for having himself elected president of her company and then creating his own company to distribute her films, thus taking both creative control and financial rewards from her.

Selznick Productions soon released films from the Herbert Brenon Film Corporation, of which Selznick was half owner and which produced films starring Nazimova; the Kitty Gordon Company; and the Norma Talmadge Film Corporation. Selznick's distributing company opened franchise exchanges* in every major city. He owned 50 percent of the individual exchange, and the local owners, such as Stanley Mastbaum in Philadelphia and Harry Garson in Detroit, owned the other 50 percent. Others stars releasing with Selznick included Constance Talmadge and Dorothy Gish.

In August 1917, Adolph Zukor secretly bought 50 percent of the company and offered the use of the Lasky Studio in Hollywood for production, with the result that Selznick still presided over the company, but its new name, Select Pictures Corporation, took Selznick's name away from public attention.

Select continued to release films of Young and the Talmadge sisters and also those of Alice Brady and Marion Davies. Arthur S. Kane was the general manager.

In January 1919, the Selznick name appeared on marquees again when Lewis's son Myron organized Selznick Pictures Corporation and began producing films starring Olive Thomas. Myron, who for several months previous had been studio manager of the Norma Talmadge Film Corporation, was backed financially by his mother. Myron's brother Howard was his assistant, and brother David was the treasurer. Eugene O'Brien became Myron's second star in films directed by Ralph Ince, and Elsie James was also featured in the company's films.

On April 10, 1919, Lewis J. Selznick bought Zukor's half of Select for over $1 million, giving Zukor and Famous Players a profit of more than $500,000. In May 1919, David Selznick, then known as David J. Selznick, became the New England manager of Select. Select went bankrupt in 1923.

BIBLIOGRAPHY

"Lewis J. Selznick Now Sole Owner of Select." *The Moving Picture World,* April 19, 1919, p. 340.
"Selznick Branches Out." *The Moving Picture World,* April 8, 1916, p. 272.
"Selznick Pictures a Family Affair." *The Moving Picture World,* March 15, 1919, p. 1477.

"Selznick Pictures Again in Field." *The Moving Picture World,* January 18, 1919, p. 316.

LIBERTY FILM COMPANY of San Mateo, California, began releasing its films early in 1915 with Kriterion*. By June 1915, it released with the Associated Service. S. Lindblom was the president.

LIBERTY FILMS, INC., was an independent production company, incorporated in January 1945 by Frank Capra (who served as president), William Wyler, George Stevens, and Sam Briskin. Its offices were located on the RKO* lot, with Marian Spitzer serving as head of the Story Department and Lou Smith as Publicity Department head. The company produced only one feature, Frank Capra's *It's a Wonderful Life* (1946); *State of the Union* was made as a Liberty Film but released as an "M-G-M Picture." Financial troubles forced the sale of Liberty Films to Paramount* in 1947 for 150,000 shares; at that time, Henry Ginsberg was named president and the principals signed contracts with Paramount.

LIBERTY MOTION PICTURE COMPANY was formed in July 1914 to make one four-reel feature per week and one- and two-reel comedies at regular intervals. Its studio was in Germantown, Pennsylvania. John Oxford was the president and Howard G. Bobb the general manager and vice president. It distributed its films through Sawyer, Inc.* In November 1914, the company reorganized, backed by a group of Alaskan millionaires. Now located in San Mateo and Glendale, California, it made comedy-dramas released by Kriterion*. Marguerite Clayton, Mona Darkfeather, and True Boardman made films for Liberty. In December 1914, a receiver was appointed for the company.

BIBLIOGRAPHY

"A Big New Enterprise." *The Moving Picture World,* July 18, 1914, pp. 438–39.
"New Liberty Film Company." *The Moving Picture World,* November 28, 1914, p. 1213.

LIFE PHOTO FILM CORPORATION was organized sometime in 1913 or 1914 and released its first film, *The Baker's Daughter,* in mid-1914. Edward M. Roskam was the president, and Jesse J. Goldburg was the secretary and general manager of the company, whose studio and laboratory were in Grantwood, New Jersey. It began releasing to the states rights* market; then, in late 1914, aligned itself with the Alco Film Corporation*; withdrew from Alco at the end of 1914 because, it complained, Alco failed to live up to the terms of its contract; and, in April 1915, began releasing through Paramount*.

An allied concern of Life Photo was the Commercial Motion Pictures Company, Inc., which in October 1913 filmed the World's Championship baseball series and the Army-Navy football game and made the films available for exhibition in nearby cities the same night as the events.

Roskam was also the president of Commercial, which had a factory at 102 West 101st Street, New York. In mid-1915, Roskam and his vice president, Leonard Abrahams, resigned at the request of the stockholders of both Life Photo and Commercial. In the reorganization, Bernard Loewenthal became president, while Goldburg remained secretary and general manager. Life Photo, with a substantial increase in capital, increased production, planning by September 1915 to release one five-reel feature every week. It planned to make adaptations of stage successes, but the company disbanded in 1916; at the end of that year it sold, outright, negatives for eight films to the Twentieth Century Film Company.

BIBLIOGRAPHY

"Life Photo Corporation Reorganized." *The Moving Picture World,* June 5, 1915, p. 1583.

LINCOLN AND PARKER FILM COMPANY of Worcester, Massachusetts, with Thomas Edison's son, Charles, on its board of directors, gained control of the Edison* Studio and plant at 2826 Decatur Avenue, New York, and over one million feet of negatives released prior to the arrangement Edison made to distribute its films through the George Kleine* system. Thomas Edison was to act as a consulting editor to the new company, which also planned to produce films. It was active late in the second decade of the twentieth century.

LINCOLN MOTION PICTURE COMPANY, the first film company to be black-owned and -managed, was formed in 1916 by actor Noble M. Johnson and his brother George P., an Omaha mailman. Noble, the president and star, ran Lincoln's studio in Los Angeles, while George—still employed by the post office—distributed the films in Omaha. By 1917, when the company incorporated with capitalization of $75,000, it had created its own exchange and had press agents working for it in the black ghettos of many major American cities.

Lincoln's first release, in 1916, the two-reel *The Realization of a Negro's Ambition,* showed the black hero overcoming discrimination through his own ambition. Its second film, *The Trooper of Troop K,* also released in 1916, portrayed the redemption of a black soldier, "Shiftless Joe," during the Mexican-American War. During the First World War Lincoln produced newsfilms of black sports and Western scenes. In 1920, when Noble Johnson left to continue with Universal*, Clarence Brooks, Lincoln's secretary, starred in *A Man's Duty.* In 1921, Booker T. Washington, Jr., appeared in a "bit" role in *By Right of Birth,* a film about racism and the situation of a black "passing" for white. Lincoln's last film was a documentary about the black 10th Cavalry at Fort Huachuca, Arizona. In 1923, Lincoln, which had always struggled to survive in an all-white industry, disbanded.

BIBLIOGRAPHY

Sampson, Henry T. *Blacks in Black and White: A Source Book on Black Films.* Metuchen, N.J.: Scarecrow Press, 1995.

LIPPERT PICTURES (also known as Lippert Productions) was the distributor/producer of the films of Robert L. Lippert (1909–1976), self-styled "King of the Bs," who specialized in low-budget features, costing an average of $75,000 each. Lippert began his film career as a theatre owner in 1942. Between 1944 and 1966, he produced some 342 films, half of which were released through Lippert Pictures before the producer signed a distribution deal with 20th Century-Fox*. Lippert's best-known production was *The Fly* (1958), and his last was *The Last Shot You Hear* (1969). Following his retirement from film production, Lippert reactivated Lippert Theatres and returned to film exhibition. Other companies controlled by Lippert included Screen Guild Productions (created in the forties), Screen Art Pictures (formed in 1954), and Regal Films (created in the late fifties).

BIBLIOGRAPHY

Okuda, Ted. *Grand National, Producers Releasing Corporation, and Screen Guild/Lippert: Complete Filmographies with Studio Histories*. Jefferson, North Carolina: McFarland, 1989.

L-KO MOTION PICTURE COMPANY, INC. Henry M. "Pathe" Lehrman was the head of the L-KO (meaning Lehrman—Knock Out) Motion Picture Company, Inc., which began production on July 14, 1914. Its average output of three reels of comedy per week was released on the Universal* program. Directors included Lehrman, David Kirkland, Harry Edwards, John B. Blystone, and Harry Matthews (who made children's films). Players included Billie Ritchie, Louise Orth, Harry Gribbin, Reggie Morris, Hank Mann, Charles Winninger, and Gertrude Selby. The L-KO studio was located at Sunset Boulevard and Gower Street in Hollywood, and Victor Heerman was its manager and Joe Morgan the head cameraman. L-KO ceased production in 1919.

LLOYD FILMS, INC., formed late in 1913, was the distributor of the three-reel "Laclede Western Features," released semimonthly. *The Pale-Faced Squaw* was its first release. Offices for the company were located in the Candler Building at 220 West 42d Street in New York, and Charles (Feature) Abrams was the general manager.

BIBLIOGRAPHY

"Abrams Handling Lloyd Films." *The New York Dramatic Mirror,* December 3, 1913, p. 31.

LOBBY CARDS. As the name suggests, lobby cards were created to promote films in theatre lobbies. They came into being in 1913, and the earliest known lobby cards were produced, in sets of four, by Universal. The early lobby cards were in shades of black and white or brown and white; color lobby cards did not appear until 1917. All lobby cards are a standard size of 11 inches by 14 inches. There is no documentation as to why this size was adopted, but it is, perhaps, connected to the fact that 8 lobby cards take up as much space as a one-sheet poster, and the size makes for easy shipping with the poster.

The standard number of lobby cards to a set is 8, with one being a title card. There were exceptions; between 1919 and 1921, the Goldwyn Company* produced 9 lobby cards to a set, and, in the twenties, Universal* produced sets of 16 lobby cards for their major productions. In the thirties, studios issued sets of 4 lobby cards for shorts and serial* releases.

BIBLIOGRAPHY

Kobal, John, and V. A. Wilson. *Foyer Pleasure: The Golden Age of Cinema Lobby Cards*. London: Aurum Press, 1982.
Scott, Kathryn Lee. *Lobby Cards: The Classic Films*. Los Angeles: Pomegranate Press, 1987
———. *Lobby Cards: The Classic Comedies*. Los Angeles: Pomegranate Press, 1988.
Slide, Anthony. *A Collector's Guide to Movie Memorabilia*. Des Moines, Iowa: Wallace-Homestead, 1983.

LOEW'S, INC. See METRO-GOLDWYN-MAYER

LOEW'S THEATRES. See METRO-GOLDWYN-MAYER

LONE PINE is a town in the Alabama Hills, north of Los Angeles, a favorite location for filmmakers from the second decade of the twentieth century through the present. Among the many Westerns shot there are *Just Tony* (1922), *Flaming Guns* (1932), *The Oregon Trail* (1936), *Under Western Skies* (1938), *High Sierra* (1941), *Nevada* (1944), *Broken Arrow* (1950), *Springfield Rifle* (1952), *Stranger Wore a Gun* (1953), *The Law and Jake Wade* (1958), *How the West Was Won* (1962), *Nevada Smith* (1966), and *Joe Kidd* (1972). Non-Westerns filmed at Lone Pine include *Lives of a Bengal Lancer* (1934), *Charge of the Light Brigade* (1936), *A Star Is Born* (1937), *Gunga Din* (1939), *The Loves of Carmen* (1948), *Samson and Delilah* (1949), *King of the Khyber Rifles* (1953), *North to Alaska* (1960), and *The Great Race* (1965).

BIBLIOGRAPHY

Holland, Dave. *On Location in Lone Pine*. Los Angeles: The Holland House, 1990.

LONE STAR FILM CORPORATION. See MUTUAL FILM CORPORATION

LONE STAR PRODUCTIONS, formed in 1933 by Paul W. Malvern and located at 9336 West Washington Boulevard in Culver City, is best known for the series of 16 Western features, starring John Wayne, beginning with *Riders of Destiny* (1933), that it produced between 1933 and

1935. The company also produced a number of minor features before it merged with Republic Pictures*.

It should not be confused with Lone Star International Pictures, a distributor that began operations in Texas in 1977. The best-known release of the Texas-based operation was *The Children of Sanchez* (1978).

LOPERT FILMS DISTRIBUTING COMPANY was formed in 1950, with Ilya Lopert (1906–1971) as president and Robert Dowling (whose company, City Investing, financially controlled the organization) as board chairman. The company was initially associated with Alexander Korda; its aim was to distribute quality British, Italian, and Hollywood product, and among Lopert's first releases in the United States were *The Tales of Hoffmann* (1951) and *Cry, the Beloved Country* (1952). In 1959, Lopert became a wholly owned, but autonomous, subsidiary of United Artists*, with the purpose of distributing films—such as the productions of the British Rank Organization—that did not fit into the United Artists schedule. In the thirties, Ilya Lopert had operated Pax Films and Juno Films, both of which distributed quality foreign productions in the United States.

LORIMAR PRODUCTIONS, founded in 1968 by Lee Rich and Merv Adelson, became a highly successful producer of such television series as *Dallas, Knots Landing, The Blue Knight, Falcon Crest,* and *The Waltons.* It entered film production in 1976 with *Twilight's Last Gleaming.* In 1977, the company created Lorimar Distribution International to handle foreign distribution of its product. A year later it moved from the Burbank Studios*, where it had made its home, to the Culver City lot of M-G-M*. In 1979, Lorimar acquired Allied Artists*. A private company, owned by Rich, Adelson, and Irwin Molasky, Lorimar Productions went public in 1981; in 1983, it merged with the New York advertising agency of Kenyon & Eckhardt. On May 20, 1984, the *Los Angeles Times* reported that Lorimar had assets of $307.5 million, with 1,130 employees. In October 1985, it merged with Telepictures to become Lorimar-Telepictures.

Lorimar retreated from film production in 1983, with Lee Rich telling the *New York Times* (May 2, 1983) that Lorimar was "basically a television company." Among the feature films it produced were *The Choirboys* (1977), *Who Is Killing the Great Chefs of Europe?* (1978), *The Fish That Saved Pittsburgh* (1979), *Cruising* (1980), *The Big Red One* (1980), *The Postman Always Rings Twice* (1981), *Second Hand Hearts* (1981), and *S.O.B.* (1981).

On January 11, 1989, Lorimar merged with Warner Communications, and later moved to the Burbank lot. Its television division was initially kept operational under the Lorimar name, but, in July 1993, for economic reasons, Warner Bros. consolidated Warner Bros. TV and Lorimar TV as a new division, Warner Bros. TV Production. Heading the new division was Leslie Moonves, the former president of Lorimar.

LORING OPERA HOUSE in Riverside, California, is famous as the site of the first screening of *The Birth of a Nation* on January 1, 1915. It was later renamed the Golden State Theater, closed in 1973, was gutted by fire on October 11, 1990, and subsequently demolished.

"LOST FILMS." "Lost films" is a term used to describe those films that are no longer known to be extant from the period prior to 1950, when films were processed on nitrate* film stock and subject to deterioration. These films may also be "lost" thanks to carelessness on the part of their original producers or distributors.

In 1970, the Museum of Modern Art published a book on the subject of lost films, among which it listed *Confessions of a Queen* (1925), *Gentlemen Prefer Blondes* (1928), *The Enemy* (1927), *The Drag Net* (1928), *The Case of Lena Smith* (1929), *Merton of the Movies* (1924), *The Divine Woman* (1928), *The Queen of Sheba* (1921), *The Patriot* (1928), and *Tess of the D'Urbevilles* (1924). Since publication of this book, some of the films included—such as *Fazil* (1928)—have been rediscovered, and, as is so often the case with eagerly sought lost films, they are far from the masterpieces that scholars and historians had thought them to be. A similar listing of lost films has been prepared by the American Film Institute* and includes *Angel of Contention* (1914), *London after Midnight* (1927), *The Man from Blankleys* (1930), *Madame Sans-Gêne* (1925), *That Royle Girl* (1925), *Cleopatra* (1917), *The Young Rajah* (1922), *The Four Devils* (1928), and *The Aryan* (1916).

In 1996, film historian Frank Thompson published his list of *Lost Films,* and in the fall of that same year, the American Film Institute announced the finding of a 1912 version of *Richard III,* which it erroneously claimed to be the first feature film, and which was hailed by the Institute and the media as one of the most important "lost films" of all time. *Richard III* was preserved thanks to a Portland, Oregon, film collector named William Buffum.

BIBLIOGRAPHY

Carey, Gary. *Lost Films.* New York: Museum of Modern Art, 1970.
Thompson, Frank. *Lost Films: Important Movies That Disappeared.* New York: Carol Publishing, 1996.

LOWVILLE, NEW YORK. See KINEMACOLOR COMPANY OF AMERICA

LUBIN MANUFACTURING COMPANY. Sigmund (sometimes spelled Siegmund) Lubin, a traveling peddler of jewelry, spectacles, and novelties, from Breslau, Germany, settled in Philadelphia and pursued an interest in lenses and photography that culminated in his association with C. Francis Jenkins to produce cameras, film printing machines, and projectors (the second model of which, manufactured in 1896, was the first projector ever advertised for sale). In 1897, Lubin produced his first film, which he remembered as being of a horse eating hay. Lubin purchased a chain of theatres in Philadelphia, and, later, these, along with others he had acquired in eastern Pennsylvania, were taken over by Stanley V. Mastbaum, who used them as the basis for the Stanley Company.

In 1897, Lubin restaged and filmed the heavyweight championship fight between James Corbett and Bob Fitzsimmons, using two Pennsylvania railwaymen. In 1899, he followed with a reenactment of the Jeffries-Fitzsimmons fight. After the 1898 filming of the German *Passion Play* proved successful, Lubin produced his own version, modeled after the earlier one, in a Philadelphia backyard. In 1904, he remade Edwin S. Porter's *The Great Bank Robbery* as *The Bold Bank Robbery*.

Although Lubin stopped making films in 1898 because of an Edison* lawsuit against him, his company later joined the Motion Picture Patents Company*, releasing through the General Film Company. Lubin opened the largest glass-enclosed studio in the country in March 1912 in the heart of Philadelphia, which could accommodate four producing companies working at the same time.

In August 1912, Lubin bought the 500-acre estate of brewer John Betz. Located in the Philadelphia suburb of Betzwood, on the Schuylkill River adjoining Valley Forge Park, the estate provided a variety of natural settings and was the site for Lubin's new studio and plant. A fire in June 1914 at the film storage vault in Lubin's plant destroyed the company's early negatives and prints.

In the winter of 1909–1910, Lubin sent a company south, to film in Nassau and Florida, headed by A. D. Hotaling. Lubin had a plant in Jacksonville, Florida, which opened in 1913. Captain Wilbert Melville took a company of players to the West and Southwest United States, in 1913, and established a studio at 4550 Pasadena Avenue, Los Angeles, in 1915. Leon D. Kent and C. C. Miller were directors of the one-, two-, three-, and six-reel pictures made there. Also in 1915, Romaine Fielding headed a Lubin company located in Phoenix, Arizona, and a studio at Coronado, near San Diego, opened in August 1915.

In April 1915, Lubin joined with Vitagraph*, Selig*, and Essanay* to form V-L-S-E* to distribute feature films. August 1916 saw the beginning of the end for Lubin, as the company was absorbed by Vitagraph. In February 1918, the Betzwood plant was purchased by the newly organized Betzwood Film Company*, of which Lubin's son-in-law and general manager, Ira M. Lowry, became the general manager.

Players of note who appeared in Lubin films included Ethel Clayton, Arthur Johnson, Lottie Briscoe, Harry Myers, Rosemary Theby, Ormi Hawley, Edwin Carewe, Billie Reeves, and Frank Borzage, who began his film career as an actor with the company.

BIBLIOGRAPHY

"Betzwood on the Perkiomen." *Motography,* August 23, 1913, pp. 121–22.
Bush, W. Stephen. "Betzwood, the Great." *The Moving Picture World,* July 11, 1914, pp. 274–75.
———. "A Day with Siegmund Lubin." *The Moving Picture World,* July 11, 1914, pp. 209–10.
Eckhardt, Joseph P., and Linda Kowall. *Peddler of Dreams.* Philadelphia: National Museum of American Jewish History, 1984.
"Get Off at Lubin." *The Moving Picture World,* September 13, 1913, pp. 1159–60.
Harrison, Louis Reeves. "Studio Saunterings." *The Moving Picture World,* March 30, 1912, pp. 1142–44.
"Lost to Film History." *The New York Dramatic Mirror,* July 8, 1914, p. 21.
"Lubin." *The Moving Picture World,* November 6, 1909, p. 641.
"Lubin Progress." *The Moving Picture World,* February 5, 1910, p. 174.
"Lubin West Coast Plant." *The Moving Picture World,* July 10, 1915, p. 246.
"New Plant of Lubin Manufacturing Company." *The Moving Picture World,* March 26, 1910, p. 473.
"Sigmund Lubin Talks." *Exhibitors' Times,* September 27, 1913, p. 11.
"S. Lubin, Philosopher." *The Moving Picture World,* March 1, 1913, p. 877.
"Studio Efficiency." *The Moving Picture World,* August 9, 1913, p. 624.

LUCASFILM, LTD., is the empirical organization of filmmaker George Lucas (born 1945), formed in 1972, and housed on a 3,000-acre ranch—Skywalker Ranch—in Marin County, California. Lucasfilm, Ltd., is the producer of the *Star Wars* series and of other features, including *Raiders of the Lost Ark* (1981).

The organization has a number of divisions, the best known of which is its special effects arm, Industrial Light & Magic, responsible for the special effects on films such as *Star Trek II, Poltergeist,* and *E.T. The Extra-Terrestrial* (all released in 1982). Its Research and Development Division is known as Sprocket Systems. In partnership with 20th Century-Fox Music, Lucasfilm operates the music publishing houses of Bantha Music and Tusken Music. The Droid Works (located at 3855 Lankershim Boulevard, North Hollywood, Calif. 91604-3417) is described in publicity as "the first fully integrated electronic post-production system, picture and sound." Among the equipment introduced by Lucasfilm is the THX Motion Picture Loud-speaker System, developed by chief audio engineer Tomlinson Holman in 1983, which enhances the quality of theatre sound; Pixar, a computer graphics machine; and EditDroid, an automated editor, introduced in 1984. In 1985, Lucas announced plans to "spin off" Droid Works and Pixar as two separate companies.

Address: P.O. Box 2009, San Rafael, Calif. 94912.

BIBLIOGRAPHY

Champlin, Charles. *George Lucas, The Creative Impulse: Lucasfilm's First Twenty-Five Years*. New York: Harry N. Abrams, 1992.

Pollock, Dale. *Skywalking: The Life and Films of George Lucas*. New York: Harmony Books, 1983.

Vax, Mark Cotta, and Shinji Hata. *From Star Wars to Indiana Jones: The Best of the Lucasfilm Archives*. San Francisco: Chronicle Books, 1994.

LUNA FILMS. See ALBUQUERQUE FILM MANUFACTURING COMPANY, INC.

Academy President Jean Hersholt presents British producer/distributor J. Arthur Rank with the Oscars won by *Hamlet* (1948).

The headquarters of the American Society of Cinematographers in Hollywood.

Grauman's Chinese Theatre (1956).

Hobart Bosworth.

Samuel Goldwyn.

An early Santa Claus Parade on Hollywood
Boulevard, looking west from Vine Street.

Republic films a 1948 Western, *The Gallant Legion*, with the Hollywoodland sign in the background.

Lucien Andriot (front) uses a Pathé camera and John van den Broek uses an Eclair camera to film Mary Pickford in *Poor Little Rich Girl* (1917) at the Paragon Studio in Fort Lee.

Actress Pauline Bush with the American Film Company logo (1912).

The Edison Studio at Bedford Park, New York, circa 1912.

Inceville.

The Finis Fox Co. (including leading lady Mae Busch, leading man Rex Lease, and cinematographer Karl Freund) about to film *A Woman Who Sinned* (1924) at the Metropolitan Studios (later Hollywood General).

Irving G. Thalberg, vice president in charge of
production at Metro-Goldwyn-Mayer.

The entrance to Metro-Goldwyn-Mayer in the 1960s.

Comedian Jack Benny (left) with M-G-M's Louis B. Mayer and 20th Century-Fox's Darryl F. Zanuck.

George Mitchell, inventor of the camera that bears his name.

The Mirisch Brothers (left to right): Harold, Walter, and Marvin.

Cinematographer William Fraker with a
Panavision camera.

The members of Our Gang in the 1920s.

Paramount Studios and the famous Paramount Gate, 1930s.

The studios of RKO Radio Pictures, 1930s.

Producer David O. Selznick.

Producer Edward Small.

Aerial view of the Fox studios in 1932.

The frontage of the 20th Century-Fox studios, 1940s.

Three Bell & Howell cameras and a Debrie camera film serial queen Ruth Roland, circa 1920.

Rita Hayworth is filmed in 3-D for *Miss Sadie Thompson* (1953).

Universal founder Carl Laemmle poses with an Akeley camera.

The Universal Studios, 1920s.

A three-strip Technicolor camera films *The Phantom of the Opera* at Universal (1943).

The United Artists studios (later known as the Goldwyn Studios) at the corner of Formosa Avenue and Santa Monica Boulevard, early 1940s.

Sound engineer George Groves supervises the production of a Vitaphone disc.

M

MABEL NORMAND FEATURE FILM COMPANY was created in April 1916 by Mack Sennett (1880–1960), with the financial backing of Adam Kessel, Jr., to produce *Mickey* (1918), starring Mabel Normand (1894–1930).

MacGUFFIN/McGUFFIN—there is no definitive spelling—is a name credited to Alfred Hitchcock, referring in his films to a deliberately mysterious plot objective, similar to a red herring in mystery novels. Perhaps coined by Hitchcock, it may also have been invented by British writer Angus McPhail (who worked on Hitchcock's *Spellbound* in 1945). According to McPhail, he overheard two men on a train from London to Scotland, discussing a strangely wrapped package. When told the parcel contained a McGuffin, the inquirer asked what it was for. "For trapping lions in the Scottish Highlands," came the reply. "But there are no lions in the Scottish Highland," said the first man, to which the other responded, "Well, then I guess that's no McGuffin." *The McGuffin* is also the title of a thriller by John Bowen, published in 1984 by Atlantic Monthly Press, which contains many of the elements of a Hitchcock drama.

BIBLIOGRAPHY

Havemann, Ernest. "We Present Alfred Hitchcock." *Theatre Arts*, vol. 40, no. 9, September 1956, pp. 27–28, 91–92.
Spoto, Donald. *The Dark Side of Genius: The Life of Alfred Hitchcock*. Boston: Little, Brown, 1983.

MAGNACOLOR. See HIRLICOLOR

MAGNA PICTURES CORPORATION was founded on March 25, 1953, to produce, distribute, and exhibit films in the Todd-AO* process. It was initially financed by producer Mike Todd (1907–1958), United Artists Theatre Circuit, UA of California, UA of New York, and American Optical, but in 1954, Kuhn, Loeb took a 20 percent interest in the corporation through a $6 million financing deal. George Skouras was the first president of the company, succeeded in 1964 by Marshall Naify. Magna released *Oklahoma!* (1955) and *South Pacific* (1958), but then remained dormant until 1964, when it announced a return to production with *Harlow* (1965). It has been inactive in production and distribution for many years.

MAIL CALL. See HOLLYWOOD VICTORY COMMITTEE

MAIN STREET, U.S.A. See HOLLYWOOD VICTORY COMMITTEE

MAJESTIC MOTION PICTURE COMPANY. See RELIANCE MOTION PICTURE COMPANY AND MAJESTIC MOTION PICTURE COMPANY

MAJESTIC PICTURES CORPORATION, active from 1932 to 1935, promised a number of screen versions of current literary successes, including *My Life* by Isadora Duncan, but in reality its films were, as its 1934 advertising proclaimed, "action type of productions in keeping with the pulse of box office demand." Among Majestic's better known "B" features were *The Vampire Bat* (1933), *Gun Law* (1933), *The World Gone Mad* (1933), and *The Scarlet Letter* (1934).

Larry Darmour (1895–1942) was in charge of production, and following Majestic's demise he created Darmour Productions, which was responsible for a number of "B" pictures released through Columbia*, including *Under Suspicion* (1937), *Crime Takes a Holiday* (1938), *Fugitive at Large* (1939), and *Ellery Queen, Master Detective* (1940).

MALPASO PRODUCTIONS was founded by actor/director Clint Eastwood (born 1930) in April 1967, and named after a creek on Eastwood's Carmel, California, property (the name is Spanish for "dangerous step"). The company's first production was *Hang 'Em High* (1968), and the first film it produced in which Eastwood did not appear was *Breezy* (1973).

Address: 4000 Warner Boulevard, Burbank, Calif. 91522.

BIBLIOGRAPHY

Plaza, Fuensanta. *Clint Eastwood: Malpaso*. Carmel Valley, Calif.: Ex Libris, 1991.
Roberts, Jerry. "Malpaso Avoids the Path of Excess." *Daily Variety*, March 27, 1995, pp. 24–30.

MANDARIN FILM COMPANY, located in Oakland, California, was the only Chinese film production company in the United States at the time of its formation in 1917. Marion E. Wong was the president of the company and the star of its first production, *The Curse of Quon Qwon*, some of which was filmed in China. The company strove to make films dealing with Chinese subjects with accurate details and settings. It had its own studio, constructed, it was stated, according to Chinese ideas.

BIBLIOGRAPHY

"Marion E. Wong, Chinese Film Producer." *The Moving Picture World,* July 7, 1917, p. 63.

MANN THEATRES CORPORATION. Founded by Ted Mann as a small Minnesota theatre chain, Mann Theatres Corporation grew with Mann's spring 1973 acquisition of the 266 theatres of the National General* chain. Mann created considerable furor by changing the name of the chain's flagship theatre, Grauman's Chinese Theatre, in Hollywood, to Mann's Chinese Theatre. With Ted Mann Productions, Mann has also been involved in the production of such films as *Buster and Billie* (1974), *Lifeguard* (1976) and *Brubaker* (1980).

In 1986, the company was sold to Gulf + Western, which, in 1987, sold 50 percent to Warner Communications, Inc.

Address: P.O. Box 20077, Encinco, Calif. 91416.

MANSON INTERNATIONAL. Founded in 1953 by Edmund Goldman and Sam Nathanson and incorporated ten years later, Manson International was, initially, a distributor of foreign films in the United States. In 1975, it began to concentrate on the marketing of independent films abroad and became one of the first Los Angeles-based international film sales agencies.

In May 1987, the company was sold to Management Company Entertainment Group (MCEG), and ceased operations in the early nineties.

MAPO. See WALT DISNEY PRODUCTIONS

MARCH OF TIME. A type of newsreel* that mixed factual footage with staged material, as in a television docudrama, March of Time was sponsored by *Time* magazine, ran approximately 20 minutes, and was narrated by Westbrook Van Voorhis. It was based on a radio series of the same name, first broadcast by CBS in 1931, and was very much the brainchild of one man, Louis de Rochemont, who produced the series until the summer of 1943, when he resigned and was succeeded by his brother, Richard.

The first episode of March of Time was released on February 1, 1935, and consisted of six items, "Saionji," "Speakeasy Street," "Belisha Beacons," "Moe Buchsbaum," "Fred Perkins," and "Metropolitan Opera." Later episodes were limited to two or three items until 1938, when March of Time featured only one story thereafter. The last March of Time, "Formosa—Island of Promise," was released in August 1951. From 1935 to 1942, March of Time was released by RKO* and from thereafter by 20th Century-Fox*. When RKO ceased to distribute March of Time, it began releasing a similar series, *This Is America,* produced by Frederick Ullman, Jr., narrated by Dwight Weist, and seen from 1942 to 1951. 16mm editions of March of Time, called Forum editions, were released, chiefly for classroom use, from 1944 onward. Some of these Forum editions had different titles;

for example, *Is Everybody Listening?* (1947) was released in a Forum edition as *Radio Broadcasting Today.*

The March of Time staff was also responsible for four feature films: *The Ramparts We Watch* (1940), *The Story of the Vatican* (1941), *We Are the Marines* (1942), and *The Golden Twenties* (1950).

BIBLIOGRAPHY

Bohn, Thomas W., and Lawrence W. Lichty. "The March of Time: News as Drama." *Journal of Popular Film* 2, 4 (Fall 1973): pp. 373–87.
Cook, Bruce. "Whatever Happened to Westbrook Van Voorhis?" *American Film,* March 1977, pp. 25–29.
Fielding, Raymond. *The March of Time, 1935–1951.* New York: Oxford University Press, 1978.
"Time Flickers Out: Notes on the Passing of the March of Time." *Quarterly of Film, Radio and Television,* Summer 1957, p. 354.

RESOURCES

Films: National Archives (reference prints and outtakes); Museum of Modern Art (reference prints).
Papers: National Archives (production files); University of Wyoming (Louis deRochemont papers).

MARINE FILM COMPANY OF LOS ANGELES, located at the old Kalem* studios in Hollywood, was organized in mid-1917. M. Phillip Hansen was the general manager, and Henry Otto was the director of the company. Frances Burnham was the leading lady, and Tyrone Power starred in Marine's first production, the six-reel *Lorelei of the Sea.*

BIBLIOGRAPHY

"Tyrone Power Signs with Marine." *The Moving Picture World,* June 30, 1917, p. 2106.

THE MARIPOSA FILM GROUP consisted of a number of San Francisco-based gays and lesbians (Peter Adair, Nancy Adair, Robert Epstein, Lucy Massie Phenix, and Veronica Selver), who came together to make the 1977 documentary feature, *The Word Is Out.* Basically consisting of interviews with 26 gays and lesbians, *The Word Is Out* is intended to present a positive view of homosexuality and homosexual culture.

BIBLIOGRAPHY

DuMont, Howard, and Jeffrey Escoffier. "*Word Is Out*: An Interview with the Mariposa Film Group." *Cineaste,* vol. 8, no. 4, 1978, pp. 8–11, 59.

MARK HELLINGER PRODUCTIONS, INC., was founded on July 27, 1945, and located on the Universal* lot. The name was changed to Mark Productions, Inc., on May 26, 1947, and the company dissolved July 1948. It produced

Swell Guy (1946), *The Killers* (1946), *Brute Force* (1947), and *The Naked City* (1948), and was financed by Bank of America*.

RESOURCES
Papers: University of Southern California.

MASCOT PICTURES CORPORATION, founded in
1927 by Nat Levine (1899–1989), is one of the "poverty row*" studios remembered with affection by film buffs for its serials, including three—*Shadow of the Eagle* (1932), *The Hurricane Express* (1932), and *The Three Musketeers* (1933)—starring John Wayne. The company did not commence producing features until the early thirties, and probably the most important of the group was *Harmony Lane* (1935). Players under contract with Mascot included Yakima Canutt, John Wayne, Joe Bonomo, and animal stars Rin-Tin-Tin, Jr., and Rex the Horse.

On January 10, 1935, Mascot moved from cramped production offices in Hollywood to the former Mack Sennett Studios in Studio City. The company was merged with Monogram* and Consolidated Laboratories to form Republic Pictures* and Levine stayed on as president of the new company. However, in February 1937, Nat Levine resigned from Republic, and Mascot was no more.

BIBLIOGRAPHY
Tuska, Jon. *The Vanishing Legion: A History of Mascot Pictures 1927–1935*. Jefferson, N.C.: McFarland, 1982.

MASTERCRAFT PHOTO-PLAY CORPORATION
was formed in January 1918, with its first production being the antisocialistic *The One Woman*, written by Thomas Dixon. Mastercraft had a studio in Boston and planned to open one in California. F. Eugene Farnsworth was the president, and Isaac Wolper, a Bostonian, was the vice president and general manager.

BIBLIOGRAPHY
"Mastercraft Forming Producing Corporation." *The Moving Picture World,* January 26, 1918, p. 491.

MASTER PICTURES CORPORATION. See BALBOA
AMUSEMENT PRODUCING COMPANY

MASTERPIECE FILM MANUFACTURING COMPANY, a production organization of 1914, made films starring
Max Figman, his wife Lolita Robinson, and Al W. Filson. M. De La Parelle and Figman directed from scenarios by Elliot J. Clawson. It released with Reliance Film Corporation. Although it purchased the Loftus Feature Studio at 1339 Gordon Street in Hollywood in December 1914, the company disbanded early in 1915 after the completion of its third film, *Jack Chanty*.

BIBLIOGRAPHY
"Masterpiece Film Men." *The Moving Picture World,* October 10, 1914, p. 171.

MAVERICK PICTURES INTERNATIONAL. See E. O. CORP.

MAYFAIR PICTURES CORP. was founded in 1932 by Ralph M. Like. Located at the former Charles Ray Studios in Hollywood, the production company was active through 1934, with its first feature being *Love in High Gear,* starring former silent performers Harrison Ford and Alberta Vaughn.

MAYFLOWER PHOTOPLAY CORPORATION was
formed in mid-1919 to produce Allan Dwan and Emile Chautard productions, released by Realart Pictures Corporation. Isaac Wolper was the president, and its first production was Dwan's *Soldiers of Fortune* (1919).

MCA, INC. The entertainment conglomerate that controls Universal*, MCA, Inc., has been frequently referred to as the "octopus" of the film industry. It was created, as Music Corporation of America, as a booking agency for dance bands in Chicago in 1924 by Jules Stein to help finance his medical training. In 1936, the corporation had grown in stature, and Stein hired Lew Wasserman (who was to become MCA's president in 1946 and chairman of the board in 1973).

Following MCA's takeover of Universal, the Justice Department intensified its investigation of the corporation, arguing that with its major television production company, Revue, and with its control of 1,400 top entertainers through its talent agency, MCA had restrained trade in violation of the Sherman Antitrust Act between 1952 and 1961. On October 18, 1962, a consent decree was signed whereby MCA agreed to divest itself of its talent agency business, but it was permitted to continue to control Universal Pictures, Revue Productions, Inc., and Decca Records and to remain as parent company of Colorado Savings and Loan Association.

In 1990, MCA was acquired by Matsushita Electric Industries, Inc., for $6.6 billion. It was a friendly takeover, but within four years, the relationship between MCA and the parent company had deteriorated, with the latter paying scant attention to the views of Wasserman or Sidney J. Sheinberg (who joined the company in 1959, and became its president in 1973). On April 9, 1995, Matsushita sold 80 percent of MCA to Edgar Bronfman, Jr., and his Seagram Co. for $5.7 billion, and on July 11 of that year, Wasserman and Sheinberg resigned from the organization with which they had been so closely associated.

In February 1996, MCA announced plans for a new studio in Osaka, Japan, and three months later, in May 1996, former Paramount* CEO Frank Biondi, Jr., took office as MCA's new CEO. In December 1996, the Seagram Co. revealed that it had decided to change the corporate name from MCA, Inc., to Universal Studios, Inc. Biondi explained that the name change "reinforces Universal's association with the excitement of Hollywood and the best in entertainment, and reflects the company's unified vision for the 21st century." Only the corporation's music division was to retain the MCA label.

Address: 100 Universal City Plaza, Universal City, Calif. 91608.

BIBLIOGRAPHY

Bart, Peter. "MCA's Man of Action." *Variety,* May 3, 1996, pp. 6, 82.
Bates, James, and Claudia Eller. "Seagram Signs MCA Agreement." *Los Angeles Times,* April 10, 1995, pp. A1, A12.
Fabricant, Geraldine, and Bernard Weinraub. "Having Gotten the Part, Bronfman Plays the Mogul." *The New York Times,* February 4, 1996, pp. F1, F13.
Gottschalk, Earl C., Jr. "If It's Show Business, Chances Are MCA Inc. Is Deeply Involved in It." *The Wall Street Journal,* July 10, 1973, pp. 1, 18.
Hiltzik, Michael, and James Flanagan. "Seagram's Big Gulp." *Los Angeles Times,* April 7, 1995, pp. D1, D4.
"The Morning After." *Newsweek,* June 19, 1995, p. 52.
Moldea, Dan E. *Dark Victory: Ronald Reagan, MCA and the Mob.* New York: Viking, 1986.

MEDFORD, MASSACHUSETTS. See HUMANOLOGY FILM PRODUCING COMPANY

MÉLIÈS MANUFACTURING COMPANY. The films of Georges Méliès, who began producing in France in 1896, were distributed in the United States by the Biograph Company* until February 1904. Georges sent his brother, Gaston, to New York, in November 1902, because of the rampant duping of his films. Gaston set up an office at 204 East 38th Street, New York, to distribute his brother's films, to which he gave what was perhaps the first brand name in film history, "Star Films," and perhaps the first trademark. Gaston Méliès joined the Motion Picture Patents Company* and contracted to release one reel per week on the American market. To help his brother meet this quota, Gaston formed a production company, the Méliès Manufacturing Company, in September 1908, with a capitalization of $75,000. The American company had its headquarters in the Criterion Theatre, Chicago.

Gaston and his son Paul took the company to Fort Lee, New Jersey*, where they produced their first film, *The Stolen Wireless,* released October 13, 1909. Early in 1910, Gaston took his company to San Antonio, Texas, and set up the Star Film Ranch there to make Westerns*. The first, *Cyclone Pete's Matrimony,* was released on April 7, 1910. The company was directed by William Haddock, the cameraman was William Paley, and the players included leads Francis Ford and Edith Storey, William Clifford, Mildred Bracken, Anne Nichols, and Daniel Reulos. Gaston occasionally played small parts.

In May 1911, the company, then called the "American Wildwest," traveled to Sulphur Mountain Springs, California. In June 1911, it opened a studio in Santa Paula, California, where it produced one and one-half reels per week, at that time the entire output released by Méliès. After making over 130 films between 1910 and 1912, Gaston traveled to the South Seas and Asia, making films as he went, but due to the poor condition that the films were in when they arrived in the United States, he was forced to close down the company, in 1913, and sold it to Vitagraph*.

BIBLIOGRAPHY

Dowling, Paul H. "He's Sixteen Years Ahead of All War Photographers." *Photoplay,* March 1917, p. 122.
Hammond, Paul. *Marvellous Méliès.* New York: St. Martin's Press, 1975.
McInroy, Patrick. "The American Méliès." *Sight and Sound,* Autumn 1979, pp. 250–54.
"Méliès Notes." *The Moving Picture World,* March 26, 1910, p. 472.
"The New Addition to the Licensed Releases. Méliès Film Takes High Rank." *The Moving Picture World,* October 23, 1909, p. 561.
Thompson, Frank. *The Star Film Ranch: Texas' First Picture Show.* Plano, Tex.: Republic of Texas Press, 1996.

MELROSE ENTERTAINMENT GROUP. See CANNON PICTURES INC.

MENTOR PICTURES, INC., incorporated in December 1932, was formed to import scientific, educational, novelty, and feature films from Europe.

MERIT FILMS. See SACK AMUSEMENT ENTERPRISES

METROCOLOR LABORATORIES, which had come into existence more than 50 years earlier as M-G-M Labs, closed on Thursday, August 24, 1989. Located on the M-G-M* studio lot, the laboratories had been acquired by Lorimar-Telepictures*, which formed a joint partnership to operate them with the Walt Disney Company* in 1987, following the U.S. Justice Department's refusal to permit the takeover of the laboratories by Technicolor*. The closure of the laboratories was forced by Disney's rescinding its partnership agreement with Lorimar-Telepictures and taking its film processing to Technicolor.

BIBLIOGRAPHY

Robb, David. "Metrocolor Lab Ends Operations after 50 Years." *Daily Variety,* August 25, 1989, pp. 1, 10.

METRO-GOLDWYN-MAYER, INC. With its trademark of a roaring lion and its logo, "Ars Gratia Artis," Metro-

Goldwyn-Mayer (M-G-M) symbolized quality film production for more than 50 years. It was the company's proud boast that it had more stars than there were in heaven, a far from outrageous claim when one recalls that under contract to the studio, at one time or another, were Greta Garbo, Norma Shearer, Jean Harlow, Joan Crawford, Katharine Hepburn, Clark Gable, Spencer Tracy, Lon Chaney, Elizabeth Taylor, the Marx Brothers, Judy Garland, Mickey Rooney, John Gilbert, Ramon Novarro, Jeanette MacDonald and Nelson Eddy, Greer Garson, and Gene Kelly. The prestige of its stars was matched by its directors—George Cukor, Clarence Brown, King Vidor, Tod Browning, Vincente Minnelli, and so on—and its films, including *Greed* (1924), *The Merry Widow* (1925), *The Big Parade* (1925), *Ben-Hur* (1926), *Grand Hotel* (1932), *Mutiny on the Bounty* (1935), *David Copperfield* (1935), *Goodbye, Mr. Chips* (1939), *The Wizard of Oz* (1939), *Mrs Miniver* (1942), *Easter Parade* (1948), *Singin' in the Rain* (1952), *Seven Brides for Seven Brothers* (1954), *Gigi* (1958), *Ben-Hur* (1959), and *2001: A Space Odyssey* (1968).

Metro-Goldwyn-Mayer's parent company, Loew's, Inc., had been formed as a theatre circuit by Marcus Loew. To assure a steady flow of product to his theatres, Loew acquired the Metro Pictures Corporation* in 1919, and the new Loew's, Inc., was organized on October 18, 1919. Loew increased the stature of Metro with the acquisition of new stars and by bringing in independent producer Louis B. Mayer (1885–1957). Nicholas Schenck, Loew's right-hand man, arranged for the company to acquire the ailing Goldwyn Pictures Corporation* and to take over Mayer's independent production company. The new organization, Metro-Goldwyn-Mayer, was created on May 17, 1924, with studios that had formerly belonged to Goldwyn in Culver City.

To supervise production, M-G-M selected Mayer's vice president Irving G. Thalberg (1899–1936), who is generally considered to have been responsible for the prestige of the company's productions. He never accepted credit on any of the films that he personally supervised, among which was *He Who Gets Slapped* (1924), *Flesh and the Devil* (1927), *The Crowd* (1928), *Anna Christie* (1930), *Freaks* (1932), *The Barretts of Wimpole Street* (1934), *A Night at the Opera* (1935), *Mutiny on the Bounty* (1935), *Romeo and Juliet* (1936), and *The Good Earth* (1937). Following Thalberg's early death, the Academy of Motion Picture Arts and Sciences* created the Irving G. Thalberg Memorial Award (first given in 1937 to Darryl F. Zanuck) "for the most consistent high level of production achievement by an individual producer." M-G-M honored Thalberg by naming its new office building, at the entrance to the lot, in his memory.

By the mid-thirties, M-G-M had some 4,000 employees under contract. There were 23 sound stages on the 117-acre lot. Its reported assets in 1939 were $144 million. Aside from its features, the studio produced short subjects, such as the Pete Smith Specialties, the "Crime Does Not Pay" series*, Tom and Jerry cartoons, and the comedies of Robert Benchley. It also released the Hal Roach Studios* output, and its best-known independent release is, of course, *Gone with the Wind* (1939), produced by David O. Selznick.

In 1937, M-G-M established a British production company with headquarters at Denham Studios, under the management of Ben Goetz and with Michael Balcon in charge of production. Here M-G-M produced *The Citadel* (1938) and *Goodbye, Mr. Chips* (1939).

As with other major studios, M-G-M faced problems in the late forties, brought on in part by the introduction of television and by declining theatre attendance. In need of a new production head, Mayer selected Dore Schary (1905–1980), who had earlier been associated with RKO*, and who was also admired by Loew's president, Nicholas Schenck, who had succeeded to the title following the death of Marcus Loew in 1926.

In 1951, following a bitter dispute between Mayer and Schenck, the former was forced to resign and was replaced by Dore Schary. Schary introduced more serious subjects to M-G-M's production schedule, beginning in 1949 with *Intruder in the Dust* and in 1950 with *The Asphalt Jungle,* but he quickly found himself in dispute with the right-wing element in Hollywood, led by gossip columnist Hedda Hopper, who accused the producer of being either too liberal, communistic, or both. At the same time, Schary was faced with the breakup of the company's theatre and production/distribution holdings following the governmental consent decree*. Loew's, Inc., continued as the parent company of M-G-M, the producer, and the distributor, but a new theatre holding company, Loew's Theatres, was formed on September 1, 1954, to control the 130 houses remaining under the company's control in the United States and Canada.

Dore Schary was fired as studio head in 1956. Meanwhile, there were extensive changes at the corporate level. Arthur Loew succeeded Nicholas Schenck as president in 1955, but a year later he was succeeded by Joseph Vogel, who successfully fended off a challenge from Stanley Meyer. Robert O'Brien was appointed president in 1963, followed by James Polk, Jr., in 1969, and then by James T. Aubrey, Jr., who was backed by M-G-M's new majority stockholder, Kirk Kerkorian.

Under Aubrey's presidency, much of the M-G-M backlot was sold off for real estate development. Aubrey disposed of M-G-M's British studios at Borehamwood, of theatres outside of the United States, and of MGM Records. In May 1970, the David S. Weisz Company held a public auction of M-G-M's collection of costumes and props. Eventually, in October 1973, Aubrey withdrew the studio from distribution, announcing that forthwith its films would be released by United Artists*.

Following Aubrey's resignation on October 31, 1973, Frank E. Rosenfelt became president, and the company once again prospered, thanks in large part to its non-film activities, such as the MGM Grand Hotel in Las Vegas. In 1981, M-G-M's majority stockholder, Kirk Kerkorian acquired United Artists* for $380 million, and in 1983, a new company, MGM/UA Entertainment was formed. It was acquired early in 1986 by Ted Turner (born 1938). He retained the film library, but sold the lot to Lorimar* for $190 million, and the production and distribution company, MGM/UA, for $480 million, to Kirk Kerkorian, who, in November 1990, sold the company to Italian financier Giancarlo Parretti for $1.38 billion. Parretti merged the company with his Pathé Communications Corp.*, and renamed it MGM-Pathé. The company quickly became mired in financial disputes between Parretti and his main financial backer, Credit Lyonnais, which, in May 1992, acquired 98.5 percent of the company, and renamed it Metro-Goldwyn-Mayer, Inc. Former Paramount Pictures* chairman Frank Mancuso was brought in as chairman, replacing Alan Ladd, Jr., who had served in that position since April 1991, and in 1994, MGM/UA was revived as the company's distribution arm. Mike Marcus was named president in April 1995.

Under U.S. bankruptcy laws, Credit Lyonnais was required to divest itself of the company by May 1997, and in July 1996, it announced that M-G-M had been acquired for $1.3 billion by a management group, financed by Kirk Kerkorian.

Address: 2500 Broadway, Santa Monica, Calif. 90404; 1350 Avenue of the Americas, New York, N.Y. 10019.

BIBLIOGRAPHY

Bart, Peter. *Fade Out: The Calamitous Final Days of MGM.* New York: William Morrow, 1990.

Carey, Gary. *All the Stars in Heaven.* New York: E. P. Dutton, 1981.

Crowther, Bosley. *The Lion's Share.* New York: E. P. Dutton, 1957.

Eames, John Douglas. *The MGM Story: The Complete History of Sixty-Five Roaring Years.* New York: Portland House, 1990.

Hay, Peter, ed. *MGM: When the Lion Roars.* Atlanta, Georgia: Turner Publishing, 1991.

Higham, Charles. *Merchant of Dreams: Louis B. Mayer, M.G.M., and the Secret Hollywood.* New York: Donald I. Fine, 1993.

Hughes, Emmet John. "M-G-M: War among the Lion Tamers." *Fortune,* August 1957, pp. 98–103, 206, 208, 210, 212, 214, 216.

King, Thomas R. "Lion in Winter." *The Wall Street Journal,* July 25, 1994, pp. A1, A6.

Knox, David. *The Magic Factory.* New York: Praeger, 1973.

"Loew's Inc." *Fortune,* August 1939, pp. 25–31, 104–6, 114.

Sheehan, Robert. "The Cliff-Hanger at M.G.M." *Fortune,* October 1957, pp. 134–35, 278, 280, 283.

RESOURCES

Music: California State University, Long Beach (Music Scores from Music Library).

Papers: Academy of Motion Picture Arts and Sciences (Art Department Records, Legal Department Records, Wardrobe Department Records, Production Materials).

Photographs: Academy of Motion Picture Arts and Sciences.

Scripts: Academy of Motion Picture Arts and Sciences (M-G-M Script Library); University of Southern California (M-G-M Television Script Library and many scripts for features and short subjects).

METROMEDIA INTERNATIONAL GROUP INC. is the holding company of billionaire chairman John W. Kluge, which owns Orion Pictures*, the Samuel Goldwyn Company* and Motion Picture Corp. of America (a producer of low-budget features, acquired by Kluge in 1995). Metromedia was originally incorporated in December 1929 as the National Fireproofing Corp., and re-incorporated in 1968 as F.I. Inc.

Address: 945 East Paces Ferry Road, Atlanta, Georgia 30326.

METRO PICTURES CORPORATION, the forerunner of M-G-M*, was incorporated on March 5, 1915, with Richard Rowland as president of the new company. It had its origins in the Alco Film Corporation*, formed a year earlier by Al Lichtman and W. H. Seeley, which served as a distributor for various producers, notably All-Star Feature Corporation. Metro also began as a distributor for the films of the Dyreda Art Film Corporation*, Popular Plays and Players*, Rolfe Photoplays, Inc.*, Quality Pictures Corporation*, and Columbia Pictures Corporation. The first release, on March 29, 1915, of the new company was *Satan Sanderson.* Within a year of its founding, Metro had become an important producer/distributor, with stars such as Francis X. Bushman, Mary Miles Minter, and Olga Petrova under contract. It was able to persuade Mr. and Mrs. Sidney Drew to leave Vitagraph* and become Metro stars. Its studios, formerly the Quality Studios, were located at 6300 Romaine Street in Hollywood, and from there, late in the second decade of the twentieth century, it produced a series of what it described as big-budget, quality features, under the brand name of Screen Classics, Inc.

Despite an average of more than 60 features a year, Metro suffered a number of financial reversals, brought on in part by the tremendous amount of money it was willing to pay for screen rights to novels such as *The Four Horsemen of the Apocalypse,* which it acquired in 1919. In 1920, Metro stock was acquired by Loews, Inc.*, the first step in the transformation of the company to Metro-Goldwyn-Mayer.

BIBLIOGRAPHY

"Metro Controls Productions." *The Moving Picture World,* March 20, 1915, p. 1745.

"Metro Plans Many Elaborate Productions." *The Moving Picture World,* August 12, 1916, p. 1086.

"Metro's First Birthday." *The Moving Picture World,* April 8, 1916, p. 237.

"Metros in the Making." *The Moving Picture World,* October 21, 1916, p. 411.

"Metro under Full Steam." *The Moving Picture World,* April 24, 1915, p. 562.

Schmidt, Jackson. "On the Road to MGM: A History of Metro Pictures Corporation, 1915–1920." *The Velvet Light Trap,* no. 19, 1982, pp. 46–52.

METROPOLITAN FILM COMPANY was organized in February 1914 to import and manufacture multireel features. Hans Bartsch was the president and H. J. Streyckmans was the sales manager. Its first release was the five-reel *The Money God,* and its offices were located in the World's Tower Building in New York.

METROPOLITAN STUDIOS. See HOLLYWOOD GENERAL STUDIOS

METROPOLITAN THEATRES CORPORATION came into being when Joseph Corwin purchased the Broadway and Metropolitan Theatres in Los Angeles in 1923. Corwin's son, Sherrill, built the chain into what was once the largest in southern California, and the corporation is presently headed by Joseph Corwin's grandson, Bruce. Its primary importance is as the operator of the great movie palaces in downtown Los Angeles, the Orpheum, the Los Angeles, the Million Dollar, and the United Artists. Metropolitan is also noted for its ownership and renovation of the Spanish-style Arlington Theatre in Santa Barbara. On August 9, 1963, the chain screened its first Spanish-language feature, and within a short space of time all its downtown Los Angeles theatres were exclusively running Spanish-language films.

Address: 8727 West Third Street, Los Angeles, Calif. 90069.

BIBLIOGRAPHY

Auerbach, Alexander. "Metropolitan Theatres—A Tradition of Service." *Boxoffice,* August 1983, pp. 14–15.

METROSCOPIX. See THREE-DIMENSIONAL FILMS

M-G-M. See METRO-GOLDWYN-MAYER, INC.

M-G-M CAMERA 65. See PANAVISION, INC.

MGM-PATHE COMMUNICATIONS CORP. See PATHE ENTERTAINMENT, INC.

MGM/UA. See METRO-GOLDWYN-MAYER, INC.

MICHEAUX FILM CORPORATION, the best known of all black-owned independent film companies, was formed in 1918 as the Micheaux Film and Book Corporation by Oscar Micheaux (1884–1951). The corporation's first production was an adaptation of Micheaux's novel, *The Homesteader* (1918). Micheaux remained active as a producer through 1940, and among his other features were *Within Our Gates* (1920), *Son of Satan* (1924), *A Daughter of the Congo* (1930), *Temptation* (1936), *God's Stepchildren* (1939), and *The Notorious Elinor* (1949).

BIBLIOGRAPHY

"Hollywood in the Bronx." *Time,* January 29, 1940, p. 67.

Jones, G. William. *Black Cinema Treasures: Lost and Found.* Denton, Tex.: University of North Texas Press, 1991.

Register, Charlene. "The Misreading and Rereading of African American Filmmaker Oscar Micheaux." *Film History,* vol. 7, no. 4, Winter 1995, pp. 426–49.

Sampson, Henry T. *Blacks in Black and White: A Source Book on Black Film.* Metuchen, N.J.: Scarecrow Press, 1995.

MIDDLETOWN, CONNECTICUT. See INTERSTATE FEATURE FILM COMPANY

MIDWEST THEATRES. See BALABAN & KATZ

MILLION DOLLAR PICTURES. See TODDY PICTURES COMPANY

MINA. See DAVID HORSLEY PRODUCTIONS

MIRAMAX FILMS CORPORATION was formed in 1979 by former rock promoter brothers, Harvey and Bob Weinstein, and named after their parents, Miriam and Max. Noted for its release of quality films from the United States and abroad, often containing serious, adult subject matter, the company enjoyed its first success in 1982 with *The Secret Policeman's Other Ball,* and its first major financial break in 1988, when British Midland Montague Bank invested $5 million and gave Miramax a $25 million credit line, enabling it to invest in the British feature *Scandal.* The following year, Miramax released *Sex, Lies and Videotape, My Left Foot,* and *Cinema Paradiso.* In May 1993, the company was purchased by the Walt Disney Company*, but it has been able to continue its policy of releasing films that do not fit the Disney image.

Address: 7920 Sunset Boulevard, Suite 230, Los Angeles, Calif. 90046.

THE MIRISCH CORPORATION was formed in 1957 by three brothers, Harold (who died in 1968), Walter, and Marvin Mirisch. It was based on the Samuel Goldwyn* studio lot, and its productions were released through United Artists*. In 1968, the corporation changed its name to Mirisch Productions, Inc., and sold its first 20 features to United Artists. This group of Mirisch productions consisted of *Sinful Davey* (1969), *How to Succeed in Business without Really Trying* (1967), *In the Heat of the Night* (1967), *Hour of the Gun* (1967), *Fitzwilly* (1967), *Hawaii* (1966), *The Fortune Cookie* (1966), *Return of* the Seven (1966), What Did You Do in the War, Daddy? (1966), The Russians Are Coming, the Russians Are Coming (1966), Cast a Giant Shadow (1966), The Satan Bug (1965), The Hallelujah Trail (1965), A Rage to Live (1965), Return from the Ashes (1965), The Pink Panther (1964), 633 Squadron (1964), A Shot in the Dark (1964), Kiss Me, Stupid (1964), and The Great Escape (1963).

The Mirisch brothers—who soon changed the name of their company back to the Mirisch Corporation—continued to release through United Artists, with later titles including Fiddler on the Roof (1971), The Private Life of Sherlock Holmes (1970), The Party (1968), The Thomas Crown Affair (1968), Gaily, Gaily (1969), and The Landlord (1970). In 1974, the brothers signed an exclusive distribution deal with Universal* and moved to the Universal lot; their first release through their new partner was Midway (1976). A new distribution deal with United Artists was signed in 1981, but the Mirisch Corporation also continued to release through Universal and remained on the Universal lot.

Address: 100 Universal City Plaza, Universal City, Calif. 91608.

RESOURCES

Papers: UCLA Special Collections.

MIRROR FILMS, INC., was formed in October 1915 with capitalization of $2.5 million and the expressed purpose of being not so much a theatrical enterprise as a commercial one. Stating, "We intend to look upon film . . . as so much canned product," Mirror, whose president was Clifford B. Harmon and treasurer was Frank S. Hastings, hired Hector J. Streychkmans to build its studio from a casino and dance hall located at Woodhaven and Myrtle streets in Glendale, Long Island, and to be its studio manager. Captain Harry L. Lambart, formerly one of Vitagraph's directors, was appointed director-general. Mirror's offices were located at 16 East 42d Street, New York.

BIBLIOGRAPHY

"Lambart Forms New Company." The Moving Picture World, October 9, 1915, p. 276.

MISSION PRODUCTIONS was formed in the fall of 1918 to produce a series of films starring child actress Gloria Joy under the direction of Sherwood Macdonald. The first, released by Pathé* on December 22, 1918, was The Fortunes of Connie.

THE MITCHELL CAMERA was for many years, and through different designs, the standard camera of the American film industry. Named after its inventor, George A. Mitchell (1889–1980), the first Mitchell camera was completed in 1920, and used by cinematographer Charles Rosher to film the Mary Pickford vehicle The Love Light. That first camera was built while Mitchell was with the National Motion Picture Camera Company; it later became the Mitchell Camera Corporation, but was never owned by the man who gave it its name. In 1929, Mitchell built the Grandeur camera for the Fox Corporation, and shortly thereafter, the latter took control of the company.

Mitchell designed and built various cameras, including the first three-strip Technicolor* camera and the NC (news camera) for Westinghouse Corporation. The successor to the NC camera, the BNC (blimped news camera), invented in 1934, was first used by Samuel Goldwyn Productions* in 1934 and 1935, and it became the camera of choice for the industry. At the 25th (1952) Academy Awards, George A. Mitchell received a honorary Oscar "for the design and development of the camera which bears his name and for his continued and dominant presence in the field of cinematography."

BIBLIOGRAPHY

Daviau, Allen. "Lights, Camera and Inaction: The Eye That Dragged Its Tail." Coast, August 1972, pp. 44–47.
Dunn, Angela Fox. "A Man and His Camera." Daily Variety, October 27, 1981, pp. 68, 83.
DiGiullo, Edmund M. "Mitchell System 35." American Cinematographer, vol. 47, no. 3, March 1966, pp. 172–75.

MITTENTHAL FILM COMPANY, INC., was organized in May 1913 by the Mittenthal brothers, to produce "Mittenthal Features," which were released by Warner's Features, Inc. Theodore Marston was the president and William Winter Jefferson was a principal actor of the company, which used the Pilot* studio in Yonkers, New York. The offices of the company were located at 1402 Broadway, New York, and its productions included The Human Bloodhound and The Prison Needle. In December 1914, it began producing single-reel films, under the brand name of "Starlight," which were released by United Film Service*, an antecedent to Warner Bros.* Mittenthal ended production in 1916.

BIBLIOGRAPHY

"Share Pilot Studio." The New York Dramatic Mirror, May 21, 1913, p. 25.

MOHAWK FILM COMPANY was a short-lived production company of 1914. Although it arranged at its formation to make 12 features, Heart of Oak, written and directed by Wray Physioc, which was distributed by Paramount*, was its only production. During a suit hearing in August 1914, officers Henry Morris, Harry Sterling Goldman, and Ben Levy stated that no more production by the company was being contemplated.

MOLE-RICHARDSON CO., founded in Hollywood in 1927 by Peter Mole, is the best-known manufacturer of studio lighting and power equipment.

Address: 937 North Sycamore Avenue, Hollywood, Calif. 90038.

MONARCH PRODUCING COMPANY. Harry Harvey, formerly with Solax*, Nestor, Broncho, and Frontier, was the managing director of the Monarch Producing Company, which was formed in November 1914 and released on the Kriterion program.

MONOGRAM PRODUCTIONS, INC. As a "B" picture producer, Monogram Productions, Inc., was relatively important, almost on a par with Republic*, with which it merged briefly. The origin of the company dates back to January 1924, when W. Ray Johnston, in collaboration with a number of independent exhibitors, formed Rayart Productions as a low-budget film production company releasing films—a reported annual schedule of 24 silent Westerns—to exhibitors who had formed themselves into a cooperative. Rayart was reorganized in 1930 as Monogram Productions, with Johnston as president and Trem Carr as head of production. The first films were produced in 1931. During 1931–1932, the company produced some 28 features, increasing to 32 in 1932–1933. In 1932, Monogram signed a distribution deal with the British Pathé company, whereby the latter released Monogram's product in the United Kingdom and Monogram released British Pathé features in the United States. By 1932, Monogram was producing 36 features a year and by the forties was producing an average of 50 titles.

When Republic Pictures was formed in 1935, it took over the Monogram exchanges, and Johnston became the new company's first president. However, in 1937, Johnston left Republic and revived Monogram as a separate production entity. When Johnston became chairman of the board in 1946, Stephen Broidy became president, and he is generally credited with increasing the quality of Monogram's films. In November 1946, Broidy created Allied Artists* as a totally owned subsidiary of Monogram, and that company's name appeared on Monogram's better features. In 1953, the Monogram name was dropped completely, and the company became Allied Artists.

The first Monogram films were shot at the studio located at 6048 Sunset Boulevard. Later, the company moved to the General Services Studio at 1040 North Las Palmas and the Talisman Studios* at 4516 Sunset Boulevard. After revival of operations in 1937, Monogram rented space at Universal*, with its final home being at 4376 Sunset Drive (which is now KCET). Monogram produced a number of series films, including those featuring the Cisco Kid (with Duncan Renaldo), Charlie Chan (with Sidney Toler), Kitty O'Day, Detective (with Jean Parker), Saddle Pals (with Jimmy Wakeley and Dennis Moore), Bomba, Jiggs and Maggie, Snuffy Smith, Joe Palooka, Mr. Wong, the High Schoolers, and Renfrew of the Royal Mounted. The best known of the Monogram series films were those starring Leo Gorcey and Huntz Hall, initially known as the East Side Kids and later as the Bowery Boys (and which had started life at Goldwyn* as the Dead End Kids). The company's first grade "A" feature is generally considered to have been *Silver Skates* (1942), starring Belita.

BIBLIOGRAPHY

Okuda, Ted. *The Monogram Checklist: The Films of Monogram Pictures Corporation, 1931–1958*. Jefferson, North Carolina: McFarland, 1987.

RESOURCES

Photographs: Academy of Motion Picture Arts and Sciences (1937–1942).

MONOPOL FILM COMPANY. When the Monopol Film Company engaged Marion Leonard, in 1912, for $1,000 a week, which may have been the largest salary any player received at that time, the company had been in existence for a few years and had produced over 30 dramas. Its offices were at 145 West 45th Street, New York. Al Lichtman was an early manager of Monopol and, when Leonard signed, Isadore Bernstein, formerly a publicist for Republic and Yankee, left the International Feature Film Company to become general manager.

Stanner E. V. Taylor took the company to Los Angeles, where he directed three-reel features starring Marion Leonard, including *As in a Looking Glass, Carmen,* and *The Dead Secret*. In June 1913, Bernstein left Monopol to manage Universal's West Coast studio. At this time, Monopol released the six-reel *The Seed of the Father,* which it claimed to be the first film of that length to be written from an original story. In September 1913, a receiver was ordered for Monopol, after creditor P. A. Powers filed an involuntary petition in bankruptcy against the company.

BIBLIOGRAPHY

"Marion Leonard Joins Monopol Company." *The Moving Picture World,* December 7, 1912, p. 988.

MONROVIA, CALIFORNIA. See CREST PICTURE COMPANY

MONROVIA FEATURE FILM COMPANY arranged to build a $200,000 plant in Monrovia, California, in 1916, which, besides a stage and studio, would include an amusement park, zoo, pool, and picnic grounds. The area was to be laid out like Universal City, and the company planned to charge 25 cents admission, with an additional fee for bathing. Officers of the company included R. M. Francisco, president; C. D. Holmes, vice president; and Edward L. Grafton, a member of the board of directors, who was president of the Grafton Film Publishing Company, which released Monrovia's product. Monrovia produced two ten-reel features, *The Argonauts of California* and *The Daughter of the Don,* directed by Henry Kabierske, a former director of pageants. In September 1916, Kabierske formed the Empire Feature Film Company, which planned to use Monrovia's studios. With three ten-reel spectacles planned, including one titled *The Ten Commandments,* Empire, in December 1916, purchased 40 acres at Murray Hill, near Grossmont in the San Diego area of California. Monrovia was declared bankrupt in October 1917.

MONUMENT VALLEY. It is generally noted that director John Ford (1894–1973) "discovered" Utah's Monument Valley, utilizing its impressively recognizable scenery in *Stagecoach* (1939), *My Darling Clementine* (1946), *Fort Apache* (1948), *She Wore a Yellow Ribbon* (1949), *Wagonmaster* (1950), *Rio Grande* (1950), *The Searchers* (1956), *Sergeant Rutledge* (1960), and *Cheyenne Autumn* (1964). In reality, Monument Valley was used as a film location as early as 1925 and *The Vanishing American.* Non-Westerns filmed in Monument Valley include *Easy Rider* (1969) and *The Eiger Sanction* (1975).

BIBLIOGRAPHY

Stanton, Bette L. *Where God Put the West: Movie Making in the Desert.* Moab, Utah: The Moab to Monument Valley Film Commission, 1994.

MOS is the term used when a sequence is to be filmed without sound. It means "mit out sound," and its origins supposedly lie in the phrase being spoken on the set by an unidentified German who spoke broken English. None of the books published in the early years of sound make reference to MOS, and it must, therefore, have originated in the thirties.

MOTION PICTURE ALLIANCE FOR THE PRESERVATION OF AMERICAN IDEALS, an anti-Communist group formed in 1944, declared itself to be a believer in the American way of life, "in sharp revolt against a rising tide of Communism[*], Fascism, and kindred beliefs." It opposed those organizations that had previously chosen to speak out against fascism on behalf of the film industry and which the Alliance labeled as Communist fronts: the Hollywood Anti-Nazi League*, the Hollywood League for Democratic Action, the Motion Picture Democratic Committee*, the Hollywood Theatre Alliance, the Hollywood Unit of the League against War and Fascism, and the American Peace Mobilization, which was earlier known as the Emergency Peace Committee. Founders of the Motion Picture Alliance included Sam Wood, King Vidor, Victor Fleming, Norman Taurog, Walt Disney, Clarence Brown, Harold S. Bucquet, and Jack Conway.

The Motion Picture Alliance quickly ran into opposition from the Screen Writers Guild, which branded it as "a subversive and dangerous organization which comforts the enemy." Nonetheless, the Alliance gained in strength, thanks to the House Un-American Activities Committee hearings. By 1950, when its president was John Wayne, the Motion Picture Alliance was demanding that the City of Los Angeles register all Communist sympathizers and that the

Hollywood Ten* not be released until they agreed to respond to questions from a congressional committee. It published a monthly newsletter, *The Vigil,* which documented the work of anyone within the film industry who might have displayed pro-Communist sympathies.

MOTION PICTURE AND TELEVISION FUND is a charitable organization, supported entirely by the film and television industries through donations, deductions from payrolls, memorial gifts, and special events. Based on the premise that the film and television industries help their own, the Fund provides financial and medical assistance to anyone in need. It also maintains a facility in Woodland Hills, California, consisting of residential cottages, a hospital, and a residential "lodge" for those not totally capable of caring for themselves. The 41-acre facility also includes the Douglas Fairbanks Lounge, the Y. Frank Freeman Library, the Louis B. Mayer Memorial Theatre, and the John Ford nondenominational chapel. The Fund's expenditures in 1985 exceeded $21 million, with financial aid to 3,300, medical aid to 4,600, and personal services aid to 4,800.

The Fund came into being on August 4, 1921, as the Motion Picture Branch of the Actors Fund of America. It was incorporated as the Motion Picture Relief Fund on December 31, 1924, and held its first annual meeting on June 30, 1925. Ground was broken for the Woodland Hills facility in 1941, with funding raised through the Screen Guild radio program. The Fund's Woodland Hills headquarters were officially opened on September 27, 1942.

Any industry member with more than 20 years of service is eligible to retire to the facility, along with his or her spouse. No preference is shown as to the member's occupation within the industry. All personal assets and income, such as Social Security, are placed in an account administered by the Fund. When and if the assets are exhausted and income does not meet the monthly costs of the member's residency, the Fund makes up the difference. After death, any monies remaining in the personal account become part of the resident's estate and are disposed of according to the terms of the individual's will.

Address: 23388 Mulholland Drive, Woodland Hills, Calif. 91364.

BIBLIOGRAPHY

Erlich, Cindy. "The Last Reel." *Rolling Stone,* December 16, 1976, pp. 67–71.
Jaynes, Gregory. "In California: A Place for Curtain Calls." *Time,* February 7, 1983, pp. 8–9.
Johnson, Sharon. "A Retirement Home That Retains a Bit of Hollywood Dazzle." *The New York Times,* June 2, 1979, p. 24.
Michaelson, Judith. "Where They Live the Last Picture Show." *Los Angeles Times,* Calendar, August 26, 1983, pp. 30–31.
Scott, Tony. "We Take Care of Our Own." *Daily Variety,* October 27, 1981, pp. 12–16, 35, 42, 46, 56.

MOTION PICTURE ARTISTS COMMITTEE was founded in 1937 to aid the Republican cause in the Spanish Civil War and to oppose fascism generally. Its organizers included Gale Sondergaard, Dashiell Hammett, Donald Ogden Stewart, Dudley Nichols, John Ford, John Garfield, Luise Rainer, Paul Muni, Fredric March, Melvyn Douglas, Lewis Milestone, and Lester Cole. The Motion Picture Artists Committee was denounced as a pro-Communist front organization by the Dies Committee*.

MOTION PICTURE ASSOCIATION OF AMERICA (MPAA) was formed in 1922 as the Motion Picture Producers and Distributors of America (MPPDA) to serve as a liaison between the industry and the public, to defend the industry against censorship (demands for which were becoming increasingly vocal following various scandals that rocked the film industry at that time), and to safeguard the producers against various demands from labor groups. To head the new group, the various producers—Marcus Loew, Lewis J. Selznick, William Fox, Carl Laemmle, Adolph Zukor, to name a few—making up the new organization selected Will H. Hays, who had served as chairman of the 1920 Republican National Committee and who was subsequently awarded with the position of postmaster general in President Warren G. Harding's administration.

Hays opened offices in New York and Hollywood and selected as his associates Governor Carl Milliken of Maine and attorneys Charles Pettijohn and Gabriel Hess. He summed up the aims of the organization: "To foster the common interests of those engaged in the motion picture industry in the United States, by establishing and maintaining the highest possible moral and artistic standards in motion picture production, by developing the education as well as the entertainment value and general usefulness of the motion picture, by diffusing accurate and reliable information with reference to the industry, by reforming abuses relative to the industry, by securing freedom from unjust or unlawful exactions, and by other lawful and proper means."

The MPPDA spoke out against a censorship bill in Massachusetts and organized its repeal in 1922. Hays addressed civic groups such as the Boy Scouts of America and the Daughters of the American Revolution. The MPPDA argued against the negative depiction of Mexicans in American films. It arranged for the registration of all bona fide film correspondents, and, in 1927, it formulated what was to become the Production Code*.

Will Hays retired and was succeeded by Eric Johnston in 1945, at which time the Motion Picture Producers and Distributors of America became the Motion Picture Association of America. At the same time, the Foreign Department of the MPPDA, which had handled the sale and distribution of American films abroad, was renamed the Motion Picture Export Association, described by Jack Valenti as "the only U.S. enterprise that negotiates on its own with foreign govern-ments." Jack Valenti succeeded Johnston as the Association's president in 1966.

One additional, recent activity of the MPAA had been the cracking down, through its Film Security Office, on film and video piracy both in the United States and abroad.

Address: 15503 Ventura Boulevard, Encino, Calif. 91436; 1600 Eye Street NW, Washington, D.C. 20006.

MOTION PICTURE BOARD OF TRADE OF AMERICA was organized in 1915 to provide an organization in which all branches of the film industry could be represented, to deal with problems concerning the industry as a whole, and to help settle disputes within the industry. The president was J. Stuart Blackton; Carl Laemmle, the manufacturers' vice president; Nicholas Power, the supply vice president; John R. Freuler, the exchanges* vice president; F. J. Rembusch, the exhibitors' vice president; W. Stephen Bush, the publication vice president; W. R. Rothacker, the miscellaneous [sic] vice president; E. A. McManus, the secretary; and Joseph W. Engel, the treasurer. In October 1915, D. W. Griffith became the first producer invited to join. The group received government recognition in 1916, when it met with President Woodrow Wilson, but that same year it disbanded and was replaced by the National Association of the Motion Picture Industry*, after various members quit because exhibitors were given only two out of the ten positions on the board.

BIBLIOGRAPHY

Bush, W. Stephen. "Motion Picture Board of Trade of America." *The Moving Picture World,* September 25, 1915, p. 2156.

MOTION PICTURE COMMITTEE COOPERATING FOR NATIONAL DEFENSE. See WAR ACTIVITIES COMMITTEE

MOTION PICTURE DEMOCRATIC COMMITTEE (MPDC) was organized in June 1938 to support radical Democrat Culbert Olsen in his California gubernatorial campaign. Among its leading members were Philip Dunne, Dudley Nichols, Allen Rivkin, Nat Perrin, and Dashiell Hammett, who served as chairman. The Committee produced a film titled *California Speaks.* Perhaps surprisingly, in view of his pro-socialist politics, Olsen won.

BIBLIOGRAPHY

Ceplair, Larry, and Steven Englund. *The Inquisition in Hollywood.* Garden City, N.Y.: Anchor Press/Doubleday, 1980.

MOTION PICTURE DIRECTORS ASSOCIATION, a fraternal organization, was incorporated first in Los Angeles on June 18, 1915. (A New York branch was incorporated on January 2, 1917.) The Association was neither a union nor a business organization; it had four aims: "to maintain the honor and dignity of the profession; to improve the moral, social, and intellectual standing of all persons connected with the motion picture producing business; to cultivate social intercourse among its members; to aid and assist all worthy distressed members."

Between 1924 and 1927, the Association published a journal titled *The Director* and later *The Motion Picture Director.* At one time, virtually every director in the industry was a member of the Association, but at its demise, in the early thirties, membership was comprised largely of "old-timers."

The following is a list of the Association's founding members: Charles W. Giblyn, Murdock J. MacQuarrie, Travers Vale, Burton King, Jay Hunt, Edward J. Le Saint, Al Christie, J. Farrell MacDonald, Henry McRae, Joseph De Grasse, Reginald Barker, Del Henderson, John O'Brien, George Morgan, William Robert Daly, Leo W. Youngsworth, Raymond B. West, Edward Dillon, Robert Z. Leonard, George Beban, Jack J. Clark, Francis Ford, Allen Curtis, Frank Lloyd, and Tom Mix.

MOTION PICTURE DISTRIBUTING AND SALES COMPANY was formed in April 1910, primarily by two independent companies, the New York Motion Picture Company* and the Independent Motion Picture Company, under the auspices of the National Independent Motion Picture Alliance, to control the output of independent films by releasing to the exchanges all independent productions through one company. While some independent producers agreed immediately to the formation, others, including Nestor, Thanhouser*, Eclair*, Capitol, Great Northern*, and Lux, formed their own alliance, the Associated Independent Manufacturers, distrusting the intentions of the companies heading the Sales Company.

After an agreement was reached in July 1910, whereby the Associated Independent Manufacturers would be fairly represented with the Sales Company, the combined group of independents had an association through which over 21 reels of film a week were to be released and which represented the product of Eclair, IMP, Nestor, Yankee, Bison, Kinograph, Lux, Powers*, Thanhouser, Ambrosio, Atlas, Champion, Electragraff, Motograph, Centaur*, Cines, Film d'Art, Defender, Capitol, Carson, Columbia, Great Northern, and Itala. The member companies sold their product directly to the Sales Company, which then dealt with the exchanges. Carl Laemmle was the president, P. A. Powers the vice president, Charles O. Baumann the treasurer, and Herbert Miles the secretary. Also on the board were William Steiner, William Swanson, and J. J. Murdock. The Sales Company also spent over $300,000 representing the independents in court over litigation brought against them by the Motion Picture Patents Company*.

The Sales Company, by acquiring the rights to the Bianchi camera, owned by the Columbia Phonograph Company, hoped to have a licensing company similar to that of the Motion Picture Patents Company, but the camera was found to

be impractical and the patents did not offer the protection promised by Columbia. Later, the Sales Company added other manufacturers to its groups, including Solax*, Reliance*, Rex, and Gaumont*.

The Sales Company came to an end in mid-1912, when the ranks of the independents split into two groups. The Film Supply Company of America announced its formation on May 14, 1912, as the releasing agency for Thanhouser, Gaumont, American*, Great Northern, Reliance, Eclair, Solax, Majestic, Lux, and Comet. In addition, the Mutual Film Corporation* was formed as a group of exchanges to handle the product of these companies. Harry E. Aitken was the organizer of both companies. Around the same time, Universal* was formed by the companies remaining in the Sales Company, including IMP, the New York Motion Picture Company, Powers, Rex, Champion, Republic*, and Nestor.

BIBLIOGRAPHY

"Alliance Executive Committee in Session. Projected Sales Co. Seeks to Regulate the Business of the Independents." *The Moving Picture World,* April 1, 1910, p. 549.

"Break in Ranks of Sales Company." *The Moving Picture World,* May 25, 1912, p. 707.

"The Motion Picture Distributing and Sales Company." *The Moving Picture World,* April 16, 1910, p. 595.

MOTION PICTURE EXHIBITORS' LEAGUE OF AMERICA, the first national exhibitors' organization, was formed at a convention in Cleveland in August 1911, due to the efforts of M. A. Neff of Cincinnati, the president of the Exhibitors' League of Ohio. In December 1909, Neff began to push for a national trade organization because of the rental exchanges' indifference to the needs of the exhibitors. The Exhibitors' League was formed in part to protect exhibitors anywhere in the country from restrictive local legislation that would be hard to fight without a national organization. Various state exhibitors' organizations existed prior to the formation of the League and continued to function during its existence, sometimes causing conflicts regarding the control and jurisdiction of the national organization.

Neff was elected president of the August 1911 convention and was reelected in 1912 (by which time the League had branches in 14 states) and 1913. The International Motion Picture Association formed as a seceding group at the July 1913 convention in New York and elected Charles H. Phillips of Milwaukee as its president. At the Exhibitors' League convention of 1914 in Dayton, Neff withdrew his nomination for reelection, and the new president, M. F. Pearce of Baltimore, effected a reconciliation with the other group.

In August 1917, another split of exhibitors occurred when Lee A. Ochs, the publisher of the new trade paper *Exhibitors' Trade Review,* which called itself the official journal of the League, was reelected president of the organization. Delegates, led by a group from Indiana, complained at the convention in Chicago that Ochs had packed the convention with stockholders of *Exhibitors' Trade Review,* in order to get himself re-elected, and that the League's distribution of voting power favored the big cities. They formed the American Exhibitors' Association*, but after a year, during which Ochs resigned from the presidency, William A. Brady, the president of the National Association of the Motion Picture Industry*, succeeded in bringing the two groups together. The resulting new national exhibitors' organization, called the National Association of the Motion Picture Industry, Exhibitors' Branch, was incorporated on September 13, 1918.

In 1920, the Motion Picture Theatre Owners of America became the dominant exhibitors' group, with a membership of 10 to 12 thousand. Led by its president, Sydney S. Cohen, and its counsel, James J. Walker (later mayor of New York), it strove to fight the wave of theatre takeovers by producers and distributors and was especially fearful of Adolph Zukor and his Famous Players-Lasky Corporation.

BIBLIOGRAPHY

"Exhibitors Form National League." *The Moving Picture World,* August 19, 1911, pp. 440–43.

"Factions Get Together in Chicago." *The Moving Picture World,* September 21, 1918, pp. 1691–95, 1727–33.

"The Motion Picture Exhibitors' League of America: How It Came into Being Told by President Neff." *The Moving Picture World,* August 17, 1912, pp. 621–23.

"Motion Picture Exhibitors' League of Greater New York Goes on Record in Favor of a National Convention of Exhibitors." *The Moving Picture World,* April 8, 1911, p. 153.

"Principles of American Association Stated." *The Moving Picture World,* August 11, 1917, p. 916.

MOTION PICTURE EXPORT ASSOCIATION. See MOTION PICTURE ASSOCIATION OF AMERICA

MOTION PICTURE GUILD. See ART HOUSES

MOTION PICTURE MOTHERS, INC., a charitable organization comprised of the mothers of film personalities, was formed on June 14, 1939, by Marie Brown. The group was initially involved in a variety of fund-raising activities but has for many years devoted itself to raising money for the Motion Picture and Television Fund*.

Address: c/o Motion Picture and Television Fund, 23388 Mulholland Drive, Woodland Hills, Calif. 91364.

BIBLIOGRAPHY

Hendrix, Kathleen. "Mothers of Stars on Memory Lane." *Los Angeles Times,* part 5, June 29, 1975, pp. 1, 16–17.

Simon, Al, and Jules Levine. "Mothers of the Stars, Inc." *Collier's,* December 23, 1944, pp. 18–19, 43.

MOTION PICTURE PATENTS COMPANY was a monopolistic organization, incorporated in New Jersey on September 9, 1908, which controlled the various patents held by Thomas Edison, the American Mutoscope and Biograph Company*, E. H. Amet, Francis Jenkins, and others, and which sought to license all film production, distribution, and exhibition. Its membership comprised the following manufacturers and importers of films: Biograph Company, Edison Manufacturing Company*, Essanay Film Manufacturing Company*, Gaumont Company* (but limited to its talking pictures only), Kalem Company*, George Kleine*, Lubin Manufacturing Company*, Gaston Méliès, Pathé* Freres, Selig Polyscope Company*, and Vitagraph Company of America*. It also licensed the following manufacturers of moving picture machines: American Moving Picture Machine Co., Armat Moving Picture Co., Edengraph Manufacturing Co., Edison Manufacturing Co., Enterprise Optical Company, Gaumont Company, Lubin Manufacturing Company, Pathé Freres, Nicholas Power Company, Eberhard Schneider, Selig Polyscope Company, George K. Spoor Company, and Vitagraph Company of America. In addition, it granted licenses to such showmen as Burton Holmes*, Lyman H. Howe, and Fred Niblo, permitting them to import films provided they paid a royalty to the company.

The Motion Picture Patents Company has its origins in the United Film Service Protective Association, formed November 16, 1907, and the Film Service Association, formed February 8, 1908. The failure of the American Mutoscope and Biograph Company, with its important patents, to join these organizations led to the formation of the new company.

Initially, the company licensed various film exchanges but, in April 1910, attempted to take them over through the creation of the General Film Company. (The Motion Picture Patents Company resolutely maintained that it did not control the General Film Company, pointing out that the two groups shared only two of the same directors.) The activities of the Motion Picture Patents Group were vigorously fought by independent producers/distributors such as Carl Laemmle and William Fox*, with the latter instituting a suit under the Sherman Antitrust Act. The Motion Picture Patents Company fought back through legal action of its own, occasionally resorting to violence in its efforts to halt the independents.

Although the Company lost the suit in 1915—and an appeal was dismissed in 1918—it was as much doomed from its lack of a clear-cut policy as regards feature-length films, which were becoming increasingly popular in the middle part of the second decade of the twentieth century, from the public interest in film personalities; from the failure of the individual member-producers to support the company's policies; and from a strong anti-Semitic bias. *Variety* (December 31, 1920) succinctly summed up the reason for the Motion Picture Patent Company or Film Trust's failure:

Put in a word, it was a matter of morale on the part of the principal men in the "trust." They were, for one thing, frenzied with money being deluged upon them; they would not take a long distance view of their interests, and they would not be subject to mutual counsel. Above all things, they were selfishly concerned with their own individual gains, jealous of each other, and imbued with the idea that their astounding success was the fruits of their own acumen rather than mostly an accident of circumstance.

If the Patents Co., or more properly speaking, the General Film Co., in the days of its greatest height of power, had had the foresight to accept into its circle the best of outside enterprise and business and artistic career, which all the time was striving for admittance, they probably would have established their huge amalgamation on a firm and permanent basis.

Aside from licensing films, the Motion Picture Patents Company also published a trade paper*, *The Film Index,* and established the first "fan" magazine in 1911, *The Motion Picture Story Magazine* (later *Motion Picture*). Its refusal to sell the former, in 1910, to *The Moving Picture World* led to its being boycotted by that trade paper, another nail in the company's coffin.

BIBLIOGRAPHY

Cassady, Ralph. *Monopoly in Motion Picture Production and Distribution: 1908–1915.* Los Angeles: Bureau of Business and Economic Research, University of California, 1959 (reprinted from *Southern California Law Review,* vol. 32, no. 4, 1959).

"General Film Company Is in No Danger of Receiver." *The Moving Picture World,* July 1, 1916, p. 64.

"The Motion Picture Patents Company and Its Work: A Retrospect and Appreciation." *The Moving Picture World,* July 17, 1909, pp. 81–84.

Thomas, Jeanne. "The Decay of the Motion Picture Patents Company." *Cinema Journal* X, 2 (Spring 1971): pp. 34–40.

MOTION PICTURE PRODUCERS AND DISTRIBUTORS OF AMERICA. See MOTION PICTURE ASSOCIATION OF AMERICA

MOTION PICTURE PUBLICISTS ASSOCIATION. See PUBLICISTS GUILD OF AMERICA

MOTION PICTURE RELIEF FUND. See MOTION PICTURE AND TELEVISION FUND

MOTION PICTURE SOCIETY FOR THE AMERICAS. Formed by the War Activities Committee* and the Office of the Coordinator of Inter-American Affairs, the Motion Picture Society for the Americas was concerned, during the Second World War, with increasing understanding and knowledge between the two Americas. South American specialists were available to offer guidance to Hollywood producers in their depiction of Latin American life and society. 16mm* projectors and films (in Spanish and Portuguese)

were available for screenings in South America. Various U.S. government agencies in cooperation with the film industry produced short subjects for South American audiences, dealing with hygiene, food, sanitation, and child nutrition. The idea, of course, was to foster a pro-American attitude in South America, rather than a pro-Axis feeling apparent in some Latin American countries. The work of the Motion Picture Society for the Americas was suspended in March 1946, and its work—on a more limited scale—was taken over by the Motion Picture Association of America*.

MOUNT VERNON, NEW YORK. See ALL-STAR FEATURE COMPANY

MOVIETIME, U.S.A., sponsored by the Council of Motion Picture Organizations (COMPO*), was a public relations project "to bring the story of Hollywood to the 'grass roots' of America." Stars (such as Greer Garson and Vera-Ellen), directors (such as Archie Mayo), and industry personnel (such as Carey Wilson and Irving Asher) were sent out on various regional tours. Celebrating the Golden Anniversary of the Motion Picture Theatre, there were 29 tours in 1951 and 9 in 1952. Movietime, U.S.A., came into existence in October 1951 and suspended operations in March 1953.

MOVIOLA. Although Moviola is often used to refer to any type of equipment used for viewing and editing motion picture films—the word appears in Webster's New World Dictionary—Moviola is, in fact, a corporate name for a specific type of editing equipment, a name registered with the U.S. Patent Office.

The Moviola and the Moviola Manufacturing Company were created by Dutch-born Iwan Serrurier, who received his first patent in April 1919. After modifying his editing equipment for use on an editing table, Serrurier sold the first Moviola Editing Machine to the Douglas Fairbanks Studio in the fall of 1924. The Mitchell Camera Company built 12 more machines for Serrurier, and the first of these, now called Moviola Midgets, was sold to M-G-M* in November 1924. With the advent of sound, Moviolas became standard equipment in the film industry, utilized for editing and synchronizing separate sound and film tracks. Moviola added a film brake to its equipment in 1936, enabling the editor to stop the film immediately without the risk of damage due to the abruptness of the halt. The Moviola Company began manufacturing rewinders in 1930 and projectors in 1931.

In the 1979 awards year—presented in 1980—the Academy of Motion Picture Arts and Sciences* presented an Award of Merit, in the form of an Oscar, "to Mark Serrurier for the progressive development of the Moviola from the 1924 invention of his father, Iwan Serrurier, to the present Series 20 sophisticated film editing equipment. The Moviola has evolved from the 1924 Midget to the complex machine necessary for the array of picture and sound formats currently employed in motion picture production. It has kept pace effectively to meet the demands of motion picture technology." The Moviola Corporation is now known as Magnasync-Moviola Corporation, a subsidiary of the Craig Corporation.

Address: Magnasync-Moviola Corporation, 1141 North Mansfield Avenue, Hollywood, Calif. 90038.

BIBLIOGRAPHY

Lehrman, Harry. "Forty Years of the Moviola." *Film World and AV News,* May 1965, p. 208.
"Moviola's New Editing Console." *American Cinematographer,* December 1970, pp. 1194–95, 1230–31.
Serrurier, Mark. "The Origins of the Moviola." *The Cinemeditor,* Winter 1965, pp. 5–7.

MPAA. See MOTION PICTURE ASSOCIATION OF AMERICA

MPDC. See MOTION PICTURE DEMOCRATIC COMMITTEE

MPPDA. See MOTION PICTURE ASSOCIATION OF AMERICA

MULBERY SQUARE PRODUCTIONS, INC. Formed in January 1971 by Joe Camp (its president) and James Nicodemus (who is no longer associated with the company) as a producer of television commercials, Mulbery Square Productions, Inc., has gained a reputation for its family features starring Benji, beginning with a film of the same name, which received its world premiere in Dallas on May 24, 1974. The company has been inactive since the late 1980s.

Address: 10300 North Central Expressway, Suite 120, Dallas, Tex. 73374.

BIBLIOGRAPHY

Camp, Joe. *Underdog.* Marietta, Georgia: Lonstreet Press, 1993.

MUSIC has always been an integral part of the motion picture. There was no such thing as a silent film, for—from 1896 onward—all films had musical accompaniment of some sort, be it a piano, an organ, or a full orchestra. "Moving pictures and music are inseparable," wrote Paul Evert Denton in *The Moving Picture World* (April 23, 1916). Cue sheets would be provided by distributors for some silent films—as early as 1910 the Edison Company* published on a regular basis lists of musical themes suitable for use with its films—while it was not uncommon for scores to be specially composed or arranged for silent features.

Perhaps the earliest example of music specially composed for a film is Camille Saint-Säens's score for the one-reel French Pathé* production of *L'Assassinat du Duc de Guise/The Assassination of the Duke of Guise* (1907). In Europe, serious composers, such as Arthur Honneger and Edmund Meisel, composed film scores during the silent era.

Among the many original scores composed or compiled for American silent features were one by Walter Cleveland Simon for *Arrah-na-Pogue* (1911); one by Joseph Carl Breil for *The Birth of a Nation* (1915), which replaced an even earlier score for the same film by Carli Elinor; one by Victor Schertzinger for *Robin Hood* (1922); one by Hugo Riesenfeld for *The Covered Wagon* (1923); and by Mortimer Wilson for *The Thief of Bagdad* (1924). Two of the busiest of silent film music composers/arrangers were David Mendoza and William Axt, who were responsible for *The Big Parade* (1925), *Ben-Hur* (1926), and *Don Juan* (1926), among many others.

Most important silent features had theme songs, several of which became popular hits. Erno Rapée and Lew Pollack wrote the theme song of "Diane" from *7th Heaven* (1927), L. Wolfe Gilbert and Mabel Wayne wrote "Ramona" for the 1928 film of the same name, and Erno Rapée composed "Charmaine" for *What Price Glory* (1926).

With the coming of sound, Hollywood producers gained total control of film music. No longer would the choice, in many cases, be left to local musicians. At the same time, film music gained a new respectability. Some producers used stock music by anonymous composers, but generally film composers were acknowledged, with many becoming associated with an individual studio. Herbert Stothart and Bronislau Kaper were with M-G-M*, Roy Webb with RKO*, Erich Wolfgang Korngold with Warner Bros.*, Cy Feuer with Republic*, and Alfred Newman with 20th Century-Fox*. Among the "serious" composers who contributed film scores were Hanns Eisler, Ernest Torch, and Aaron Copland.

Some composers were associated with a particular production or a group of films. Marvin Hatley is remembered as the composer of the Laurel and Hardy theme music; Bernard Herrmann's name is associated with *Citizen Kane* (1941) and scores for some of Hitchcock's films; Erich Wolfgang Korngold with the lush scores of Warner Bros. adventure films such as *The Adventures of Robin Hood* (1938) and *The Sea Hawk* (1940); David Raksin with the theme song from *Laura* (1944); Miklos Rozsa and Max Steiner with lush, romantic scores; and Ernest Gold with the theme from *Exodus* (1960). The best known of contemporary composers is John Williams, thanks to his instantly recognizable scores for *Jaws* (1975), *Star Wars* (1977), *E.T. The Extra-Terrestrial* (1982), and *Return of the Jedi* (1983). Other contemporary composers with high reputations among their peers are Leonard Rosenman, Jerry Goldsmith, Giorgio Moroder, and Bill Conti, successors to such memorable earlier film composers as John Green, Ray Heindorf, Morris Stoloff, Franz Waxman, and Victor Young.

Academy Awards for Best Music Scores have been given since 1934, when the winner was the Columbia Studio Music Department (Louis Silvers, head) for *One Night of Love.* The award points up the early practice of crediting music departments or their heads for film scores, rather than the actual composers or arrangers.

BIBLIOGRAPHY

Anderson, Gillian B. *Music for Silent Films, 1894–1929: A Guide*. Washington, D.C.: Library of Congress, 1988.

Atkins, Irene Cahn. *Source Music in Motion Pictures*. Rutherford, N.J.: Associated University Presses, 1983.

Bell, Donald A. *Getting the Best Score for Your Film: A Filmmakers' Guide to Music Scoring*. Los Angeles: Silman-James, 1994.

Benjamin, Ruth. *Movie Song Catalog: Performers and Supporting Crew for the Songs in 1460 Musical and Nonmusical Films, 1928–1988*. Jefferson, N.C.: McFarland, 1993.

Carlin, Don. *Music in Film and Video Productions*. Boston: Focal Press, 1991.

Darby, William, and Jack Du Bois. *American Film Music: Major Composers, Techniques, Trends, 1915–1990*. Jefferson, N.C.: McFarland, 1990.

Ehrenstein, David, and Bill Reed. *Rock on Film*. New York: Delilah Books, 1982.

Eisler, Hans. *Composing for the Films*. New York: Oxford University Press, 1947.

Evans, Mark. *Soundtrack: The Music of the Movies*. New York: Hopkinson and Blake, 1975.

Faulkner, Robert S. *Hollywood Studio Musicians*. Chicago: Aldine Atherton, 1971.

Flinn, Caryl. *Strains of Utopia: Gender, Nostalgia, and Hollywood Film Music*. Princeton, N.J.: Princeton University Press, 1992.

Gorbman, Claudia. *Unheard Melodies: Narrative Film Music*. Bloomington, Ind.: Indiana University Press, 1987.

Huntley, John. *The Technique of Film Music*. New York: Hastings House, 1957.

Kalinak, Kathryn. *Settling the Score: Music and the Classical Hollywood Film*. Madison, Wis.: University of Wisconsin Press, 1992.

Karlin, Fred. *Listening to Movies: The Film Lover's Guide to Film Music*. New York: Schirmer, 1994.

Karlin, Fred, and Rayburn Wright. *On the Track: A Guide to Contemporary Film Scoring*. New York: Schirmer, 1990.

Limbacher, James L. *Film Music from Violins to Video*. Metuchen, N.J.: Scarecrow Press, 1974.

————. *Keeping Score: Film Music, 1972–1979*. Metuchen, N.J.: Scarecrow Press, 1981.

London, Kurt. *Film Music*. London: Faber and Faber, 1936.

McCarty, Clifford. *Film Composers in America*. Glendale, Calif.: John Valentine, 1953.

Meeker, David. *Jazz in the Movies*. New York: Da Capo, 1982.

Scharf, Walter. *The History of Film Scoring*. Studio City, Calif.: Cinema Songs, 1988.

Stubblebine, Donald J. *Cinema Sheet Music: A Comprehensive Listing of Published Film Music from Squaw Man (1914) to Batman (1989)*. Jefferson, N.C.: McFarland, 1991.

Thomas, Tony. *Music for the Movies*. New York: A. S. Barnes, 1973.

MUSICALS. "What is a musical?" asked critic John Russell Taylor. "All talking, all singing, all dancing? Well, yes, preferably. But a lot more, and sometimes a lot less. A film musical is, essentially, just that: a film which, in whole or in part, has its shape, its movement, its whole feeling dictated by music."

The musical genre is as old as the sound film itself. *The Jazz Singer* (1927), generally considered the first sound feature, was a musical. The sound era began with all singing, all talking, all dancing revues, such as *Hollywood Revue of 1929* from M-G-M*, *Show of Shows* (1929) from Warner Bros.*, *Paramount on Parade* (1930), and *The King of Jazz* (1930) from Universal*. The first film musical with an original score, by Arthur Freed and Nacio Herb Brown, was *Broadway Melody* (1929) from M-G-M, starring Bessie Love, Charles King, and Anita Page. The first musical in Technicolor* was Warner Bros.' *On with the Show* (1929), starring Betty Compson, Arthur Lake, and Ethel Waters. The first operetta written specially for the screen was Sigmund Romberg and Oscar Hammerstein's *Viennese Nights* (1930), produced by Warner Bros. and starring Vivienne Segal, Alexander Gray, and Walter Pidgeon.

Following the initial enthusiasm for musicals, there was a period in the early thirties when the public turned against the genre. It returned to popularity with Warner Bros.' *42nd Street* (1932), Eddie Cantor's comedy musicals at the Goldwyn* studios, and with the Fred Astaire-Ginger Rogers musicals at RKO*, the first of which (although the two were not its stars) being *Flying Down to Rio* (1933). Maurice Chevalier was Paramount's musical star of the early thirties, usually partnered with Jeanette MacDonald, who moved over to M-G-M to costar with Nelson Eddy in a series of operettas from the mid-thirties through the mid-forties. At Warner Bros., the "Gold Diggers" series* was popular, thanks largely to the winsome charm of Ruby Keeler and Dick Powell and the extravagant routines choreographed by Busby Berkeley.

Shirley Temple was 20th Century-Fox's first musical star, to be followed by Alice Faye and Betty Grable. Deanna Durbin was responsible for a new form of musical, which embraced serious music for dramatic effect, at Universal, in features such as *100 Men and a Girl* (1937). M-G-M had introduced the "Broadway Melody" series with the 1929 feature of that name; it continued the series with the Broadway Melodies of 1936, 1938, and 1940. Also at M-G-M, Eleanor Powell became the leading exponent of tap dancing (with strong competition from

Ann Miller at Columbia*). Judy Garland starred in *The Wizard of Oz* (1939) and was cofeatured with Mickey Rooney in a delightful series of musical comedies such as *Babes in Arms* (1939) and *Strike Up the Band* (1940). Gene Kelly came into his own at M-G-M in the forties, while Mario Lanza dominated the musical scene at the studio in the early fifties, during which period M-G-M's female musical stars included Kathryn Grayson and Betty Hutton. The fifties also saw lyricist Arthur Freed consolidating his reputation as the studio's greatest musical producer with films such as *Annie Get Your Gun* (1950), *An American in Paris* (1951), *Singin' in the Rain* (1952), *The Band Wagon* (1953), *Silk Stockings* (1957), and *Gigi* (1958).

There were five screen versions of Richard Rodgers and Oscar Hammerstein II stage musicals: *Oklahoma!* (1955), *Carousel* (1956), *The King and I* (1956), *South Pacific* (1958), and *Flower Drum Song* (1961).

All-black musicals have failed to make much of an impact, with the best known being *Cabin in the Sky* (1943), *Stormy Weather* (1943), *Carmen Jones* (1954), *Porgy and Bess* (1959), and *The Wiz* (1978). A more enduring subgenre has been that of the biographical musical, which can be devoted to entertainers, as with *The Helen Morgan Story* (1957), *The Jolson Story* (1946), and *Jolson Sings Again* (1949), *Yankee Doodle Dandy* (1942), and *The Story of Vernon and Irene Castle* (1939); to band leaders, as with *The Glenn Miller Story* (1954); and to composers, as with the highly fanciful Richard Rodgers and Lorenz Hart biography, *Words and Music* (1948).

"Modern" musicals can embrace the strictly entertainment values of their predecessors, as with *The Music Man* (1962), *Mary Poppins* (1964), *The Sound of Music* (1965), *Camelot* (1967), and *Hello, Dolly!* (1969), and can also be new and original, as was evidenced by *West Side Story* (1961), and *All That Jazz* (1979). With so few film musicals in recent times, 1996 proved to be a bumper year, presenting Woody Allen's first musical venture, *Everyone Says I Love You*, and the musical feature-film debut of Madonna in *Evita*, directed by Alan Parker.

Only nine musicals have won Academy Awards for Best Picture: *Broadway Melody* (1929), *The Great Ziegfeld* (1936), *An American in Paris* (1951), *Gigi* (1958), *West Side Story* (1961), *My Fair Lady* (1964), *The Sound of Music* (1965), *Oliver!* (1968), and *Amadeus* (1984).

BIBLIOGRAPHY

Barrios, Richard. *A Song In the Dark: The Birth of the Musical Film*. New York: Oxford University Press, 1995.
Bloom, Ken. *Hollywood Song: The Complete Film & Musical Companion*. New York: Facts on File, 1995.
Chaplin, Saul. *The Golden Age of Movie Musicals and Me*. Norman, Okla.: University of Oklahoma Press, 1994.
Fehr, Richard, and Frederick G. Vogel. *Lullabies of Hollywood: Movie Music and the Movie Musical, 1915–1992*. Jefferson, N.C.: McFarland, 1993.
Feuer, Jane. *The Hollywood Musical*. Bloomington, Ind.: Indiana University Press, 1993.
Green, Stanley. *Encyclopedia of the Musical Film*. New York: Oxford University Press, 1981.
Koerner, Julie. *Hollywood Musicals*. New York: Friedman/Fairfax, 1993.
Kreuger, Miles. *The Movie Musical*. New York: Dover, 1975.
Mast, Gerald. *Can't Help Singin': The American Musical on Stage and Screen*. Woodstock, N.Y.: The Overlook Press, 1987.
Mordden, Ethan. *The Hollywood Musical*. New York: St. Martin's Press, 1981.
Parish, James Robert, and Michael R. Pitts. *The Great Hollywood Musical Pictures*. Metuchen, N.J.: Scarecrow Press, 1992.
Stacy, Jan, and Ryder Syvertsen. *Rockin' Reels: An Illustrated History of Rock & Roll Movies*. Chicago: Contemporary Books, 1984.
Taylor, John Russell, and Arthur Jackson. *The Hollywood Musical*. New York: McGraw-Hill, 1971.

THE MUTOGRAPH was an early camera, developed in 1895 by Herman Casler (1867–1939).

MUTUAL FILM CORPORATION was organized in March 1912 as an independent exchange system to function in a manner similar to that of the General Film Company. Harry E. Aitken, (1870–1956) Mutual's president—who later in 1912 formed the Film Supply Company of America as an alliance of independent film manufacturers to challenge the Carl Laemmle-controlled Motion Picture Distributing and Sales Company*—and John R. Freuler, Mutual's vice president, interested financiers Crawford Livingston and Otto Kahn (of Kuhn, Loeb, and Company) in the enterprise. With a capitalization of $2.5 million, Mutual eventually succeeded in signing half of the members of the Motion Picture Distributing and Sales Company. Shortly after Mutual's creation, the Universal Film Manufacturing Company was created and it became Mutual's rival independent exchange.

Mutual handled films for Thanhouser*, Gaumont*, American*, Great Northern*, Reliance, Eclair*, Solax*, Majestic, Lux, Comet, and the New York Motion Picture Company*, supervised by Thomas H. Ince, which controlled Kay-Bee, Broncho, and Domino Films. Adam Kessel and Charles O. Baumann, who owned the New York Motion Picture Company and Reliance, formed the Keystone Film Company* in 1912, with Mack Sennett, to produce films for Mutual. In October 1913, Mutual hired D. W. Griffith to be in charge of the amalgamated Reliance-Majestic studio. The next month, Griffith's cameraman, Billy Bitzer, joined Mutual, along with directors Edward Dillon and W. Christy Cabanne, actor Courtenay Foote, and scenarist Frank Woods. Griffith soon established his company at the former Kinemacolor studio at

4500 Sunset Boulevard in Hollywood (when it became known as Fine Arts*).

The Continental Feature Film Company was formed as a subsidiary to Mutual in late 1913, to release features made by Reliance. W. C. Toomey was its manager, and its offices were 219 Sixth Avenue, New York.

In January 1914, Mutual contracted with Pancho Villa for his permission and cooperation regarding the filming of the battles of the Mexican war. According to Terry Ramsaye (in *A Million and One Nights*), Villa was so camera struck that he held off fighting battles until Mutual's camera team was set up, fought during the day rather than at night, and made sure he was always prominent in the picture. Later, Mutual used some of this footage in the fictional *The Life of Villa,* which starred Raoul Walsh.

Mutual instituted a series of features called "Mutual Masterpieces" early in 1915. In May 1915, a split between, on one side, Aitken, Kessel, and Baumann, and, on the other, Freuler and America's head Samuel S. Hutchinson resulted in Freuler's succeeding Aitken as president. The latter left Mutual, and, two months later, Aitken, Kessel, and Baumann formed the Triangle Film Corporation* to release the films of D. W. Griffith, Thomas H. Ince, and Mack Sennett. Freuler appointed J. C. Graham as his general manager and signed David Horsley's Centaur Film Company and the Bostock Jungle and Film Company* to release with Mutual.

On February 26, 1916, Mutual signed Charles Chaplin, for $670,000, to produce comedies for it. His new company, Lone Star Film Corporation, produced 12 films and ended in 1917, when Chaplin signed with First National*. In early 1917, Mutual secured the rights to release the Charles Frohman plays, produced with the Charles Frohman stars by the newly formed Empire All Star Corporation, which was incorporated with $2.5 million capital.

Freuler, who complained that he did not have the backing of his associates to make much needed changes, resigned May 1, 1918, and was replaced by James M. Sheldon. On November 6, 1918, the Affiliated Distributors' Corporation* acquired 51 percent of Mutual, which was then losing money at an alarming rate. The Exhibitors' Mutual Distributing Corporation, formed later in 1918, was an outgrowth of Mutual and the Affiliated.

BIBLIOGRAPHY

"Mutual Film Corporation." *The Moving Picture World,* April 6, 1912, p. 34.

"Mutual Withdraws from Film Supply." *The Moving Picture World,* December 12, 1912, p. 1280.

THE MUTUAL WEEKLY. See NEWSREELS

NAGRA was the first portable and battery-operated sound recorder, using three-quarter inch magnetic tape, to gain widespread popularity and use in the film industry. It was invented in 1958 by Stefan Kudelski, who, in 1965 received a Class II Scientific or Technical Award from the Academy of Motion Picture Arts and Sciences*.

THE NASH MOTION PICTURE COMPANY, INC.
Thomas Nash, formerly a producer of one- and two-reel animal films for the Selig Polyscope Company*, formed his own company in mid-1914 and built a studio and zoo in Edendale, California, to make three- to five-reel wild animal features. It released on the Kriterion* program at the beginning, later releasing to the states rights* market.

BIBLIOGRAPHY

"New Wild Animal Company Formed." *The Moving Picture World,* July 4, 1914, p. 87.

NATIONAL ASSOCIATION OF THEATRE OWN-ERS, INC. (NATO), came into being on January 1, 1965, with the merger of Theatre Owners of America and the Allied States Association of Motion Picture Exhibitors. According to its constitution, its concerns are the maintenance of a strong, national trade organization; the promotion and protection of interests of motion picture exhibitors; and the cultivation of the highest possible standards in all film industry matters in general and in film exhibition in particular. NATO serves as a spokesperson for all matters affecting exhibitors. It also organizes an annual convention, at which exhibitors can see the latest in products relating to theatre operations, including technical equipment, the latest studio productions, and food and equipment relating to the concessions counter. Also at its convention, NATO presents awards to the stars of the year and the stars of tomorrow and the Sherill C. Corwin Award (named after a former president of NATO) for contributions to theatre exhibition.

Address: 4605 Lankershim Boulevard, Suite 340, North Hollywood, Calif. 91602.

NATIONAL ASSOCIATION OF THE MOTION PIC-TURE INDUSTRY (NAMPI) was formed in July 1916 as a successor to the Motion Picture Board of Trade of America*. Its objectives were to foster trade and commerce among members, promote business interests of the industry, provide information about the industry, settle difficulties within the industry, and secure freedom from unjust government exactions. The membership represented producers and importers, the Motion Picture Exhibitors' League of America*, manufacturers, dealers and importers of motion picture supplies, distributors, and others connected with the industry. The exhibitors, who wanted a bigger representation on the board of the previous organization, voted to join the National Association of the Motion Picture Industry at its first meeting on July 25, 1916. A few months later, William A. Brady was elected president, Jules Brulatour treasurer, Thomas Furniss the first vice president, and Adolph Zukor the second vice president. After the United States entered the First World War in 1917, NAMPI responded to a letter of President Woodrow Wilson and appointed various members to act in conjunction with the various government departments. NAMPI went out of existence when the stronger Motion Picture Producers and Distributors of America, Inc., headed by Will Hays, came into existence early in 1922.

BIBLIOGRAPHY

"Film Men Form Temporary Organization." *The Moving Picture World,* July 22, 1916, p. 612.
"Motion Pictures Mobilized for War." *The Moving Picture World,* August 11, 1917, p. 918.

NATIONAL BOARD OF CENSORSHIP OF MOTION PICTURES, a precursor to the National Board of Review of Motion Pictures*, was formed in October 1909, after an earlier organization, the Board of Censorship, experimented for five months censoring the product of most of the early companies. The Board of Censorship was established by the People's Institute, a New York civic organization, in response to a petition from the Motion Picture Exhibitors of New York State, which financed its operations and had two members on the Board's executive committee. The exhibitors wanted a censorship board to prevent hostility from vigilance groups and to limit the danger of losing exhibitors' licenses as a result of being taken to court—the result of the negative reaction to some of the films that they screened.

The Board's governing body was composed of individuals from nine public-interest bodies, such as the Public Education Association and the City Vigilance League. Dr. George William Knox of the Union Theological Seminary was the chairman. At its formation, the Board had made arrangements with every company in the Motion Picture Patents Company* and a few of the independents to censor their films before they were sent to the exchanges. The Board was opposed to the depiction of crime or violence for its own sake, indecency, and immoral suggestiveness. The Board also emphasized that it would try to encourage the use of motion pictures for educational purposes. It carried no legal weight, and, in its most publicized case, the Board refused to censor D. W. Griffith's *The Birth of a Nation* (1915). In 1916, its name was changed to the National Board of Review of Motion Pictures.

BIBLIOGRAPHY

"An Eloquent Record." *The Moving Picture World,* December 4, 1915, p. 1821.

"The Board of Censorship." *The Moving Picture World,* March 6, 1909, pp. 265–66.

"Censorship of Film Subjects." *The Moving Picture World,* March 20, 1909, p. 325.

"National Board of Censorship of Motion Pictures." *The Moving Picture World,* October 16, 1909, p. 524.

NATIONAL BOARD OF REVIEW OF MOTION PICTURES, INC.,

founded in 1909 as the National Board of Censorship of Motion Pictures*, served as a citizens' group concerned with the evaluation of films. It was initially formed to discourage official censorship of motion pictures and enjoyed the financial support of the film industry. All films were submitted to the Board—it became the National Board of Review of Motion Pictures, Inc., in 1916—for a seal of approval, consisting of the words, "Passed by the National Board of Review," which would appear on the main titles. The Board charged a fee, per reel, for the review and approval of each film.

With the creation of local censorship boards, the National Board of Review's approval became valueless, and by January 1938 only Providence, Rhode Island, still required films to carry the Board's seal of approval—and then only for Sunday screenings.

The National Board of Review is probably better known today for its selection of "Ten Best Films," which it has undertaken since 1930, with the inclusion—in more recent years—of citations for Best Actor, Actress, Director, Foreign Language Film, and so on. It is also noted for its publications: *Film Program* (1917–1926), *Exceptional Photoplays* (1920–1925), *Photoplay Guide to Better Movies* (1924–1926), *National Board of Review Magazine* (1926–1942), *New Movies* (1942–1949), and *Films in Review* (1950 to present). As of its July/August 1996 issue, *Films in Review* has been published in association with Then and There Media.

Address: P.O. Box 589, New York, N.Y. 10021.

BIBLIOGRAPHY

Fisher, Robert. "Film Censorship and Progressive Reform: The National Board of Censorship of Motion Pictures, 1909–1922." *Journal of Popular Film* 4, 2 (1975): pp. 143–56.

Hochman, Stanley, ed. *From Quasimodo to Scarlett O'Hara: A National Board of Review Anthology 1920–1940.* New York: Frederick Ungar, 1982.

"National Board of Review Facing Test on Continuance of Activity." *Motion Picture Herald,* January 29, 1938, pp. 16, 18, 28.

Ramsaye, Terry. "Forty Years of the National Board." *Films in Review,* February 1950, pp. 23–24.

Warfield, Nancy. "A Film Students Index to the National Board of Review Magazine 1926–1948." *The Little Film Gazette of N.D.W.,* vol. 5, no. 2, December 1974.

NATIONAL CAMERAPHONE COMPANY,

an early producer of "talking pictures," began leasing its machines across the country at the beginning of 1908, after two years of experimentation. During the company's two-year existence, a number of other processes for producing talking pictures, including Gaumont's Chronophone, Powers's Fotophone, and the Cinephone, were presented to an interested public, prompting a journalist to predict that "the speaking picture will soon be as common as the moving picture now."

E. E. Norton of Bridgeport, Connecticut, formerly a mechanical engineer with the American Gramophone Company, invented the Cameraphone, a combination of a motion picture projector and the gramophone. The company's factory was located in Bridgeport, at 423 Water Street, and its offices were at 1161 Broadway, New York, where the films were first produced in its "gallery." In May 1908, the company converted a five-story warehouse at 573–579 Eleventh Avenue, New York, into a studio and exhibition hall. Carl Herbert was Cameraphone's general manager.

Although the National Cameraphone Company never lived up to its claim to have perfected synchronization between sound and picture, it did please audiences throughout the country for a short time. Successful exhibitions were reported in Kalamazoo, Michigan; Oakland, California; Pueblo, Colorado; Baltimore, Maryland; Youngstown, Ohio; Helena, Montana; Columbus, Georgia; and New York City. One show consisted of a song, a scene in a Turkish bath, and a dramatic enactment of *The Corsican Brothers.* Another included an impersonation of George M. Cohan.

The company purchased the projectors and gramophones used in the exhibitions from manufacturers and leased them to theatres. The gramophone, which was placed behind the screen, could be turned on and off by the projectionist, to keep the sound reasonably in sync with the picture. Although critics complained that synchronization often was not achieved, and that the sound had a harsh, metallic ring, the company hoped that improvements could be made. However, the Cameraphone Company went out of business in May 1910.

BIBLIOGRAPHY

"The Cameraphone." *The Moving Picture World,* January 16, 1909, p. 71.

"Cameraphone Experiments." *The Moving Picture World,* January 23, 1909, p. 90.

"Cameraphone Hits." *The Moving Picture World,* July 25, 1908, p. 63.

"Cameraphone the Latest Wonder." *The Moving Picture World,* April 25, 1908, pp. 369–70.

NATIONAL CATHOLIC OFFICE FOR MOTION PICTURES. See NATIONAL LEGION OF DECENCY

THE NATIONAL CHILDREN'S FILM LIBRARY was created in 1946 by the Motion Picture Association of America to keep in circulation film versions of "ageless juvenile stories and classics." By 1950 it was boasting that 57 feature films were available for children's screenings, including *The Adventures of Robin Hood, Gallant Bess, Green Grass of Wyoming, Nanook of the North, The Secret Garden,* and *The Wizard of Oz.*

NATIONAL DRAMA CORPORATION. After the success of *The Birth of a Nation* (1915), Thomas Dixon, author of *The Clansman,* upon which the film was based, formed the National Drama Corporation in 1915, so that he might produce and direct his first film. *The Fall of a Nation* (1916), a warning against disarmament and women's suffrage, was the result. Dixon hired composer Victor Herbert to write the score, which was performed by a 60-piece orchestra under the direction of Harold Sanford at the film's New York premiere in June 1916 at the Liberty Theatre. After *The Fall of a Nation,* National contracted with Dixon for the rights to his literary output for the next five years. P. D. Gold, Jr., was the president of the company, William R. Perkins the vice president, Dixon the director-general and treasurer, Bartley Cushing the head producing director, and William C. Thompson and John W. Boyle the cameramen.

NATIONAL FILM AND PHOTO LEAGUE. Radical young filmmakers and film enthusiasts formed the National Film and Photo League (sometimes referred to as the Workers' Film and Photo League and sometimes as simply the Film and Photo League) in 1931. The group included Lewis Jacobs, David Platt, Leo T. Hurwitz, Jay Leyda, Irving Lerner, and Ralph Steiner. It had its origins in the Workers' International Relief, the Workers' Camera League, and the Labor Defender Photo Group.

The League was organized into city groups. It produced a newsreel and documentary shorts; organized protests against anti-Communist Hollywood productions and the screening of pro-Nazi films from Germany; held meetings; and published a magazine, *Film Front,* from 1934–1935. The New York group produced *Albany Hunger March* (1931), *The Strike against Starvation* (1931), *The Fight for the Bonus* (1932), *Hands Off Ethiopia* (1935), among others. From Detroit came *The Ford Massacre* (1932); from Chicago, *The Great Depression* (1934); from Los Angeles, *Tom Mooney Run* (1932) and *Bloody Memorial Day* (1934). Unfortunately, these films gained only very limited screenings, and those chiefly for committed radicals.

By 1937, the National Film and Photo League had basically ceased to exist, although one breakaway group, the Photo League, was still around as late as 1951. Another breakaway group was Nykino, which became the film division of the Theatre of Action and which produced such films as *Pie in the Sky* (1935), *Black Legion* (1936), and *The World Today* (1936). From Nykino emerged Frontier Films*.

BIBLIOGRAPHY

Campbell, Russell. *Cinema Strikes Back.* Ann Arbor, Mich.: UMI Research Press, 1982.

Rosenzweig, Roy. "Working Class Struggles in the Great Depression: The Film Record." *Film Library Quarterly,* vol. 13, no. 1, 1980, pp. 5–14.

Seltzer, Leo. "Documenting the Depression of the 1930s." *Film Library Quarterly,* vol. 13, no. 1, 1980, pp. 15–22.

RESOURCES

Films: Museum of Modern Art (16mm reference prints).

NATIONAL FILM CORPORATION OF AMERICA was formed in 1915 by comedian "Smiling" Bill Parsons. The following year, Paul Gilmore became associated with the company, which announced plans for a move from Los Angeles to Tampa, Florida, where it was to build a new studio. Despite valid claims by many of the corporation's stockholders as to irregularities in its affairs, National prospered for quite a while. It produced the first "Tarzan" feature, *Tarzan of the Apes* (1918), and two sequels, *The Romance of Tarzan* (1918) and a 15-chapter serial*, *The Son of Tarzan* (1920). At its Hollywood studio, at Santa Monica Boulevard and Gower Street, the corporation produced a series of comedies featuring Parsons, his wife Billie Rhodes, Mr. and Mrs. Carter De Haven, and Eddie Flanagan and Neely Edwards as "The Hall Room Boys," as well as dramas with Ann Little, Jack Hoxie, and Henry B. Walthall. Its films were released by Goldwyn*, Pioneer Film Corporation*, and the W. W. Hodkinson Corporation*. Following Parsons's death in 1919, National was acquired by R. E. Frey, who moved the corporation to new studios at 1116 Lodi Street. It lost much of its importance as Frey attempted to make John Bunny's brother, George, into a comedy star. National ceased operations in 1923.

BIBLIOGRAPHY

"National Film Corporation of America." *The Moving Picture World,* July 10, 1915, p. 254.

Nelson, Richard Alan. " 'High Flyer' Movie Finance and the Silver Screen: The Rise and Fall of the National Film Corporation of America." *Film & History,* vol. 13, no. 4, December 1983, pp. 73–83, 93.

NATIONAL GENERAL CORPORATION. When 20th Century-Fox* was required by the consent decree* to divest itself of its theatre chain, the 549 theatres that it controlled in 1951 became National General Corporation. The number of theatres gradually declined, and in 1973 the remaining 266 were sold to Mann Theatres Corporation*.

NATIONAL LEGION OF DECENCY (often erroneously referred to as the Legion of Decency) was formed in April 1934 as an agency of the Catholic Bishops of the United States. Its purpose was to assure that motion pictures conformed to the accepted and traditional morality upon which the home and civilization were founded. The Legion rated films into four categories, with the rating undertaken by the Motion Picture Department of the International Federation of Catholic Alumnae: Class A, Section I, Unobjectionable for General Patronage; Class A, Section II, Unobjectionable for Adults; Class B, Objectionable in Part; Class C, Condemned.

An editorial in the Catholic journal *America* (December 13, 1941) pointed out that "the Legion has no legal authority, and wishes none. Its appeal is to the decent citizens in every country, and this, it is confident, will not go unheeded." However, the Legion was the subject of considerable criticism for its ludicrous condemnation of films such as *The Private Life of Henry VIII* (1933), on the grounds that it condoned divorce, and its approval of 120 Nazi films submitted between 1936 and 1937, as well as its refusal to condemn films on the ground of anti-Semitism.

The National Legion of Decency became the National Catholic Office for Motion Pictures in January 1966, and the name was again changed, in January 1971, to the U.S. Catholic Conference—Division of Film and Broadcasting. By 1981, films were rated A–1 of General Patronage, A–2 for Adults and Adolescents, A–3 for Adults, and A–4 for Adults with reservations. A new category "O was added to signify "morally offensive," and, in addition, "recommended," in parenthesis, was placed after some titles. In 1994, the U.S. Catholic Conference began providing film reviews and ratings via a telephone service.

Address: 3211 4th Street N.E., Washington, D.C. 20017-1194.

BIBLIOGRAPHY

Black, Gregory D. *Hollywood Censored: Morality Codes, Catholics, and the Movies.* New York: Cambridge University Press, 1994.
Facey, Paul W. *The Legion of Decency.* New York: Arno Press, 1974.
Skinner, James M. *The Cross and the Cinema: The Legion of Decency and the National Catholic Office for Motion Pictures.* Westwood, Conn.: Greenwood Press, 1993.

NATIONAL SCREEN SERVICE is the country's major provider of promotional materials—such as lobby cards,* still photographs,* posters, and trailers*—to theatres. Through the thirties, the studios produced their own advertising matter. But, in 1940, National Screen Service (which had been in existence since 1919) took over the distribution of such materials for Paramount and RKO, and gradually all the major studios turned over the production and distribution of theatrical advertising matter to National Screen Service (NSS).

The company operates a printing facility in Cleveland, a studio for the production of trailers in London, Advertising Industries for the creation and manufacture of frames and display cases, and Continental Lithograph Corporation for the printing of posters. It does not handle advertising material for small distributors, and is licensed to provide materials only to theatres.

Address: 40 Rockwood Place, Englewood, N.J. 07631.

BIBLIOGRAPHY

"The NSS Story of Service." *Motion Picture Herald,* March 14, 1959, pp. 18–21.
"The 'Prize Baby' Remembers." *Motion Picture Herald,* November 7, 1959, pp. 16–17.

NATIONAL TELEFILM ASSOCIATES. See REPUBLIC PICTURES CORPORATION (NEW)

NATIONAL THEATRES CORPORATION. See FOX WEST COAST THEATRES CORPORATION

NATIONAL THEATRES, INC. See FOX WEST COAST THEATRES CORPORATION

NATO. See NATIONAL ASSOCIATION OF THEATRE OWNERS, INC.

NATURAL VISION. See THREE-DIMENSIONAL FILMS

NAVAJO FILM MANUFACTURING COMPANY, formed in late 1914 to make films for the Kriterion* program, erected a studio in Edendale, California. W. H. Bissell was the president, Charles K. French, formerly with Bison, the head of production, and Fred Granville the cameraman. Leading players for Navajo were Wallace MacDonald, Lucille Young, and William Parsons. After Kriterion's demise, Navajo and seven other West Coast companies combined to form the Associated Service to release their films.

NELSON FILM COMPANY. See SMALLWOOD FILM CORPORATION

NESTOR FILM COMPANY. See CENTAUR FILM COMPANY

NEVADA MOTION PICTURE COMPANY, organized by wealthy men of Reno, built a studio at 40 West Mountain Street in Pasadena in 1916. Its production of *The Planters,* starring Tyrone Power, was filmed partly in Guatemala. F. W. Manson, a millionaire, was the company's president, and John Ince the production manager. Nevada's studio burned down on March 24, 1917.

NEWHALL RANCH. Less than 30 miles from Hollywood*, the Newhall Ranch, with its 38,000 acres, stretching from Newhall to Simi Valley, was considered the largest and most important location area for Hollywood-produced films and television programs. It offers a variety of scenery, as well as an airstrip, a river, a South American or Asian village, two golf courses, oil wells, a military base, and various standing sets. Founded by Henry Mayo Newhall (1825–1882) in the 1850s, the Newhall Ranch has remained intact largely because Newhall's will forbade the sale of any of his real estate. To supplement the income from oil wells and cattle ranching, the Newhall Ranch has been rented out as a film location from the mid-forties. It was while *The Twilight Zone* (1984) was being filmed at the Newhall Ranch that actor Vic Morrow and two young children were killed. The ranch has been little used in the 1990s.

NEW HORIZON PICTURES CORPORATION. See CONCORDE PICTURES CORPORATION

NEW HUDSON, MICHIGAN. See LABADIE-DETROIT MOTION PICTURE COMPANY

NEW LINE CINEMA was founded by Robert Shaye in 1967 as a specialized New York-based distributor, later entering film production. In 1992, the company was acquired by Ted Turner in a $550 million deal, at which time it was making 11 films a year. New Line's first major success was *Polyester* (1981), but in the 1990s, it has come to be known for more commercially oriented features, such as *Teenage Mutuant Ninja Turtles* (1990) and *The Mask* (1994). In August 1996, it announced a three-year production and distribution deal with the Samuel Goldwyn Company*.

Address: 116 North Robertson Boulevard, Suite 200, Los Angeles, Calif. 90048.

BIBLIOGRAPHY

Young, Josh. "New Line Cinema: It Was a Very Good Year." *New York Times,* September 18, 1994, pp. 13, 20–21.

"NEW MAJESTIC." See RELIANCE MOTION PICTURE COMPANY AND MAJESTIC MOTION PICTURE COMPANY

NEW ORLEANS. See COQUILLE FILM COMPANY

NEWSREELS. The most succinct description of a newsreel is probably given by Raymond Fielding in his definitive volume *The American Newsreel 1911–1967:* "a ten-minute potpourri of motion picture news footage, released twice a week to motion picture theaters throughout the country. For more than half a century, from 1911 to 1967, it survived intact and unchanged, during which time it was as predictably a part of every theater's program as the Walt Disney cartoon and the Fitzpatrick travelogue."

The earliest of films were actualities, in themselves a form of newsreel. News events were filmed as early as 1895, and when cameramen were unable to be present the events could easily be faked. Equally, from the earliest years, newsreels have presented a biased view of an event, influenced by the political or social leanings of the newsreel's makers.

The first regular newsreel to be released in the United States was *Pathé's Weekly,* first seen on August 8, 1911, and which later became *Pathé News,* and, in 1947, *Warner-Pathé News.* It was followed in 1912 by *The Gaumont Animated Weekly.* The middle of the second decade of the twentieth century saw the birth of most of the newsreels, including *The Mutual Weekly, Kinograms, The Hearst-Selig News Pictorial, Fox News* (introduced in 1919), and *The Universal Animated Weekly* (which was introduced in 1913 and later became *Universal News*). William Randolph Hearst later was to lend his name to *Hearst-Pathé News* and—in 1927—*Hearst Metrotone News,* which was co-produced with M-G-M*. Hearst had also introduced *The International Newsreel.*

The final group of major newsreels appeared in 1927: *Paramount News, Fox-Movietone News,* and the aforementioned *Hearst-Metrotone News.* An all-black newsreel, *All-American News,* was introduced in 1942.

Warner-Pathé News ceased in 1956, followed by *Paramount News* a year later. *Fox Movietone News* ceased in 1963. *Hearst-Metrotone* produced its last issue in 1967, and, in December of that year, America's last newsreel, *Universal News,* appeared for the final time. The National Archives in Washington, D.C., has the *Universal News,* along with the occasional issues of many silent newsreels. *Fox Movietone News* is still controlled by 20th Century-Fox. *Pathé News* and *Paramount News* are owned by Sherman Grinberg*. *Hearst-Metrotone* was acquired by King Features and has been turned over to the UCLA Film and Television Archive. *See also* March of Time.

BIBLIOGRAPHY

Ballantyne, James, ed. *Researcher's Guide to British Newsreels.* London: British Universities Film & Video Council, 1983.

Fielding, Raymond. *The American Newsreel 1911–1967.* Norman, Okla.: University of Oklahoma Press, 1972.

NEW WORLD PICTURES. After leaving American International Pictures*, Roger Corman founded New World Pictures in 1970; he chose the name because he wanted a company that was worldwide in scope, and, in time, New World became America's largest independent producer/distributor. As critic David Chute has commented, New World quickly gained a "reputation for soft-core action pictures and gilt-edged foreign product." New World's first success came with the "Nurse" series of "R"-rated films, beginning with *The Student Nurses* (1970). Its small budgets and short production schedules helped the company enjoy a first year profit of $3.2 million.

Among the directors who began their careers with New World were Andrew Meyer, Stephanie Rothman, Jonathan Kaplan, and Peter Bogdanovich, who both directed and starred in *Targets* (1968) for New World and returned to the company in 1979 to direct *Saint Jack*. Beginning with *Cries and Whispers* (1973), New World also gained a reputation for the release of outstanding foreign films.

In February 1983, Corman sold the company to Harry E. Sloan, Lawrence E. Kuppin, and Larry A. Thompson for $16.5 million. He subsequently formed a new company, Concorde Pictures Corporation*. According to Robert Rehme, who joined the company in the fall of 1983 as co-owner and chief executive officer, the new New World was "gonna make hit pictures, high concept pictures." However, the first in-house production, *Angel* (1984), bore a striking similarity to the type of films with which New World had been associated under Roger Corman.

In April 1989, the Andrews Group purchased the company for $145 million, selling the theatrical and video assets to Sloan and Kuppin in January 1990, at which time the couple formed TransAtlantic Pictures. Television assets were acquired by TriStar Television and Turner Program Services in 1991 and 1992. The company continues as New World Entertainment.

Address: 1440 South Sepulveda Boulevard, Los Angeles, Calif. 90025.

BIBLIOGRAPHY

Caufield, Deborah. "What's New Is Old at the New New World." *Los Angeles Times,* Calendar, February 19, 1984, pp. 3–5.

Chute, David. "The New World of Roger Corman." *Film Comment,* March–April 1982, pp. 27–32.

Corman, Roger, and Jim Jerome. *How I Made a Hundred Movies in Hollywood and Never Lost a Dime.* New York: Random House, 1990.

di Franco, J. Philip, ed. *The Movie World of Roger Corman.* New York: Chelsea House, 1979.

Naha, Ed. *The Films of Roger Corman: Brilliance on a Budget.* New York: Arco, 1982.

NEW YORK. New York City was the first home of the film industry in the United States. Here D. W. Griffith directed his first shorts at the American Biograph* studios on East 14th Street. Thanks largely to the presence of the Astoria Studios*, filmmaking continued on a moderate scale in New York through the thirties. The revitalization of the Astoria plant in the mid-seventies led to a resurgence of filmmaking in the city, as filmmakers such as Robert De Niro, Martin Scorsese, Sidney Lumet, and Bob Fosse expressed their preference for filmmaking in New York. Among the major features produced in New York in recent years are *Taxi Driver* (1976), *The Wiz* (1978), *All That Jazz* (1979), *Kramer vs. Kramer* (1979), *Hair* (1979), *Wolfen* (1981), *Arthur* (1981), *They All Laughed* (1981), *Ragtime* (1981), *Raging Bull* (1981), *Tootsie* (1982), *The Verdict* (1982), *Author! Author!* (1982), *The King of Comedy* (1983), and, of course, the films of Woody Allen.

Although the films might have been produced in Hollywood, the streets and landmarks of New York have been immensely popular with filmmakers. Among the "classic" American films with a New York background are *The Crowd* (1928), *Lonesome* (1928), *The Broadway Melody* (1929), *Applause* (1929), *The Struggle* (1931), *King Kong* (1933), *Dead End* (1937), *The Naked City* (1948), *Sorry, Wrong Number* (1948), *On the Town* (1949), *On the Waterfront* (1954), *The Blackboard Jungle* (1955), and *Midnight Cowboy* (1969).

Most filmmaking in the city is coordinated through the Mayor's office of Film, Theatre & Broadcasting, 1697 Broadway, 6th Floor, New York, N.Y. 10019.

BIBLIOGRAPHY

Alleman, Richard. *The Movie Lover's Guide to New York.* New York: Perennial Library, 1988.

Haskell, Molly. "Movie Boomtown." *New York,* December 5, 1977, pp. 43–47.

Jacobson, Mark. "New York's Love Affair with the Movies." *New York,* December 29, 1975, pp. 33–44.

Johnson, Hillary. "Hollywood East." *New York,* June 28, 1982, pp. 32–37.

McCourt James. "City of Your Dreams." *Film Comment,* March–April 1976, pp. 52–54.

Stern, Ellen. "How To Make a Movie in New York." *New York,* December 29, 1976, pp. 55–60.

NEW YORKER FILMS takes its name from the New Yorker Theatre on New York's upper East side, films for which Dan Talbot began programming in 1960. Talbot entered film distribution in 1964, when the only way he could screen Bernardo Bertolucci's *Before the Revolution* was by acquiring the U.S. rights. By 1981, Talbot had a library of 200 films from around the world.

Address: 16 West 61st Street, New York, N.Y. 10023.

NEW YORK FILM FESTIVAL. Sponsored by, and always held at, the Lincoln Center for the Performing Arts, the New York Film Festival was first held September 10–19, 1963. It now takes place in either September or October. A noncompetitive festival, the number of films screened at New York is small in comparison with other festivals, but the quality is always very high. The Festival also usually includes several vintage films (often supplied by the Cinémathèque Française). In its formative years, the New York Film Festival was closely linked with the London Film Festival, with both screening the same films and sharing a common director in Richard Roud (1929–1989), who eventually parted with the London Film Festival, but remained program director for New York until 1988.

Address: Film Society of Lincoln Center, 140 West 65th Street, New York, N.Y. 10023.

RESOURCES

Papers: Boston University (Richard Roud Collection).

NEW YORK MOTION PICTURE COMPANY

(NYMPC), one of the first independent production companies formed after the creation of the Motion Picture Patents Company*, was organized by Adam Kessel, Jr., who earlier formed a combination of exchanges* in New York with six or seven exchange owners, and Charles O. Baumann, Kessel's partner and the head of the International Film Exchange, a subexchange created by Kessel. When Kessel was dismissed from the combination for forming the subexchange, he and Baumann created the New York Motion Picture Company to produce films since their supply was stopped. They teamed with cameraman Fred J. Balshofer to make their first film, *Disinherited Son's Loyalty,* released on May 21, 1909. NYMPC's films, known as "Bison" Life Motion Pictures, carried the emblem of a bison in their advertising. The company's first offices were located at 426 Sixth Avenue, New York. It has been called the first to issue multiple-reel weekly releases on a regular program. According to Robert Grau, it was also the first manufacturer to supply exchanges with posters. Later in 1909, NYMPC became the American releasing agent of the Itala* and Ambrosio companies of Italy. In 1910, its offices were in the Lincoln Building at One Union Square, and H. J. Streyckmans was its press agent.

Kessel and Baumann participated in the organization of the Motion Picture Distributing and Sales Company*, the first grouping of independent manufacturers, in April 1910. In April 1912, Kessel and Baumann left the Sales Company and with other manufacturers organized the Universal Film Manufacturing Company, but they left it after six weeks. A few weeks later, they became affiliated with the Mutual Film Corporation*.

In the fall of 1909, a company of 17 was sent to Los Angeles under the direction of cameraman Fred Balshofer to produce one-reel Bison films. Included in the group were J. Barney Sherry, Charles K. French, Jane Darrell, Evelyn Graham, William Edwards, William Gibbons, Charles Avery, Charles Inslee, James Youngdeer, and Red Wing. The company established itself in a bungalow and barn in the Edendale suburb, which later became the site of the Keystone* studio.

The Reliance Moving Picture Company*, created by Kessel and Baumann and affiliated with the New York Motion Picture Company, offered its first release in October 1910. Two years after the Edendale company began producing, Kessel and Baumann sent Thomas H. Ince from New York to take over the directing chores. He made only a few films before taking possession of a ranch in the Santa Mon-

ica Mountains, which became known as Inceville*. At this time Ince suggested that Kessel and Baumann contract to use the Miller Brothers' 101 Ranch, a popular traveling Wild West show, spending the winter in Los Angeles. After the company left Universal and had to give up the brand names of Bison and Bison 101, for the films made with the Miller Brothers' ranch, it created the new brand names of Kay-Bee and Broncho.

In July 1912, Kessel and Baumann created the Keystone Film Company* with Mack Sennett. In the Spring of 1913, a reorganization created the New York Motion Picture Corporation, with Kessel as president, Baumann as vice president, Charles Kessel as secretary, Charles J. Hite as treasurer, and Harry E. Aitken as assistant treasurer.

NYMPC created a new brand, "Domino," in September 1913. In 1915, with the creation of the Triangle Film Corporation* and the termination of NYMPC's contract with Mutual, the Ince studios moved to Culver City. Ince formed his own production company to produce Artcraft releases for Famous Players-Lasky Corporation.

BIBLIOGRAPHY

Balshofer, Fred J., and Arthur C. Miller. *One Reel a Week.* Berkeley, Calif.: University of California Press, 1967.

Blaisdell, George. "New York Motion Picture Company." *The Moving Picture World,* July 10, 1915, p. 233.

"Charles Baumann Goes West." *The Moving Picture World,* August 13, 1910, p. 344.

"C. O. Baumann Talks of Plans." *The Moving Picture World,* September 5, 1914, p. 1349.

Kessel, A., Jr. "When the Field Was Fresh." *The Moving Picture World,* March 10, 1917, pp. 1523–24.

"New York Motion Picture Company." *The Moving Picture World,* May 15, 1909, p. 632.

von Harleman, G. P. "Motion Picture Studios of California." *The Moving Picture World,* March 10, 1917, pp. 1599–1600.

NFL FILMS was created in 1964 by the National Football League to exploit and license footage from NFL games. The idea came about as a result of the League's satisfaction with footage of game highlights shot between 1962 and 1964 by Blair Productions. Ed Sabol, who had founded Blair Productions in the late fifties, was hired to head NFL Films, initially located in Philadelphia, and to produce a series of game highlight documentaries. As NFL Films expanded, it produced *Inside the NFL* for HBO, *Game of the Week* for ESPN, and other programming. It moved outside of the National Football League in 1980 with the production of *The Greatest Adventure,* a television program on the U.S. space program, narrated by Orson Welles, and in 1984, NFL Entertainment was created, as a division of NFL Films, to produce music documentaries.

Address: 330 Fellowship Road, Mt. Laurel, N.J. 08054.

BIBLIOGRAPHY

Conger, Elizabeth. "NFL Films." *In Motion,* January/February 1985, pp. 42–44.

NICKELODEONS were the first theatres in the United States to exhibit films exclusively. As the name suggests, the price of admission was five cents. According to *The Moving Picture World* (November 20, 1907), the first nickelodeon was opened in Pittsburgh by Harris Davis in 1905. By 1908, there were between four and five thousand, and, according to *The Saturday Evening Post,* over two million people, a third of whom were children, attended nickelodeons annually. The heyday of the nickelodeon was from 1908 to 1911, but, by the middle of the second decade of the twentieth century, the nickelodeon had been supplanted by a more standard type of theatre.

The following description of a typical nickelodeon appeared in the November 23, 1907, edition of the *The Saturday Evening Post:* "The nickelodeon is usually a tiny theatre, containing 199 seats, giving from twelve to eighteen performances a day, seven days a week. Its walls are painted red. The seats are ordinary kitchen chairs, not fastened. The only break in the red color scheme is made by half a dozen signs in black and white, No Smoking, Hats Off, and sometimes, but not always, "Stay as Long as You Like."

BIBLIOGRAPHY

Bowers, Q. David. *Nickelodeon Theatres and Their Music.* Vestal, N.Y.: Vestal Press, 1986.
"The First Nickelodeon in the States." *The Moving Picture World,* November 20, 1907, p. 629.
Haskin, Frederick J. "The Popular Nickelodeon." *The Moving Picture World,* January 18, 1908, pp. 36–37.
———. "Nickelodeon History." *Views and Film Index,* February 1, 1908, pp. 5, 14.
Patterson, Joseph Medill. "The Nickelodeons." *The Saturday Evening Post,* November 23, 1907, reprinted in *The Moving Picture World,* January 11, 1908, pp. 21–22.

"NIGGER" was the name given in the silent era to a black shield of wood used to keep the rays of the Kleig lights from the camera lens. The "nigger" was also known as the "elephant ear," "gobo" and "flat." To remove the shield, the cry was "Kick the nigger down." The origin of the term is obvious, but it may also date back to the nineteenth-century "nigger boards," which were temporary platforms set on the ground for use in theatrical open-air productions.

NILES, CALIFORNIA. See ESSANAY FILM MANUFACTURING COMPANY

NILES CINEMA, located in South Bend, Indiana, was a popular sales outlet for 8mm* prints for collectors. It was purchased in June 1978 by Louis Freitag, and went out of business on September 17, 1981.

9.5mm. was developed as a substandard film gauge in 1921 by the French Pathé* Company; a 9.5mm hand-cranked projector was introduced in 1922, and the following year saw the invention of a 9.5mm camera. By the late twenties, 9.5mm had become a popular film gauge for amateur film enthusiasts throughout Europe. Because the sprocket holes appeared between each frame of film, rather than on the sides (as in the better-known substandard gauges of 8mm* and 16mm*), there was a larger picture image and resultant increase in picture quality when the film was projected. Also, Pathé devised a method of notching the film when titles appeared; these notches stopped the projector mechanism for sufficient time to allow the viewer to read the titles and thus saved a considerable amount of film.

Sound was added to 9.5mm in the thirties, and the gauge continued in popularity through the fifties, when the increase in appeal of 8mm heralded the end of 9.5mm as a viable commercial proposition. Despite the demise of the Pathéscope Company, which marketed 9.5mm, there remains a hard-core group of enthusiasts for the gauge, and equipment and films continue to be manufactured. Regardless of its success in Europe, 9.5mm had little impact in the United States.

BIBLIOGRAPHY

Pedler, Garth. "The Silent Picture Guide to 9.5mm." *The Silent Picture,* no. 11/12, Summer–Autumn 1971, unpaged.
———. *The Encyclopedia of 9.5mm Silent Film Releases, Vol. I: 160,000 feet.* South Croydon, England: The Author, 1972.

NITRATE FILM. Although Eastman Kodak* had developed safety film as early as 1908, it was not until 1949, and the introduction of a new, improved safety-based film stock, that nitrate film ceased to be used in commercial motion picture production. (The acetate film* introduced in 1908 proved too brittle and too liable to shrinkage.) Nitrate film had two major drawbacks: it was highly flammable and it would eventually decompose. Its chemical composition is similar to that of guncotton, used in the manufacture of explosives, and nitrate film can burn 20 times as fast as wood, contains sufficient oxygen to continue burning under water, and will self-ignite at 300 degrees or less. Further, burning nitrate film gives off a gas that can form nitric acid in the lungs and lead to death. A major nitrate fire took place at the Ferguson Building, Pittsburgh, in 1909, and a number of fires were attributed to nitrate during a 1949 heatwave in New York.

Nitrate film is chemically unstable and is in a perpetual state of decomposition, which begins with fading of the image, followed by the film becoming sticky, forming bubbles, and eventually turning to a brownish powder. Decomposing nitrate film can also affect other film stored in close proximity to it. If kept at low temperature and humidity, nitrate can be safely stored; some nitrate film from the 1890s is still in excellent condition, while some from the Second World War, made from inferior stock, quickly decomposed. *See also* "Lost Films."

"NOLA" BRAND. See COQUILLE FILM COMPANY

NONINFLAMMABLE FILM. See ACETATE FILM

NORBIG FILM MANUFACTURING COMPANY. Frank E. North owned all the stock, was the president, and supervised all production at the Norbig Film Manufacturing Company, whose studio was on Allesandro Street in Edendale, between the Selig* and Keystone* studios. Although Norbig did not produce until 1915, it had a functioning laboratory and leased its studio during the previous two years. Norbig made Western and Indian pictures with James Young Deer and Bebe Daniels. In 1916, Harry T. De Vere produced the three-reel drama *Darkness,* starring Margaret Darwin, for Norbig.

NORFOLK, VIRGINIA. See SUBMARINE FILM COMPANY

NORMAN FILM MANUFACTURING COMPANY was founded by white businessman Richard E. Norman, Sr.

(1891–1961), to produce all-black films for all-black audiences. The company was located in Jacksonville, Florida, but usually filmed in Boley, Oklahoma*, "an all-colored city." Its productions include *The Green-Eyed Monster* (1920), *The Crimson Skull* (1921), *The Bull-Dogger* (1921), *Regeneration* (1923), *A Debtor to the Law* (1924), *The Flying Ace* (1926), and *The Black Gold* (1928).

BIBLIOGRAPHY

Sampson, Henry T. *Blacks in Black and White: A Source Book on Black Film.* Metuchen, N.J.: Scarecrow Press, 1995.

NORTH MIAMI. See IVAN TORS STUDIO

NOSOTROS is an advocacy group, founded in 1970 by Gil Avila and Ricardo Montalban, to improve the image of Latinos in the entertainment industry. It also sponsored an annual award show, the Golden Eagles. The organization was embroiled in a bitter leadership dispute in the late 1980s and early 1990s, until Montalban was unanimously elected board chairman in 1994.

Address: 1314 North Wilton Place, Hollywood, Calif. 90028.

NYKINO. See NATIONAL FILM AND PHOTO LEAGUE

OCCIDENTAL STUDIOS. See ALDRICH STUDIOS

OCEAN FILM CORPORATION was a short-lived company formed in November 1915. James D. Goldburg was the general manager and vice president and John L. Dudley the president. It planned to make five-reel features to be released to the states rights* market and had no stock company of players. Its offices were at the Candler Building at 220 West 42d Street, New York, and its only production, *Life without Soul,* from Mary Wollstonecraft Shelley's *Frankenstein,* was marketed after its demise by the Raver Film Corporation*.

BIBLIOGRAPHY

"Ocean Film Corporation Formed." *The Moving Picture World,* November 13, 1915, p. 1316.

OCTOBER FILMS is a New York-based distributor of films intended primarily for the art house market. It was founded in March 1991 by Jeff Lipsky, the former president of the motion picture division of Skouras Pictures, and Bingham Ray from Avenue Entertainment. Amir Malin became a partner in September 1991, and John Schmidt became a partner in May 1992. Lipsky resigned from the company in April 1995. In November 1992, October launched Mad Dog Pictures to distribute exploitation films* and signed a ten-year agreement with Cinecom Entertainment Group to distribute its library. In June 1995, it linked up with Hallmark Home Entertainment, creating October Films Home Entertainment as a video distributor. October's first release was Mike Leigh's *Life Is Sweet;* other releases include *Kika* (1994), *The Last Seduction* (1994), *Secrets and Lies* (1996), and *Breaking the Waves* (1996). In May 1997, Universal* announced it was acquiring a majority interest in the company. The purchase involved an immediate cash figure plus a variable payout over five years, estimated to be worth as much as $60 million.

Address: 65 Bleeker Street, 2nd Floor, New York, N.Y. 10012.

BIBLIOGRAPHY

Dawtrey, Adam. "Oct Films Comes in from the Cold." *Daily Variety,* May 15, 1992, p. 22.
Eller, Claudia. "Universal Says It Will Acquire October Films." *Los Angeles Times,* May 1, 1997, pp. D1, D4.
Young, Josh. "The Fall of Our Content." *Esquire,* October 1996.

OFFICIAL FILMS, INC. Based in New York and later New Jersey, Official Films, Inc., was organized in 1939 to produce 16mm* instructional, sponsored, and entertainment shorts for outright sale. It also sold 20- and 30-minute edited versions of features films, Soundies*, and early Charlie Chaplin shorts with music and sound effects. By the forties, the company was also selling films in 8mm*, and, in 1948, listed some 300 titles for sale. Official Films also published a booklet on "The Film Rental Library," indicating to purchasers how they might form their own libraries with films purchased from the company. Official Films remained active through the seventies. In 1945, the company was sold by founder Leslie Winick to a syndicate headed by George A. Hirliman, Harry J. Rothman, and Aaron Katz.

OGDEN PICTURES CORPORATION, located at Ogden, Utah, and backed by Ogden capital, claimed to be, at its formation in 1917, the first motion picture studio between Chicago and the West Coast. Albert Scowcroft, a leading Utah businessman, was the president. Lillian Walker was signed to star in Ogden's five-reel comedy-dramas, which were to be directed by Harry Revier and written by playwright Aaron Hoffman.

BIBLIOGRAPHY

"Lillian Walker Going to Utah." *The Moving Picture World,* April 7, 1917, p. 82.

OLIVER MOROSCO PHOTOPLAY COMPANY was organized on November 9, 1914, with theatrical producer Morosco (1876–1945) as president and Frank A. Garbutt, a California sportsman and millionaire who was treasurer of Bosworth, Inc.*, as vice president. By arrangement with John Cort, who owned a chain of theatres in the West and Northwest, Morosco was to get first call to film Cort's productions and to use his stars. In addition, Morosco's three Los Angeles theatres provided plays and actors for the new company to use.

The Morosco productions were released on the Paramount* program, and the studios were located at 201 North Occidental Boulevard in Los Angeles, studios that were later shared by Pallas Pictures*, a company also releasing with Paramount and that was formed in August 1915. William Desmond Taylor was director of the Morosco films. Although Morosco merged with the Famous Players-Lasky Corporation in October 1916, the name continued to be used through 1923.

BIBLIOGRAPHY

"Morosco and Cort Enter Picture Field." *The Moving Picture World,* November 21, 1914, p. 1093.

"Morosco in Film Field." *The New York Dramatic Mirror,* November 11, 1914, p. 25.

OMNIMAX. See IMAX

OMNI-ZOETROPE. See ZOETROPE

ORION PICTURES CORPORATION. Generally considered a major among contemporary Hollywood companies, Orion Pictures Corporation was formed in January 1978 when five former members of the top management at United Artists*—Arthur Krim, Robert S. Benjamin, Eric Pleskow, William Bernstein, and Mike Medavoy—left following a policy dispute. Krim, who became Orion's president, gave the new company its name—Orion is a five-star constellation. Orion describes itself as "a financing and distribution organization," with close ties to Warner Bros.*, on whose studio lot it was initially located.

In 1982, Orion merged with Filmways, Inc., a production company founded by Martin Ransohoff, which was also involved in magazine and paperback publishing and television syndication, and which had acquired the publishing house of Grosset & Dunlap in 1974. Filmways' distribution arm was Sigma III. Filmways was in financial trouble, brought on, in part, by a March 1979 merger with American International Pictures*.

In October 1996, John Kluge announced that he was consolidating his ownership of Orion Pictures and the Samuel Goldwyn Company* under the name of Metromedia Entertainment Group, Inc. Orion was to operate as the Group's distribution arm, with Leonard White (who had been president and CEO at Orion since 1992) as president and CEO.

Address: 1888 Century Park East, Suite 1777, Los Angeles, Calif. 90067.

BIBLIOGRAPHY

Kilday, Gregg. "Orion: A Humanistic Production." *Los Angeles Times,* part 4, January 5, 1979, pp. 13, 26, 28.

McGilligan, Patrick. "Breaking Away, Mogul Style." *American Film,* June 1980, pp. 28–32.

Stimac, Elias. "Leonard White." *Drama-Logue,* April 18, 1996, p. 28.

ORO PICTURES COMPANY, INC., was formed in late 1917 and planned to make one six-reel feature per month. H. Grossman was the president and Isadore Bernstein was the production supervisor. Oro, whose motto was "Pictures for the Clean Minded," had offices at 729 Seventh Avenue in New York and took over the plant of Bernstein Productions, Inc., in Los Angeles. Oro's productions include *Humility* (1917), *Loyalty* (1918) and *When Destiny Wills* (1921).

ORTHOCHROMATIC FILM was the stock in use during most of the silent era. Unlike Panchromatic Film*, which replaced it in 1927 and which is sensitive to all visible wavelengths, Orthochromatic film is sensitive to blue and green light but not to red. It was much slower than modern film stock and thus required cinematographers be particularly accurate with focus and exposure.

OSHKOSH, WISCONSIN. See EBONY PICTURES CORPORATION

OUR GANG SERIES. The most popular of all series featuring children, some 169 *Our Gang* comedy shorts were produced by Hal Roach Studios* between 1922 and 1938, with a final 52 being produced by M-G-M* from 1938 to 1944. The first short in the series, titled *Our Gang,* was released by Pathé* on November 5, 1922; the last, *Tale of a Dog,* was released by M-G-M on April 15, 1944. Among the children featured in the series were Mickey Daniels, Johnny Downs, Joe Cobb, Carl "Alfalfa" Switzer, Jean Darling, Mary Kornman, Spanky McFarland, Darla Hood, Allen "Farina" Hoskins, Bobby "Wheezer" Hutchins, Jackie Cooper, and Matthew "Stymie" Beard. When the films were released to television, Hal Roach was forced to change the series title to *The Little Rascals,* as the rights to the title *Our Gang* had been acquired by M-G-M (which had distributed the films from 1927 onward; previously they were distributed by Pathé).

BIBLIOGRAPHY

Bond, Tommy "Butch," with Ron Genini. *Darn Right It's Butch: Memories of Our Gang, the Little Rascals.* Wayne, Penn.: Morgin Press, 1994.

Maltin, Leonard, and Richard W. Bann. *The Little Rascals: The Life and Times of Our Gang.* New York: Crown, 1992.

Smith, Leon. *Following the Comedy Trail: A Guide to Laurel and Hardy and Our Gang Film Locations.* Los Angeles: Pomegranate Press, 1988.

OUR GIRLS, also known as Our Club, was an informal social group of the twenties. Mary Pickford was honorary president and Helen Ferguson was secretary and treasurer. The club members in 1927 included Mildred Davis, Billie Dove, Pauline Garon, Carmelita Geraghty, Laura La Plante, May McAvoy, Patsy Ruth Miller, Edna Murphy, Carmel Myers, Gertrude Olmstead, ZaSu Pitts, Ruth Roland, and Claire Windsor.

OZ FILM MANUFACTURING COMPANY. L. Frank Baum, the creator of the "Oz" books, opened his own production company, the Oz Film Manufacturing Company, in June 1914, to produce films from his books. It had a studio on Santa Monica Boulevard, between Gower and Lodi

Streets, in Hollywood, and Baum was the president and general manager. Composer Louis F. Gottschalk, the vice president and works manager, wrote music and played the piano as the films were being shot. Oz's first film, *The Patchwork Girl of Oz,* was directed by J. Farrell MacDonald and released by Paramount*. After *The Magic Cloak of Oz,* the studio closed temporarily in November 1914, and the Oz players were disbanded. In the spring of 1915, the Oz studio reopened under another brand name, managed by Frank J.

Baum, and it released features directed by Francis Powers on the Alliance program.

BIBLIOGRAPHY

Karr, Kathleen. "Oz Lives." In *The American Film Heritage.* Washington, D.C.: Acropolis Books, 1972, pp. 162–67.

"Oz Film Company Starts in Los Angeles." *The Moving Picture World,* June 13, 1914, p. 1531.

PACIFIC INTERNATIONAL ENTERPRISES, INC., was founded in 1969 by president Arthur R. Dubs (born 1930) as a producer of family adventures films, such as *The Adventures of the Wilderness Family* (1975), *The Further Adventures of the Wilderness Family* (1978), and *Mountain Family Robinson* (1980). It also co-produced *Windwalker* (1980) with Santa Fe International (a Phoenix-based company).

Address: 1133 South Riverside, Medford, Ore. 97501.

PALLAS PICTURES, INC., active from 1915 to 1917, maintained a studio at 201 North Occidental Boulevard in Los Angeles, which it shared with the Oliver Morosco Photoplay Company*. Its features, which were released on the Paramount* program, were scripted and produced by Julia Crawford Ivers.

PALMER PHOTOPLAY CORPORATION. Active in the second half of the second decade of the twentieth century and early twenties, the Palmer Photoplay Corporation was formed in August 1918 by Frederick Palmer as a clearinghouse for story materials to be considered for film production and to offer extensive courses, by mail, in screenwriting. There were many such schools of screenwriting operating at this time, but none had the prestige of the Palmer Photoplay Corporation, which boasted an advisory board including Cecil B. DeMille, Lois Weber, Jesse L. Lasky, Thomas H. Ince, and Allan Dwan. The organization published a variety of pamphlets by prominent individuals within the industry, as well as many volumes by Frederick Palmer.

PALO ALTO, CALIFORNIA. See EXACTUS PHOTO-FILM CORPORATION

"PANAMA" BRAND. See BALBOA AMUSEMENT PRODUCING COMPANY

PANAVISION, INC., was formed in 1953 by Robert Gottschalk (who was murdered in 1982 at the age of 64). Gottschalk developed the M-G-M Camera 65, which utilized an anamorphic lens* and 65mm film in the camera for a widescreen system. It was first utilized on *Raintree County*, which received its world premiere at the Brown Theatre in Louisville, Kentucky, on October 2, 1957. *Raintree County* was released in 35mm*, and the system was seen to better advantage in *Ben-Hur* (1959), which was released in 70mm*. In 1972, Gottschalk introduced the Panaflex silent motion picture, followed by the Panaglide floating camera mechanism. In 1978, Gottschalk received a Scientific or Technical Award of Merit (Oscar statuette) "for the concept, design and continuous development of the Panaflex Motion Picture Camera System." Today, Panavision is highly regarded as a leading source of cameras and lenses. Although Gottschalk remained as president of the company, Panavision was sold in 1965 to producer Sy Weintraub, who sold it three years later to Kinney National Service, Inc., which, in turn, sold it in 1985 to a consortium headed by Chicago newspaper and department store heir Frederick Field. In 1988, the company was acquired by a British concern, Lee International, for $100 million.

Address: 18618 Oxnard Street, Tarzana, Calif. 91356.

BIBLIOGRAPHY

Harris, Kathryn. "Panavision Seen as Field's Ticket to Hollywood." *Los Angeles Times,* business section, January 24, 1985, pp. 1, 5.
Henderson, Scott. "The Panavision Story." *American Cinematographer,* April 1977, pp. 414–15, 422–23, 432–33.
"Mr. Panavision Speaks Out." *American Cinematographer,* April 1977, pp. 417–18, 424–25, 434–35.
Pizzello, Stephen. "40 Years in Focus." *The Hollywood Reporter,* June 10, 1994, pp. P1–P4.

PANCHROMATIC FILM replaced Orthochromatic* as the standard film in the industry. Conceived by Eastman Kodak* as early as 1913, it was used in the United States as early as 1919. Eastman Kodak began manufacturing Panchromatic film on a regular basis in 1923, and the previous year, it was utilized in the photography of *The Headless Horseman*. When Panchromatic film was priced lower than Orthochromatic stock, its sales increased in 1926, and by 1927, it was in general studio use. In the filming of some late silent films, both Panchromatic and Orthochromatic stock was used, and as a result, an actor's hair color, for example, might change from dark to light and back again within the same scene.

PAPER PRINTS. Prior to 1912, there was no way by which motion picture producers could copyright their films as films with the Library of Congress. Therefore, to protect their work, producers deposited motion pictures in the form of paper prints, with the film printed directly on to paper as opposed to celluloid. The first film to be copyrighted—on January 7, 1894—in this fashion was *Edison Kinetoscopic*

Record of a Sneeze, a few feet of film recording Fred Ott sneezing made by Thomas Edison's associate, W. K. L. Dickson. Paper prints continued to be deposited for copyright purposes as late as 1916. According to Kemp R. Niver, "Producers of motion picture films obtained the paper to make the copies of their negatives from various sources. The type that had the best photographic propensities was normal bromide paper cut into strips the same width as the negative and perforated so that a contact print could be made on the same equipment as was used to make the nitrate prints."

Because so few films from the early years of the cinema have survived, the paper print collection offers valuable documentation of this period. The problem of transferring the paper prints back to film was first considered by Carl Louis Gregory of the National Archives in 1943. In 1947, Howard Walls, the first archivist of the Academy of Motion Picture Arts and Sciences*, was able to persuade the Academy to sponsor the project, and Carl Gregory undertook some initial experimentation. The project did not begin in earnest until 1954, when Kemp R. Niver undertook the conversion program with his Los Angeles-based Renovare Film Company. For his work, Niver received a special Academy Award in 1955. Funding was provided by the Academy, the U.S. government, and Eastman Kodak*, which donated raw film stock for the project.

Niver's conversion consisted of transferring the films from paper to 16mm* film. Since 1982, the paper print conversion project has been undertaken by the UCLA Film and Television Archive, and for the first time the paper prints have been converted to 35mm* film.

BIBLIOGRAPHY

Niver, Kemp R. *Early Motion Pictures: The Paper Print Collection in the Library of Congress.* Washington, D.C., Library of Congress, 1985.

PARAGON. See WORLD FILM CORPORATION

"PARAGON" BRAND. See CROWN CITY FILM MANUFACTURING COMPANY

PARALTA PLAYS, INC., was founded on March 22, 1917, with Carl Anderson as president, Herman Katz as treasurer, Robert T. Kane as vice president, Nat L. Brown as secretary and general manager, and Herman Fichtenberg as chairman of the board. It announced in *The Moving Picture World* (April 14, 1917) that it would produce films that would be sold to exhibitors for a period of one year, during which time the films could be screened as often as the exhibitor might wish.

Production of Paralta's first film, *A Man's Man,* began at the company's Los Angeles studios on June 4, 1917. Oscar Apfel was the director and J. Warren Kerrigan the star. Other Paralta productions included *Madame Who, Within the Cup, Carmen of the Klondyke, His Robe of Honor, Humdrum Brown, An Enemy Alien,* and *Shackled,* all released in 1918. The initial Paralta studios were located on the south side of Melrose Avenue in Hollywood, but in the spring of 1918 the company completed the building of a new studio, directly opposite, at Melrose and Van Ness (studios that are now part of Paramount*). Among the stars under contract were Henry B. Walthall, J. Warren Kerrigan, Bessie Barriscale, and Louise Glaum; Paralta's directors included Rex Ingram, Wallace Worsley, Raymond B. West, and Reginald Barker. The company ceased production in the fall of 1918, and its studios were taken over by Robert Brunton.

BIBLIOGRAPHY

"Carl Anderson Produces Splendid Plays." *The Moving Picture World,* April 6, 1918, p. 69.
Slide, Anthony. "The Paralta Company." In *Aspects of American Film History prior to 1920.* Metuchen, N.J.: Scarecrow Press, 1978, pp. 79–86.
"Work on Paralta Studios Progressing." *The Moving Picture World,* April 13, 1918, p. 256.

PARAMOUNT ACTING SCHOOL. See ASTORIA STUDIOS

PARAMOUNT-BRAY PICTOGRAPH. See BRAY STUDIOS, INC.

PARAMOUNT LABORATORY. See CONSOLIDATED FILM INDUSTRIES

PARAMOUNT NEWS. See NEWSREELS

PARAMOUNT PICTURES, INC., with its familiar trademark of a snow-capped mountain, surrounded by stars, came into being thanks to three men, of whom only one usually receives the credit. Paramount Pictures Corporation was founded, on May 8, 1914, strictly as a distribution organization by W. W. Hodkinson. As a production company, it had its origins in the Famous Players Film Company, incorporated on June 1, 1912, by Adolph Zukor (1873–1976) and in the Jesse L. Lasky Feature Play Company, incorporated on November 26, 1913, by Lasky (1880–1958).

The Famous Players Film Company was responsible for the importation of the French feature *Queen Elizabeth/Les Amours de la Reine Elizabeth* (1912), starring Sarah Bernhardt, the first major film to give the industry respectability and one of the first feature-length productions to be screened in the United States. The Jesse L. Lasky Feature Film Company produced *The Squaw Man* (1914), directed by Cecil B. DeMille and Oscar Apfel, which was the first important feature-length production to be filmed in Hollywood*.

As a distributor, Paramount handled not only the films of Lasky and Famous Players but also those of Bosworth* and Oliver Morosco*. In May 1916, 50 percent of the stock in Paramount was acquired by Zukor and Lasky, and a month later Hodkinson resigned as president of the company (to be succeeded by Hiram Abrams). On June 19, 1916, Famous

Players-Lasky Corporation was incorporated, with Zukor as president, but the name Paramount was retained for trade purposes and by the late twenties had become the familiar name to filmgoers. Indeed, the company's slogan was "If It's a Paramount Picture, It's the best show in town."

On July 19, 1916, the company organized Artcraft Pictures Corporation for the release of the films of Mary Pickford, but later the Artcraft name was utilized for any major Paramount release. On May 28, 1919, Realart Pictures Corporation was incorporated to handle lesser Paramount productions. The use of the name ended in July 1922.

Adolph Zukor is the best-known "name" associated with Paramount, and it was he who was responsible for the company's financial success. He built up a theatre chain and tried, unsuccessfully, to give Paramount a monopoly of the film industry. Jesse L. Lasky was the creative force behind the studio, responsible for signing stars such as Mary Pickford, Rudolph Valentino, Geraldine Farrar, Wallace Reid, Pola Negri, Gloria Swanson, and Thomas Meighan; and directors such as Cecil B. DeMille (virtually all of whose career was at Paramount), Maurice Tourneur, and D. W. Griffith. Both men were able to steer the studio through a series of major scandals in the early twenties, involving the rape and manslaughter charges against Paramount star Roscoe "Fatty" Arbuckle, the murder of Paramount director William Desmond Taylor and the implication in it of contract star Mary Miles Minter, and the death from drug addiction of Paramount leading man Wallace Reid.

The studio suffered a major financial setback in the early thirties through losses from the Paramount-Publix theatre chain, and, in 1933, the company was forced to enter bankruptcy. Jesse L. Lasky was forced out, but under the 1935 reorganization the company reemerged as Paramount Pictures, Inc., with Adolph Zukor as chairman of the board.

Despite the setbacks, the thirties were arguably Paramount's greatest decade. Its staff of directors was headed by Ernst Lubitsch and included Rouben Mamoulian (who directed the studio's first major artistic sound success in 1929, *Applause*), George Cukor, Norman Taurog, Norman Z. McLeod, Josef von Sternberg, and Mitchell Leisen. Paramount stars of the thirties included Mae West, Jeanette MacDonald, Maurice Chevalier, the Marx Brothers, W. C. Fields, Charlie Ruggles, Marlene Dietrich, Bing Crosby, George Burns and Gracie Allen, Claudette Colbert, and Gary Cooper. The decade ended with Paramount's elevating screenwriter Preston Sturges to director, a move that resulted in some of the greatest screwball comedies* of all time. Although not as memorable a decade as the thirties, the forties saw Paramount's producing *The Lady Eve* (1941), *Holiday Inn* (1942), *For Whom the Bell Tolls* (1943), *Going My Way* (1944), *The Lost Weekend* (1945), *The Blue Dahlia* (1946), and *The Heiress* (1949).

Prior to a major involvement in television production, Paramount sold all rights to its 1929–1949 features to MCA* in 1958. On October 19, 1966, Paramount was acquired by Gulf + Western* and became a wholly owned subsidiary of the Charles Bludhorn conglomerate. By the

fifties, the star system* was basically over, and Jerry Lewis and Dean Martin were, arguably, the only two major stars under contract to the studio. Production heads such as Howard W. Koch, Martin Rackin, and Robert Evans tried, with varying degrees of success, to steer Paramount into a new era, with films such as *Ordinary People* (1980), *Raiders of the Lost Ark* (1981), and *Terms of Endearment* (1983).

On September 20, 1993, Barry Diller and the QVC television home shopping network launched a hostile takeover bid for Paramount. It was unsuccessful, and on February 14, 1994, the company was taken over by Viacom Inc.*

Aside from the Astoria* studios in New York, and an earlier New York studio on 26th Street (which was destroyed by fire in September 1915), Paramount's studios were in Hollywood, initially at Sunset Boulevard and Vine Street, until 1926, when the company moved to its present location. The famous Paramount Gate, immortalized in *Sunset Boulevard,* is located on Marathon Street. It is no longer used, and the studio has built a new gate on Melrose Avenue.

Address: 5555 Melrose Avenue, Hollywood, Calif. 90038.

BIBLIOGRAPHY

Daily Variety, special Paramount issue, July 26, 1945.

Eames, John Douglas. *The Paramount Story.* New York: Crown, 1985.

Edmonds, I. G., and Reiko Mimura. *Paramount Pictures and the People Who Made Them.* San Diego: A. S. Barnes, 1980.

Halliwell, Leslie. *Mountain of Dreams.* New York: Stonehill Publishing, 1976.

The Hollywood Reporter, special Paramount issue, July 27, 1945.

Irwin, Will. *The House That Shadows Built.* Garden City, N.Y.: Doubleday, Doran, 1928.

Lasky, Jesse L., with Don Weldon. *I Blow My Own Horn.* Garden City, N.Y.: Doubleday, 1957.

Luft, Herbert G. "Remembering Adolph Zukor." *Films in Review,* vol. 27, no. 10, December 1976, pp. 595–98.

O'Donnell, Pierce, and Dennis McDougal. *Fatal Subtraction: The Inside Story of Buchwald v. Paramount.* New York: Doubleday, 1992.

"Paramount." *Fortune,* vol. 15, no. 3, March 1937, pp. 86–96, 194–211.

Parish, James Robert. *The Paramount Pretties.* New Rochelle, N.Y.: Arlington House, 1972.

Taylor, John Russell. "Paramount." *Films and Filming,* June 1984, pp. 7–10, and July 1984, pp. 7–10.

Zukor, Adolph. "Triumph of the Motion Picture." *Theatre,* May 1925, pp. 38, 92.

Zukor, Adolph. with Dale Kramer. *The Public Is Never Wrong.* New York: G. P. Putnam's Sons, 1953.

RESOURCES

Films: Library of Congress (extant Paramount silent features and preservation elements on 1929–1949 titles); UCLA

Film and Television Archive (35mm nitrate studio prints, 1929–1949).

Papers: Academy of Motion Picture Arts and Sciences (budget and production records, 1930s–1950s; pressbooks).

Photographs: Academy of Motion Picture Arts and Sciences (1914–1970).

Scripts: Academy of Motion Picture Arts and Sciences.

PARAMOUNT-PUBLIX CORP. See PUBLIX THEATERS CORPORATION

THE PARAMOUNT THEATRE, located "at the crossroads of the world," at the intersection of New York's Broadway and 43d Street, was the flagship theatre of Paramount Pictures*. It opened on November 19, 1926, with *God Gave Me 20 Cents,* directed by Herbert Brenon, and starring Lya de Putti and Jack Mulhall. Mayor James J. Walker, Thomas Edison, Will H. Hays, and Florenz Ziegfeld, Jr., were among the invited guests at the opening, treated to a stage gala, produced by John Murray Anderson and featuring Marguerite Ringo singing "The Star Spangled Banner" and Jesse Crawford performing "Organs I Have Played." The initial seating capacity was 3,650. The theatre was built on the site of the Putnam Building, acquired by Paramount in 1922, and construction began in November 1925.

Following the consent decree* in 1949, Paramount leased the theatre to American Broadcasting-Paramount Theatres, Inc. The Paramount Theatre closed on August 4, 1964, and reopened on September 4 of the same year under the ownership of Webb & Knapp. The last film screened under the Paramount ownership was *The Carpetbaggers.*

BIBLIOGRAPHY

Frederick, Robert B. "Epitaph for Paramount, Publix Flagship." *Variety,* July 29, 1964, pp. 27, 30.

Hall, Ben M. "The Paramount Goes Dark." *New York Herald Tribune,* August 9, 1964, p. 11.

PASADENA. See CROWN CITY FILM MANUFACTURING COMPANY, NEVADA MOTION PICTURE COMPANY, and SIGNAL FILM COMPANY

PASSING PARADE. Also known as *John Nesbitt's Passing Parade,* this series of shorts had its origin in Nesbitt's radio series of the same name and was produced by M-G-M* from 1938 to 1949. One reel in length, each short dealt with a topical subject—sometimes more than one—and was narrated in John Nesbitt's inimitable style.

BIBLIOGRAPHY

Maltin, Leonard. *The Great Movie Shorts.* New York: Crown, 1972.

PATHÉ. Pathé Freres, established in France in 1896 by Charles Pathé with $2,000 in capital, became the largest film company in the world, producing, in addition to motion pictures, cameras and film stock (including a noninflammable film used in most of Pathé's European productions). J. A. Berst, who began working for Pathé as a boy in 1896, was sent to the United States in 1904 with the four-reel film *Passion Play* to develop a market there for Pathé's films. Later, Pathé joined the American trust companies in the Motion Picture Patents Company*. In 1907 or 1908, at Berst's suggestion, Arthur Roussel, the technical head of Pathé's studio at Vincennes, was sent to the United States to build and equip a studio in Bound Brook, New Jersey, which was formerly a cash register factory.

Pathé used the Bound Brook studio to produce weekly releases of Westerns*, comedies, and dramas to suit American tastes. The first American-made film was *The Girl from Arizona,* released on May 16, 1910. Louis J. Gasnier was the director-general of the Bound Brook studio, where the *Pathé Weekly* newsreel, edited by H. C. Hoagland, was also produced. In 1912, Pathé built a new studio at One Congress Street, Jersey City, and this became Pathé's major American studio. Early Pathé stars included Paul Panzer, Pearl White, Octavia Handworth, and Crane Wilbur. In 1912, Pathé sent James Youngdeer to Los Angeles to make films, and, by mid-1914, Pathé's West Coast company was producing comedies at the Zodiak* studio, under the direction of P. C. Hartigan and featuring Peggy Hart.

In 1914, when General Film Company began releasing the competing *Hearst-Selig Newsreel,* Pathé stopped releasing through General. It sold its American production facilities to Merrill, Lynch & Company, and began its own exchange organization. Its serial, *The Perils of Pauline,* produced in conjunction with the Eclectic Film Company* and the Hearst newspapers, was a great box office success. Pathé and Eclectic followed with further serials, short subjects, and a few features, and late in 1914 combined to form Pathé Exchange, Inc.

As an exchange, Pathé was involved in the productions of a number of companies, including Balboa*, Astra*, Wharton*, and Arrow*. Pathé also released the animated cartoons of J. C. Bray and the "Lonesome Luke" comedies featuring Harold Lloyd, produced by Rolin.

In March 1918, J. A. Berst, who had been the head of Pathé's American branch for most of its existence, resigned as vice president and general manager. Paul Brunet replaced him, and, in 1919, Pathé moved its headquarters to New York.

The twenties saw Pathé as the distributor of the Hal Roach shorts and features (including the *Our Gang* series*), of Robert Flaherty's *Nanook of the North* (1922), and, from 1923, of the Mack Sennett productions. In 1923, Merrill, Lynch & Company purchased a controlling interest in Pathé, which it retained until October 1926, when it sold such interest to Blair and Company.

In the spring of 1927, Pathé took over Producers Distributing Corporation* and for a short time Cecil B. DeMille, who was involved in the latter company, became a Pathé producer. With the acquisition of Producers Distributing Corporation, Pathé also acquired what became the Laird* studios in Culver City. Joseph P. Kennedy became involved with Pathé in 1928, becoming its chairman of the board the following year. It was Kennedy who was primarily responsible for the sale of Pathé, as a producer and distributor, to RKO* in 1931 (although rights to certain of Pathé's sound features, notably *Holiday,* were sold to Columbia*). Despite the demise of Pathé as a producer/distributor, the company continued to exist and actively financed other production companies and operated a laboratory.

BIBLIOGRAPHY

Blaisdell, George. "Charles Pathé, Film Producer." *The Moving Picture World,* November 14, 1914, pp. 904–5.
"Charles Pathé—World Promoter of the Photoplay." *The Film Index,* January 21, 1911, p. 1.
"The Daddy of Them All." *Photoplay,* April 1918, pp. 61–62.
Everett, Eldon K. "Frank Leon Smith Remembers the Pathé Serials." *Classic Images,* November 1981, pp. 10–11.
"The Great Works of Pathé Freres." *The Moving Picture World,* March 10, 1917, pp. 1529–30.
"Pathé Freres." *Views and Film Index,* May 19, 1906, p. 8.
"Pathé's American Film." *The Moving Picture World,* May 14, 1910, p. 777.
"Pathé's American Productions." *The Moving Picture World,* June 18, 1910, p. 1043.
Sadoul, Georges. "Napoleon of the Cinema." *Sight and Sound,* Spring 1958, p. 183.
"25th Anniversary Marks Outstanding Production Schedule of Pathé." *Exhibitors Herald-World,* July 6, 1929, pp. 91, 106.

RESOURCES

Papers: Academy of Motion Picture Arts and Sciences (1927–1931 business records).

PATHE ENTERTAINMENT, INC., had a short life as one of America's largest film companies. It was created on January 30, 1989, with Italian financier Giancarlo Parretti's acquisition of the Cannon Group*, and with Alan Ladd, Jr. (born 1937), as its chairman and CEO. In March 1990, Parretti agreed to purchase MGM/UA for $1.38 billion, and the deal was finalized in November 1990, with the new company renamed MGM-Pathé Communications Corp. Continually mired in financial problems, MGM-Pathé Communications was taken over by Parretti's major creditor, Credit Lyonnais, in May 1991, and it became a corporate shell in June 1992. According to Standard and Poor's, as of December 31, 1994, Pathé Entertainment, Inc., "had no operating assets or sources of income."

Address: 10 East 40th Street, New York, N.Y. 10016.

PATHÉ NEWS. See NEWSREELS

PATHÉ STUDIOS. See LAIRD INTERNATIONAL STUDIOS

PATHÉ'S WEEKLY. See NEWSREELS

PATSY AWARDS were established in 1951 by the American Humane Association (organized in 1877) to honor Hollywood's animal stars. The first winners were Francis the Talking Mule (First Place); California, the horse (Second Place); Pierre the Chimp (Third Place); Jerry Brown, the horse (Richard C. Craven Award, named after AHA's first western regional director); and Flame, the dog; Lassie; Black Diamond, the horse; and Jackie, the lion (all of whom received Awards of Excellence). From 1958, awards were also given to animals working in television, with Lassie being the first winner. Currently, awards are presented in the Wild Animal Category, the Canine Category, the Special Category (including birds, domestic cats, farm animals, and so on), and the Human/Animal Bond Award (given to a production best typifying the bond between animals and people). The American Humane Association also sponsors a "Hall of Fame." "Patsy" stands for "Picture Animal Top Star of the Year."

Address: 63 Inverness Drive East, Englewood, Colo. 80112; 15503 Ventura Boulevard, Encino, Calif. 91436.

PAX FILMS. See LOPERT FILMS DISTRIBUTING COMPANY

PDC. See PRODUCERS DISTRIBUTING CORPORATION

"PEACEFUL RAFFERTY" SERIES. See ALL-CELTIC FILM COMPANY

PEDIGREED PICTURES, INC., formed in 1936 by Mrs. Milton Erlanger, Mrs. Sylvester Stern, and Thomas Frelinghuysen, announced plans to produce a series of short subjects on the breeding and care of thoroughbred dogs, for release by Paramount. At least one film, *The Chesapeake Bay Retriever,* was produced in 1936.

PEERLESS FEATURE FILM COMPANY. See WORLD FILM CORPORATION

"PELICAN" BRAND. See EASTERN FILM COMPANY

THE PERMANENT CHARITIES COMMITTEE OF THE ENTERTAINMENT INDUSTRIES is the organization through which members of the entertainment industries contribute to various charities, either through pledges or payroll deductions. It was conceived in 1940, when Samuel Goldwyn called a meeting of industry leaders to consider the question of multiple charitable contributions from the various studios. In 1942, Permanent Charities set up its own campaign organization, and in 1968 it merged with the Radio-Television-Recording-Advertising Charities (which had been formed in 1950).

Address: 11132 Ventura Boulevard, Suite 401, Studio City, Calif. 91604.

PETER STARK MOTION PICTURE PRODUCTION PROGRAM is probably the best-known film industry-related course offered by an American university. Founded with a 1979 endowment by producer Ray Stark, father of the late Peter Stark, the course at the University of Southern California covers all aspects of film production and is taught by various active members of the film community. A. D. Murphy was the program's director from its inception through 1990.

PETROVA PICTURE COMPANY. See SUPERPICTURES, INC.

THE PHILHARMONIC AUDITORIUM opened at 5th and Olive (with a street address of 421–433 W. 5th Street), Los Angeles, on November 8, 1906; it operated as the "Theatre Beautiful" by the Auditorium Company, whose major stockholder was the Temple Baptist Church. From 1914 to 1919, it operated as Clune's "Theatre Beautiful," the largest motion picture theatre west of New York, with Carli Elinor as its musical director, and notable as the premiere site of many of D. W. Griffith's classic films, including *The Birth of a Nation* and *Hearts of the World*. The Philharmonic Auditorium was demolished in 1985.

PHOENIX, ARIZONA. See LUBIN MANUFACTURING COMPANY

PHOENIX PICTURES was founded in November 1995 by Mike Medavoy and Arnold W. Messer as an independent production company. Seventy percent of the financing for the new company was provided by Canadian airline foods and auto parts company Onex Corp., British Pearson Television, and Sony Pictures Entertainment.

Address: 10125 West Washington Boulevard, Culver City, Calif. 90232.

BIBLIOGRAPHY

Eller, Claudia, and James Bates. "2 Veteran Movie Producers Unveil Phoenix Pictures." *Los Angeles Times,* November 28, 1995, p. D6.

PHONOFILMS. See DE FOREST PHONOFILM

PHOTO DRAMA PRODUCING COMPANY of Turin, Italy, established a company in the United States in August 1914, a company that was later owned by George Kleine. Bill Steiner was the general manager, and Pierce Kingsley

was hired to direct and to find players and subjects. After filming *After the Ball* and *Prohibition* in the Centaur* studio at Bayonne, New Jersey, Kingsley took the company to Los Angeles. Photo Drama ceased operations in 1924.

PHOTOPLANE was a short-lived system of unknown technical worth that supposedly allowed films to be screened in theatres without the necessity of turning down the house lights. It was first reported in the November 19, 1910, issue of *Variety*. In January 1911, the Motionplane Co. was formed in New York, with John J. Murdock as its president, to exploit the system.

PHOTOPLAY. The word "photoplay" was first used to describe a motion picture in the fall of 1910 by the Essanay Company*. Essanay had conducted a newspaper contest "with the object of finding a suitable synonym which would not only be descriptive, but would sum up in one word the spectacular entertainment afforded by picture theatres." The winning word, "photoplay," was contributed by Mr. Edgar Strakosh, and the house organ of the Essanay Company was promptly named *The Photoplay Review*. *Photoplay* was also the title of the motion picture's best-known "fan" magazine, published from 1911 to 1980.

PHOTOPLAY AUTHORS' LEAGUE was formed in 1914 to organize scenarists, story writers, playwrights, writers of fiction whose work had been adapted for films, and story editors to deal with issues of importance to the photoplay writer. Early in its existence, it exposed fake photoplay schools, proposed a copyright bill in favor of photoplays, demanded payment for authors from magazines that printed film plots, and fought for protection for writers treated unjustly by producing concerns. Frank E. Woods was the president and Richard Harding Davis the vice president. The Photoplay Authors' League published an official organ, *The Script,* which was edited by William M. Ritchey.

BIBLIOGRAPHY

Wing, William E. "Photoplay Authors' League." *The Moving Picture World,* July 10, 1915, p. 268.

THE PHOTOPLAYERS, a social club similar to the Screen Club*, was organized in Los Angeles in December 1912 under the initial title of the Reel Club. Fred Mace was elected the first president, and the original membership stood at 150, consisting of producers, directors, actors, trade paper journalists, scenario writers, studio managers, and film importers. The group met at the Gamut Club on South Hope Street in downtown Los Angeles. The Photoplayers would appear to have been disbanded by 1920.

PHOTO PLAY PRODUCTIONS COMPANY. E. K. Lincoln was the president and lead actor of the Photo Play Productions Company, which was founded in April

1914. Frank A. Tichener was the general manager, Edgar Lewis the director, Philip Rosen the cameraman, and Edward Peple the scenarist. Its first production was *The Littlest Rebel*. Photo Play's offices were located in the Candler Building, 220 West 42d Street, New York.

BIBLIOGRAPHY

"Another Feature Company." *The Moving Picture World,* April 25, 1914, p. 531.

PICTURE PLAYHOUSE FILM COMPANY began in 1914 as the sole American agent for the films of the Pasquali Company of Turin, Italy. In addition to releasing films from other foreign companies, Picture Playhouse distributed films from the Interstate Feature Film Company. Its offices were at 71 West 23d Street, New York.

PIERROT FILM COMPANY, INC., was formed in mid-1914 to produce one-reel comedies with vaudeville comedian Louis Simon. Edgar Allan Woolf was the scenarist and Charles Marks was the general manager. Later Caryl Fleming appeared in juvenile leads. Pierrot began using the Reliance Studios at Yonkers but later moved to a studio in Tappan, New York. In December 1914, a U.S. district judge enjoined the company from manufacturing, selling, or leasing films made with a camera held to constitute infringement of the patent rights of the Motion Picture Patents Company*.

BIBLIOGRAPHY

"New Company Plans Big Things." *The Moving Picture World,* June 6, 1914, p. 1418.

PIKE'S PEAK FILM COMPANY, located at the Garden of the Gods studio in Colorado Springs, Colorado, was formed in December 1914. Otis B. Thayer, formerly with Selig*, was the director. George Gebhart and Josephine West were the leading players at the company's inception, and later Gertrude Bonehill starred in two-reel Westerns*, biblical films, and poetic dramas under the "Lariat" brand. Pike's Peak released through the United Film Service* at first, and later it released on the Standard program.

PILOT FILMS CORPORATION was formed early in 1913, with Lottie Pickford as one of its stars. Its first production, *The Blacksmith's Story,* was directed by Travers Vail. Later in 1913, it made the four-reel feature *Across the Continent*.

PINE-THOMAS CORPORATION was formed as an independent producer in 1940 by two former publicists, William C. Thomas and William H. Pine. Based on the Paramount* lot, it produced some 81 features for Paramount release, beginning with *Power Drive* (1941). Among its other productions were *Tokyo Rose* (1945), *Caged Fury* (1948), *El Paso* (1949), *Tripoli* (1950), *Crosswinds* (1951),

Hong Kong (1951), and *Passage West* (1951). The team broke up with Pine's death in 1955.

All Pine-Thomas productions were low-budget "A" features or Westerns. Its best-known stars were John Payne and Rhonda Fleming. The producers' publicist was A. C. Lyles, who later became an independent producer.

BIBLIOGRAPHY

English, Richard. "Gaudiest Producers in Hollywood." *The Saturday Evening Post,* January 3, 1953, pp. 22, 76–78.
"It's Not Art But . . . " *Time,* August 6, 1941, pp. 82–84.
Reddy, John. "Hollywood's Double Bills." *Esquire,* June 1945, pp. 64, 140–43.

PIONEER FILM CORPORATION. The Pioneer Feature Film Company, incorporated in March 1915 by Julian Belman, Nathan Hirsch (its president), and Augusta Hirsch, purchased the exchanges of the Cosmo Feature Film Corporation, which Nathan Hirsch had owned since 1912. Pioneer purchased the rights to the Polar Bear features of the Great Northern Film Company*, and the New York State rights to Thomas H. Ince's *Civilization* (1916). In 1918, the company was reorganized and renamed Pioneer Film Corporation. Its policy was to buy negatives of features from independent producers and sell them to the states rights* market. In January 1919, Nathan Hirsch resigned from the company, and M. H. Hoffman merged his releasing company with Pioneer and became its general manager.

PIONEER PICTURES, INC., was organized in 1933 by John Hay "Jock" Whitney and his cousin Cornelius Vanderbilt "Sonny" Whitney to produce Technicolor* films for release through RKO*. The Whitneys became enthusiastic about the possibilities of Technicolor thanks to the efforts of producer Merian C. Cooper, who was also instrumental in persuading the Whitneys to purchase a large block of Technicolor stock.

The first Pioneer production was also the first live-action Technicolor short, *La Cucaracha* (1934), produced by Kenneth Macgowan and with color direction by Robert Edmond Jones. In cost $65,000 to produce, compared with $15,000 for the typical two-reel short of the period. *La Cucaracha* was followed by the first three-strip Technicolor feature, *Becky Sharp* (1935), again produced by Kenneth Macgowan and with color design by Robert Edmond Jones, direction by Rouben Mamoulian, and with Miriam Hopkins in the title role. Pioneer Pictures produced only one other film, *The Dancing Pirate* (1936), the first musical feature to be filmed in three-strip Technicolor, starring Steffi Duna, who had also been the star of *La Cucaracha. The Dancing Pirate* was not successful, and Pioneer quietly faded from the scene.

BIBLIOGRAPHY

Ayer, Fred. "New Name, New Money, New Notion Given Industry with Jock Whitney." *Motion Picture News,* January 12, 1935, pp. 39–40.

"What? Color in the Movies Again?" *Fortune,* October 1934, pp. 92–97, 161–71.

"Whitney Colors." *Time,* May 27, 1935, pp. 28–34.

P.I.T.S. See EMBASSY COMMUNICATIONS

PIXAR. See LUCASFILM, LTD.

PLANET FILM CORPORATION, incorporated in Delaware on March 1, 1916, was formed by Harry B. Raver, its vice president and general manager, who allied himself with various banking interests. It produced at Raver's studios in Rockville, Long Island, and planned to make one five-reel feature a month from a popular play or book, to be released to states rights* buyers contracting on a yearly basis. It planned to make its profits on its four special eight-reel productions for each year.

BIBLIOGRAPHY

"Raver Forms New Company." *The Moving Picture World,* May 20, 1916, p. 1346.

PLASTICON. See THREE-DIMENSIONAL FILMS

PLIMPTON EPIC PICTURES, INC. Horace G. Plimpton, formerly in charge of the Edison studios* for some seven years, formed Plimpton Epic Pictures, Inc., in 1915. Its studio was located at 250th Street, between Yonkers and Mount Vernon, in New York, and it released through the Authors' Film Company, which had been formed to distribute films through express companies rather than exchanges. Gertrude McCoy was featured in Plimpton films.

In December 1918, Plimpton-Fischer Photoplays, Inc., was formed, with William J. Reed as president, Horace G. Plimpton as vice president and general manager, David G. Fischer as the director-general, and Stanley G. Mason as cameraman. It used the Plimpton Epic studios.

PLIMPTON-FISCHER PHOTOPLAYS, INC. See PLIMPTON EPIC PICTURES, INC.

PLITT THEATRES, INC., came into being in 1978 when Henry G. Plitt (1919–1993), a former ABC executive, along with a group of investors, acquired the theatre chain owned by ABC Television for $45 million. It was then the fourth largest chain and the largest privately owned circuit in the United States. In 1985, Plitt Theatres established a $100,000 fellowship at UCLA to provide grants for students with a desire to enter the field of film exhibition, and on November 22 of that year, it was sold to Cineplex Odeon Corp. At that time, it operated 711 theatres.

"POKES AND JABBS" SERIES. See WIZARD MOTION PICTURE CORPORATION

"POLAR BEAR FEATURES." See GREAT NORTHERN FILM COMPANY

POLAROID. See THREE-DIMENSIONAL FILMS

POLYGRAM N.V. is a Dutch company, majority owned by Philip Electronics N.V. and primarily active in the field of popular music through the ownership of A&M Records, Inc., Decca Record Co. Ltd., etc. It has also quietly become a prominent figure in the American film industry through its subsidiary, PolyGram Filmed Entertainment. The latter has its origins in PolyGram Pictures, formed in March 1980 from Casablanca Record & FilmWorks (which was founded in 1976 with the merger of Peter Gruber's FilmWorks Inc. and Neil Bogart's Casablanca Records). Gruber and Peters disposed of their interest in PolyGram Pictures in January 1982. In July 1989, Polygram created Manifesto Film Sales as a joint venture with Propaganda Films* and Working Title Films in which it had purchased partial interest in 1988 and 1989 respectively, and which it totally acquired in 1992. Also in 1989, the company took over ownership of A&M Films. In May 1992, PolyGram founded Gramercy Pictures as a distribution co-venture with Universal*, and in December 1994, it purchased Island Pictures.* In February 1995, PolyGram acquired ITC Entertainment Group, giving it a major library of films and television programming. PolyGram also owns Jodie Foster's Egg Pictures, Interscope Pictures, and the Benelux producer and distributor, Movies Films Prods.

Address: 825 8th Avenue, New York, N.Y. 10019 (Poly-Gram N.V.); 9348 Civic Center Drive, Suite 300, Beverly Hills, Calif. 90210 (PolyGram Filmed Entertainment).

POPULAR PLAYS AND PLAYERS COMPANY. Charles O. Baumann formed the Popular Plays and Players Company, incorporated in 1914 for $1 million, to produce high-class features of varying lengths according to the needs of their stories. Directors of the company were Baumann (the president), C. A. "Doc" Willat, A. Butler, Harry J. Cohen (the general manager and treasurer), and L. Lawrence Weber. Offices were at 1600 Broadway, New York. Using the players and facilities of the Lubin Film Manufacturing Company*, Popular Plays and Players produced its first two releases, *Michael Strogoff,* with Jacob P. Adler, and *The Ragged Earl,* with Andrew Mackin and directed by Lloyd B. Carleton. Its subsequent productions were shot at the Willat Studios and Laboratories in Fort Lee, New Jersey*. Olga Petrova was a featured player. The company released first with the Alco Film Corporation* and later with Metro Pictures Corporation, when Alco went bankrupt. By the end of 1914, Popular Plays and Players had changed from producing features to releasing 28 reels per week of one-, two-, and three-reel films, representing 14 brands, including Cee-O-Bee, Willat,

Niagara, Palisade, Longacre, Canyon, and Continental (all dramas), and Jester, Luna, Owl, Frolic, Gayety, O.K., and Pastime (all comedies). Metro absorbed the company on May 25, 1917.

BIBLIOGRAPHY

"C. O. Baumann Talks of Plans." *The Moving Picture World,* September 5, 1914, p. 1349.
"Popular Plays and Players Company." *The Moving Picture World,* June 6, 1914, p. 1396.

POPULAR SCIENCE. See JERRY FAIRBANKS PRODUCTIONS

POST PICTURES CORPORATION, founded by Clyde E. Elliott (1885–1959), was active from 1919 to 1921 in the production of scenic and travelogue shorts under the series titles of Post Travel Pictures, Post Scenics, and Post Nature Pictures. Elliott became known in the thirties and forties for the direction of a number of animal features, including *Bring 'Em Back Alive* (1932).

POVERTY ROW was the name initially bestowed on the area of Hollywood around Sunset Boulevard and Gower Street, where might be found such once minor producers as Columbia*, whose films were noted for the cheap manner in which they were produced. In time, Poverty Row came to refer not to an area of the city but to a type of production from a minor company, such as Mascot*, Tiffany*, or Grand National*. The name was in common usage in the film industry as early as 1924.

BIBLIOGRAPHY

Donnell, Dorothy. "Poverty Row." *Motion Picture Classic,* April 1925, pp. 16–17, 78–79.
Fernett, Gene. *Poverty Row.* Satellite Beach, Fla.: Coral Reef Publications, 1973.

POWERS COMPANY, an early independent manufacturer, began operations in 1909 at a building adapted into a studio at 241st Street and Richardson Avenue, Wakefield, New York. Headed by P. A. "Pat" Powers, who later was a cofounder of the Universal Film Manufacturing Company, the Powers Company, with capital of $250,000, began releasing "Columbia Licensed Motion Pictures" in late 1909, using a non-patent-infringing camera developed by Joseph Bianchi, a recording expert for the Columbia Phonograph Company. Powers was the vice president of the Motion Picture Distributing and Sales Company*, formed in April 1910, which planned to use the Bianchi camera to license independent manufacturers in a manner similar to that of the Motion Picture Patents Company*. But because the camera proved to be impractical and the patents, held by Columbia, did not offer the protection promised, Powers and the others switched to using infringing equipment and gave up their licensing plan.

Powers changed the name of its releases to "Powers Picture Plays." Joseph Golden was an early Powers director, Ludwig G. B. Erb was its cameraman and technical expert, and Irving Cummings the leading man. In April 1910, the Power Company came out with talking pictures, which it made for the American Fotofone Company. In January 1912, Juliet Shelby, later known as Mary Miles Minter, made *The Nurse,* her first film, for Powers.

Powers became a part of Universal* at its formation. In May 1913, it reincorporated as Powers Photoplays, Inc., and produced in Hollywood, at which time its directors included J. Farrell MacDonald and Harry C. Matthews. It continued production through 1917. In May 1918, the Powers-Cameron Film Company was formed, and it purchased the plant of the Fireproof Film Company in Rochester, New York, to make, among other things, 3-D talking pictures, with the financial backing of Rochester businessmen.

BIBLIOGRAPHY

"P. A. Powers Heads New Rochester Concern." *The Moving Picture World,* May 25, 1918, p. 1125.
"Picture Plays and Their Production: A Visit to the Powers Factory at Wakefield." *The Moving Picture World,* April 23, 1910, pp. 636–37.
"The Powers Company." *The Moving Picture World,* October 2, 1909, p. 444.
"Powers Photoplays Studio." *The New York Dramatic Mirror,* May 21, 1913, p. 25.
"Talking Moving Pictures by the Powers Company." *The Moving Picture World,* April 16, 1910, p. 605.

POWER'S PEERLESS PROJECTOR, developed in 1897 or 1898 by Nicholas Power (1854–1921) was the first in a series of Power's Projectors numbered one through five, the first projectors produced in the United States on a commercial basis.

P.R.C. In the late thirties, producer Ben Judell had formed a couple of independent production companies, Progressive Pictures Corporation and Producers Distributing Corporation (PDC), which had no connection with the earlier Cecil B. DeMille organization of the same name. PDC produced a number of films, notably *Hitler, Beast of Berlin* (1940, retitled for political reasons *Goose Step*). When the company went heavily in debt in 1940, with its major creditor being Pathé Laboratories, the latter decided to reform PDC as P.R.C. (Producers Releasing Corporation), with studios at 6404 Hollywood Boulevard and George Batcheller in charge of production.

One of the company's first productions was *Misbehaving Husbands* (1940), a pathetic comedy featuring two former silent stars, Betty Blythe and Harry Langdon, and which indicated the type of features with which P.R.C. would be associated. Indeed, the company was so denigrated within the industry that it was crudely referred to as "Prick Productions." Aside from cheap melodramas and comedies, P.R.C. produced three Western series, under the guidance of Sigmund Neufeld, *Billy the Kid, Frontier Marshall,* and *Lone Rider.* Producing an average of 30 features a year, P.R.C. continued as a production entity through the late forties, when it merged with Eagle-Lion*. However, as a corporate name, P.R.C. existed until 1953, as a subsidiary of Pathé Industries, Inc., a successor to Pathé Laboratories.

BIBLIOGRAPHY

Okuda, Ted. *Grand National, Producers Releasing Corporation, and Screen Guild/Lippert: Complete Filmographies with Studio Histories.* Jefferson, North Carolina: McFarland, 1989.

PRE-CINEMA is a term used to describe the various events and discoveries that led to the invention of the motion picture. More specifically, it relates to the invention of the magic lantern, on which a treatise was first published by the Jesuit priest Athanasius Kircher in 1646; to the concept of projection*, which is interrelated to the discovery of concave glass, first discussed in John Baptista Porta's *Natural Magick* (1589); and to the theory of persistence of vision, developed in the early nineteenth century by Peter Mark Roget and Joseph Antoine Ferdinand Plateau. Because of its own importance outside of the development of the motion picture, the invention of photography is not usually discussed as an aspect of pre-cinema.

Magic lanterns and other optical toys from the Victorian era are the most generally known items discussed under the heading of pre-cinema. Indeed, it might be argued that were it not for the popularity of magic lantern entertainments in the mid- through late 1800s, the discovery of the motion picture might not have proceeded so quickly.

Other important events in pre-cinema history include Dr. John Ayrton Paris's invention of the Thaumatrope, William George Horner's invention of the Zoetrope, and Emile Reynaud's invention of the Praxinoscope, all of which relate to persistence of vision; Eadweard Muybridge's photographic experiments in the mid-1870s and his invention of the Zoopraxiscope; Alexander Parkes's invention of celluloid in 1855; the Reverend Hannibal Goodwin's perfection of nitro-cellulose film in 1887; and Etienne Jules Marey's experiments with a gun-like photographic camera in 1882.

BIBLIOGRAPHY

Ceram, C. W. *Archaeology of the Cinema.* New York: Harcourt, Brace & World, 1981.
Cook, Olive. *Movement in Two Dimensions.* London: Hutchinson, 1963.
Deslandes, Jacques. *Histoire Comparée du Cinéma: 1826–1896.* Paris: Casterman, 1966.
Hecht, Herman. *Pre-Cinema History: An Encyclopedia and Annotated Bibliography of the Moving Image Before 1896.* London: Bowker-Saur, 1993.
Quigley, Martin Jr. *Magic Shadows.* Washington, D.C.: Georgetown University Press, 1948.

PRE-EMINENT FILMS, LTD., began producing in mid-1915. Its first film, *The Running Fight,* starred Violet Hemming and was directed by James Durkin. W. E. Green was the company's president and general manager.

PREFERRED PICTURES. When B. P. Schulberg (1892–1957) left Famous Players-Lasky* in 1920, he formed his own company, Preferred Pictures (also known as Famous Attractions Corporation), with J. G. "Jack" Bachmann (who served as president) and Al Lichtman. The new company's first star was Katharine MacDonald (with Preferred through 1923), but a more important leading lady with the company was Clara Bow, whom Schulberg spotted in *Down to the Sea in Ships* (1923) and featured in three Preferred features: *Maytime* (1923), *Poisoned Paradise* (1924), and *Capital Punishment* (1925). When Famous Players-Lasky's head, Adolph Zukor, asked Schulberg to return to the studio, he did, and Preferred Pictures released its last films in 1926. It should not be confused with a minor company of the same name formed in November 1937 by J. G. Bachmann, Joe Goldberg, and Julius Schlein.

BIBLIOGRAPHY

Schulberg, Budd. *Moving Pictures.* New York: Stein and Day, 1981.

"PREMIER" BRAND. See ST. LOUIS MOTION PICTURE COMPANY

PREMIER COMPANY made two-reel Westerns released with United Film Service* in 1915. Lillian Hamilton and Fred Church were the leading players, Mr. and Mrs. Al Garcia played supporting roles, and Joseph J. Franz was the director.

PREMO FEATURE FILM COMPANY released its first film, *The Master Hand,* through the World Film Corporation* in August 1915. Nat Goodwin was the film's star.

"PREQUELS" is a word coined to describe film sequels that take place prior to the original film. For example, *Another Part of the Forest* (1947) tells of the earlier life of the Hubbard family from *The Little Foxes* (1941); *The Night Comers* (1971) is the story of Peter Quint and Miss Jessel, who had been seen only as ghosts in *The Innocents* (1961); Robert Redford and Paul Newman starred in *Butch Cassidy and the Sundance Kid* (1969), but Butch and Sundance were seen as younger men, portrayed by Tom Berenger and

William Katt, in *Butch and Sundance: The Early Days* (1979).

PREVUES. See TRAILERS

PRIMOGRAF COMPANY produced multi-reel films from its studios at 302 East 38th Street in New York in 1914. Irving Billig was the managing director, and its first production was *The Black Cross,* directed by Frank Coygne.

PRINCIPAL PRODUCTIONS, INC., also known as Principal Pictures, was the name of Sol Lesser's (1890–1980) production company from 1922 to 1941. For it, he produced the Baby Peggy silent dramas, the Jackie Coogan comedies, the Tarzan features, the Smith Ballew musical Westerns, and the Bobby Breen musicals, as well as many other features. Associated companies, of which Lesser was also president, were Principal Theatres Corporation of America and Principal Distributing Corporation.

PRIZMA COLOR. A forerunner of Cinecolor*, Magnacolor, and Multicolor, Prizma color was invented by William Van Doren Kelley. It is described by Adrian Cornwell-Clyne in *Colour Cinematography* (London: Chapman and Hall, 1951):

> Negatives were exposed at a speed of 32 pictures per second in a normal camera equipped with a rotating filter carrying the usual two-color taking filters. Prints were made on double-coated film, the alternate frames being selected by a skipping contact printer. One side of the film was toned blue-green by an iron solution, and the opposite side was toned red-orange with uranium. Prizma color was first demonstrated at the Museum of Natural History in New York on February 8, 1917. Its best-known use was in J. Stuart Blackton's production of *The Glorious Adventure,* starring Lady Diana Manners and shot in England in 1921.

Prizma, Inc., began producing a weekly one-reel educational film late in 1918; *Kilauea,* a film about a Hawaiian volcano, was shown at the Rivoli Theatre, New York, the week of December 29, 1918. In November 1919, the company—by then known as Prizma Natural Color Pictures—took over the contract of child actress Madge Evans from the World Film Corporation* and produced two-reel and longer films featuring the actress. H. W. Saulsbury was the president and Carroll H. Dunning the vice president of the company.

BIBLIOGRAPHY

"How Prizma Films Are Made and Why They Are Practical." *The Moving Picture World,* April 26, 1919, p. 508.
"Prizma to Use Standard Projectors." *The Moving Picture World,* January 11, 1919, p. 190.

PRODUCERS' DISTRIBUTING CORPORATION. Frank G. Hall, an exhibitor in New Jersey, was the president of the Producers' Distributing Corporation, which was formed in September 1918 to furnish exhibitors with 12 special productions a year at the fixed prices of 10 dollars, 20 dollars, or 30 dollars a day, depending on the age of the subject, no matter how successful the film became. Franchise holders would sign for all 12 films but could cancel by giving a two-picture notice. The Loew circuit, along with exchanges of Moss, Mastbaum, Keith, and the Ascher Brothers signed with Producers' shortly after its formation. Producers' offices were located at 126–130 West 46th Street, New York. Its first release was *Her Mistake,* featuring Evelyn Nesbit.

PRODUCERS DISTRIBUTING CORPORATION (PDC), formed in 1924 by Jeremiah Milbank, took over the former Ince Studios in Culver City (Laird International*), and between 1924 and 1927 produced more than 100 features. Cecil B. DeMille joined the corporation in 1925, and, at that time, Cinema Corporation of America was formed as a holding company to control the stock of Producers Distributing Corporation and Cecil B. DeMille Pictures Corporation, with the stock jointly owned by DeMille and Realty and Securities Company.

DeMille was responsible for the Culver City studios, while F. C. Munro (president) and John C. Flinn (vice president and general manager) were based at the New York office. The corporation published its own house journal, *The Dotted Line.* The corporation was taken over by Pathé in 1928.

BIBLIOGRAPHY

Hayne, Donald, ed. *The Autobiography of Cecil B. DeMille.* Englewood Cliffs, N.J.: Prentice-Hall, 1959.

PRODUCERS FILM COMPANY, founded by Henry W. Laugenour and based in Oroville, California, was active in the early twenties in the production of the one-reel "Betty June Comedies."

PRODUCERS GUILD OF AMERICA, INC. In an effort to gain some recognition as the ultimate creator of a motion picture, a group of producers banded together in April 1950 to establish the Screen Producers Guild, whose original objectives were to represent producers in industry matters, to promote the professional interests of members, and to increase the value and importance of the industry. Among the founding members were Buddy Adler, Irwin Allen, Sam Bischoff, Bryan Foy, Edmund Grainger, Joe Pasternak, and Jerry Wald. William Perlberg was the Guild's first president.

Founded initially as little more than a social club, the Guild became a bargaining organization for the producers in their dealings with the studios in 1966. The following year, the Guild changed its name to the Producers Guild of America, Inc. Its efforts to gain recognition as a bargaining agent were never entirely successful, and, in December 1984, the Guild affiliated with the Western Conference of the Teamsters, an action that many viewed as a final endeavor to obtain industrywide contracts from Hollywood studios and gain recognition as a bargaining agent for *all* producers.

From 1952 to 1977, the Guild published a journal, which examined various aspects of the film and television industries in some detail.

Address: 400 South Beverly Drive, Suite 211, Beverly Hills, Calif. 90212.

PRODUCERS' PROTECTIVE ASSOCIATION. On October 18, 1917, 14 independent states rights* producers organized the Producers' Protective Association to regulate the states rights field. Directors of the Association were William L. Sherrill, the president; Harry Rapf the vice president; Jesse J. Goldburg, secretary and treasurer; Leopold Wharton; M. A. Schlesinger, and I. N. Chadwick. The organization was formed because of the unsettled state of business in the states rights market and the doubtful aspect with which banking institutions doing business with states rights producers viewed the present manner of regulating the states rights market. The Association sought to regulate advertising, pass judgment on grievances, institute a central sales exchange, and attempt the complete systemization of states rights production and distribution. Members included the Frohman Amusement Corporation*, Mayfair Film Corporation, Harry Rapf Productions, Ivan Film Productions, Inc.*, Duplex Film Corporation, Crystal Film Corporation, Ogden Pictures Corporation*, and John W. Noble, Inc.

BIBLIOGRAPHY

"Independent Producers Organize." *The Moving Picture World,* September 29, 1917, p. 2013.
"Producers' Protective Association Formed." *The Moving Picture World,* November 3, 1917, p. 714.

PRODUCERS RELEASING CORPORATION. See P.R.C.

PRODUCERS STUDIO. See CALIFORNIA STUDIOS

PRODUCTION CODE. Described as a "moral document," the Production Code encompassed three general principles:

1. No picture shall be produced which will lower the moral standards of those who see it. Hence the sympathy of the audience shall never be thrown to the side of crime, wrongdoing, evil, or sin.
2. Correct standards of life, subject only to the requirements of drama and entertainment, shall be presented.
3. Law, natural or human, shall not be ridiculed, nor shall sympathy be created for its violation.

The Production Code's origins date back to 1927, when Will H. Hays, president of the Motion Picture Producers and Distributors of America (later the Motion Picture Association of America*) formulated a group of directives for producers, consisting of 11 "don'ts" and 26 "be carefuls." A more formal "Code to Maintain Social and Community Values" was adopted by the Association and ratified by its board of directors on March 31, 1930. It was not mandatory for producers to adhere to the Code and the majority did not.

However, in the next couple of years, the Motion Picture Producers and Distributors of America came under increasing pressure from the public to adopt a formal code. In 1934, the National Legion of Decency* was created and threatened a Catholic boycott unless some rigid form of internal censorship was imposed on the film industry. Through his publication *Motion Picture Herald,* a leading Catholic layman, Martin Quigley, urged the industry to take action, and he, along with Daniel A. Lord, a Jesuit professor at the University of St. Louis, was largely responsible for drafting the new Production Code. Joseph I. Breen was selected to head the newly created Production Code Administration, which came into being on July 1, 1934.

All producers belonging to the Motion Picture Producers and Distributors of America were obligated to submit scripts and finished films for Code approval. Most independent and foreign productions were also submitted for voluntary approval. An additional Code governing things such as advertising and still photographs* was introduced in 1935. The provisions of the Production Code, initially published in a 19-page booklet, could vary from year to year. An up-to-date copy of the Code appeared annually in *International Motion Picture Almanac.*

In the fifties, theatres began screening films that did not have the Code seal of approval. United Artists* released *The Moon Is Blue* (1953) and *The Man with the Golden Arm* (1955) without Code approval, and increasingly important films, such as *Who's Afraid of Virginia Woolf?* (1966) and *Alfie* (1966), were produced whose subject matter precluded approval by the Production Code Administration. In 1966, the Code was revised and a new heading, "Suggested for Mature Audiences," introduced. Eventually, the Code became obsolete with the introduction—in 1968—of the ratings* system.

BIBLIOGRAPHY

Gardner, Gerald C. *The Censorship Papers: Movie Censorship, Letters from the Hays Office, 1934–1968.* New York: Dodd, Mead, 1987.
Leff, Leonard J., and Jerold L. Simmons. *The Dame in the Kimono: Hollywood, Censorship, and the Production Code from the 1920s to the 1960s.* New York: Grove Weidenfeld, 1990.
Ramsaye, Terry. *What the Production Code Really Says.* New York: Motion Picture Herald, 1934 (reprinted from the August 11, 1934, issue).

"Rethinking the Production Code." *Quarterly Review of Film and Video,* special issue, vol. 15, no. 4, March 1995.

Shurlock, Geoffrey. "The Motion Picture Production Code." In *The Annals of the American Academy of Political and Social Science.* Philadelphia: The American Academy of Political and Social Science, 1947, pp. 140–46.

RESOURCES

Papers: Academy of Motion Picture Arts and Sciences (Review Files of the Production Code Administration), Indiana University Lilly Library (Will Hays Collection).

PROGRESSIVE PICTURES CORPORATION. See P.R.C.

PROJECTION, one of the crucial elements in motion pictures, is possible as a result of the discovery of "concave glass," first discussed in John Baptista Porta's *Natural Magick* (1589), which permits the projection of objects and forms the basis for Leonardo da Vinci's camera obscura.

Thanks to projection, motion pictures are given the illusion of movement. Film transport is necessary to carry the motion picture from an upper reel, through the projector gate, to a lower reel. The beam from a light source is directed through a condensing lens or a mirror (which can sometimes be adjusted manually to sharpen the image), and motion on the film is synthesized by use of a two-shutter movement, which prevents the eye from perceiving flicker and cuts off the light source during the movement from one frame to the next. The film then moves through a second gate, through which a beam is directed at the sound track, and a photoelectric or a solar cell converts the light waves to sound waves.

Reels of film were one reel (running between 8 and 11 minutes) in length until 1933, when 2,000-foot reels were introduced (which, despite their name, usually hold only 1,700 feet of film). Reel changes, indicated by a visual cue in the right-hand corner of the picture, would be made manually by the projectionist. To prevent a break in the presentation, all theatres needed to be equipped with a minimum of two projectors. However, in the seventies, automated projection was introduced whereby the entire feature could be mounted on one single platter—to hold up to 20,000 feet of film—with the lead of the show spliced to the tail, thereby giving a continuous performance. Virtually all theatres are equipped with front projection, although back projection through a translucent screen is occasionally used.

PROMOTIONAL FILMS, INC. See ASTOR PICTURES CORPORATION

PROPAGANDA FILMS, founded in 1986 by Steve Golin and Joni Sighvatsson, was initially known as a music video producer. It expanded its activities in 1990 with the making of the David Lynch feature *Wild at Heart* and the Fox television series *Beverly Hills 90210.*

Address: 940 N. Mansfield Avenue, Hollywood, Calif. 90038.

BIBLIOGRAPHY

Rohter, Larry. "Producers Find Success on Their Terms." *New York Times,* October 15, 1990, pp. B1, B7.

PROVIDENCE, RHODE ISLAND. See EASTERN FILM COMPANY

PUBLICISTS GUILD OF AMERICA. The negotiating body for various types of publicists working within the industry, the Publicists Guild of America was chartered on July 11, 1955, as IATSE Local 818. It has jurisdiction over the entire country, including New York Publicists Local 872.

The Publicists Guild has its origins in the Screen Publicists Guild, organized on June 2, 1937. Because the original Guild sided with the Conference of Studio Unions*, IATSE* chartered the Motion Picture Publicists Association to replace it, but the Screen Publicists Guild was able to organize sufficient support to declare a "closed shop" within the studios in 1950. The Screen Publicists Guild produced a popular radio series in the early fifties and presented annual "Tom-Tom" awards from 1953. The name survives as that of the New York-based Screen Publicists Guild, which is a member of District 65 of the Distributive Workers of America.

The Publicists Guild presents a variety of awards: the Bob Yeager Award (first given in 1977 to Julian Myers), the Les Mason Award (first given in 1965 to Nat James), the Max Weinberg Publicist Showmanship Award (first given in 1982 to Kim Rowley and Margaret Scott), the Motion Picture Showmanship Award (first given in 1964 to Stanley Kramer), the Television Showmanship Award (first given in 1970 to Kragen-Smothers-Fritz), and the Press Award (first given in 1964 to Don Carle Gillete).

Address: 13949 Ventura Boulevard, Suite 302, Sherman Oaks, Calif. 91423.

PUBLIX THEATERS CORPORATION was created by Adolph Zukor in 1925 with the merger of the Balaban & Katz theatres with those owned by Paramount*. In 1930, the company was renamed Paramount Publix Corp., at which time it consisted of 1,210 theatres in the United States and Canada. On January 1, 1950, United Paramount Theatres, Inc., was formed to take over all theatre chains owned by Paramount in order to comply with the governmental consent decree*. At that time, the company controlled 1,424 theatres under a variety of circuit names.

BIBLIOGRAPHY

Ayer, Fred. "1,210 Theatres under Paramount's Control." *Motion Picture Herald,* January 5, 1935, pp. 9–12.

Gomery, Douglas. "The Movies Become Big Business: Publix Theatres and the Chainstore Strategy." In *The American Movie Industry: The Business of Motion Pictures*. Carbondale, Ill.: Southern Illinois University Press, 1982, pp. 104–16.

PUPPETOONS was a form of animated cartoon created by George Pal (1908–1980) that utilized miniaturized wooden figures instead of drawings. Pal first began making Puppetoons at a studio in Eindhoven, the Netherlands, in 1934. The films he made there were advertising shorts for either Philips or Horlicks, with the first Puppetoon being *The Ship of the Ether* (1934). George Pal came to the United States in 1939 and opened a studio in Santa Monica, California, where he produced his Puppetoons, for release through Paramount*, until 1947. He created the Negro boy Jasper as a favorite Puppetoon character in shorts such as *Jasper and the Watermelons* (1942), *Jasper Goes Fishing* (1943), and *Jasper in a Jam* (1946). The black folk hero, John Henry, was featured in the 1946 Puppetoon *John Henry and the Inky Poo*. In 1943, Pal received a Special Academy Award "for the development of novel methods and techniques in the production of the series of short subjects known as Puppetoons."

BIBLIOGRAPHY

Hickman, Gail Morgan. *The Films of George Pal*. South Brunswick and New York: A. S. Barnes, 1977.

Schepp, Ole, and Fred Kamphuis. *George Pal in Holland 1934–1939*. The Hague: Kleinoffsetdrukkerij Kapsenberg, 1983.

Taylor, Frank J. "Pal of the Puppets." *Collier's*, January 16, 1943, pp. 15, 61.

PURITAN SPECIAL FEATURES COMPANY, located in Boston, produced the 1914 feature *Quincy Adams Sawyer*. Charles F. Atkinson was the company's president.

BIBLIOGRAPHY

"Pictures Stimulate Interest in Play." *The Moving Picture World,* January 10, 1914, p. 153.

PUSSYCAT THEATRES. The best known of adult theatre chains, with theatres throughout California, the Pussycat circuit was formed in 1968 by Vincent Miranda (1933–1985). Miranda had acquired his first theatre, the Lyric, in Huntington Beach, California, in 1961, and to ease his advertising costs began acquiring additional theatres, all of which he managed as "safe," clean theatres for a middle-class white clientele. The advent of adult films on home video led to its demise.

PYRAMID PICTURES, INC., was formed in mid-1915 to make features, serials, and occasional industrial films under contract to various distributors. Arthur N. Smallwood was the president and general manager, and Pyramid's studio was at Ridgefield Park, New Jersey.

QUAKERS, or the Society of Friends, were seen on screen as early as 1903 in Siegmund Lubin's production of *Quaker Dance*. Clara Bow was a surprisingly demure Quaker in *Down to the Sea in Ships* (1922), featuring the Quaker-whaling community of New Bedford, Massachusetts. The closest that the Quakers ever came to production was in August 1969, when the Quaker Oats Company diversified into film through an arrangement with David L. Wolper Productions, Inc. The best-known film of Quaker life is William Wyler's *Friendly Persuasion* (1956), based on Jessamyn West's 1954 novel, *The Friendly Persuasion*. The novel was also the basis for a 1975 television feature, *Except for Me and Thee*.

There is an interesting footnote relative to *Friendly Persuasion*. One of the principal writers on the film was Michael Wilson, who refused to reveal whether he was a Communist before the House Un-American Activities Committee. The Writers Guild* ruled that Wilson should receive sole credit for the screenplay but also pointed out to the film's distributor, Allied Artists, that if the writer had ever taken the Fifth Amendment before a congressional committee vis-à-vis his being a member of the Communist Party, Allied Artists was not required to give that individual credit. And so Allied Artists released *Friendly Persuasion* with no screenplay credit. Thirty-six years later, in 1992, President Ronald Reagan, on a visit to the Soviet Union, presented Mikhail Gorbachev with a videotape of *Friendly Persuasion,* praising it for the American values the film espoused. Friends and collagues of Michael Wilson were quick to denounce Reagan's hypocrisy in his praise, as a staunch conservative, for a film written by a Communist.

QUALITY PICTURES CORPORATION was organized on March 1, 1915, by Fred J. Balshofer, formerly the head of the original Bison Company. Charles "Feature" Abrams was the company's business manager, and its studios were at the old Nestor plant at Sunset Boulevard and Gower Street in Hollywood. Quality began by producing films featuring Francis X. Bushman and Marguerite Snow, with William Bowman as director and William Alder as cameraman. Beverly Bayne joined Quality soon after release of its first film, *The Second in Command*. The company released on the Metro* program. It fell into other hands in 1916 and continued producing through 1922.

BIBLIOGRAPHY

"Amusement Feast for Public Is Quality's Hope." *Motion Picture News,* September 11, 1915, p. 47.
"Quality Pictures Corporation." *The Moving Picture World,* July 10, 1915, pp. 240–41.

QUINTEX ENTERTAINMENT, INC. See RHI ENTERTAINMENT, INC.

R

RADIO AND TELEVISION DIRECTORS GUILD. See DIRECTORS GUILD OF AMERICA, INC.

RADIO CITY MUSIC HALL. The foremost film showplace in the country, designed by Donald Deskey and with seating for 6,200, Radio City Music Hall opened at New York's Rockefeller Center on December 27, 1932, under the direction of S. L. "Roxy" Rothapfel. The opening-night program was strictly a vaudeville presentation. The first feature to be screened at the Music Hall was Frank Capra's production of *The Bitter Tea of General Yen*. Increasing financial problems led to the closure of Radio City Music Hall on April 12, 1978, with the feature *Crossed Swords*. However, the Music Hall was saved from demolition thanks to the efforts of various concerned groups and reopened as an entertainment center with occasional live shows and film presentations, on May 31, 1979. The traditional Christmas shows continue to be presented at Radio City, and its famed dancers, the Rockettes, remain in residence, making frequent tours with their precision dance routines, including their specialty, "Parade of the Wooden Soldiers," to the music of Victor Herbert.

Address: 50th Street and Avenue of the Americas, New York, N.Y. 10020.

BIBLIOGRAPHY

Ansen, David. "Radio City Redux." *Time,* June 11, 1979, p. 60.

Francisco, Charles. *The Radio City Music Hall.* New York: E. P. Dutton, 1979.

Morris, Joe Alex. "The Music Hall." *The Saturday Evening Post,* January 11, 1959, pp. 35, 90–92.

Shepard, Richard F. "Radio City Music Hall Returns." *The New York Times,* June 1, 1979, pp. C1, C6.

RADIO-TELEVISION-RECORDING-ADVERTISING CHARITIES. See THE PERMANENT CHARITIES COMMITTEE OF THE ENTERTAINMENT INDUSTRIES

RAILROAD SCREENINGS. As early as 1914, the Chicago and Northwest Railroad began screening films on some of its passenger runs. The following year, Kinetic Films was founded in Buffalo to supply films to passenger trains. On September 3, 1920, *Variety* reported that film screenings had been instituted on the New York-New Orleans Limited: "The idea is to amuse passengers en route." In 1947, the Chesapeake and Ohio Railroad introduced "the Chessie Theatre," a 16mm film theatre in a converted dining car on the Newport News to Cincinnati run. The first presentation was the world premiere of Universal-International's *Swell Guy.*

RALEIGH STUDIOS. See CALIFORNIA STUDIOS

RAMO FILMS, INC., began as the brand name of the pictures produced by the Directors Film Corporation in February 1913. It made two releases per week: a split-reel comedy directed by Epes Winthrop Sargent and a dramatic film directed by Wray B. Physioc. Its studios, called Ramo's Perfect Studios, were located at 102 West 101st Street, New York, and it released with the Exclusive Film Corporation. In May 1914, Ramo Films, Inc., was formed as an enlargement of the previous company. Homer H. Snow became director of the company, and C. Lang Cobb, Jr., became chief advisor. Directors during this period included George Gebhart and Will S. Davis, the cameraman was John Arnold, and Paul M. Potter was the scenarist. It moved to a studio in Flushing, Long Island, in August 1914, after the New York Fire Department forced Ramo to leave its previous studio, and, because it planned to confine its activities to the production of features, it got rid of its stock company. However, in 1915, it contracted to make one- and two-reel films under the brand name "Regent" for the United Film Service*. Ramo ceased operations on January 1, 1916.

BIBLIOGRAPHY

"Ramo Films Expanding." *The Moving Picture World,* May 9, 1914, p. 831.

"Ramo Films Soon." *The New York Dramatic Mirror,* February 5, 1913, p. 26.

RAMPART PRODUCTIONS, INC., was an independent production company, headed by William Dozier, that released through Universal-International*. It produced two features in 1948, *Letter from an Unknown Woman* and *You Gotta Stay Happy,* both of which starred Dozier's then wife Joan Fontaine, who was vice president of Rampart. A third feature, *A Very Remarkable Fellow,* was announced but unproduced. In the sixties, Dozier again had its own independent production company, Greenaway Productions.

RASTAR is the umbrella name for four companies created by producer Ray Stark (born 1914), the earliest of which dates back to 1966: Rastar Films, Rastar Features, Rastar Productions, and Rastar Television (formed in 1981, the best-known series from which is *Ripley's Believe It or Not*). Rastar Productions was acquired by Columbia* in 1974 (although the acquisition did not become generally known until 1978), and Rastar Films was purchased by the same studio in 1980.

Ray Stark serves as chairman of the board of Rastar, which has been responsible for more than 50 popular features, including such Neil Simon titles as *The Goodbye Girl* (1977), *California Suite* (1978), and *The Cheap Detective* (1978), as well as *Funny Girl* (1968), *The Way We Were* (1973), *Funny Lady* (1975), *The Electric Horseman* (1979), and *Annie* (1982). In 1983, it was announced that all personally produced Stark films would be known as Ray Stark Productions, while all others would be called Rastar Productions.

Address: 10202 West Washington Boulevard, Culver City, Calif. 90232.

RATHS-SEAVOLT FILM MANUFACTURING COMPANY was the first industrial film producer in the United States, founded in St. Paul, Minnesota, in 1910 by Otto N. Raths and Edward Seavolt. In 1921, W. R. Mills acquired partial ownership of the company, and it was renamed Raths, Mills & Bell. Four years later, Reid H. Ray took over management and changed the name to Ray-Bell Films, Inc. When Bell retired in 1947, the company became Reid H. Ray Industries, and in 1975, it was sold to Zitek & Associates of Minneapolis.

RATINGS SYSTEM. The system of rating motion pictures was introduced by the Motion Picture Association of America* on November 1, 1968. It is a voluntary service, open to all and generally supported by most producers within the industry. The rating system is sponsored by the Motion Picture Association of America, the International Film Importers & Distributors of America, and the National Association of Theatre Owners*. It is supervised by the Motion Picture Association, and the actual rating is undertaken by a board in Hollywood*. The primary purpose of the rating system is to advise patrons, particularly parents, as to the type of material in a particular film. The Ratings Board is not a censorship board, and its ratings are not intended to indicate the quality or artistry of any motion picture.

There are five categories of ratings. "G" indicates the film is for general audiences of all ages. "PG" indicates that parental guidance is suggested, but all ages can be admitted. Films rated "PG" contain some material that parents may consider too mature for preteenagers. "PG-13" (introduced in 1984 after criticism of a number of "PG"-rated films with excessively violent sequences) suggests, but does not require, that children under 13 be accompanied by a parent or guardian. "R" indicates the film is restricted and that those under 17 must be accompanied by a parent or adult guardian; the film has an adult theme or treatment. "NC-17" (introduced in 1990 to replace the "X" rating) indicates that no children under 17 are to be admitted.

BIBLIOGRAPHY

"Highlights of the New Voluntary Rating Plan." *Motion Picture Herald,* October 23, 1968, p. 25.
Motion Picture Association of America. *The Motion Picture Code and Rating Program: A System of Self-Regulation.* New York: Motion Picture Association of America, 1968.
Sandler, Adam. "Controlling the Content." *Daily Variety,* April 27, 1995, p. 42.
Sublett, Scott. "'Indiana' and 'Gremlins' Stir Up Ratings Squabble." *The Washington Times,* June 22, 1984, pp. 4D–6D.
Tusher, Will. "Censorship's a Horrid Word to Religious Leaders, But on the Other Hand Films Are a Target of Growing Criticism." *Daily Variety,* October 30, 1984, pp. 58, 106, 108, 110, 114, 118.

RAVER FILM CORPORATION. Harry R. Raver organized the Raver Film Corporation, of which he was president, in October 1915, after he obtained the rights to produce a number of well-known plays, including a collection of 29 by Augustus Thomas, also formerly associated with All-Star. Raver first used the W. Lindsay Gordon studios on Staten Island, New York, and later moved to Rockville, Long Island. The company's first production was *The Other Girl,* directed by Percy Winter. In February 1916, it took over the exploitation of productions of the Ocean Film Corporation*. Later, under the new name of Harry Raver, Inc., the company released films to the states rights* market through 1921.

BIBLIOGRAPHY

"River [*sic*] Film Corporation." *The Moving Picture World,* October 15, 1915, p. 589.

RAYART PRODUCTIONS, INC. See MONOGRAM PRODUCTIONS, INC.

RAYBERT PRODUCTIONS. See BBS PRODUCTIONS

R.C.M. PRODUCTIONS. See SOUNDIES

READER, SMITH AND BLACKTON COMBINATION. See VITAGRAPH COMPANY OF AMERICA

REDLANDS, CALIFORNIA. See DUDLEY MOTION PICTURE MANUFACTURING COMPANY and FUJIYAMA FEATURE FILM COMPANY

REEL CLUB. See THE PHOTOPLAYERS

REEL PHOTOPLAY COMPANY. See GOTHAM FILM COMPANY

REGAL DISTRIBUTING CORP. was a New York-based company, headed by Sherman S. Krellberg, and active from

1934 through 1939. It released only minor features and foreign imports. During the life of Regal Distributing Corp., Krellberg produced the serial *The Lost City* (1935), through his Regal Pictures.

"REGENT" BRAND. See RAMO FILMS, INC.

REGENT FILM COMPANY, INC., of which S. L. Warner was the president and general manager, was organized in January 1915 to produce one- and two-reel society dramas under the brand name "Tams" Pictures, starring Irene Tams. It leased the Centaur Studios in Bayonne, New Jersey, with its first release being the two-reel *Rebellious Irene,* directed by Walter Edwin and written by Lawrence McGill. Regent released with the United Film Service*.

THE REGULARS, an informal social club for the younger female members of the film community in the twenties, met every Monday night in rotation at a member's home. Among its members were Mary Astor, Margerie Bonner, Priscilla Bonner, Mary Brian, Sue Carol, Virginia Brown Faire, Pauline Garon, Mary Philbin, Esther Ralston, and Jobyna Ralston.

BIBLIOGRAPHY

Slide, Anthony. "The Regulars." *Films in Review,* April 1978, pp. 222–24.

RELIANCE MOTION PICTURE COMPANY AND MAJESTIC MOTION PICTURE COMPANY. Charles O. Baumann and Adam Kessel, Jr., formed the Reliance Motion Picture Company in 1910 at a Coney Island plant. Reliance's first film, *In the Gray of the Dawn,* released October 22, 1910, featured Arthur Johnson, Marion Leonard, Henry B. Walthall, James Kirkwood, Frances Burns, Gertrude Robinson, and Phillips Smalley, many of whom were hired away from the Biograph Company*.

The Majestic Motion Picture Company, formed the first week of September 1911 by Harry E. Aitken, acquired Mary Pickford, her husband Owen Moore, and general manager Thomas D. Cochrane from the IMP Company, while IMP's owner Carl Laemmle was on vacation in Europe. Majestic's offices were located at 145 West 45th Street, New York, and its first film, *The Courting of Mary,* starring Mary Pickford, was released on November 18, 1911, by the Motion Picture Distributing and Sales Company*. The Majestic Company, with Moore and David Miles directing, traveled to California, where its players included Mabel Trunnelle, Herbert Prior, George Loane Tucker, Paul Scarolon, and Charles Craig. Its Christmas release, *Little Red Riding Hood,* starred Mary Pickford and was directed by Owen Moore. Pickford left Majestic to return to Biograph in 1912. By January of that same year, Majestic had increased its release schedule to two reels per week.

In October 1911, Baumann sold the Reliance Company to J. C. Graham, who was formerly associated with Aitken in the Western Film Exchange. Both Reliance and Majestic joined the Mutual Film Corporation* upon its formation in 1912. Reliance produced its first three-reeler, *The Man from Outside,* with Irving Cummings, directed by Oscar Apfel, in February 1913. In July 1913, the company acquired the site for a new studio, The Pines, a four-acre estate of actress Clara Morris, overlooking the Hudson River on the Yonkers-Manhattan line at 262d Street and Riverdale Avenue. Later in 1913, Reliance signed D. W. Griffith to be director-in-chief of all its productions, which included those made at the Morris estate, at a studio located at 29 Union Square at the corner of 16th Street and Broadway, New York, and at its newest acquisition, the former Kinemacolor Company* studios at 4500 Sunset Boulevard in Hollywood. Aitken incorporated Reliance for $1 million (apparently it had earlier been part of the Carlton Motion Picture Company) in December 1913. Majestic, at this time, was producing under the name "New Majestic" from its studio at 651 Fairview Avenue, Los Angeles.

In March 1914, Majestic, with directors John Adolfi and Frederick Vroom, joined the Reliance studio at 4500 Sunset Boulevard, which under Griffith's supervision expanded greatly over the next 15 months. The studio became known as the Reliance-Majestic Studio and remained such until the creation of Fine Arts* in 1915.

BIBLIOGRAPHY

"New Reliance Studio." *The Moving Picture World,* July 26, 1913, p. 433.
"Reliance a Million Dollar Company." *The Moving Picture World,* January 3, 1914, p. 32.
"Reliance-Majestic." *The Moving Picture World,* July 10, 1915, p. 249–50.
"Reliance under New Management." *The Moving Picture World,* October 14, 1911, p. 135.
von Harleman, G. P. "Motion Picture Studios of California." *The Moving Picture World,* March 10, 1917, pp. 1605–6.

RELIANCE PICTURES, INC. See EDWARD SMALL PRODUCTIONS, INC.

"REMBRANDT LIGHTING" is the term given to lighting that emphasizes highlights and shadows, similar to that used by the Dutch painter (1606–1669). It was introduced by Cecil B. DeMille (1881–1959) and his cameraman Alvin Wyckoff in *The Warrens of Virginia* (1914), in an effort to escape from the flat lighting of early films. In *The Autobiography of Cecil B. DeMille* (Prentice-Hall, 1959), the producer/director wrote, "What I was after was naturalism: if an actor was sitting beside a lamp, it was crudely unrealistic to show both sides of his face in equal light, so, with portable spotlights borrowed from the Mason Opera House in downtown Los Angeles, we began to make shadows where shadows would appear in nature."

RENFAX FILM COMPANY, INC., was organized in January 1914 to make talking pictures illustrating popular songs. Exhibitors who owned a phonograph and who would purchase an attachment to synchronize the phonograph and the projector could show these novelties, which were released four to a reel. Known vaudeville performers were featured in the films. By the end of its first year, Renfax had opened exchanges in New York; Columbus, Ohio; Chicago; and Pittsburgh. Its main offices were in the World's Tower Building, New York; Arthur M. Hess was the president and treasurer, and DeWitt Fox was the vice president.

BIBLIOGRAPHY

"Renfax Musical Pictures a Year Old." *The Moving Picture World,* February 6, 1915, p. 833.
"Renfax Talking Pictures." *The Moving Picture World,* January 17, 1914, p. 298.

REOL MOTION PICTURE COMPANY, an early producer of black films, was owned by Robert J. Levy, a white backer of the Lafayette Players, a Harlem theatre group that appeared in Reol's films. Reol produced at least six features, one of which, *The Call of His People,* was released in 1921.

REPUBLIC DISTRIBUTING CORPORATION. Lewis J. Selznick, the head of Select* Pictures Corporation, took over the entire list of 22 exchanges* from the World Film Corporation* and formed the Republic Distributing Corporation, in the fall of 1919, to have no connection with Select. Republic's offices were located at 130 West 46th Street, New York. Although Britton N. Busch was president and general manager, Selznick was in full control in his official role as advisory director. Republic planned to handle the highest grade independent films, including high-class short subjects. The company ended in 1921.

BIBLIOGRAPHY

"Selznick Absorbs a Corporation." *The Moving Picture World,* November 8, 1919, p. 3472.

REPUBLIC FILM LABORATORIES. See CONSOLIDATED FILM INDUSTRIES

REPUBLIC PICTURES CORPORATION. The most important and influential studio in the history of the "B" movie*, Republic Pictures Corporation was also the one studio that made a conscious and at times successful effort to raise its status. Throughout its life, Republic was controlled by only one man, Herbert John Yates (1880–1966), a former executive with the American Tobacco Company who had been involved with various film laboratories, notably Consolidated Film Industries*, from the middle of the second decade of the twentieth century.

Republic's staple product included Westerns and serials (some 66 of the latter), and among the best-known stars under contract were Gene Autry, Roy Rogers, John Wayne, and ice skater Vera Hruba Ralston (whom Yates married in 1952). Louella Parsons's daughter, Harriet, began her career as a feature-film producer with Republic. From 1937 to 1947, Republic produced the musical revue "Hit Parade" series. In the forties, Yates worked hard to improve Republic's image. Among the directors he placed under contract were such prominent names as Orson Welles, Allan Dwan, Frank Borzage, John Ford, and Ben Hecht, all lured with promises of directorial freedom. Among the "class" features produced by Republic in the late forties and early fifties were *Spectre of the Rose* (1946), *Macbeth* (1948), *Sands of Iwo Jima* (1949), *The Red Pony* (1949), *Rio Grande* (1950), and *The Quiet Man* (1952).

The company was formed on March 29, 1935, when Yates merged Mascot*, Monogram*, and Liberty companies, with headquarters at the former Mascot Studios (earlier the Mack Sennett Studios) at Ventura Boulevard and Radford Avenue in Studio City. Nat Levine, formerly at Mascot, was named first president. Monogram's exchanges were the basis for Republic's distribution setup. After only a few months, M. H. Hoffman withdrew his Liberty Pictures; on August 6, 1936, Trem Carr and Ray Johnston left to reform Monogram, and in 1937 Nat Levine resigned. Yates was left very much in sole command of the company, and its success was entirely to his credit.

Republic prospered, enjoying its most financially successful year in 1946. Its sound department was noted throughout the industry, and, in 1945, Republic received a Special Technical Award from the Academy of Motion Picture Arts and Sciences* "for the building of an outstanding musical scoring auditorium which provides optimum recording conditions and combines all elements of acoustic and engineering design." The studio's profits fell in the fifties, partially because of the increasing popularity of television but also, ironically, because of Yates's promotion of prestige productions that failed to gain an adequate audience and, above all, his promotion of his wife, Vera Hruba Ralston, as a major star.

On July 1, 1959, Yates resigned as Republic's president. Los Angeles industrialist Victor M. Carter took over the company, but, for all intents and purposes, Republic had ceased to exist. The studios were leased first to Lippert* and then to CBS*, which purchased them in 1967, renaming the lot CBS Studio Center. (The studios are still utilized by CBS but were acquired in 1984 by Mary Tyler Moore Productions.)

Republic Corporation continues as the parent company of Consolidated Film Industries. In 1984, National Telefilm Associates, which had purchased the library of Republic films in 1967, voted to change its name to Republic and to utilize the Republic logo of the American eagle as its trademark.

BIBLIOGRAPHY

Barbour, Alan G. *Selected Papers from the Republic Reporter 1939–40.* Kew Gardens, N.Y.: Screen Facts, 1975.

Hurst, Richard Maurice. *Republic Studios: Between Poverty Row and the Majors.* Metuchen, N.J.: Scarecrow Press, 1979.

Mathis, Jack. *Valley of the Cliffhangers.* Northbrook, Ill.: Jack Mathis Advertising, 1975.

———. *Republic Confidential: The Players.* Barrington, Ill.: Jack Mathis Advertising, 1992.

O'Connor, Edward. "The Golden Age of Republic Serials." *Screen Facts,* no. 17, 1968, pp. 48–61.

———. "The Golden Age of Republic Serials, Part 2." *Screen Facts,* no. 18, 1968, pp. 20–36.

Swann, Thomas Burnett. *The Heroine or the Horse: Leading Ladies in Republic's Films.* New York: A. S. Barnes, 1977.

Whalen, David B. "Republic Pictures." In *The Film Daily Cavalcade.* New York: The Film Daily, 1939, pp. 176–82.

RESOURCES

Films: UCLA Film and Television Archives (nitrate master elements and some safety negatives and prints).

Scripts: UCLA Special Collections.

REPUBLIC PICTURES CORPORATION (NEW). National Telefilm Associates, formed in 1952, claimed to be the world's leading independent distributor of film and television programs, with one of its major assets being the entire Republic film library, which it acquired in 1965. Recognizing the importance of the latter, the company in December 1994 changed its name to Republic Pictures Corporation. In 1986, it was purchased by a group headed by Russell Goldsmith for $8.7 million, and the following year made a modest entry into film and television production. In January 1993, Blockbuster Entertainment* acquired a 35 percent stake in the company, and in April 1994 arranged for its merger with the Spelling Entertainment Group*.

Address: 5700 Wilshire Boulevard, Suite 525, Los Angeles, Calif. 90036.

RHI ENTERTAINMENT, INC., a producer of television and feature films, was formed in 1956 by Robert Halmi (born 1924), a Hungarian who came to the United States in the late 1940s. In June 1988, RHI and Hal Roach Studios, Inc.*, merged to form Quintex Entertainment, Inc., but in 1990, the latter declared bankruptcy and Halmi was able to purchase back his company along with the assets of Hal Roach Studios, Inc. In 1992, New Line* acquired a 52 percent interest in RHI, and in 1994, Hallmark Cards Inc. purchased the company for $378 million plus assumption of $50 million in debt.

RIALTO DE LUXE PRODUCTIONS was formed by Jesse J. Goldburg early in 1918 to produce one adaptation of a novel or play, five reels or more in length, per month, to be released to the states rights* market. Its first release was *The Unchastened Woman* with Grace Valentine. Rialto, which was located in New York, remained active through 1923.

RIALTO STAR FEATURES. See GAUMONT COMPANY

RIDGEFIELD PARK, NEW JERSEY. See PYRAMID PICTURES, INC.

RKO-PATHÉ STUDIOS. See LAIRD INTERNATIONAL STUDIOS

RKO RADIO PICTURES, INC., one of the smaller of the major Hollywood studios, is best known for the Fred Astaire-Ginger Rogers musicals of the thirties, for *King Kong* (1933), for *Citizen Kane* (1941), and for the Val Lewton low-budget "horror" productions of the early forties. It helped advance the careers of Orson Welles, George Stevens, Katharine Hepburn, Robert Wise, Val Lewton, David O. Selznick, and George Cukor. As Richard B. Jewell wrote in *The RKO Story,* it "generated more than 1000 pictures—some forgettable, some too awful to contemplate, and a handful of the best movies ever made."

RKO, which stands for Radio-Keith-Orpheum, had its origin in the Film Booking Office of America (FBO), which was formed in 1922 from Robertson-Cole* and which produced and released minor action, melodramatic, and Western features, many starring Yakima Canutt and Strongheart the dog. The company was acquired in 1926 by Joseph P. Kennedy, but there was little change in the quality of its films. With the coming of sound, David Sarnoff, president of Radio Corporation of America (RCA), joined forces with Kennedy, perceiving FBO as a suitable production company showcase for his RCA Photophone sound system. FBO was merged with the vaudeville circuit of Keith-Albee-Orpheum, which provided the company with theatres in which to screen its product, and on October 23, 1928, RKO Radio Pictures came into being. Its trademark, seen at the start of each film, was a radio tower perched on top of the world, beaming out the letters "R K O." The company's first film was *Syncopation* (1929), directed by Bert Glennon and starring Fred Waring and His Pennsylvanians.

David O. Selznick became head of production in the autumn of 1931, and to him goes the credit for some of the studio's best early films, including *What Price Hollywood?* (1932), *A Bill of Divorcement* (1932), *The Animal Kingdom* (1932), and *King Kong* (1933). When Selznick left for M-G-M* in 1933, he was replaced by Merian C. Cooper, and when he resigned, a year later, the position was taken over by B. B. Kahane. In 1935, Kahane was replaced by Samuel Briskin, who was, in turn, replaced, in 1938, by Pandro S. Berman. Berman, who had produced many of RKO's successes in the thirties, quit in 1939, and with his departure, a new president, George Schaefer, began bringing freelance talent to the studio and signing "new" names, such as Orson Welles. Although the films produced under the Schaefer regime were of superior quality, many failed to make money, and when Schaefer left in 1942 the company was financially in trouble.

Charles Koerner took over as production head, followed, on his death in 1946, by Peter N. Rathvon and, in 1947, by Dore Schary. In 1948, RKO was acquired by Howard Hughes, whose bad judgment as a producer led to the studio's downfall. He sold the studios in 1955 to General Teleradio, Inc., which was more interested in RKO's library of films for possible television use than in turning out new products. However, under William Dozier's leadership, as head of production, RKO continued to produce features through 1957, with its last film being *The Unholy Wife,* directed by John Farrow and starring Diana Dors. RKO continued to release films, some of which were produced by its British arm, through 1960.

In 1987, Ted Turner acquired the RKO film library, while the corporate entity was taken over by Wesray-Capital, Inc. In August 1989, RKO was purchased by Pavilion Communications, Inc., founded in 1987 by Ted Hartley and Dina Merrill. The new company, initially known as RKO/Pavilion, but later renamed RKO Pictures, Inc., owns remake and sequel rights to almost 650 films, together with rights to a handful of features produced by RKO in recent years. The value of the new company was placed at $20 million by *Daily Variety* (August 29, 1989).

The RKO studio was located at 780 Gower Street in Hollywood, and is now part of the Paramount* lot.

Address: 1875 Century Park East, Suite 2140, Los Angeles, Calif. 90067.

BIBLIOGRAPHY

Jewell, Richard B., with Vernon Harbin. *The RKO Story.* New York: Arlington House, 1982.
Lasky, Betty. *RKO, the Biggest Little Major of Them All.* Englewood Cliffs, New Jersey: Prentice-Hall, 1984.
Neibaur, James L. *The RKO Features: A Complete Filmography of the Feature Films Released or Produced by RKO Radio Pictures, 1929–1960.* Jefferson, North Carolina: McFarland, 1994.
Parish, James Robert. *The RKO Gals.* New Rochelle, New York: Arlington House, 1974.
Walsh, James. "Dina and Ted's Excellent Adventure." *California Business,* April 1990, pp. 88–92.

RKO THEATRES CORPORATION. When RKO* was required by the consent decree* to divest itself of its theatre chain, the 124 theatres that it controlled in 1948 became RKO Theatres Corporation. The theatres were resold in 1953 to List Industries, which merged with Glen Alden Corp. in 1959. Later, the theatres became part of the RKO Century Warner Theatres, and are now owned by the Cineplex Odeon Corp.

RESOURCES

Films: Library of Congress.

Photographs: Academy of Motion Picture Arts and Sciences.

"ROAD MOVIES." To older filmgoers, the term "road movies" refers to the series of comedy features starring Bing Crosby, Bob Hope, and Dorothy Lamour and produced by Paramount*: *Road to Singapore* (1940), *Road to Zanzibar* (1941), *Road to Morocco* (1942), *Road to Utopia* (1946), *Road to Rio* (1948), and *Road to Bali* (1953). (There was also one final "road" picture, in which Lamour made only a cameo appearance and which was released by United Artists*; that was the 1962 feature *Road to Hong Kong.*)

There is also the new genre of "road movies," of which Mark Williams writes, "Broadly speaking, there are two types of road movie; those that simply pander to car chauvinism, and those that exploit a nation's belief in the freedom that lies across a state line or two, with a car being the means to that end." Among such varied types of "road movies" are *The Grapes of Wrath* (1940), *They Drive by Night* (1940), *Bonnie and Clyde* (1967), *Hells Angels on Wheels* (1967), *Easy Rider* (1969), *Cycle Savages* (1970), *Paper Moon* (1973), *Eat My Dust* (1976), and *Bobby Deerfield* (1977).

BIBLIOGRAPHY

Mielke, Randall G. *Road to Box Office: The Seven Film Comedies of Bing Crosby, Bob Hope and Dorothy Lamour 1940–1962.* Jefferson, North Carolina: McFarland, 1997.
Williams, Mark. *Road Movies.* New York: Proteus, 1982.

ROAD SHOW ATTRACTIONS was founded by veteran exploitation showman Dwain Esper (1893–1982) to present his features *Maniac* (1934), *Modern Motherhood* (1934), and *Marijuana* (1936).

ROBERT BRUNTON STUDIOS, INC. Located at 5341–5601 Melrose Avenue in Hollywood, the Robert Brunton Studios, Inc., was one of the major rental studios late in the second decade of the twentieth century, with seven covered stages, 300,000 props, and 30 acres of land available for exterior scenes. Twenty production companies could operate there at one time. Formerly the home of Paralta, the Brunton Studios became the United Studios in the early twenties and eventually the home of Paramount Pictures*.

ROBERTSON-COLE COMPANY was an importer and later producer/distributor out of which came RKO*. Indeed, the RKO studios were the former Robertson-Cole studios, which the company built in 1921 at the junction of Gower Street and Melrose Avenue in Hollywood on 13.5 acres of land that had previously been owned by the Hollywood Cemetery. Robertson-Cole was formed by the English-born Harry F. Robertson and the American Rufus Sidman Cole as an import/export company for which films were a sideline to Rohmer automobiles. Among the first films acquired by the company were *His Birthright* and *The Temple of Dusk,* both produced by 1918 by Haworth Pictures Corporation and starring Sessue Hayakawa. Robertson-Cole continued to distribute Haworth/Hayakawa films through 1920, initially through Exhibitors Mutual Distributing Corp. and later through Robertson-Cole Distributing Corporation. Robertson-Cole also released films produced by B. B. Features (starring Bessie Barriscale and her husband Howard Hickman), National Film Corporation of America*, Jesse D. Hampton Feature Corp. (starring William Desmond), and Brentwood Film Corporation* (starring either ZaSu Pitts or Florence Vidor and directed by King Vidor or Henry Kolker).

After the building of its studio, Robertson-Cole entered production, with its first Hollywood feature being *Kismet,* starring Otis Skinner in a recreation of his famous stage role. (The first Robertson-Cole production was actually *The Wonder Man,* shot at the former Solax* studios in Fort Lee and starring Georges Carpentier.) Both *Kismet* and *The Wonder Man* were released in 1920, with the interior scenes being shot at the Haworth Pictures studios.

In 1922, Robertson-Cole became Film Booking Offices of America (FBO)*, which was the immediate predecessor of RKO.

BIBLIOGRAPHY

Jewell, Richard B., with Vernon Harbin. *The RKO Story.* New York: Arlington House, 1982.

ROCKVILLE, LONG ISLAND. See PLANET FILM CORPORATION and RAVER FILM CORPORATION

ROCKY GLEN, PENNSYLVANIA. See FEDERAL FEATURE FILMS CORPORATION

ROGERS & COWAN, INC. Possibly the best-known public relations company in the United States, Rogers & Cowan, Inc., was founded in 1935 by Henry C. Rogers. Rogers's first major client—in 1939—was Rita Hayworth. In 1945, Rogers joined forces with Warren Cowan, and Rogers & Cowan was created. Among the company's clients have been Audrey Hepburn, Doris Day, Robert Redford, Paul Newman, Kirk Douglas, Shirley MacLaine, Natalie Wood, the Ford Motor Company, and Exxon. In the fifties, Rogers & Cowan was involved in a long-running feud with gossip columnist Hedda Hopper.

Address: 10000 Santa Monica Boulevard, Suite 400, Los Angeles, Calif. 90067.

BIBLIOGRAPHY

Rogers, Henry C. *Walking the Tightrope.* New York: William Morrow, 1980.
"'Work for the Press' PR Firm's Slogan." *Editor & Publisher,* June 26, 1965, pp. 28, 30.

ROLANDS FEATURE FILM COMPANY. George K. Rolands was the director of films made by the Rolands Feature Film Company, which began in February 1914 to manufacture, import, and export films. Samuel Q. Edelstein was the manager of the company, which was located at 145 West 45th Street, New York, and whose first production was the police thriller *Trapped in the Great Metropolis.* Rolands's 1915 release *The Frank Case,* based on a case still in the courts at that time, was refused approval by the National Board of Review* but was, nevertheless, shown in New York.

BIBLIOGRAPHY

"New Feature Film Company." *The Moving Picture World,* February 7, 1914, p. 687.

ROLFE PHOTOPLAYS, INC. See B. A. ROLFE PHOTOPLAYS, INC.

ROLFE PRODUCTIONS, INC. See B. A. ROLFE PHOTOPLAYS, INC.

ROLIN FILM COMPANY. See HAL ROACH STUDIOS, INC.

ROMAYNE SUPER-FILM COMPANY. H. Y. Romayne was the president of the Romayne Super-Film Company, which was organized in July 1918 to produce five- and six-reel features for the states rights* market without using big names. Betty Burbank was the company's leading actress, Josephine Crowell played supporting roles, and Wyndham Gettins directed. Its first production was *Me und Gott.* Romayne used the David Horsley* studios in Los Angeles, with offices in the Marsh Strong Building, also in the city.

ROTHACKER-ALLER FILM LABORATORIES, INC. One of the major film laboratories of the silent era, with offices in Chicago and New York, the Rothacker-Aller Film Laboratories, Inc., plant opened at 5515 Melrose Avenue in Los Angeles on June 1, 1921. Under the presidency of Watterson R. Rothacker, it could handle up to three million feet of film a week, and among its customers were Mary Pickford, Marshall Neilan, Louis B. Mayer, William S. Hart, and Sessue Hayakawa.

ROTHACKER FILM MANUFACTURING COMPANY. See INDUSTRIAL FILM COMPANY

ROTHAPFEL PICTURES CORPORATION. Samuel L. Rothapfel, formerly the manager of the Stand*, Rialto*, and Rivoli theatres in New York, became a producer in February 1919, when he organized Rothapfel Pictures Corporation to supply exhibitors with complete screen programs, which he called "Rothapfel Unit Programs," containing a feature, shorts, scenics, and music, all related to each other. Frank G. Hall was vice president, and Hall's distributing organization, the Independent Sales Corporation, handled the productions. Rothapfel himself selected the stories, engaged actors, and supervised the production.

The feature in the first "Unit" was *False Gods,* codirected by Wally Van.

BIBLIOGRAPHY

"Rothapfel's Unit Idea Progressing." *The Moving Picture World,* May 3, 1919, p. 674.

"Samuel Rothapfel, Program Producer." *The Moving Picture World,* February 22, 1919, p. 1048.

ROXY THEATRE, located at 50th Street and Seventh Avenue in New York, was one of America's greatest movie palaces, advertised as "The Cathedral of the Motion Picture." When it opened on March 11, 1927, with Gloria Swanson's first United Artists* release, *The Love of Sunya,* it was billed as the largest film theatre in the world. With its 5,920 seats it was surpassed only when the Radio City Music Hall* opened. It was named for its first managing director (until 1931), S. L. Rothapfel (1882–1936), and was noted for its lavish stage productions that preceded the feature presentation. The theatre became the venue of New York premieres of Fox* features. Live presentations ceased in February 1960, and a month later—on March 29, 1960—the theatre closed with *The Wind Cannot Read.* It was demolished that same year.

BIBLIOGRAPHY

Marquee, vol. 2, no. 1, first quarter 1979, special issue devoted to the Roxy.

RUBY FEATURE FILM COMPANY. Leon J. Rubenstein was the principal owner of the Ruby Feature Film Company, which was formed early in 1914. Its "twinplex" studio, which it rented to other companies, was located at 217 East 24th Street, New York. Frank Coygne was the director and Julia Kellity the company's star.

BIBLIOGRAPHY

"The Ruby Feature Studio." *The Moving Picture World,* January 24, 1914, p. 423.

RUDDER PRODUCTIONS was a Santa Monica-based film company set up by the FBI in 1985 as part of a five-year operation to expose the influence of organized crime over labor unions in the film industry. The operation was titled DRAMEX (Drama Exposé). FBI agent Garland Schweickhardt spent 12 weeks studying film production at UCLA before changing his name to David Rudder and setting up the company. The FBI actually purchased four film scripts and came close to producing one, *Cartunes,* in Rhode Island.

BIBLIOGRAPHY

Lieberman, Paul. "FBI's Venture into Film Business Less Than Boffo." *Los Angeles Times,* November 23, 1994, pp. 1, 24–26.

RUGOFF AND BECKER. See CINEMA 5

RUNAWAY PRODUCTION is the term used to describe a film produced by an American company entirely abroad, taking advantage of cheap labor costs and/or tax breaks. It originated in the forties, when film companies began producing in Europe to take advantage of impounded funds.

RYDER SOUND SERVICES was founded on October 20, 1948, quickly becoming a leading expert in all areas of sound. Founder Loren L. Ryder, who designed the original magnetic film used for motion picture sound, sold his company to Leo Chaloukian and Mel Sawelson in 1976, and the former acquired sole ownership in 1986.

Address: 1161 North Vine Street, Hollywood, Calif. 90038.

BIBLIOGRAPHY

"Ryder Sound Services Marks Its 40th Anni." *Daily Variety,* November 21, 1988, pp. 11–12.

RYNO FILM COMPANY, INC. John Noble was the principal director of Ryno Film Company, Inc., a production company formed in February 1913. Its manufacturing plant was located at 189 Terrace Place, City Island, New York. Albert Roscoe was assistant director, Emmett Williams the cameraman, and the players included Julia Bruns, Jane Fernley, and Glenn White.

SACK AMUSEMENT ENTERPRISES, initially formed in 1920 by Alfred N. Sack, was a major producer/distributor of all-Negro features and shorts, starring and produced for black Americans. The company remained in existence through the seventies. In addition, Sack organized Merit Films in 1946 as a 16mm subsidiary, Sack Television Enterprises in 1948, and Vogue Films in 1952 as a distributor of foreign art films in the South. He also opened in Dallas—where his various companies had their headquarters—the Coronet Theatre, in 1948, which he claimed to be the first art- and foreign-film theatre in the Southwest.

SAFETY FILM. See ACETATE FILM

ST. AUGUSTINE, FLORIDA. See STELLAR PHOTO-PLAY COMPANY

ST. LOUIS MOTION PICTURE COMPANY began in 1913 making Westerns starring George W. "Buck" Conner in "Frontier" brand films for the Universal* program. Gilbert P. Hamilton was the head of the company, and Eugenie Forde and Victoria Forde also appeared in the films. In November 1913, Hamilton and Conner became involved in the newly formed Albuquerque* Motion Picture Company, and by October 1914 O. E. Goebel was president of St. Louis. In January 1915, the "Frontier" brand was replaced by the "Premier" brand, released with the United Film Service*. Its studio at this time was at Santa Paula, outside of Los Angeles. Willis L. Robards and Lillian Hamilton starred in the later productions, which Hal Clements directed and for which his wife Olga Printzlau wrote scenarios.

ST. PAUL, MINNESOTA. See RATHS-SEAVOLT FILM MANUFACTURING COMPANY

THE "SAINT" SERIES. Based on the stories by Leslie Charteris, the "Saint" series featured three leading men in the role of Simon Templar (alias the Saint): Louis Hayward, George Sanders, and Hugh Sinclair. Hayward played the Saint in the first film in the series, *The Saint in New York* (1938), and in the last, *The Saint's Girl Friday* (1954). George Sanders, who is the best-known Saint, played the role in the second through sixth films in the series: *The Saint Strikes Back* (1939), *The Saint in London* (1939), *The Saint's Double Trouble* (1940), *The Saint Takes Over* (1940), and *The Saint in Palm Springs* (1941). Hugh Sinclair played the Saint in two features: *The Saint's Vacation* (1941) and *The Saint Meets the Tiger* (1943). The last was produced by Republic Pictures*. All of the other Saint features were produced by RKO*. The Saint was later played on television by Roger Moore (1967–1969) and by Ian Ogilvy (1978).

BIBLIOGRAPHY

Zinman, David. *Saturday Afternoon at the Bijou.* New Rochelle, N.Y.: Arlington House, 1973.

THE SAMUEL GOLDWYN COMPANY, an independent film and television distributor and producer, founded in 1978 by Samuel Goldwyn, Jr., when his father's estate was settled, began with a library of 52 classic Goldwyn titles and by 1985 had distribution rights to some 500 films. The company's chief involvement is in distribution, with only limited interest in production. In 1985, it financed a four-screen theatre complex in west Los Angeles. The first feature to be distributed by Goldwyn on a first-run theatrical basis was the Dutch film *Spetters* in 1981. It merged with the financially troubled Heritage Entertainment, Inc., on December 6, 1991, and became a public company. On January 31, 1996, it was announced that the company had been acquired by John W. Kluge's Metromedia International Group, Inc., for $115 million. The Samuel Goldwyn Company operated out of the former Goldwyn Studios until their sale in 1982, when it moved to Century City.

Address: 10203 Santa Monica Boulevard, Los Angeles, Calif. 90067.

BIBLIOGRAPHY

Bates, James. "Metromedia To Buy Goldwyn for $115 Million." *Los Angeles Times,* February 1, 1996, pp. D1, D10.
Berkowitz, Stan. "Old Studios Never Die." *Los Angeles,* January 1982, pp. 87–96.
Block, Alex Ben. "No Shareholders." *Forbes,* June 3, 1985, p. 228.
Harmetz, Aljean. "Sam Goldwyn's Little Studio That Could." *The New York Times,* October 18, 1992, pp. 13, 23.

SAMUEL GOLDWYN, INC. Following his ouster by the stockholders of the Goldwyn Pictures Corporation*, Samuel Goldwyn (1882–1974) formed a new production company, of which he had absolute control. Samuel Goldwyn, Inc., was to become synonymous with quality entertainment in the years ahead, as Goldwyn displayed an uncanny knack for placing under contract upcoming film stars, such as Vilma

Banky, Ronald Colman, Gary Cooper, Eddie Cantor, David Niven, and Danny Kaye. His writers were always of the highest calibre, as were his directors, notably William Wyler, whose association with Goldwyn lasted from 1937 to 1946. Goldwyn's one error in judgment was in signing the Russian-born actress Anna Sten and attempting to build her into a major Hollywood star.

The first feature to bear the words "Samuel Goldwyn Presents" was *The Eternal City* (1923), directed by George Fitzmaurice and starring Lionel Barrymore and Barbara LaMarr. Its release led to an action by Goldwyn Pictures Corporation to prevent Goldwyn's use of his name on screen; initially, Goldwyn was required to add "Not now connected with the Goldwyn Pictures Corporation" to his main titles, but by private agreement, in 1924, the qualification was no longer sought.

Goldwyn eventually took over the former Mary Pickford-Douglas Fairbanks Studios at 7200 Santa Monica Boulevard, which had become known by the thirties as the United Artists Studios—Goldwyn was a major stockholder in United Artists*. In 1949, Goldwyn lost a bitter fight with Mary Pickford over control of the studio lot, and it was not until after many years of litigation that Goldwyn was able to purchase the studios for $1,920,000, with the name officially changing to the Goldwyn Studios on April 21, 1955.

Goldwyn's second wife, Frances, was very active in the running of the company with her husband, and on her death, in 1976, the studio was left to the Motion Picture and Television Fund*. Later that same year, the lot was sold to Warner Bros.* for $35 million and renamed the Warner Hollywood Studios.

Following Goldwyn's last feature, *Porgy and Bess,* in 1959, the Goldwyn studios were used as a rental lot. It suffered a number of disastrous fires, beginning with two small ones in 1972. The lot was struck by a $1 million fire in May 1974 and a $3 million fire in December 1975. There was also a much smaller fire in June 1976.

BIBLIOGRAPHY

Berg, A. Scott. *Goldwyn: A Biography.* New York: Alfred A. Knopf, 1989.

Easton, Carol. *The Search for Sam Goldwyn: A Biography.* New York: William Morrow, 1976.

Epstein, Lawrence J. *Samuel Goldwyn.* Boston: Twayne, 1981.

Goldwyn, Samuel. *Behind the Screen.* New York: George H. Doran, 1923.

Griffith, Richard. *Samuel Goldwyn: The Producer and His Films.* New York: Museum of Modern Art, 1956.

Johnston, Alva. *The Great Goldwyn.* New York: Random House, 1937.

Marill, Alvin H. *Samuel Goldwyn Presents.* Cranbury, N.J.: A. S. Barnes, 1976.

Marx, Arthur. *Goldwyn: A Biography of the Man behind the Myth.* New York: W. W. Norton, 1976.

RESOURCES

Papers: Academy of Motion Picture Arts and Sciences.

SAN ANTONIO, TEXAS. See MÉLIÈS MANUFACTURING COMPANY and SUNSET MOTION PICTURE CORPORATION

SAN DIEGO and vicinity was the home to a number of early film companies. In August 1911, director Allan Dwan brought members of the American Film Manufacturing Company* to La Mesa, and filmed there through the summer of 1912. The Essanay Film Manufacturing Company* was also located in La Mesa from January through April 1912, filming a number of "Broncho Billy" Westerns and "Alkali Ike" comedies. In 1911, a group of San Diego businessmen financed the Amex Motion Picture Manufacturing Company, headed by president Charles Oesting. With a studio at the National Bank Building in National City, the company's first production was *The Trail of Guilt,* released on August 28, 1912. On September 24, 1915, the Lubin Manufacturing Company* opened a studio in Coronado, across the bay from San Diego. Also in 1915, the Dudley Motion Picture Manufacturing Company was founded in San Diego. The Pollard Comedy Company had a studio on the grounds of the Panama-California Exposition in Balboa Park, but it was asked to leave by city officials in 1917.

The Exposition was featured in a number of films, notably *Fatty and Mabel at the San Diego Exposition,* starring Roscoe "Fatty" Arbuckle and Mabel Normand, produced by Keystone, and released on January 28, 1915. San Diego's best-known hotel, the Del Coronado, has been seen to advantage in *Some Like It Hot* (1959) and *The Stunt Man* (1980).

SAN FRANCISCO. San Francisco has been featured by name, if not physically, in a number of classic Hollywood features. Perhaps the best known is *San Francisco* (1936), with its title song performed by Jeanette MacDonald. Al Jolson was seen singing at San Francisco's Coffee Dan's in *The Jazz Singer* (1927). *The Maltese Falcon* (1941) is set in San Francisco, with Sam Spade's office located at 111 Sutter Street. Other films with San Francisco locations include *More Pay, Less Work* (1926), *One Way Passage* (1931), *Klondike Annie* (1936), *After the Thin Man* (1936), *Flame of the Barbary Coast* (1945), and *Sudden Fear* (1952).

The first major feature to include scenes actually shot on location in San Francisco was probably *Greed* (1924). As of 1985, major producers with headquarters in San Francisco included John Korty, Francis Ford Coppola with his Zoetrope* Studios, and George Lucas with Lucasfilm* in nearby San Rafael.

BIBLIOGRAPHY

Knowles, Eleanor. "A Late-Movie Buff's Guide to San Francisco." *Passages,* April 1977, pp. 16–17.

SAN MATEO, CALIFORNIA. See LIBERTY MOTION PICTURE COMPANY

SAN RAFAEL, CALIFORNIA. See DOUGLASS NATURAL COLOR FILM COMPANY, LTD., OF SAN RAFAEL, CALIFORNIA

SANTA BARBARA. See AMERICAN FILM MANUFACTURING COMPANY

SANTA BARBARA MOTION PICTURE COMPANY. Dr. Elmer J. Boeske, a prominent Santa Barbara dentist, socialite, polo player, and two-time mayor, organized the Santa Barbara Motion Picture Company in association with other Santa Barbara businessmen. Production commenced on July 29, 1914, with Lorimer Johnston, formerly with American*, as director-general. Johnston brought his best cameraman from American, Roy F. Overbaugh, with him, and Overbaugh, in turn, brought his assistant cameraman, Victor Fleming. Johnston's wife, Caroline Francis Cooke, an actress formerly with Selig*, was the leading lady, while Jack Nelson played opposite her. Jane Scott was the ingenue, Baron Erik von Ritzau was the "heavy," and Harry T. DeVere played character roles. Santa Barbara planned to make four-reel features from well-known novels and plays, with Sawyer* as its initial distributor.

The company's first production, *The Envoy Extraordinary,* was written and directed by Johnston, who left the company soon after, in September 1914. Henry W. Otto, formerly with Selig and American, signed to replace him, but he too left shortly thereafter, to return to American. Cameraman Overbaugh, reminiscing many years later, explained that the reason he and some of the others associated with Santa Barbara left after such short stays was that "the local gentry that put up the money felt that they should be able to get their sons and daughters and wives to play principal parts," and the resulting films were simply no good.

In November 1914, Santa Barbara contracted to release two brands, a comedy and a drama, with the Mica Film Corporation on the Kriterion* program. Aubrey M. Kennedy became the general manager. William Robert Daly directed the dramatic company, headed by Fritzi Brunette, and Bert Angeles directed comedies with Reta Williams. Santa Barbara became the principal producing company for Kriterion, but in June 1915, after the latter's demise, it became part of the Associated Service. Dr. Boeske, at that time, claimed he had lost $25,000 in the year of his ownership.

BIBLIOGRAPHY

"New Producing Company." *The New York Dramatic Mirror,* July 8, 1914, p. 24.

SANTA PAULA, CALIFORNIA. See ST. LOUIS MOTION PICTURE COMPANY

SARATOGA SPRINGS, NEW YORK. See SAWYER, INC.

SAVOY PICTURES ENTERTAINMENT INC. is a production/distribution company, founded in 1992 by former TriStar* and Columbia* executives Victor A. Kaufman and Lewis J. Korman, with financial backing from the investment firm of Allen & Co. The company was criticized for its inability to produce or distribute an adequate number of films, and in its first full year, it lost $12.5 million. The first major success was *Shadowlands* (1993), followed by *Serial Mom* (1994) and *Tales from the Hood* (1994). The company went public in March 1993. In November 1995, it was purchased by Barry Diller's Silver King Communications for $210 million in stock.

Address: 2425 Olympic Boulevard, Santa Monica, Calif. 90404.

BIBLIOGRAPHY

Fabrikant, Geraldine. "Savoy Pictures' High and Low Road." *The New York Times,* January 30, 1995, pp. D1, D8.
Harris, Kathryn. "Savoy's Slim Pickings Annoy Investors." *Los Angeles Times,* August 2, 1994, p. D4.

SAWYER, INC. A. H. Sawyer resigned as the general manager of the Kinemacolor* Company of America and formed Sawyer, Inc., in May 1914, to produce short comedies, no longer than two reels in length, featuring celebrities such as De Wolf Hopper, and to distribute these as well as films from other producers. It used an open-air studio in Asbury Park, New Jersey, and one in Saratoga Springs, New York, and its offices were located at 1600 Broadway, New York. William H. Rudolph was the general manager. Its first big release was the seven-reel feature *The Lightning Conductor,* with Dustin Farnum, directed by William Elliott.

The distribution wing became known as "Sawyer Film Mart," and among the companies releasing through it were the Santa Barbara Motion Picture Company*, the Liberty Motion Picture Company*, Bosburn Photoplay Company, the Canadian Bioscope Company, Esanja Film Company of Detroit, Trans-Oceanic Films, Ltd., the Japanese-American Film Company*, and the Phoenix Film Company. In December 1914, the company increased its capitalization, changed its name to Sawyer Film Corporation, and began a new policy of purchasing negatives outright and financing production companies releasing through it exclusively. It went out of business in March 1915.

BIBLIOGRAPHY

"Sawyer, Inc., Quarters Superb." *The Moving Picture World,* July 11, 1914, pp. 258–59.

SCENTOVISION. See AROMARAMA AND SMELL-O-VISION

SCIENCE FICTION FILMS. A genre that overlaps into the field of the horror film* and that is generally conceded to have been introduced by French filmmaker Georges Méliès (1861–1938), science fiction was of little interest to American silent filmmakers. Universal and the Williamson Brothers produced a 1916 version of Jules Verne's *20,000 Leagues under the Sea,* and, in 1929, M-G-M* eventually released a screen version of Verne's *The Mysterious Island.* Willis O'Brien provided the special effects* for *The Lost World* (1925). One of the most unusual of silent science fiction films was *The Last Man of Earth* (1924), a Fox* feature directed by J. G. Blystone, with Earle Fox in the title role; it takes place after an epidemic of "masculitis" in 1954 has killed off all men over the age of 14.

The first science fiction film from the sound era was *Just Imagine* (1930), one of the few examples of an intentionally funny science fiction subject, with interpolated musical numbers. Also in 1930, Cecil B. DeMille's *Madame Satan* was released; it was not supposed to be funny, but was. In 1933, RKO* released *King Kong,* directed by Merian C. Cooper and Ernest Schoedsack, a classic of the subgenre of monster films that was revived in the fifties with such productions as *The Thing* (1951), *Them!* (1954), *Tarantula* (1956), and *The Fly* (1958). The last was responsible for two sequels, *Return of the Fly* (1959) and *The Curse of the Fly* (1965), and a 1986 remake.

The science fiction genre is very much reminiscent of a comic strip, and nowhere is this more apparent than in the area of serials*, which have frequently utilized science fiction backgrounds. Among the best known of such serials are *The Phantom Empire* (1935), *Flash Gordon* (1936), *Dick Tracy* (1937), *Flash Gordon's Trip to Mars* (1938), *Buck Rogers* (1939), *Flash Gordon Conquers the Universe* (1940), *Captain Midnight* (1942), *Jack Armstrong* (1947), *King of the Rocket Men* (1949), and *Radar Men from the Moon* (1952).

On a more serious level, science fiction films have dramatized the dangers of nuclear war and the evils that the future may hold with the "Planet of the Apes" series* from 20th Century-Fox* and *On the Beach* (1959). Stanley Kubrick presented a lyrical view of the future in *2001: A Space Odyssey* (1968), a tragically comical one in *Dr. Strangelove or How I Learned to Stop Worrying and Love the Bomb* (1964), and a disturbingly violent view in *A Clockwork Orange* (1971).

Novelist Jules Verne's view of a world of science fiction adventure has continued to appeal to filmmakers, notably with *20,000 Leagues under the Sea* (1954), *Journey to the Center of the Earth* (1959), and *Master of the World* (1961).

With his background in puppet films and special effects, George Pal (1908–1980) was a major figure in science fiction films of the fifties and early sixties. Among his productions were *Destination Moon* (1950), *When Worlds Collide* (1951), *War of the Worlds* (1953), *The Conquest of Space* (1955), *The Time Machine* (1960), and *Atlantis the Lost Continent* (1961). A pupil of Pal's who has a consid-

erable cult following is Ray Harryhausen (born 1920), whose films include *The Beast from 20,000 Fathoms* (1953), *Earth vs. the Flying Saucers* (1956), *The 7th Voyage of Sinbad* (1958), and a dozen other films produced in the United Kingdom.

Prior to 1950, science fiction films were relatively juvenile in appeal—a typical example was *Dr. Cyclops* (1940), with Albert Dekker in the title role of a mad scientists miniaturizing a group of American explorers in the Peruvian jungle. *The Day the Earth Stood Still* (1951) heralded a new era for the genre. Director Robert Wise presented a believable story of an alien from outer space who lands in Washington, D.C., to warn the world of the dangers of nuclear war. Thanks to the lead this film showed, even what might have been an immature feature, *Invasion of the Body Snatchers* (1956), became another frighteningly realistic production dealing with visitors from another planet.

In *The Birds* (1963), Alfred Hitchcock presented a typically terrifying view of a world in which birds take their revenge. Miniaturization—a favorite topic with filmmakers—allowed a group of scientists to explore the human body internally in *Fantastic Voyage* (1966). *Logan's Run* (1976) presented a view of a future world in which no one lived beyond the age of 30. Equally disturbing glimpses at the world of the future were offered by *Silent Running* (1972), *Westworld* (1973), *Soylent Green* (1973), and *Rollerball* (1975). However, there was also Woody Allen to provide an amusing one in *Sleeper* (1973).

A new era of special effects in science fiction films was heralded in 1977 by *Star Wars.* The eighties saw the production of science fiction films in which the special effects rather than the actors were the stars, as exemplified by *Altered States* (1980), *The Empire Strikes Back* (1980), *Blade Runner* (1982), *E. T.: The Extra-Terrestrial* (1985), *Robocop* (1986), *Total Recall* (1991), and *Jurassic Park* (1994). Also worthy of mention is *Cocoon* (1986), which introduced a strong element of pathos to the genre, and the series *James Bond, Superman* and *Star Trek.*

BIBLIOGRAPHY

Anderson, Craig W. *Science Fiction Films of the Seventies.* Jefferson, N.C.: McFarland, 1985.
Baxter, John. *Science Fiction in the Cinema.* New York: A. S. Barnes, 1970.
Benson, Michael. *Vintage Science Fiction Films, 1896–1949.* Jefferson, N.C.: McFarland, 1985.
Brosnan, John. *Future Tense.* New York: St. Martin's Press, 1978.
Everman, Welch D. *Cult Science Fiction Films: From The Amazing Colossal Man to Yog—Monster from Space.* Secaucus, N.J.: Citadel Press, 1995.
Hardy, Phil. *Science Fiction.* New York: William Morrow, 1984.
Johnson, William, ed. *Focus on the Science Fiction Film.* Englewood Cliffs, N.J.: Prentice-Hall, 1972.

Landon, Brooks. *The Aesthetics of Ambivalence: Rethinking Science Fiction Film in the Age of Electronic (Re)Production.* Westport, Conn.: Greenwood Press, 1992.

Lentz, Harris M., III. *Science Fiction, Horror & Fantasy Film and Television Credits.* Jefferson, N.C.: McFarland, 1983.

————. *Science Fiction, Horror & Fantasy Film and Television Credits Supplement: Through 1987.* Jefferson, N.C.: McFarland, 1989.

Lucamio, Patrick. *Them or Us: Archetypal Interpretations of Fifties Alien Invasion Films.* Bloomington, Ind.: Indiana University Press, 1987.

Meyers, Richard. *S-F2: A Pictorial History of Science Fiction Films from Rollerball to Return of the Jedi.* Secaucus, N.J.: Citadel Press, 1984.

Parish, James Robert, and Michael R. Pitts. *The Great Science Fiction Pictures.* Metuchen, N.J.: Scarecrow Press, 1977.

————. *The Great Science Fiction Pictures II.* Metuchen, N.J.: Scarecrow Press, 1990.

Searles, Baird. *Films of Science Fiction and Fantasy.* New York: Harry N. Abrams, 1988.

Senn, Bryan, and John Johnson. *Fantastic Cinema Subject Guide: A Topical Index to 2500 Horror, Science Fiction, and Fantasy Films.* Jefferson, N.C.: McFarland, 1992.

Sobchack, Vivian. *Screening Space: The American Science Fiction Film.* New York: Ungar, 1987.

Telotte, J. P. *Replications: A Robotic History of the Science Fiction Film.* Urbana, Ill.: University of Illinois Press, 1995.

Warren, Bill. *Keep Watching the Skies!* Jefferson, N.C.: McFarland, 1982.

Wright, Gene. *The Science Fiction Image.* New York: Facts on File, 1983.

SCOPITONE. See SOUNDIES

SCREEN ACTORS GUILD, with more than 44,000 members, is active in both film and television, negotiating collective bargaining contracts, providing pension and welfare benefits, and regulating relationships between actors and agents. It has taken strike action in 1952–1953, 1955, 1960, and 1980. The organization was founded as a result of poor working conditions for actors and the March 1933 order by film producers that all contract players take a 50 percent cut in salaries and all independent performers take a 20 percent cut. Eighteen actors met to conceive of the notion of a Screen Actors Guild, which was officially incorporated on June 30, 1933. The first president was Ralph Morgan, but he served only briefly in 1933 before yielding office to the better known Eddie Cantor (who served from 1933 to 1935). Since its inception, the Guild has published *The Screen Guild Magazine* (first known as *The Screen Player* 1934–1938, *Official Bulletin of the Screen Actors Guild* (1938–1940), *Screen Actor* (1938–1947), and *Screen Actor* (1959 to present).

Address: 5757 Wilshire Boulevard, Los Angeles, Calif. 90036.

BIBLIOGRAPHY

Screen Actor, "Sixtieth Anniversary Issue," vol. 34, no. 1, March 1995.

SCREEN CLASSICS, INC., was formed in 1918 to release and present features of the highest quality for first-run presentation. Although connected in some manner with Metro*, Screen Classics also handled films made by other producers, with its first two releases being *Revelation,* with Nazimova, and *Lest We Forget,* about the sinking of the *Titanic,* starring a survivor of the tragedy, Rita Jolivet. Later, Screen Classics marketed a series of Nazimova features. Its offices were at 1476 Broadway, New York.

BIBLIOGRAPHY

"Screen Classics Takes Over Metro Specials." *The Moving Picture World,* April 27, 1918, p. 552.

THE SCREEN CLUB began in a Broadway café on Labor Day, 1912, with the "triple purpose of unity, advancement, and preservation of the motion picture art, and composed of those allied in the development of the art," which at its inception meant managers, directors, actors, authors, cameramen, and photoplay newspapermen. Those attending the first meeting were Dell Henderson, Lawrence McGill, Pierce Kingsley, Frank Powell, C. A. "Doc" Willat, Herbert Brenon, William E. Shay, King Baggot, William Camp, Frank Russell, H. C. Judson, George F. Blaisdell, Thomas Malloy, P. C. Carroll, and Calder Johnston. By the fourth meeting, on September 14, 1912, the membership, which required a $20 deposit, had risen to 101.

King Baggot, the first president, was credited with having initiated the idea for the club. John Bunny was the first vice president. The club, which sought "to raise the industry to the highest status of respectability and dignity," and to eliminate existing evils, served also as a social club, holding annual balls and Thanksgiving dinners. The first clubhouse, located at 163 West 45th Street, New York, contained a library, smoking room, music room, dining hall, café, and meeting hall. The clubhouse acquired the following year was a mansion located at 165 West 47th Street. In 1917, the Club was located at 117 West 45th Street. James Kirkwood succeeded Baggot as president in 1914, and other presidents included Billy Quirk and Joseph W. Farnham. In later years, Screen Clubs were established in other cities, including San Francisco, Pittsburgh, and Montreal.

BIBLIOGRAPHY

"Screen Club a Winner." *The Moving Picture World,* September 28, 1912, p. 1283.

"The Screen Club Is a Fact." *The Moving Picture World,* September 21, 1912, p. 1163.

"Screen Club Opens Its Door." *The Moving Picture World,* November 23, 1912, p. 778.

SCREEN DIRECTORS GUILD INCORPORATED. See DIRECTORS GUILD OF AMERICA, INC.

SCREEN DIRECTORS INTERNATIONAL GUILD. See DIRECTORS GUILD OF AMERICA, INC.

SCREEN EXTRAS COALITION. See SCREEN EXTRAS GUILD

SCREEN EXTRAS GUILD (SEG) was formed in 1945 as a breakaway from the Screen Actors Guild (SAG)*. It acts as a negotiating agent with producers regarding appropriate pay for extras, although it was never able to operate a closed-shop situation as far as the hiring of extras was concerned. It helped to increase the wage scales for extras; in 1959, a general extra could earn $22.05 for an eight-hour day and a dress extra (one who could provide a suitable wardrobe) could earn $29.04, an increase from $15.56 a day in 1950. By 1965 the daily wage for an extra was $27.31, and by 1976 the average daily wage was $47.50. Through the years, extras who are members of the Guild have included famous stuntman Richard Talmadge and former silent star Franklin Farnum (who was the Guild's president from 1956 to 1959). In 1992, the extras rejoined the Screen Actors Guild.

SCREEN PRODUCERS GUILD. See PRODUCERS GUILD OF AMERICA, INC.

SCREEN PUBLICISTS GUILD. See PUBLICISTS GUILD OF AMERICA

SCREEN WRITERS GUILD. See WRITERS GUILD OF AMERICA

SCREWBALL COMEDY. There is no agreement as to exactly what constitutes a screwball comedy. The term is used, basically, to describe a type of comedy that includes whimsy or the more pleasant aspects of insanity. It is the genre of "daffy" comedies in which the heroes and heroines are "wacky." It emerged from the American Depression in the mid-thirties and had its origins, frequently, in stage comedies, particularly those of Philip Barry. The best-known directors associated with screwball comedies are Frank Capra, Leo McCarey, and Preston Sturges, and its better-known stars are Cary Grant and Carole Lombard. Screwball comedies include *My Man Godfrey* (1936), *The Awful Truth* (1937), *Nothing Sacred* (1937), *Bringing Up Baby* (1938), *Holiday* (1938), *You Can't Take It with You* (1938), and *The Lady Eve* (1941). *The Thin Man* series, starring William Powell and Myrna Loy, is a blend of thriller and screwball comedy. The genre lost its popularity in the forties but has been revived with features such as Peter Bogdanovich's *What's Up Doc?* (1972).

BIBLIOGRAPHY

Byrge, Duane. *The Screwball Comedy Films: A History and Filmography, 1934–1942.* Jefferson, N.C.: McFarland, 1991.

Cavell, Stanley. *Pursuits of Happiness.* Cambridge, Mass.: Harvard University Press, 1981.

Gehring, Wes D. *Screwball Comedy: A Genre of Madcap Romance.* Westport, Conn.: Greenwood Press, 1986.

Sarris, Andrew. "The Sex Comedy without Sex." *American Film,* March 1978, pp. 8–15.

Sennett, Ted. *Lunatics and Lovers.* New Rochelle, N.Y.: Arlington House, 1973.

Sikov, Ed. *Screwball: Hollywood's Madcap Romantic Comedies.* New York: Crown, 1989.

SCRIPT DOCTOR is the name given to a writer who helps to "polish," rewrite, or make a screenplay produceable after the original writer or writers are finished with it. Script doctors, who generally are anonymous and do not receive screen credit, can contribute as little as a few lines or as much as many new scenes to a film, and have been part of the film industry since the twenties.

BIBLIOGRAPHY

Corliss, Richard. "Miracle Surgery." *Times,* July 25, 1994, pp. 60, 62.

"SEE AMERICA FIRST." See KINEMACOLOR COMPANY OF AMERICA

SELECT FILM BOOKING AGENCY was created early in 1915 by the Famous Players Film Company to exploit and distribute its prestigious film *The Eternal City* and other films that were too long or expensive to be released as program pictures. Select aligned important legitimate and motion picture theatres throughout the country to present its elaborate features, at the minimum admission price of 25 cents, for indefinite engagements to be determined by each film's popularity. Adolph Zukor, in announcing the formation of Select, stated that its operation would put motion pictures "on the plane of legitimate theatrical offerings of the most serious type. The adoption of this policy will greatly dignify the public aspects of the trade, as it will now assume every iota of systemization associated with the business methods of the theater." *The Eternal City* opened at Philadelphia's Chestnut Street Opera House. Although Select announced it was ready to release any producer's feature, if it was distinctive enough to warrant its elaborate exploitation, it refused to consider *The Birth of a Nation,* presumably because it was thought that its subject matter would demean the presumably more pristine *The Eternal City.*

BIBLIOGRAPHY

"First Move for Higher Prices." *The Moving Picture World,* February 13, 1915, p. 966.

"Select Film Booking Agency." *The Moving Picture World,* March 20, 1915, p. 1744.

SELECTO FILM COMPANY, INC., was founded in Los Angeles by Richard Wallace (1894–1951) to produce one-reel comedies; it was unsuccessful and abandoned in April 1916.

SELECT PICTURES CORPORATION. See LEWIS J. SELZNICK PRODUCTIONS, INC.

SELIG POLYSCOPE COMPANY. William N. Selig (1864–1948), formerly a traveling magician and minstrel show operator, known as the Colonel, formed one of the earliest motion picture companies on April 9, 1896, at 43 Peck Court (later Eighth Street) in Chicago, when he and a partner developed a projector called the Polyscope and a camera, both modeled on drawings of the Lumière camera-projector. First called the Mutoscope & Film Co., the company's name changed after a year to W. N. Selig Co., and finally, six months later, to the Selig Polyscope Company. Selig's first films were slapstick comedies less than 50 feet in length. To avoid the patent suits of the Edison Company*, Selig shot travel films in the Southwest during the first years of the company's operations. In April and May 1901, Selig made films for Armour and Company, of the Chicago stockyards, to document the operations of its slaughterhouse and meat-packing plant. Selig later claimed that this was the first time that motion pictures had been taken by artificial light. In the spring of 1904, Selig produced what he called his "really first" picture, the 700-foot comedy *Humpty Dumpty.* Also in 1904, G. M. Anderson, who was later to found the Essanay Company*, convinced Selig to let him produce Westerns* in western settings.

When Edison brought Selig to court, Philip D. Armour provided free legal representation to Selig, during 1905–1907, in return for prints of the films Selig had previously made, to be used for public relations purposes, because at that time Armour suffered from the attack made on the meat industry by Upton Sinclair in *The Jungle.* Selig joined with Edison and the other trust companies to form the Motion Picture Patents Company* and released its films through the General Film Company.

In September 1907, Selig moved into a new plant at Irving Park Road and Western Avenue, where Thomas S. Nash, who had been with the company since 1907 as an electrician and cameraman, became the general superintendent. Former stage director Francis Boggs was sent west to direct for Selig (in 1911, he was murdered in the Selig Edendale studio by a Japanese gardener). Boggs and his company, which included Thomas Santschi, James L. McGee, James Crosby, Harry Todd, Gene Ward, and Mrs. Boggs, went to California, where, in the early spring of 1908, they shot some scenes for *The Count of Monte Cristo,* thus claiming to be the first motion picture company to shoot a narrative film in the Los Angeles area. By 1909, Boggs had established a permanent company in the West, and he wrote and directed what is claimed to be the first film made completely in Los Angeles, *The Heart of a Race Tout.* The Selig studio in Edendale, on Allesandro Street, constructed in 1909–1910, was managed by James L. McGee. At this time, Otis Turner wrote and directed the films produced at the Chicago plant.

Selig's first release of 1,000 feet in length was *The Female Highwayman,* made in the fall of 1906. Selig's two-reel *Damon and Pythias,* released in June 1908, may have been the first film of that length produced in the United States. Its *The Coming of Columbus,* made in the fall of 1911 and released May 1912, was claimed to be the first three-reel picture filmed in America. *The Two Orphans* and *Cinderella,* each three-reelers, were produced soon after.

Selig's *Hunting Big Game in Africa,* shot at its Chicago studio with its own animals and released in May 1909, was an early animal picture, which recreated ex-President Theodore Roosevelt's hunting expedition at the time, and enjoyed great success. In 1911, the Selig Jungle Zoo, located opposite Eastlake Park on Mission Road in Los Angeles, was started with a nucleus of animals owned by showman Big Otto, which had been featured in Selig films shot in Jacksonville, Florida. The zoo grew to be the largest collection of wild animals in the world, containing, in 1915, 700 animals and birds on its 32 acres. A Glendale studio opened later, and there Tom Mix directed and starred in Westerns. Thomas A. Persons was the supervisor of all of Selig's Western studios.

On December 29, 1913, Selig released the first episode of what is considered to be the first true motion picture serial*, *The Adventures of Kathlyn,* starring Kathlyn Williams. In 1914, the company produced *The Spoilers,* the first screen version of the popular Rex Beach novel.

Selig, along with Vitagraph*, Lubin*, and Essanay*, formed V-L-S-E* in April 1915 to distribute its features. In the next year, the distribution group, K-E-S-E, with Kleine* and Edison replacing Vitagraph and Lubin, was formed to continue distributing features. The Selig Company stopped production in 1918, although Colonel Selig continued to be involved in various film activities through the thirties.

Directors who worked for Selig include Colin Campbell, Tom Mix, Lawrence Marston, Thomas Santschi, George Nicholls, Lloyd Carleton, Marshall Neilan, Jack Le Saint, and Frank Beal. Players include Kathlyn Williams, Thomas Santschi, Tom Mix, Wheeler Oakman, Charles Clary, Hobart Bosworth, Betty Harte, William V. Mong, Al Garcia, Herbert Rawlinson, Bessie Eyton, Nick Cogley, Baby Lilian Wade, Myrtle Stedman, Eugenie Besserer, and Harold Lockwood.

BIBLIOGRAPHY

Blaisdell, George. "Great Selig Enterprise." *The Moving Picture World,* July 10, 1915, pp. 227–28.

Bosworth, Hobart. "The Picture Forty-Niners." *Photoplay,* December 1915, pp. 75–81.

Edwards, Leo. "An Afternoon at the Selig Studio." *Feature Movie Magazine,* April 15, 1915, pp. 34–39, 56–57.

Lahue, Kalton C. *Motion Picture Pioneer: The Selig Polyscope Company.* South Brunswick, N.J.: A. S. Barnes, 1973.

"Making Selig Pictures." *The Film Index,* November 20, 1909, pp. 4–6.

"The Selig at Edendale." *The Moving Picture World,* July 10, 1915, p. 230.

"Twenty-One Years in the Business." *The Moving Picture World,* May 12, 1917, pp. 948–49.

RESOURCES

Papers: Academy of Motion Picture Arts and Sciences.
Photographs: Academy of Motion Picture Arts and Sciences.

SELZNICK INTERNATIONAL PICTURES was formed as an independent production company by David O. Selznick (1902–1965) in 1935. The company set up office at what became the Laird International Studios* in Culver City, utilizing the colonial front of the studios as a trademark. The first film to be produced by the new organization was *Little Lord Fauntleroy* (1936), directed by John Cromwell and starring Dolores Costello and Freddie Bartholomew. It was released by United Artists*, as were the following Selznick International films: *The Garden of Allah* (1936), *A Star Is Born* (1937), *The Prisoner of Zenda* (1937), *Nothing Sacred* (1937), *The Adventures of Tom Sawyer* (1938), *The Young in Heart* (1938), *Made for Each Other* (1939), *Intermezzo* (1939), and *Rebecca* (1940). The best known of all Selznick International Pictures, *Gone with the Wind* (1939), was released by M-G-M*.

Following a legal dispute with United Artists in 1946, Selznick set up his own distribution company, Selznick Releasing Organization (SRO), through which he released his final independent productions: *Duel in the Sun* (1947), *The Paradise Case* (1948), and *Portrait of Jennie* (1949). Prior to a protracted European trip, Selznick closed down his production company in 1949. With the exception of *Gone with the Wind,* the rights to all the Selznick independent productions were eventually acquired by ABC Television.

BIBLIOGRAPHY

Behlmer, Rudy, ed. *Memo from David O. Selznick.* New York: Viking Press, 1972.

Haver, Ronald. *David O. Selznick's Hollywood.* New York: Alfred A. Knopf, 1980.

Leff, Leonard J. *Hitchcock and Selznick: The Rich and Strange Collaboration of Alfred Hitchcock and David O. Selznick in Hollywood.* New York: Weidenfeld & Nicolson, 1987.

Thomson, David. *Showman: The Life of David O. Selznick.* New York: Alfred A. Knopf, 1992.

RESOURCES

Films: University of Texas at Austin (Selznick's personal prints); Museum of Modern Art (35mm preservation).
Papers: University of Texas at Austin.

SELZNICK INTERNATIONAL STUDIOS. See LAIRD INTERNATIONAL STUDIOS

SELZNICK PICTURES CORPORATION. See LEWIS J. SELZNICK PRODUCTIONS, INC.

SELZNICK RELEASING CORPORATION. See SELZNICK INTERNATIONAL PICTURES

SENSURROUND is the trademark of a special effects* system developed by Universal Pictures* in 1974, initially to enhance the tremor sequences in *Earthquake.* The system is one that adds air vibrations (low frequency signals) to the soundtrack of a film during the dubbing process. Special equipment installed in theatres decodes the signals on the soundtrack, triggering a series of audible and sub-audible effects, and the vibration of air movement against the bodies and ears of the audience creates the illusion of participating in an event such as an earthquake. Since its introduction, Universal has considerably enhanced the system, and its potential has been realized in features such as *Midway* (1976), *Rollercoaster* (1977), and *Battlestar Galactica* (1979). By 1981, more than 700 theatres had been equipped with the special decoding units, amplifiers, and speakers necessary to reproduce the effect of Sensurround, but Universal appears to have no plans for continued use of the system.

BIBLIOGRAPHY

Leonard, Robert. "Recording *Rollercoaster* Sound in Sensurround." *American Cinematographer,* June 1977, pp. 648–49.

SERIAL FILM COMPANY. William Steiner was the supervising director and the head of the Serial Film Company, formed in 1916. Its studio was in Cliffside, New Jersey, and its first production was the serial *The Yellow Menace,* which was released by the Unity Sales Corporation*. Following this, the company made a series of two-reel comedy-dramas about amateur detective Philo Gubb, which was filmed in Jacksonville, Florida. Serial also produced a seven-reel feature directed by Pierce Kingsley.

SERIALS. A genre almost exclusively limited to the United States and France, serials were produced from 1912 to 1956. They were generally cheaply made with shoddy production values, but they enjoyed an appeal that has continued long after the last serial was released. Divided into chapters, serials were intended to hold the interest of their audiences from one week's release through the next. Thus, the concept of ending a chapter, or an episode, with a "cliff-hanger" was conceived. Some serials were comprised of self-contained weekly episodes, and these are more correctly identified as serials.

The first serial, which was actually a series, was *What Happened to Mary?,* starring Mary Fuller and released by the Edison Company* in 1912. As with many silent serials, it was produced in association with a popular magazine—in this case McClure's *Ladies World*—which published the story concurrently with the serial's release. The first true serial was *The Adventures of Kathlyn,* directed by F. J. Grandon, starring Kathlyn Williams, and produced by the Selig Polyscope Company* for release from 1913 to 1914. *The Adventures of Kathlyn* was released in 13 episodes; during the silent era there was no uniformity as to the number of episodes to a serial. *The Hazards of Helen,* which the Kalem Company* produced for release from 1914 to 1916, had two leading ladies, first Helen Holmes and later Helen Gibson, and was 119 episodes long. (However, it was not a cliff-hanger serial.) With the coming of sound, serials were limited to either 12 or 15 episodes. The length of each episode could vary from one to two reels during the silent era, but with the coming of sound it was usual for the first episode to be three reels in length and the remainder to comprise two reels each.

Silent serial stars were usually women. The best known was Pearl White (1889–1938), whose serials included *The Perils of Pauline* (1914), *The Exploits of Elaine* (1915), *The Fatal Ring* (1917), and *Plunder* (1923). Second in popularity to Pearl White was Ruth Roland (1892–1937), whose serials included *The Red Circle* (1915), *Hands Up!* (1918), and *The Adventures of Ruth* (1919). Other silent "serial queens" included Allene Ray, Mollie King, Marie Walcamp, Arline Pretty, and Grace Darmond. The best known of male serial stars were Eddie Polo, Ben Wilson, Harry Houdini, Elmo Lincoln, Joe Bonomo, and William Desmond.

Just as Pathé was the leading producer of silent serials so was Republic Pictures* during the sound era. As with the silent era, the serials were intended largely for a juvenile audience—for screenings at Saturday afternoon matinees—and plot lines were suitably ludicrous, with no subtle shading in the depiction of heroism and villainy.

Men were more prominent than women in sound serials, with the best-known heroes of the genre having been Reed Howes, Tom Tyler, Johnny Mack Brown, Larry "Buster" Crabbe, Ray "Crash" Corrigan, and Buck Jones. The sound serial also became a refuge for the former silent stars, such as Jack Mulhall. Frequently, their producers would turn to comic-strip heroes, such as Superman or Flash Gordon, for inspiration.

Republic made its last serial in 1955, and the honor of producing the final American serial went to Columbia Pictures* for *Blazing the Overland Trail,* released in the summer of 1956. It was directed by Spencer Gordon Bennet, the best-known name in serial direction.

BIBLIOGRAPHY

Barbour, Alan G. *Days of Thrills and Adventure.* New York: Macmillan, 1970.
———. *Cliffhanger.* New York: A & W, 1977.
Cline, William C. *In the Nick of Time.* Jefferson, N.C.: McFarland, 1984.
———. *Serials-ly Speaking: Essays on Cliffhangers.* Jefferson, N.C.: McFarland, 1994.
Harmon, Jim. *Radio Mystery and Adventure: And Its Appearances in Film, Television, and Other Media.* Jefferson, N.C.: McFarland, 1992.
Harmon, Jim, and Donald F. Glut. *The Great Movie Serials.* Garden City, N.Y.: Doubleday, 1972.
Hayes, R. H. *The Republic Chapterplays: A Complete Filmography of the Serials Released by Republic Pictures Corporation, 1934–1955.* Jefferson, N.C.: McFarland, 1991.
Lahue, Kalton C. *Continued Next Week: A History of the Moving Picture Serial.* Norman, Okla.: University of Oklahoma Press, 1964.
Landrum, Larry N., and John Nachbar. "The Serials: A Selected Checklist of Published Materials." *Journal of Popular Film* 3, 3 (Summer 1974): pp. 273–276.
Rainey, Buck. *Those Fabulous Serial Heroines: Their Lives and Films.* Metuchen, N.J.: Scarecrow Press, 1990.
Schutz, Wayne. *The Motion Picture Serial: An Annotated Bibliography.* Metuchen, N.J.: Scarecrow Press, 1992.
Stedman, Raymond William. *The Serials.* Norman, Okla.: University of Oklahoma Press, 1971.
Weiss, Ken, and Ed Goodgold. *To Be Continued.* New York: Crown, 1972.
Whitney, William. *In a Door, into a Fight, out a Door, into a Chase: Moviemaking Remembered by the Guy at the Door.* Jefferson, N.C.: McFarland, 1996.

SEVEN ARTS PRODUCTIONS, LTD. See WARNER BROS. PICTURES, INC.

70mm. The widest film gauge in general use and double the size of the standard 35mm* film gauge, 70mm film currently is used for printing only. It is the basis for most widescreen systems and dates back to the twenties. The film was actually shot on 65mm and printed on 70mm, with the additional 5mm being utilized for the soundtracks (generally six multitrack stereophonic). Special projectors are needed to screen 70mm film and, as of 1985, there were some 600 theatres in the United States so equipped. In 1963, a system was introduced whereby 35mm films could be blown up to 70mm for exhibition, and since then, fewer than 30 features have been shot in 70mm as opposed to more than 230 shot in 35mm and blown up to 70mm.

BIBLIOGRAPHY

Belton, John. *Widescreen Cinema*. Cambridge, Mass.: Harvard University Press, 1992.

SHERMAN GRINBERG FILM LIBRARIES, INC., the best-known stock shot library in the United States, was founded by Grinberg (1928–1982) in 1957, moving to its present Hollywood location in 1965. Suppliers of film footage to all types of film and video productions, the Sherman Grinberg Film Libraries include the Pathé* and Paramount* newsreel collections, and, in the past, Grinberg has represented the stock footage libraries of 20th Century-Fox*, M-G-M*, and ABC network news (for which it first served as sole representative beginning in 1963). Grinberg became involved in the film industry in 1950, when he joined 20th Century-Fox as an accountant. His first involvement with stock footage came when he persuaded Darryl F. Zanuck to accept his plan for the marketing of 20th Century-Fox's stock footage. With David Wolper, Grinberg produced the 1961 television series *Biography,* and his other documentary television series included *Greatest Headlines of the Century* (1960), *Sportfolio* (1961), *Battleline* (1964), *Survival* (1965), and the specials *Bogart* (1969) and *Hollywood: The Selznick Years* (1969).

Address: 1040 North McCadden Place, Hollywood, Calif. 90038; 630 Ninth Avenue, New York, N.Y. 10036.

SHERPIX was founded by Louis K. Sher, president of the Art Theatre Guild Circuit (established in 1954) in the summer of 1965 to distribute theatrical features of an adult or pornographic nature. The New York-based company quickly became known as America's leading distributor of better class pornographic subjects, such as *A History of the Blue Movie* (1970), *Adultery for Fun and Profit* (1971), *Meat Rack* (1971), *The Stewardesses* (1969), *Mona* (1970), and *The Nurses* (1972). The company also distributed Alex De Renzy's marijuana documentary, *Weed* (1972); a British lowbrow comedy, *On the Buses* (1972); Arch Oboler's 3-D feature, *The Bubble* (1966); and Andy Warhol's *Lonesome Cowboys* (1968) and *Flesh* (1969). Following Sher's conviction on obscenity charges, in Washington, D.C., in the winter of 1973—charges that were eventually dismissed on appeal in August 1975—Sherpix ceased operations on March 1, 1974.

BIBLIOGRAPHY

MacDonough, Scott. "The Story of Sherpix: Soft-Core, Hard-Core, Encore." *Show,* vol. 2, no. 5, July 1971, pp. 18–21.
Verrill, Addison. "Sherpix, Top Nat'l Distrib of Hardcore Pix, Shutting March 1, Will Keep Theatres." *Daily Variety,* January 16, 1974, pp. 1, 19.
———. "Shiffrin Heir to 'Milder' Sherpix." *Variety,* February 20, 1974, p. 5.

SHERWOOD FOREST and LAKE SHERWOOD, located north of Los Angeles, have been utilized for location filming of *Tarzan, the Ape Man* (1932), *The Charge of the Light Brigade* (1936), *Way Out West* (1937), *Gunga Din* (1939), *Tell Them Willie Boy Is Here* (1970), among many other productions. Appropriately, Sherwood Forest was used for filming both *Robin Hood* (1922) and *The Adventures of Robin Hood* (1938).

SHORTS AND FEATURES. There is no definite ruling as to what constitutes a short film and what a feature-length production. Prior to 1910, all American films were short subjects, but many were featured on a theatre program. Arguably the first American feature-length film was Vitagraph's *The Life of Moses,* released late 1909 and early 1910 in five self-contained reels. Vitagraph* intended that each reel be screened as a separate entity, but many exhibitors chose to show the five reels together at one presentation.

Among the earliest of American feature-length films were *Oliver Twist* (1912), *From the Manger to the Cross* (1912, an American production filmed on location in Palestine), *In the Bishop's Carriage* (1913), *The Count of Monte Cristo* (1913), and *Traffic in Souls* (1913). Cecil B. DeMille's *The Squaw Man* (1914), which was codirected with Oscar Apfel, is often cited as the first feature-length film to be shot in Hollywood. This is not true, although it is certainly the first major feature-length production to come out of Los Angeles.

The Academy of Motion Picture Arts and Sciences defines any film not more than 30 minutes in running time to be a short subject. The British Board of Trade defines any film running less than 40 minutes to be a short subject. Because it is difficult to conceive of a film under one hour in length being a feature, the term "featurette" has been coined to describe films that are too long to be shorts and too short to be features.

SHOWSCAN, developed by special effects expert Douglas Trumbull in the late seventies and early eighties, is a revolutionary process that offers the viewer enhanced clarity and dramatic realism with a sensation of three-dimensionality. It involves the shooting of films in 70mm* and their projection at 60 frames per second, as opposed to the normal rate of 24 frames per second. Showscan also requires the use of a special projection system. It has yet to be used for any commercial feature film.

Address: Showscan Entertainment, 3939 Landmark Street, Culver City, Calif. 90232.

SHUBERT FILM CORPORATION. See WORLD FILM CORPORATION

SID OLCOTT INTERNATIONAL FEATURES. Sidney Olcott (1872–1949), formerly the director of the Gene Gauntier Feature Players Company, formed his own company in January 1914 to release his "Sidfilms" through Warner's Features. With Valentine Grant as his leading lady, Olcott shot three-reel features in Jacksonville, Florida, until June 1914 and then went to Ireland to shoot. Fred C. "Wid" Gunning, who later founded the trade journal *The Film Daily,* was Olcott's assistant director.

BIBLIOGRAPHY

"New Picture Making Company." *The Moving Picture World,* January 10, 1914, p. 181.

SIGMA III. See ORION PICTURES CORPORATION

SIGNAL FILM COMPANY was formed in October 1915 to produce at the old Western Lubin* studio at 4560 Pasadena Avenue, Pasadena. It produced railroad serials featuring Helen Holmes and nonrailroad dramas, such as the five-reel *The Diamond Runner,* filmed in Honolulu. J. P. McGowan directed the serials and J. Murdock McQuarrie directed the features. S. S. Hutchinson, the president of Signal, was also the president of the American Film Manufacturing Company*. Signal's films were released by the Mutual Film Corporation*, and the company disbanded late in 1917.

SILLY SYMPHONIES was a term coined by Walt Disney Productions* to refer to short subjects that combined animation and music in perfect unison, but that did not feature continuing characters (such as Mickey Mouse). The term was first used to describe *Skeleton Dance* in 1928. The first Silly Symphony to be filmed in color, and also the first Disney-animated cartoon shot in Technicolor*, was *Flowers and Trees* (1932). After 1939, Disney did not use the term Silly Symphonies on his cartoons.

BIBLIOGRAPHY

Geis, Darlene, ed. *Walt Disney's Treasury of Silly Symphonies.* New York: Harry N. Abrams, 1981.
Maltin, Leonard. *The Disney Films.* New York: Hyperion, 1995.

SILVER SCREEN LIMITED PARTNERSHIPS was organized by E. F. Hutton & Co. to obtain public investment in feature-film production, and was first associated with Home Box Office, Inc., in 1983. The first offering raised $83 million. Beginning with Silver Screen Partners II, which raised $193 million, subsequent offerings were associated with Walt Disney Productions*. In 1991, Silver Screen Partners IV completed its $600 million investment obligations to Disney.

SIRITZKY INTERNATIONAL PICTURES, INC., was founded in October 1945 by Sam and Joe Siritzky, who ran the Squire, Majestic, and Ambassador theatres in New York. It distributed French films in the United States, including, for the first time, Marcel Pagnol's Marseilles trilogy, and Maurice

Tourneur's *Volopone* (1938). Italian films were added in 1949. In April 1950, Films International of America acquired U.S. distribution rights to all of Siritzky's 26 films.

16mm. The Eastman Kodak* company introduced 16mm film in 1923 as a film gauge for amateur moviemaking. By the thirties, 16mm was used as an audiovisual aid in educational institutions, churches, hospitals, and prisons. Following their theatrical release, most feature films were released nontheatrically in 16mm. Silent 16mm film has perforations at both edges, while 16mm sound film has only one row of perforations, with the soundtrack printed on the other edge of the film. For bulk printing, 32mm film stock is usually utilized, with the film being slit in two to create two rolls of 16mm film.

Up until fairly recent times, 16mm was not considered suitable for projection before a large audience, although it was utilized for professional filmmaking from the thirties onward, usually in the fields of documentary, educational, instructional, sponsored, and industrial films. Some feature films were shot in 16mm and then blown up to 35mm*. In 1971, a new 16mm frame size, Super 16mm, was introduced, which made available 40 percent more picture image for blow up to the 35mm aspect ratio of 1.75:1. The first feature-length entertainment film to be shot in 16mm is generally considered to have been *Sundown Riders,* filmed in Kodachrome in 1944, by Major 16mm Productions. The film was directed and written by Lambert Hillyer, photographed by Alan Stensvold, and featured Russell Wade, Jay Kirby, and Andy Clyde.

The major 16mm film libraries include Ideal (founded in the 1920s), Films Inc. (founded 1935), Castle Films (founded 1924), Brandon Films (founded 1940), Audio Film Center (founded 1951), Blackhawk Films (founded 1939), Roa's Films (founded 1926), Pyramid Films (founded 1960), Budget Films (founded 1950), Festival Films (founded 1975), and Kit Parker Films (founded 1971).

BIBLIOGRAPHY

Happé, L. Bernard. *Basic Motion Picture Technology.* New York: Hastings House, 1975.
Kruse, William F. "The Feature Film in 16mm." *Film News,* September 1966, pp. 6–7.
Offenhauser, William H., Jr. *16mm Sound Motion Pictures.* New York: Interscience, 1949.
Provisor, Henry. *8mm/16mm Movie-Making.* New York: Amphoto, 1970.
Trojan, Judith, and Nadine Covert, comp. *16mm Distribution.* New York: Educational Film Library Association, 1977.

SKOURAS PICTURES was founded in 1983 by Dimitri Skouras as a distributor of low-budget, quality productions, such as the Swedish *My Life As a Dog* (1987).

Address: 335 North Maple Drive, Suite 248, Beverly Hills, Calif. 90210.

SLAPSTICK COMEDY. Slapstick, also known as "low" or knockabout, comedy is a comic form that ridicules authority or dignity through physical humor involving, in its most basic form, a custard pie* in the face or a slip on a banana peel.* The origins of American slapstick film comedy lie in turn-of-the-century European film comedy and in music hall or vaudeville humor. The greatest name in American slapstick comedy was Mack Sennett (1880–1960), whose Keystone* comedies contained all of the elements common to slapstick humor. In his classic piece on "Comedy's Greatest Era" (published in *Life,* September 3, 1949), critic James Agee wrote, "Mack Sennett made two kinds of comedy: parody laced with slapstick, and plain slapstick. The parodies were the unceremonious burial of a century of hamming. . . . The plain slapstick, at its best, was even better: a profusion of hearty young women in disconcerting bathing suits, frisking around with a gaggle of insanely incompetent policemen and of equally certifiable male civilians sporting museum-piece mustaches. All these people zipped and caromed about the pristine world of the screen as jazzily as a convention of water bugs."

The physical humor of slapstick comedy was best suited to the early years of the silent motion picture. It did not easily make a transition to sound films, although a 1935 Warner Bros.* short, *Keystone Hotel,* successfully gathered together all of the elements of a good slapstick comedy. The slapstick tradition continued in such television series as *Laugh-In* (1979) and Stanley Kramer's *It's a Mad Mad Mad Mad World* (1963). The word slapstick originated in the nineteenth century, and comes from the fastening together of two flat pieces of wood that when used by one comic to hit another created a lot of noise but no physical damage.

BIBLIOGRAPHY

Lahue, Kalton C., and Terry Brewer. *Kops and Custards: The Legend of Keystone Films.* Norman, Okla.: University of Oklahoma Press, 1967.

S.-L. PICTURES CORPORATION. Arthur H. Sawyer and Herbert Lubin, previously involved together in General Enterprises, Inc., formed S.-L. Pictures Corporation late in 1918 as both a producer and distributor. S.-L. released the films of Ralph Ince Film Attractions, and its first such release was *Virtuous Men,* directed by Ince.

BIBLIOGRAPHY

"New Combination Outline Project." *The Moving Picture World,* November 16, 1918, p. 746.

THE SMALL AGENCY. See EDWARD SMALL PRODUCTIONS, INC.

SMALL-LANDAU AGENCY. See EDWARD SMALL PRODUCTIONS, INC.

SMALLWOOD FILM CORPORATION. Arthur N. Smallwood was the president and general manager of the Smallwood Film Corporation, which in 1913 absorbed the U.S. Film Corporation, with which Smallwood had been associated since 1908. The U.S. Film Corporation began operations in Cincinnati and made Westerns*. Later, it opened an office in New York and specialized in industrial, advertising, and educational films. After Smallwood's takeover, the U.S. Film Corporation began making dramatic films for release through Warner's Features. It led an intermittent existence during 1914, opening and closing several times. Finally, J. Arthur Nelson, U.S. Film's vice president and head of the Nelson Film Company, was arrested early in 1915 for misappropriation of stockholders' funds.

As far as can be ascertained, it was this same Smallwood Film Corporation with which Ray Smallwood became involved in 1914, producing, directing, photographing, and editing one-reel films featuring his wife Ethel Grandin. The brand name "Grandin Films" was incorporated as Grandin Films, Inc., early in 1915. In the beginning, Smallwood worked without studio facilities, using a newly developed portable lighting system that could be set up in any room. In April 1915, it used a studio in Cliffside, New Jersey, where society and psychological dramas starring Edwin August and Ruth Blair were produced. L. B. "Pop" Hoadly was in charge of the scenario department, and A. R. Mariner was the technical director. When United Film Service* replaced Warner's Features, Smallwood released through the new organization.

SMELL-O-VISION. See AROMARAMA AND SMELL-O-VISION

SNUFF FILMS. Rumors of the existence of "snuff films," in which an individual, usually female, is killed and mutilated on camera, have routinely circulated since the sixties, despite a report in the September 1984 edition of *Playboy* that the New York Police Department is "not aware of any authentic snuff films in the U.S. . . . at any time." Such rumors reached their peak in October 1975, when it was reported that private screenings of a snuff film were taking place in New York, with admission tickets selling at $200 apiece. The object of this gossip turned out to be an 82-minute feature titled *Snuff.*

The film, featuring a Charles Manson-like character and obviously influenced by contemporary "slasher" productions, opens with two women on motorbikes capturing a third. It concludes with the script girl on the set, telling the director how much she admires his work; she is invited to have sex with him on camera and then cut apart. "This scene is well presented and alone justifies all the shouting," reported the trade paper, *Boxoffice* (April 19, 1976). When *Snuff* opened at New York's National Theatre on February 17, 1976, there was such a public outcry that the New York District Attorney was forced to investigate. That investigation revealed that the film was, in the words of *Playboy* critic Bruce Williamson

(June 1976), a "dreary trifling hoax." *Snuff* was, in reality, a 1970 film, *The Slaughter,* shot in South America, at a cost of $33,000, by Roberta and Michael Findlay. The final four-minute killing segment was filmed in New York by Allan Shackleton. The Findlays claimed to know nothing of what had happened to their film until the release of *Snuff,* and worked out a financial settlement with Shackleton.

Snuff was distributed by Shackleton's Monarch Releasing Corporation, which advertised in *Boxoffice* (November 10, 1975), "The film that could only be made in South America . . . Where life is cheap." To which *Hustler* (July 1976) responded, "Not only is life cheap in South America, but apparently so is talent." *Snuff* received its world premiere at the Uptown Theatre, Indianapolis, on January 16, 1976, before an audience of fewer than two dozen and primarily consisting of the media and police officers. The Los Angeles premiere took place at Mann's Hollywood Theatre on March 17, 1976.

Snuff films have figured prominently in at least two mystery novels, Joseph Wambaugh's *The Glitter Dome* (William Morrow, 1981) and Richard Nehrbass's *A Perfect Death* (HarperCollins, 1991). The subject is also central to Gregory Mcdonald's novel, *The Brave* (Barricade Books, 1991), which chronicles the last days of Rafael Brown, an impoverished slum dweller with a wife and two children, after he has agreed to "star" in a snuff film. Rafael wastes the "advance" he is paid on toys his children cannot play with and on food his wife cannot cook, and at the book's conclusion, it is revealed that the contract the illiterate Rafael has signed for his wife to receive $30,000 after the film is made is worthless. The third chapter of *The Brave* contains a graphic and gruesome description of Rafael's death, as the producer tells him what will take place, from the pulling of the first fingernail to the disemboweling. In 1995, Johnny Depp announced plans to direct and star in a screen adaptation of *The Brave.*

SOCIETY FOR THE PRESERVATION OF FILM MUSIC, founded in Los Angeles in 1984, is devoted to the salvaging and protection of film music. It has 650 members in 18 countries. In October 1996, the Society completed a joint venture with Paramount Pictures*, cleaning, cataloging, and preserving the studio's library of orchestral scores and parts for 1,500 feature films and short subjects.

Address: P.O. Box 93536, Hollywood, Calif. 90093-0536.

SOCIETY OF MOTION PICTURE AND TELEVISION ART DIRECTORS. A professional society that acts as a bargaining agency, the Society of Motion Picture and Television Art Directors was founded in 1937—the name was changed to include television in January 1968. It is Local 876 of IATSE*. The Society published a journal, *Production Design,* in the fifties.

Address: 11365 Ventura Boulevard, Suite 315, Studio City, Calif. 91604.

SOCIETY OF MOTION PICTURE AND TELEVISION ENGINEERS. The Society of Motion Picture Engineers was formed on January 24, 1916, in Washington, D.C., by ten motion picture engineers, including C. F. Jenkins, Donald J. Bell, and W. Burton Wescott. The Society's basic aim, which has remained the same through the years, was the standardization of motion picture (and later television) technology and the publication of the research of its members. In the first issue of its publication *Transactions* (July 1916) (now titled *SMPTE Journal*), the Society gave as its goals the "advancement in the theory and practice of motion picture engineering and the allied arts and sciences, the standardization of the mechanisms and practices employed therein, and the maintenance of a high professional standing among its members."

The Society's name was changed to include Television in January 1950. It organizes an annual technical conference, at which papers are read and which includes a major exhibit of current film and television equipment; holds monthly regional meetings; and publishes the monthly *SMPTE Journal.* Membership in the Society of Motion Picture and Television Engineers (SMPTE) is open to qualified members of the film and television industries.

Address: 595 West Hartsdale Avenue, White Plains, N.Y. 10607.

SOCIETY OF MOTION PICTURE FILM EDITORS was incorporated on May 20, 1937, and ratified its first contract in November of that year. It became affiliated with IATSE* in 1944 as Local 776, and its membership was instrumental in the formation of the American Cinema Editors* and the Motion Picture Sound Editors (founded 1953).

SOCIETY OF OPERATING CAMERAMEN was formed in 1981 by 120 members of the International Photographers Local 659 of the International Alliance of Theatrical Stage Employes*, as a professional organization concerned with gaining recognition for the craft of operating cameramen. The first president was Bob Marta.

Address: P.O. Box 2006, Toluca Lake, Calif. 91610.

BIBLIOGRAPHY

"Operating Cameramen Form New Society." *International Photographer,* July 1981, pp. 12, 16.

SOLAR PRODUCTIONS was formed in 1961 by actor Steve McQueen (1930–1980) and his partner, executive producer Robert E. Relyea, with Jack Reddish as production manager. It produced *Adam at 6 A.M.* (1970), starring Michael Douglas, and the following Steve McQueen features: *Soldier in the Rain* (1963), *Baby the Rain Must Fall* (1965), *The Cincinnati Kid* (1965), *Nevada Smith* (1966), *The Sand Pebbles* (1966), *Bullitt* (1968), and *Le Mans* (1971). All but the last two were financed by Warner Bros.*

BIBLIOGRAPHY

"McQueen Adds 7th Solar Film; Total CCF Budget $20 Mil." *Daily Variety,* April 29, 1969, pp. 1, 4.

SOLAX COMPANY was founded on September 7, 1910, by Madame Alice Guy Blaché, the world's first woman director, in association with her husband, Herbert Blaché, and George A. Magie. Its first release—on October 21, 1910—was *A Child's Sacrifice.* The first Solax studios were located in Flushing, New York, but, in 1912, the company built a new studio complex in Fort Lee, New Jersey*. Alice Guy Blaché directed the more important of the company's productions, including its first major film and its first three-reel feature, *Fra Diavolo,* released on July 12, 1912, and among the players in the Solax stock company were Magda Foy, Billy Quirk, Marion Swayne, Darwin Karr, and Blanche Cornwall. The Solax Company went out of existence in 1914, when Herbert Blaché established Blaché Features and the United States Amusement Company*.

BIBLIOGRAPHY

Blaché, Alice Guy. *The Memoirs of Alice Guy Blaché.* Lanham, Md.: Scarecrow Press, 1996.
Gates, Harvey. "Alice Blaché, a Dominant Figure in Pictures." *The New York Dramatic Mirror,* November 6, 1912, p. 28.
Harrison, Louis Reeves. "Studio Saunterings." *The Moving Picture World,* June 15, 1912, pp. 1007–11.

SOLDIERS WITH WINGS. See HOLLYWOOD VICTORY COMMITTEE

SONG SLIDES. With the popularity of the nickelodeon* in the early twentieth century, a number of manufacturers—such as the St. Louis (Missouri) Calcium Light Company, DeWitt C. Wheeler, Scott and Van Altena, A. L. Simpson, and Henry B. Ingram—began producing song slides, illustrating the lines of popular "hits" of the day. They were utilized as a vocalist or pianist accompanied the numbers in theatres, with the audiences joining in the chorus. Song slides were not unique to nickelodeons but had been utilized earlier in vaudeville and as part of stereopticon entertainments. They were distributed, for purchase, by film exchanges and were sometimes loaned to nickelodeons by song publishers.

Among the models who appeared in song slides—"live model" slides were generally considered to have been introduced by George H. Thomas, a stage electrician at a Brooklyn theatre—were many future film stars, including Francis X. Bushman, Patricia Collinge, Priscilla Dean, Ethel Grandin, Alice Joyce, Florence La Badie, Anita Stewart, Norma Talmadge, Florence Turner, and Lillian Walker.

BIBLIOGRAPHY

Ripley, John W. "Romance and Joy, Tears and Heartache, and All for a Nickel." *Smithsonian,* March 1982, pp. 77–82.
"Slide Makers Organizing." *The Moving Picture World,* January 4, 1908, pp. 6–7.
"Song Slides: How They Are Produced." *Views and Film Index,* July 28, 1906, p. 10.
"The Song Slide Situation." *Views and Film Index,* March 7, 1908, pp. 13–15.

SONO ART-WORLD WIDE PICTURES, INC., was a New York-based company, headed first by J. Douglas Watson and later by E. W. Hammons, which was operational from 1929 to 1932. Among the more than 30 features produced by the company, the best known are *The Great Gabbo* (1929), directed by James Cruze and starring Erich von Stroheim as a ventriloquist driven insane through jealous love, and *Reno* (1930), the first sound feature of former serial queen Ruth Roland. The company was not involved with short films and, as far as can be ascertained, had some link with Educational Pictures* and Tiffany Productions*.

SONY CORP. OF AMERICA is the parent company of Columbia Pictures*, which it acquired in November 1989. Following that acquisition, the studios of Columbia—the former M-G-M* lot in Culver City—were renamed the Sony Pictures Studios. To handle its film- and television-related interests, Sony Pictures Entertainment Inc. was created, responsible for Columbia Pictures*, TriStar Pictures*, Sony Pictures Classics, Triumph Films, Sony Pictures Releasing, Columbia TriStar Film Distributors International, Columbia TriStar International Television, Columbia TriStar Television, TriStar Home Video, Sony Pictures Studios, and Culver Studios.

Sony Corporation of America is owned by the Japanese video and electronics giant, incorporated in Japan in 1946 as Tokyo Telecommunications Engineering Corp. The company adopted the name Sony in January 1958. The head office is located at 7-35 Kitashinagawa 6-chome, Shinagawa-Ku, Japan.

Address: 555 Madison Avenue, 33rd Floor, New York, N.Y. 10022.

BIBLIOGRAPHY

Lyons, Nick. *The Sony Vision.* New York: Crown, 1976.

SONY PICTURES ENTERTAINMENT. See COLUMBIA PICTURES.

SOUND DESIGNER is a title first used by Walter Murch on *Apocalypse Now* (1979) to credit an individual totally responsible for *all* sound in a production. In more recent years, it has been used as a credit by technicians who might better be described as sound editors or sound effects creators.

BIBLIOGRAPHY

Cohen, Laura. "Who or What Is a Sound Designer?" *American Cinemeditor,* vol. 39, no. 4, Winter 1989–90, pp. 28–29.

SOUNDIES was the name given to a film jukebox presentation popular in the early forties. For a nickel, patrons could view a three-minute musical short on a 24-by-18-inch plastic screen. The film was projected by mirrors within the jukebox, called a Panoram, and this required that the film by printed in reverse (the reason why when film collectors purchase Soundies today the titles are always reversed). The musical entertainment might be a novelty number; a jazz number with Hoagy Carmichael, "Fats" Waller, or Duke Ellington; or a popular favorite performed by a minor celebrity. All-black soundies were produced exclusively for Negro neighborhoods.

Soundies were introduced in 1940 by the Mills Novelty Company of Chicago. The initial films were produced by James Roosevelt's Globe Productions in Hollywood. They were later produced by Minoco Productions, Inc., a Mills subsidiary in New York, and R.C.M. Productions in Hollywood. The initials R.C.M. stood for (James) Roosevelt; (Sam) Coslow, a songwriter whose Cameo Productions was part of R.C.M.; and (Gordon) Mills, the president of the Mills Novelty Company.

Customers could not select individual numbers but had to be content with any one of eight titles in a reel-long program. By 1941, it was reported that more than 4,000 Panoram jukeboxes were in operation. Soundies lost their appeal at the end of the Second World War, and the films became available to private collectors (often offering a unique record of a popular musical personality's performance). In the sixties, a new version of Soundies, titled Scopitone, was introduced.

BIBLIOGRAPHY

Terenzio, Maurice, Scott MacGillivray, and Ted Okuda. *The Soundies Distributing Corporation of America: A History and Filmography.* Jefferson, North Carolina: McFarland, 1991.

SOUTHERN CALIFORNIA MOTION PICTURE COUNCIL. Incorporated in 1936, the Southern California Motion Picture Council previews and grades films and television programs for the Parent-Teacher Association (PTA) and church and youth groups. It is not a censorship board but seeks to encourage the production of family entertainment by awarding Golden, Silver, and Bronze halos initially on a monthly and since 1980 on a bimonthly basis. It was involved in a major 1975 dispute with a breakaway organization, the Film Advisory Board*.

Address: 400 South Burnside Avenue, Suite 12-D, Los Angeles, Calif. 90036.

THE SOUTH ON FILM. The romantic image of the Old South had appealed to American filmmakers long before D. W. Griffith made *The Birth of a Nation* in 1915. Many of Griffith's earlier films for the American Biograph Company* have southern themes, while the Kalem Company* produced a variety of films concerning Confederate spies, many filmed on location in Florida*. Harriet Beecher Stowe's *Uncle Tom's Cabin* was filmed as early as 1903, and later versions were released in 1909, 1913, 1914, 1918, 1927, and 1965. In 1927, the Duncan Sisters filmed their parody of the classic *Topsy and Eva.*

D. W. Griffith presented a further romanticized view of the South in *A Romance of Happy Valley* (1919), and *The White Rose* (1923). A far more realistic view of southern life was presented by Karl Brown in *Stark Love* (1927), a study of the isolated mountain people of Kentucky, filmed on location in Robbinsville, North Carolina. The rural South was the theme of Henry Hathaway's *The Trail of the Lonesome Pine* (1936). Al Capp is said to have based his character L'il Abner on Henry Fonda's characterization of Dave Tolliver in this film. There have been two versions of *L'il Abner*—in 1940 and 1959—and comic figures of the rural South have been represented by "Sis Hopkins" (first in Kalem* shorts and later by Judy Canova at Republic*) and by Pa and Ma Kettle.

With the coming of sound, the motion picture's view of the South changed little. It was a sentimental land of friendly Negroes, as seen in King Vidor's *Hallelujah* (1929), Paul Sloane's *Hearts in Dixie* (1929), and John Ford's *Judge Priest* (1934), *Steamboat round the Bend* (1935), and *The Sun Shines Bright* (1953). A change in attitude toward the South was first evidenced in *Cabin in the Cotton* (1932), followed by *Jezebel* (1938), *Tobacco Road* (1941), *The Little Foxes* (1941), *The Southerner* (1945), *All the King's Men* (1949), *The Glass Menagerie* (1950), *A Streetcar Named Desire* (1951), *Baby Doll* (1956), *Cat on a Hot Tin Roof* (1958), *The Defiant Ones* (1958), *The Long Hot Summer* (1958), *Suddenly Last Summer* (1959), *Sweet Bird of Youth* (1962), *To Kill a Mockingbird* (1963), and *In the Heat of the Night* (1967).

By the seventies, the South served as a background for crusading cops, as in *Walking Tall* (1973); for a new brand of black women, such as Cicely Tyson in *Sounder* (1972); for womanizers, such as Burt Reynolds in *Smokey and the Bandit* (1977); for political drama, as in *Nashville* (1975); and for unionization, as in *Norma Rae* (1979). At the same time, the old stereotypes were retained in films such as *Mandingo* (1975) and *Drum* (1976), and there can be little question that that is the image of the old, romantic South that remained predominant with filmgoers through the 1970s, thanks to *Gone with the Wind* and, to a lesser extent, *Song of the South* (1947). The eighties and nineties presented audiences with a very different, harsher Southern view, with racism often a strong theme, in films such as *The Color Purple* (1986), *Crimes of the Heart* (1987), *Biloxi Blues* (1989), *Mississippi Burning* (1989), *Driving Miss Daisy* (1990),

Steel Magnolias (1990), *Fried Green Tomatoes* (1992), and *Ghosts of Mississippi* (1996).

BIBLIOGRAPHY

Campbell, Edward D. C., Jr. *The Celluloid South.* Knoxville, Tenn.: University of Tennessee Press, 1981.

French, Warren, ed. *The South and Film.* Jackson, Miss.: University Press of Mississippi, 1981.

Karby, Jack Temple. *Media-Made Dixie: The South in the American Imagination.* Baton Rouge, La.: Louisiana State University Press, 1978.

Williamson, J. W. *Southern Mountaineers in Silent Films: Plot Synopses of Movies about Moonshining, Feuding, and Other Mountain Topics, 1904–1929.* Jefferson, N.C.: McFarland, 1994.

SPEAKING OF ANIMALS. See JERRY FAIRBANKS PRODUCTIONS

SPECIAL EFFECTS is a term used to describe a multitude of specialist creative works, from the burning of Chicago in *In Old Chicago* (1938) to the parting of the Red Sea in Cecil B. DeMille's *The Ten Commandments* (1956). It is primarily a visual field, and many times the term *special visual effects* rather than simply *special effects* is used. The Academy of Motion Picture Arts and Sciences* has presented Academy Awards for Special Effects or Special Visual Effects since 1938, when a Special Award was given to those responsible for the special photographic and sound effects in Paramount's *Spawn of the North.* Among the films honored by the Academy for their special effects are *The Rains Came* (1939), *The Thief of Bagdad* (1940), *Mighty Joe Young* (1949), *War of the Worlds* (1953), *tom thumb* (1958), *Ben-Hur* (1959), *Mary Poppins* (1964), *2001: A Space Odyssey* (1968), *Earthquake* (1974), *Superman* (1978), *Alien* (1979), *The Empire Strikes Back* (1980), *E. T.: The Extra-Terrestrial* (1982), *Return of the Jedi* (1983), and *Indiana Jones and the Temple of Doom* (1984).

Because most special effects involve the use of the camera or optical printing by a laboratory, the area of expertise is one that has primarily been held by cinematographers, among whom were Linwood G. Dunn, John P. Fulton, Fred Sersen, and L. B. Abbott.

The earliest film to include a special effect is believed to be Edison's production of *The Execution of Mary, Queen of Scots* (1895), which uses a freeze frame to show the decapitation. A freeze frame allows for the stopping of the camera while one object, in this case a dummy, is substituted for another, in this case the actress portraying the Queen. Freeze frames, double exposures, and other similar and simplistic special effects devices were utilized by the French filmmaker Georges Méliès in the early years of the twentieth century. J. Stuart Blackton used the same methods for the production of *Princess Nicotine* (1909) and other early Vita-graph* films. Freeze frame has now come to mean freezing a frame optically for projected effect.

One of the more basic types of special effects is a matte shot, which permits a portion of the frame to be matted out, with another picture substituted for that part of the frame. A similar type of special effect is the glass shot, which involves a painted scene on glass through which the actors are filmed; they thus appear to be within the scene represented on the glass. The glass shot is thought to have originated with Norman Dawn in 1905.

Puppet animation is another form of special effect animation that was utilized in such early films as *The Lost World* (1925), in which the model prehistoric animals that were created by Willis O'Brien, who had been active in the field from the middle of the second decade of the twentieth century. Willis O'Brien was also involved in the special effects for *King Kong* (1933), which uses animated puppet models, optical printing, miniatures and other such devices.

Optical printing is a form of special effect undertaken in the laboratory. Rear projection, which first became popular in the early thirties, permits the projection of a scene behind the players, thus allowing them to appear to be riding in a car, traveling on a plane, or whatever. The same effect can also be obtained—many argue more realistically—with front projection. Miniatures have long been used when the building of a full-scale castle or town is obviously impossible. Some films—for example, Cecil B. DeMille's *Cleopatra* (1933)—contained scenes made up of both miniatures and full-scale sets.

The most elaborate and complex of special effects were introduced in the seventies, when electronics and animation were increasingly a part of the special effects field. The new era of special effects was heralded by the films of Steven Spielberg and George Lucas, such as *Star Wars* (1977) and *Close Encounters of the Third Kind* (1977). The seventies also saw new names entering the special effects field, such as Carlo Rambaldi, John Dykstra, Richard Edlund, Robert Blalack, H. R. Giger, and Dennis Muren, who dominated the Academy Awards nominations for Special Visual Effects. At the same time, a new type of special effect was introduced by Benjamin Burtt, Jr., with his creation of alien creature and robot voices in *Star Wars.* Arguably the end of the old era of special effects and the beginning of the new came in 1976, when the Special Visual Effects Award was shared by *King Kong* and *Logan's Run,* with the winners including "old" names, such as Frank Ven Der Veer and L. B. Abbott, and "new" names, represented by Carlo Rambaldi and Matthew Yuricich.

BIBLIOGRAPHY

Abbott, L. B. *Special Effects: Wire, Tape and Rubber Style.* Hollywood, Calif.: American Society of Cinematographers, 1984.

Baker, Christopher W. *Computer Illusion in Film & TV.* Indianapolis, Ind.: Alpha Books, 1994.

Culhane, John. *Special Effects in the Movies.* New York: Ballantine Books, 1981.

Dunn, Linwood G., and George E. Turner, ed. *The ASC Treasury of Visual Effects*. Hollywood, Calif.: American Society of Cinematographers, 1983.

Fielding, Raymond. *The Technique of Special Effects Cinematography*. New York: Hastings House, 1972.

Finch, Christopher. *Special Effects: Creating Movie Magic*. New York: Abbeville Press, 1984.

Hayes, R. M. *Trick Cinematography: The Oscar Special Effects Movies*. Jefferson, N.C.: McFarland, 1986.

Imes, Jack, Jr. *Special Visual Effects*. New York: Van Nostrand Reinhold, 1984.

McAlister, Michael J. *The Language of Visual Effects*. Los Angeles: Lone Eagle Publishing, 1993.

McCarthy, Robert E. *Secrets of Hollywood Special Effects*. Boston: Focal Press, 1992.

———. *Special Effects Sourcebook*. Boston: Focal Press, 1992.

Millar, Dan. *Cinema Secrets: Special Effects*. Secaucus, N.J.: Chartwell Books, 1990.

O'Connor, Jane, and Katy Hall. *Magic in the Movies*. Garden City, N.Y.: Doubleday, 1980.

Perisic, Zoran. *Special Optical Effects*. Boston: Focal Press, 1980.

Schecter, Harold, and David Everitt. *Film Tricks*. New York: Harlin Quist, 1980.

Wilkie, Bernard. *Creating Special Effects for TV and Film*. Boston: Focal Press, 1991.

SPECIALTY STORES. The notion of exploiting copyrighted films and trademarked characters through merchandising originated with the Walt Disney Company*, which operates specialty stores at both Disneyland and Disney World. In 1988, the Walt Disney Company opened its first store outside of its theme parks in Glendale, California, and by 1990, it had almost 80 stores open (including one non-American outlet on London's Regent Street). Hanna-Barbera* opened its first store at the Universal Studios Tour in Florida in 1990, followed the same year by stores in West Los Angeles and Torrance, California. Also in 1990, Jim Henson Productions entered into a licensing agreement with a Toronto-based chain of stores called Muppet Stuff, and the Children's Television Workshop agreed to the use of its name for the Sesame Street General Store chain. The most active of studios in the field of store merchandizing is Warner Bros.*, which opened its first specialty store at the Beverly Center in Los Angeles on September 15, 1991. As of 1997, it operated 138 stores in the United States, 11 in Europe, 10 in Asia, and 2 in Australia.

BIBLIOGRAPHY

Sanchez, Jesus. "Specialty Shops Giving Studios a New Showcase." *Los Angeles Times*, November 24, 1990, pp. D1, D2.

SPELLING ENTERTAINMENT, INC., was founded in August 1969 as Aaron Spelling Productions, and is primarily associated with television production. In November 1988, the company merged with Worldvision Enterprises, Inc., the television subsidiary of Great American Communications, and Spelling Entertainment, Inc., was formed as a holding company for both concerns. Aaron Spelling retained 31 percent of the company, but in April 1991, he sold out to Carl Lindner, owner of Great American. A controlling interest in the company was purchased by Blockbuster Entertainment Corp.* in March 1993, and in April 1994, Blockbuster merged it with Republic Pictures Corp.* Spelling Films International had been created in November 1990 to acquire international rights to feature films.

Address: 5700 Wilshire Boulevard, Suite 575, Los Angeles, Calif. 90036.

SPROCKET SYSTEMS. See LUCASFILM, LTD.

STAMFORD, CONNECTICUT. See AMERICAN CORRESPONDENT FILM COMPANY, INC.

STANDARD PICTURES, INC. See UNITED FILM SERVICE

STAND-INS, as the name suggests, are used by production companies to stand in for stars during the lighting of scenes. They should not be confused with stunt people or with body doubles, a fairly new innovation. Selected either by the player or by the studio, stand-ins were paid on the same salary scale as dress extras. They were required to have the same coloring, facial contours, and approximate height and weight of the stars for whom they were standing in. The idea of a stand-in originated in the twenties, when Pola Negri demanded such an individual and was supplied with a dummy. In 1939, stand-ins formed their own fraternal organization, Hollywood Standin Players, Inc., and the following year, they introduced their own awards, the Elmers.

The name stand-in was in common usage except at Warner Bros.* While filming *Disraeli* there in 1929, star George Arliss referred to his stand-in as "my step-in," and from then onward that name stuck at the studio.

Some stand-ins stood in for multiple stars, but generally a stand-in remained with one specific player for many years. The following is a listing of some stars from Hollywood's "golden age," together with their stand-ins:

Richard Barthelmess ("Dutch" Pettit), Warner Baxter (Frank McGrath), Charles Boyer (Fig Newton), George Brent (Don Turner), James Cagney ("Red" Breen), Ronald Colman (Buddy Roosevelt), Joan Crawford (Ann Dvorak, who later became a star), Bing Crosby (Leo Lynn), Bette Davis (Sally Sage), Olivia de Havilland (Ann Robinson), Dolores Del Rio (Carmen La Rue), Deanna Durbin (Marie Osborne, who had been a child star in silent films), Irene Dunne (Kathryn Stanley), Alice Faye (Helene Holmes), Barry Fitzgerald (Gus

Tallon), Errol Flynn (James Fleming), Judy Garland (Bernice Webb), Cary Grant (Mal Merrihugh), Ann Harding (Julie Haydon, who later became a leading lady), Sonja Henie (Lillian Baer and, for skating scenes, Bert Clark), Katharine Hepburn (Adeline and Katharine Doyle), Bob Hope (Jack Robbins), Edward Everett Horton (Eddie Hall), Alan Ladd (Tommy Summers), Hedy Lamarr (Sylvia Lamarr, no relation), Charles Laughton (Bill Hoover), Fredric March (Bill Meader), Joel McCrea (Arnold Grey), Margaret O'Brien (Carol Ann Saunders), May Robson (Mae Warren), Ginger Rogers (Dorothy Panter and Marie Osborne, who also stood in for Deanna Durbin), Rosalind Russell (Mildred Crawford), C. Aubrey Smith (Brigadier General R. D. Napier-Raikes), Barbara Stanwyck (Patsy Doyle), Shirley Temple (Mary Lou Isleib), and Mae West (Edna Eckert Noyer).

BIBLIOGRAPHY

Jones, Grover. "Star Shadows." *Collier's,* April 30, 1938, pp. 18, 44–46.
"Movie Stand-Ins." *Life,* June 27, 1944, pp. 49–51.
"They Also Serve in Realm of Motion Pictures Who Only Stand In and Wait." *Los Angeles Times,* March 21, 1936, p. 24.

STANLEY BOOKING CORPORATION OF PHILADELPHIA, headed by Stanley and Jules Mastbaum, took over the extensive theatre holdings of Lubin* throughout eastern Pennsylvania. Acting as a "booking combine" for its theatres, Stanley was able to program the theatres and exact a 5 to 10 percent fee above the rental prices. Some exhibitors claimed they were forced into the Booking Corporation, and in 1918 Stanley was ordered by the Federal Trade Commission, in the first order of its kind in the motion picture industry, to cease its unfair methods of competition.

Jules Mastbaum became the president after Stanley's death, and in 1919 the organization was incorporated, with a capitalization of $15 million, as the Stanley Company of America. It fought for an open-booking system, and Adolph Zukor, who served on the Board of Directors, wanted to make the Stanley Company a booking combine for all parts of the country, using the thousands of exhibitors belonging to the First National* Exhibitors Circuit, but the First National exhibitors rejected the idea.

BIBLIOGRAPHY

"Stanley Corporation Is Enjoined." *The Moving Picture World,* September 28, 1918, p. 1869.

STANLEY WARNER CORPORATION. When Warner Bros.* was required by the consent decree* to divest itself of its theatre chain, the 436 theatres that it controlled in 1951 became the Stanley Warner Corporation. The latter merged with the Glen Alden Corp. in 1967, which merged the Stanley Warner Corporation with RKO Theatre Corporation and, in 1971, sold the circuit to Cinerama, Inc.

"STAR" BRAND. See MÉLIÈS MANUFACTURING COMPANY

STARLIGHT COMEDY COMPANY. See UNITED FILM SERVICE

STARS OVER AMERICA. See HOLLYWOOD VICTORY COMMITTEE

STATEN ISLAND, NEW YORK. See ALL-STAR FEATURE COMPANY

STATES RIGHTS. States rights distribution was a system that developed in the days prior to national distribution organizations. To distribute a film across the country, an independent producer would lease the rights to the film to independent exchanges in each territory of the United States, with the territory usually being a state (hence the name). The exchanges had the exclusive rights to the film in their territories and then rented the film to exhibitors in the area and handled the physical chores of distribution, such as booking and cleaning prints, collecting rentals, and so on.

This distribution system, while dominant through the second decade of the twentieth century, was not the most efficient system for producers, for three main reasons: (1) most exchanges were owned by exhibitors and they were not eager to let their competition have films they might be able to use; (2) exchanges handled films from many different producers and could not give much attention to promoting any one film; and (3) there was always the probability of dishonesty by the exchange, either by not reporting rentals (when the film was leased on a percentage basis) or by "bicycling" the print to unlicensed exhibitors and keeping the rentals.

As states rights distribution depended on an industry that was fragmented, it began to disappear when the vertical integration of the industry, begun by Adolph Zukor, became dominant and national distribution systems were formed. Yet, it has never totally disappeared and probably will not as long as there are independent producers around to make films for regional and minority audiences.

BIBLIOGRAPHY

Lewis, Howard T. *The Motion Picture Industry.* New York: D. Van Nostrand, 1933.
Whole Distribution/Motion Picture Films. Washington, D.C.: U.S. Department of Commerce, Bureau of the Census, 1932.

STATES RIGHTS DISTRIBUTORS, INC. Sol Lesser headed States Rights Distributors, Inc., which was organized on August 22, 1917, by 15 distributors representing most of the United States, to purchase the negative rights on pictures in a manner similar to the then recently formed First National* organization. Each franchise holder was to be taxed a pro-rata share on any film purchased. Louis Haas was the vice president of the organization, and Louis B. Mayer was the treasurer.

THE STATIC CLUB OF AMERICA. James Crosby, who owned a studio and a laboratory in Los Angeles, was the founder, in 1913, of the Static Club of America, whose membership was limited to active cameramen. Its headquarters were at 406 Court Street, Los Angeles, and Leonard H. Smith was the president in April 1913 and William F. Alder the secretary. In 1915, the Static Club, with a membership of 100, attempted to see that the names of cameramen were included in the credits of films. Its offices at that time were at 1839 Santa Cruz Street, Los Angeles, overlooking Echo Park, and its president was E. G. Ullman. *Static Flashes,* its official weekly paper, was edited by "Captain Jack" Poland, who later became the first editor of *American Cinematographer,* and it ran for about six months before ceasing publication in September 1915.

BIBLIOGRAPHY

Poland, Captain "Jack." "The Static Club." *The Moving Picture World,* July 10, 1915, pp. 272–73.

STEADICAM is the trade name for a lightweight, portable stabilizer for cameras that permits a steady picture image when the camera is in motion. Invented and developed by Garrett Brown—who received an Academy Award in 1977—and marketed by Cinema Products Corporation, Steadicam revolutionized filmmaking in the late seventies. For the first time, a cinematographer—utilizing a 35mm,* 16mm, or video camera—was able to walk or run and maintain a steady image.

BIBLIOGRAPHY

Brown, Garrett. "The Steadicam and 'The Shining.'" *American Cinematographer,* August 1980, pp. 786–89, 826–27, 850–54.
McDonough, Tom. "The Fabulous Flying Robot Camera." *The Movies,* July 1983, pp. 88–90, 119.

STELLAR PHOTOPLAY COMPANY. Frank J. Carroll, previously with the Selig Polyscope Company*, formed the Stellar Photoplay Company as a production organization late in 1913. Carroll was the president, C. A. "Doc" Willat was vice president, and William A. McManus was secretary and treasurer. Its first release, the melodrama *Forgiven; or, The Jack of Diamonds,* with Edwin Forsberg and directed by William Robert Daly, was shot at the Ruby Twinplex studio in New York and at St. Augustine. Stellar's offices were in the Candler Building, New York.

BIBLIOGRAPHY

"F. J. Carroll Will Make Pictures." *The Moving Picture World,* January 3, 1914, p. 54.

STERLING CAMERA AND FILM COMPANY was formed late in 1913 by Fred J. Balshofer and ceased production in January 1915. Ford Sterling and George Nichols were the featured players in the company's films, released by Universal*, and Robert Thornby directed a company of children for Sterling.

STILLS is the term used for still photographs of scenes from films used for publicity purposes. Except on the cheapest of productions (which cannot afford a still photographer), stills are posed shots of scenes from the film or production shots showing the cast and crew at work. Frame enlargements from the film itself are only utilized as stills when no still photographer is present. The standard size of a still photograph is eight inches by ten inches, and this has been the standard since the second decade of the twentieth century. There is no documentation as to when stills, as opposed to frame enlargements, were first used to promote films, but as early as 1907 both the Edison* and Vitagraph* companies were utilizing stills.

Some still photographers became associated with individual studios. Clarence Sinclair Bull and George Hurrell are best known for their work for M-G-M*, while Roman Freulich was Universal's* chief still photographer. These still photographers were also responsible for posed portrait stills of the studio's personalities, both stars and technicians. Prior to the studios' use of an in-house portrait photographer, such Los Angeles photographers as Melbourne Spurr, Lansing Brown, and the houses of Evans, Hartsok, and Witzel would provide portrait stills of the stars.

It is only in recent years that the art of the studio still photographer has come to be recognized, and the value of original still photographs has risen. However, from 1941 to 1947 the Academy of Motion Picture Arts and Sciences* organized exhibits of the work of still photographers and awarded medals to the best.

BIBLIOGRAPHY

Johnston, John LeRoy. "Stillmen Mustn't Stand Still." *International Photographer,* February 1939, pp. 9–12.
Kobal, John. *The Art of the Great Hollywood Portrait Photographers, 1925–1940.* New York: Alfred A. Knopf, 1980.
Slide, Anthony. *A Collector's Guide to Movie Memorabilia.* Des Moines, Iowa: Wallace-Homestead, 1983.
Willinger, L. "Still Please." *International Photographer,* January 1940, pp. 9–11.

STOCK SHOT LIBRARIES provide footage for film or television productions that the producer would either be unwilling to film himself because of cost or time or unable to film because the objects or the events in the stock footage can no longer be duplicated. Stock footage may be in black-and-white or color and can include anything from footage of the 1932 Olympic Games in Los Angeles to a shot of a pride of lions in Kenya. With the preponderance of color films and television programs, color stock footage is the most sought after and utilized, particularly color footage of landmarks or events from the forties and earlier.

It was common practice for studios to operate their own stock footage libraries, in which they deposited surplus footage from their current productions, but it was footage that did not show any identifiable player. If a film was cancelled after certain footage had already been shot, that footage usually finished up in a stock footage library. For example, the film that Orsen Welles shot in Brazil for his abortive 1941–1942 project *It's All True* was sold by the studio, RKO*, as stock footage to Paramount*, where it remained for many years until it was deposited in 1985 with the UCLA Film and Television Archive.

The earliest known stock footage library was created by Abram Stone in 1908, and remained active through the Second World War. It was known simply as The Film Library. The two most prominent stock footage libraries in the first half of the century were the Progress Film Library and the General Film Library. The former opened in New York in 1914 as the Joe Miles Library; it was sold to Maurice Zouary early in 1957. The General Film Library was operated, in both New York and Los Angeles, by Sidney Kandel and Morris Landres, and founded in 1920. It was acquired by Ziv Television in the late forties.

BIBLIOGRAPHY

"Stock Footage Libraries." In *Nitrate Won't Wait: A History of Film Preservation in the United States,* by Anthony Slide. Jefferson, N.C.: McFarland, 1992, pp. 134–44.

STRATFORD PICTURES CORPORATION. See ALLIED ARTISTS

STUDIO BASIC AGREEMENT. See INTERNATIONAL ALLIANCE OF THEATRICAL STAGE EMPLOYES AND MOVING PICTURE MACHINE OPERATORS OF THE UNITED STATES AND CANADA

THE STUNTMEN'S ASSOCIATION is a fraternal organization, to which membership is open by invitation. It came into being as a result of a staged fight on the set of the 1961 Mickey Rooney vehicle *Everything's Ducky.* Loren Jones and Dick Geary were concerned that they were the only two professional stuntmen involved in the sequence, and realized the need for an organization of professionals to coordinate and do stunts. With a charter membership of 46, the Stuntmen's Association held its first meeting at the Screen Actors Guild* in 1961. A number of similar organizations came along later, including an International Stunt Association and the Stuntwomen's Association; these various groups were united by Tony Epper of the Screen Actors Guild in 1992 under the umbrella title of National League of SAG Stunt Performers.

Address: 4810 Whitsett Avenue, North Hollywood, Calif. 91607.

BIBLIOGRAPHY

Setlowe, Richard. "Biz's Fall Guys Join Hands." *Daily Variety,* December 6, 1996, pp. 28, 30.

STUNTS/STUNTMEN. The use of stuntmen to perform dangerous or specialized feats dates back to circa 1908. Although many silent actors and actresses—particularly the comedians—performed their own stunts, stunt doubles were also used when necessary. Richard Talmadge and Harvey Parry doubled for Harold Lloyd. Talmadge doubled for Douglas Fairbanks. Jean de Kay doubled for Norma Phillips in the 1914 Mutual* serial* *Our Mutual Girl.* A number of male stuntmen doubled for Pearl White in her serials. Generally, however, the names of stunt doubles were not publicized, and the industry clung to the myth that stars performed their own stunts.

With the popularity of the "B" Western*, with its frequent and sometimes dangerous action sequences, stuntmen became an established part of the film community. These men called a stunt "a gag," and the doyen of Hollywood stuntmen was Yakima Canutt 1895–1986. Canutt was also featured in "B" Westerns (usually as a villain), became noted for his second unit direction work, particularly the chariot race from *Ben-Hur* (1959), and received an Honorary Academy Award in 1966, "for achievements as a stunt man and for developing safety devices to protect stunt men everywhere."

Stunt flying was at its height in the late twenties with *Wings* (1927) and *Hell's Angels* (1930). *The Lost Squadron* (1932) depicted a typical group of stunt flyers, all of whom were members of various flying circuses. Ormer Locklear was the first to become well known as a stunt pilot, and he died in 1920 while filming *The Skywayman.* Probably the best known of all stunt flyers was Dick Grace, who wrote three books on his exploits: *I Am Still Alive* (Rand, McNally, 1931), *Squadron of Death* (The Sun Dial Press, 1937), and *Visibility Unlimited* (Longman's Green, 1950).

Thanks to the 1980 feature film, *The Stunt Man,* and to the Lee Major television series, *The Fall Guy,* the public has become increasingly aware of the work of stunt men and women, with Hal Needham, who has been closely associated with Burt Reynolds, one of the best known. There is also a Stuntmen's Hall of Fame, founded in 1973.

BIBLIOGRAPHY

Baur, Tassilo. *Special Effects and Stunt Guide.* Los Angeles: Lone Eagle Publishing, 1993.
Baxter, John. *Stunt.* Garden City, N.Y.: Doubleday, 1974.
Canutt, Yakima, with Oliver Drake. *Stunt Man.* New York: Walker, 1979.
Dwiggins, Don. *The Air Devils.* Philadelphia: J. B. Lippincott, 1966.
Farmer, James H. *Broken Wings: Hollywood's Air Crashes.* Missoula, Mont.: Pictorial Histories Publishing Company, 1984.

Greenwood, Jim, and Maxine Greenwood. *Stunt Flying in the Movies.* Blue Ridge Summit, Pa.: TAB Books, 1982.

Johnson, John. *Cheap Tricks and Class Acts: Special Effects, Makeup, and Stunts from the Films of the Fantastic Fifties.* Jefferson, N.C.: McFarland, 1996.

Sullivan, George, and Tim Sullivan. *Stunt People.* New York: Beaufort Books, 1983.

Wiener, David Jon. *Burns, Falls, and Crashes: Interviews with Movie Stunt Performers.* Jefferson, N.C.: McFarland, 1996.

Wise, Arthur, and Derek Ware. *Stunting in the Cinema.* New York: St. Martin's Press, 1973.

SUBMARINE FILM COMPANY. Captain Charles Williamson spent 30 years perfecting his invention, the Williamson Submarine Tube, which his sons, J. Ernest and George M., used to make underwater films for their company called, at various times, the Submarine Film Company and the Williamson Submarine Film Company, of Norfolk, Virginia. Carl Louis Gregory, who had been a cameraman for Edison* and Thanhouser*, and a producer of Mutual's "Princess" pictures, was selected to film the company's productions, which would be released through the Thanhouser Film Company on the Mutual* program. Its first release, *The Terrors of the Deep,* was made in 1914 in the waters off the Bahamas and Bermuda. The film was screened at the Smithsonian Institute, at New York's Museum of Natural History, and at Broadway's Rose Gardens before touring large cities. A company was formed at Universal* early in 1915 to take the films produced by the company throughout the United States with a lecturer. The Williamson brothers' second film, *Twenty Thousand Leagues under the Sea,* shot by Eugene Gaudio, was made in collaboration with Universal. Later in that same year, 1916, the company made *The Submarine Eye,* again in association with Universal, with whom the Williamson brothers were to be connected for some time. In 1917, Harry Houdini signed with the Williamsons to demonstrate on film that he could escape the Williamson Tube without breaking the two-inch-thick glass.

BIBLIOGRAPHY

"Under Water Photography." *The Moving Picture World,* April 25, 1914, p. 497.

SUBTITLES. The word *subtitles* can be used to refer either to the titles that appear at the bottom of the screen on foreign-language films or to narrative or descriptive titles in silent films. The latter are usually described today as intertitles, but during the silent era they were always called subtitles.

In an average silent feature film, one-fifth of the production consisted of subtitles. Many subtitles in silent films could be quite florid, while others were intelligently witty, and some title writers—such as Ralph Spence—became noted for their humorous titles. Very occasionally, subtitles in silent films were superimposed over the action, but this was most unusual. *The Old Swimmin' Hole* (1921) utilized no subtitles to tell its story but rather explained the action through entries in the diary of the leading man, Charles Ray. The best known of silent films without subtitles was F. W. Muranu's *The Last Laugh,* made in Germany in 1925, which had only one title to explain the "happy ending" tacked on the end of the feature.

The first foreign-language feature to be subtitled in English is believed to have been *Two Hearts in Waltz Time/Zwei Herzen in 3/4 Takt,* produced in Germany in 1930, which was subtitled in the United States by Herman G. Weinberg (1908–1983). Weinberg is the best known of all subtitle writers, with a reported 400 films to his credit. Through the thirties, subtitles on foreign-language films were kept to a minimum, used from time to time to explain the plotline. It was not until the late forties that distributors began providing detailed subtitles for foreign-language features.

BIBLIOGRAPHY

Silent Films

"Artistic Subtitles." *The Moving Picture World,* December 30, 1916, p. 1966.

Bradlet, John W. "On Subtitles." *The Moving Picture World,* February 27, 1909, p. 235.

Bush, Stephen W. "Perfection in Titles." *The Moving Picture World,* October 4, 1913, p. 1261.

Richardson, Dorothy M. "Continuous Performance: Captions." *Close Up,* September 1927, pp. 52–56.

"What Is a Subtitle?" *The American Cinematographer,* December 15, 1921, p. 12.

Williams, Lawrence. "The Making of Photoplay Titles." *Motion Picture,* March 1919, p. 86.

Foreign-Language Films

Salemson, H. J. "She Walks like a Church." *Action,* November–December 1978, pp. 44–49.

SUNDANCE INSTITUTE. Opened in 1980 by Robert Redford (born 1937), the Sundance Institute, located in the mountains of Utah, serves to encourage and train serious young directors, producers, writers, and actors, working basically in a laboratory situation each summer. Young filmmakers are encouraged to submit scripts to be made utilizing a Sundance co-production fund, and an average of 400 are received each year. A preliminary reading of the best 50 takes place in October, and the final selection of 7 is made in April. Sundance Institute operates with a reported annual budget of $625,000, with funding provided by Redford, the National Endowment for the Arts, and private foundations and corporations. In 1995, the Sundance Film Channel was created as a 50-50 venture between Robert Redford and Showtime Network Inc. Robert Redford serves as president of the Institute, with a board of creative individuals from the film industry.

Address: P.O. Box 16450, Salt Lake City, Utah 84116.

BIBLIOGRAPHY

Greenberg, James. "Sundance Institute Shot in Arm for Indie Prod'n." *Daily Variety,* June 11, 1984, pp. 22, 36.
Lombardi, John. "Redford's Film Lab in the Rockies." *The New York Times Magazine,* October 23, 1983, pp. 48–51, 54, 58–61.
Perry, Gerald. "Sundance." *American Film,* October 1981, pp. 46–51.
Pollock, Dale. "Robert Redford and the Sundance Kids." *Los Angeles Times,* Calendar, July 4, 1982, pp. 1, 26, 27, 30, 31, 33.
"Robert Redford's Summer Camp." *Vogue,* February 1984, pp. 114, 116.

SUNN CLASSICS See JENSEN-FARLEY PICTURES, INC.

SUNSET COMEDY COMPANY, based in Youngstown, Ohio, under the presidency of H. C. Kunkleman, produced a series of one-reel comedies in the second decade of the twentieth century and early twenties, released on a states rights* basis and featuring "Fatty Beilstein" (an obvious copy of Roscoe "Fatty" Arbuckle).

SUNSET MOTION PICTURE COMPANY. The directors and stockholders of the Sunset Motion Picture Company included such distinguished men as U.S. Senator James B. Phelan; Judge B. V. Sargent of the Superior Court; bankers Herbert Fleischhocker and C. L. Smith; J. H. Henry, one of California's wealthiest men; and Charles K. Field, the editor of *Sunset Magazine,* from which the company got its name. Sunset was formed in 1914, with M. E. Cory as general manager, and had offices in the World's Tower Building at 110 West 40th Street, New York. For its first film, *Rescue of the Stefansson Arctic Expedition,* it sent cameraman Fred LeRoy Granville to Kamchatka and Siberia to document the Arctic explorers' expedition.

SUNSET MOTION PICTURE CORPORATION began producing films on five acres of land and an open-air stage on the outskirts of San Antonio, Texas, in September 1918. Frank Powell directed the company's films, which were released by the W. W. Hodkinson Corporation*.

SUNSHINE COMEDY COMPANY. William Fox was the president and Harry "Pathe" Lehrman was the vice president and general manager of the Sunshine Comedy Company, formed in March 1917 and also referred to as Sunshine Comedies, Inc. Four companies were put in operation to make two reels of comedy every two weeks. Lehrman supervised all the productions and also directed his own company and one featuring Mildred Lee. David Kirkland directed a company featuring Billie Rhodes, and Noel

Smith directed H. I. Symonds. By mid-1919, Hampton Del Ruth had taken over supervision of the company, which included directors Eddie Cline, Roy Del Ruth, Mal St. Clair, Vin Moore, Jack Blystone, and Frank Griffin and stars Chester Conklin, Polly Moran, Slim Summerville, Jack Cooper, Alice Davenport, Laura La Varnie, and Ethel Teare.

BIBLIOGRAPHY

"Fox Has New Comedy Company." *The Moving Picture World,* March 31, 1917, p. 2130.
"Sunshine Comedies Live Up to Name." *The Moving Picture World,* July 19, 1919, p. 356.

SUNSHINE FILM CORPORATION. See UNITED FILM SERVICE

"SUPERBA" BRAND. See FREDERICK DOUGLASS FILM COMPANY

SUPERBA COMPANY. See UNITED FILM SERVICE

SUPER 8mm was introduced by the Eastman Kodak Company* in 1965 in the form of Kodachrome II film in an easy-loading cartridge and instamatic movie cameras and projectors. The Super 8mm format provided approximately 50 percent more image area per frame than standard 8mm*. The use of the system was licensed to other manufacturers by Eastman Kodak, and for its development of the format the company received the Albert S. Howell Award from Bell & Howell*. Super 8mm virtually ended the use of standard 8mm, and, in turn, Super 8mm has largely been superseded by the use of videotape. This area of filmmaking was covered from 1972 to 1981 by *Super 8 Filmmaker* magazine.

BIBLIOGRAPHY

Foreign Correspondence: The International Super 8 Phenomenon. Somerville, Mass.: The International Center for 8mm Film and Video, Inc., 1986.
Glenn, George D. *Super 8 Handbook.* Indianapolis, Ind.: Howard W. Sams, 1974.
Lipton, Lenny. *The Super 8 Book.* San Francisco: Straight Arrow Books, 1975.
McClain, Bebe Ferrell. *Super 8 Filmmaking from Scratch.* Englewood Cliffs, N.J.: Prentice-Hall, 1978.
Matzkin, Myron A. *The Super 8 Film Maker's Handbook.* New York: Amphoto, 1976.

SUPERLATIVE PICTURES CORPORATION, whose formation was announced on June 1, 1917, consisted of two subsidiary producing companies working independently of each other to produce high-class features: Irving Cummings Pictures, Inc., and Lois Meredith Pictures, Inc. Morris F. Tobias was president and Irving Cummings was vice president. Lois Meredith was the vice president of her own company and had the privilege of approving any stories before they were accepted for production.

BIBLIOGRAPHY

"Superlative Company Launched." *The Moving Picture World,* June 16, 1917, p. 1793.

SUPERPICTURES, INC., was incorporated in Delaware in November 1916, with a capitalization of $9 million, to encourage, finance, and distribute films of quality. W. W. Hodkinson, formerly the head of Paramount*, was the president; Frederick L. Collins, the president of McClure Publications, was the vice president; and Raymond Pawley, of Paramount, was the treasurer. In keeping with Hodkinson's belief that distributors should not produce films, Superpictures planned to pick and choose its releases from the product of the best studios and provide capital to producers to make films of the highest quality. The McClure publications were to publicize Superpictures releases.

Superpictures acquired a substantial interest in Paramount and in the Progressive Motion Picture Company, the Western distributing concern of Paramount. Soon after its inception, Superpictures joined with the Triangle Film Corporation* to form the Triangle Distributing Corporation, which operated 22 exchanges* and handled productions of Triangle-Fine Arts, Kay Bee, and Keystone. Hodkinson was the president and general manager of the new concern, whose offices were at 1454 Broadway, New York.

In 1917, the Superpictures Distribution Corporation was formed to distribute films made by the Petrova Picture Company, the star of which was Olga Petrova, a partner with Frederick L. Collins. Ralph Ince directed its productions, beginning with *Daughter of Destiny,* at the Bacon-Backer studio at 230 West 38th Street, New York.

BIBLIOGRAPHY

"Hodkinson to Head Superpictures." *The Moving Picture World,* November 25, 1916, p. 1140.

SUPERSCOPE. See CINEMASCOPE

SUPER TECHNIRAMA 70. See TECHNIRAMA

SUPREME PICTURES CORP. was founded in 1934 by A. W. Hackel to produce two Western series starring Johnny Mack Brown and Bob Steele. Its last production, in 1940, was the all-black feature, *Am I Guilty?,* starring Ralph Cooper.

SUTHERLAND STUDIOS. See ALDRICH STUDIOS

SYMBOL PRODUCTIONS was formed by actor/director Cornel Wilde (1915–1989). It produced only one film, *No Blade of Grass* (1970).

BIBLIOGRAPHY

Coen, John. "Producer/Director Cornel Wilde." *Film Comment,* vol. 16, no. 1, Spring 1970, pp. 52–61.

SYNCHRONOPHONE MOTION PICTURE COMPANY OF NEW YORK was formed early in 1913 to promote the Synchronophone and the Cinematophone, two talking picture devices. These were exhibited at Sherwood's Picture Theatre, Fulton Street, New York.

BIBLIOGRAPHY

"Talking Picture Devices." *The Moving Picture World,* March 29, 1913, p. 1318.

TAFT INTERNATIONAL PICTURES. See JENSEN-FARLEY PICTURES, INC.

TALISMAN STUDIOS was the name given to the former Fine Arts* Studios, with a postal address of 4516 Sunset Boulevard, from 1934 to 1942. From 1935 onward, John F. Meehan held the position of studio manager. The studio had previously been owned from 1932 to 1933 by Bert Kelly, Sam Bischoff, and Bill Saul. During the period that the lot was controlled by Talisman Pictures Corporation, it was used by Monogram*, Crescent Pictures, Benny Zeidman, Jam Handy*, Majestic Pictures*, and Splay Commercials.

BIBLIOGRAPHY

Hearn, Marjorie. "Talisman Studios." In *The Film and Daily Cavalcade.* New York: The Film Daily, 1939, p. 281.

TALKING PICTURE EPICS, INC., formed in 1929 as a New York-based company and with Frank R. Wilson as president, was one of the more impressive sounding of the smaller independent producer/distributors from the early years of sound. In an advertisement in the 1931 edition of *The Film Daily Year Book,* it promised "features and short subjects vibrant with strange realities, pulsing with the fascination of nature's wonder and changing moods, and human and animal oddities."

Indeed, its films were unusual. Among the company's feature-length releases (some of which were also released as serials) were *Around the World via Graf Zeppelin* (1929), *Hunting Tigers in India* (1929), *Across the World with Mr. and Mrs. Martin Johnson* (1930), *The Bottom of the World* (1930), *Break-Up* (1930), *South Seas* (1930), *Wild Men of Kalihari* (1930), *Lost Gods* (1930), and *In the South Seas with Mr. and Mrs. Pinchot.* Talking Picture Epics also produced the 1931 *Intimate Interview* series of one-reel shorts, which featured conversations with such Hollywood personalities as James Cagney, Mae Clarke, and Bela Lugosi. The company ceased operations in 1932.

TAMPA, FLORIDA. See BIOSCOPE FILM COMPANY

"TAMS" PICTURES. See REGENT FILM COMPANY, INC.

TANDEM. See EMBASSY COMMUNICATIONS

TAPPAN, NEW YORK. See DRACO FILM COMPANY, INC., and PIERROT FILM COMPANY, INC.

T.A.T. COMMUNICATIONS. See EMBASSY COMMUNICATIONS

TEC-ART STUDIO, located at 5360 Melrose Avenue, Hollywood, at the junctions of Melrose and Bronson Avenue, was one of the major rental studios of the twenties. It was opened in 1913 by William H. Clune (who also operated Clune's Auditorium in downtown Los Angeles), and the first important film to be shot there was *Ramona* (1916). In the early twenties, the studio became known as Tec-Art, and among the films shot there were *Timothy's Quest* (1922), *Soul-Fire* (1925), *Ramona* (1928), *She Goes to War* (1929), *Hell Harbor* (1930), and *Mamba* (1930). Among the sound shorts produced there were the Meglin Kiddie Revues and the "Voice of Hollywood"* series. Although Tec-Art was not known as a producer, all but three of the films in the latter series were copyrighted by the studio. As far as can be ascertained, Tec-Art ceased to exist in 1931. *See also* California Studios.

TECHNICOLOR. The best-known name in the history of color motion pictures, Technicolor has been applied to several different processes since the introduction of the name by Dr. Herbert T. Kalmus (1881–1963). The name Technicolor was chosen by Kalmus, because he, along with other physicists who worked on the invention, were graduates of the Massachusetts Institute of Technology.

The first Technicolor process was an additive one. The camera photographed a pair of images through red and green filters, and when the one strip of film with these two images was projected through red and green filters they merged on the screen. The first and only film to be shot in the additive process by Technicolor was *The Gulf Between,* supervised by C. A. Willat and starring Grace Darmond and Niles Welch, which was filmed in the summer of 1917 in Jacksonville, Florida. A special passenger car was purchased and remodeled by the Technicolor Corporation* to serve as both a laboratory and an office while the film was being shot on location. *The Gulf Between* was first screened, privately, at New York's Aeolian Hall on September 21, 1917.

Technicolor developed a two-color process utilizing a special camera, which photographed objects in two of the three primary colors—red and green. The camera contained a beam-splitter prism that made red and green exposures on two frames simultaneously, with one of the frames inverted. The film moved through the camera two frames at a time, using twice as much film as with regular black-and-white production. Two prints were made from the negative—one for each primary color—utilizing stocks of half the normal thickness. These two pieces of film were then cemented together and dyed complementary colors.

The first film to be shot in Technicolor's new two-color process was *The Toll of the Sea,* which was originally intended to be a short subject but which cameraman Ray Rennahan persuaded Technicolor to release as a five-reel feature. Filmed in Santa Monica, California, in 1921, and released in 1922, *The Toll of the Sea* starred Anna May Wong and Kenneth Harlan in a version of *Madame Butterfly,* which was directed by Chester Franklin. The Technicolor process was first utilized for a sequence in a major feature—the exodus of the Israelites from Egypt—in Cecil B. DeMille's *The Ten Commandments* (1923), and was subsequently used in other features. The first interior use of Technicolor was for a sequence in George Fitzmaurice's *Cytherea* (1924). The first major commercial feature to be filmed entirely in two-color Technicolor was Paramount's *Wanderer of the Wasteland* (1924), followed by Douglas Fairbank's *The Black Pirate* (1926). It was also used for sequences in *The Phantom of the Opera* (1925), *Ben-Hur* (1926), and *The King of Kings* (1927), among others. The first sound feature to be shot entirely in Technicolor—although the sound was limited to music and effects—was *The Viking* (1928). Subsequently, Warner Bros.* utilized Technicolor for many of its early sound features, including *On with the Show* (1929), the first all-Technicolor, all-talking, all-singing, all-dancing production.

In 1928, Technicolor introduced two-color imbibition prints, which did not require two strips of film cemented together, but which could be printed using the imbibition (or dye transfer) process on one strip of film.

The full-color or three-color Technicolor process—utilizing the primary colors of blue, red, and green (which in the printing process became the subtractive primary colors of yellow, cyan, and magenta)—was introduced in 1932, following the completion of the building of the first three-strip camera under the direction of J. A. (Joseph Arthur) Bell, who became the company's director of research following the 1932 death of Dr. Leonard T. Troland. As Dr. Kalmus recalled in a December 1938 article,

By May 1932, Technicolor had completed the building of its first three-component camera, and had one unit of its plant equipped to handle a moderate amount of three-color printing. The difference between this three-component process and the previous two-component process was truly extraordinary. Not only was the accuracy of tone and color reproduction greatly improved, but definition was markedly better. However, we could not offer the three-component product to one customer without offering it to all, which required many more cameras, and the conversion of much of our plant. To allow time for this

and to prove the process beyond any doubt, we sought first to try it out in the cartoon field. But no cartoonist would have it. We were told cartoons were good enough in black-and-white, and that of all the departments of production, cartoons could least afford the added expense. Finally Walt Disney tried it as an experiment on one of his "Silly Symphonies." The first attempt was *Flowers and Trees,* following which Disney contracted for a series.

Flowers and Trees was released in 1932. *La Cucaracha,* the first live-action subject photographed in Technicolor, was released in 1934, and *Becky Sharp,* the first full-length feature to be shot in the Technicolor three-strip process, was released in 1935. *Thunderhead,* the first all-Monopak (Kodachrome converted to Technicolor in the printing process) Technicolor feature, was released in 1944.

Technicolor quickly became the industry standard for color. It was expensive, with Technicolor's providing not only the camera and the cameraman (the best known of which was Ray Rennahan) but also a color consultant in the person of Natalie Kalmus, the ex-wife of the company's founder. As explained by the company, "The credit phrase, Color by Technicolor, is used for motion pictures in color which have been controlled from the developing of the original negative or 'taking' film to the manufacture of the positive release prints by a Technicolor company." The phrase "Print by Technicolor" was utilized to describe release prints made by Technicolor but not necessarily photographed in Techicolor. In 1975, economic reasons forced the demise of imbibition printing by Technicolor, and all films after that date were simply printed by the Technicolor laboratory but generally photographed in Eastman Color*. The only laboratory capable of printing in the original three-strip Technicolor process is the dye transfer processing plant built by Technicolor in Peking in 1979.

BIBLIOGRAPHY

Basten, Fred E. *Glorious Technicolor.* San Diego: A. S. Barnes, 1980.

Behlmer, Rudy. "Technicolor." *Films in Review,* June–July 1964, pp. 333–51.

Haines, Richard W. *Technicolor Movies: The History of Dye Transfer Printing.* Jefferson, North Carolina: McFarland, 1993.

Kalmus, H. T. "Technicolor Adventures in Cinemaland." *Journal of the Society of Motion Picture Engineers* (December 1938): pp. 564–68.

Kalmus, Herbert T., and Eleanore King Kalmus. *Mr. Techicolor.* Absecon, New Jersey: MagicImage Filmbooks, 1993.

Kalmus, Natalie. "Color Consciousness." *Journal of the Society of Motion Picture Engineers* (August 1935): pp. 139–47.

Penfield, Cornelia. "Joseph's Coat for the Silver Screen?" *Stage,* July 1936, pp. 49–50.

Taylor, Frank J. "Mr. Technicolor." *The Saturday Evening Post,* October 22, 1949, pp. 26–27, 131–34.

"The Three Color Process." *Academy Technicians Branch Technical Bulletin,* May 31, 1935, special issue.

"What? Color in the Movies Again?" *Fortune,* October 1934, pp. 92–97, 161–71.

TECHNICOLOR CORPORATION had its origins in the company of Kalmus, Comstock & Wescott, Inc., founded by Dr. Herbert Thomas Kalmus (1881–1963), Dr. Daniel F. Comstock, and W. Burton Wescott in 1912. This research and development group was approached by a Boston lawyer named William H. Coolidge to investigate a new motion picture projector called the Vanoscope. The trio persuaded Coolidge to invest in the design of a motion picture camera that would photograph color, and, in 1915, Coolidge and C. A. Hight provided the $10,000 necessary to establish the Technicolor Motion Picture Corporation. In 1920, William Travers Jerome replaced Coolidge as Technicolor's principal backer, and that same year Marcus Loew became involved in the corporation.

Wescott left the corporation in 1921, followed in 1925 by Comstock. Initially a Boston corporation, Technicolor began the removal of its headquarters to Hollywood in 1930 with the opening of Plant No. 4 at 1016 North Cole Avenue—a postal address that was later changed to 6311 Romaine Avenue—which was to become the corporation's headquarters. (In 1973, Technicolor moved its laboratory to new premises on the Universal* lot, while maintaining corporate headquarters in Century City.) John Hay Whitney became interested in the Technicolor* process in the early thirties, when he formed Pioneer Pictures* and purchased a considerable amount of Technicolor stock.

A British Technicolor laboratory was established in 1936, with the first British Technicolor feature being *Wings of the Morning* (1937). In 1938, Technicolor's J. Arthur Ball received a Special Academy Award "for his outstanding contributions to the advancement of color in motion picture photography."

As of 1933, the corporation had processed 9 million feet of Technicolor film stock. The amount increased to 80 million feet by 1940 and 125 million by 1943. As of 1956, it was reported that Technicolor had processed some 5 billion feet of film, with 41 million feet of that footage being used for prints of *Gone with the Wind* (1939).

In May 1947, the U.S. government filed an antitrust suit against both Technicolor and Eastman Kodak*, a suit perhaps prompted by the government's control of a German color process developed by General Analine that was making little headway in the United States thanks to Technicolor's monopoly. A consent decree between Technicolor and the Justice Department was signed in 1950. The increase in the use of Eastman Color* led to Technicolor's diversification with Technirama*, its introduction of 8mm cassette projectors; the creation of a television syndication company, Gold Key Media (which was sold in 1982); and its eventual move into video.

On June 30, 1956, the Technicolor Motion Picture Corporation was renamed Technicolor Corporation. (Technicolor, Inc., was incorporated in New York in 1922.) The Technicolor Corporation was acquired by Patrick J. Frawley, Jr., in 1961, but a stockholders' group, led by producer Harry Saltzman, wrested control away from Frawley in 1970. In 1982, the corporation was acquired by MacAndrews and Forbes Group, Inc., of New York. It was purchased by the U.K.-based Carlton Communications in 1988 for $780 million.

Address: 4050 Lankershim Boulevard, North Hollywood, Calif. 91608.

TECHNIRAMA, developed by the Technicolor Corporation*, was a widescreen process utilizing an anamorphic lens and 35mm* film traveling horizontally through the camera (as with VistaVision*), thus, according to Technicolor, photographing approximately 50 percent more of the horizontal dimension. The first film to be shot in Technirama was *The Monte Carlo Story,* which received its premiere at the Reposi Cinema in Turin, Italy, on December 19, 1956. A 70mm* version of Technirama was introduced as Super Technirama 70 with *Spartacus* (1960).

BIBLIOGRAPHY

Mascelli, Joseph V. "Technirama." *International Photographer,* June 1957, pp. 5–8.

TED MANN PRODUCTIONS. See MANN THEATRES CORPORATION

TELEVIEW. See THREE-DIMENSIONAL FILMS

TELEVISION PRODUCTIONS OF AMERICA, INC. See EDWARD SMALL PRODUCTIONS, INC.

TELLURIDE FILM FESTIVAL. A small yet exclusive—some might say elitist—film festival, the Telluride Film Festival takes place each Labor Day weekend. It is held in the small Victorian mining town of Telluride, with a population of little over 1,000, located some 320 miles southwest of Denver, with Telluride's Sheridan Opera House serving as the focal point of the festival. Because of its location and limited housing facilities, attendance at Telluride remains small and tickets are eagerly sought. It offers a blend of the best of new and old world cinema.

The Telluride Film Festival was founded in 1974—it was first held from August 30 to September 2 that year—by Bill Pence, and the first celebrity guests were Gloria Swanson, Francis Ford Coppola, and Leni Riefenstahl. Pence's codirector is Tom Luddy (with James Card and William K. Everson also serving at various times as codirector).

Address: P.O. Box B1156, Hanover, N.H. 03755.

TERRYTOONS was organized as an animated film production company in 1930 by Paul Terry (1887–1971), who had commenced his career as an animator in 1915. The best-known series to be produced by Terrytoons was "Mighty Mouse," which was a rodent version of Superman and which, for its first cartoons, had been known as Supermouse. The first of the series, "The Mouse of Tomorrow, was released by 20th Century-Fox* on October 16, 1942.

Paul Terry sold his company to CBS in 1955, but Terrytoons continued to produce cartoons through the seventies, with one of its best-known later animators being Ralph Bakshi (who became supervising director in 1966). The company was located in New Rochelle, New York, from 1935 through 1972, when it moved to the New York headquarters of Viacom*, which eventually acquired CBS Films, including Terrytoons.

BIBLIOGRAPHY

Klein, I. "On Mighty Mouse." In *The American Animated Cartoon,* ed. Gerald Peary and Danny Peary. New York: E. P. Dutton, 1980, pp. 171–77.
Maltin, Leonard. "Paul Terry and Terrytoons." In *Of Mice and Magic.* New York: McGraw-Hill, 1980, pp. 121–53.

THALIA THEATER at Broadway and 95 Street, New York, is one of the best-known art houses* in the United States. It was designed by a 26-year-old novice architect named Ben Schlanger and experienced theatre architect Raymond Irrera, and opened in 1931 as a 292-seat theatre in the basement of a public market owned by Vincent Astor. (Schlanger, who also designed the Sutton Theater, opened in 1933, was responsible for the Thalia's much discussed "parabolic reversed floor," with the dip in the middle of the auditorium.) The theatre was initially operated as a conventional movie house, but in 1939, Martin J. Lewis began a policy of programming international films; that policy continued after Lewis's death in 1955 until 1987, when the Thalia closed. It reopened on June 8, 1993, under the ownership of Roy Ennacheril.

THANHOUSER FILM CORPORATION was formed by theatrical entrepreneur Edwin Thanhouser (1865–1956) in 1909, with studios located at Grove and Warren streets and Crescent Avenue in New Rochelle. Thanhouser's first film, *The Actor's Children,* featured Orilla Smith and Yale Boss and was directed by one of Thanhouser's first two contract directors, Barry O'Neil or Lloyd B. Carleton. It was released on March 15, 1910. As the title suggests, Thanhouser often featured children in its films, and among those it had under contract were Helen Badgley (the Thanhouser Kidlet), Marie Eline (the Thanhouser Kid), and Marion and Madeline Fairbanks (the Thanhouser Twins). Other actors under contract included Florence La Badie, Mignon Anderson, Marguerite Snow, James Cruze, and William Russell.

In 1912, Thanhouser opened a winter studio in Jacksonville, Florida, and that same year the company was acquired by a syndicate headed by C. J. Hite. The year 1913 saw the destruction of Thanhouser's New Rochelle studios by fire, the

signing of noted stage actress Maude Fealy, and the release of the company's first serial, *The Million Dollar Mystery.* When C. J. Hite was killed in a 1914 automobile accident, Edwin Thanhouser returned as head of the studio. The company had always released its films independently, but in 1916 Pathé took over the distribution of its product, which, in that year, included the two films in which Jeanne Eagels made her screen debut, *The World and the Woman* and *Fires of Youth.*

Edwin Thanhouser retired in February 1918, and the studio was loaned out to Clara Kimball Young. In 1919, it was sold to Crawford Livingston and Wilbert Shallenberger, and later that same year it was acquired as the site for B. A. Rolfe Photoplays*. In 1995, Edwin W. Thanhouser, grandson of the company's founder, formed Thanhouse Company Film Preservation, Inc., a nonprofit organization, with the goal of acquiring, preserving, and restoring Thanhouser's heritage; it is located at 705 NW Albemarle Terrace, Portland, Ore. 97210.

BIBLIOGRAPHY

"A Day with Thanhouser." *The Moving Picture World,* April 24, 1915, p. 563.
Duncan, Robert C. "Forty-Five Minutes from Broadway." *Picture Play,* January 1917, pp. 90–96.
Harrison, Louis Reeves. "Studio Saunterings." *The Moving Picture World,* July 13, 1912, pp. 123–26.
Photoplay Arts Portfolio of Thanhouser Moving-Picture Stars. New York: Photoplay Arts, 1914.
Slide, Anthony. "The Thanhouser Company." In *Aspects of American Film History prior to 1920.* Metuchen, N.J.: Scarecrow Press, 1978, pp. 68–78.
Thanhouser, Edwin. "Reminiscences of Picture's Babyhood Days." *The Moving Picture World,* March 10, 1917, pp. 1524–25.
"Thanhouser Company: A New Film Producer." *The Moving Picture World,* March 12, 1910, p. 374.

THEADOROA PRODUCTIONS was created in 1955 by actor Cornel Wilde (1915–1989) and his second wife, Jean Wallace (1921–1990); the best film produced by the company was *The Naked Prey* (1966), which Wilde directed and starred in.

THEATRE OWNERS OF AMERICA. See NATIONAL ASSOCIATION OF THEATRE OWNERS, INC.

THEATROFILM. See ELECTRONOVISION

"THE THIN MAN" SERIES. A series of six features produced by M-G-M* between 1934 and 1947, "The Thin Man" starred William Powell and Myrna Loy as the husband-and-wife detective team of Nick and Nora Charles. The first four films in the series, which were noted for their witty dialogue, were directed by W. S. Van Dyke. The characters, which were based on a couple created by Dashiell Hammett, lived in New York, were wealthy socialites, and owned a wire-haired fox terrier named Asta. They were also featured on radio and in a 1957–1959 NBC television series, on which they were played by Peter Lawford and Phyllis Kirk. The following is a complete list of "The Thin Man" films: *The Thin Man* (1934), *After the Thin Man* (1936), *Another Thin Man* (1939), *Shadow of the Thin Man* (1941), *The Thin Man Goes Home* (1944), and *Song of the Thin Man* (1947).

BIBLIOGRAPHY

Zinman, David. *Saturday Afternoon at the Bijou.* New Rochelle, N.Y.: Arlington House, 1973.

35mm is the standard gauge used in professional filmmaking and has been such since the 1890s. It is 35mm in width, with four perforations on each side of the film frame and 16 frames to one foot of film.

THIS IS AMERICA. See MARCH OF TIME

"THISTLE" BRAND. See CROWN CITY FILM MANUFACTURING COMPANY

THOMAS A. EDISON, INC. See EDISON MANUFACTURING COMPANY

THOMAS H. INCE CULVER CITY STUDIOS. See LAIRD INTERNATIONAL STUDIOS

THREE-DIMENSIONAL FILMS. The British film pioneer William Friese-Greene is generally credited with the creation of the first three-dimensional films, although there is little, if any, factual documentation to back up the claim. He utilized the theory behind stereoscopic viewers, popular in Victorian households and whose contemporary equivalent would be the Viewmaster. Images were photographed twice, with the camera being moved 2 1/2 inches for the second photograph. The 2 1/2 inches represented the average distance between the eyes of the viewer, and when the two photographic images were viewed through the stereoscopic device, a three-dimensional effect was obtained. In the late 1890s, Friese-Greene used the same principle but applied it to motion picture film.

Early three-dimensional experiments used what is known as the anaglyphic process, which, simply explained, uses two cameras to photograph the same image. The film representing the left eye is dyed red and the film representing the right eye is dyed green. In processing, these two pieces of film are placed on top of each other, and when viewed through red and green glasses a three-dimensional effect is obtained.

On September 27, 1922, Harry K. Fairall screened the first major 3-D production, a five-reel feature titled *The Power of Love,* starring Barbara Bedford and Noah Berry. William Van Doren Kelley (who invented Prizma Color*) exhibited his 3-D process, known as Plasticon in the fall of 1922, and, some two years later, Frederick Eugene Ives and J. F. Leventhal produced a series of 3-D shorts called Plastigrams. Film pioneer George K. Spoor, who cofounded the Essanay Company*, worked throughout the twenties on a three-dimensional process called Natural Vision and shot at least one feature, *Danger Lights* (1930), and one short, *Campus Sweethearts* (1930), utilizing his system, which, apparently, also boasted widescreen and some form of stereophonic sound.

Slightly different from the anaglyphic process was the Teleview, invented by Laurens Hammond and William F. Cassidy, which required the spectator to view the film through a glass screen fitted with a shutter that operated in synchronization with the shutter on the one projector required for the process. One six-reel feature, *Mars* (also known as *Radio-Mania,* 1923) was filmed in Teleview; directed by Roy William Neill and starring Grant Mitchell and Margaret Irving, it told of an inventor who tries to manufacture a radio to contact Mars and, in his dreams, meets a group of Martians.

Abel Gance considered using 3-D for his production of *Napoléon* (1927) but had to content himself instead with a triple-screen effect; most producers during the twenties and thirties displayed little interest in 3-D. The anaglyphic process reappeared in the mid-thirties with a couple of shorts, *Audioskopics* (1936) and *The New Audioskopics* (1938), produced by Pete Smith for M-G-M*. With a budget of $3,000, and using two Bell & Howell* cameras with specially matched Bausch and Lomb lenses, technicians Irving Ries and A. G. Wise, director George Sidney, and Pete Smith produced a parody of the Frankenstein story titled *Third Dimension Murder* (1941), for which the 3-D process was rechristened Metroscopix by M-G-M.

The invention of the polaroid process by Edwin H. Land in 1932 heralded a new era for the three-dimensional film. Using Land's original concept, John A. Norland developed a polarizing three-dimensional film system. Two cameras, representing the human eyes, photograph the object, as in the anaglyphic process. However, two projectors are used to screen the two pieces of film, with polaroid filters in front of each projector lens. One filter passes light waves vibrating vertically, while the other passes light waves vibrating horizontally. The polaroid glasses worn by the viewer operate in a similar fashion, and as each eye sees the image, as in a natural binocular effect, a three-dimensional picture is obtained. Unlike the anaglyphic process, the new polaroid process permitted the use of color film. However, it had one major disadvantage in that two projectors were required, running in precise synchronization, something that many contemporary projectionists and theatres seem incapable of handling.

The first American film to use the new process was a 15-minute short produced by J. A. Norling for the Chrysler Corporation exhibit at the 1939 New York World's Fair. A 3-D feature, *Beggar's Weekend,* was produced in Italy in 1936, and two 3-D features were filmed in Germany: *You Can Nearly Touch It* (1937) and *Six Girls Drive into the Weekend* (1939). The Soviets used the polaroid process but did away with the need for glasses by placing a grille of 30,000 copper wires in front of the screen on which the film was projected. The Moscow Cinema was set up for this purpose, and the first Russian 3-D film, *Land of Youth,* filmed partly in color, was screened there in 1941.

It was not until ten years later that the film industry again showed an interest in 3-D, when, in 1951, a three-dimensional abstract short, *Around Is Around,* directed by Norman McLaren for the National Film Board of Canada, was screened at the annual convention of the Society of Motion Picture and Television Engineers*. A Hollywood entrepreneur, Milton Gunzburg, was the first to realize the dormant commercial potential of 3-D, and in 1952 he and Arch Oboler produced *Bwana Devil,* a shoddy melodrama starring Robert Stack and Barbara Britton. Three-dimensional films were revived in the United Kingdom for the 1951 Festival of Britain; the 1953 British Coronation was filmed in 3-D; and two Italian features, *Beauty to Measure* and *Odessey,* were screened in 3-D. The most important and successful 3-D feature of the fifties was Warner Bros.' *House of Wax* (1953), starring Vincent Price and directed by Andre de Toth. Other 3-D features include *It Came from Outer Space* (1953), *Man in the Dark* (1953), *Charge at Feather River* (1953), *Creature from the Black Lagoon* (1954), *Kiss Me Kate* (1953), and *Dial M for Murder* (1954), which was not actually seen in 3-D until 1979.

CinemaScope* effectively ended the industry's interest in 3-D until the seventies, when there was a minor revival with *The Stewardesses* (1970), *Prison Girls* (1972), *Andy Warhol's Frankenstein* (1974), and a major reissue of *Creature from the Black Lagoon.* The year 1982 marked another return for 3-D with *Friday the 13th Part III.* Murray Lerner produced a 17-minute 3-D short, *Journey into the Imagination,* for the Eastman Kodak* Pavilion at the new EPCOT Center at Disney World in Florida, and *Jaws 3-D* (1983) was released. However, the failure of the last at the box office may prove another stumbling block in the continued exploitation of three-dimensional films.

BIBLIOGRAPHY

Connor, Edward. "3-D on the Screen." *Films in Review,* March 1966, pp. 159–74.
Hayes, R. M. *3-D Movies: A History and Filmography of Stereoscopic Cinema.* Jefferson, N.C.: McFarland, 1989.
Kerbel, Michael. "3-D or Not 3-D." *Film Comment,* November–December 1980, pp. 11–20.
Quigley, Martin, Jr. *New Screen Techniques.* New York: Quigley Publishing Company, 1953.
Slide, Anthony. "3-D Back Again and Again and Again." In *Film Review 1983–84,* ed. F. Maurice Speed. London: W. H. Allen, 1983, pp. 17–21.
"Strictly for the Marbles." *Time,* June 1953, pp. 66–74.

THX MOTION PICTURE LOUDSPEAKER SYSTEM. See LUCASFILM, LTD.

TIFFANY FILM CORPORATION. Herbert Brenon left the Universal Film Manufacturing Company in October 1914 to become the head of the Tiffany Film Corporation, which planned to release with the Alco Film Corporation*. Intending to make films that would enjoy long runs on Broadway, Brenon signed Mrs. Leslie Carter to play in the Civil War drama *The Heart of Maryland,* in which she had appeared on Broadway and around the country for some 3,500 performances for the previous 20 years. The film was shot at the Oz* studio in Hollywood, with William Shay in the male lead. When it was released by Metro* in March 1915, the film was the first feature to be shown at the New York Hippodrome, the largest theatre in the world, seating 5,400. Although Brenon planned to make his next film at Tiffany with actress Nance O'Neil, instead he went to the newly formed Fox Film Corporation, taking O'Neil and Shay with him.

BIBLIOGRAPHY

"Brenon to Produce for Tiffany." *The Moving Picture World,* October 31, 1914, p. 619.

TIFFANY PRODUCTIONS, incorporated in 1921, was a minor film producer, but one that eschewed the types of features—"B" Westerns and the like—that one might expect from such a company. It specialized in society dramas and melodramas, notably *Peacock Alley,* starring Mae Murray, which Tiffany produced both as a silent feature (1922) and as a part-talkie with a Technicolor sequence (1930). From 1927 to 1929, director John Stahl was associated with the company, which became known during that period as Tiffany-Stahl Productions.

The most important of all Tiffany films was *Journey's End* (1930), directed by James Whale; it was the first Anglo-American sound co-production. *Journey's End* brought such prominence to Tiffany that in 1930 an injunction against the use of the name was filed by the jewellers Tiffany and Company. Unfortunately, *Journey's End* also marked the end of quality production at Tiffany, with the exceptions of *Lucky Boy* (1929), a part-talkie starring George Jessel; *The Medicine Man* (1930), starring Jack Benny; and *Mamba* (1930), a Technicolor feature. In an effort to overcome its financial problems, Tiffany began to turn out the staple of the "B" movie* producers: "B" Westerns, featuring Ken Maynard and Bob Steele, and short subjects such as The Tiffany Talking Chimps series, The Voice of Hollywood*, Paul Hurst comedies, *Al Mannon's Sports Folio, Screen Book of Knowledge, Romance of the Old and New World,* and *Screen Novelties* series. It ceased operations in 1932. (From 1927 onward, Tiffany was located at the former Fine Arts* studio on Sunset Boulevard.)

BIBLIOGRAPHY

Fernett, Gene. *Poverty Row.* Satellite Beach, Fla.: Coral Reef Publications, 1973.

THE TILFORD CINEMA CORPORATION, headed by W. F. Tilford, was a New York-based producer, active from

1922 to 1924. Its films appear to have been entirely shot in Florida.

TIME-LIFE FILMS, INC., a division of Time, Inc., was formed in 1973 by the merger of Time-Life Films, Time-Life Video, and Time-Life Entertainment. It was chiefly noted for its exclusive distribution of BBC Television productions in the United States, a ten-year partnership that terminated on April 30, 1981. In 1973, the company signed an agreement for the nontheatrical distribution of films produced by the American Film Institute, and that same year it acquired worldwide rights to the Harold Lloyd films. It financed a number of theatrical features: *They All Laughed* (1981), *Loving Couples* (1980), and *Fort Apache, the Bronx* (1981). There was talk early in 1981 of the sale of the company to 20th Century-Fox*, but, in August 1981, its assets were acquired by Columbia Pictures*. The sale became necessary following a loss of some $9 million, after taxes, in 1980.

TIME WARNER INC. In March 1989, Warner Communications, Inc., and Time Inc. (incorporated on November 28, 1922) announced plans for a merger, which would create the world's largest communications organization. Paramount* attempted an abortive takeover of Time Inc., but on January 10, 1990, the $14.9 billion merger of the two companies became official. On June 30, 1992, Time Warner Inc. formed Time Warner Entertainment Co., responsible for the activities of Warner Bros.*, HBO, and Time Warner cable interests. In 1995, Time Warner announced the $8 billion acquisition of the Turner Broadcasting System*, approved by the Federal Trade Commission on September 11, 1996.

Address: 75 Rockefeller Plaza, New York, N.Y. 10019.

BIBLIOGRAPHY

Bruck, Connie. *Master of the Game: Steve Ross and the Creation of Time Warner.* New York: Simon & Schuster, 1994.
Landler, Mark, and Judith H. Dobrzynski. "Time Warner." *Business Week,* July 22, 1991, pp. 70–74.
"Main Men." *Newsweek,* July 29, 1996, pp. 42–43, 46.

TINTING AND TONING was a popular method of coloring silent films. Tints could be used to indicate changes in mood, while green and blue tints might be utilized for night scenes. By the mid-twenties, tinting and toning was used less frequently, and it virtually disappeared with the coming of sound because of problems in printing the sound track on tinted film stock. (However, tinting is used to advantage in a number of early sound films, notably in two 1932 features, *One Hour with You* and *Bird of Paradise*.)

Tinting involved the dipping of the film in the appropriate colored dye, which gave an overall color to the film stock. Toning involved the conversion of the silver in a black-and-white film through chemical toning. Thus, the black image could be changed to any color, while the white image remained unaffected. Unfortunately, the "tinting" of silent films today is usually handled by copying the original print on to Eastman Color* stock, which captures the essence of the original tinting but loses much of its delicacy and can even slightly change the coloring.

BIBLIOGRAPHY

Eastman Kodak Company. *Tinting and Toning of Eastman Positive Motion Picture Film.* Rochester, N.Y.: Eastman Kodak, 1924.
"Toning and Tinting as an Adjunct to the Picture." *The Moving Picture World,* March 18, 1911, p. 574.

THE TITLE REGISTRATION BUREAU was created in 1925, and is operated by the Motion Picture Association of America*. Producers can register potential film titles with the Bureau and so avoid duplication or any harmful degree of similarity in titles. The registration of titles has no legal significance and no effect upon copyrights; in reality, titles cannot be copyrighted. As of 1946, it was reported that the Bureau had 13,500 unreleased titles on register and 41,500 released titles, both features and short subjects. The Title Registration Bureau's best-known employee was Margaret Ann Young, who was there from 1934 to 1969.

BIBLIOGRAPHY

Hill, Gladwyn. "Any Titles To Spare?" *The New York Times,* March 16, 1947.
Menagh, Fred. "Monitor of Movie Titles." *The Saturday Evening Post,* August 7, 1948.
"MPA Title Bureau Proves Its Worth." *Motion Picture Herald,* December 7, 1946, p. 52.

TODD-AO, a widescreen system developed by Dr. Brian O'Brien of the American Optical Company, utilized a single camera, with four lenses, and a single projector. The width of the film in the camera was 65mm, and the width of the projected film was 70mm*. The first film to be shot in Todd-AO was *Oklahoma!,* which received its premiere at the Rivoli Theatre, New York, on October 13, 1955. *Oklahoma!* was released by Magna Pictures Corporation* (which also released *South Pacific* in 1958 and *Harlow* in 1965), of which Todd-AO became a wholly owned subsidiary until 1976. The second Todd-AO feature is probably the best known, and that was *Around the World in 80 Days,* produced by the man who gave the system its name, showman Mike Todd, and which received the 1956 Academy Award for Best Picture.

BIBLIOGRAPHY

Rowan, Arthur. "Todd-AO—Newest Wide-Screen System." *American Cinematographer,* October 1954, pp. 494–96, 526.
Williams, Kathryn. "The Rich History of Todd-AO." *Post,* vol. 3, no. 1, January 1988, pp. 62–63.

TODDY PICTURES COMPANY. One of the most important producers of all-black films strictly for black American audiences was Toddy Pictures Company, formed in 1941 by its president Ted Toddy by merging his other companies, Dixie Film Exchange of Atlanta, Million Dollar Pictures, and Consolidated National Film Exchanges. It produced both features and shorts, starring celebrities such as Lena Horne, Joe Louis, Nine Mae McKinney, Ralph Cooper, and Louise Beavers, with a production office at 6406 Sunset Boulevard in Los Angeles, New York headquarters, and film exchanges in Atlanta, Dallas, Chicago, and Los Angeles. In the April 12, 1947, issue of *Motion Picture Herald,* Toddy explained the nature of his product: "Negro audiences do not care for heavy emotional dramas. Their choice in film entertainment is the picture which features light comedy, outdoor adventures, musical comedies with an abundance of singing and dancing, and comedy romances." Toddy Pictures remained in existence through the early seventies.

TONING. See TINTING AND TONING

TOUCHSTONE FILMS was created in February 1984 by Walt Disney Productions* to produce films separate from the studio's typical entire family-oriented fare. Touchstone, meaning a test of quality, was selected from some 1,200 suggested names, and the first film to be released under the Touchstone banner was *Splash* (1984).

Address: 500 South Buena Vista Street, Burbank, Calif. 91521.

TRADE PAPERS are the means by which those within the industry keep abreast of matters relating to all aspects of the motion picture—production, distribution, and exhibition. The oldest surviving and best known of all such papers is *Variety,* which has been published weekly in New York since December 16, 1905. Often referred to as the "Bible of Show Business," *Variety* began life as a publication chiefly concerned with vaudeville, and it was not until the twenties that motion pictures began to take up half of each issue. The earliest of trade papers exclusively devoted to film was *The Film Index,* which was founded as *Views and Film Index* on April 25, 1906, and which ceased publication on July 1, 1911, when it merged with *The Moving Picture World.*

The Moving Picture World is the best known of silent film trade papers to those studying the history of the motion picture. First published on March 9, 1907, it was published as a separate entity until December 31, 1927, when it merged with *Exhibitor's Herald* to become *Exhibitor's Herald World.* In time, the latter, along with the other major trade papers from the silent era—*Motion Picture News* (May 1908–December 27, 1930) and *Motography* (which began life as *The Nickelodeon* in January 1909 and ceased publication on July 13, 1918)—became *Motion Picture Herald.* A Quigley publication, *Motion Picture Herald* was the first published January 3, 1931, and ended life May 5, 1973, as *QP Herald.* Quigley Publications was also responsible for the *International Motion Picture Almanac* and for *Motion Picture Daily* (which began life as *Exhibitor's Trade Review* on December 9, 1916).

Certainly the first major and possibly one of the best known of daily trade papers was *The Film Daily,* which began publication as *Wid's Films and Film Folks* in October 1915. *The Film Daily* along with its annual publication, *The Film Daily Year Book,* ceased publication in 1970. Presently, there are two daily trade papers, published five days a week: *The Hollywood Reporter* and *Daily Variety.* Both are published in Hollywood, the former since September 3, 1930, and the latter since September 6, 1933.

BIBLIOGRAPHY

D'Agostino, Annette M. *An Index to Short and Feature Film Reviews in the Moving Picture World: The Early Years, 1907–1915.* Westport, Conn.: Greenwood Press, 1995.
———. *Filmmakers in The Moving Picture World: An Index of Articles, 1907–1927.* Jefferson, North Carolina: McFarland, 1997.
Slide, Anthony. *International Film, Radio, and Television Journals.* Westport, Conn.: Greenwood Press, 1985.

TRAILERS, also known as coming attraction trailers and prevues, are utilized to "sell" a new film to a theatre audience by providing a brief outline of the star or emphasizing the most commercial aspects of the production (that is, its stars, director, or unusual theme). Trailers data back to the early part of the second decade of the twentieth century, when they consisted of nothing more than the film's main title and one or two important scenes. Extensive new artwork to promote a film was not introduced until the twenties.

By the thirties, trailers had become an integral part of a film presentation and remained so through the sixties. Research has indicated that trailers constitute 25 or 35 percent of the motivating force that encourages people to see a film, and as such producers are generally willing to spend between $10,000 and $30,000 on the production of individual trailers. Distributed to theatres by National Screen Service*, trailers are almost always prepared by independent production companies, with M-G-M* being the only studio to have had its own trailer department.

It is almost unprecedented for a film's maker to prepare a trailer, but, in recent years, directors such as Michael Cimino, Francis Ford Coppola, and Paul Schrader have overseen production of trailers promoting their current releases. Some trailers have attained "classic" stature, notably the one for *Citizen Kane* (1941), Cecil B. DeMille's lengthy promotional trailer for *The Ten Commandments* (1956), and a number of Alfred Hitchcock's trailers. Among the last, the best known is the trailer for *Rope* (1948), which introduces a character who is dead at the start of the film itself, and Hitchcock's personal tour of the Bates Motel in an eight-minute promotional trailer for *Psycho* (1960). In 1983, John

Landis prepared a 60-minute compilation of Universal trailers for pay television under the title of *Coming Soon*.

The average trailer is two to three minutes in length. In addition, trailers from 10 to 90 seconds are prepared for promotional purposes on television.

BIBLIOGRAPHY

Blair, Iain. "Film Trailers: Attracting Audiences with Flair." *On Location,* January 1983, pp. 39–49.
Fadden, James. "Trailers: Hollywood's Recreational Vehicle." *Back Stage,* August 19, 1983, pp. 5, 8, 10, 18, 29, 38.
Francis, Barbara. "Movie Trailers: The Lure of the Filmstrip Tease." *Los Angeles Times,* Calendar, October 7, 1979, p. 7.
Goodwin, Michael. "The Lost Films of Alfred Hitchcock." *New West,* April 1981, pp. 84–87, 142.
Lees, David, and Stan Berkowitz. "The True Story behind Those 'Coming Attractions' (You'll Laugh! You'll Cry!)." *Los Angeles,* January 1979, pp. 94–99.

TRANSATLANTIC PICTURES was formed by British theatre magnate Sidney Bernstein and Alfred Hitchcock (1899–1980) in April 1946, with Victor Peers as production manager and offices in London. Financed by Bankers Trust, the company produced *Rope* (1948) and *Under Capricorn* (1949), both directed by Hitchcock.

BIBLIOGRAPHY

"Transatlantic Is Planning Three Pictures a Year." *Motion Picture Herald,* May 17, 1947, p. 50.

RESOURCES

Papers: Academy of Motion Picture Arts and Sciences (Alfred Hitchcock Collection).

TRANS-LUX CORPORATION was founded in 1920 by Percy N. Furber, who had invented a rear projection screen that made possible the showing of motion pictures in daylight and that formed the basis for the screen utilized for the projection of the ticker tape on the New York Stock Exchange. In the early thirties, Trans-Lux expanded its operations to include the management of newsreel theatres, and the name quickly became synonymous with newsreel* presentations, the Trans-Lux theatres becoming known as "Luxers." The corporation—which changed its name in 1937 from Trans-Lux Daylight Screen Corporation to Trans-Lux Corporation—operated newsreel theatres in New York at 58th Street, 49th Street and Broadway, 60th Street and Madison Avenue, 52th Street and Lexington Avenue, and 85th Street and Madison Avenue.

In time, some of the theatres began screening second-run features in competition with a young man named Harry Brandt (who was president of the Independent Theatre Owners Association, formed in 1933), who persuaded Trans-Lux, in 1939, to form Film Alliance of the U.S., Inc., to import and exhibit films from the United Kingdom and France. The new endeavor was not successful, but Brandt remained associated with Trans-Lux, gaining control of the corporation in the late forties. He transformed the Trans-Lux theatres at 60th Street and Madison Avenue, 52d Street and Lexington Avenue, and 85th Street and Madison Avenue into art houses. In 1955, Trans-Lux Distributing Corporation was created, with its first film being Federico Fellini's *La Strada*.

Trans-Lux operated two exhibits at the 1964 New York World's Fair, which led to the corporation's later involvement with the multimedia attractions, the New York Experience, and the Seaport Experience. It sold its theatres to Paramount* in 1986.

Address: 110 Richards Avenue, Norwalk, Conn. 06856-5090.

TRIANGLE FILM CORPORATION. Leading figures associated with the Mutual Film Corporation* met in La Junta, California, on July 20, 1915, and created the Triangle Film Corporation, with a capitalization of $5 million, to produce and market films. Harry A. Aitken was the president, Adam Kessel was the treasurer, and producers D. W. Griffith, Thomas H. Ince, and Mack Sennett, along with Charles O. Baumann, were vice presidents. The company was formed to produce and release multiple-reel films made by the separate companies of the three producers and to lease a chain of first-class theatres in major U.S. cities to exhibit the company's more elaborate productions. Triangle's offices were in the Brokaw Building, Broadway and 42d Street, New York.

Triangle's first release, which on September 23, 1915, opened New York's Knickerbocker Theatre, was composed of *The Lamb*, Douglas Fairbanks' first feature, nominally supervised by D. W. Griffith; *The Iron Strain*, produced by Ince and starring Dustin Farnum; and Keystone's *My Valet*, starring Raymond Hitchcock. Triangle attracted stars from the legitimate stage, vaudeville, and musical comedy to its three production entities: Sir Herbert Beerbohm Tree, Mary Anderson de Navarro, Weber and Fields, DeWolf Hopper, William Collier, Billie Burke, Mario Doro, Elliott Dexter, Texas Guinan, Helen Ware, Jane Grey, Joe Jackson, Eddie Foy, Mary Boland, and Julia Dean.

In 1916, the Triangle Distributing Corporation, which was jointly owned by the Triangle Film Corporation and Superpictures, Inc.*, was created to handle the productions of Fine Arts*, Kay-Bee, and Keystone*. W. W. Hodkinson was the president and general manager, and Raymond Pawley was the treasurer. Its offices were located at 1454 Broadway. Early in 1917, Allan Dwan became supervising director of Triangle's Yonkers, New York, studios. After Hodkinson left in mid-1917, Stephen A. Lynch gained control. When Griffith, Ince, and Sennett left the organization at the same time, Triangle retained control of the Keystone trademark, and H. O. Davis assumed control of the company.

Paralta* distributed through Triangle for a short period in the latter half of 1917. In September 1917, there was an announcement that Triangle was planning to produce films in India, China, and Buenos Aires, but nothing came of these plans, and a year later the company dismissed its stock company of 75. In mid-1919, Goldwyn* purchased the Triangle studio in Culver City.

BIBLIOGRAPHY

"H. E. Aitken Announces Triangle Merger." *Motion Picture News,* March 25, 1916, p. 1767.

"Kessel-Baumann-Aitken." *The Moving Picture World,* July 3, 1915, p. 42.

Lahue, Kalton C. *Dreams for Sale.* South Brunswick, N.J.: A. S. Barnes, 1971.

Milne, Peter. "The First Knickerbocker Triangle Program." *Motion Picture News,* October 9, 1915, pp. 84–85.

"Triangle Film Incorporated." *The Moving Picture World,* July 31, 1915, p. 824.

"Triangle Opening Announced." *The Moving Picture World,* September 4, 1915, pp. 1622–23.

"Triangle's Auspicious Opening." *The Moving Picture World,* October 9, 1915, pp. 233–34.

TRIANGLE PRODUCTIONS, INC. See COMET PRODUCTIONS, INC.

TRICOLORE FILMS, INC., was formed in 1946 by Alexander Korda (1893–1956) to distribute French films in the United States. It was headed by Landy Lawrence, and its first release was *Les Enfants du Paradis* (1944).

TRISTAR was formed on November 30, 1982, by CBS, Home Box Office, and Columbia Pictures* as a major Hollywood producer/distributor. Initially known by the code name Nova, the company was originally called Tri-Star, but the hyphen was dropped in 1981. Gary Hendler (1939–1989) was TriStar's first president—he resigned in December 1994—responsible for its first two features, *The Natural* and *Places in the Heart,* and the company's logo was a white horse. TriStar and Columbia merged in 1987, but the former continued as a separate production arm of Sony Pictures Entertainment, and as late as 1991, TriStar Television was formed.

Address: 10202 West Washington Boulevard, Culver City, Calif. 90232.

BIBLIOGRAPHY

Kilday, Gregg. "How Dare They." *Esquire,* February 1985, pp. 121–25.

Pollock, Dale. "Just What Is This 'Eighth Studio'?" *Los Angeles Times,* Calendar, December 13, 1982, pp. 1–2.

Salmans, Sandra. "Tri-Star's Bid for Movie Stardom." *The New York Times,* May 13, 1984, pp. F1, F12–F13.

TRIUMPH FILM CORPORATION. See WORLD FILM CORPORATION

TRIUMPH FILMS was formed in February 1982 by Columbia Pictures* as a separate corporate entity for the specialized release of foreign and American independent features. Shortly after its creation, Triumph became closely associated with the French Gaumont Company, whose films it distributed in the United States. Charles Schreger was named Triumph's first president—he resigned in 1984—and the company's first release was the German feature *Das Boot* (1982). In November 1985, Triumph Films was totally absorbed by Columbia Pictures' Classics Division (which had been founded in 1971 by Dennis Doph).

BIBLIOGRAPHY

Jacobson, Harlan. "How the Classics Kids Snatched the Foreign Film." *The Village Voice,* November 22, 1983, pp. 74–76.

TROMA, INC., founded in New York in 1974 by Lloyd Kaufman and Michael Herz, is a low-budget production company, noted for its "camp" films, including *The Toxic Avenger* (1986), *Surf Nazis Must Die* (1987), and *Teenage Catgirls in Heat* (1994). By the early 1990s, it had produced more than 100 such films with budgets of between 2 and 4 million each. In 1993, Troma formed 50th Street Films to distribute productions that did not fit its traditional style.

Address: 733 Ninth Avenue, New York, N.Y. 10019.

BIBLIOGRAPHY

Grimes, William. "Troma, the Film Studio That Says Low Is Good and Bad May be Better." *The New York Times,* July 20, 1992, pp. C11, C13.

TRUART FILM CORPORATION, active from the early through mid-twenties, was a New York-based producer and states rights* distributor, formed by L. A. Young. It had three minor stars under contract: Larry Semon, Elaine Hammerstein, and Richard Talmadge.

TRUCOLOR. See CINECOLOR

TUCSON, ARIZONA. See AL JENNINGS PRODUCTION COMPANY

TURNER BROADCASTING SYSTEM, INC., is the umbrella company for the activities of Robert E. "Ted" Turner (born 1938). Through a subsidiary, Turner Entertainment Co., the company controls the rights to all M-G-M* films from 1924 through June 1986; the RKO* film library from 1930 to 1957; all Warner Bros.* features and shorts from 1918 to 1950; the entire Hanna-Barbera* library; and the output of Turner Pictures. Turner Broadcasting System also owns New Line Cinema* and Castle Rock Entertainment*. The entire Turner library consists of approximately 900 color features, 2,500 black-and-white features, 3,000 short subjects, 2,200 hours of television programming, and 900 animated shorts and 1,500 hours of animated television programming. In 1995, Time Warner* acquired Turner Broadcasting System, Inc., for $8 billion; the acquisition was approved by the Federal Trade Commission on September 11, 1996.

Address: 1050 Techwood Drive, N.W., Atlanta, Ga. 30318; 1888 Century Park, East Los Angeles, Calif. 90067 (Turner Entertainment Co.).

TURNER PICTURES, INC., was founded by Ted Turner (born 1938) in 1989 to produce films for the TNT cable channel. It later expanded into theatrical film production, and its first theatrical release was *Gettysburg* (1993). In 1994, Amy Pascal was named president and she announced that the company would produce six to eight features a year. With the acquisition of the Turner Broadcasting System by Time Warner*, Turner Pictures was phased out of existence in November 1996, ironically as it enjoyed its greatest commercial success with the John Travolta vehicle *Michael*.

BIBLIOGRAPHY

Bibb, Porter. *It Ain't As Easy As It Looks: Ted Turner's Amazing Story*. New York: Crown, 1993.
Fabrikant, Geraldine. "New Time Warner To Combine Film Units." *The New York Times*, November 15, 1996, p. D5.
Goldberg, Peter, and Gerald Jay Goldberg. *Citizen Turner: The Wild Rise of an American Tycoon*. New York: Harcourt Brace, 1995.

TUSKEN MUSIC. See LUCASFILM, LTD.

20TH CENTURY-FOX FILM CORPORATION. By 1935 the Fox Film Corporation* was in need of new corporate blood, and on May 28 of that year its merger with Twentieth Century Pictures* was announced, with the new company named 20th Century-Fox Film Corporation. Darryl F. Zanuck (1902–1979) became vice president and head of production, Joseph M. Schenck was named chairman of the board, and Sidney Kent continued over from the Fox Film Corporation as president.

Zanuck took over a company with two major stars, Shirley Temple and Will Rogers, but lost the latter in a plane crash the first year of the new studio's existence. Tyrone Power became the company's new major male star, and Zanuck embarked on an ambitious production schedule that included *Lloyds of London* (1936), *Alexander's Ragtime Band* (1938), *Suez* (1938), *In Old Chicago* (1938), *Jesse James* (1939), *Stanley and Livingstone* (1939), and *Drums Along the Mohawk* (1939). Don Ameche played the inventor of the telephone in *The Story of Alexander Graham Bell* (1939) and Stephen Foster in *Swanee River* (1939). Zanuck produced the popular series of Charlie Chan, Mr. Moto, and The Country Doctor, featuring Jean Hersholt and the Dionne quintuplets. New female stars, such as Alice Faye, Betty Grable, and Sonja Henie, were created.

In the forties, Zanuck produced the commercially and critically unsuccessful biographical feature—one of his favorite genres—*Wilson* (1944), but he was also responsible for such important social dramas as *The Grapes of Wrath* (1940), *Gentleman's Agreement* (1947), and *The Snake Pit* (1948). In the fifties, it was Zanuck and 20th Century-Fox that made Marilyn Monroe a star, in a decade that also saw the company introduce the widescreen system of CinemaScope*.

In 1956, Darryl F. Zanuck left the company he had worked so hard to create, and he was succeeded by Buddy Adler (who died in 1960). Spyros Skouras, who had been the head of the studio since 1942, found himself in financial difficulties with *Cleopatra*, the costly Elizabeth Taylor-Richard Burton epic, which was eventually released in 1963. In 1962, Zanuck returned to the studio as its president and with his son, Richard, embarked on a production program that included the highly successful *The Sound of Music* (1965), *Patton* (1970), and *M*A*S*H* (1970) and also the poorly received *Doctor Doolittle* (1967) and *Star!* (1968).

Zanuck resigned as president in 1969, and, after an interim period during which his son ran the company, Dennis C. Stanfill took over in 1971. He became chairman of the board, and Gordon T. Stulberg stepped in as president, to be succeeded in 1975 by Stanfill (who also served as chairman of the board and chief executive officer). That same year Alan Ladd, Jr., became head of production and did much to help the studio's financial position with the *Star Wars* trilogy. In 1981, Alan Hirschfield became chairman of the board, with Sherry Lansing as president, succeeded a year later by Joe Wizan.

Denver oilman Marvin Davis acquired the company in 1981, selling 50 percent of it to Rupert Murdoch in 1985. Alan Hirschfield resigned in October 1984; he was succeeded by Barry Diller, and Lawrence Gordon became president. Rupert Murdoch acquired Davis's half of the company in October 1985 for a reported $325 million, plus real estate.

In 1985, the company was purchased by Rupert Murdoch's News Corp. Ltd. A new corporation, Fox, Inc., was created, with the production arm named Fox Film Corporation, and the hyphen quietly dropped from the 20th Century Fox. As of 1995, 20th Century Fox had four distinct production units: 20th Century Fox, Fox 2000 Pictures, Fox Family Films (which includes its animation division), and Fox Searchlight (making "art house" films). In May 1996, Rupert Murdoch announced plans for a new 20th Century Fox studio in Sydney, Australia.

The 20th Century Fox studio lot, which began life as Movietone City and which was initially part of Westwood, before becoming part of the newly developed Century City, was sold to Alcoa Corporation in 1961. The bulk of the backlot was used for the Century City development, with 20th Century Fox leasing back some 63 acres for its production needs. The entrance to the lot is notable for the *Hello, Dolly!* New York street set, constructed in 1968.

In response to an oft-asked question, 20th Century Fox plans to keep its name and its familiar logo into the twenty-first century.

Address: 10201 West Pico Boulevard, Los Angeles, Calif. 90035.

BIBLIOGRAPHY

Behlmer, Rudy, ed. *Memo from Darryl F. Zanuck: The Golden Years at Twentieth Century-Fox.* New York: Grove Press, 1993.

Dunne, John Gregory. *The Studio.* New York: Farrar, Straus & Giroux, 1969.

Parish, James Robert. *The Fox Girls.* New Rochelle, New York: Arlington House, 1971.

Silverman, Stephen M. *The Fox That Got Away: The Last Days of the Zanuck Dynasty at Twentieth Century-Fox.* Secaucus, New Jersey: Lyle Stuart, 1988.

Solomon, Aubrey. *Twentieth Century-Fox: A Corporate and Financial History.* Metuchen, New Jersey: Scarecrow Press, 1988.

Thomas, Tony, and Aubrey Solomon. *The Films of 20th Century-Fox.* Secaucus, New Jersey: Citadel Press, 1979.

RESOURCES

Films: Museum of Modern Art, UCLA Film and Television Archives (35mm nitrate studio prints).

Papers: Columbia University (archives of the Research Department), UCLA (Production Records).

Photographs: University of Southern California (Set Stills, 1932–1953).

Scripts: University of Southern California (1916–1971).

20TH CENTURY-FOX MOVIE RANCH, now the Malibu Creek State Park, was utilized in the location filming of many studio productions, including *Brigham Young* (1940), *How Green Was My Valley* (1941), *My Friend Flicka* (1943), *Viva Zapata!* (1952), *Love Is a Many Splendored Thing* (1955), *Love Me Tender* (1956), *Butch Cassidy and the Sundance Kid* (1969), and *M*A*S*H* (1970). In the late eighties and early nineties, a Hollywood-based group, The Silent Society, regularly screened silent films there in the open during the summer months.

TWENTIETH CENTURY PICTURES. When Daryl F. Zanuck (1902–1979) resigned as production head of Warner Bros.* in the spring of 1933, he joined with Joseph Schenck to form a new company, utilizing $100,000 that Louis B. Mayer had given to Zanuck in order that Mayer's son-in-law, William Goetz, would be Zanuck's executive assistant. The company was called Twentieth Century Pictures at the suggestion of Samuel G. Engel, who supposedly told Zanuck that he had a name for him that would be good for 67 years.

Twentieth Century Pictures owned no studio and leased space at the United Artists* lot. The first production was *The Bowery* (1933), directed by Raoul Walsh and starring Wallace Beery and Fay Wray. The company produced 17 further features: *Broadway through a Keyhole* (1933), *Blood Money* (1933), *Advice to the Lovelorn* (1933), *Gallant Lady* (1934), *Moulin Rouge* (1934), *The House of Rothschild* (1934), *Looking for Trouble* (1934), *Born to Be Bad* (1934), *The Affairs of Cellini* (1934), *Bulldog Drummond Strikes Back* (1934), *The Last Gentleman* (1934), *The Mighty Barnum* (1934), *Clive of India* (1935), *Folies Bergere* (1935), *Cardinal Richelieu* (1935), *Les Miserables* (1935), and *The Call of the Wild* (1935). On May 29, 1935, Twentieth Century Pictures merged with the Fox Film Corporation* to become 20th Century-Fox*.

21ST CENTURY FILM CORP. began life in New York in 1976 as 21st Century Distribution, Inc. That company was acquired in 1989 by Giancarlo Parretti and renamed Cannon Pictures*. However, as part of the deal for Menahem Golan's departure from the Cannon Group, Inc.*, which Parretti had earlier acquired, Golan was given the name and logo of 21st Century Distribution, which he renamed 21st Century Film Corp. In August 1993, it was announced that Melrose Entertainment, owned by Golan's former partner, Yoram Globus, would distribute 21st Century's films, and in December of the same year, the company filed for reorganization under Chapter XI of the Bankruptcy Code, at which time, Golan lost control of the company's assets.

Address: 1925 Century Park East, Los Angeles, Calif. 90067.

22mm was a home movie film gauge, utilizing three images printed side by side, developed by Thomas A. Edison, Inc., in 1912.

UA. SEE UNITED ARTISTS CORPORATION

UIP (Universal International Pictures) was created in London in the early 1980s as the European distributor for Paramount*, Universal*, and MGM/UA (now superceded by Turner Entertainment Co.), by which it is jointly owned.

Address: 45 Beadon Road, London W6 0EG, England, United Kingdom.

UNION PHOTOPLAY COMPANY. Charles R. Macauley, cartoonist for the *New York Evening World,* was the head of the Union Photoplay Company, which was formed in 1914. It produced *Alice in Wonderland,* followed by a series of half-reel cartoons.

BIBLIOGRAPHY

"Charles R. Macauley Making Pictures." *The Moving Picture World,* October 17, 1914, p. 315.

UNITED ARTISTS (UA) CLASSICS was the first division to be established by a major studio to acquire and release "art" or noncommercial films, generally from abroad. United Artists Classics was formed in 1980 from the old UA Classics, established to handle bookings from revival houses for the Warner Bros.* features and shorts controlled by United Artists Corporation*. The first film to be acquired by the newly reorganized division was François Truffaut's *The Last Metro* (1981). As a result of UA's success with its Classics Division, Columbia Pictures* formed Triumph Film*, Universal* created Universal Classics, and 20th Century-Fox* established Twentieth Century Fox International Classics. With the merger between M-G-M* and United Artists, United Artists Classics became MGM/UA Classics.

BIBLIOGRAPHY

Springer, Alica. "Sell It Again, Sam!" *American Film,* March 1983, pp. 50–55.

UNITED ARTISTS CORPORATION. The formation of United Artists Corporation (UA) marked the first time that a group of artists rather than businessmen had come together to create a major distribution corporation for their films. The four principals in the new company were Mary Pickford, Douglas Fairbanks, Charles Chaplin, and D. W. Griffith; a fifth, William S. Hart, was involved in the original discussions as to the corporation's formation but later dropped out.

On January 15, 1919, United Artists came into being, and Richard A. Rowland, president of Metro Pictures Corporation*, made his famous remark to the effect that "the lunatics have taken charge of the asylum."

United Artists was established to market films produced by its four stockholders, each of whom received 1,000 shares of preferred stock, with an additional 1,000 going to UA's general counsel, William Gibbs McAdoo. The corporation was incorporated on April 17, 1919, with headquarters in New York, and the first feature it released—on September 1, 1919—was Douglas Fairbanks's *His Majesty, the American.*

Despite early financial problems, the company prospered by the mid-twenties. D. W. Griffith left the organization when his contract expired in December 1924, but at the same time Joseph Schenck joined the group as its new chairman of the board. It was Schenck who was instrumental in forming the United Artists Theatre Circuit, Inc., in 1926, a theatre circuit that at last gave the company guaranteed screenings for its releases. To United Artists Schenck brought Norma Talmadge and Gloria Swanson. Rudolph Valentino's *The Eagle* (1925), and *The Son of the Sheik* (1926) were released by United Artists. Samuel Goldwyn agreed, in 1925, to release his productions through the organization, and two years later he became a partner. Howard Hughes and Buster Keaton released their films through United Artists.

With the coming of sound the company faced a crisis. D. W. Griffith had rejoined the group in 1927, but his later films were not particularly successful. Fairbanks and Pickford were in decline, and Chaplin was producing fewer and fewer features. The only major addition to UA's producers was Walt Disney, who agreed, in 1931, to release his cartoons through the company, followed by the newly formed Twentieth Century Pictures* and Alexander Korda's British-based London Film Productions.

The year 1935 was a crucial one for United Artists. Schenck resigned, Alexander Korda became a partner, and David O. Selznick agreed to release eight features through UA. Walter Wanger Productions was formed in 1936 to release through UA, and that same year A. H. Giannini, chairman of the Bank of America, became the company's new president.

The Second World War heralded the beginning of the end for the old United Artists as its partners fought over the company—there was a particularly bitter dispute between Goldwyn and Pickford over the United Artists Studios in Hollywood, which the former utilized as a production center—and product became scarce, despite UA's release of some of the

J. Arthur Rank British productions. In 1950, after three consecutive years of losses of almost a million dollars, Arthur B. Krim and Robert S. Benjamin (of the law firm of Phillips, Nizer, Benjamin & Krim) took over the company, and a new United Artists was created. (Chaplin sold his remaining stock to Krim and Benjamin in 1955, and Mary Pickford followed suit a year later.)

Benjamin and Krim went into partnership with new producers, whose films they were willing to finance partially. In the fifties, United Artists released more than 50 features a year, including such memorable productions as *The African Queen* (1951), *High Noon* (1953), *The Night of the Hunter* (1955), *Marty* (1955), *Witness for the Prosecution* (1957), *Some Like It Hot* (1959), *Exodus* (1960), and *The Apartment* (1960). In 1957, the company acquired the Warner Bros.* library of 800 pre-1950 features and 1,500 shorts and cartoons.

In that same year, United Artists became a public company, and some ten years later 98 percent of its stock was acquired by the TransAmerica Corporation, which continued to run the organization, under the guidance of Benjamin and Krim, as a wholly owned subsidiary. Following a policy dispute with TransAmerica, Krim, Benjamin, and three other top executives left United Artists to form Orion Pictures Corporation* in January 1978. In July 1981, United Artists was acquired by Metro-Goldwyn-Mayer*, and in 1983 the two companies were merged as MGM/UA Entertainment Co.* In 1986, Ted Turner acquired MGM/UA, but kept only the M-G-M film library, selling other assets, including UA to Kirk Kerkorian, who, in turn, sold MGM/UA to Italian financier Giancarlo Parretti. The latter allowed UA to become a dormant company until 1993, when Credit Lyonnais, which gained control of UA after Parretti defaulted on loans, announced that Frank Mancuso (former chairman of Paramount Pictures*) would head a revamped United Artists. In August 1993, Mancuso named John Calley to be president of UA, and the company released its first film in many years, *Son of the Pink Panther*. Calley was replaced by Lindsay Doran in November 1996. United Artists unveiled a new logo with its 1995 release of *Rob Roy*.

Address: 2500 Broadway, Santa Monica, Calif. 90404; 1350 Avenue of the Americas, New York, N.Y. 10019.

BIBLIOGRAPHY

Balio, Tino. *United Artists*. Madison, Wis.: University of Wisconsin Press, 1976.

———. *United Artists: The Company That Changed the Film Industry*. Madison, Wis.: University of Wisconsin Press, 1987.

Bergan, Ronald. *The United Artists Story*. New York: Crown, 1986.

RESOURCES

Papers: Wisconsin Center for Film and Theater Research.
Photographs: Academy of Motion Picture Arts and Sciences (1950–1981).

UNITED COSTUME COMPANY. See WESTERN COSTUME CO.

UNITED FILM SERVICE was a releasing program of Warner's Features, Inc., which began on November 8, 1914. Later, by court order, the name of Warner's Features was changed to the United Film Service. United released 16 brands of short films, including those made by the Gaumont Company, Regent Film Company*, Sunshine Film Corporation (which made Juno, Mars, and Magnet single-reel comedies), Colonial Motion Picture Corporation, Pyramid Pictures, Inc., Superba Company (which made one-reel comedies with Edith Thorton, directed by Frank Hutchinson), Starlight Comedy Company (which produced comedies in the Mittenthal brothers' studio in Yonkers with Jimmy Aubrey and Walter Kendig), Lariat Company, Premier Company, and Luna Company. P. A. Powers was the first president of United. Later, J. C. Graham became the president and general manager.

In December 1914, a group of production companies organized to form United Motion Picture Producers, Inc., to supply the United Film Service with a daily volume of films. The affiliated producers were Albuquerque Film Manufacturing Company*, Crystal Film Company (which produced the Superba brand of comedies), Features Ideal, Gene Gauntier Feature Players Company (which produced two-reel dramas written by and starring Gauntier), Mittenthal Film Company, Inc., Nelson Film Corporation, St. Louis Motion Picture Company, and Smallwood Film Corporation. Ludwig G. B. Erb was the president of the producers group, and Gilbert P. Hamilton, the head of Albuquerque, was the vice president.

In June 1915, when United went bankrupt, the group of producers organized a new combination called the Combined Photoplay Producers, Inc. Producing companies included were Crystal, Gaumont, Erbograph Company, Ideal Company (which produced dramas from directors Frank Beal, Carl Levinus, and Webster Cullison and starred Edna Payne, George Larkin, and Fred Hearn), Pike's Peak Film Company*, St. Louis, Albuquerque, Grandin Films, Inc., Smallwood, and Mittenthal. Erb was the president. At the same time, A. and H. M. Warner, formerly with Warner's Features, Inc., and Al Lichtman, formerly with Paramount* and Alco*, formed Standard Pictures, Inc., to handle the product of the Combined Photoplay Producers. Standard planned to sell its pictures outright to its exchange connections rather than lease them. Standard signed a contract with the producing organization that gave Standard control of the quality of the films that it handled.

BIBLIOGRAPHY

"New Combination Formed." *The Moving Picture World,* July 3, 1915, p. 43.

"United Motion Picture Producers." *The Moving Picture World,* December 12, 1914, p. 1500.

"United's Affairs Aired in Court." *The Moving Picture World,* August 14, 1915, p. 1140.

"Warner's to Inaugurate New Service." *The Moving Picture World,* November 14, 1914, p. 947.

UNITED FILM SERVICE PROTECTIVE ASSOCIATION. See MOTION PICTURE PATENTS COMPANY

UNITED KEANOGRAPH FILM MANUFACTURING COMPANY

COMPANY was founded in Fairfax, California, in 1915 by James Keane, who was responsible for the production, direction, and writing of its first effort, *Money* (1915), starring Matt Synder. It was succeeded by James Keane Feature Photoplay Productions, which ceased operations in 1921.

BIBLIOGRAPHY

"New California Producing Co. Formed." *The Moving Picture World,* July 18, 1914, p. 448.

UNITED MOTION PICTURE PRODUCERS, INC. See UNITED FILM SERVICE

UNITED PARAMOUNT THEATRES, INC. When Paramount* was required by the consent decree* to divest itself of its theatre chain, the 1,424 theatres that it controlled in 1949 became United Paramount Theatres, Inc. American Broadcasting Companies, Inc., merged with United Paramount Theatres in 1953, and when ABC decided to leave the theatre circuit business in 1978, the chain was sold to Plitt Theatres*.

UNITED PHOTOPLAYS COMPANY was a Chicago-based producing company of 1915. Although it specialized in topical and educational films, such as *Ming Tombs and Camel Trail into Mongolia* and *Nara, the Cradle of Japanese Art,* United did produce a five-reel dramatic feature, *The Victory of Virtue,* featuring Gerda Holmes and Wilmuth Merkyl, directed by Harry McRae Webster, which was released late in 1915.

UNITED PICTURE THEATRES OF AMERICA, INC., a cooperative to distribute films that were owned, financed, and controlled by exhibitors, commenced operations on March 1, 1918. Lee A. Ochs, United's president, was also the president of the Motion Picture Exhibitors' League of America*. C. R. Seelye, former business manager of Pathé*, Vitagraph*, and World*, was United's vice president. In its first statement to the press, United announced that it planned to "reduce the film rentals by about thirty percent, giving producers a larger and quicker revenue than under the present expensive exchange system." It announced that its method of financing its operations would be to divide the cost of the film negative proportionately among as large a number of exhibitors as it could align. There would be five grades of exhibitors, each paying a different rate of the cost of the negative. Profits would be paid to the exhibitors who were United's stockholders. Early in January 1919, United merged with the World Film Corporation, which was to distribute films made for United by the Peerless Company. At that time there were 1,300 moving picture houses that were members of United, and J. A. Berst was the organization's president.

BIBLIOGRAPHY

"New Company Outlines Working Plans." *The Moving Picture World,* March 16, 1918, p. 1496.
"United Pictures Theatres Formed." *The Moving Picture World,* March 2, 1918, p. 1219.
"World and United Theatres Merge." *The Moving Picture World,* February 1, 1919, p. 599.

UNITED PRODUCTIONS OF AMERICA was formed in 1945 by a young animator named Stephen Bosustow from an earlier company, Industrial Films and Poster Service. In 1948, Bosustow signed a long-term distribution agreement with Columbia*, and his company's cartoon characters, Gerald McBoing-Boing and Mister Magoo, became two of the most popular with filmgoers, thanks to the quality of the films with their unusual storylines and lack of assembly-line approach. The company was also noted for many of its other cartoons, such as *Magic Flute* (1949), *Man Alive!* (1952), and *The Tell Tale Heart* (1953).

On January 1, 1956, the company changed its name to UPA Pictures, Inc., and around the same time it was sold to Henry G. Saperstein. In 1959, UPA's contract with Columbia ended, but it continued to produce cartoons for television into the sixties.

BIBLIOGRAPHY

Hine, Al. "McBoing-Boing and Magoo." *Holiday,* June 1951, pp. 6, 8–9, 11.
Langsner, Jules. "UPA." *Arts and Architecture,* December 1954, pp. 12–15.
Lee, Walter W., Jr. "UPA." *Pendulum,* Spring 1953, pp. 42–50.
Penney, Ed. "U.P.A. Animated Art." *The Arts,* March 1953, pp. 12–13.

UNITED STATES AMUSEMENT CORPORATION. Herbert Blaché, the president of Blaché Features, Inc., and the Exclusive Supply Corporation*, formed the United States Amusement Corporation in April 1914 to produce large feature films, five or more reels in length, based on well-known novels and plays. Other directors of the company were Madame Alice Blaché, the president of Solax*, Joseph M. Shear; Charles D. Lithgow; Joseph Borries; Henri Menessier; and Jules E. Brulatour. The company used the newly enlarged Blaché studio and laboratory at Fort Lee, New Jersey*, and its first production was Charles Dickens's *The Chimes,* starring Tom Terriss and directed by Terriss and Blaché. Productions of the United States Amusement Corporation were first released by World* and later by Art Dramas, Inc., of which Blaché was treasurer. Madame Blaché began directing the company's films in 1917.

BIBLIOGRAPHY

"Blaché Forms New Company." *The Moving Picture World,* May 2, 1914, p. 653.

UNITED STATES EXHIBITORS' BOOKING COR-PORATION. Frank G. Hall and William Oldknow formed the United States Exhibitors' Booking Corporation late in 1917 to buy special productions directly from producers and then, through M. H. Hoffman's Four Square Exchanges, to rent them to exhibitors. By not selling to territorial buyers, it planned to eliminate the middleman and thus reduce rental fees to exhibitors. Both Hall, the president and general manager, and Oldknow, the secretary and treasurer, had previously been exhibitors. Each production was sold separately, with the organization's first release being Thomas H. Ince's *The Zeppelin's Last Raid* (1918). In June 1918, it terminated its agreement with Foursquare and signed with regional independent exchanges to handle the films that it bought. The company went out of existence early in 1919.

BIBLIOGRAPHY

"Bill Oldknow and Frank Hall Hook Up." *The Moving Picture World,* November 3, 1917, p. 682.

UNITED STATES GOVERNMENT COMMITTEE ON PUBLIC INFORMATION: DIVISION OF FILMS. On September 25, 1917, the Division of Films of the United States Government Committee on Public Information was established by presidential order. Under the direction of Charles S. Hart, who had been an advertising manager at *Hearst's Magazine,* the Division of Films produced three feature-length propaganda documentaries concerning the First World War: *Pershing's Crusaders* (1918), *America's Answer* (1918), and *Under Four Flags* (1919). The Division also produced the one-reel weekly newsreel, *The Official War Review,* released by Pathé Exchange, Inc., which commenced on July 1, 1918, and continued for 31 issues.

The Division of Films' Advisory Board of Motion Picture Directors included J. Searle Dawley (who served as chairman), James Vincent (secretary), Maurice Tourneur, Captain E. H. Calvert, Edwin Carewe, Charles Giblyn, Raoul Walsh, Sidney Olcott, George Irving, and Travers Vale. In addition to producing, the Division, with the help of the motion picture industry, succeeded in stopping German propaganda films from being exhibited in neutral European countries. American producers demanded that their exported films be screened only if the Division's propaganda films were shown with them. Because of the popularity of the American films, furnished at cost, German productions were unwanted. The Committee and its Division of Films were disbanded by an Order of Congress on June 30, 1919.

BIBLIOGRAPHY

Creel, George. *How We Advertised America.* New York: Harper & Brothers, 1920.

"Film Division Names Director Advisers." *The Moving Picture World,* July 20, 1918, p. 363.
"Government Forging Ahead in Picture Making." *The Moving Picture World,* March 2, 1918, p. 1228.
"Hart to Dissolve Division of Films." *The Moving Picture World,* February 22, 1919, p. 1056.
"U.S. Film Division Makes Vast Plans." *Motion Picture News,* June 29, 1918, p. 3863.

UNITED STATES MOTION PICTURE CORPORA-TION built its studio between the Susquehanna River and the Blue Mountains in Wilkes-Barre, Pennsylvania, in August 1915. Fred W. Hermann, a Wilkes-Barre exhibitor, was the company's vice president, and James O. Walsh was the president. Playwright Daniel L. Hart was the scenario editor and Leatrice Joy the leading woman. The company made single-reel Black Diamond comedies, which were released by Paramount*, and ended operations early in 1918.

BIBLIOGRAPHY

"New Studio in Pennsylvania." *The Moving Picture World,* August 14, 1915, p. 1141.
"Wilkes-Barre Company Enlarging." *The Moving Picture World,* June 30, 1917, p. 2126.

UNITED STUDIOS. See ROBERT BRUNTON STU-DIOS, INC.

UNITED TALENT AGENCY, headed by president Marty Bauer, was established in 1991 with the merger of Bauer Benedict and Leading Artists. It is regarded as one of Hollywood's fastest growing agencies.

Address: 8560 Wilshire Boulevard, Suite 500, Beverly Hills, Calif. 90212.

BIBLIOGRAPHY

Citron, Alan. "United Talent Agency's Star Ascends." *Los Angeles Times,* July 26, 1994, p. D4.

UNITED THEATRICAL WAR ACTIVITIES COM-MITTEE. See HOLLYWOOD VICTORY COMMITTEE

UNITED WORLD FILMS. Recognizing the increasing importance of 16mm film*, Universal* established a wholly owned 16mm division, United World Films, in 1946, in which year it also took over the 16mm Bell & Howell Film-sound Library and Castle Films. United World Films ceased operations in 1967, becoming Universal 16, which has also now ceased to exist. With no 16mm library of its own, Universal currently rents 16mm prints of a selection of its films through Swank Motion Pictures of St. Louis and Clem Williams Films of Pittsburgh.

UNITY SALES CORPORATION. The distributor Unity Sales Corporation was formed in May 1916, with Andrew J.

Cobe as president and general manager. Among the films that it handled were the serial *The Yellow Menace,* starring Edwin Stevens, produced by the Serial Film Company; *My Country First,* produced by the Tom Terriss Film Corporation; and the "Tweedledum and Tweedledee" series, produced by the Eagle Film Company of Jackonsville, Florida. Unity disbanded early in 1917.

BIBLIOGRAPHY

"First Month of Unity Sales." *The Moving Picture World,* June 10, 1916, p. 1892.

THE UNIVERSAL ANIMATED WEEKLY. See NEWS-REELS

UNIVERSAL-INTERNATIONAL. See UNIVERSAL PICTURES

UNIVERSAL NEWS. See NEWSREELS

UNIVERSAL PICTURES. For more than one-third of its existence, Universal Pictures was associated with one man, Carl Laemmle (1867–1939), who created a distinctive company and whose films had a definite studio style. He aimed for a studio with a family atmosphere, with himself as the genial "Uncle Carl." A pioneer of the modern film industry, Laemmle began his motion picture career with a nickelodeon*, the White Front Theatre, located at 909 Milwaukee Avenue in Chicago, which he opened on February 24, 1906. With his partner, Robert Cochrane, Laemmle established the Laemmle Film Service, which by 1909, had become one of the largest film exchanges in the country. When the Motion Picture Patents Company* began questioning his independence, Laemmle fought back by turning to production and, in 1909, formed the IMP Corporation (Independent Motion Picture Corporation). IMP's first film was a one-reel version of Longfellow's "Hiawatha," directed by William V. Ranous and starring Gladys Hulette. A year later, Laemmle was able to lure Florence Lawrence away from the Biograph Company*, of which she was the leading lady. Mary Pickford also worked for a short period as an IMP actress.

On June 8, 1912, Carl Laemmle formed a new organization, Universal, by merging IMP with Pat Powers's Picture Plays, Adam Kessel and Charles Baumann's Bison Life Motion Picture Company, William Swanson's Rex Company, and Nestor and Champion. Legend has it that Laemmle selected the name Universal after seeing it on the side of a truck belonging to Universal Pipe Fittings. The first Universal production was *The Dawn of Netta,* a two-reel short directed by Tom Ricketts.

Universal operated two studios in Los Angeles, one in Edendale and the former Nestor Studios on Sunset Boulevard at Gower Street. Among some of the company's best-known early films were *Traffic in Souls* (1913), *Neptune's Daughter* (1914), and *Damon and Pythias* (1914).

On March 15, 1915, Universal City was opened on the site of the 250-acre Taylor Ranch in the San Fernando Valley; it remains as the present headquarters of Universal, the oldest continuously operating studio in the country and the only city in the world purpose-built as a film studio. It was at Universal City that John Ford made his directorial debut in 1917; Irving Thalberg was studio manager from 1918 to 1923; Erich von Stroheim made the first of his screen masterpieces, *Blind Husbands* (1919) and *Foolish Wives* (1922); and Lon Chaney became a star and made *The Hunchback of Notre Dame* (1923) and *The Phantom of the Opera* (1925).

With the coming of sound, Universal made the obligatory all-talking, all-singing, all-dancing revue, *The King of Jazz* (1930). A year earlier, Carl Laemmle, Jr. (generally known as Junior Laemmle), had been appointed head of production by his father, leading Ogden Nash to comment that "Uncle Carl Laemmle has a very large faemmle." Despite considerable adverse criticism, Junior Laemmle was responsible for many fine films, including *All Quiet on the Western Front* (1930), and a series of classic horror films such as *Dracula* (1931), *Frankenstein* (1932), *The Mummy* (1932), *The Invisible Man* (1933), *The Black Cat* (1934), and *The Bride of Frankenstein* (1935).

Carl Laemmle lost control of the studio in 1936, when it was taken over by Charles Rogers and J. Cheever Cowdin, with the former as head of production. The studio was financially in trouble, and it was saved thanks almost entirely to one child star, Deanna Durbin, who delighted thirties and forties audiences with *Three Smart Girls* (1936), *100 Men and a Girl* (1937), and *First Love* (1939), among others. Cliff Work replaced Charles Rogers in 1938 and embarked on a production schedule that consisted of low-budget, quality features, including a continuing batch of horror subjects, exotic features with Maria Montez, a group of W. C. Fields titles, the Sherlock Holmes series with Basil Rathbone and Nigel Bruce, and the classic Abbott and Costello comedies.

On November 12, 1946, Universal was merged with the independent International Pictures production company to become Universal-International. William Goetz and Leo Spitz took over production, and they introduced a new logo to replace the ultra-modern glass logo, which had, in turn, replaced the original logo of a biplane encircling the world in 1936. A year earlier, Universal became associated with the British producer J. Arthur Rank and began releasing his prestige features in the United States. Low-budget features, such as the "Ma and Pa Kettle" series, formed a prominent part of the new production schedule.

Universal was taken over by Decca Records in 1952, and Edward Muhl became head of production, introducing glamorous Technicolor* features, often directed by Douglas Sirk. In the late fifties, MCA, Inc.*, began acquiring a controlling interest in Decca, and, by 1962, Universal had become part of the MCA empire, headed by Dr. Jules Stein and Lew Wasserman. Universal-International became Universal once again, with a new, modern logo. Celebrities, such as Alfred Hitchcock and Edith Head, were lured to the studio from

Paramount*. Universal became the home of such major productions as *The Sting* (1973), *Jaws* (1975), *E.T. the Extraterrestrial* (1982), and the "Airport" series. Universal Pictures is a division of Universal City Studios, Inc., which is a subsidiary of MCA, Inc.*

Address: Universal City, Calif. 91608.

BIBLIOGRAPHY

Brunas, Michael, John Brunas, and Tom Weaver. *Universal Horrors: The Studio's Classic Films, 1931–1946.* Jefferson, North Carolina: McFarland, 1990.

Dettman, Bruce. *The Horror Factory.* New York: Gordon Press, 1976.

Edmonds, I. G. *Big U.* Cranbury, N.J.: A. S. Barnes, 1977.

Fitzgerald, Michael G. *Universal Pictures.* New Rochelle, N.Y.: Arlington House, 1977.

Hirschhorn, Clive. *The Universal Story.* New York: Crown, 1983.

Koszarski, Richard. *Universal Pictures: 65 Years.* New York: The Museum of Modern Art, 1977.

Perry, Jeb H. *Universal Television.* Metuchen, N.J.: Scarecrow Press, 1983.

RESOURCES

Films: Library of Congress (preservation elements and some reference prints), UCLA Film and Television Archives (selected titles).

Papers: University of Southern California (business records).

Photographs: Academy of Motion Picture Arts and Sciences (negatives, 1946–1956), Lincoln Center Library of the Performing Arts (still books).

UNIVERSAL STUDIOS TOUR. One of the best-known tourist attractions in Los Angeles, and second in popularity only to Disneyland, the new Universal* Studios Tour opened on June 17, 1964. It was intended only as a summertime operation but proved so successful that it continued through the winter months. Visitors are taken through the tour by tram and get to see some of the stars' dressing rooms and standing sets, and visit various rides and attractions. In 1993, more than eight million visitors toured the facility, compared to 39,000 in 1964. In 1993, Universal opened CityWalk, a shopping and restaurant complex adjacent to the tour.

Tours of the studio originated in 1915 when Universal City opened. Visitors were permitted to watch filming from bleacher seats built above the dressing rooms and were provided with box lunches. These original tours ended when the coming of sound made visiting the set impracticable.

Address: 100 Universal City Plaza, Universal City, Calif. 91608.

BIBLIOGRAPHY

Harmetz, Aljean. "Why Studio Tour Focuses on Big Films." *The New York Times,* June 25, 1984, p. C11.

Marple, Albert. "A Solution for the 'Movie' Visitor Problem." *Motion Picture Magazine,* March 1916, p. 143.

Scheuer, Philip K. "So You Want to Visit a Studio?" *Los Angeles Times,* Calendar, July 19, 1964, p. 3.

Stoddard, Maynard Good. "420 Acres of Make-Believe." *The Saturday Evening Post,* May/June 1984, pp. 62–63, 100–101.

Sutton, Horace. "A Traveler in Flickville." *Saturday Review,* January 9, 1965, pp. 61–62.

UNUSUAL OCCUPATIONS. See JERRY FAIRBANKS PRODUCTIONS

UPA PICTURES, INC. See UNITED PRODUCTIONS OF AMERICA

URINE. In 1994, *USA Today* suggested that Hollywood films have been "flush with scenes of urination," mentioning toilet scenes featuring Demi Moore in *Indecent Exposure,* Burt Reynolds in *Cop and a Half,* Huey Lewis in *Short Cuts,* Richard Harris and Robert Duvall in *Wrestling Ernest Hemingway,* Ralph Fiennes in *Schindler's List,* Tom Hanks in *A League of Their Own,* and Danny Glover in *Lethal Weapon 2.*

The best-known incident in Hollywood's past concerning urination involved Lee Tracy, a Broadway actor who had caught Hollywood's attention after playing Hildy Johnson in the original 1928 production of *The Front Page,* and who had been featured in two prominent M-G-M productions of 1933, *Dinner at Eight* and *Bombshell.* In November 1933, M-G-M sent Tracy to Mexico City to play reporter Johnny in *Viva Villa.* Tracy had long had a drinking problem, and he did not take kindly to being awakened on the morning of November 19 by Mexican soldiers marching outside his hotel window. What happened next is subject to speculation. "The wildest exaggerations were circulated and published," said Tracy some years later. "When I came back to Hollywood, I heard that I had stood on a hotel balcony, and deliberately insulted the Mexican flag." What is known is that Tracy did stand on the hotel balcony and, clothed or unclothed, urinate on the troops below.

The Mexican government reacted angrily to the incident, making Tracy a scapegoat in its opposition to the filming of the life story of Pancho Villa, and taking the opportunity generally to excoriate the film industry for its continued portrayal of Mexicans as villains on screen. "It seems fantastic that a professional actor, built after years of endeavor, should summarily be tossed on the ash heap for so trivial an offense," editorialized *Photoplay* (February 1934).

"If the Tracy incident had occurred in the United States, the whole matter would have blown over in a week. Undoubtedly Mexican newspaper enterprise was largely, if not altogether, responsible for the attitude taken by the Mexican government. The parading cadets, whom Tracy is alleged to have insulted, appeared to have taken the matter lightly but when the press of the capital found good copy in the incident, the hue and cry for the *Americano's* scalp arose."

Lee Tracy was summarily discharged by M-G-M on November 23, 1933, and his part reassigned to Stuart Erwin. Tracy never worked again for the studio, but did continue to work on screen through *The Best Man* in 1964.

There is something about location shooting that brings out the worst in Hollywood actors. Less known than the Lee Tracy affair was the time when Victor McLaglen was shooting *South of Pago Pago* in 1940. While telling a joke to producer Edward Small's brother, he took the opportunity to take a pee—on the man's leg.

BIBLIOGRAPHY

"Close-Ups and Long-Shots." *Photoplay,* vol. 45, no. 3, February 1934, p. 25.
Ergenbright, Eric L. "The Most Startling Confession Any Star Ever Made." *Photoplay,* vol. 51, no. 1, January 1937, pp. 24–25, 110.
Wloszcyna, Susan. "Hollywood Answers the Call of Nature." *USA Today,* January 4, 1994, p. D1.

USA FILM FESTIVAL. The first completely American film festival, the USA Film Festival is held annually on the campus of Southern Methodist University in Dallas, with the films being selected by a group of American film critics. It was first held from March 8 to 14, 1971, under the directorship of L. M. Kit Carson and William Jones. (A year earlier Carson and Jones had organized The Screen Generation Film Festival.) The first director to be honored was George Stevens, and the USA Film Festival has honored one director a year ever since. From 1974, beginning with Gregory Peck, it has also presented a Master Screen Artist Award. From 1980, with a salute to Gene Kelly and the American musical, it has presented special tributes. Until 1973, the Festival was competitive, but since then it has served as a showcase. In 1981, it expanded its activities to include year-long screenings in the Dallas area.

Address: 2917 Swiss Avenue, Dallas, Tex. 75204.

U.S. ARMY PICTORIAL CENTER. See ASTORIA STUDIOS

U.S. ARMY PICTORIAL SERVICE. See ASTORIA STUDIOS

U.S. CATHOLIC CONFERENCE—DIVISION OF FILM AND BROADCASTING. See NATIONAL LEGION OF DECENCY

U.S. FILM CORPORATION. See SMALLWOOD FILM CORPORATION

VAN BEUREN CORPORATION. In existence from 1928 to 1937, the New York-based Van Beuren Corporation produced a number of features, including Frank Buck's *Bring 'Em Back Alive* (1932), but is better known for its short subjects, the Aesops Fables and Tom & Jerry cartoons, Bill Corum Sports Review, the World on Parade, the Struggle to Live, and the Chaplin shorts from the second decade of the twentieth century released with added music and sound effects. All Van Beuren films were released through RKO*. President of the corporation was Amadee J. Van Beuren, who also owned Condor Pictures during this same period.

VANGUARD FILMS, INC., was a production company formed by David O. Selznick in 1945, with Daniel T. O'Shea as president and Dore Schary as head of production. Films, such as *Duel in the Sun* (1946), were advertised as both Selznick* productions and Vanguard productions. The company was liquidated on June 9, 1951.

VENUS FEATURES COMPANY was formed in mid-1913 with a studio in Hollywood. Thomas W. Evans was manager of its productions, the first of which was the three-reel *Sleeping Beauty,* directed by H. C. Matthews. Later, J. Farrell MacDonald began directing three-reel Venus productions, and, in October 1913, Richard Willis was hired to write a series of films for MacDonald to direct.

VIACOM INC. was spun off from CBS in 1971 as a diversified communications and entertainment company, initially known for its distribution and syndication of television programming such as *I Love Lucy, The Honeymooners,* and *All in the Family.* In 1979, it paid $30 million for 28 feature films owned by CBS and a defunct subsidiary, Cinema Center Films. In 1985, Viacom purchased MTV and Showtime Network Inc., and between 1986 and 1988, it acquired a 15 percent share in Orion Pictures Corporation*. On November 10, 1986, the company was merged with Arsenal Holdings, Inc., which took Viacom's name, and expanded its holdings to include Nickelodeon, USA Network, Cinamerica, and Spelling Entertainment Inc.*. On February 14, 1994, Viacom took over Paramount Communications (including Paramount Pictures*); even prior to that acquisition, the company's holdings included 7,000 television programs, 1,500 feature films, 5 television stations, 14 radio stations, and assorted cable networks.

On September 29, 1994, Viacom acquired Blockbuster Entertainment Corp., and in March 1995, it sold off Madison Square Garden Corp. As of 1997, Viacom's subsidiary companies are Paramount Communications, Inc., Blockbuster Entertainment Group, Spelling Entertainment, Inc., the Showtime Networks, Inc., Games Productions, Inc., Music by Video, Inc., Remote Productions, Inc., LT Holdings, Inc., Nickelodeon Huggins UK Ltd., Nickelodeon Magazines, Inc., United Cinemas International Multiplex B.V., Cinema International Corporation N.V., USA Networks, Comedy Central, All News Channel, Cinamerica, Discovery Zone, Viacom International, Inc., Film Intex Corp., Viacom Productions, Inc., VJK, Inc., Glendale Property Corp., Cable TV of Marin, Inc., Clear View Cable Systems, Inc., Com-Cable TV, Inc., Marin Cable Television, Inc., Television Signal Corp., Tele-Vue Systems, Inc., Broadcast Leasing, Inc., Riverside Broadcasting Co., Inc., KBSG, KYSR, WMQZ, WNYT, and WVIT. Viacom's chairman and chief executive officer is Sumner M. Redstone.

Address: 1515 Broadway, New York, N.Y. 10036.

VICTOR FILM COMPANY. Florence Lawrence, earlier known as "The Biograph Girl," and her husband, Harry Salter, formed the Victor Film Company, located in Fort Lee, New Jersey*, in 1912. Salter directed Lawrence in one-, two-, and three-reel films, with Owen Moore as her leading man. Victor's first film, *Not Like Other Girls,* was released on June 14, 1912. Shortly after its formation, Victor joined the newly organized Universal Film Manufacturing Company, and by 1914 Universal* had absorbed the company. The brand name "Victor" was no longer used after 1917.

VICTORY PICTURES CORPORATION, founded by Sam Katzman (1901-1973), was active from 1935 through 1940 as a producer of "B"* Westerns starring Tom Tyler and Tim McCoy. It was also responsible for the 1937 serial, *Blake of Scotland Yard.*

VIDEO. The Japanese Sony Corporation* introduced the first commercially viable home videotape systems, Betamax, in 1975, and a year later, another Japanese company, JVC, came out with the VHS or Video Home System, which subsequently supplanted Betamax. The video revolution has affected the film industry in a number of ways. Home video is a new and important market for both theatrical features and documentaries. Video has found a place in the editing room, and also enables directors instantly to view "rushes." Whereas once, films were provided for airing to television stations in the form of 35mm and, more often,

16mm prints, they are now distributed in the form of video masters. In May 1959, Acme Film Laboratories in Los Angeles became the first to be equipped with Ampex recorders for film to tape and tape to film transfers.

VIDIENCE is a word introduced in the mid-1920s to describe the audience for silent films as opposed to the audience for spoken stage productions, who came to *hear* a performance.

VIGILANT PICTURES CORPORATION. See ASTOR PICTURES CORPORATION

VIM COMEDY COMPANY typified the short-lived expansionist studios of the middle of the second decade of the twentieth century movie boom. By the sheer number of films released (156 one-reelers) as well as the personalities making them, Vim historically is one of the more interesting of the early studios producing comedy shorts. Founded in late 1915 by two flamboyant figures of the early industry, Louis Burstein and Mark Dintenfass, Vim controlled production facilities in both New Jersey and Florida. Former Lubin*, Sterling, and Wizard* stars, Bob "Pokes" Burns and Walter "Jabbs" Stull continued their pratfall series as headliners with Vim. The new "Pokes and Jabbs" comedies entered the market in November 1915 to replace MinA ("Made in America") films on the General Film Company program, when a dispute between General and MinA head David Horsley led him to disband the company, form other brands, and move his releasing program to Mutual*.

To increase its teamed offerings, Vim also quickly obtained the services of Oliver "Babe" Hardy, another Lubin veteran, to perform opposite diminutive Billy Ruge in a second unit of 35 slapstick "Plump and Runt" pictures released in 1916. Surviving films show the series was important in developing Hardy's comedy style critical to his much later teaming with Stan Laurel.

Other regulars at Vim included Harry Myers and Rosemary Theby, who specialized in domestic comedies, plus talented performers such as Kate Price, Billy Bletcher, his wife Arline Roberts, ingenue Ethel Burton, and others. Including casts, directors, cameramen, crew, and administrative personnel, the Vim southern studio in Jacksonville (at 740–750 Riverside Drive, where most of the pictures were made) employed nearly 50 people plus extras in 1916, with a regular weekly payroll of approximately $3,800.

A number of expansion companies collapsed in 1917 because of market uncertainties connected with the First World War, but Vim might have continued indefinitely had the two owners not tried to cheat each other. The resulting legal battles ended the partnership, with the bulk of Vim's interests eventually being taken over by the Amber Star Film Corporation, a subsidiary of Eastern Film Company of Providence, Rhode Island. Burstein (later Burston) retained control of the former Vim northern studio in Bayonne and used it to make early Billy West comedies under his new King-Bee Films

Corporation brand with the help of Hardy and other ex-Vim supporting players before moving everything to Hollywood.

BIBLIOGRAPHY

Nelson, Richard Alan. "Before Laurel: Oliver Hardy and the Vim Company, a Studio Biography." In *Current Research in Film: Audience, Economics and Law,* ed. Bruce A Austin. Norwood, N.J.: Ablex Publishing, 1986.
"Scenes at the Vim Studio." *Florida Times-Union* (Jacksonville), January 16, 1916, section 3, p. 5.
Young, Jordan R. "Early Ollie: The Plump and Runt Films." *Pratfall,* vol. 1, no. 12, 1975, pp. 3–7.

VISTAVISION was Paramount's answer to the widescreen CinemaScope* system. It utilized a camera through which the 35mm* film traveled horizontally, rather than vertically, with eight sprocket holes per frame (instead of four). This resulted in a negative image with an area three times that of a normal 35mm negative. The film was then processed in a normal way and optically reduced. (At first, in a few key theatres, the films were shown via horizontal projection.)

The VistaVision process received its premiere presentation on April 27, 1954, at New York's Radio City Music Hall*, with *White Christmas*. All major Paramount features of the succeeding few years were shot in VistaVision, and the process was also used for productions from other studios, such as *High Society* (1956) from M-G-M*. For the invention of VistaVision, Paramount Pictures*, Loren L. Ryder, and John R. Bishop received a Class I Scientific or Technical Award (an Oscar statuette) in 1954, and Paramount was also honored with a Class III Award in 1956 for the introduction of a lightweight, horizontal movement VistaVision camera. *One Eyed Jacks* (1961) was the last major feature to be shot in VistaVision.

BIBLIOGRAPHY

Daily, C. R. "New Paramount Lightweight Horizontal-Movement VistaVision Camera." *Journal of the SMPTE* (May 1956): pp. 279–81.
Easey, Bert. "Production in VistaVision." *Journal of the British Film Academy* (Spring 1955): pp. 14–15.

VITAGRAPH COMPANY OF AMERICA was the most important of the early film producers. It was the first to build up a stable of stars, the first to experiment successfully with animated and trick films, the first to film the classics from Shakespeare to Dickens, and the first to use the motion picture for propaganda purposes.

Founded by J. Stuart Blackton (1875–1941) and Albert E. Smith (1875–1958), the Vitagraph Company had its origins in the Reader, Smith and Blackton Combination (formed circa 1894), the Edison Vitagraph Company (formed 1897), the Commercial Advertising Bureau (formed 1897), and the American Vitagraph Company (formed 1898). Associated with Smith and Blackton in those early companies were Ronald A. Reader and William T. "Pop" Rock. In 1898, the company produced two of its most important early films, *The Burglar on the Roof* and *The Battle of Manilla Bay,* both shot at Vitagraph's first studio on the roof of the Morse Building on New York's Nassau Street.

Vitagraph opened its own studio in the Flatbush area of Brooklyn in 1905 and shortly thereafter began building up a stock company of players and directors, including Florence Turner, Maurice Costello, Paul Panzer, Lawrence Trimble (who owned Jean, the Vitagraph Dog), John Bunny (who became the most famous of early screen comedians), and Gladys Hulette (who starred in the 1909 trick film *Princess Nicotine*). Norma and Constance Talmadge began their screen careers at Vitagraph, as did Anita Stewart and Corinne Griffith.

In 1913, Vitagraph established a West Coast Studio at 1438 2d Street in Santa Monica, California, under the direction of Rollin Sturgeon. Later, the company opened new studios at Prospect and Talmadge Avenues in Hollywood (now the ABC Television Center). From 1914 to 1916, the Criterion Theatre became the Vitagraph Theatre and was the New York showcase for Vitagraph productions. Vitagraph helped Theodore Roosevelt's "preparedness" efforts prior to the American entry into the First World War with the production of *The Battle Cry of Peace* (1915), the first major use of film for propaganda purposes.

In 1915, Vitagraph consolidated its importance by establishing V-L-S-E* to release the feature-length productions of Lubin*, Selig*, Essanay*, and itself. In 1919, it took over what was left of the Kalem Company*.

Blackton left Vitagraph in 1917 to pursue independent production, but he returned to the studio in 1923. By that time Vitagraph had lost much of its importance, thanks to the rise of Paramount* and Metro*, among others, but it still had major stars such as Antonio Moreno, Larry Semon, Alice Calhoun, and Jean Paige under contract and continued to produce important features such as *Black Beauty* (1921), *The Clean Heart* (1924), and *Captain Blood* (1924). However, on April 20, 1925, an agreement was signed with Warner Bros.* for the purchase of the company for $735,000. The Vitagraph name continued to be used as a trademark by Warner Bros. through the fifties.

BIBLIOGRAPHY

Musser, Charles. "American Vitagraph: 1897–1901." *Cinema Journal* 22, 3 (Spring 1983): pp. 4–46.

Slide, Anthony, with Alan Gevinson. *The Big V: A History of the Vitagraph Company.* New and revised ed. Metuchen, N.J.: Scarecrow Press, 1987.

Trimble, Marian Blackton. *J. Stuart Blackton: A Personal Biography by His Daughter.* Metuchen, N.J.: Scarecrow Press, 1985.

Uricchio, William, and Roberta E. Pearson. *Reframing Culture: The Case of the Vitagraph Quality Films.* Princeton, N.J.: Princeton University Press, 1993.

RESOURCES

Films: The largest collection of Vitagraph films is held by the National Film Archive, London.

Papers: Academy of Motion Picture Arts and Sciences (J. Stuart Blackton Collection), UCLA Special Collections (Albert E. Smith papers), University of Southern California (some corporate papers in the Warner Bros. Collection).

VITAGRAPH-LUBIN-SELIG-ESSANAY, INC. See V-L-S-E

VITAPHONE. Although it was neither the first nor the ultimate sound film system, Vitaphone is possibly the best known, largely because the 1927 Vitaphone feature *The Jazz Singer,* starring Al Jolson, is generally lauded as the feature that gave the motion picture a voice. The Vitaphone sound-on-disc system was created by Western Electric, utilizing the audion tube (invented by Dr. Lee De Forest in 1906 and acquired by Western Electric in 1913) and an electromagnetic phonograph reproducer (invented in 1913 by Western Electric scientists, Dr. Irving B. Crandall and F. W. Kranz). These two inventions were of importance to Western Electric in terms of their value to the Bell Telephone system, but Western Electric also utilized them in the twenties for experimentation into sound-on-film and sound-on-disc motion pictures.

In 1925, Western Electric's Nathan Levinson demonstrated the sound-on-disc process to Sam Warner of Warner Bros.*, which viewed the new invention as a possible solution to its financial problems. Warner Bros. created the Vitaphone Corporation on April 20, 1926, taking the name from its then recently acquired Vitagraph Company of America*. The first Vitaphone shorts were produced at the former Vitagraph studios in Brooklyn, but because of lack of soundproofing, new studios were created at the Manhattan Opera House on New York's West 34th Street. The first feature to utilize the Vitaphone system was *Don Juan,* starring John Barrymore, which opened at the Warners Theatre, New York, on August 6, 1926. The program also included a series of short subjects, commencing with an address by Will H. Hays, followed by the overture to *Tannhauser* played by the New York Philharmonic, Mischa Elman, Roy Smeck, Marion Talley, Efrem Zimbalist, Giovanni Martinelli, and Anna Case. The first Vitaphone all-talking feature was *Lights of New York,* which received its premiere at the Mark Strand Theatre, New York, on July 6, 1928.

The Vitaphone system discs, manufactured by the Victor Talking Machine Company and later RCA, were recorded at 33⅓ r.p.m. and were played from the inside out. The 16-inch records were the equivalent of one reel of film. The projectionist was required to place the stylus on the disc when he had the picture frame marked "Start" in the gate of the projector. Quite obviously such a system was subject to synchronization problems, and, by the early thirties, Vitaphone was no longer in use and Warner Bros. had joined all other studios in releasing its motion pictures with sound on film.

BIBLIOGRAPHY

Bandy, Mary Lea, ed. *The Dawn of Sound*. New York: Museum of Modern Art, 1989.
Institute of the American Musical, Inc. *The 50th Anniversary of Vitaphone 1926–1976*. New York: The Author, 1976.
"The Vitaphone—Pro and Con." *The Literary Digest,* September 25, 1926, pp. 28–29.
"Vitaphone's Third Anniversary." *Motion Picture News,* August 10, 1929, pp. 531–39, 596.

RESOURCES

Films: Library of Congress and ULCA Film and Television Archive.
Papers: University of Southern California (Warner Bros. Collection).

VITARAMA. See CINERAMA

V-L-S-E. Vitagraph-Lubin-Selig-Essanay, Inc., or V-L-S-E, was incorporated on April 5, 1915, to release features made by the member companies that could not be adequately handled by the exchanges of the General Film Company. The company's creation marked the acceptance by these member companies of the Motion Picture Patents Company* of the importance of longer films, for which independent companies had earlier created a market. Most of the features released by V-L-S-E were five or six reels in length. Albert E. Smith of Vitagraph* was V-L-S-E's president, William N. Selig was treasurer, George K. Spoor of Essanay* was secretary, and Walter W. Irwin was general manager. The company released mostly films based on successful novels or plays, beginning with *The Carpet from Bagdad*. V-L-S-E was dissolved on August 17, 1916, when the Selig* and Essanay companies withdrew and joined the George Kleine* and Edison* companies to form the Kleine-Edison-Selig-Essanay Service.

BIBLIOGRAPHY

"Scope of the V-L-S-E." *The Moving Picture World,* May 1, 1915, pp. 703–4.

VOGUE FILMS. See SACK AMUSEMENT ENTERPRISES

VOGUE FILMS, INC., also known as the Vogue Motion Picture Company, began producing comedies at the old Lubin* studio at 4560 Pasadena Avenue, Los Angeles, in October 1915. It released on the Mutual program. Samuel S. Hutchinson, the president of the American Film Manufacturing Company*, was also the president of Vogue. In 1916, the company used a studio at the corner of Santa Monica Boulevard and Gower Street in Hollywood and produced two-reel comedies with two companies: Rube Miller directed the Ben Turpin and Gypsy Abbott unit, and R. E. Williamson directed the Patsy McGuire and Lillian Hamilton unit. Vogue disbanded in 1917.

THE VOICE OF HOLLYWOOD. A series of shorts produced by Louis Lewyn for Tiffany* in 1930–1931, the Voice of Hollywood was supposedly presented by a fictitious radio station, STAR, and featured Hollywood celebrities filmed at official functions and brief items with personalities whose stars were fading. Each short was hosted by a minor celebrity, such as Reginald Denny or Lloyd Hamilton.

BIBLIOGRAPHY

Maltin, Leonard. *The Great Movie Shorts*. New York: Crown, 1972.

"WALL STREET LAYS AN EGG" is perhaps the most famous headline from *Variety*. It was published on the front page of the October 30, 1929, edition, in reference to the Wall Street crash.

WALT DISNEY PRODUCTIONS. Although he was not himself a great animator, Walt Disney (1901–1966) has come to stand for the best in animated art, or at least the best known and the most easily understood. Thanks to Mickey Mouse and Donald Duck, to features such as *Snow White and the Seven Dwarfs* and *Mary Poppins,* and to one of the longest-running of television shows, Walt Disney is a household name. As *The New York Times* reported at Disney's death, he "founded an empire on a mouse," but it was such an empire that it survived and prospered after he was gone thanks largely to the legacy of his films, cartoon characters, and the entertainment enterprises that he created and so successfully promoted.

Walt Disney's company began as Laugh-O-Gram Films, a Kansas City partnership with Ub Iwerks, which produced animated short subjects for the Newman Theatre Company and which was incorporated on May 23, 1922. In the summer of 1923, Walt Disney went to Hollywood and that same year, with his brother Roy, formed the Disney Bros. Studio to produce Alice cartoons, which combined both live action and animation and were distributed by a minor company, M. J. Winkler. Early in 1926, the brothers moved to a new studio on Hyperion Avenue in the Silverlake district of Los Angeles, and the Walt Disney Studio, later Walt Disney Productions, came into being. (When the company outgrew the Hyperion Avenue studios, the brothers purchased land for a new studio, in August 1938, on Buena Vista Street in Burbank.)

In 1929, Walt Disney Productions was incorporated. It was "re-incorporated" in 1938, with its stock shared between Walt and his wife, Lillian, and Roy and his wife, Edna. Stock in Walt Disney Productions was first offered for public sale in April 1940.

The first Mickey Mouse cartoon, *Plane Crazy,* was produced in 1928; the third Mickey Mouse cartoon, also released in 1928, was *Steamboat Willie,* which was Disney's first sound subject. Donald Duck was first seen in *The Wise Little Hen* (1934). In 1932, Walt Disney first used Technicolor*—for *Flowers and Trees*—and from that point onward all of his Silly Symphony* films were in color. The first Disney animated feature was *Snow White and the Seven Dwarfs* (1937).

The first completely live-action Disney feature was *So Dear to My Heart* (1949). With *The Living Desert* (1953) Disney also became noted for its "true-life" nature features, which included *The Vanishing Prairie* (1954) and *Perri* (1957). On television, Walt Disney Productions was represented by *Disneyland, The Mickey Mouse Club, Davy Crockett,* and *Zorro.*

Following Disney's death, the company came under the management of E. Cardon Walker, who had joined the organization in 1938 and who, in 1976, became president and chief executive officer. He was faced with a 1979 defection by a group of Disney animators, led by Don Bluth, who felt that the company's artistic standards had deteriorated. The company also experienced financial problems with some of its new films, notably *Tron,* and increasingly received the bulk of its income from its theme parks, Walt Disney World and Disneyland.

A new president, Ron Miller, introduced major changes—against the wishes of majority shareholder Roy Disney, Walt's nephew, who resigned from the board in April 1984. It was Miller who created the new Touchstone Films* to produce films outside of the normal type of Disney product and who sought to improve the quality of programming on the pay-television service, the Disney Channel.

The Walt Disney name is also synonymous with two entertainment complexes, both of which are unique theme parks, accurately described as world's fairs of the imagination. Disneyland opened as the Magic Kingdom brought to reality on July 17, 1955, in Anaheim, California. Walt Disney had conceived of the idea for such a park as early as 1928. Disneyland features Main Street America, Adventureland, Fantasyland, Frontierland, and Tomorrowland. A similar, but more ambitious, undertaking is Walt Disney World in Florida, which opened on October 23, 1971. Some 11 years later EPCOT, the experimental prototype community of tomorrow, opened as part of Walt Disney World. Both the latter and Disneyland were built by WED Enterprises, founded in 1952, which is described as "the creative laboratory" for Walt Disney Productions. A sister manufacturing and production company to WED is MAPO, named after the most commercially successful Disney film at the time of its formation, *Mary Poppins* (1964).

A new "golden age" of animation began for Disney in the 1990s with *Beauty and the Beast* (1991), followed by *Aladdin* (1992) and *The Lion King* (1994). The company also witnessed commercial failure with Euro Disneyland (which opened in France in 1992), and tragedy with the death of its

CEO and president Frank Wells in 1994. Wells had been half of the leadership team with Michael Eisner (chairman) since 1984. Jeffrey Katzenberg, who was chairman of Walt Disney Studios, expected to be named by Eisner as the replacement for Wells, but when he was not, he resigned, and on April 9, 1996, Katzenberg filed a lawsuit, claiming he was owed $250 million in bonuses. Instead of Katzenberg, Eisner named Michael Ovitz, founder of Creative Artists Agency*, as president of the company. Ovitz left Creative Artists Agency in August 1995, two weeks after it had been announced that Walt Disney was to acquire Capital Cities/ABC, Inc., for $19 billion. The formal acquisition of Capital Cities/ABC, Inc., was approved by the U.S. Justice Department in January 1996 after Disney agreed to sell Los Angeles television station KCAL (which it had purchased for $200 million in 1988). In December 1996, Michael Ovitz announced he was stepping down as president, effective January 31, 1997, and his $90 million stock and cash severance deal created considerable controversy in and out of the industry.

Address: 500 South Buena Vista Street, Burbank, Calif. 91521.

BIBLIOGRAPHY

Bailey, Adrian. *Walt Disney's World of Fantasy*. New York: Everest House, 1982.

Bain, David, and Bruce Harris. *Mickey Mouse: Fifty Happy Years*. New York: Harmony Books, 1977.

Beard, Richard. *Walt Disney's EPCOT Center*. New York: Harry N. Abrams, 1982.

Blitz, Marcia. *Donald Duck*. New York: Harmony Books, 1979.

Bryman, Alan. *Disney and His Worlds*. New York: Routledge, 1995.

Disney, Walt. *Walt Disney's Parade*. New York: Garden City Publishing, 1940.

———. *The Life of Donald Duck*. New York: Random House, 1941.

Eliot, Marc. *Walt Disney: Hollywood's Dark Prince*. New York: Carol Publishing, 1993.

Field, Robert D. *The Art of Walt Disney*. New York: Macmillan, 1942.

Finch, Christopher. *Walt Disney's America*. New York: Abbeville Press, 1978.

———. *The Art of Walt Disney: From Mickey Mouse to the Magic Kingdoms*. New York: Harry N. Abrams, 1995.

Grant, John. *Encyclopedia of Walt Disney's Animated Characters*. New York: Hyperion, 1993.

Grover, Ron. *The Disney Touch: How a Daring Management Team Revived an Entertainment Empire*. Homewood, Ill.: Business One Irwin, 1991.

Hahn, Don. *Animation Magic: A Behind-the-Scenes Look at How an Animated Film Is Made*. New York: Disney Press, 1996.

Hollis, Richard, and Brian Sibley. *The Disney Studio Story*. New York: Crown, 1988.

Jackson, Kathy Merlock. *Walt Disney: A Bio-Bibliography*. Westport, Conn.: Greenwood Press, 1993.

Maltin, Leonard. *The Disney Films*. New York: Hyperion, 1995.

Miller, Diane Disney, as told to Pete Martin. *The Story of Walt Disney*. New York: Henry Holt, 1957.

Munsey, Cecil. *Disneyana*. New York: Hawthorn Books, 1974.

Schickel, Richard. *The Disney Version*. New York: Simon and Schuster, 1968.

Shale, Richard. *Donald Duck Grows Up: The Walt Disney Studio during World War II*. Ann Arbor, Mich.: UMI Research Press, 1982.

Shows, Charles. *Walt: Backstage Adventures with Walt Disney*. La Jolla, Calif.: Communication Creativity, 1979.

Smith, Dave. *Disney A to Z: The Official Encyclopedia*. New York: Hyperion, 1996.

Solomon, Charles. *The Disney That Never Was: The Stories and Art from Five Decades of Unproduced Animation*. New York: Hyperion, 1995.

Taylor, John. *Storming the Magic Kingdom: Wall Street, the Raiders, and the Battle for Disney*. New York: Alfred A. Knopf, 1987.

Thomas, Bob. *Walt Disney: The Art of Animation*. New York: Simon and Schuster, 1958.

———. *Walt Disney: Magician of the Movies*. New York: Grosset & Dunlap, 1966.

Thomas, Frank, and Ollie Johnston. *Disney Animation: The Illusion of Life*. New York: Abbeville Press, 1981.

West, John G., Jr. *The Disney Live-Action Productions*. Milton, Wash.: Hawthorne & Peabody, 1994.

RESOURCES

Papers: Walt Disney Archives.
Photographs: Walt Disney Archives.

WALT DISNEY WORLD. See WALT DISNEY PRODUCTIONS

WALTER READE ORGANIZATION. With its beginnings in a Port Chester, New York, vaudeville house that Walter Reade, Sr., acquired in 1908, the Walter Reade Organization grew from 1945, when Walter Reade, Jr.—who died in 1973 at the age of 56—assumed control of the company. It operated a major theatre circuit, with more than 70 screens in 1970, and was also involved in educational and nontheatrical film distribution, in independent co-production—of features such as *Ulysses* (1967)—and in theatrical distribution through Continental Releasing.

The company merged with Sterling Television in 1961 to become Walter Reade-Sterling, Inc., and in September 1966 adopted the name of the Walter Reade Organization. In 1970, the company sold off its theatrical and television distribution divisions, including Continental Distributing (with the latter's library being acquired in 1982 by Kino International*). In

1977, the Walter Reade Organization filed for reorganization under Chapter XI of the Federal Bankruptcy Act, reorganization that was fully approved by the courts in 1981. Its theatres were acquired by Cineplex Odeon in 1987.

WALTER WANGER PRODUCTIONS, INC. Walter Wanger (1894–1968) formed Walter Wanger Productions, Inc., incorporated on July 24, 1936, with funding provided by United Artists* and the Bank of America. Located at what became known as the Samuel Goldwyn Studios in Hollywood, Walter Wanger Productions was responsible for many memorable features, including *You Only Live Once* (1937), *History Is Made at Night,* (1937), *Algiers* (1938), *Stagecoach* (1939), *Foreign Correspondent* (1940), and *The Long Voyage Home* (1940). Walter Wanger Productions ceased to exist in November 1941, when it was renamed United Artists Productions, Inc.

BIBLIOGRAPHY
Bernstein, Matthew. *Walter Wanger: Hollywood Independent.* Berkeley, Calif.: University of California Press, 1994.

WAMPAS BABY STARS. See WESTERN ASSOCIATED MOTION PICTURE ADVERTISERS

WAR ACTIVITIES COMMITTEE. Organized in June 1940, with the fall of France to the Nazis during the Second World War, as the Motion Picture Committee Cooperating for National Defense, the War Activities Committee officially came into being on December 12, 1941. Presidents of 34 motion picture organizations formed a national committee to coordinate the activities of seven working divisions. The Theatres Division consisted of 16,486 theatres pledged to screen approved government- or industry-produced trailers and short subjects and to participate in bond drives and scrap drives. The Distributors Division had 352 film exchanges in 31 cities to handle releases of approved films without charge to the government. The Hollywood Division was made up of 30,000 studio workers involved in various war duties. The Newsreel Division consisted of the five major newsreel* companies and *March of Time** with the responsibility of filming the war at home and abroad. The Trade Press Division was made up of the entire staffs of 16 trade papers* concerned with the reporting of war activities within the motion picture industry and providing free advertising. The Foreign Managers Division was concerned with the distribution of gifts and appropriate films to the Allied forces. The Public Relations Division, as its name suggests, consisted of 1,800 publicity and public relations men promoting the activities of the Committee. The War Activities Committee was liquidated on January 7, 1946.

WAR FILM HEARINGS. A Senate subcommittee was appointed at the instigation of Senator Gerald P. Nye to investigate war propaganda produced by the film industry in the form of films that attacked Nazi Germany and supported the British war effort. Serving on the committee, which began its hearings on September 8, 1941, were five isolationist senators, D. Work Clark (chairman), Homer T. Bone, Charles W. Tobey, C. Wayland Brooks, and Ernest W. McFarland.

The motion picture industry appointed Wendell Wilkie as its spokesman and legal counsel, although the industry needed little support, for the subcommittee was thoroughly castigated as little more than a Nazi tool by all except Father Coughlin. Anti-Semitic comments by the subcommittee regarding Jewish control of the industry were the subject of many editorials. The subcommittee recessed after two weeks of hearings.

WARNER BROS. HISTORICAL SERIES. In the thirties, Warner Bros. produced a number of short subjects on the theme of American history: *The Song of a Nation* (1936, 17 minutes, director Frank McDonald) on the writing of the "Star Spangled Banner"; *Give Me Liberty!* (1937, 20 minutes, director B. Reeves Eason) on the period 1765–1775 and Patrick Henry; *The Romance of Louisiana* (1937, 16 minutes, director Crane Wilbur) on the period 1802–1803 and the Louisiana Purchase; *Under Southern Stars* (1937, 15 minutes, director Nick Grinde) on the Civil War and emphasizing the Battle of Chancellorsville; *The Man without a Country* (1938, 18 minutes, director Crane Wilbur) on the 1805–1835 period and Lieutenant Philip Nolan; and *Sons of Liberty* (1939, 20 minutes, director Michael Curtiz) on the period 1776–1781 and Jewish patriot Haym Salomon.

WARNER BROS. PICTURES, INC. Although Warner Bros. Pictures was not incorporated until 1923, the history of the four Warner Bros.—Harry, Albert, Sam, and Jack—in the film industry goes back a lot further, to 1907 when the boys opened the Duquesne Amusement Supply Company, with offices in Pittsburgh, Pennsylvania, and Norfolk, Virginia. The company folded in 1909, and three years later Warner Bros. moved to the West Coast, producing its first important feature, *My Four Years in Germany,* in 1918.

In 1925, Warner Bros. acquired the Vitagraph Company*, which gave the brothers a studio in Brooklyn, an additional studio in Hollywood, and Vitagraph's 34 exchanges. With *Don Juan* (1926) and *The Jazz Singer* (1927), Warner Bros. pioneered the sound motion picture and also acquired sufficient funding to purchase, in 1929, First National Pictures* and Fox West Coast Theatres*. With the acquisition of First National, Warner Bros. moved to its Burbank Studios*, although it continued for a time to operate the former Vitagraph Studios and its own studios on Sunset Boulevard in Hollywood (which became the home of the independent television station KTLA). (Through the early forties the name First National appeared on many Warner Bros. productions, just as Vitagraph continued to be used as a trademark.)

The thirties may well be considered as Warner Bros.' "golden age," when the studio's name was associated with

Busby Berkeley musicals, gangster pictures, social dramas, action spectacles, and soap operas. Darryl F. Zanuck, who had been the studio's production chief under Jack L. Warner, resigned in 1933, following the studio's refusal to rescind, on a specified date, the 50 percent pay cuts advocated by the Academy of Motion Picture Arts and Sciences*. Zanuck had been responsible for keeping the studio alive in the twenties, with his Rin-Tin-Tin features, and is generally considered the person to whom credit should go for Warner Bros.' early success. He was replaced by Hal Wallis, who was, in turn, replaced in 1941 by Steve Trilling, who had less authority.

In the fifties, Warner Bros. became involved in television production, but it experienced financial difficulties in the early sixties. In 1956, rights to almost all of the pre-1950 features were sold to Associated Artists, which in turn sold them to United Artists*. In 1966, Seven Arts Productions, Ltd., a Toronto-based company acquired Warner Bros. outright. Warner Bros.-Seven Arts, Ltd., became known chiefly as a television distributor, with not only the Warner Bros. features but also films from 20th Century-Fox*, Allied Artists*, and Universal*. In addition, Seven Arts operated the record companies of Atlantic, Warner, and Reprise.

On July 9, 1969, the company changed hands again when it was acquired by Kinney National Services, Inc., a New York-based operation previously known for its parking lots and funeral homes. Ted Ashley, of another Kinney-owned company, Ashley-Famous Agency, became the new head of Warner Bros. Kinney subsequently formed Warner Communications, Inc., to supervise its entertainment activities, including Warner Bros.

In 1989, Warner Communications was acquired by Time, Inc., in an $18 billion merger, and a new company, Time Warner, Inc.*, was formed. A new division, Warner Bros. Family Entertainment, was created in 1993, to produce films for a general audience.

BIBLIOGRAPHY

Beck, Jerry, and Will Friedwald. *Looney Tunes and Merrie Melodies: A Complete Illustrated Guide to the Warner Bros. Cartoons.* New York: Henry Holt, 1989.

Behlmer, Rudy. *Inside Warner Bros.* New York: Viking Press, 1985.

Freedland, Michael. *The Warner Brothers.* New York: St. Martin's Press, 1983.

Gustafson, Robert. "What's Happening to Our Pix Biz? from Warner Bros. to Warner Communications, Inc.," in *The American Film Industry,* ed. Balio Tino. Madison, Wis.: University of Wisconsin Press, 1985, pp. 574–602.

Higham, Charles. *Warner Brothers.* New York: Charles Scribner's Sons, 1975.

Hirschhorn, Clive. *The Warner Bros. Story.* New York: Crown, 1979.

Horak, Jan-Christopher. *Dream Merchants: Making and Selling Films in Hollywood's Golden Age.* Rochester, N.Y.: George Eastman House, 1989.

Jerome, Stuart. *Those Crazy Wonderful Years When We Ran Warner Bros.* Secaucus, N.J.: Lyle Stuart, 1983.

Meyer, William A. *Warner Brothers Directors.* New Rochelle, N.Y.: Arlington House, 1978.

Roddick, Nick. *A New Deal in Entertainment: Warner Brothers in the 1930s.* London: British Film Institute, 1983.

Schreider, Steve. *That's All Folks!: The Art of Warner Bros. Animation.* New York: Henry Holt, 1988.

Sennett, Ted. *Warner Brothers Presents.* New Rochelle, N.Y.: Arlington House, 1971.

Silke, James R. *Here's Looking at You, Kid.* Boston: Little, Brown, 1976.

Sperling, Cass Warner, Cork Milner, and Jack Warner, Jr. *Hollywood Be Thy Name: The Warner Brothers Story.* Rocklin, Calif.: Prima Publishing, 1994.

Thomas, Bob. *Clown Prince of Hollywood: The Antic Life and Times of Jack L. Warner.* New York: McGraw-Hill, 1990.

Warner, Jack L., with Dean Jennings. *My First Hundred Years in Hollywood.* New York: Random House, 1965.

Wilson, Arthur, ed. *The Warner Bros. Golden Anniversary Book.* New York: Film and Venture, 1973.

Woolley, Lynn, Robert W. Malsbary, and Robert G. Strange, Jr. *Warner Bros. Television: Every Show of the Fifties and Sixties: Episode by Episode.* Jefferson, N.C.: McFarland, 1985.

RESOURCES

Films: Library of Congress (35mm preservation elements and some reference prints of pre-1950 titles), UCLA Film and Television Archive (35mm nitrate studio prints and safety elements on some Vitaphone short subjects), Wisconsin Center for Film and Theater Research (16mm viewing prints of pre-1950 titles).

Papers: University of Southern California (legal, story and production files, etc.).

Photographs: George Eastman House.

WARNER BROS.-SEVEN ARTS, LTD. See WARNER BROS. PICTURES, INC.

WARNER COMMUNICATIONS, INC. See WARNER BROS. PICTURES, INC.

WARNER'S FEATURES, INC. See UNITED FILM SERVICE

WARNERSUPERSCOPE. See CINEMASCOPE

WAYNE-FELLOWS PRODUCTIONS. See BATJAC PRODUCTIONS, INC.

WEBER-FIELDS-KINEMACOLOR. See KINEMACOLOR COMPANY OF AMERICA

WED ENTERPRISES. See WALT DISNEY PRODUCTIONS

WEINTRAUB ENTERTAINMENT GROUP, INC., was founded in 1986 by Jerry Weintraub after his dismissal as chairman of United Artists*. In May 1987, the company purchased for $90 million the British Thorn/EMI Library, including the Pathé News Library of footage from 1896–1970. By 1989, Weinbtraub was reporting heavy financial losses; it sold the Pathé News Library to Parkfield Entertainment in the United Kingdom for $16 million, filed for Chapter XI bankruptcy protection on September 14, 1990, and two weeks later, Jerry Weintraub resigned as chairman and CEO of the company bearing his name. In January 1994, Weintraub's library was acquired by the French Initial Group for $85 million.

BIBLIOGRAPHY

Turner, Richard. "Losing the Touch." *The Wall Street Journal,* June 14, 1989, pp. A1, A9.

THE WESTERN. One of the American film industry's favorite genres from the early years of the twentieth century through the fifties, the Western has generated its own stars, writers, and directors. It is the genre of William S. Hart, Tom Mix, Buck Jones, John Wayne, Roy Rogers, Gene Autry, Ken Maynard, George "Gabby" Hayes, and George O'Brien, and of director John Ford, who succinctly summed up his career with the words, "I make Westerns."

Although it was not the first Western, Edwin S. Porter's *The Great Train Robbery* (1903) is usually considered as the starting point for a study of the American Western film. It was pioneer producer Thomas H. Ince who legitimized the genre in the second decade of the twentieth century, and it was Broncho Billy Anderson and William S. Hart who created the Western hero. In the twenties, Tom Mix glamorized the image of the West, and Mix's view of the genre was perpetuated by the singing cowboy heroes of the thirties and forties, such as Gene Autry and Roy Rogers, whose films were the staple of Republic Pictures* and who, along with Hopalong (William Boyd) Cassidy, carried the image to radio and television.

The epic Western can be dated back to James Cruze's *The Covered Wagon* (1923) and John Ford's *The Iron Horse* (1924). Raoul Walsh's *In Old Arizona* (1929) was the first sound Western to make effective use of outdoor locations, but it was Raoul Walsh's *The Big Trail* (1930) that was the first epic talkie Western. The most popular Western story is, arguably, *The Virginian,* based on a novel by Owen Wister and a play by Kirke La Shelle, which had been filmed in 1914, 1923, 1929, and 1946. Another favorite stage Western was Edwin Royle's *The Squaw Man,* which Cecil B. DeMille filmed in 1914 (codirected by Oscar Apfel), 1918, and 1931.

For much of the thirties, the Western was relegated to the level of a "B" movie*, but that changed with John Ford's *Stagecoach* (1939), starring John Wayne and a good example of the brilliant stuntwork of Western veteran Yakima Canutt (who was featured in many "B" Westerns and also served as second unit director on many more). The Western genre prospered in the forties with *Santa Fe Trail* (1940), *Virginia City* (1940), *The Westerner* (1940), *Western Union* (1941), *The Ox-Bow Incident* (1943), *The Outlaw* (1946), *My Darling Clementine* (1946), *Fort Apache* (1948), *Three Godfathers* (1948), *Red River* (1948), and *She Wore a Yellow Ribbon* (1949).

John Ford continued to make his inimitable Westerns into the fifties, with *Wagonmaster* (1950) and *Rio Grande* (1950), but a new, more adult Western came on the scene, as represented by Henry King's *The Gunfighter* (1950), Fred Zinnemann's *High Noon* (1952), Fritz Lang's *Rancho Notorious* (1952), Nicholas Ray's *Johnny Guitar* (1954), Anthony Mann's *The Man from Laramie* (1955), Samuel Fuller's *Run of the Arrow* (1956), and Howard Hawk's *Rio Bravo* (1959). Violence became a more prominent aspect of the Western genre with the films of Sam Peckinpah, including *Major Dundee* (1964), *The Wild Bunch* (1969), *The Ballad of Cable Hogue* (1970), and *Pat Garrett and Billy the Kid* (1973).

John Ford continued to direct Westerns into the sixties, with *Sergeant Rutledge* (1960), *Two Rode Together* (1961), *The Man Who Shot Liberty Valance* (1962), and *Cheyenne Autumn* (1964). Other major Westerns of the sixties and seventies include *The Alamo* (1960), *How the West Was Won* (1962), *Cat Ballou* (1965), *El Dorado* (1966), *True Grit* (1969), *Butch Cassidy and the Sundance Kid* (1969), *A Man Called Horse* (1970), *Soldier Blue* (1970), *Rio Lobo* (1971), and the Western spoof *Blazing Saddles* (1974). Elvis Presley became a new-style Western hero in *Flaming Star* (1960) and *Charro!* (1969).

The Western lost its appeal for American filmmakers in the seventies, but the genre continued chiefly in the so-called spaghetti Westerns produced in Italy and Spain, of which Sergio Leone is the best-known director. *City Slickers* (1992) and *City Slickers II* (1995), both starring Billy Crystal and Jack Palance, introduced a comedic aspect to the Western. At the same time, the genre was taken very seriously in *Dances with Wolves* (1991) and *Unforgiven* (1993).

Among the most popular Western figures to have been portrayed on film were Billy the Kid (William H. Bonney), Wyatt Earp, the James brothers, and Wild Bill Hickok (James Butler Hickok). Billy the Kid was played by Johnny Mack Brown in *Billy the Kid* (1930), by Roy Rogers in *Billy the Kid Returns* (1938), by Buster Crabbe in *Billy the Kid Wanted* (1941), by Robert Taylor in *Billy the Kid* (1941), by Jack Beutel in *The Outlaw* (1946), by Lash LaRue in *Son of Billy the Kid* (1949), by Paul Newman in *The Left-Handed Gun* (1958), by Michael Pollard in *Dirty Little Billy* (1972) and by Kris Kristofferson in *Pat Garrett and Billy the Kid.* (1973).

Wyatt Earp has been played by George O'Brien in *Frontier Marshall* (1934), by Randolph Scott in *Frontier Marshall* (1939), by Richard Dix in *Tombstone—the Town Too Tough to Die* (1942), by Henry Fonda in *My Darling Clementine* (1946), by Joel McCrea in *Wichita* (1955), by Burt Lancaster in *Gunfight at the O.K. Corral* (1957), by James Stewart in *Cheyenne*

Autumn (1964), by James Garner in *Hour of the Gun* (1967), and by Harris Yulin in *Doc* (1971). In the self-produced *Wyatt Earp* (1995), Kevin Costner played the title character, with Dennis Quaid as Doc Holliday.

The James brothers have been featured in more than 20 films, including *Jesse James* (1927), in which Fred Thomson played the title role; *Jesse James* (1939), in which Tyrone Power played the title role and Henry Fonda played Frank James; *Return of Frank James* (1940), in which Henry Fonda played the title role; *Jesse James at Bay* (1941), in which Roy Rogers played the title role; *Jesse James Rides Again* (1947), a serial in which Clayton Moore (better known as the Lone Ranger) played the title role; *The Return of Jesse James* (1950), in which John Ireland played the title role; *Alias Jesse James* (1958), in which Bob Hope played the title role; *Jesse James Meets Frankenstein* (1961), in which Jack Beutel played James; *I Shot Jesse James* (1949), in which Reed Hadley played James; *Kansas Raiders* (1950), in which Audie Murphy played Jesse James; and *The Long Riders* (1980), in which James Keach played Jesse and Stacy Keach played Frank James.

Wild Bill Hickok has been featured in *Wild Bill Hickok* (1923), *Aces & Eights* (1936), *Great Adventures of Wild Bill Hickok* (1938), *Wild Bill Hickok Rides* (1941), *Prairie Gunsmoke* (1942), *Deadwood '76* (1965), *the Plainsman* (1966), and *The White Buffalo* (1977), among others.

BIBLIOGRAPHY

Buscombe, Edward, ed. *The BFI Companion to the Western.* New York: Atheneum, 1988.

Cameron, Ian, and Douglas Pye, eds. *The Book of Westerns.* New York: Continuum, 1996.

Cusic, Don. *Cowboys and the Wild West: An A-Z Guide from the Chisholm Trail to the Silver Screen.* New York: Facts on File, 1994.

Davis, Robert Murray. *Playing Cowboys: Low Culture and High Art in the Western.* Norman, Okla.: University of Oklahoma Press, 1992.

Eyles, Allen. *The Western.* Cranbury, N.J.: A. S. Barnes, 1975.

Everson, William K. *The Hollywood Western: 90 Years of Cowboys and Indians, Train Robbers, Sheriffs and Gunslingers, and Assorted Heroes.* New York: Carol Publishing.

Fenin, George N., and William K. Everson. *The Western.* New York: Grossman, 1973.

French, Philip. *Westerns: Aspects of a Movie Genre.* New York: Viking Press, 1973.

Hardy, Phil. *The Western.* New York: William Morrow, 1983.

Hitt, Jim. *The American West from Fiction (1823–1976) into Film (1909–1986).* Jefferson, N.C.: McFarland, 1990.

Holland, Ted. *B Western Actors Encyclopedia: Facts, Photos and Filmographies for More Than 250 Familiar Faces.* Jefferson, N.C.: McFarland, 1989.

Langman, Larry. *A Guide to Silent Westerns.* Westport, Conn.: Greenwood Press, 1992.

Nachbar, Jack G. *Western Films: An Annotated Critical Bibliography.* New York: Garland, 1975.

Nachbar, Jack G., Jackie R. Donath, and Chris Foran. *Western Films 2: An Annotated Critical Bibliography from 1974 to 1987.* New York: Garland, 1988.

Parish, James Robert, and Michael R. Pitts. *The Great Western Pictures.* Metuchen, N.J.: Scarecrow Press, 1976.

———. *The Great Western Pictures II.* Metuchen, N.J.: Scarecrow Press, 1988.

Parks, Rita. *The Western Hero in Film and Television.* Ann Arbor, Mich.: UMI Research Press, 1982.

Pitts, Michael R. *Western Movies: A TV and Video Guide to 4200 Genre Films.* Jefferson, N.C.: McFarland, 1986.

Place, J. A. *The Western Films of John Ford.* Secaucus, N.J.: Citadel Press, 1974.

Rainey, Buck. *Heroes of the Range: Yesterday's Saturday Matinee Movie Cowboys.* Metuchen, N.J.: Scarecrow Press, 1987.

———. *Sweethearts of the Sage: Biographies and Filmographies of 258 Actresses Appearing in Western Movies.* Jefferson, N.C.: McFarland, 1992.

———. *The Reel Cowboy: Essays on the Myth in Movies and Literature.* Jefferson, N.C.: McFarland, 1996.

Sennett, Ted. *Great Hollywood Westerns.* New York: Harry N. Abrams, 1990.

Smith, Packy, and Ed Hulse, eds. *Don Miller's Hollywood Corral: A Comprehensive B-Western Roundup.* Burbank, Calif.: Riverwood Press, 1993.

Thomas, Tony. *The West That Never Was.* New York: Carol Publishing, 1989.

Tuska, Jon. *The Filming of the West.* New York: Doubleday, 1976.

WESTERN ASSOCIATED MOTION PICTURE ADVERTISERS (WAMPAS), founded in 1920, was comprised of professional publicists in the film industry. With fewer than 20 members in 1920, the organization had grown to more than 100 by 1933. According to an early press release, "The WAMPAS founders were animated by a spirit of fraternity and cooperation. Their aims were both social and professional. Their objectives, as stated in their constitution, which remains unchanged, were to foster comradeship, promote the ethics of the profession, and encourage cooperation among the members."

The best-known activity of the Association was the annual selection of 13 young actresses with potential star power, an idea that was conceived in 1921 and first undertaken in 1922. Among those actresses selected as WAMPAS Baby Stars were Mary Astor, Joan Blondell, Mary Brian, Dolores Del Rio, Janet Gaynor, Laura La Plante, Bessie Love, Colleen Moore, Karen Morley, Sally Rand, Ginger Rogers, Lupe Velez, Fay Wray, and Loretta Young.

The Association merged with the Writers Club in 1930, but it retained its separate identity. No WAMPAS Baby Stars were selected in 1933, and in 1934 the "stars" included freelance actresses as well as studio contract players. The winners, none of whom achieved any prominence in the industry, were featured in two films, *Kiss and Make Up* and *Young and Beautiful*. The following year, the WAMPAS Baby Stars idea was discarded, and the Western Associated Motion Picture Advertisers disbanded. In 1955 the idea of naming WAMPAS Baby Stars was revived unsuccessfully.

BIBLIOGRAPHY
Uselton, Roi A. "The WAMPAS Baby Stars." *Films in Review*, February 1970, pp. 73–97.

WESTERN AUDIO VISUAL ENTERPRISES. See JERRY FAIRBANKS PRODUCTIONS

WESTERN COSTUME CO., the best-known supplier of film costumes in the world, dates back to the second decade of the twentieth century, when a former Indian trader named L. L. Burns was asked by Western star William S. Hart to provide authentic costumes for his films. Burns acquired Fisher's Costume House and opened his first company at 7th and Figueroa in downtown Los Angeles. As more Hollywood producers turned to Western Costume to provide clothing, the company moved, in 1924, to a new ten-story building.

Through heavy competition from United Costume Company, created by his former employees, Burns was forced into bankruptcy, and Western Costume Co. was acquired, in 1928, by Dan, Joe, and Ike Greenberg. The Greenberg brothers moved the company in 1932 to Hollywood. Joe and Abe Schnitzer acquired the company in 1934, and in 1937 a consortium of major Hollywood studios acquired Western, after its competitor, United Costume Company, had been taken over by Warner Bros.* and its assets merged with the studio's wardrobe department. G. B. Howe was named president of the company in 1950, and upon his retirement, John Golden took over.

In March 1989, Western Costume was sold to the AHS Trinity Group, a holding company whose principles are Sidney Sheldon and Bill Haber. The company's building adjacent to Paramount* was demolished in 1991, and the previous year, Western Costume moved to North Hollywood. An outlet store opened there in 1994. In June 1996, Western Costume was purchased from AHS Trinity Group by partner Bill Haber.

Address: 11041 Vanowen Street, North Hollywood, Calif. 91605.

BIBLIOGRAPHY
Scott, Tony. "Future Uncertain for Western Costume, Fabulous Repository of Motion Picture History." *Daily Variety,* October 25, 1988, pp. 17, 20, 22, 42, 76, 78, 80, 82, 85, 88, 94, 104, 106, 108, 110, 116, 118.

WESTERN ELECTRIC. See VITAPHONE

WESTERN PHOTOPLAYS, INC., began producing for Pathé in mid-1918. Joseph A. Golden and A. Alperstein were the company's officers. Western produced two-reel Westerns* starring Helen Gibson and a serial*, *Wolves of Kultur,* with Leah Baird and Sheldon Lewis, which Golden wrote, produced, and directed. The company went out of business late in 1918, and Astra Film Corporation completed production of the remaining episodes of the serial.

WGA. See WRITERS GUILD OF AMERICA

WHARTON, INC. Theodore W. Wharton (1875–1931), who earlier was scenario editor and studio supervisor for the Edison Company*, established the Kalem Company's first indoor studio and started Pathé Freres's American studio and became its first director. He went to Ithaca, New York, in the fall of 1912 to produce a football picture for Essanay* and decided to make the city his home. He convinced Essanay to send a company under his direction for the summer of 1913; when he saw that Essanay was not interested in sending one there again, he left the company and formed Wharton, Inc., with his brother Leopold, previously an actor and director with Pathé, and with the assistance of the Ithaca business community.

The company began production on May 1, 1914, using the glass ball cage of Cornell University as a temporary studio. Later in that year, it built its own studio and plant in the city. Wharton, Inc., was a contracting producer for Pathé, for which it made the serials* *The Exploits of Elaine, The New Exploits of Elaine, The Romance of Elaine* (all starring Pearl White), and *The New Adventures of J. Rufus Wallingford.* Early in 1916, it began producing for other companies and made the serials *Beatrice Fairfax* and *Patria* for the International Film Service*. By the beginning of 1919, Wharton had ceased production.

BIBLIOGRAPHY
Stainton, Walter R. "Pearl White in Ithaca." *Films in Review,* May 1951, pp. 19–25.
"Wharton Incorporated." *The Moving Picture World,* April 18, 1914, p. 349.
"Whartons, of Ithaca, Rest on Oars." *The Moving Picture World,* January 25, 1919, p. 470.

WHITE EAGLE ENTERPRISES is the production company of Sylvester Stallone (born 1946). Upon its foundation in 1986, the company committed to a ten-film deal with United Artists*, but was released from that arrangement in January 1989, and signed a similar deal with Carolco*.

Address: 8800 Sunset Boulevard, 5th Floor, Los Angeles, Calif. 90069.

BIBLIOGRAPHY

Tusher, Will. "Stallone's Eagle Perches at Carolco for 10 Films." *Daily Variety,* January 24, 1989, pp. 1, 54.

WHITESTONE, LONG ISLAND. See KINEMACOLOR COMPANY OF AMERICA

WHITMAN BENNETT STUDIOS, the home of Whitman Bennett Productions (released through First National* and United Artists*), were the former East Coast studios of Fine Arts*, located at 537 Riverdale Avenue in Yonkers. Operating from 1919 to 1925, the Whitman Bennett Studios were also used by other independent producers.

WHITMAN FEATURES COMPANY, which began producing in 1914, had Martin J. Faust, formerly with Lubin*, as its director and John William Kellette as its scenario editor. Its productions included the three-reel *His Flesh and Blood* (1914), about recent gang troubles in New York; the five-reel *Lena Rivers* (1914), starring Violet Horner; and the four-reel *Jane Eyre* (1914). Blinkhorn Photoplays Corporation released Whitman's films to the states rights* market.

"WHY WE FIGHT" SERIES. The most successful and the best-known series of documentaries to be produced by the U.S. government during the Second World War was "Why We Fight," supervised by Major (later Lieutenant-Colonel) Frank Capra. Chief of Staff George C. Marshall placed Capra in charge of the project, and the former Hollywood director set about producing a series of films that blended actuality footage with staged theatrical scenes. There were seven films in the series: *Prelude to War* (1942), *The Nazis Strike* (1942), *Divide and Conquer* (1943), *The Battle of Britain* (1943), *The Battle of Russia* (1943), *The Battle of China* (1944), and *War Comes to America* (1945). In addition, Capra's unit also created a newsreel, *Army-Navy Screen Magazine,* and produced a number of other documentaries, notably *The Negro Soldier* (1944).

BIBLIOGRAPHY

Barnouw, Erik. *Documentary.* New York: Oxford University Press, 1974.
Capra, Frank. *The Name above the Title.* New York: Macmillan, 1971.
Murphy, William Thomas. "The Method of *Why We Fight.*" *The Journal of Popular Film* 1, 3 (Summer 1972): pp. 185–96.

WIDESCREEN. See CINEMASCOPE, CINEMIRACLE, CINERAMA, SHOWSCAN, TODD-AO, and VISTA-VISION

WILDING PICTURE PRODUCTIONS, founded in 1914 by traveling salesman Norman E. Wilding (1891–1947), be-

came one of the largest nontheatrical film producers in the United States. Founded in Detroit, it was incorporated in 1927. In July 1967, the company was acquired by Bell & Howell*, and subsequently sold in 1980 to Maritz, Inc.

WILDWOOD ENTERPRISES was formed in 1969 by actor Robert Redford (born 1937) in association with his ex-agent, Richard Gregson. The company's first production was *Downhill Racer* (1969), followed by *The Candidate* (1972), *Three Days of the Condor* (1975), and *All the President's Men* (1976). In 1995, a subsidiary company, South Fork Pictures, was created to develop and produce independent films.

Address: 101 Montana Avenue, Suite E, Santa Monica, Calif. 90403.

WILKES-BARRE, PENNSYLVANIA. See UNITED STATES MOTION PICTURE CORPORATION

WILLIAM A. BRADY PICTURE PLAYS, INC. See WORLD FILM CORPORATION

WILLIAM L. SHERRY SERVICE. William L. Sherry (1874–1951) opened the William L. Sherry Feature Film Company of New York on March 15, 1913, to distribute *The Prisoner of Zenda* and, later, other productions of the Famous Players Film Company and the Jesse L. Lasky Feature Play Company in the state and city of New York. On September 26, 1916, Sherry, formerly vice president of Paramount*, opened his own offices and exchanges nationwide. In May 1918, the William L. Sherry Service was started to distribute Frank A. Keeney Productions, starring Catherine Calvert, and soon the Service added Edgar Lewis Productions, De Luxe Pictures, Inc.*, and features of Gilbert M. "Broncho Billy" Anderson. In late 1918, Sherry used the physical apparatus of the General Film Company to release his films but, in May 1919, switched to using the Film Clearing House.

WILLIAM MORRIS AGENCY, INC., the oldest talent agency in the world, was founded on New York's 14th Street in 1898 by William Morris, Sr. Its best-known employee was Abe Lastfogel, who joined the staff in 1912 and remained with the agency until his death in 1984 at the age of 86. William Morris, Jr., became president on the death of his father in 1932, and remained president until 1952. In 1992, William Morris acquired Triad Artists. As of 1997, Norman Brokaw was chairman and CEO, and Jerry Katzman was president. The William Morris Agency had 200 agents worldwide, with half that number working in Los Angeles, and its clients included Alec Baldwin, Bill Cosby, Clint Eastwood, Whoopi Goldberg, Roseanne, Sylvester Stallone, Quentin Tarantino, John Travolta, and Bruce Willis.

Address: 151 El Camino, Beverly Hills, Calif. 90212.

BIBLIOGRAPHY
Rose, Frank. *The Agency.* New York: HarperBusiness, 1995.
Weinraub, Bernard. "Dusted and Muscled Up: A New William Morris Agency." *The New York Times,* March 9, 1995, pp. C13, C17.

WILLIAMSON SUBMARINE FILM COMPANY. See SUBMARINE FILM COMPANY

WILL ROGERS MEMORIAL FUND. The financial branch of the Will Rogers Memorial Hospital and the Will Rogers Institute, the Will Rogers Memorial Fund has its origins in the National Vaudeville Association (NVA) Lodge at Saranac Lake, New York, which came into being in 1925. Established as a hospital for those suffering from tuberculosis, the NVA Lodge was turned over to the Will Rogers Memorial Commission in 1936. As drugs against and treatment of tuberculosis became standardized, the Will Rogers Memorial Hospital became concerned with pulmonary research and health education, for which the funds are now used. Since the thirties, the film industry has supported the Will Rogers Memorial Fund through radio and motion picture appeals by Hollywood personalities. The Will Rogers Memorial Fund should not be confused with the Will Rogers Memorial in Claremore, Oklahoma, which serves as a repository of Rogers's papers and artifacts.

Address: 785 Mamaroneck Avenue, White Plains, N.Y. 10605.

BIBLIOGRAPHY
Daniels, Bill. "Will Rogers Institute: Caring for Medical Needs of Showbiz." *Daily Variety,* December 3, 1984, pp. 3, 6.

WILMINGTON, NORTH CAROLINA. See DEG STUDIOS

WINCHESTER PICTURES CORPORATION. In existence through the fifties, and with offices at 780 North Gower Street in Hollywood, Winchester Pictures Corporation was the production company of director Howard Hawks (1896–1977)—Winchester was his middle name. It produced Hawks's 1952 feature *The Big Sky* and the 1951 feature *The Thing,* directed by Christian Nyby (probably with uncredited help from Hawks).

WIZARD MOTION PICTURE CORPORATION was formed in mid-1915 to produce the "Pokes and Jabbs" comedy series starring Bob Burns and Walter Stull as two henpecked husbands. Burns, Stull, and general manager Louis Burstein organized the company, whose films were distributed through the World Comedy Stars Film Corporation*. The company disbanded later in 1915, with Burstein, Burns, and Stull continuing the "Pokes and Jabbs" series for Vim*.

BIBLIOGRAPHY
"Pokes and Jabbs." *The Moving Picture World,* September 11, 1915, p. 1811.

WOMEN FILMMAKERS. Writing in the December 1923 issue of *The Business Woman,* Myrtle Gebhart commented,

> Excluding acting, considering solely the business possibilities, the positions are held by women in the Hollywood studios as typists, stenographers, secretaries to stars and executives, telephone operators, hairdressers, seamstresses, costume designers, milliners, readers, script girls, scenarists, cutters, film retouchers, film splicers and other laboratory work, set designers and set dressers, librarians, artists, title writers, publicity writers, plaster moulder, casting director, musicians, film editors, executives and department managers, directors and producers.

Gebhart ended her article by noting, "We are here, sisters, and we're so stubborn that we're going to make our mark—indeed many of our sisterhood are already making it, and indelibly, too."

There was nothing that unusual about women directors in the American silent film industry. The first female director in the world was Alice Guy, who made her first film for Gaumont in the 1890s, and, with her husband Herbert Blaché, came to the United States in 1907, establishing the Solax Company* and working as a director until 1920. Screenwriters such as Frances Marion, Anita Loos, June Mathis, Beulah Marie Dix, Bess Meredyth, and Lenore Coffee dominated the silent film industry. Frances Marion directed three features—*The Love Light, Just around the Corner,* and *The Song of Love*—between 1921 and 1923, and other female screenwriters who tried their hand at direction included Marguerite Bertsch, Mrs. George Randolph Chester, Julia Crawford Ivers, Marion Fairfax, Jane Murfin, and Elizabeth Pickett.

The most important of all women film directors in America was Lois Weber, whose career extended from the teens to the early thirties. She was an uncompromising filmmaker, whose productions dealt with social issues such as abortion, birth control, capital punishment, and anti-Semitism. Margery Wilson, one of D. W. Griffith's leading ladies in *Intolerance,* was active as a director in the early twenties. Another D. W. Griffith star, Lillian Gish, directed one feature, *Remodeling Her Husband* (1920). Other actresses who tried their hand at directing included Gene Gauntier, Kathlyn Williams, and Mabel Normand.

At one time or another, nine women directors were at work at Universal*, including Ida May Park, Ruth Ann Baldwin, Grace Cunard, Cleo Madison, and Ruth Stonehouse. With the death of her husband, Wallace Reid, in 1923, Dorothy Davenport (better known as Mrs. Wallace Reid) took to production and direction and was to remain active through the fifties. The only American female director to make a successful transition from silent features to talkies was Dorothy Arzner, who began her directorial career in 1927 and made her last feature, *First Comes Courage,* in 1943.

Aside from Arzner, only one other woman directed an American feature in the thirties, and that was Wanda Tuchock, who codirected *Finishing School* in 1934. Women did not come into their own as directors again until Ida Lupino codirected *Not Wanted* in 1949. In more recent years, Shirley Clarke came to prominence with *Portrait of Jason* (1967). Stephanie Rothman is noted for her exploitation films*, such as *It's a Bikini World* (1966), *The Student Nurses* (1970), and *Working Girls* (1974). Ruth Orkin cowrote and codirected three features with her husband Morris Engel: *The Little Fugitive* (1953), *Lovers and Lollipops* (1956), and *Weddings and Babies* (1958). Elaine May directed *A New Leaf* (1970) and *Heartbreak Kid* (1972). Other American women directors active from the sixties onward include Mary Ellen Bute, Claudia Weill, Martha Coolidge, Nell Cox, Storm de Hirsch, Lynne Littman, Joan Micklin Silver, Joan Rivers, Barbara Kopple, Francine Parker, Faith Hubley, Kathleen Dowdey, Penny Marshall, Julia Dash, Susan Seidelman, and Betty Thomas. As a result of the success of *The Piano* (1993), for which she received an Academy Award nomination for Best Director, Australian filmmaker Jane Campion was invited to direct the U.S. feature *Portrait of a Lady* (1996).

In 1980, the Directors Guild of America* reported that in the previous 30 years only 7 women had directed features and only 23 women had been employed as directors of prime-time television. Since then the position has improved somewhat, but women have yet to gain the prominence they held in the American film industry during the silent era.

BIBLIOGRAPHY

Acker, Ally. *Reel Women: Pioneers of the Cinema, 1896 to the Present.* New York: Continuum, 1991.

Foster, Gwendolyn Audrey. *Women Film Directors: An International Bio-Critical Dictionary.* Westport, Conn.: Greenwood Press, 1995.

Heck-Rabi, Louise. *Women Filmmakers: A Critical Reception.* Metuchen, N.J.: Scarecrow Press, 1984.

Kay, Karyn, and Gerald Peary, eds. *Women and the Cinema.* New York: E. P. Dutton, 1977.

Kuhn, Annette, and Susannah Redstone. *The Women's Companion to International Film.* Berkeley, Calif.: University of California Press, 1994.

Miller, Lynn Fieldman. *The Hand That Holds the Camera: Interviews with Women Film and Video Directors.* New York: Garland, 1988.

Quart, Barbara Koenig. *Women Directors: The Emergence of a New Cinema.* Westport, Conn.: Greenwood Press, 1988.

Seger, Linda. *When Women Call the Shots.* New York: Henry Holt, 1996.

Slide, Anthony. *The Silent Feminists: America's First Women Directors.* Lanham, Md.: Scarecrow Press, 1996.

Smith, Sharon. *Women Who Make Movies.* New York: Hopkinson and Blake, 1975.

WOMEN IN FILM was formed, by 12 women, on March 2, 1973, as a nonprofit organization for professional women in the film industry. Tichi Wilkerson, editor-in-chief of *The Hollywood Reporter,* was the organization's first president. Women in Film organizes workshops, conferences, publishes a newsletter, and, since 1977, has presented Crystal Awards to honor outstanding individuals "whose professional careers have been distinguished by their excellence, endurance and expansion of the role given women within the entertainment industry." (Lucille Ball, Nancy Malone, Eleanor Perry, and Norma Zarky were the first honorees.) Membership in Women in Film requires sponsorship by two current members and is limited to those with three years or more experience in the industry.

Address: 6464 Sunset Boulevard, Suite 530, Hollywood, Calif. 90028.

WOMEN OF THE MOTION PICTURE INDUSTRY. Formed in 1953, Women of the Motion Picture Industry (WOMPI) is a nationwide organization, with chapters in various cities, concerned with community and industry service. It is involved in fundraising and charitable work and sponsors a room at the Will Rogers Memorial Hospital.

Address: P.O. Box 900, Beverly Hills, Calif. 90213.

WONDERGRAF PRODUCTION COMPANY, founded by C. H. Gowman in December 1920, and based in Los Angeles, produced a series of novelty shorts, under the headings of "Wondergrafs," "Stay-at-Home Tourists," "The Little Players," and "Cameo Playlets."

WORCESTER, MASSACHUSETTS. See LINCOLN AND PARKER FILM COMPANY

WORKERS' FILM AND PHOTO LEAGUE. See NATIONAL FILM AND PHOTO LEAGUE

WORLD COMEDY STARS FILM CORPORATION was formed early in 1915 by Phil Gleichman to produce one-reel comedies with famous stars of the legitimate and vaudeville stages. Edmund Lawrence, formerly with Kalem*, was the director, William W. Jefferson was associate director, and Mark Swan, Roy McCardell, Paul Arlington, Herbert Hall Winslow, and Robert Broderick were hired to write scenarios. The comedy team of Weber and Fields appeared in *Two of the Bravest* (1915), and other players with the company included Jeff De Angelis, Lulu Glaser, Florence Tempest, Paula Tempest, Katherine Osterman, Richard Carle, and Tom Wise. After distributing a series of "Pokes and Jabbs" comedies made by the Wizard Motion Picture Corporation*, the World Comedy Stars Film Corporation went out of business in August 1915.

BIBLIOGRAPHY

"Gleichman Heads New Company." *The Moving Picture World,* February 6, 1915, p. 806.
"To Make Comedies." *The Moving Picture World,* March 6, 1915, p. 1422.

WORLD FILM CORPORATION was formed on February 16, 1914, when E. Mandelbaum and Philip Gleichman, the founders of the World Special Films Corporation (which the year before had brought to the United States the Italian films *The Last Days of Pompeii* and *Protea* and released two films per month until its demise two days before World's formation), interested Wall Street bankers W. A. Pratt, Van Horn Ely, and others in their enterprise. G. L. P. Vernon was the president, Mandelbaum the first vice president, Gleichman the second vice president, and Britton Busch the secretary and treasurer. World's offices were at 130 West 46th Street.

On June 10, 1914, World and the Shubert Theatrical Company, representing the interests of the William A. Brady, Charles A. Blaney, and Owen Davis enterprises, formed a $3 million corporation to film the theatrical successes of the Shubert Company. The Shubert Film Corporation, which had been formed a few months earlier to produce and distribute Shubert-Brady productions, planned to produce one feature-length film a week, to be released by World.

When Mandelbaum sold his interest in World in mid-1914, the company became incorporated for $2 million, and Lewis J. Selznick became vice president and general manager in July 1914. In September 1914, Selznick signed Clara Kimball Young and her husband, James, to produce films for the Peerless Feature Film Company, which was formed in July by Jules Brulatour to produce Brady and Blaney plays with former Eclair* players such as Barbara Tennant, Alec B. Francis, and Stanley Walpole. Peerless built a studio at which four companies worked in Fort Lee, New Jersey*. World had by this time secured 24 distributing offices throughout the country.

In October 1914, Gleichman left the company. World next formed an alliance with Liebler and Company to produce its big stage successes, including *Alias Jimmy Valentine.* World added the product of the Dyreda Art Film Corporation*, the Colonial Motion Picture Corporation, the California Motion Picture Corporation*, and the Frohman Amusement Corporation* to its releases. At the end of the year, Al Lichtman became the general manager of a Special Attractions Department, which imported *Salambo,* among other films, from Italy.

In May 1915, World took over completely the Shubert Film Corporation, which owned Peerless, which, in turn, owned half of William A. Brady Picture Plays, Inc., earlier having split the ownership with the Shuberts. The Equitable Motion Picture Corporation was formed in June 1915 and incorporated for $2 million to produce two features and two comedies per month, which World would release. Arthur Spiegel was president, Selznick the vice president, and Isadore Bernstein the technical director. In July 1915, the Wizard Motion Picture Corporation* was formed to release comedies through World. In August 1915, World gained control of the new Paragon studios in Fort Lee, which were to be the largest studios in the East. Maurice Tourneur was the vice president and general manager of Paragon, which planned to make 24 five-reel features a year, plus three to four longer features. The Triumph Film Corporation, a subsidiary of Equitable, came into existence in September 1915 and took over the old Horsley studio in Bayonne, New Jersey. Julius Steger was the president, Joseph Golden was the director-in-chief, and Eve Unsell was in charge of adaptations.

In February 1916, World reorganized again. Arthur Spiegel, who died a few months later, was elected president. Selznick left the company and took World's leading star, Clara Kimball Young, with him and formed Lewis J. Selznick Productions, Inc. World acquired all the stock of Equitable, and William A. Brady assumed active control of World's producing units.

In October 1917, the Famous Players-Lasky Corporation bought the Paragon studio. Brady resigned as head producer in February 1918 and became an independent producer. In January 1919, World, with which Selznick was again associated, merged with the United Picture Theatres of America, Inc. World's distribution system was used for United productions, and Peerless was used to make special productions for United. Later in 1919, the Republic Distributing Corporation, which was controlled by Selznick, took over World's entire list of exchanges.

Directors of note who made films for World included Maurice Tourneur, Albert Capellani, Emile Chautard, Stanner E. V. Taylor, Edwin August, Oscar Apfel, J. Searle Dawley, Edwin Carewe, Romaine Fielding, and O. A. C. Lund. Writers for World included Frances Marion, Joseph Franklin Poland, Clara S. Beranger, Harry O. Hoyt, and Giles R. Warren. World's players included Clara Kimball Young, Alice Brady, Kitty Gordon, Robert Warwick, Carlyle Blackwell, Madge Evans, Vivian Martin, Lillian Russell, Marie Dressler, Doris Kenyon, Edwin August, and Elaine Hammerstein.

BIBLIOGRAPHY

"Selznick Absorbs a Corporation." *The Moving Picture World,* November 8, 1919, p. 3472.
"Shuberts and World Film in Best Deal." *The Moving Picture World,* June 20, 1914, p. 1700.
Spehr, Paul C. *The Movies Begin.* Newark: The Newark Museum, 1977.
"Wall Street Bankers Enter Film Business." *The Moving Picture World,* February 21, 1914, p. 966.
"World and United Theatres Merge." *The Moving Picture World,* February 1, 1919, p. 599.
"World Film Anniversary." *The Moving Picture World,* February 20, 1915, p. 1153.
"World Film Reorganizes." *The Moving Picture World,* February 12, 1916, p. 931.

WORLD NORTHAL FILM CORP. was founded in 1977 by Al Schwartz and Imre Rosenthal as the New York-based Northal Film Distribution. It changed its name in March 1978, when two new partners, Frank Stanton and Victor Elmaleh of World-Wide Holdings Corp., joined the company. It began life as a distributor of quality foreign films, such as *Cousin, Cousine* (1975), but then began releasing action movies. The company ceased operations in 1990.

WORLD PICTURES CORP., a New York-based distributor of minor U.S. films and foreign imports, was founded in 1932 by Irvin Shapiro (1907–1989). Shapiro quit as the company president in 1941, and it ceased operations shortly thereafter.

WORLD'S BEST FILM COMPANY produced animal pictures in Florida, early in 1913, for release by Universal*. Harold M. Shaw was the company's director.

WRATHER CORPORATION had its origins in Jack Wrather Pictures, Inc., formed in 1946 by Jack D. Wrather (1918–1984). It controlled the *Queen Mary* and the Spruce Goose tourist attractions in Long Beach, California, the Disneyland Hotel, television series such as *Lassie, The Lone Ranger,* and *Sergeant Preston of the Yukon,* and films based on those characters, as well as other independently produced feature films. It went public in June 1961, and was acquired by the Walt Disney Company* in September 1987.

WRITERS CLUB. See WRITERS GUILD OF AMERICA

WRITERS GUILD OF AMERICA (WGA) has its origins in the Writers Club, a social group popular in the twenties for its annual revues and presided over for many years by Rupert Hughes. From the Writers Club, the Screen Writers Guild was organized, as part of the Authors League of America, with 173 charter members. John Howard Lawson was elected the non-profit organization's first president on April 6, 1933. The Guild was open to all writers and was extremely vocal in its opposition to the Academy of Motion Picture Arts and Sciences*, which it saw as a tool of the producers. The thirties were bitter years for the new Guild as it fought for unionization and recognition by the studios. Its members were blasklisted, accused of being Communists, and it was, at times, split by internal bickering between left- and right-wing elements. (Certainly it is worth noting that the bulk of the members of the Hollywood Ten* were screenwriters.) It was not until the summer of 1938 that the Guild was recognized by the National Labor Relations Board as the collective bargaining agent for writers within the film industry.

In the early fifties, the Guild was once more under attack with regard to Communist infiltration and the refusal of certain members to support the signing of a loyalty oath. At the same time, it was anxious to claim the right to negotiate on behalf of television and radio writers and, during 1953 and 1954, discussed merger with the Radio Writers Guild and the Television Writers of America. In the summer of 1954, a new organization was formed from the Screen Writers Guild called the Writers Guild of America, which quickly gained recognition as the negotiating body for writers in film, radio, and television and which was divided into two national chapters: WGA/East in New York, and WGA/West in Hollywood.

The Writers Guild of America has been involved in four major strike actions against producers: in 1959–1960, in February–June 1973, in April–July 1981, and in March 1985.

It also presents a number of annual awards. The Laurel Award for Screen Writing Achievement was first given in 1953 to Sonya Levien and is for the Guild member who has, in the opinion of the board of directors, "advanced the literature of the motion picture through the years, and who has made outstanding contributions to the profession of the screen writer." The Laurel Award for TV Writing Achievement (now called the Paddy Chayefsky Laurel Award) was first given in 1976 to Rod Serling and honors members in the field of television literature. The Valentine Davies Award, first presented in 1962 to Mary McCall, Jr., is given to the person(s) "whose contribution to the motion picture community has brought dignity and honor to writers everywhere." The Morgan Cox Award, first given in 1970 to Barry Trivers, is presented "to that member or group of members whose vital ideas, continuing efforts and personal sacrifices best exemplify the ideal of service to the Guild which the life of Morgan Cox so fully represented." The previous awards were presented by WGA/West. WGA/East presented three memorial awards: The John Merriam Memorial Award, first given in 1977 to Ralph D. Buglass; the Evelyn F. Burkey Memorial Award, first given in 1978 to Fred Coe; and the Richard B. Jablow Memorial Award, first given in 1978 (in memoriam) to Richard B. Jablow.

Addresses: Writers Guild/West, 8955 Beverly Boulevard, Los Angeles, Calif. 90048; Writers Guild/East, 555 West 57th Street, New York, N.Y. 10019.

BIBLIOGRAPHY

Academy of Motion Picture Arts and Sciences and the Writers Guild of America West. *Who Wrote the Movie and What Else Did He Write?* Los Angeles: The Authors, 1970.

Ceplair, Larry. "The Writers Guild Redeems Itself." *Emmy,* January/February 1983, pp. 6, 44.

Schwartz, Nancy Lynn. *The Hollywood Writers' War.* New York: Alfred A. Knopf, 1982.

W. W. HODKINSON CORPORATION. W. W. Hodkinson (1881–1971), who earlier founded Paramount Pictures Corporation* and was its president until June 1916, formed W. W. Hodkinson Corporation in November 1917 as a distribution company. Hodkinson obtained the use of the General Film Company exchange organization, through which to distribute its product physically, and installed its own salesmen in each of the 28 exchanges. Hodkinson, a longtime advocate of separation of control in the industry between producers, distributors, and exhibitors, maintained that his company was not controlled by producers or exhibitors, but he promulgated a plan whereby, through his company, exhibitors would advance money to producers to make films but would retain no financial interest in the production companies. Later, the exhibitors would acquire the completed films on a percentage basis.

Some of the companies that released through Hodkinson included Paralta*, Artco Productions, Deitrich-Beck*, Great Authors Pictures, Zane Grey Pictures, and companies formed to produce features starring Bessie Barriscale, J. Warren Kerrigan, Henry B. Walthall, Louise Glaum, and Lillian Walker. Although Hodkinson announced, early in 1918, the proposed marketing plan of "Motion Picture Plus"—an invention of the Photo Motion Company of Kansas City, Missouri, which, by exposing pictures sideways on the negative and having images twice as wide as the then present height and the same height as the then present width, promised a widescreen format—there is no indication that the theatres or the public were very interested. At the end of 1918, Hodkinson began to release through Pathé* exchanges. The company lasted until 1924.

BIBLIOGRAPHY

"Hodkinson Comes Back." *The Moving Picture World,* November 10, 1917, p. 843.

"What 'Motion Picture Plus' Is." *The Moving Picture World,* January 12, 1918, p. 214.

Y

YANKEE FILM COMPANY, an independent producer, released its first film, *Jeffries on His Ranch,* on June 15, 1910, just before the July 4th Heavyweight Championship fight between ex-champion James J. Jeffries and his successor, Jack Johnson. Afterward, Yankee released one reel every Monday with the Motion Picture Distributing and Sales Company, until December 1910, when it began releasing two films a week. William Steiner was the director-general, and Isadore Bernstein rose from publicity man to become general manager of the company, whose offices were at 344 East 32d Street, New York. Its last film, *The Two Rooms,* was released on November 17, 1911.

BIBLIOGRAPHY

"Growth of the Yankee." *The Moving Picture World,* November 19, 1910, p. 1182.

YARNS FOR YANKS. See HOLLYWOOD VICTORY COMMITTEE

YIDDISH PRODUCTIONS. See COLLECTIVE FILM PRODUCERS, INC., JEWISH TALKING PICTURES, and JUDEA PICTURES

YUKON PICTURES, INC. See JERRY FAIRBANKS PRODUCTIONS

Z

ZANUCK-BROWN PRODUCTIONS was formed in August 1972 by Richard Zanuck (born 1934) and David Brown (born 1916), and was responsible for a string of commercial successes, beginning with *The Sting* (1973) and including *Jaws* (1975) and *Cocoon* (1985). The company was first located at Universal*, moving to 20th Century-Fox* in 1980, to Warner Bros. in 1983, and to M-G-M* in 1986. On October 1, 1988, in an amicable split, Brown ceased to be a partner in the company, which was renamed the Zanuck Company.

BIBLIOGRAPHY

Robison, Diane Dowsing, and Terri Frankle-Smith. "A Power Dinner Every Night." *POV,* vol. 1, no. 1, January 1990, pp. 62–66.

ZION FILMS, INC., produced the feature *Broken Barriers,* starring Alice Hastings and directed by Charles E. Davenport, from the Sholom Aleichem story "Khavah," in 1919. Although it planned to produce a series of Jewish and Russian pictures written by Jewish and Russian authors, Zion's plans never materialized. S. Adler was Zion's president.

BIBLIOGRAPHY

"Zion Company to Produce Russian and Jewish Films." *The Moving Picture World,* April 19, 1919, p. 394.

ZODIAC ENTERTAINMENT was founded in Studio City, California, in 1989 by the British company Central Television plc as a producer of animated children's programming. Its first series was *Widget* (1990), followed by *Mr. Bogus* (1991).

Address: 4400 Coldwater Canyon, Suite 200, Studio City, Calif. 91604.

ZODIAK FILM MANUFACTURING COMPANY took over one of the largest and best-equipped studios and laboratories on the West Coast when it purchased, in mid-1914, the J.A.C. plant located at Hill and Court streets in downtown Los Angeles. J. A. Crosby, who formerly was in charge of the technical operations for the Selig Polyscope Company*, New York Motion Picture Company, Reliance Motion Picture Company, and Universal*, began his own studio and laboratory, the J.A.C. Film Manufacturing Company, in 1913, in the old Bradbury mansion on South Hill Street. Companies that used the J.A.C. studios included the Albuquerque Film Manufacturing Company*, Pathé's* Western company, the Nash Motion Picture Company*, Bosworth, Inc.*, and the Famous Players Film Company, which produced many of its Mary Pickford features there. Thomas S. Nash acquired the plant and renamed it Zodiak. Albert S. Ruddell was secretary and general manager of the new company.

BIBLIOGRAPHY

"J.A.C. Film Company." *The New York Dramatic Mirror,* May 28, 1915, p. 26.

ZOETROPE. Impressed by independent producer John Korty's facility in San Francisco, director/producer Francis Ford Coppola (born 1939) created his own independent production company, American Zoetrope, in San Francisco in 1969. The first film of the new company was *The Rain People* (1969), followed by *THX 1138* (1971) and *Apocalypse Now* (1979). Coppola's *The Conversation* (1974) was produced by his Directors Company.

In 1973, Coppola purchased his present headquarters; in 1979, he changed the name of his company to Omni-Zoetrope, and, a year later, he purchased the former Hollywood General Studios,* renaming them the Zoetrope Studios (and dropping the Omni). Coppola planned his new studios to be a state-of-the-art facility, to be run along the lines of the old Hollywood studios. The same year he acquired the studios, he hired Gene Kelly to put together a musical unit, he announced plans for a Performing Arts High School on the lot, and he brought in veteran British director Michael Powell as "Senior Director in Residence." Wim Wenders's *Hammett* was the first film to go into production at the new studio but proved to be plagued with problems and was not released until 1982. It was followed by *One from the Heart* (1982), *The Outsiders* (1983), and *Rumble Fish* (1983). Aside from his own productions, Coppola used his company to sponsor the first screenings of Kevin Brownlow's restoration of Abel Gance's *Napoleon* (1927) and to sponsor the release of new films by foreign directors, such as Akira Kurosawa.

Unfortunately, financial problems forced Coppola to curtail his operations, and, in 1984, the Zoetrope Studios were sold at a bankruptcy auction. Coppola was forced to retrench at his San Francisco headquarters, from where he coproduced *The Cotton Club* (1984).

Address: 916 Kearny Street, San Francisco, Calif. 94123.

BIBLIOGRAPHY

Bock, Audie. "Zoetrope and Apocalypse Now." *American Film,* September 1979, pp. 55–60.

Linck, David. "Zoetrope Takes Cue from Studios of '30s and '40s." *Boxoffice,* May 4, 1980, pp. 1–2, 4.

Myles, Lynda. "The Zoetrope Saga." *Sight and Sound,* Spring 1982, pp. 91–93.

Pollock, Dale. "Has Coppola Won Battle for Studio?" *Los Angeles Times,* Calendar, March 5, 1980, pp. 1, 4–5.

Ross, Lillian. "Onwards and Upwards with the Arts." *The New Yorker,* November 8, 1982, pp. 48–87.

ZOOM LENS. Although it is often confused with different kinds of camera movement, the zoom stands in direct opposition to traditional moving shots. In a dolly or trucking shot, for example, the camera moves bodily through space, producing an image that reflects, through changes in perspective and the presence of parallax, the original filming process in which the camera actually traversed a three-dimensional space. A zoom lens, on the other hand, produces the illusion of movement *optically* through continuous changes in the focal length of the lens rather than through actual movement of the camera; it creates an image that progressively alters the original space being photographed, either flattening (by zooming out to the telephoto focal lengths) or elongating it (by zooming in to the wide-angle range of the lens).

Prototypes of the modern zoom lens were developed in the late twenties and the early thirties. The first zoom lenses consisted of two optical elements that moved in relation to one another. They had extremely small apertures for the period (f/11 or f/8) and, though they required a great deal of high key light and the negative required longer development than usual, they possessed good depth of field. Bell & Howell's Cooke Vara Lens (circa 1932) was a three-element lens possessing a slightly larger aperture (f/8 to f/3.5) and a greater range. The elements of the lens were moved in relation to one another mechanically by a series of cams, operated by a crane.

Contemporary zoom lens technology dates from the development of the Zoomar lens by Dr. Frank G. Back in 1946. Unlike the earlier variable focal length lenses, the Zoomar had no cams with which to contend. It was entirely optical, employing four lens elements. Movable lens elements were mounted in a common barrel; manual movement of the barrel to any position in the housing produced a change in image size, creating a zoom effect. The uniqueness of the Zoomar lens related to the lens's aperture or iris diaphragm. In earlier zoom lenses, the iris diaphragm had to be changed each time there was a change in focal length, a procedure that required a complex mechanical linkage between the cams operating the focal length and the aperture. By placing the iris diaphragm *behind* all the movable elements of the lens, the Zoomar eliminated the need for coordinating the changes in focal length with the aperture setting; the aperture was merely set for the shot and remained constant during it.

Initially associated with television and newsreel work, where it enabled continuous coverage of events, such as baseball games, without time-consuming changes by the camera operator of lenses of different, fixed focal lengths to capture action at different distances, the zoom lens quickly became a staple of documentary filmmaking in the late fifties and early sixties and of feature-film production in the sixties and seventies. Filmmakers most frequently associated with innovative use of the zoom included Roberto Rossellini, Michael Snow, Robert Mulligan, Claude Chabrol, Blake Edwards, and Robert Altman.

BIBLIOGRAPHY

Belton, John. "The Bionic Eye: Zoom Esthetics." *Cineaste,* vol. 11, no. 1, Winter 1980–81, pp. 20–27.

Lightman, Herb A. "Some Interesting Facts about Zoom Lenses." *American Cinematographer,* March 1975, pp. 324–25.

Resource Libraries and Institutions

Academy of Motion Picture Arts and Sciences, Margaret Herrick Library, 333 South La Cienega Boulevard, Beverly Hills, Calif. 90211.

American Film Institute, 2021 North Western Avenue, Hollywood, Calif. 90027.

Arizona State University, Charles Trumbull Hayden Library, Tempe, Ariz. 85281.

Brigham Young University, Harold B. Lee Library, Provo, Utah 84602.

Columbia University Library, Department of Special Collections, 116th Street and Broadway, New York, N.Y. 10027.

Edison National Historic Site, Box 126, Orange, N.J. 07051.

George Eastman House (International Museum of Photography at George Eastman House), 900 East Avenue, Rochester, N.Y. 14607.

Historical Society of Long Beach, Rancho Los Alamitos, 6400 Bixby Hill Road, Long Beach, Calif. 90815.

Indiana University, Lilly Library, Bloomington, Ind. 47405.

Library of Congress, Washington, D.C. 20540.

Museum of Modern Art, 11 West 53d Street, New York, N.Y. 10019.

National Archives and Records Service, Washington, D.C. 20408.

National Film Archives 21 Stephen Street, London W1P 1PL, England, United Kingdom.

New York State Archives, Albany, N.Y. 12230.

Ohio State Historical Society, 1-71 and 17th Avenue, Columbus, Ohio 43211.

Stanford University Libraries, Stanford, Calif. 94305.

UCLA Film and Television Archive, 1015 North Cahuenga Boulevard, Hollywood, Calif. 90038.

UCLA (University of California at Los Angeles), Department of Special Collections, 405 Hilgard Avenue, Los Angeles, Calif. 90024.

University of Southern California, Doheny Memorial Library, University Park, Los Angeles, Calif. 90007.

University of Texas, Hoblitzelle Theatre Arts Library, Box 7219, Tex. 78712.

University of Wyoming, Division of Rare Books and Special Collections, Box 3334, Laramie, Wyo. 82071.

Walt Disney Archives, 500 South Buena Vista Street, Burbank, Calif. 91521.

Wisconsin Center for Film and Theater Research, 816 State Street, Madison, Wis. 53706.

Index

About the Author

Anthony Slide has been described as "a one-man publishing phenomenon" by the *Los Angeles Times* and "a meticulous scholar" by *Variety*. He is the author or editor of more than sixty books on the history of popular entertainment and editor of the Filmmakers Series published by Scarecrow Press. Among the many pioneering works that he has authored on the history of cinema are *Early American Cinema* (1970, revised and reprinted 1994), *Early Women Directors* (1977, revised and reprinted as *The Silent Feminists*, 1996), *The Cinema and Ireland* (1988), *Nitrate Won't Wait: A History of Film Preservation in the United States* (1994), and *Lois Weber: The Director Who Lost Her Way in History* (1996). His 1994 book, *The Encyclopedia of Vaudeville*, was named an outstanding academic book of the year by *Choice* magazine, a best reference book of the year by *Library Journal*, and outstanding reference source of the year by the American Library Association.

In 1990, in recognition of his work on the history of popular culture, Anthony Slide was awarded an honorary doctorate of letters by Bowling Green University, and was hailed by Lillian Gish as "our preeminent historian of the silent film."

Anthony Slide has served as associate archivist of the American Film Institute and resident film historian of the Academy of Motion Picture Arts and Sciences. He has lectured widely and also has produced a number of documentaries on silent film personalities, including the feature length *The Silent Feminists: America's First Women Directors*.